COLLINS

SUPERSCAL
LONDON
ATLAS

CONTENTS

HarperCollins*Publishers*

Published by Collins
An imprint of HarperCollins*Publishers*
77-85 Fulham Palace Road, Hammersmith, London W6 8JB

The HarperCollins website address is:
www.**fire**and**water**.com

Mapping generated from Bartholomew digital databases

Bartholomew website address is:
www.bartholomewmaps.com

London Underground Map by permission of London Regional Transport
LRT Registered User No. 99/3054

Printed in Hong Kong

ISBN 0 00 448857 1   NM10532   CUNN

e-mail: roadcheck@harpercollins.co.uk

Key to Map Symbols

3

Symbol	Description	Symbol	Description
A40(M) Dual	Motorway	POL	Police station
A4 Dual	Primary route	Fire Sta	Fire station
A40	'A' road	PO	Post office
B504	'B' road	Lib	Library
	Other road		Cinema
→	One way street*		Theatre
	Street market	⊠	Major hotel
	Pedestrian street	USA	Embassy
	Access restriction	+	Church
-------	Track/Footpath	☾	Mosque
– – –	Pedestrian ferry	✡	Synagogue
CITY	Borough boundary	Mormon	Other place of worship
EC2	Postal district boundary		Leisure/Tourism
⇄	Main railway station		Shopping
⇄	Other railway station		Administration/Law
⊖	Underground station		Health/Welfare
–⊖–	DLR station		Education
	Bus/Coach station		Industry/Commerce
P	Car park		Public open space
WC	Public toilet		Park/Garden/Sports ground
i	Tourist information centre	↑↑↑	Cemetery

Scale 1:7,500 (8.45 inches to 1 mile)

0	0.25	0.5	0.75 Kilometres

0	¼	½ Miles

* One way arrows are shown on all roads in the centre of London and on classified roads in the outer areas.

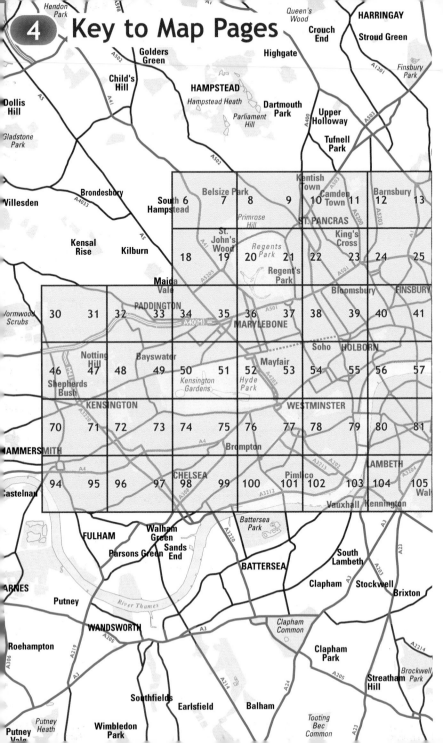

Key to Map Pages

4

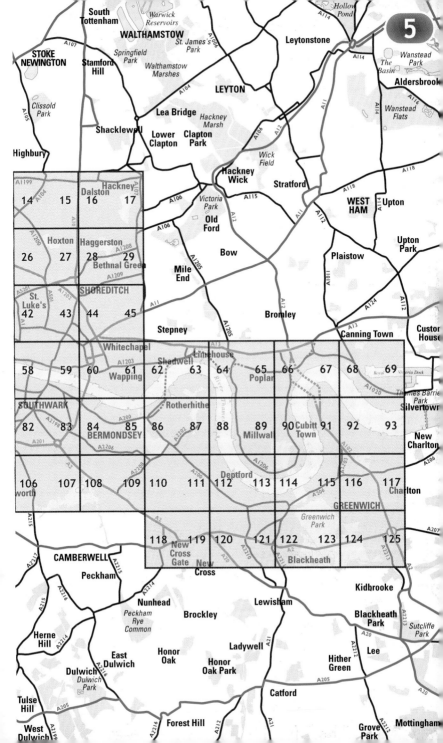

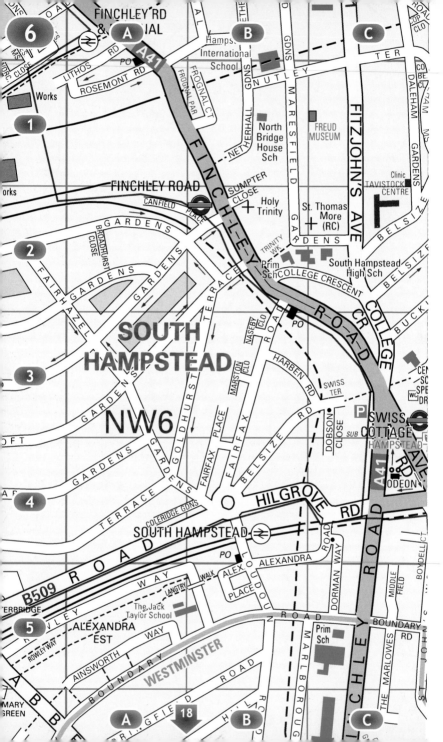

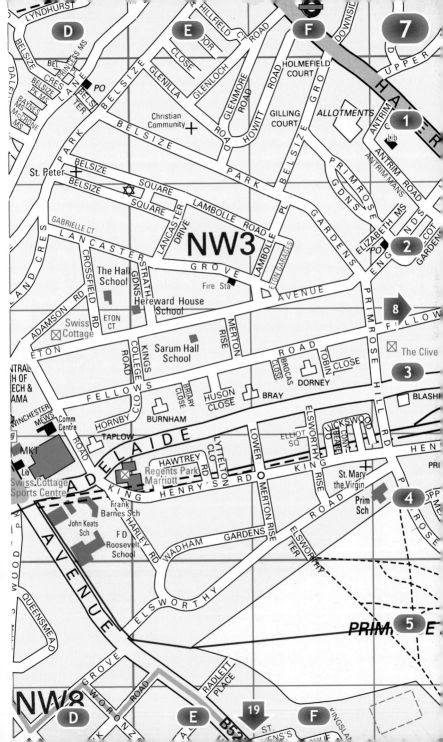

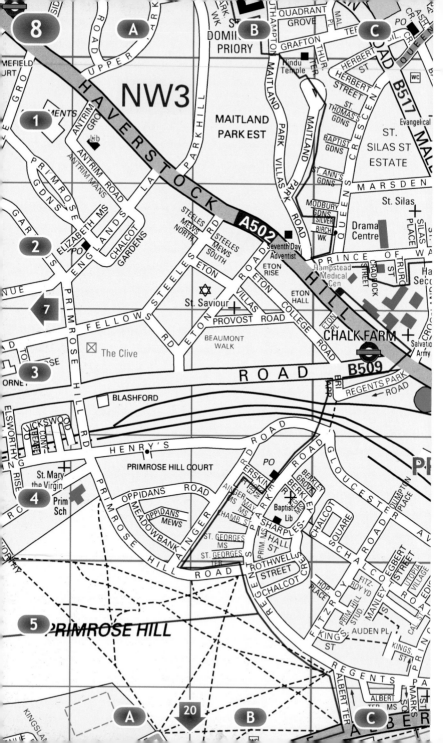

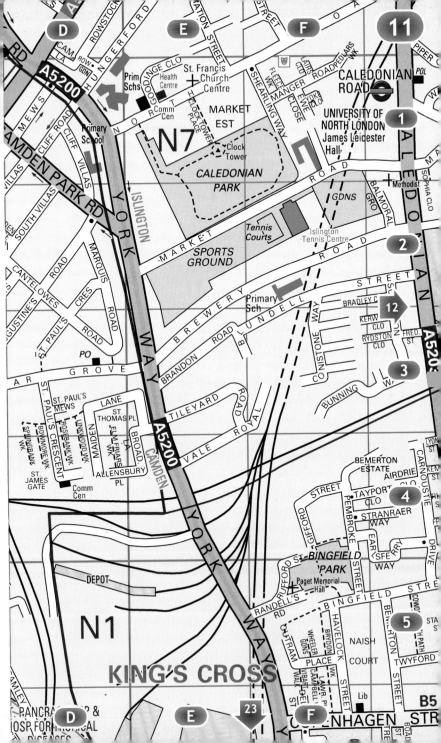

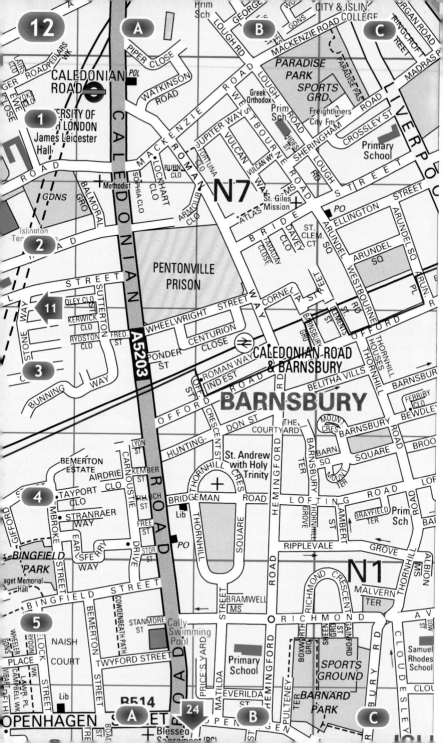

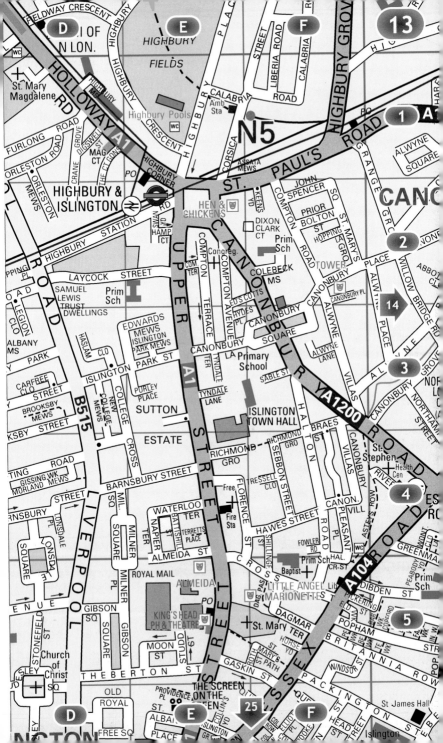

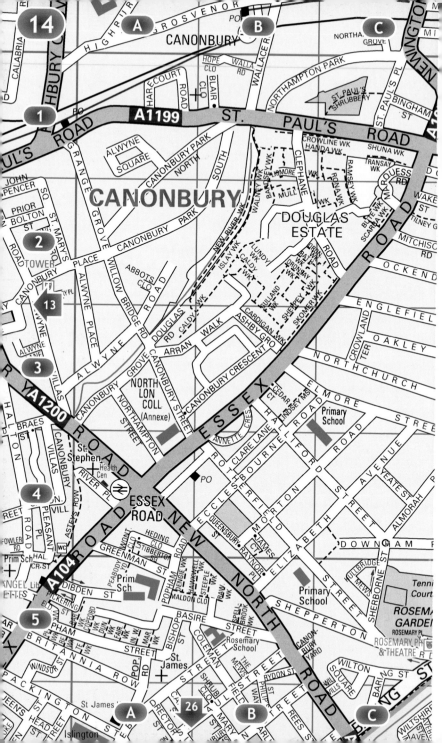

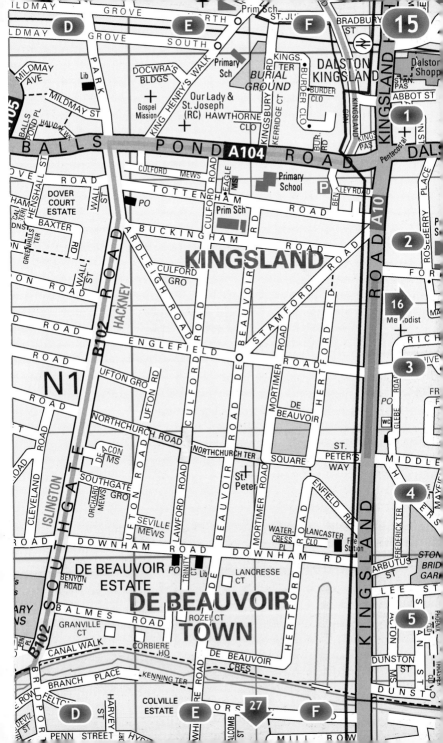

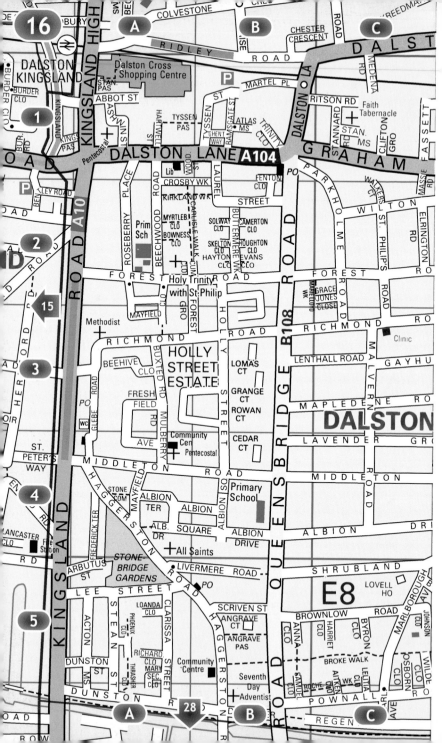

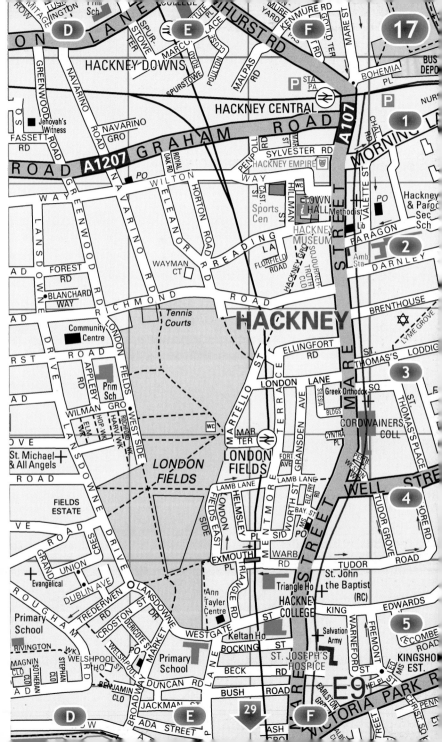

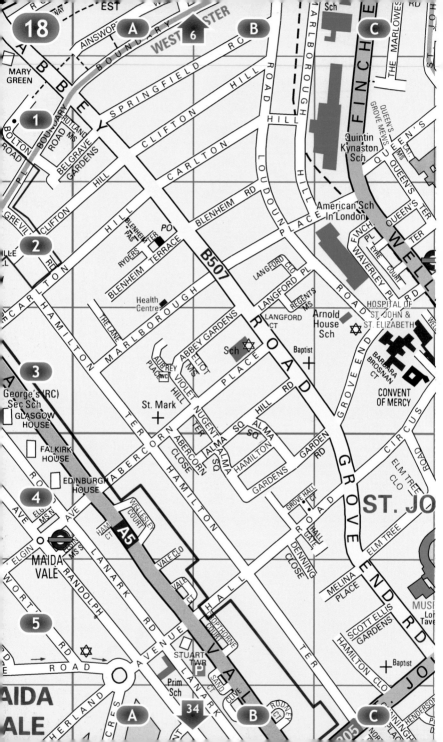

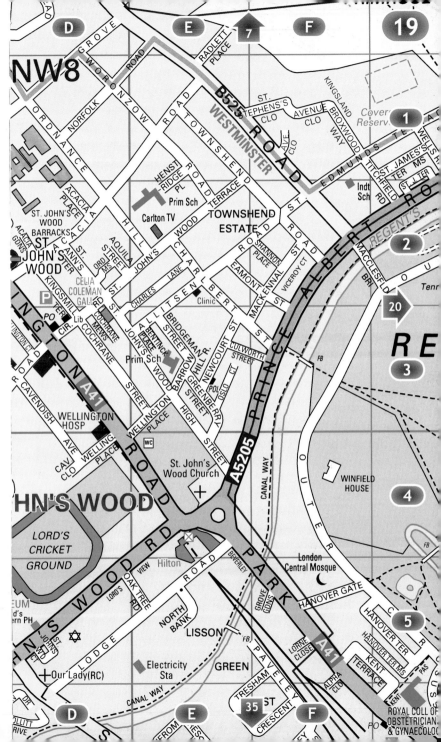

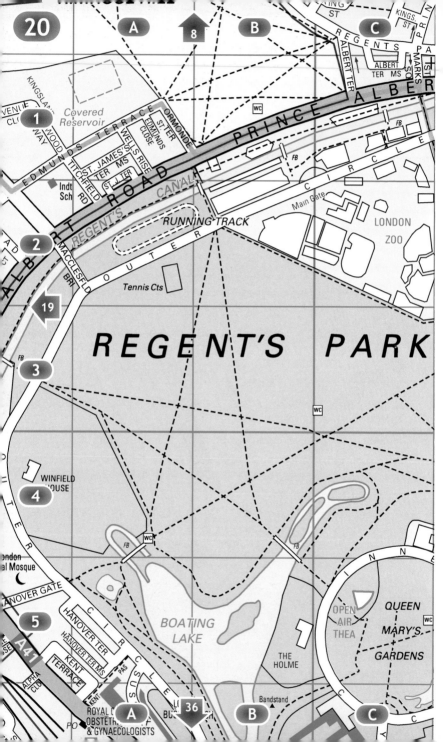

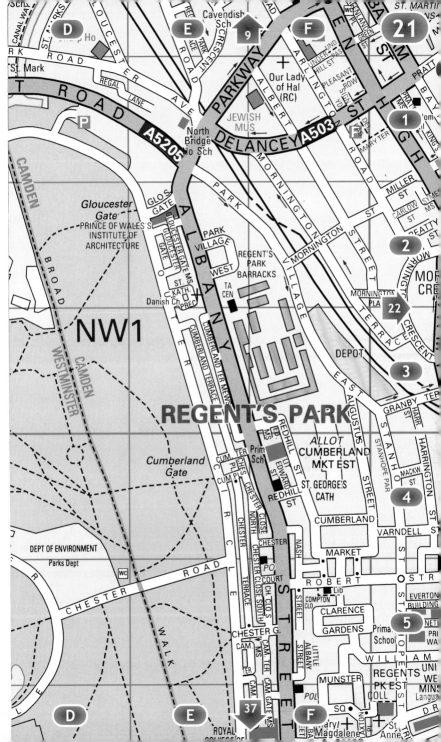

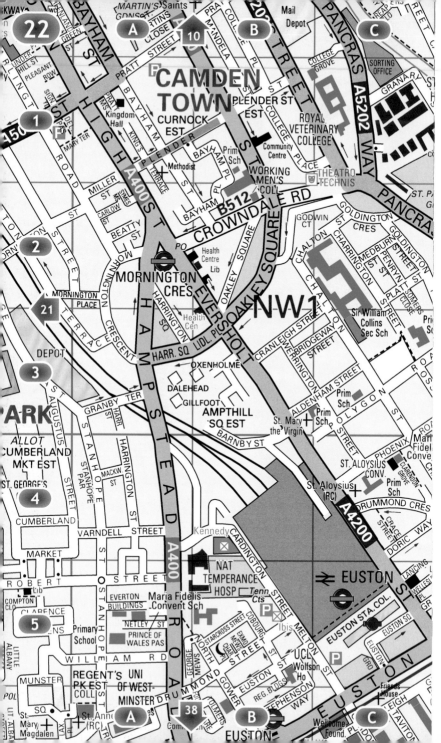

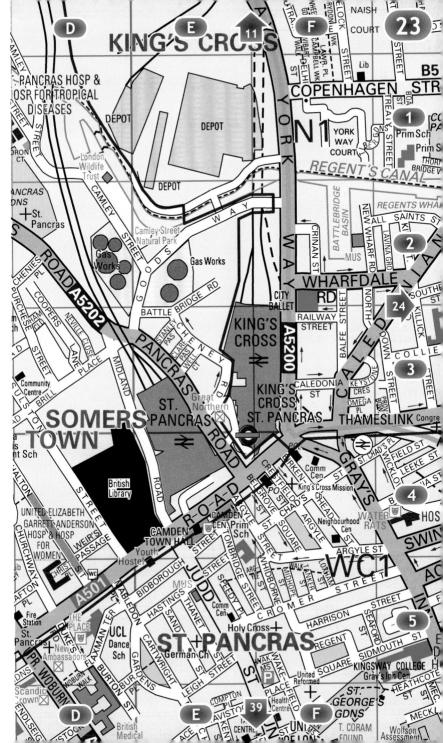

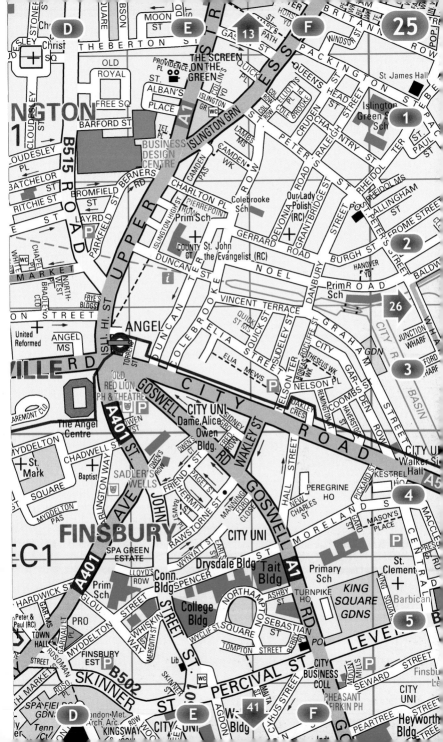

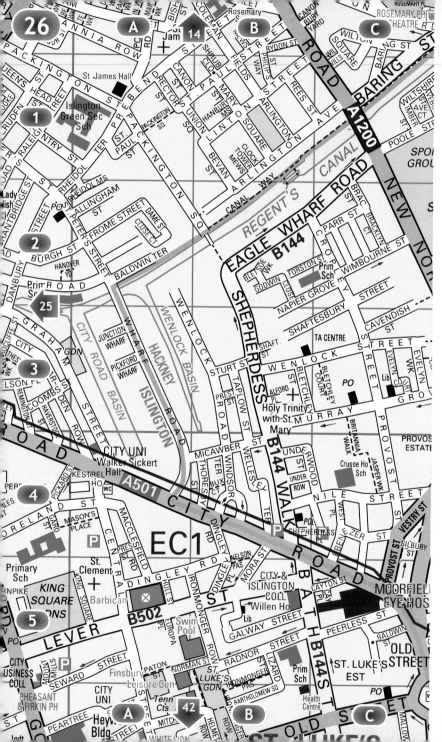

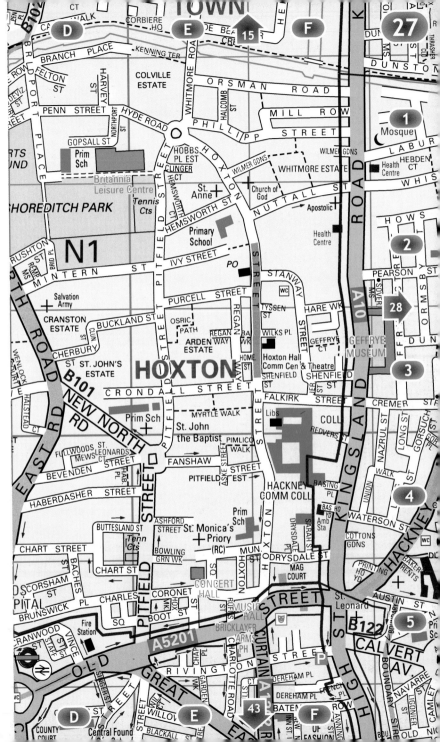

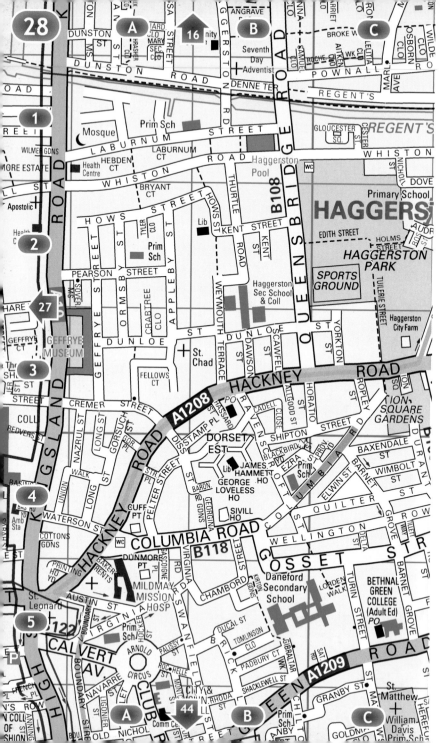

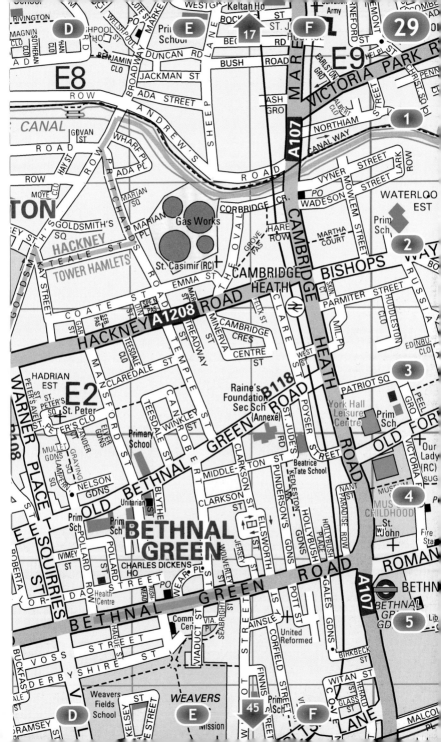

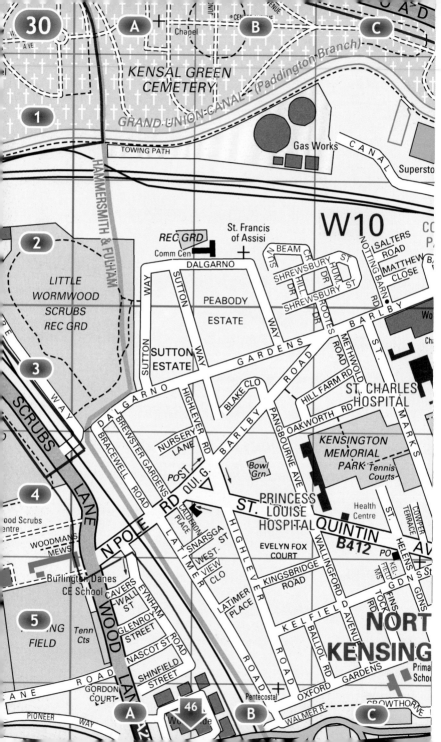

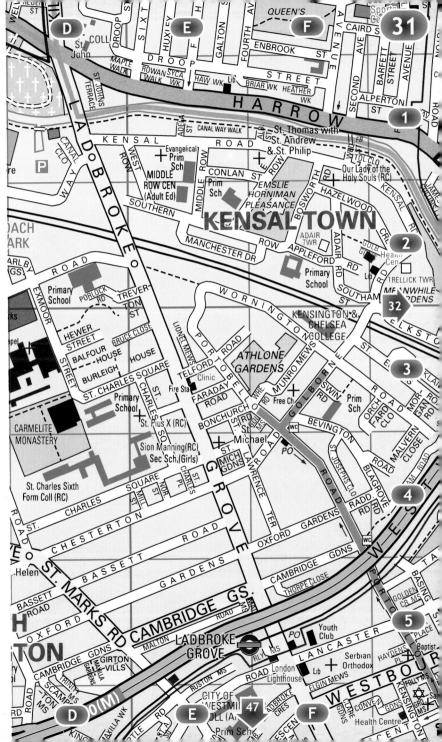

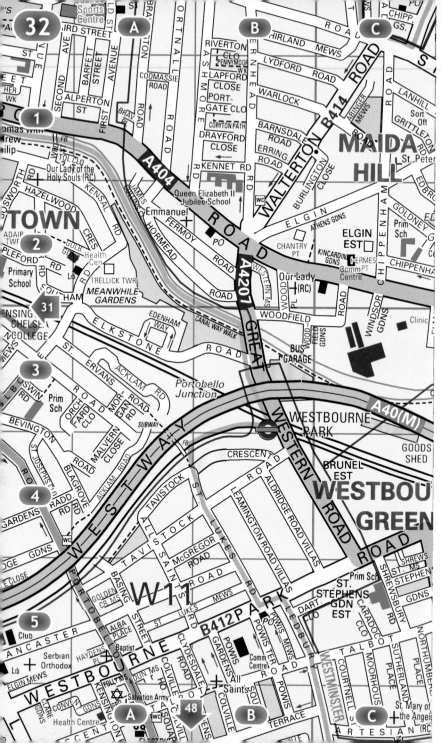

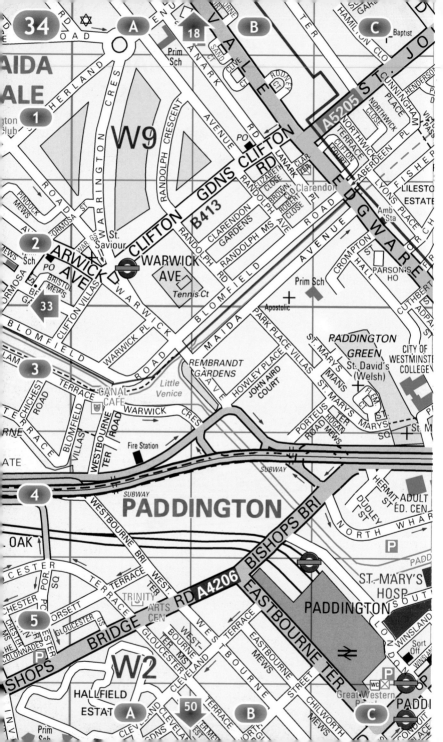

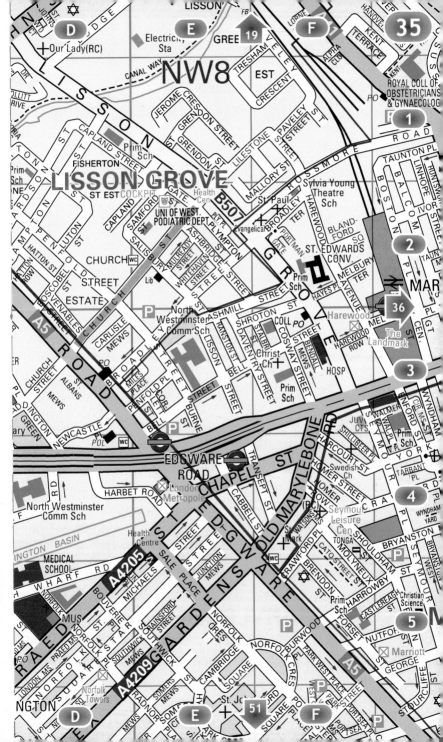

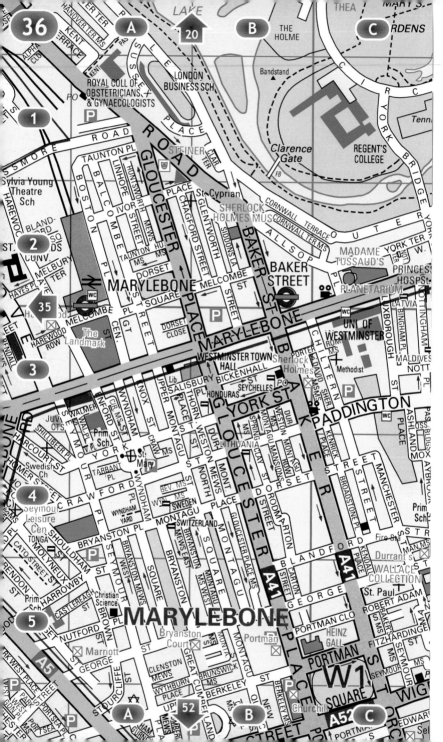

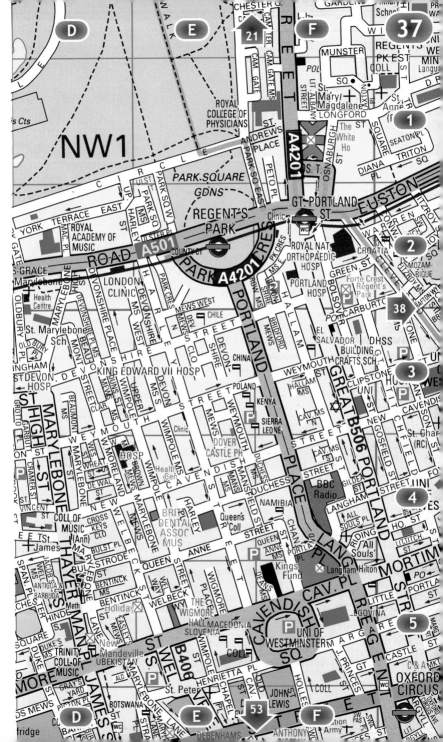

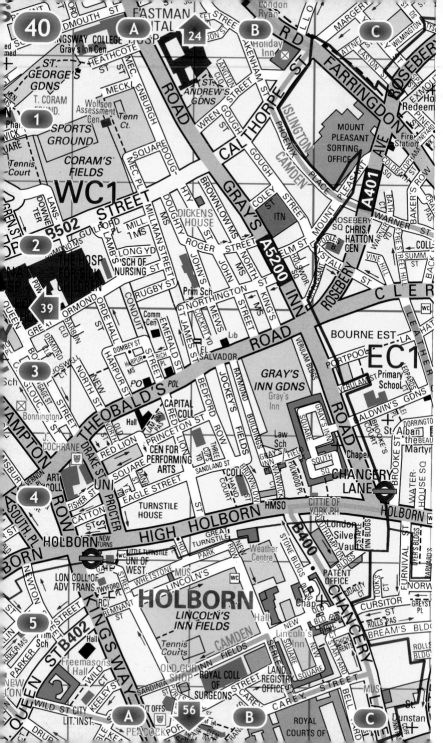

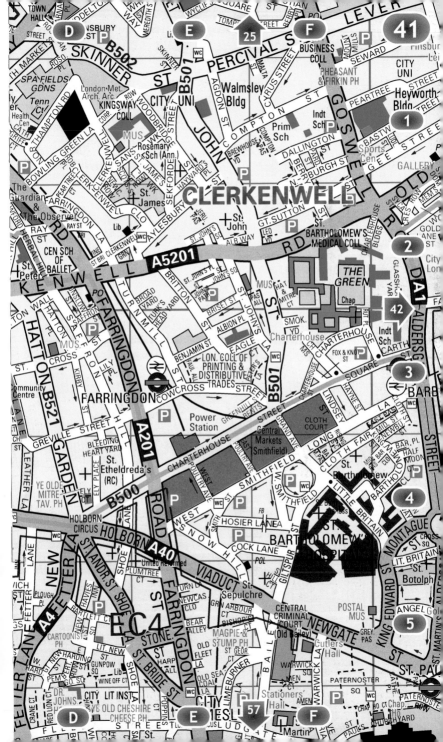

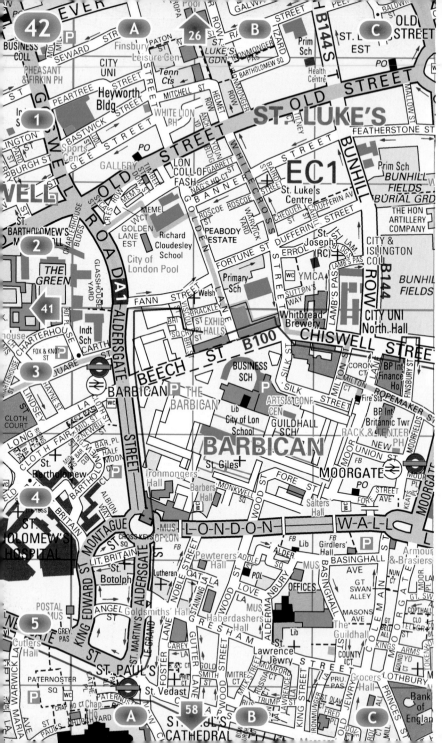

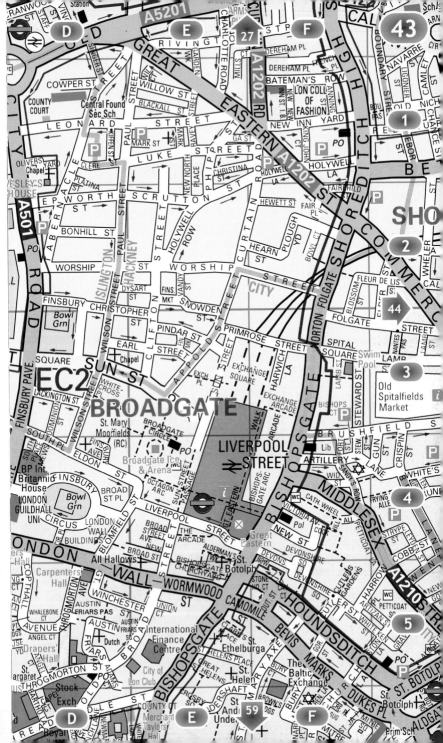

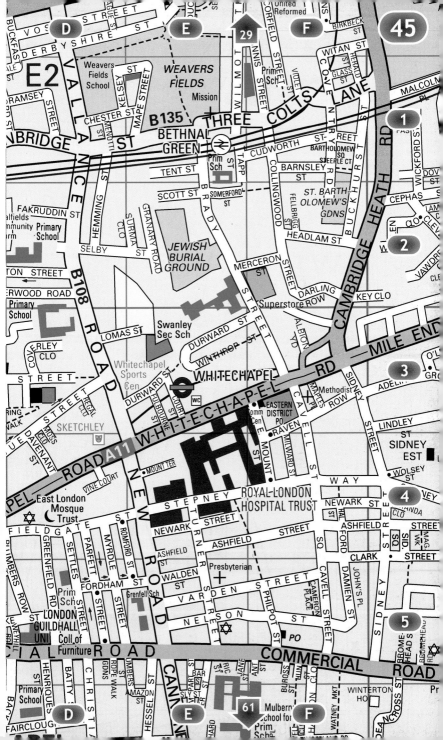

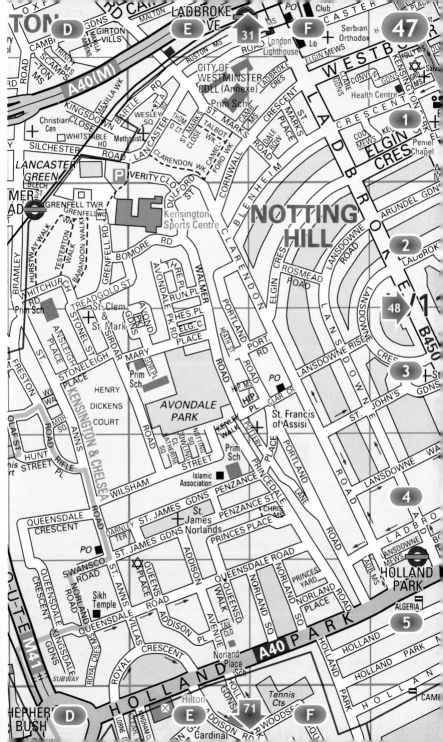

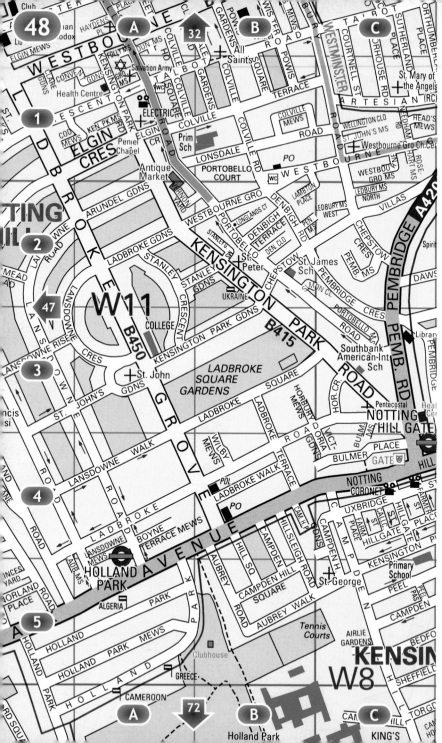

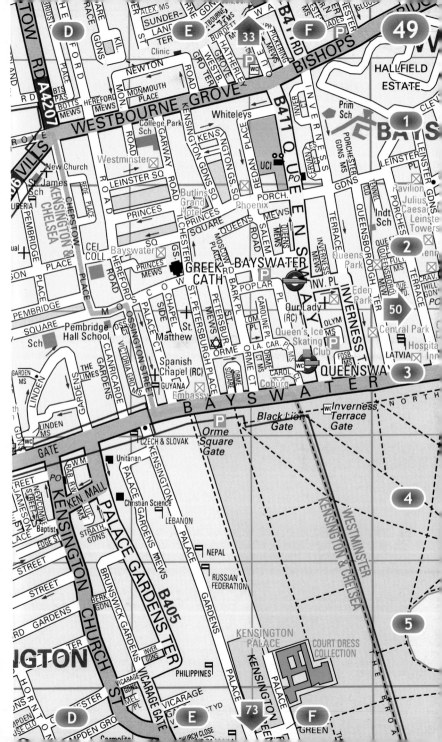

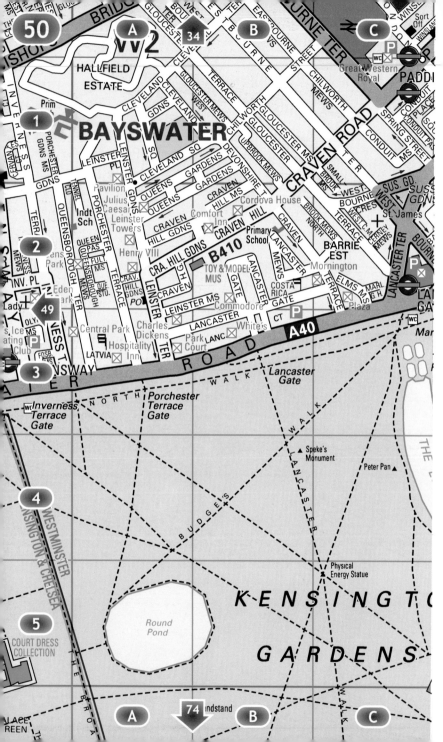

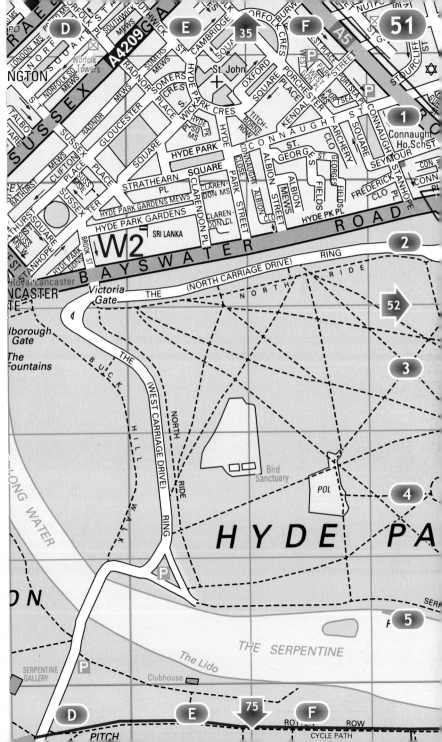

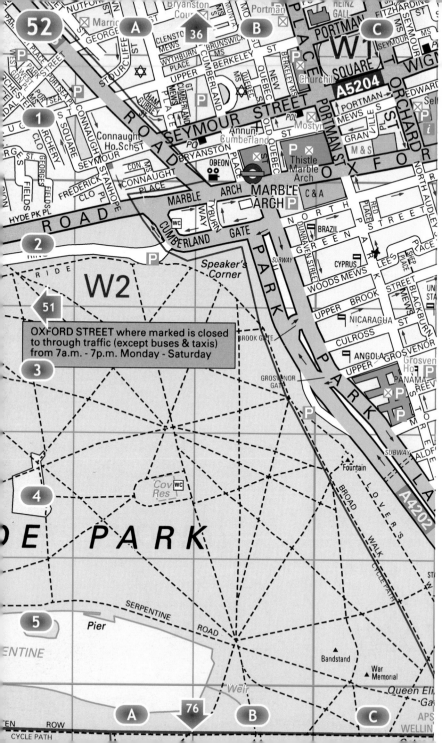

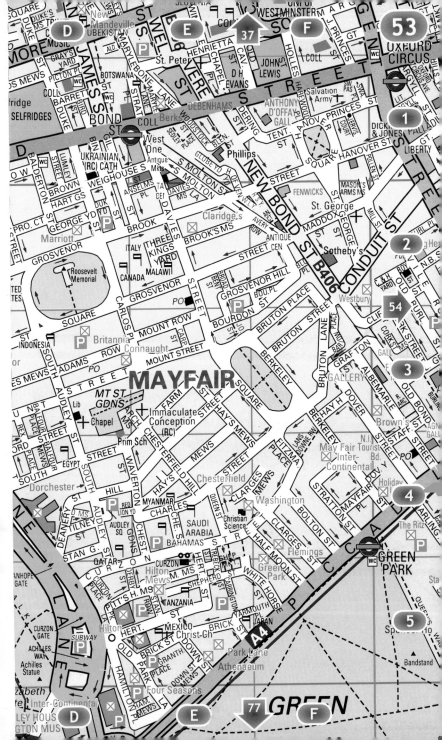

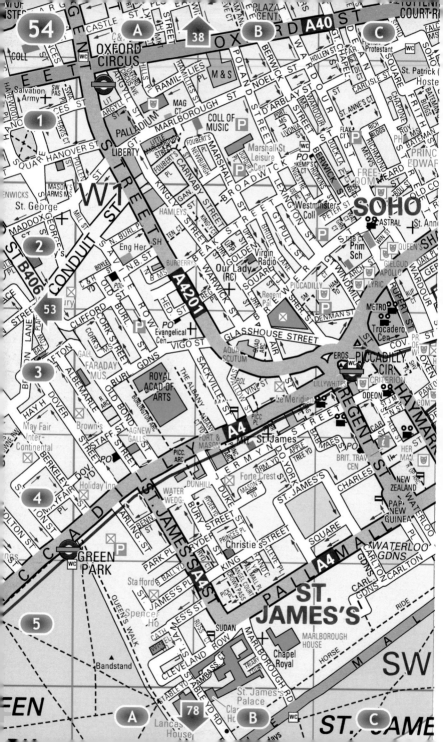

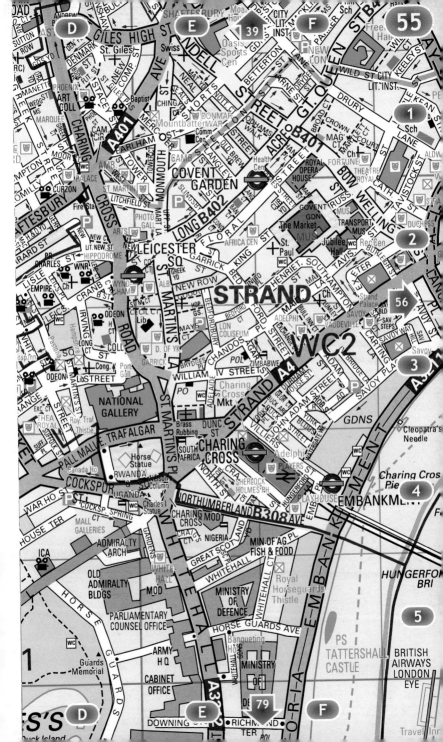

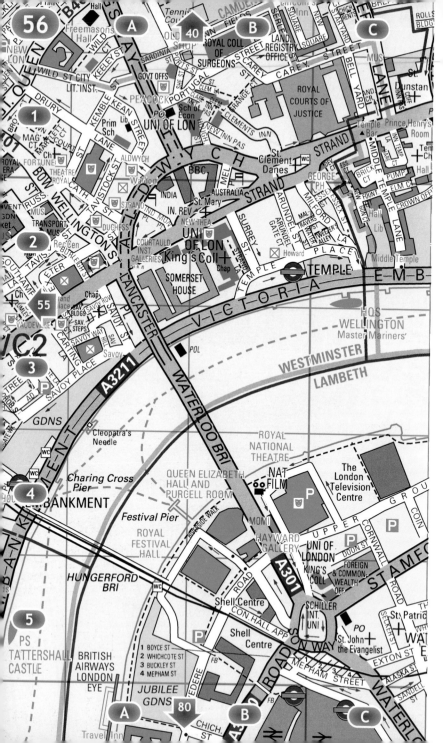

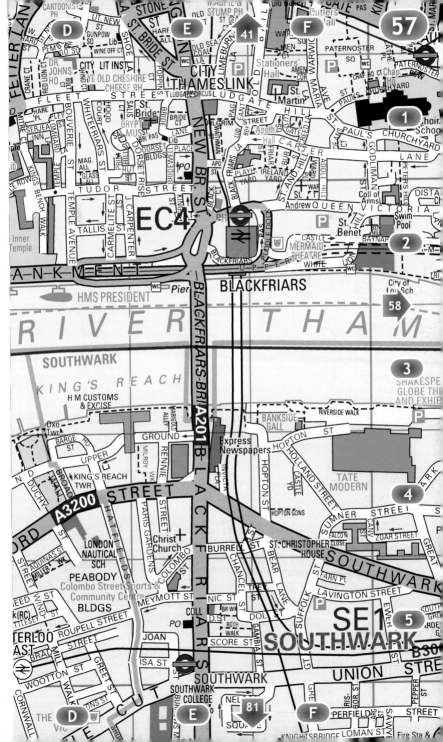

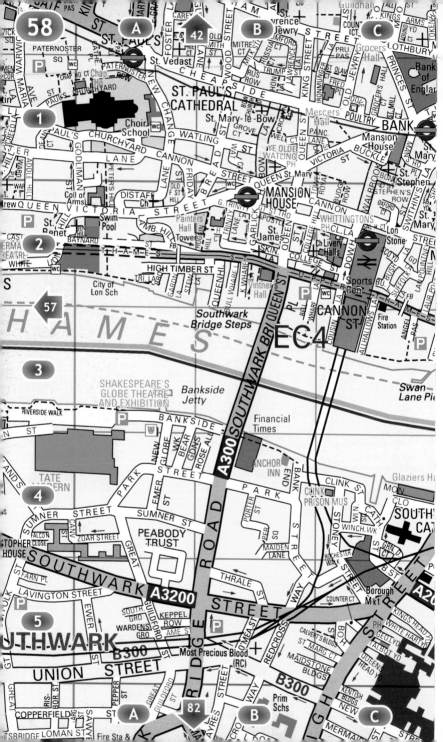

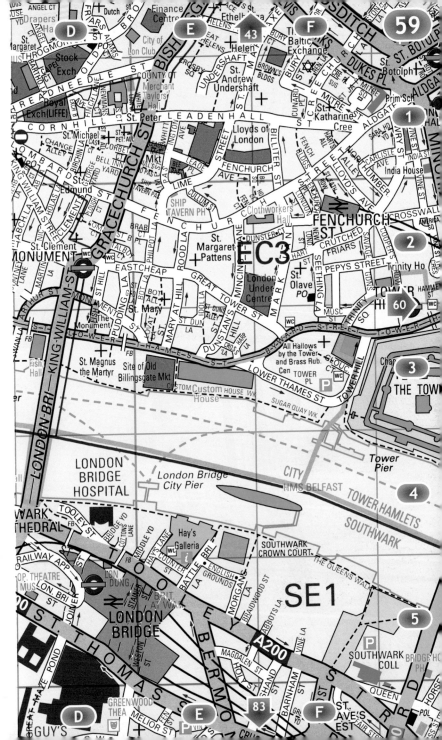

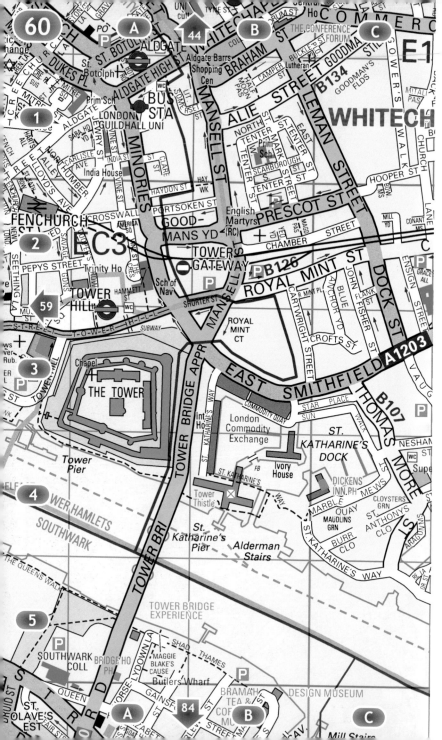

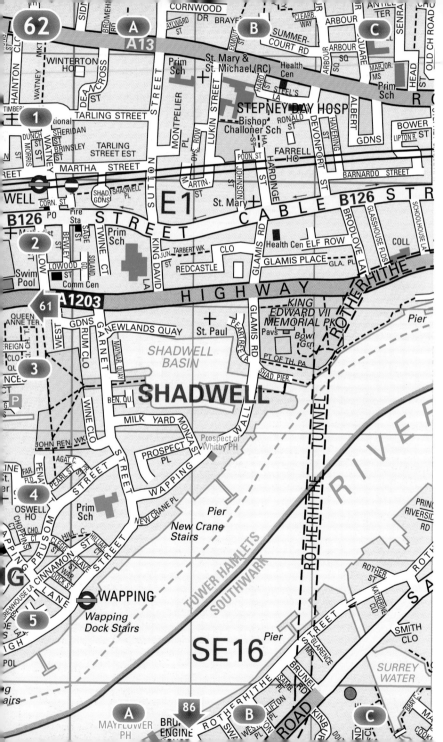

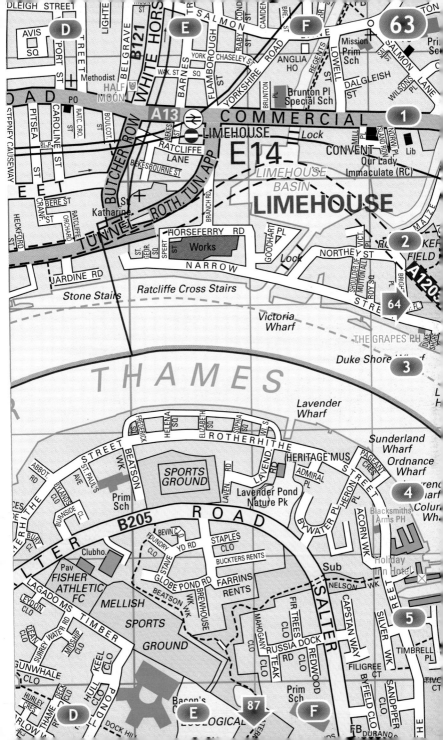

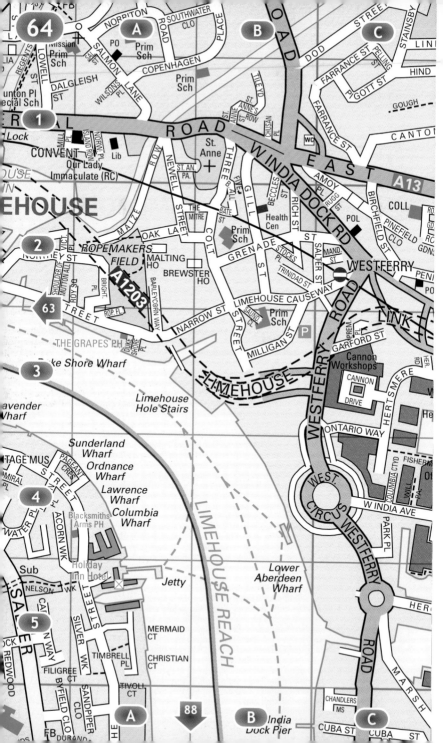

NORBITON
SOUTHWATER CLO
ROAD
PLACE
A
STREET
STAINSBY
C
DOD
SALMON
LINI
B
LOWELL ST
Mission Prim Sch
PO
Prim Sch
FARRANCE ST
PELLING
HIND
REGENTS
Prim Sch
COPENHAGEN
GOTT ST
LIA
DALGLEISH ST
WILSONS PL
LANE
TILE YD
ANNE'S ROW
GOUGH
FARRANCE ST
Special Sch
nton Pl
1
ROAD
EAST
A13
CANTON
Lock
CONVENT
ISLAND ROW
St. Anne
WINDIA DOCK RD
WC
Lib
St. Anne
AMOY PL
COLL
Our Lady Immaculate (RC)
ST. AN. PA.
RUGG
BIRCHFIELD ST
PINEFIELD CLO
RO GDN
EHOUSE
THE MITRE
NEWELL STREET
THREE BALL
GILL ST
BECCLES ST
RICH ST
POL
PINEFIELD CLO
2
ROPEMAKERS FIELD
OAK LA
COLT ST
Prim Sch
Health Cen
SALTER ST
MAND ST
WESTFERRY
PENI
NORTHEY ST
VICT.
MALTING HO
GRENADE ST
STOCKS PL
63
A1203
BRIGHT.
BREWSTER HO
BARLEYCORN WAY
TRINIDAD ST
LIMEHOUSE CAUSEWAY
ROP. FL.
NARROW ST
SAUND CL
Prim Sch
GARFORD ST
THE GRAPES PH
DUKE SHORE PL
MILLIGAN ST
P
Cannon Workshops
LINK
3
ke Shore Wharf
LIMEHOUSE
WESTFERRY ROAD
CANNON DRIVE
HERTSMERE
avender Wharf
Limehouse Hole Stairs
ONTARIO WAY
He
Sunderland Wharf
TAGE MUS
PAGEANT CRES
Ordnance Wharf
STREET
COLUMBIA CTYD
FISHERN
4
Lawrence Wharf
ACORN WK
Blacksmiths Arms PH
Columbia Wharf
LIMEHOUSE REACH
WEST CIRCUS
W INDIA AVE
PARK PL
WATER PL
Sub
Holiday Inn Hotel
NELSON WK
SILVER WK
STREET
Jetty
Lower Aberdeen Wharf
WESTFERRY
HER
SALE
5
CAT
N WAY
MERMAID CT
CHRISTIAN CT
TIMBRELL PL
ROAD
REDWOOD
FILIGREE CT
BYFIELD CLO
SANDPIPER CLO
TIVOLI CT
A
88
B
India Dock Pier
CHANDLERS MS
CUBA ST
CUBA
C
FB
DURAND
MARSH

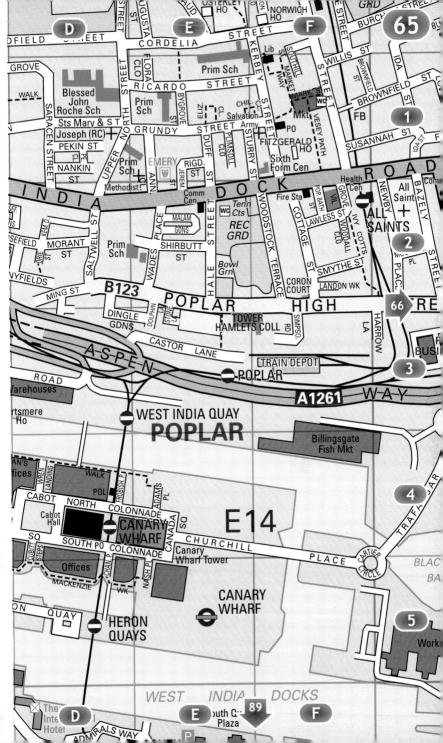

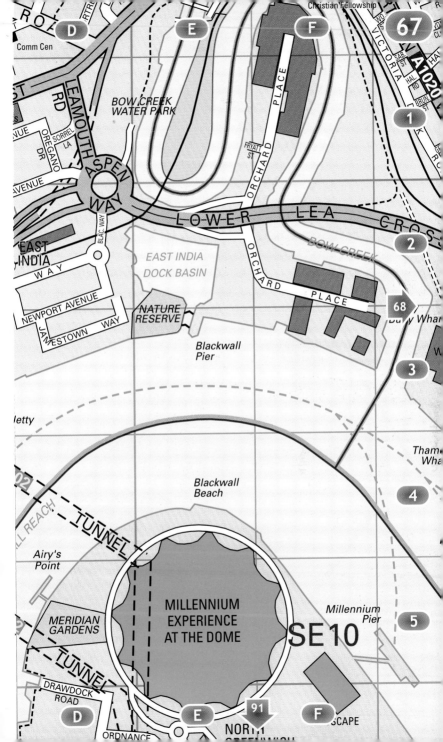

Christian Fellowship

Comm Cen

LEAMOUTH RD

ROAD

BOW CREEK
WATER PARK

OREGANO
DR

SORREL
LA

AVENUE

ASPEN WAY

FRYATT ST.

ORCHARD PLACE

VICTORIA

A1020

SAB ST

HAL
RD

BRUN
ST

1

LOWER LEA CROS.

EAST INDIA WAY

BLAC. WAY

W A Y

EAST INDIA
DOCK BASIN

ORCHARD PLACE

BOW CREEK

2

NEWPORT AVENUE

JAMESTOWN WAY

NATURE
RESERVE

ORCHARD PLACE

68

Du y Whar

Blackwall
Pier

3

Jetty

Tham
Wha

A102

Blackwall
Beach

4

ALL REACH

TUNNEL

Airy's
Point

MERIDIAN
GARDENS

Millennium
Pier

5

TUNNEL

MILLENNIUM
EXPERIENCE
AT THE DOME

SE10

DRAWDOCK
ROAD

D

E

91

NOR H

F

SCAPE

ORDNANCE

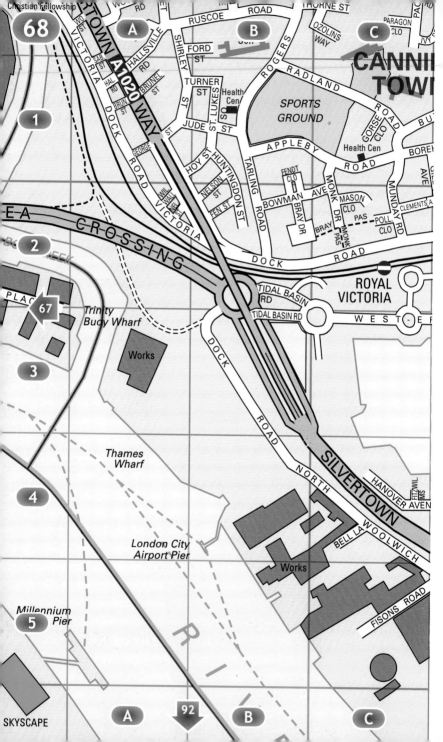

Christian Fellowship

A

B

C

CANNII
TOW

1

RUSCOE ROAD

THORNE ST

PARAGON
CLO

PAC

OZOLINS
WAY

WOOD

RD

CANNING TOWN A1020 WAY

VICTORIA

HALLSVILLE

SAB
ST

HAL
RD

BRUNEL ST

BRUN
ST

GEORGE

DOCK ROAD

WILL WALL

VICTORIA

SHIRLEY ST

FORD
ST

TURNER
ST

JUDE ST

ST. LUKES ST

HOY ST

NELSON ST

FEN ST

HUNTINGDON ST

Health
Cen

ROGERS ST

RADLAND ROAD

SPORTS
GROUND

GORSE
CLO

HEALTH CEN

APPLEBY ROAD

BOWMAN

FENDT
CLO

BRAY DR

BRAY

MASON
CLO

PAS

MONK
PAS

POLL.
CLO

MONK DR

MUNDAY RD

GOSE
CLO

BORE

AVE

BUI

CLEMENTS A

1

EA

CROSSING

CREEK

2

PLAC

67

Trinity
Buoy Wharf

Works

3

TARLING ROAD

DOCK

ROAD

TIDAL BASIN
RD

TIDAL BASIN RD

ROYAL
VICTORIA

WEST E

DOCK

ROAD

Thames
Wharf

4

London City
Airport Pier

NORTH

SILVERTOWN

HANOVER AVEN

FITZ WIL MS

WOOLWICH

BELL LA

Works

FISONS ROAD

Millennium
Pier

5

R I V E

SKYSCAPE

A

B

C

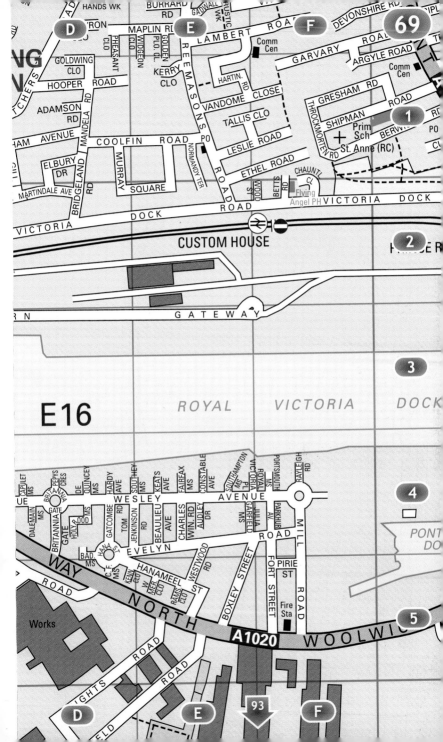

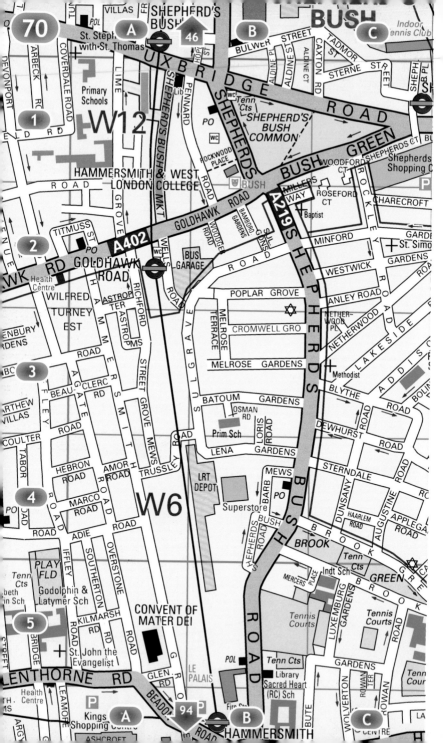

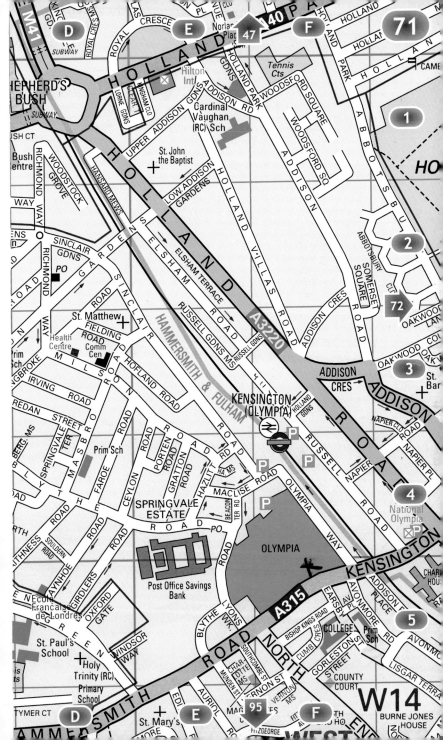

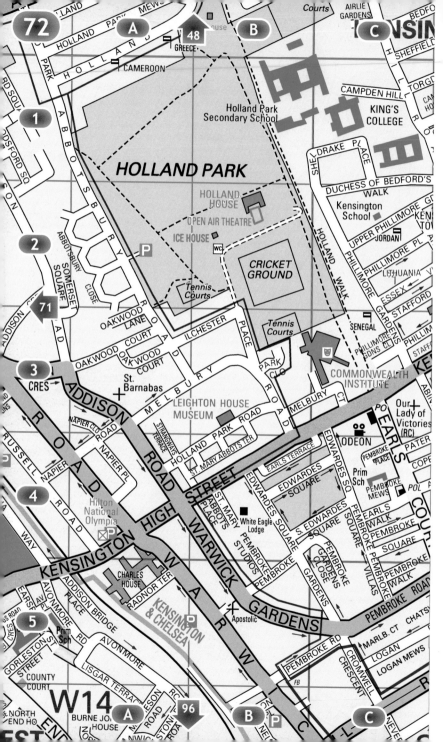

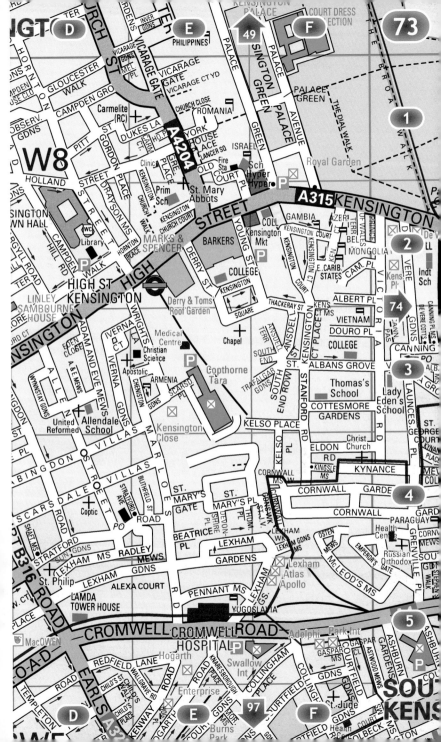

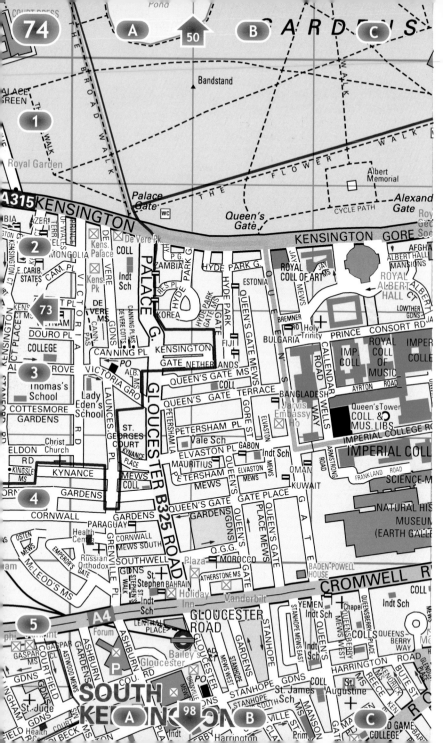

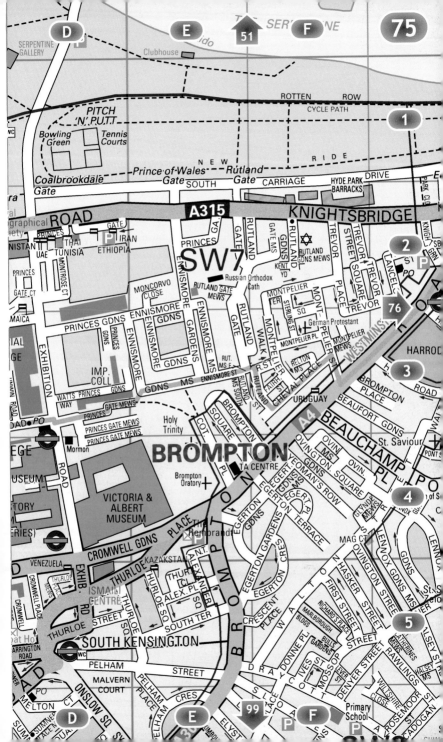

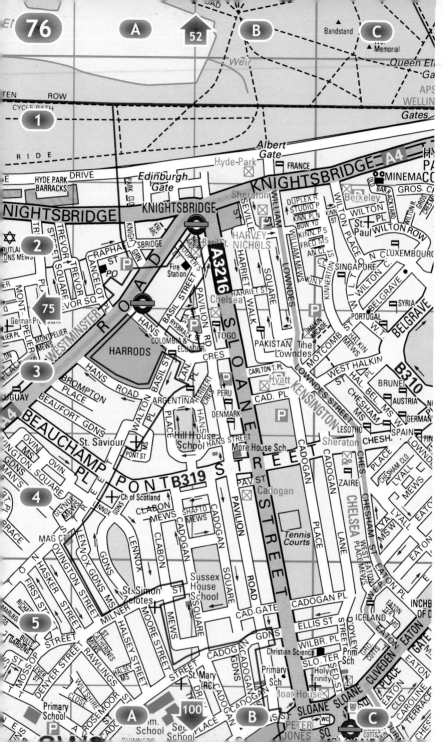

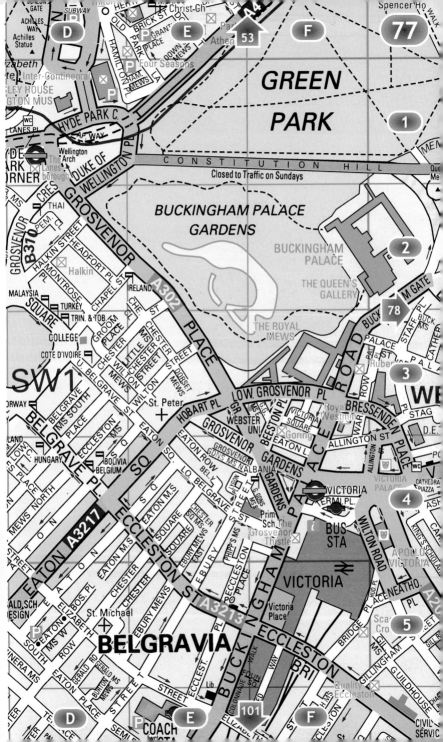

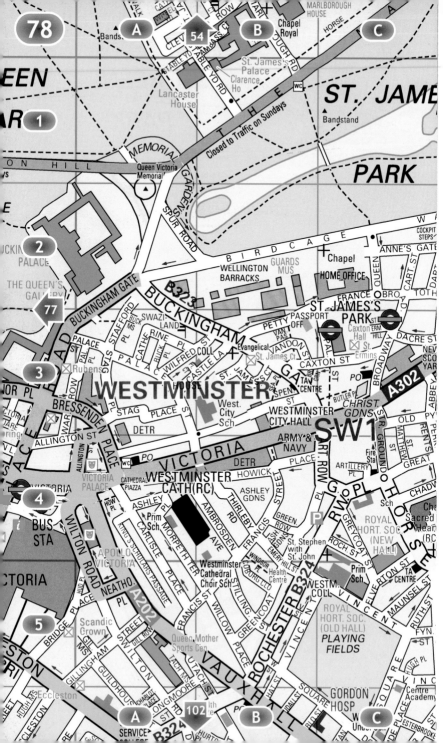

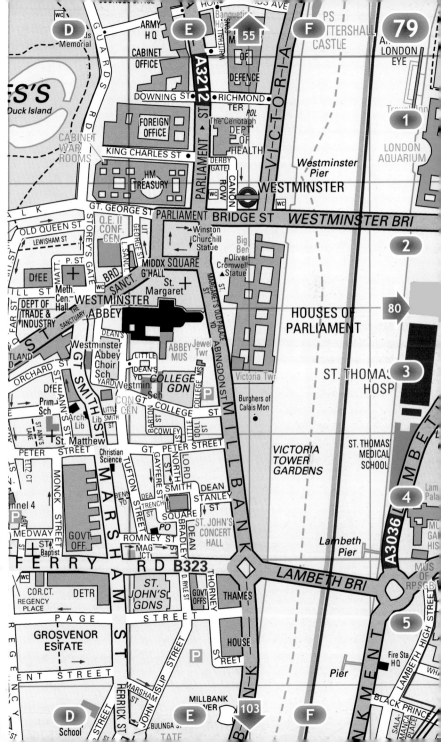

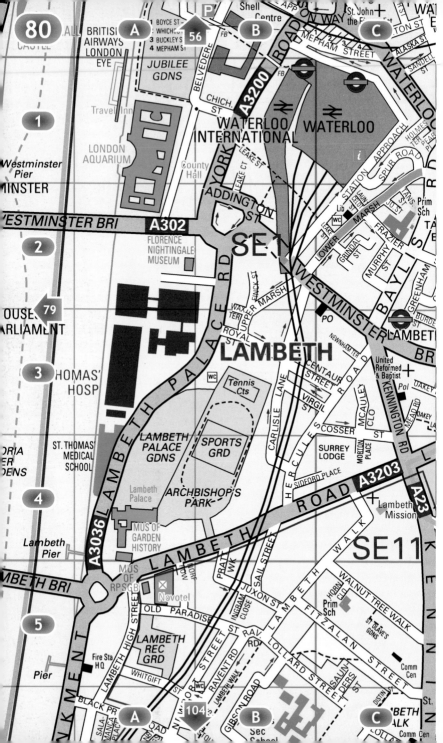

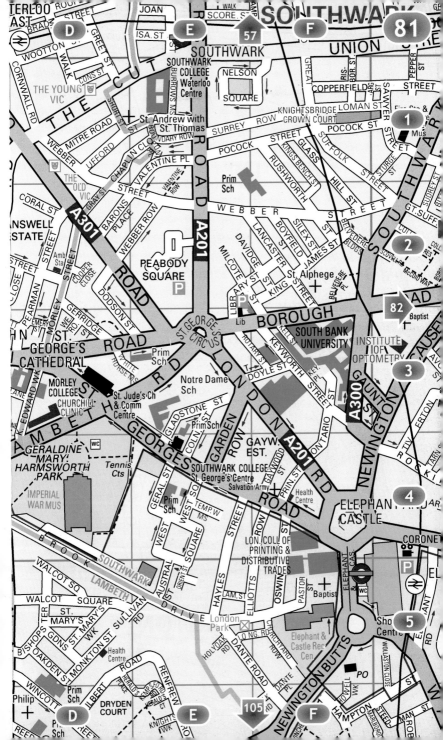

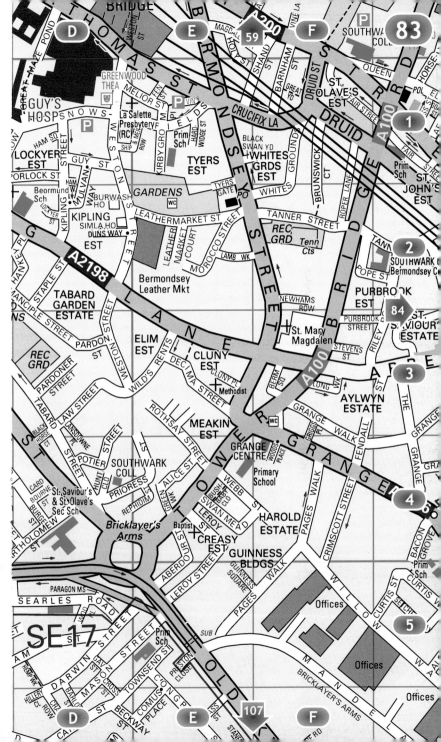

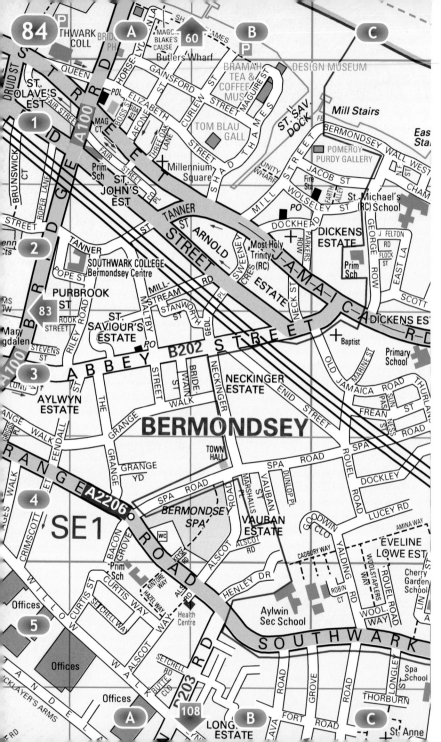

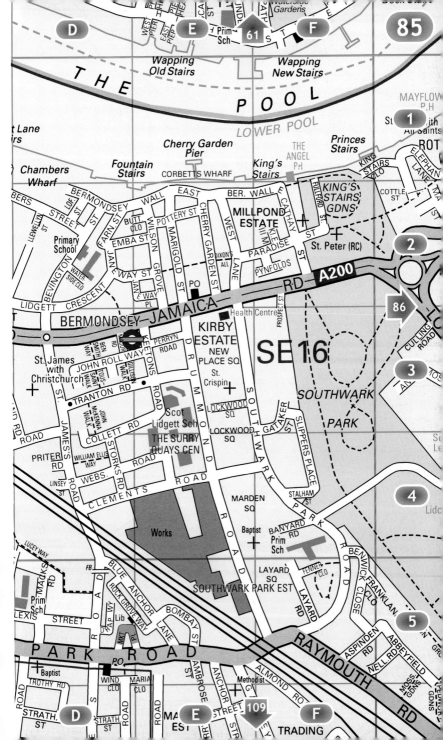

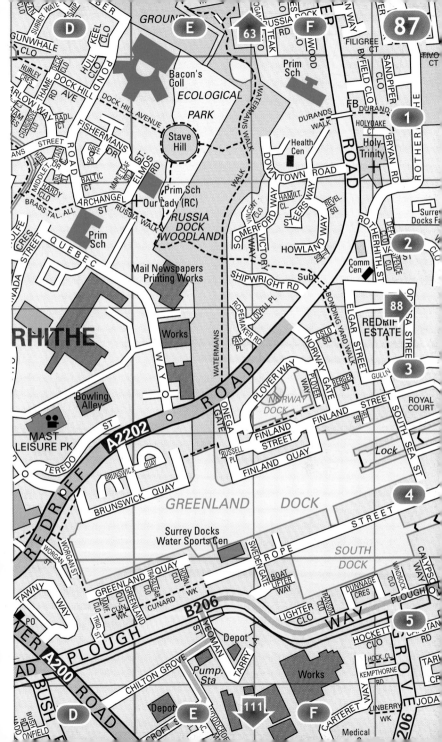

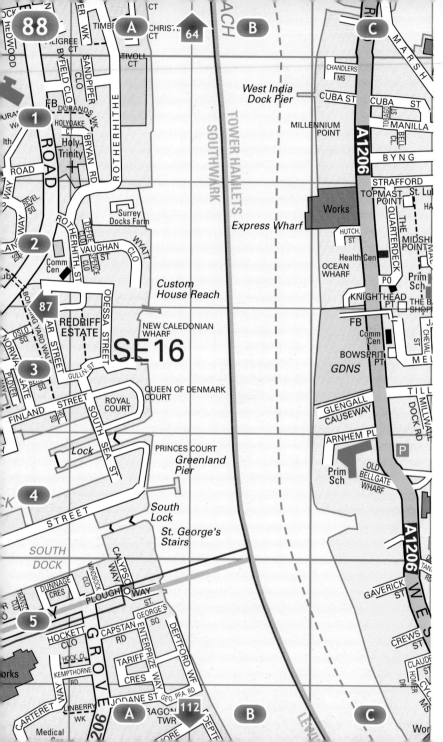

A

CT

CHRIST
CT

64

B

C

MARSH

REDWOOD

TIMBER
WK

FILIGREE
CT

BYFIELD CLO

SANDPIPER WK

TIVOLI
CT

ROTHERHITHE

CHANDLERS
MS

West India
Dock Pier

CUBA ST

CUBA ST

MANILLA

FB

DURAND'S WK

1

HOLYOAKE
CT

BRYAN RD

HOLY-
TRINITY

Holy-
Trinity

MILLENNIUM
POINT

LOBLEY

TOBAGO ST

BELL CL

BYNG

A1206

ROAD

ROAD

WAY

REVEL
SQ

WAY

2

ROTHERHITHE ST

DEFOE

Surrey
Docks Farm

WYATT

CLO

STRAFFORD

Works

Express Wharf

HUTCH.
ST

TOPMAST
POINT

St. Lu

HA

THE QUARTERDECK

THE
MIDSHI
POINT

VAUGHAN

SPENCE

ST

CLO

ST

Comm
Cen

ODESSA

STREET

Custom
House Reach

Health Cen

OCEAN
WHARF

PO

Prim
Sch

THE B
SHOP

87

REDRIFF
ESTATE

NEW CALEDONIAN
WHARF

KNIGHTHEAD
PT

FB

Comm
Cen

CHEVAL

OSLO SQ

NORWAY

AR STREET

SE 16

BOWSPRIT
PT

ME

3

GATE

GULLIN ST

STREET

BERG
SQ

SOUTH SEA ST

ROYAL
COURT

QUEEN OF DENMARK
COURT

GDNS

GLENGALL
CAUSEWAY

TILL

MILLWALL DOCK RD

FINLAND

PLOVER

ST

PRINCES COURT

ARNHEM PL

Lock

Greenland
Pier

P

4

STREET

South
Lock

St. George's
Stairs

Prim
Sch

OLD
BELLGATE
WHARF

A1206

SOUTH
DOCK

CALYPSO WAY

WINDSOCK CLO

DUNNAGE
CRES

PLOUGH WAY

ST.
GEORGE'S
SQ

GAVERICK ST

WE

5

HOCKETT
CLO

GROVE

CAPSTAN
RD

ENTERPRIZE WAY

DEPTFORD WF RD

CREWS

CLAUDE

HOMER

DR

HOCK CL

TARIFF
CRES

KEMPTHORNE
RD

LINBERRY
WK

CARTERET

JODANE ST

GEO. BEA. RD

A

DRAGON
TWR

112

B

C

Medical

LEWIS

orks

SOUTHWARK

TOWER HAMLETS

902

Wor

D E F 89

WEST INDIA DOCKS

65

The International Hotel

South Quay Plaza

Thames Quay (L.D.D.C.)

1

MERIDIAN GATE

ADMIRALS WAY

SOUTH QUAY

P

WALL STREET

LEN ST.

NUSON CLO.

STREET

SAVANNAH ST

ke
+

Comm Cen

BAR

ST

ARKANTINE PING PAR

THANET ST

ENGLISH

ER

ALPHA

GROVE

E14

MASTMAKER RD

MARSH

MERIDIAN PL

LORD AMORY WAY

WAL

ISLE

Guardian Newspaper Print Works

LIGHTERMANS RD

INDESCON COURT

Tate & Lyle Sugar Works

LANTERNS COURT

STREET

CORD WAY

Swim Pool

OMEGA CLO.

ROAD

STARB. WAY

CLAIRE PL.

MILLHARBOUR

MILLWALL

INNER

OF

DOCK

COLL

MUIRFIELD CRE

PEPPER ST.

MUIRFIELD CRES.

HARBOUR EX SQUARE

Great Eastern Enterprise Cen

2

AST

ROFFEY ST

CHIP ST

FERR

90

CAB ST

HICK ST

EAST LA

PLEVNA

BRAIT

LimeHARBOUR

London Arena

P

3

CROSSHARBOUR & LONDON ARENA

GLENGALL

Lib

ST

PEPPER ST.

TURNBERRY QUAY

LANARK SQ.

SELSDON

SELSDON WAY

P

WAY

Health Cen

Comm Cen

P

GREEN. VW PL

GREENWICH VIEW PL.

Daily Telegraph

ROAD

FERRY

4

Superstore

P

Dockland Sailing Cen

MILLWALL   OUTER   DOCK

DOGS

Comm Cen

ARDEN CRES

SEVERNAKE CL.

DARTM WK

CHARNWOOD GDNS

EPPING CLO.

MUS

THAMES CIRCLE

OPS

IRONMONGERS

ASHDOWN WK

ROTH WK

RADNO. WK

RINGWOOD GDNS

INGLEW.

COPE. DR

SHERW.

BARNSDALE AVE

St. Edmund(RC)

Prim Sch

Medical Cen

MILLWALL

WHEAT SHEAF CLO

TELEGRAPH PL.

SPINDRIFT

BARNFIELD PL.

TAEPING ST

TAEPING STREET

TAEPING ST

TAEPING ST

TAEPING ST

WHITEADDER WAY

FALCON WAY

UNDI. RD

UNDINE RD

UN. RD

UN. RD.

AVENUE

ROAD

EAST

5

IU

ALLOT

MUDCHUTE

GLOBE

GLOBE

RO

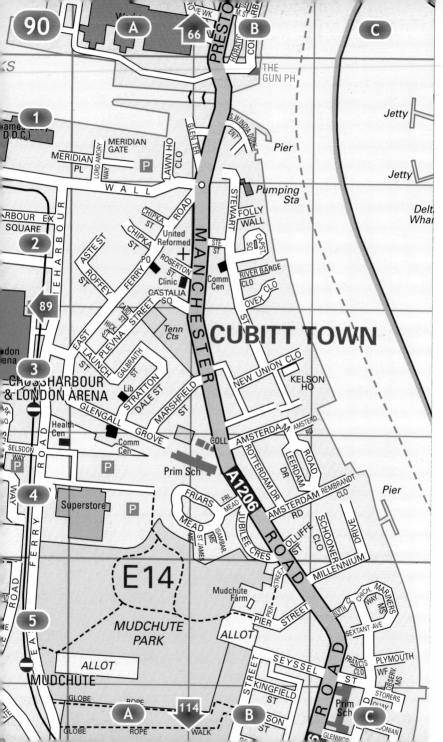

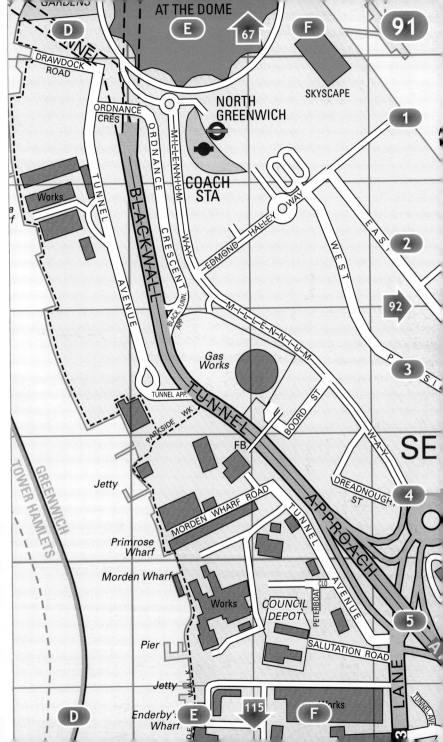

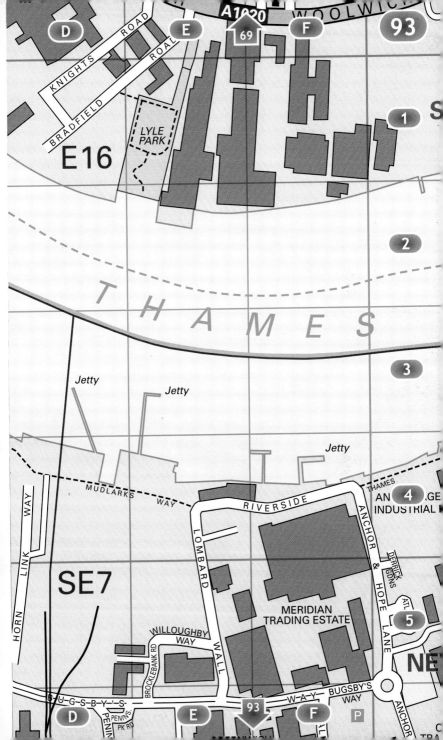

KNIGHTS ROAD

BRADFIELD ROAD

69

LYLE PARK

E 16

S

1

2

T H A M E S

3

Jetty

Jetty

Jetty

MUDLARKS WAY

RIVERSIDE

THAMES

AN 4 GE INDUSTRIAL

LOMBARD

ANCHOR &

DERRICK GDNS

SE7

HORN LINK WAY

WILLOUGHBY WAY

BROCKLEBANK RD

WALL

HOPE LANE

ATL

5

MERIDIAN TRADING ESTATE

NE

B-U-G-S-B-Y-'-S

PENINS PK RD

W-A-Y BUGSBY'S WAY

ANCHOR

P

TR

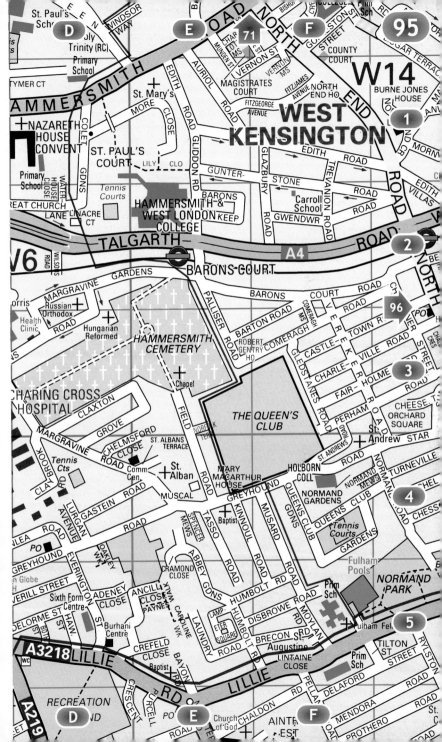

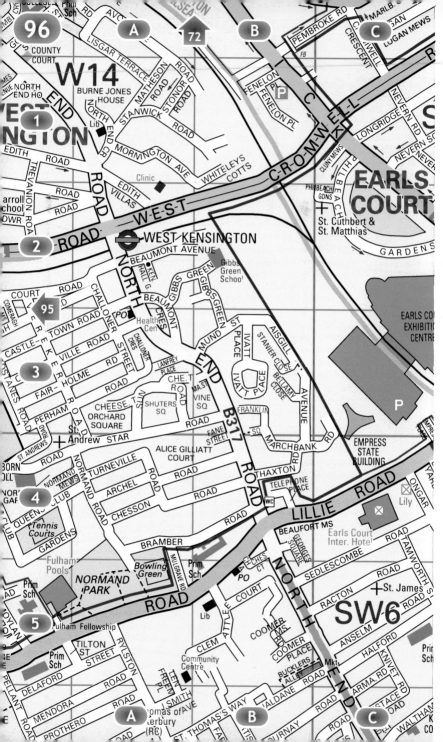

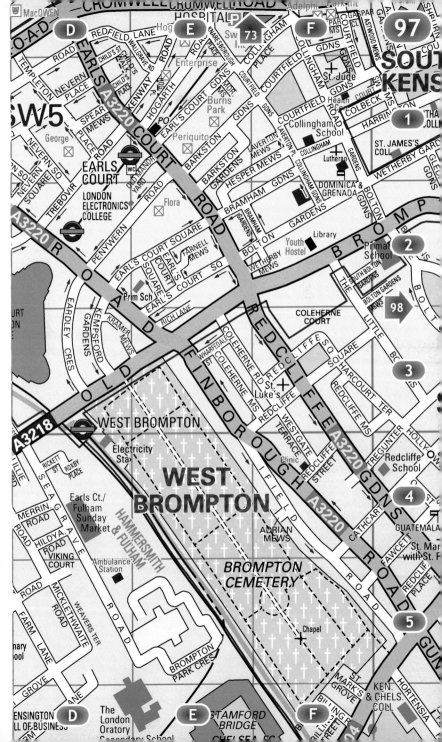

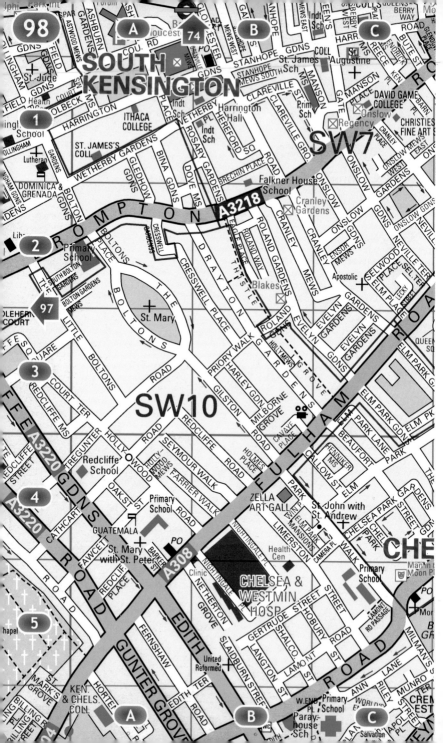

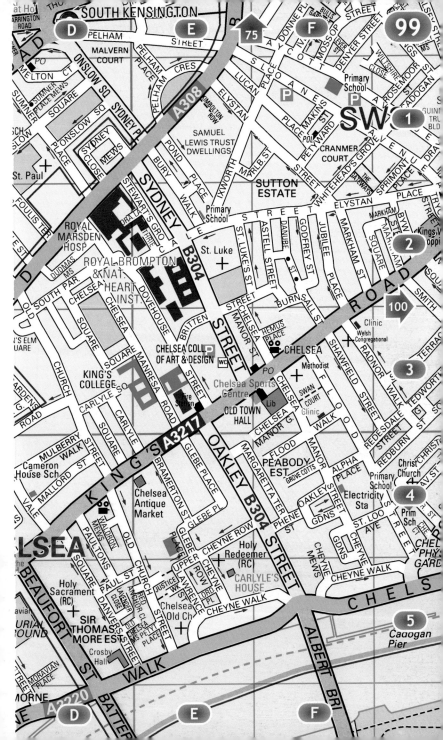

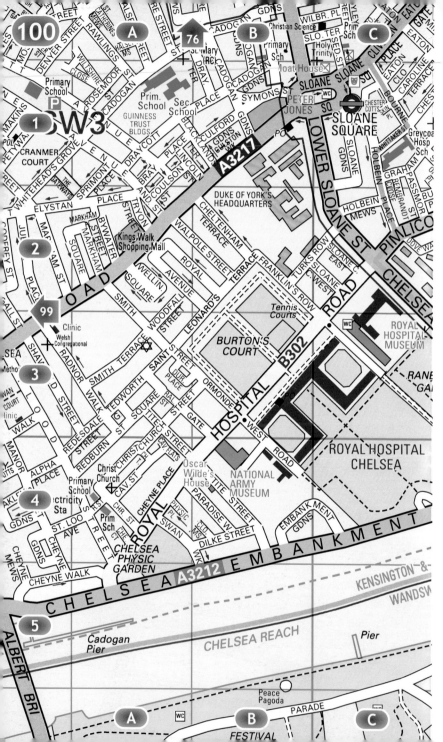

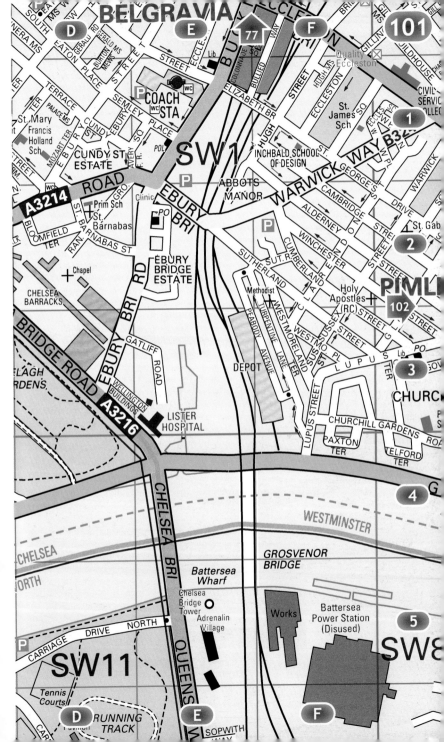

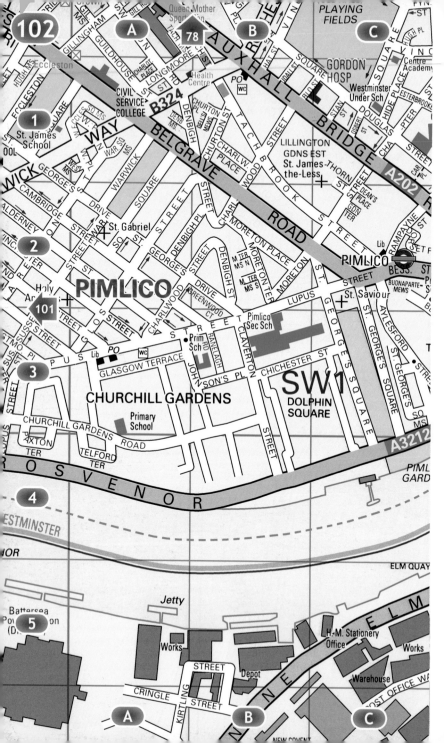

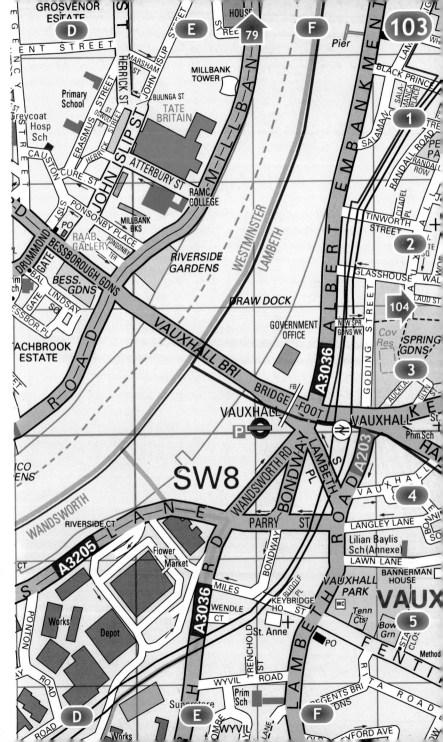

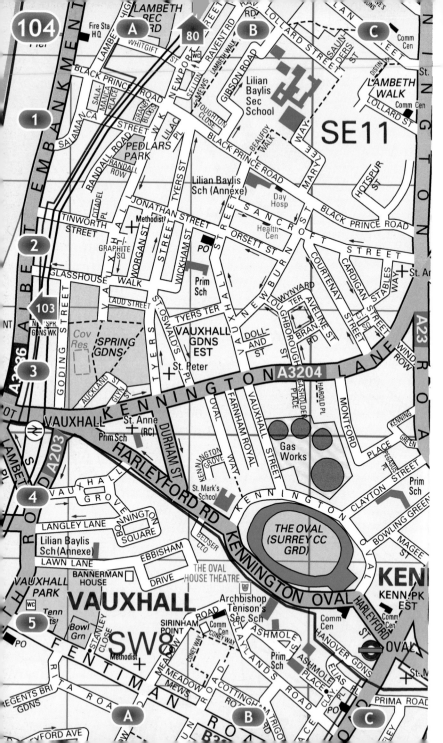

D
E
81
F

1

2

106

3

4

5

BISHOP GDNS ST
OAKDEN ST
Health Centre
GILBERT ST
WILTON ST
RENFREW ROAD
HERALD'S
KEMPSFORD
HOLYOAK RD
DANTE PL
RICHARDSON
HOWELL
PO
MAROE
MAN ST
WINDSOR CLOSE
ST

Philip
WINCOTT
Prim Sch
DRYDEN COURT
KNIGHTS WK
HERALD'S CT
KEMPSFORD
WINCHESTER
HAMPTON ST
STREET
MARLBOROUGH CT
MARBLE
WA

STREET
Prim Sch
GILBERT
KEMP RD
A3204
CRICKETERS CT
CANTERBURY PLACE
CANTERBURY PL
IND EST
CUM MUS & Lib

REEDWORTH STREET
Health Centre
NEWINGTON BUTTS
WESLEY CLO
CANTERBURY PL
PEACOCK ST
CRAMPTON
STREET
W

DENNY STREET
CHESTER WAY
KENNINGTON LANE
A3 ROAD
PENTON
GUINNESS TRUST BLDGS
PEACOCK YD
Prim Sch
ILIFFE STREET
ILIFFE YARD
DENNY CRES
OPAL STREET
St. Mary Newington
STREET
AMELIA
2

WHITE HART ST
COTT ST
OTHELLO CLO
BERRYFIELD RD
MANOR
DE
SE

Lib
nselm
CLEAVER ST
TATE CLO
SEATON CLO
KENNINGTON
ALBERTA
ALBERTA
AMBER
GATE ST
TARVER RD
DEL RD
PLACE
STOPFORD
MARS
PEN

COUNTY COURT
KENNINGS WAY
ALBERTA ST
EST
106
PASLEY CLO

BOWDEN
CLEAVER SQUARE
BRAGANZA STREET
GAZA ST
TA CENTRE
MANOR RD
CHAPTER
3

METHLEY ST
RAVENSDON ST
SOUTHWARK
LAUNE STREET
SHARSTED ST
Primary School
Walworth (City Fm)
ROAD
Prim Sch

WTG PL
IVERTON ST
AULTON PLACE
DODDINGTON GROVE
WESTCOTT
PAUL'S TER
FRED RD
CARTER STREET

STANNARY
VAUXHALL·COLL Kennington Rd Cen
DE
HARMSWORTH ST
TAUNCE ST
DODDING PL
FLEMING RD
LORRIMORE
St. Paul
SQUARE
EGLINGTON
CT
NEY

STANN
RIFLE PL
KENNINGTON PARK PL
COOKS RD
FORSYTH GDNS
GREIG
TER
LORRIMORE
ROAD
4

PO
KENNINGTON PARK
ROYAL ROAD
ST. AGNES PL
COOKS
RD
St. Wilfred (RC)
OLNEY ROAD
SLADE WALK

WC
Tenn Cts
RILEY CLO
OTTO
BRANDON ESTATE
HERON
HILLINGDON
DIGHTON CT

ST
PO
Aspen House School
St. Agnes
BATEMAN HO
MADDOCK WAY
PO
Lib
ST
5

NINGTON
MEADCROFT
CORNISH HO
WALTERS HO
BRAWNE HO
ANDREWS WALK
DALE
CHILLES CT
GROSVENOR

Open Air Pool
SPORTS GROUND
ST. AGNES PLACE
KENNINGTON PARK
CRUDEN HO
PRESCOTT HO
STREET
RUSKIN
GROSVENOR

Mark
BOLTON CRES
HILLINGDON ROAD
BETHWIN

CAMBE
D
E
F

Evangelical

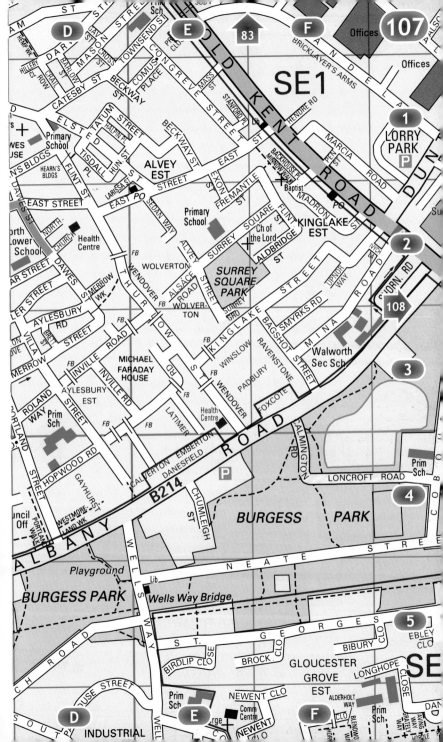

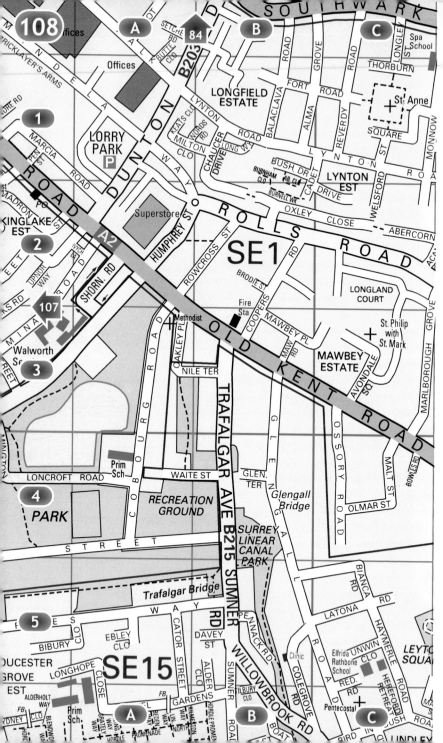

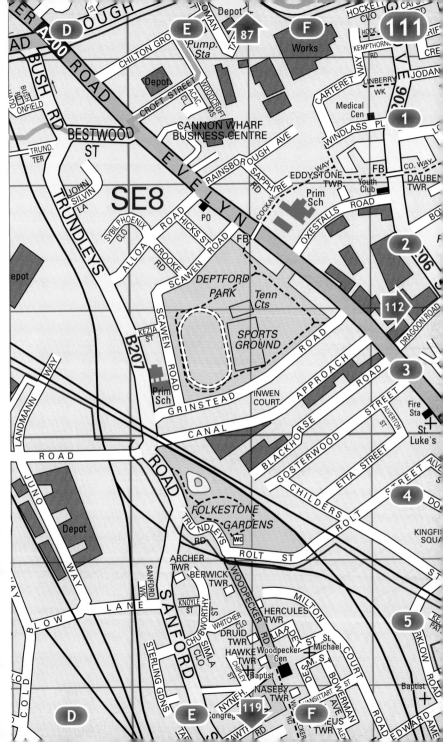

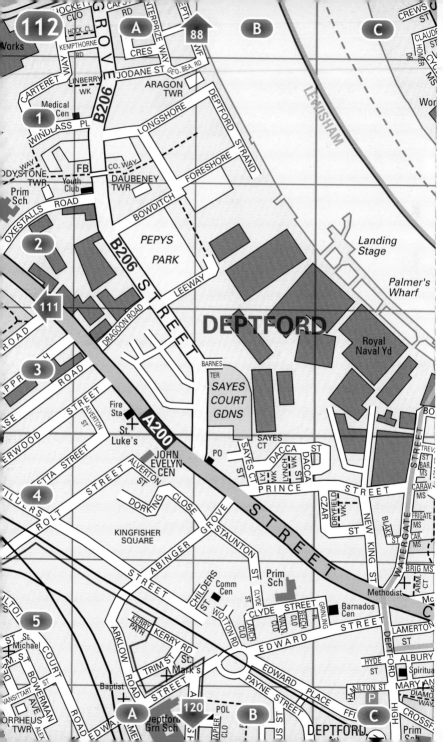

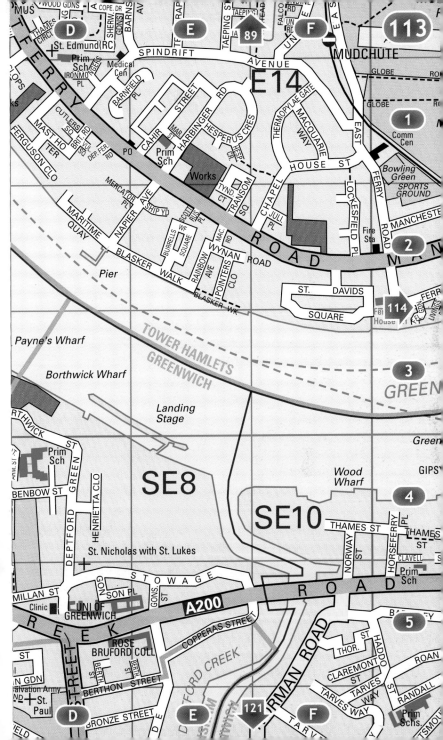

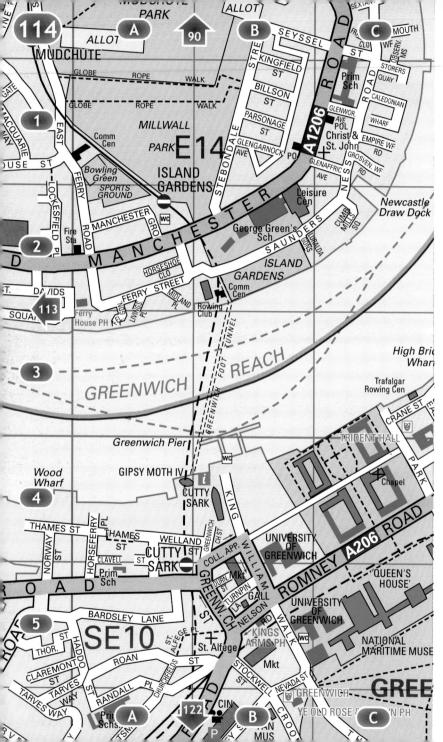

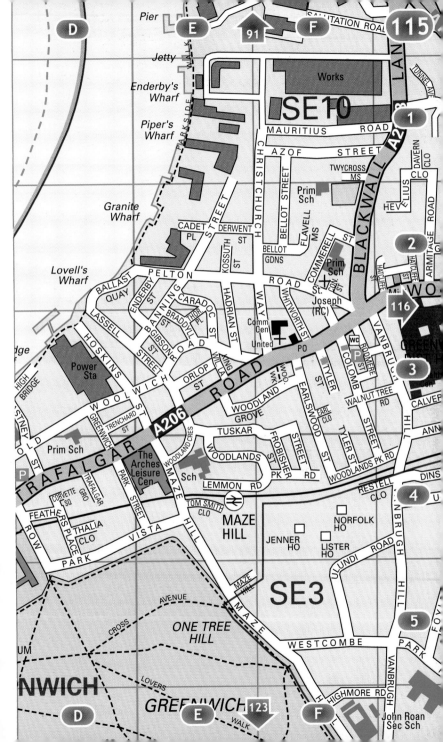

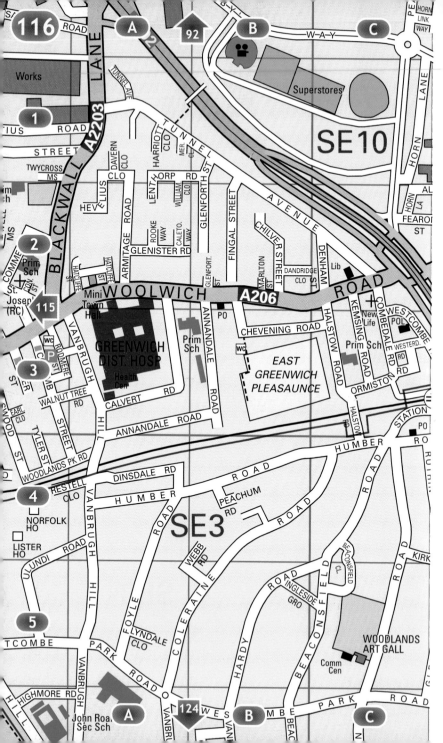

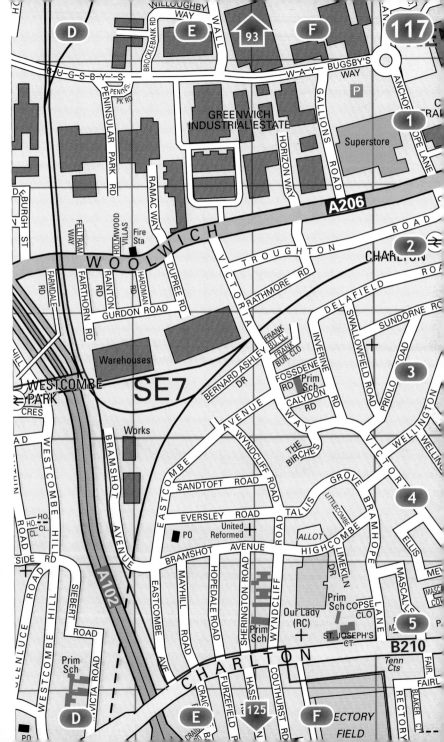

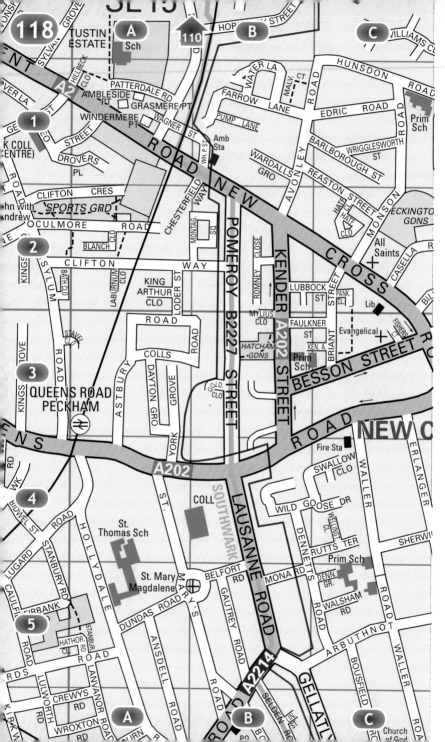

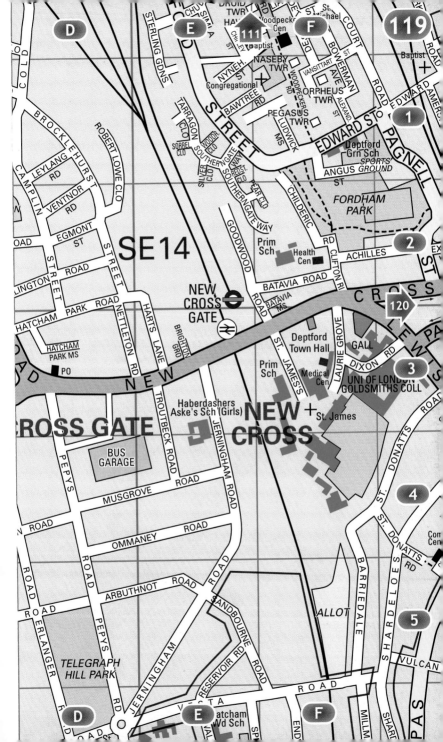

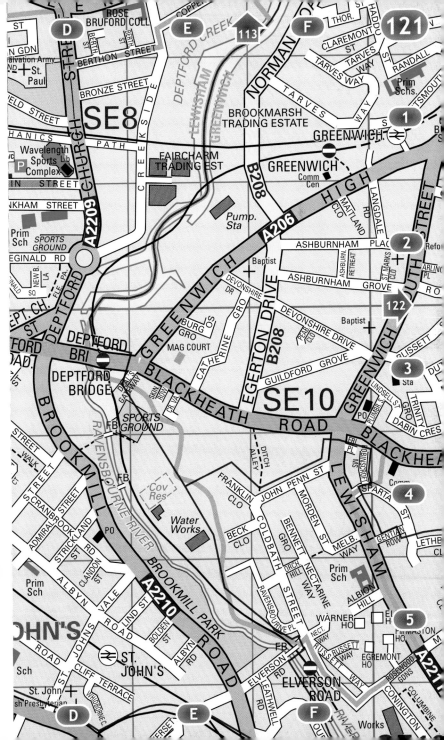

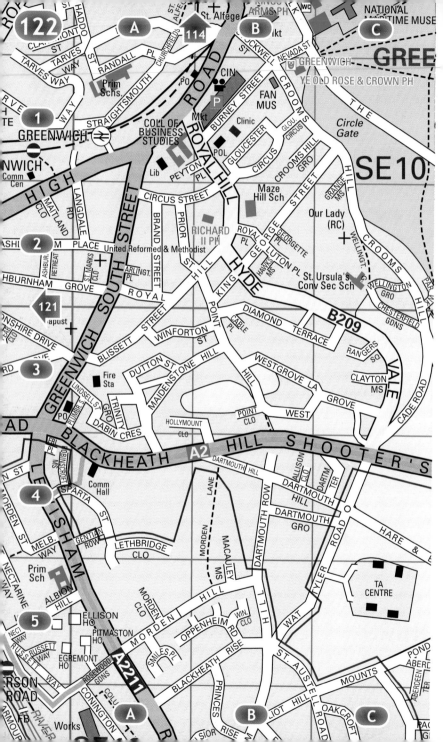

D **E** HILL F WESTCOMBE

123

GREENWICH

115

GREENWICH

LOVERS WALK

HIGHMORE RD

John Roan Sec Sch

FLAMSTEED HOUSE
(OLD ROYAL OBSERVATORY)

PARK

MAZE

FIELDS

1

AVENUE

BLACKHEATH

GREAT CROSS AVENUE

AVENUE

VANB

VAN B

HILL

THE GARDENS

2

Croom's
Hill Gate

Cov
Res

THE WILDERNESS
(DEER PARK)

124

Tenn
Cts

AVENUE

BOWER

B21

CONDUIT AVENUE

CHESTERFIELD

RANGER'S
HOUSE

Blackheath Gate

CHARLTON

DUKE HUMPHREY RD

ROAD

3

GENERAL WOLFE ROAD

WC

WALK

HILL

A2

BLACKHEA

4

WHITFIELD ROAD

GOFFERS

LONG

POND

ROAD

ROAD

SE3

DUKE HUMPHREY ROAD

BILLET ROAD

ROAD

TALBOT

PLACE

Prim Sch

ROAD

5

MOUNTS POND
RD

BLACKHEATH
VALE

PRINCE

HARE & BILLET ROAD

THE
ORCHARD

ORCHARD
DR

ORCHARD DR

ROAD

ALL SAINTS DR

ALL SAINTS
DR

All Saints

DEEN TER

ELIOT
VALE

ELIOT PLACE

ELIOT COT

GROTES

GROTES PLACE

TRY

ROYAL PAR

M.V.
MS

PAGODA
DNS

D **E** **F** VALE

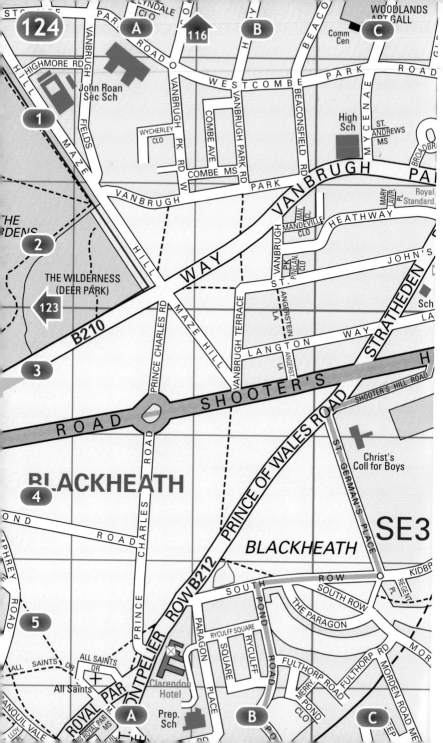

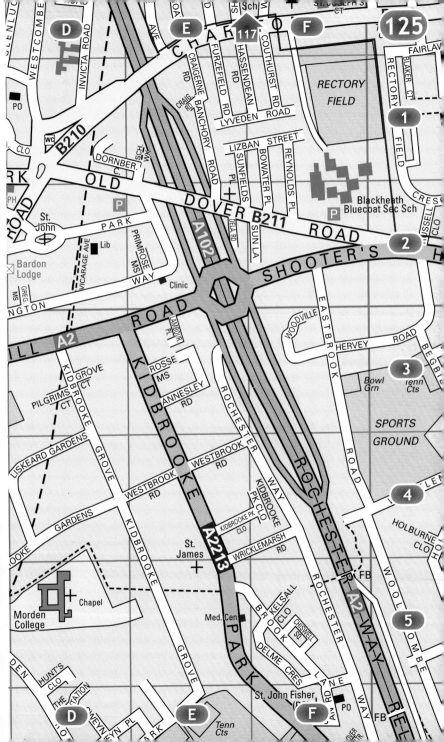

Index to Hospitals

Note

Those hospitals shown in red have an Accident and Emergency Department.

Index to Railway Stations

Index to London Regional Transport Stations

Index to Places of Interest

Index to Street Names

Note

The figures and letters following a street name indicate the Postal District, page and map square where the name can be found.

General Abbreviations

All.	Alley	Est.	Estate	Pas.	Passage
Allot.	Allotments	Ex.	Exchange	Pav.	Pavilion
Amb.	Ambulance	Exhib.	Exhibition	Pk.	Park
App.	Approach	F.B.	Footbridge	Pl.	Place
Arc.	Arcade	F.C.	Football Club	Pol.	Police
Av., Ave	Avenue	Fld.	Field	Prec.	Precinct
Bdy.	Broadway	Flds.	Fields	Prim.	Primary
Bk.	Bank	Fm.	Farm	Prom.	Promenade
Bldgs.	Buildings	Gall.	Gallery	Pt.	Point
Boul.	Boulevard	Gar.	Garage	Quad.	Quadrant
Bowl.	Bowling	Gdn./Gdns	Garden/Gardens	R.C.	Roman Catholic
Br., Bri	Bridge	Govt.	Government	Rd.	Road
C. of E.	Church of England	Gra.	Grange	Rds.	Roads
Cath.	Cathedral	Grd.	Ground	Rec.	Recreation
Cem.	Cemetery	Grds.	Grounds	Res.	Reservoir
Cen.	Central, Centre	Grn.	Green	Ri.	Rise
Cft.	Croft	Grns.	Greens	S.	South
Cfts.	Crofts	Gro.	Grove	Sch.	School
Ch.	Church	Gros.	Groves	Sec.	Secondary
Chyd.	Churchyard	Ho.	House	Shop.	Shopping
Cin.	Cinema	Hos.	Houses	Sq.	Square
Circ.	Circus	Hosp.	Hospital	St.	Saint
Cl., Clo	Close	Hts.	Heights	St.	Street
Co.	County	Ind.	Industrial	Sta.	Station
Coll.	College	Int.	International	Sts.	Streets
Comm.	Community	Junct.	Junction	Sub.	Subway
Conv.	Convent	La.	Lane	Swim.	Swimming
Cor.	Corner	Las.	Lanes	T.A.	Territorial Army
Coron.	Coroners	Lib.	Library	T.H.	Town Hall
Cors.	Corners	Lo.	Lodge	Tenn.	Tennis
Cotts.	Cottages	Lwr.	Lower	Ter.	Terrace
Cov.	Covered	Mag.	Magistrates	Thea.	Theatre
Crem.	Crematorium	Mans.	Mansions	Trd.	Trading
Cres.	Crescent	Mem.	Memorial	Twr.	Tower
Ct.	Court	Mkt.	Market	Twrs.	Towers
Cts.	Courts	Mkts.	Markets	Uni.	University
Ctyd.	Courtyard	Ms.	Mews	Vil.	Villa, Villas
Dep.	Depot	Mt.	Mount	Vw.	View
Dev.	Development	Mus.	Museum	W.	West
Dr.	Drive	N.	North	Wd.	Wood
Dws.	Dwellings	N.T.	National Trust	Wds.	Woods
E.	East	Nat.	National	Wf.	Wharf
Ed.	Education	P.H.	Public House	Wk.	Walk
Elec.	Electricity	P.O.	Post Office	Wks.	Works
Embk.	Embankment	Par.	Parade	Yd.	Yard

Alderney St. SW1	101	F2
Aldersgate St. EC1	42	A3
Alderson St. W10	31	F1
Aldford St. W1	52	C4
Aldgate EC3	59	F1
Aldgate Ave. E1	44	A5
Aldgate High St. EC3	60	A1
Aldine Ct. W12	46	B5
Aldine Pl. W12	70	B1
Aldine St. W12	70	B1
Aldridge Rd. Vil. W11	32	B4
Aldsworth Clo. W9	33	E2
Aldwych WC2	56	A2
Alexa Ct. W8	73	D5
Alexander Ms. W2	33	E5
Alexander Pl. SW7	75	E5
Alexander Sq. SW3	75	E5
Alexander St. W2	33	D5
Alexandra Cotts. SE14	120	B4
Alexandra Est. NW8	6	A5
Alexandra Pl. NW8	6	B5
Alexandra Rd. NW8	6	B4
Alexandra St. SE14	119	F1
Alexis St. SE16	85	D5
Alford Pl. N1	26	B3
Alfred Ms. W1	38	C3
Alfred Pl. WC1	38	C3
Alfred Rd. W2	33	D3
Alice Gilliatt Ct. W14	96	A4
Alice St. SE1	83	E4
Alie St. E1	60	B1
All Saints Dr. SE3	124	A5
All Saints Rd. W11	32	A4
All Saints St. N1	24	A2
All Souls Pl. W1	37	F4
Allen St. W8	73	D3
Allensbury Pl. NW1	11	D4
Allgood St. E2	28	B3
Allhallows La. EC4	58	C3
Allingham St. N1	26	A2
Allington St. SW1	77	F4
Allison Clo. SE10	122	B4
Allitsen Rd. NW8	19	E3
Alloa Rd. SE8	111	D2
Allsop Pl. NW1	36	B2
Alma Gro. SE1	108	B1
Alma Sq. NW8	18	B4
Alma St. NW5	9	F1
Almeida St. N1	13	E4
Almond Rd. SE16	85	F5
Almorah Rd. N1	14	C4
Alperton St. W10	31	F1
Alpha Clo. NW1	19	F5
Alpha Gro. E14	89	D2
Alpha Pl. SW3	99	F4
Alpha Rd. SE14	120	B3
Alpine Rd. SE16	110	C2
Alsace Rd. SE17	107	E2
Alscot Rd. SE1	84	B5
Alscot Way SE1	84	A5
Alverton St. SE8	112	A3
Alvey Est. SE17	107	E1
Alvey St. SE17	107	E2
Alwyne La. N1	13	F3
Alwyne Pl. N1	14	A2
Alwyne Rd. N1	14	A3
Alwyne Sq. N1	14	A1
Alwyne Vil. N1	13	F3
Amazon St. E1	61	E1
Ambassador's Ct. SW1	54	B5
Ambergate St. SE17	105	F2
Amberley Rd. W9	33	D3
Ambrosden Ave. SW1	78	B4
Ambrose St. SE16	85	E5
Amelia St. SE17	106	A2
Amen Cor. EC4	57	F1
Amen Ct. EC4	41	F5
America Sq. EC3	60	A2
America St. SE1	58	A5
Amersham Gro. SE14	120	A1
Amersham Rd. SE14	120	A2
Amersham Vale SE14	120	B1
Amina Way SE16	84	C4
Amor Rd. W6	70	A4
Amoy Pl. E14	64	C1
Ampthill Sq. Est. NW1	22	B3
Ampton Pl. WC1	24	A5
Ampton St. WC1	24	A5
Amsterdam Rd. E14	90	B4
Amwell St. EC1	24	C4
Anchor & Hope La. SE7	93	F4
Anchor St. SE16	85	E5
Anchor Yd. EC1	42	B1
Ancill Clo. W6	95	E5
Anderson St. SW3	100	A2
Andrew Borde St. WC2	39	D5
Andrews Crosse WC2	56	C1
Andrew's Rd. E8	29	E1
Andrews Wk. SE17	105	F5
Angel All. E1	44	B5
Angel Ct. EC2	43	D5
Angel Ct. SW1	54	B5
Angel Ms. N1	25	D3
Angel Pas. EC4	58	C3
Angel Pl. SE1	82	C1
Angel St. EC1	42	A5
Angel Wk. W6	94	A1
Angerstein La. SE3	124	B3
Angler's La. NW5	9	F1
Anglia Ho. E14	63	F1
Angrave Ct. E8	16	B5
Angrave Pas. E8	16	B5
Angus St. SE14	119	F1
Anley Rd. W14	70	C2
Ann Moss Way SE16	86	A3
Anna Clo. E8	16	B5
Annabel Clo. E14	65	E2
Annandale Rd. SE10	116	A3
Annesley Rd. SE3	125	E3
Annette Cres. N1	14	B4
Anning St. EC2	43	F1
Ann's Clo. SW1	76	B2
Ann's Pl. E1	44	A4
Ansdell Rd. SE15	118	A5
Ansdell St. W8	73	F3
Ansdell Ter. W8	73	F3
Anselm Rd. SW6	96	C5
Ansleigh Pl. W11	47	D3
Anthony St. E1	45	F5
Antrim Gro. NW3	8	A1
Antrim Mans. NW3	8	A1
Antrim Rd. NW3	8	A1
Apothecary St. EC4	57	E1
Apple Tree Yd. SW1	54	B4
Appleby Rd. E8	17	D3
Appleby Rd. E16	68	B1
Appleby St. E2	28	A3
Appleford Rd. W10	31	F2
Applegarth Rd. W14	70	C4
Appold St. EC2	43	E3
Apsley Way W1	77	D1
Aquila St. NW8	19	D2
Aquinas St. SE1	57	D5
Aragon Ms. E1	60	C4
Arbour Sq. E1	62	C1

Arbuthnot Rd. SE14	118	C5
Arbutus St. E8	16	A5
Arcade, The EC2	43	E4
Arch St. SE1	82	A4
Archangel St. SE16	87	D2
Archel Rd. W14	96	A4
Archer St. W1	54	C2
Archery Clo. W2	51	F1
Archibald Ms. W1	53	E3
Arden Cres. E14	89	D5
Arden Est. N1	27	E3
Ardleigh Rd. N1	15	E2
Argent St. SE1	81	F1
Argyle Sq. WC1	23	F4
Argyle St. WC1	23	E4
Argyle Wk. WC1	23	E5
Argyle Way SE16	109	D3
Argyll Rd. W8	73	D2
Argyll St. W1	54	A1
Ariel Way W12	46	B4
Arklow Rd. SE14	112	A5
Arlington Ave. N1	26	B2
Arlington Pl. SE10	122	A2
Arlington Rd. NW1	9	E5
Arlington Sq. N1	26	B1
Arlington St. SW1	54	A4
Arlington Way EC1	25	D4
Armada Ct. SE8	112	C5
Armada St. SE8	113	D4
Armitage Rd. SE10	116	A2
Armour Clo. N7	12	A2
Armstrong Rd. SW7	74	C4
Arne St. WC2	55	F1
Arneway St. SW1	79	D4
Arnhem Pl. E14	88	C4
Arnold Circ. E2	28	A5
Arnold Est. SE1	84	B2
Arnside St. SE17	106	B4
Arran Wk. N1	14	A3
Artesian Rd. W2	48	C1
Arthur Ct. W2	33	E5
Arthur St. EC4	59	D2
Artichoke Hill E1	61	E3
Artillery La. E1	43	F4
Artillery Pas. E1	43	F4
Artillery Pl. SW1	78	C4
Artillery Row SW1	78	C4
Artizan St. E1	43	F5
Arundel Gdns. W11	48	A2
Arundel Great Ct. WC2	56	B2
Arundel Pl. N1	12	C2
Arundel Sq. N7	12	C2
Arundel St. WC2	56	B2
Ash Gro. E8	29	F1
Ashbridge St. NW8	35	E2
Ashburn Gdns. SW7	74	A5
Ashburn Pl. SW7	74	A5
Ashburnham Gro. SE10	121	F2
Ashburnham Pl. SE10	121	F2
Ashburnham Retreat SE10	121	F2
Ashby Gro. N1	14	B3
Ashby St. EC1	25	F5
Ashcroft Sq. W6	94	A1
Ashdown Wk. E14	89	D5
Asher Way E1	61	D4
Ashfield St. E1	45	E4
Ashford St. N1	27	E4
Ashland Pl. W1	36	C3
Ashley Gdns. SW1	78	B4
Ashley Pl. SW1	78	A4
Ashmead Rd. SE8	120	C5
Ashmill St. NW1	35	E3
Ashmole Pl. SW8	104	B5
Ashmole St. SW8	104	B5
Ashmore Rd. W9	32	B1
Ashton St. E14	66	B2
Ashwin St. E8	16	A1
Aske St. N1	27	E4
Aspen Way E14	65	D3
Aspenlea Rd. W6	94	C4
Aspinden Rd. SE16	85	F5
Assam St. E1	44	C5
Assata Ms. N1	13	F1
Astbury Rd. SE15	118	A3
Aste St. E14	90	A2
Astell St. SW3	99	F2
Asteys Row N1	13	F4
Astrop Ms. W6	70	A3
Astrop Ter. W6	70	A2
Astwood Ms. SW7	73	F5
Athens Gdns. W9	32	C2
Atherstone Ms. SW7	74	B5
Athlone St. NW5	9	D1
Athol Sq. E14	66	B1
Atlas Ms. E8	16	B1
Atlas Ms. N7	12	B2
Atterbury St. SW1	103	E1
Attneave St. WC1	24	C5
Aubrey Pl. NW8	18	A3
Aubrey Rd. W8	48	B5
Aubrey Wk. W8	48	B5
Auckland St. SE11	104	A3
Auden Pl. NW1	8	C5
Audley Dr. E16	69	E4
Audley Sq. W1	53	D4
Audrey St. E2	29	D2
Augustine Rd. W14	70	C4
Augustus St. NW1	21	F3
Aulton Pl. SE11	105	D3
Auriol Rd. W14	95	E1
Austin Friars EC2	43	D5
Austin Friars Pas. EC2	43	D5
Austin Friars Sq. EC2	43	D5
Austin St. E2	28	A5
Austral St. SE11	81	E5
Ave Maria La. EC4	57	F1
Avebury Ct. N1	26	C1
Avebury St. N1	26	C1
Aveline St. SE11	104	C3
Avenue, The SE10	122	C1
Avenue Clo. NW8	19	F1
Avenue Rd. NW3	6	C4
Avenue Rd. NW8	7	D4
Averill St. W6	95	D5
Avery Fm. Row SW1	101	E1
Avery Row W1	53	F2
Avon Pl. SE1	82	B2
Avondale Pk. Gdns. W11	47	E3
Avondale Pk. Rd. W11	47	E2
Avondale Sq. SE1	108	C3
Avonley Rd. SE14	118	B2
Avonmore Pl. W14	71	F5
Avonmore Rd. W14	71	F5
Avonmouth St. SE1	82	A3
Aybrook St. W1	36	C4
Aylesbury Est. SE17	107	D3
Aylesbury Rd. SE17	107	D3
Aylesbury St. EC1	41	E2
Aylesford St. SW1	102	C3

Aylton Est. SE16	86 B2
Aylwyn Est. SE1	83 F3
Aynhoe Rd. W14	71 D5
Ayres St. SE1	82 B1
Ayrton Rd. SW7	74 C3
Azof St. SE10	115 F1

B

Babmaes St. SW1	54 C4
Bacchus Wk. N1	27 E3
Baches St. N1	27 D5
Back Ch. La. E1	61 D1
Back Hill EC1	40 C2
Backhouse Pl. SE17	107 F1
Bacon Gro. SE1	84 A4
Bacon St. E1	44 B1
Bacon St. E2	44 B1
Baden Pl. SE1	82 C1
Badminton Ms. E16	69 D4
Bagshot St. SE17	107 F3
Baildon St. SE8	120 C2
Bainbridge St. WC1	39 D5
Baird St. EC1	42 B1
Baker St. NW1	36 B2
Baker St. W1	36 B3
Baker's Ms. W1	36 C5
Baker's Rents E2	28 A5
Baker's Row EC1	40 C2
Balaclava Rd. SE1	108 B1
Balcombe St. NW1	36 A1
Balderton St. W1	53 D1
Baldwin St. EC1	26 C5
Baldwin Ter. N1	26 A2
Baldwin's Gdns. EC1	40 C3
Balfe St. N1	23 F3
Balfour Ho. W10	31 D3
Balfour Ms. W1	53 D4
Balfour Pl. W1	53 D3
Balfour St. SE17	82 C5
Balkan Wk. E1	61 E3
Ballast Quay SE10	115 D2
Balliol Rd. W10	30 C5
Balls Pond Pl. N1	15 D1
Balls Pond Rd. N1	15 D1
Balmes Rd. N1	15 D5
Balmoral Gro. N7	12 A2
Balniel Gate SW1	103 D2
Baltic Ct. SE16	87 D1
Baltic St. E. EC1	42 A2

Baltic St. W. EC1	42 A2
Bamborough Gdns. W12	70 B2
Banbury Ct. WC2	55 E2
Banchory Rd. SE3	125 E1
Bank End SE1	58 B4
Bankside SE1	58 A3
Banner St. EC1	42 B2
Bannerman Ho. SW8	104 A5
Banning St. SE10	115 E3
Banyard Rd. SE16	85 F4
Baptist Gdns. NW5	8 C1
Barandon Wk. W11	47 D2
Barb Ms. W6	70 B4
Barbara Brosnan Ct. NW8	18 C3
Barbican, The EC2	42 A3
Barbon Clo. WC1	39 F3
Bard Rd. W10	46 C2
Bardsey Wk. N1	14 B2
Bardsley La. SE10	114 A5
Barfett St. W10	32 A1
Barford St. N1	25 D1
Barge Ho. St. SE1	57 D4
Baring St. N1	26 C1
Bark Pl. W2	49 E2
Barkantine Shop. Par.,The E14	88 C2
Barker Dr. NW1	10 B4
Barker St. SW10	98 A4
Barkston Gdns. SW5	97 E1
Barkworth Rd. SE16	109 F3
Barlborough St. SE14	118 C1
Barlby Gdns. W10	30 C2
Barlby Rd. W10	30 B4
Barley Mow Pas. EC1	41 F4
Barleycorn Way E14	64 A2
Barlow Pl. W1	53 F3
Barlow St. SE17	107 D1
Barnaby Pl. SW7	98 C1
Barnardo St. E1	62 C1
Barnard's Inn EC1	40 C5
Barnby St. NW1	22 B4
Barnes St. E14	63 E1
Barnes Ter. SE8	112 B3
Barnet Gro. E2	28 C4
Barnett St. E1	45 E5

Barnfield Pl. E14	113 D1
Barnham St. SE1	83 F1
Barnsbury Gro. N7	12 B3
Barnsbury Pk. N1	12 C3
Barnsbury Rd. N1	24 C2
Barnsbury Sq. N1	12 C3
Barnsbury St. N1	13 D4
Barnsbury Ter. N1	12 B4
Barnsdale Ave. E14	89 D5
Barnsdale Rd. W9	32 B1
Barnsley St. E1	45 F1
Barnston Wk. N1	13 F5
Barnwood Clo. W9	33 E2
Baron St. N1	24 C3
Baroness Rd. E2	28 B4
Barons Ct. Rd. W14	95 F2
Barons Keep W14	95 E2
Barons Pl. SE1	81 D2
Barque Ms. SE8	112 C4
Barrett St. W1	53 D1
Barrie Est. W2	50 C2
Barriedale SE14	119 F5
Barrow Hill Rd. NW8	19 E3
Barter St. WC1	39 F4
Bartholomew Clo. EC1	42 A4
Bartholomew La. EC2	59 D1
Bartholomew Pl. EC1	42 A4
Bartholomew Rd. NW5	10 B2
Bartholomew Sq. E1	45 F1
Bartholomew Sq. EC1	42 B1
Bartholomew St. SE1	83 D4
Bartholomew Vil. NW5	10 A2
Bartle Rd. W11	47 D1
Bartlett Ct. EC4	41 D5
Bartletts Pas. EC4	41 D5
Barton Rd. W14	95 E3
Barton St. SW1	79 E3
Basil St. SW3	76 A3
Basing Ho. Yd. E2	27 F4
Basing Pl. E2	27 F4
Basing St. W11	32 A5
Basinghall Ave. EC2	42 C4

Basinghall St. EC2	42	C5
Basire St. N1	14	A5
Bassett Rd. W10	31	D5
Bassett St. NW5	8	C1
Bastwick St. EC1	42	A1
Batavia Ms. SE14	119	F2
Batavia Rd. SE14	119	F2
Batchelor St. N1	25	D2
Bate St. E14	64	B2
Bateman Ho. SE17	105	E5
Bateman St. W1	54	C1
Bateman's Bldgs. W1	54	C1
Bateman's Row EC2	43	F1
Bath Ct. EC1	40	C2
Bath St. EC1	26	B5
Bath Ter. SE1	82	A4
Bathurst Ms. W2	51	D2
Bathurst St. W2	51	D2
Batoum Gdns. W6	70	B3
Battishill St. N1	13	E4
Battle Bri. La. SE1	59	E5
Battle Bri. Rd. NW1	23	E3
Batty St. E1	45	D5
Bawtree Rd. SE14	119	E1
Baxendale St. E2	28	C4
Baxter Rd. N1	15	D2
Bayford Ms. E8	17	F4
Bayford St. E8	17	F4
Bayham Pl. NW1	22	B1
Bayham St. NW1	10	A5
Bayley St. WC1	38	C4
Baylis Rd. SE1	80	C2
Baynes Ms. NW3	7	D1
Baynes St. NW1	10	B4
Bayonne Rd. W6	95	E5
Bayswater Rd. W2	49	E3
Bazely St. E14	66	A2
Beaconsfield Clo. SE3	116	C4
Beaconsfield Rd. SE3	116	B5
Beaconsfield Rd. SE17	107	D3
Beaconsfield Ter. Rd. W14	71	E4
Beadon Rd. W6	94	A1
Beak St. W1	54	B2
Bear All. EC4	41	E5
Bear Gdns. SE1	58	A4
Bear La. SE1	57	F5
Bear St. WC2	55	D2

Beatrice Pl. W8	73	E4
Beatrice Rd. SE1	109	D1
Beatson Wk. SE16	63	E4
Beatty St. NW1	22	A2
Beauchamp Pl. SW3	75	F3
Beauchamp St. EC1	40	C4
Beaufort Gdns. SW3	75	F3
Beaufort Ms. SW6	96	B4
Beaufort St. SW3	99	D5
Beaufoy Wk. SE11	104	B1
Beaulieu Ave. E16	69	E4
Beaumont Ave. W14	96	A2
Beaumont Cres. W14	96	A2
Beaumont Ms. W1	37	D3
Beaumont Pl. W1	38	B1
Beaumont St. W1	37	D3
Beaumont Wk. NW3	8	B3
Beccles St. E14	64	B2
Beck Clo. SE13	121	E4
Beck Rd. E8	17	E5
Becket St. SE1	82	C3
Beckford Pl. SE17	106	B3
Beckway St. SE17	107	E1
Bedale St. SE1	58	C5
Bedford Ave. WC1	39	D4
Bedford Ct. WC2	55	E3
Bedford Gdns. W8	48	C5
Bedford Pl. W1	38	B3
Bedford Pl. WC1	39	E3
Bedford Row WC1	40	B3
Bedford Sq. WC1	39	D4
Bedford St. WC2	55	E2
Bedford Way WC1	39	D2
Bedfordbury WC2	55	E2
Bedser Clo. SE11	104	B4
Bedwin Way SE16	109	E3
Beech Clo. SE8	112	B5
Beech St. EC2	42	A3
Beechwood Rd. E8	16	A2
Beehive Clo. E8	16	A3
Beehive Pas. EC3	59	E1
Beeston Pl. SW1	77	F4
Bekesbourne St. E14	63	E1
Belfort Rd. SE15	118	B5
Belgrave Ms. N. SW1	76	C2

Belgrave Ms. S. SW1	77	D3
Belgrave Ms. W. SW1	76	C3
Belgrave Pl. SW1	77	D3
Belgrave Rd. SW1	102	A1
Belgrave Sq. SW1	76	C3
Belgrave St. E1	63	D1
Belgrave Yd. SW1	77	E4
Belgrove St. WC1	23	F4
Belitha Vil. N1	12	C3
Bell Inn Yd. EC3	59	D1
Bell La. E1	44	A4
Bell La. E16	68	C4
Bell St. NW1	35	E3
Bell Wf. La. EC4	58	B2
Bell Yd. WC2	56	C1
Bellamy Clo. E14	88	C1
Bellamy Clo. W14	96	B3
Bellot Gdns. SE10	115	F2
Bellot St. SE10	115	F2
Belmont St. NW1	9	D3
Belsize Ave. NW3	7	D1
Belsize Cres. NW3	7	D1
Belsize Gro. NW3	7	F1
Belsize La. NW3	6	C2
Belsize Pk. NW3	6	C2
Belsize Pk. Gdns. NW3	7	D1
Belsize Pk. Ms. NW3	7	D1
Belsize Pl. NW3	7	D1
Belsize Sq. NW3	7	D1
Belsize Ter. NW3	7	D1
Belvedere Bldgs. SE1	81	F2
Belvedere Pl. SE1	81	F2
Belvedere Rd. SE1	80	B1
Bemerton Est. N1	11	F4
Bemerton St. N1	12	A5
Ben Smith Way SE16	85	D3
Benbow St. SE8	113	D4
Bendall Ms. NW1	35	F3
Benjamin Clo. E8	29	D1
Benjamin St. EC1	41	E3
Bennet's Hill EC4	57	F2
Bennett Gro. SE13	121	F4
Bennett St. SW1	54	A4
Bennetts Yd. SW1	79	D4
Benson Quay E1	62	A3
Bentinck Ms. W1	37	D5
Bentinck Pl. NW8	19	E3

Bracklyn St. N1	26	C2
Brad St. SE1	57	D5
Braddyll St. SE10	115	E3
Braden St. W9	33	E2
Bradenham Clo. SE17	106	C4
Bradfield Rd. E16	93	D1
Bradley Clo. N7	11	F2
Bradley's Clo. N1	25	D2
Brady St. E1	45	E2
Braes St. N1	13	F3
Braganza St. SE17	105	E3
Braham St. E1	60	B1
Braidwood St. SE1	59	E5
Bramber Rd. W14	96	A4
Bramcote Gro. SE16	110	A2
Bramerton St. SW3	99	E4
Bramham Gdns. SW5	97	E2
Bramhope La. SE7	117	F4
Bramley Rd. W10	47	D2
Bramshot Ave. SE7	117	D4
Bramwell Ms. N1	12	B5
Branch Pl. N1	15	D5
Branch Rd. E14	63	E2
Brand St. SE10	122	A2
Brandon Est. SE17	105	F5
Brandon Rd. N7	11	E3
Brandon St. SE17	106	B1
Brangton Rd. SE11	104	B3
Brass Tally All. SE16	87	D2
Bratley St. E1	44	C2
Bravington Pl. W9	32	A1
Brawne Ho. SE17	105	F5
Bray NW3	7	F3
Bray Cres. SE16	86	C1
Bray Dr. E16	68	B2
Bray Pas. E16	68	C2
Bray Pl. SW3	100	A1
Brayfield Ter. N1	12	C4
Bread St. EC4	58	B2
Bream's Bldgs. EC4	40	C5
Brechin Pl. SW7	98	B1
Brecon Rd. W6	95	F5
Breezers Hill E1	61	D3
Bremner Rd. SW7	74	B3
Brendon St. W1	35	F5
Bressenden Pl. SW1	77	F3
Brettell St. SE17	107	D3
Brewer St. W1	54	B2
Brewer's Grn. SW1	78	B3
Brewers Hall Gdns. EC2	42	B4
Brewery Rd. N7	11	E3
Brewhouse La. E1	61	F5
Brewhouse Wk. SE16	63	E5
Brewhouse Yd. EC1	41	E1
Brewster Gdns. W10	30	A3
Brewster Ho. E14	64	B2
Briant St. SE14	118	C3
Briar Wk. W10	31	F1
Briary Clo. NW3	7	E3
Brick Ct. EC4	56	C1
Brick La. E1	28	B5
Brick La. E2	44	B2
Brick St. W1	53	E5
Bricklayer's Arms SE1	83	F5
Bride Ct. EC4	57	E1
Bride La. EC4	57	E1
Bride St. N7	12	B2
Bridewain St. SE1	84	A3
Bridewell Pl. E1	61	F5
Bridewell Pl. EC4	57	E1
Bridford Ms. W1	37	F3
Bridge App. NW1	8	C3
Bridge Ave. W6	94	A2
Bridge Ho. Quay E14	66	B5
Bridge Meadows SE14	110	C4
Bridge Pl. SW1	77	F5
Bridge St. SW1	79	E2
Bridge Vw. W6	94	A2
Bridge Yd. SE1	59	D4
Bridgefoot SE1	103	F3
Bridgeland Rd. E16	69	D2
Bridgeman Rd. N1	12	A4
Bridgeman St. NW8	19	E3
Bridgeport Pl. E1	61	D4
Bridgewater Sq. EC2	42	A3
Bridgewater St. EC2	42	A3
Bridgeway St. NW1	22	B3
Bridle La. W1	54	B2
Bridport Pl. N1	27	D2
Bridstow Pl. W2	33	D5
Brig Ms. SE8	112	C5
Brightlingsea Pl. E14	64	A2
Brighton Gro. SE14	119	E3
Brill Pl. NW1	23	D3
Brindley St. SE14	120	A4
Brinklow Ho. W2	33	D4
Brinsley St. E1	61	F1
Brinton Wk. SE1	57	E5
Briset St. EC1	41	E3
Bristol Gdns. W9	33	F2
Bristol Ms. W9	33	F2
Britannia Gate E16	69	D4
Britannia Rd. E14	113	D1
Britannia Row N1	13	F5
Britannia St. WC1	24	A4
Britannia Wk. N1	26	C4
Britten St. SW3	99	E3
Britten's Ct. E1	61	E3
Britton St. EC1	41	E2
Broad Ct. WC2	55	F1
Broad La. EC2	43	E4
Broad Sanctuary SW1	79	D2
Broad St. Ave. EC2	43	E4
Broad St. Pl. EC2	43	D4
Broad Wk. NW1	21	D2
Broad Wk. W1	52	C4
Broad Wk., The W8	74	A1
Broad Yd. EC1	41	E2
Broadbent St. W1	53	E2
Broadbridge Clo. SE3	124	C1
Broadfield La. NW1	11	E4
Broadgate Circle EC2	43	E3
Broadhurst Clo. NW6	6	A2
Broadley St. NW8	35	D3
Broadley Ter. NW1	35	F2
Broadmayne SE17	106	C2
Broadstone Pl. W1	36	C4
Broadwall SE1	57	D4
Broadway SW1	78	C3
Broadway Mkt. E8	29	E1
Broadwick St. W1	54	B2
Brocas Clo. NW3	7	F3
Brockham St. SE1	82	B3
Brocklebank Rd. SE7	117	E1
Brocklehurst St. SE14	119	D1
Brockley Gdns. SE4	120	A5
Brodie St. SE1	108	B2

Campden Hill Rd. W8	48 C4	
Campden Hill Sq. W8	48 B4	
Campden Ho. Clo. W8	73 D1	
Campden St. W8	48 C5	
Camperdown St. E1	60 B1	
Camplin St. SE14	119 D1	
Canada Est. SE16	86 B3	
Canada Sq. E14	65 E4	
Canada St. SE16	86 C2	
Canal App. SE8	111 E3	
Canal Clo. W10	31 D1	
Canal Gro. SE15	109 D4	
Canal St. SE5	106 C5	
Canal Wk. N1	15 D5	
Canal Way NW1	9 D5	
Canal Way W10	30 C1	
Canal Way Wk. W10	31 E1	
Canary Wf. E14	65 D4	
Candover St. W1	38 A4	
Canfield Pl. NW6	6 A2	
Canning Pas. W8	74 A3	
Canning Pl. W8	74 A3	
Canning Pl. Ms. W8	74 A3	
Cannon Dr. E14	64 C3	
Cannon St. EC4	58 A1	
Cannon St. Rd. E1	45 E5	
Cannon Wf. Business Cen. SE8	111 E1	
Canon Beck Rd. SE16	86 B1	
Canon Row SW1	79 E1	
Canon St. N1	26 A1	
Canonbury Cres. N1	14 A3	
Canonbury Gro. N1	14 A3	
Canonbury La. N1	13 E3	
Canonbury Pk. N. N1	14 A2	
Canonbury Pk. S. N1	14 A2	
Canonbury Pl. N1	13 F2	
Canonbury Rd. N1	13 E2	
Canonbury Sq. N1	13 F3	
Canonbury St. N1	14 A3	
Canonbury Vil. N1	13 F4	
Canonbury Yd. N1	14 B5	
Canrobert St. E2	29 E3	
Cantelowes Rd. NW1	11 D2	
Canterbury Pl. SE17	105 F1	
Canton St. E14	64 C1	
Canute Gdns. SE16	86 C5	
Canvey St. SE1	57 F4	
Cape Yd. E1	61 D4	
Capel Ct. EC2	59 D1	
Capener's Clo. SW1	76 C2	
Capland St. NW8	35 D1	
Capper St. WC1	38 B2	
Capstan Rd. SE8	88 A5	
Capstan Sq. E14	90 B2	
Capstan Way SE16	63 F5	
Capulet Ms. E16	69 D4	
Caradoc Clo. W2	32 C5	
Caradoc St. SE10	115 E2	
Caravel Ms. SE8	112 C4	
Carburton St. W1	37 F3	
Cardale St. E14	90 A3	
Cardigan St. SE11	104 C2	
Cardigan Wk. N1	14 B3	
Cardinal Bourne St. SE1	83 D4	
Cardington St. NW1	22 B4	
Carey La. EC2	42 A5	
Carey Pl. SW1	102 C1	
Carey St. WC2	56 B1	
Carfree Clo. N1	13 D3	
Carlisle Ave. EC3	60 A1	
Carlisle La. SE1	80 B4	
Carlisle Ms. NW8	35 D3	
Carlisle Pl. SW1	78 A4	
Carlisle St. W1	54 C1	
Carlisle Wk. E8	16 A2	
Carlos Pl. W1	53 D2	
Carlow St. NW1	22 A2	
Carlton Gdns. SW1	54 C5	
Carlton Hill NW8	18 A1	
Carlton Ho. Ter. SW1	54 C5	
Carlton St. SW1	54 C3	
Carlton Twr. Pl. SW1	76 B3	
Carlyle Sq. SW3	99 D3	
Carmel Ct. W8	73 E1	
Carmelite St. EC4	57 D2	
Carnaby St. W1	54 A1	
Carnegie St. N1	24 A1	
Carnoustie Dr. N1	12 A4	
Carol St. NW1	10 A5	
Caroline Clo. W2	49 F3	
Caroline Pl. W2	49 F2	
Caroline Pl. Ms. W2	49 F3	
Caroline St. E1	63 D1	
Caroline Ter. SW1	100 C1	
Caroline Wk. W6	95 E5	
Carpenter St. W1	53 E3	
Carriage Dr. N. SW11	101 D5	
Carrick Ms. SE8	112 C4	
Carrington St. W1	53 E5	
Carter La. EC4	57 F1	
Carter Pl. SE17	106 B3	
Carter St. SE17	106 A4	
Carteret St. SW1	78 C2	
Carteret Way SE8	111 F1	
Carthusian St. EC1	42 A3	
Cartier Circle E14	65 F5	
Carting La. WC2	55 F3	
Carton St. W1	36 B5	
Cartwright Gdns. WC1	23 E5	
Cartwright St. E1	60 B3	
Casella Rd. SE14	118 C2	
Casson St. E1	44 C4	
Castalia Sq. E14	90 A2	
Castellain Rd. W9	33 E1	
Casterton St. E8	17 F2	
Castle Baynard St. EC4	57 F2	
Castle Ct. EC3	59 D1	
Castle La. SW1	78 A3	
Castle Ms. NW1	9 E2	
Castle Pl. NW1	9 F2	
Castle Rd. NW1	9 E2	
Castle Yd. SE1	57 F4	
Castlebrook Clo. SE11	81 E5	
Castlehaven Rd. NW1	9 F2	
Castlereagh St. W1	35 F5	
Castletown Rd. W14	95 F3	
Castor La. E14	65 E3	
Catesby St. SE17	107 D1	
Cathay St. SE16	85 F2	
Cathcart Rd. SW10	97 F4	
Cathcart St. NW5	9 E1	
Cathedral Piazza SW1	78 A4	
Cathedral Pl. EC4	42 A5	

Charterhouse St. EC1	41	E4
Chaseley St. E14	63	E1
Chatham St. SE17	82	C5
Chatsworth Ct. W8	72	C5
Chaucer Dr. SE1	108	B1
Chauntler Clo. E16	69	F1
Cheapside EC2	58	A1
Cheesemans Ter. W14	96	A3
Chelmsford Clo. W6	95	D4
Chelsea Bri. SW1	101	E4
Chelsea Bri. SW8	101	E4
Chelsea Bri. Rd. SW1	100	C2
Chelsea Embk. SW3	99	F5
Chelsea Manor Gdns. SW3	99	F3
Chelsea Manor St. SW3	99	F3
Chelsea Pk. Gdns. SW3	98	C4
Chelsea Sq. SW3	99	D2
Cheltenham Ter. SW3	100	B2
Cheney Rd. NW1	23	E3
Chenies Ms. WC1	38	C2
Chenies Pl. NW1	23	D2
Chenies St. WC1	38	C3
Cheniston Gdns. W8	73	E3
Chepstow Cres. W11	48	C2
Chepstow Pl. W2	49	D2
Chepstow Rd. W2	33	D5
Chepstow Vil. W11	48	B2
Chequer St. EC1	42	B2
Cherbury St. N1	27	D3
Cherry Gdn. St. SE16	85	E2
Chesham Clo. SW1	76	C4
Chesham Ms. SW1	76	C3
Chesham Pl. SW1	76	C4
Chesham St. SW1	76	C4
Cheshire Clo. SE4	120	A5
Cheshire St. E2	44	B1
Chesson Rd. W14	96	A4
Chester Clo. SW1	77	E2
Chester Clo. N. NW1	21	F4
Chester Clo. S. NW1	21	F5
Chester Cotts. SW1	100	C1
Chester Ct. NW1	21	F4
Chester Gate NW1	21	E5
Chester Ms. SW1	77	E3
Chester Pl. NW1	21	E4
Chester Rd. NW1	21	D5
Chester Row SW1	100	C1
Chester Sq. SW1	77	D5
Chester Sq. Ms. SW1	77	E4
Chester St. E2	45	D1
Chester St. SW1	77	D3
Chester Ter. NW1	21	E4
Chester Way SE11	105	D1
Chesterfield Gdns. SE10	122	C2
Chesterfield Gdns. W1	53	E4
Chesterfield Hill W1	53	E4
Chesterfield St. W1	53	E4
Chesterfield Wk. SE10	123	D3
Chesterfield Way SE15	118	A2
Chesterton Rd. W10	31	D4
Chestnut All. SW6	96	B4
Chestnut Ct. SW6	96	B4
Chestnuts, The SE14	120	A3
Chettle Clo. SE1	82	C3
Cheval Pl. SW7	75	F3
Cheval St. E14	88	C3
Chevening Rd. SE10	116	B3
Cheyne Ct. SW3	100	A4
Cheyne Gdns. SW3	99	F4
Cheyne Ms. SW3	99	F4
Cheyne Pl. SW3	100	A4
Cheyne Row SW3	99	E5
Cheyne Wk. SW3	99	F5
Chicheley St. SE1	80	B1
Chichester Rents WC2	40	C5
Chichester Rd. W2	33	F3
Chichester St. SW1	102	B3
Chichester Way E14	90	C5
Chicksand St. E1	44	B4
Chigwell Hill E1	61	E3
Chilcot Clo. E14	65	E1
Childeric Rd. SE14	119	F2
Childers St. SE8	111	F4
Child's Pl. SW5	97	D1
Child's St. SW5	97	D1
Child's Wk. SW5	97	D1
Chiltern St. W1	36	C3
Chilton Gro. SE8	111	D1
Chilton St. E2	44	B1
Chilver St. SE10	116	B2
Chilworth Ms. W2	50	C1
Chilworth St. W2	50	B1
Ching Ct. WC2	55	E1
Chipka St. E14	90	A2
Chipley St. SE14	111	E5
Chippenham Ms. W9	32	C2
Chippenham Rd. W9	32	C2
Chiswell Sq. SE3	125	F5
Chiswell St. EC1	42	C3
Chitty St. W1	38	B3
Choppins Ct. E1	61	F4
Christ Ch. Pas. EC1	41	F5
Christchurch St. SW3	100	A4
Christchurch Ter. SW3	100	A4
Christchurch Way SE10	115	F1
Christian Ct. SE16	64	A5
Christian St. E1	45	D5
Christina St. EC2	43	E1
Christopher Clo. SE16	86	C1
Christopher Pl. NW1	23	D5
Christopher St. EC2	43	D2
Christopher's Ms. W11	47	F4
Chubworthy St. SE14	111	E5
Chumleigh St. SE5	107	E4
Church Ave. NW1	9	F2
Church Clo. W8	73	E1
Church Pl. SW1	54	B3
Church St. NW8	35	D3
Church St. W2	35	D3
Church St. Est. NW8	35	D2

Crinan St. N1   23 F2
Cripplegate St.   42 A3
   EC2
Crisp Rd. W6   94 A3
Crispin St. E1   44 A4
Croft St. SE8   111 E1
Crofters Way NW1   10 C5
Crofts St. E1   60 C3
Crogsland Rd. NW1   8 C3
Cromer St. WC1   23 F5
Crompton St. W2   34 C2
Cromwell Clo. E1   61 D4
Cromwell Cres.   72 C5
   SW7
Cromwell Gdns.   75 D4
   SW7
Cromwell Gro. W6   70 B3
Cromwell Ms. SW7   75 D5
Cromwell Pl. SW7   75 D5
Cromwell Rd. SW5   73 D5
Cromwell Rd. SW7   74 C5
Crondall St. N1   27 E3
Crooke Rd. SE8   111 E2
Crooms Hill SE10   122 B1
Crooms Hill Gro.   122 B1
   SE10
Cropley St. N1   26 C2
Cropthorne Ct. W9   18 B5
Crosby Ct. SE1   82 C1
Crosby Row SE1   82 C1
Crosby Sq. EC3   59 E1
Crosby Wk. E8   16 A1
Cross Ave. SE10   115 D5
Cross Keys Clo. W1   37 D4
Cross Keys Sq. EC1   42 A4
Cross La. EC3   59 E3
Cross St. N1   13 E5
Crossfield Rd. NW3   7 D2
Crossfield St. SE8   120 C1
Crosslet St. SE17   83 D5
Crosslet Vale   121 E3
   SE10
Crossley St. N7   12 C1
Crosswall EC3   60 A2
Croston St. E8   17 D5
Crowder St. E1   61 E2
Crowland Ter. N1   14 C3
Crowline Wk. N1   14 B1
Crown Ct. EC2   58 B1
Crown Ct. WC2   55 F1
Crown Office Row   56 C2
   EC4
Crown Pas. SW1   54 B5
Crown Pl. NW5   9 F1

Crowndale Rd.   22 B2
   NW1
Crowthorne Rd.   46 C1
   W10
Crucifix La. SE1   83 E1
Cruden Ho. SE17   105 E5
Cruden St. N1   25 F1
Cruikshank St.   24 C4
   WC1
Crutched Friars   59 F2
   EC3
Cuba St. E14   88 C1
Cubitt Steps E14   65 D4
Cubitt St. WC1   24 B5
Cubitts Yd. WC2   55 F2
Cudworth St. E1   45 F1
Cuff Pt. E2   28 A4
Culford Gdns.   100 B1
   SW3
Culford Gro. N1   15 E2
Culford Ms. N1   15 E1
Culford Rd. N1   15 E3
Culling Rd. SE16   86 A3
Culloden Clo.   109 D3
   SE16
Cullum St. EC3   59 E2
Culross St. W1   52 C3
Culworth St. NW8   19 E3
Cumberland Clo.   16 A2
   E8
Cumberland Cres.   71 F5
   W14
Cumberland Gdns.   24 B4
   WC1
Cumberland Gate   52 A2
   W1
Cumberland Mkt.   21 F4
   NW1
Cumberland Mkt.   21 F4
   Est. NW1
Cumberland Mills   114 C2
   Sq. E14
Cumberland Pl.   21 E4
   NW1
Cumberland St.   101 F2
   SW1
Cumberland Ter.   21 E3
   NW1
Cumberland Ter.   21 E3
   Ms. NW1
Cumming St. N1   24 B3
Cunard Pl. EC3   59 F1
Cunard Wk. SE16   87 D5
Cundy St. SW1   101 D1

Cundy St. Est.   101 D1
   SW1
Cunningham Pl.   34 C1
   NW8
Cureton St. SW1   103 D1
Curlew St. SE1   84 A1
Curnock Est. NW1   22 A1
Cursitor St. EC4   40 C5
Curtain Rd. EC2   27 F5
Curtis St. SE1   84 A5
Curtis Way SE1   84 A5
Curzon Gate W1   53 D5
Curzon Pl. W1   53 D5
Curzon St. W1   53 D5
Custom Ho. Reach   88 A2
   SE16
Custom Ho. Wk.   59 E3
   EC3
Cut, The SE1   81 D1
Cuthbert St. W2   34 C3
Cutler St. E1   43 F5
Cutlers Gdns. E1   43 F5
Cutlers Sq. E14   113 D1
Cyclops Ms. E14   88 C5
Cygnet St. E1   44 B1
Cynthia St. N1   24 B3
Cyntra Pl. E8   17 F4
Cypress Pl. W1   38 B2
Cyrus St. EC1   41 F1
Czar St. SE8   112 C4

D

Dabin Cres. SE10   122 A3
Dacca St. SE8   112 B4
Dacre St. SW1   78 C3
Dagmar Pas. N1   13 F5
Dagmar Ter. N1   13 F5
Dalby St. NW5   9 E2
Dale Rd. SE17   105 F5
Dale Row W11   47 F1
Daleham Gdns.   6 C1
   NW3
Daleham Ms. NW3   7 D1
Dalehead NW1   22 A3
Dalemain Ms. E16   69 D4
Dalgarno Gdns.   30 A3
   W10
Dalgarno Way W10   30 A2
Dalgleish St. E14   63 F1
Dallington St. EC1   41 F1
Dalston Cross Shop.   16 A1
   Cen. E8
Dalston La. E8   16 A1

Devonshire Ms. N. W1   37 E3
Devonshire Ms. S. W1   37 E3
Devonshire Ms. W. W1   37 E2
Devonshire Pl. W1   37 D2
Devonshire Pl. W8   73 E4
Devonshire Pl. Ms. W1   37 D2
Devonshire Row EC2   43 F4
Devonshire Row Ms. W1   37 F2
Devonshire Sq. EC2   43 F4
Devonshire St. W1   37 D3
Devonshire Ter. W2   50 B1
Dewey Rd. N1   24 C2
Dewhurst Rd. W14   70 C3
Dewsbury Ter. NW1   9 F5
Diadem Ct. W1   54 C1
Dial Wk., The W8   73 F1
Diamond Ter. SE10   122 B3
Diamond Way SE8   120 C1
Diana Pl. NW1   37 F1
Dibden St. N1   13 F5
Dickens Est. SE1   84 C2
Dickens Est. SE16   84 C3
Dickens Sq. SE1   82 B3
Dighton Ct. SE5   106 A5
Digswell St. N7   13 D1
Dilke St. SW3   100 B4
Dilston Gro. SE16   86 A5
Dingle Gdns. E14   65 D3
Dingley Pl. EC1   26 B5
Dingley Rd. EC1   26 A5
Dinmont St. E2   29 E2
Dinsdale Rd. SE3   116 A4
Disbrowe Rd. W6   95 F5
Discovery Wk. E1   61 E4
Disney Pl. SE1   82 B1
Disney St. SE1   82 B1
Diss St. E2   28 A4
Distaff La. EC4   58 A2
Distillery La. W6   94 B3
Distillery Rd. W6   94 B3
Distin St. SE11   104 C1
Ditch All. SE10   121 F4
Ditchburn St. E14   66 B3
Dixon Clark Ct. N1   13 F2
Dixon Rd. SE14   119 F3
Dixon's All. SE16   85 E2
Dobson Clo. NW6   6 C4
Dock Hill Ave. SE16   87 D1

Dock Rd. E16   68 B3
Dock St. E1   60 C2
Dockers Tanner Rd. E14   88 C4
Dockhead SE1   84 B2
Dockley Rd. SE16   84 C4
Docwra's Bldgs. N1   15 E1
Doddington Gro. SE17   105 E4
Doddington Pl. SE17   105 E4
Dodson St. SE1   81 D2
Dolben St. SE1   57 F5
Dolland St. SE11   104 B3
Dolphin Clo. SE16   86 C1
Dolphin La. E14   65 E3
Dolphin Sq. SW1   102 B3
Dombey St. WC1   40 A3
Domingo St. EC1   42 A1
Dominion St. EC2   43 D3
Donegal St. N1   24 B3
Donne Pl. SW3   75 F5
Doon St. SE1   56 C4
Doric Way NW1   22 C4
Dorking Clo. SE8   112 A4
Dorman Way NW8   6 C5
Dornberg Clo. SE3   125 D1
Dorney NW3   7 F3
Dorrington St. EC1   40 C3
Dorset Bldgs. EC4   57 E1
Dorset Clo. NW1   36 A3
Dorset Est. E2   28 B4
Dorset Ms. SW1   77 E3
Dorset Pl. SW1   102 C2
Dorset Ri. EC4   57 E1
Dorset Sq. NW1   36 A2
Dorset St. W1   36 B4
Doughty Ms. WC1   40 A2
Doughty St. WC1   40 A1
Douglas Est. N1   14 B2
Douglas Rd. N1   14 A3
Douglas St. SW1   102 C1
Douglas Way SE8   120 B2
Douro Pl. W8   73 F3
Douthwaite Sq. E1   61 D4
Dove Ct. EC2   58 C1
Dove Ms. SW5   98 A1
Dove Rd. N1   14 C1
Dove Row E2   28 C1
Dove Wk. SW1   100 C2
Dovehouse St. SW3   99 E2
Dover St. W1   53 F3
Dover Yd. W1   53 F4
Dovercourt Est. N1   15 D2

Dowgate Hill EC4   58 C2
Down St. W1   53 E5
Down St. Ms. W1   53 E5
Downfield Clo. W9   33 E2
Downham Rd. N1   15 D4
Downing St. SW1   79 E1
Downtown Rd. SE16   87 F1
Dowrey St. N1   12 C5
Doyce St. SE1   82 A1
D'Oyley St. SW1   76 C5
Draco St. SE17   106 A4
Dragoon Rd. SE8   112 A3
Drake Clo. SE16   87 D1
Drake St. WC1   40 A4
Drappers Way SE16   85 D5
Drawdock Rd. SE10   67 D5
Draycott Ave. SW3   75 F5
Draycott Pl. SW3   100 A1
Draycott Ter. SW3   100 B1
Drayford Clo. W9   32 B1
Drayson Ms. W8   73 D2
Drayton Gdns. SW10   98 B2
Dreadnought St. SE10   91 F4
Droop St. W10   31 E1
Druid St. SE1   83 F1
Drum St. E1   44 B5
Drummond Cres. NW1   22 C4
Drummond Gate SW1   103 D2
Drummond Rd. SE16   85 E3
Drummond St. NW1   38 A1
Drury La. WC2   39 F5
Dryden Ct. SE11   105 D1
Dryden St. WC2   55 F1
Dryfield Wk. SE8   112 C4
Drysdale Pl. N1   27 F4
Drysdale St. N1   27 F4
Dublin Ave. E8   17 D5
Ducal St. E2   28 B5
Duchess Ms. W1   37 F4
Duchess of Bedford's Wk. W8   72 C2
Duchess St. W1   37 F4
Duchy St. SE1   57 D4
Duck La. W1   54 C1
Dudley St. W2   34 C4
Dudmaston Ms. SW3   99 D2
Duff St. E14   65 E1

Dufferin Ave. EC1	42	C2
Dufferin St. EC1	42	B2
Dufour's Pl. W1	54	B1
Duke Hill Rd. SE1	57	E4
Duke Humphrey Rd. SE3	123	F4
Duke of Wellington Pl. SW1	77	D1
Duke of York St. SW1	54	B4
Duke Shore Pl. E14	64	A3
Duke Shore Wf. E14	63	F3
Duke St. SW1	54	B4
Duke St. W1	37	D5
Duke St. Hill SE1	59	D4
Dukes La. W8	73	D1
Duke's Ms. W1	37	D5
Dukes Pl. EC3	59	F1
Duke's Rd. WC1	23	D5
Duke's Yd. W1	53	D2
Dulford St. W11	47	E2
Dumpton Pl. NW1	8	C4
Dunbridge St. E2	44	C1
Duncan Rd. E8	17	E5
Duncan St. N1	25	E2
Duncan Ter. N1	25	E3
Duncannon St. WC2	55	E3
Dunch St. E1	61	F1
Dundas Rd. SE15	118	A5
Dundee St. E1	61	E5
Dunloe St. E2	28	B3
Dunlop Pl. SE16	84	B4
Dunmore Pt. E2	28	A5
Dunmow Wk. N1	14	A5
Dunnage Cres. SE16	87	F5
Dunns Pas. WC1	39	F5
Dunraven St. W1	52	B2
Dunsany Rd. W14	70	C4
Dunstable Ms. W1	37	D3
Dunster Ct. EC3	59	E2
Dunsterville Way SE1	83	D2
Dunston Rd. E8	28	A1
Dunston St. E8	16	A5
Dunton Rd. SE1	108	A2
Dunworth Ms. W11	32	A5
Duplex Ride SW1	76	B2
Dupree Rd. SE7	117	E2
Durands Wk. SE16	87	F1
Durant St. E2	28	C4
Durham Ho. St. WC2	55	F3
Durham Pl. SW3	100	A3
Durham St. SE11	104	A3
Durham Ter. W2	33	E5
Durnford St. SE10	114	B5
Durward St. E1	45	E3
Durweston Ms. W1	36	B3
Durweston St. W1	36	B4
Duthie St. E14	66	B3
Dutton St. SE10	122	A3
Dyer's Bldgs. EC1	40	C4
Dyott St. WC1	39	D5
Dysart St. EC2	43	E2

E

Eagle Ct. EC1	41	E3
Eagle Ms. N1	15	E2
Eagle Pl. SW1	54	B3
Eagle Pl. SW7	98	B2
Eagle St. WC1	40	A4
Eagle Wf. Rd. N1	26	B2
Eamont St. NW8	19	E2
Eardley Cres. SW5	97	D2
Earl Rd. SE1	108	A2
Earl St. EC2	43	D3
Earlham St. WC2	55	D1
Earls Ct. Gdns. SW5	97	E1
Earls Ct. Rd. SW5	73	D5
Earls Ct. Rd. W8	72	C3
Earls Ct. Sq. SW5	97	E2
Earls Ter. W8	72	B4
Earls Wk. W8	72	C4
Earlsferry Way N1	12	A4
Earlstoke St. EC1	25	E4
Earlston Gro. E9	29	F1
Earlswood Clo. SE10	115	F3
Earlswood St. SE10	115	F3
Early Ms. NW1	9	F5
Earnshaw St. WC2	39	D5
Earsby St. W14	71	F5
Easley's Ms. W1	37	D5
East Ferry Rd. E14	89	F5
East Harding St. EC4	41	D5
East India Dock Rd. E14	64	C1
East La. SE16	84	C2
East Mt. St. E1	45	F3
East Parkside SE10	92	A2
East Pas. EC1	42	A3
East Pier E1	61	E5
East Poultry Ave. EC1	41	E4
East Rd. N1	27	D4
East Row W10	31	F1
East Smithfield E1	60	B3
East St. SE17	106	B2
East Tenter St. E1	60	B1
Eastbourne Ms. W2	34	B5
Eastbourne Ter. W2	34	B5
Eastbrook Rd. SE3	125	F2
Eastcastle St. W1	38	A5
Eastcheap EC3	59	D2
Eastcombe Ave. SE7	117	E4
Eastney St. SE10	114	C3
Easton St. WC1	24	C5
Eaton Clo. SW1	100	C1
Eaton Gate SW1	76	C5
Eaton La. SW1	77	F4
Eaton Ms. N. SW1	76	C4
Eaton Ms. S. SW1	77	E4
Eaton Ms. W. SW1	77	D5
Eaton Pl. SW1	76	C4
Eaton Row SW1	77	E4
Eaton Sq. SW1	77	D5
Eaton Ter. SW1	76	C5
Eaton Ter. Ms. SW1	76	C5
Ebbisham Dr. SW8	104	A5
Ebenezer St. N1	26	C4
Ebley Clo. SE15	108	A5
Ebor St. E1	44	A1
Ebury Bri. SW1	101	E2
Ebury Bri. Est. SW1	101	E2
Ebury Bri. Rd. SW1	101	D3
Ebury Ms. SW1	77	E5
Ebury Ms. E. SW1	77	E4
Ebury Sq. SW1	101	D1
Ebury St. SW1	101	D1
Ecclesbourne Rd. N1	14	B4
Eccleston Bri. SW1	77	F5
Eccleston Ms. SW1	77	D4
Eccleston Pl. SW1	77	E5
Eccleston Sq. SW1	101	F1
Eccleston Sq. Ms. SW1	101	F1
Eccleston St. SW1	77	D4

Epworth St. EC2	43	D2
Erasmus St. SW1	103	D1
Erlanger Rd. SE14	118	C4
Errington Rd. W9	32	B1
Errol St. EC1	42	B2
Erskine Ms. NW3	8	B4
Erskine Rd. NW3	8	B4
Esmeralda Rd. SE1	109	D1
Essex Ct. EC4	56	C1
Essex Rd. N1	25	F1
Essex St. WC2	56	C2
Essex Vil. W8	72	C2
Esterbrooke St.	102	C1
SW1		
Ethel Rd. E16	69	E1
Ethel St. SE17	106	B1
Ethnard Rd. SE15	109	E5
Eton Ave. NW3	7	D3
Eton College Rd.	8	B2
NW3		
Eton Ct. NW3	7	D3
Eton Garages NW3	7	F2
Eton Hall NW3	8	B2
Eton Pl. NW3	8	C3
Eton Ri. NW3	8	B2
Eton Rd. NW3	8	B3
Eton Vil. NW3	8	B2
Etta St. SE8	111	F4
Eugenia Rd. SE16	110	B1
Europa Pl. EC1	26	A5
Euston Cen. NW1	38	A1
Euston Gro. NW1	22	C5
Euston Rd. N1	38	C1
Euston Rd. NW1	37	F2
Euston Sq. NW1	22	C5
Euston Sta.	22	C5
Colonnade NW1		
Euston St. NW1	22	B5
Evans Clo. E8	16	B2
Eveline Lowe Est.	84	C4
SE16		
Evelyn Ct. N1	26	C3
Evelyn Fox Ct. W10	30	B4
Evelyn Gdns. SW7	98	C3
Evelyn Rd. E16	69	E4
Evelyn St. SE8	111	E1
Evelyn Wk. N1	26	C3
Evelyn Yd. W1	38	C5
Everilda St. N1	24	B1
Everington St. W6	95	D4
Eversholt St. NW1	22	B2
Eversley Rd. SE7	117	E4
Everton Bldgs.	22	A5
NW1		
Evesham St. W11	46	C3
Ewe Clo. N7	11	F1
Ewer St. SE1	58	A5
Excel Ct. WC2	55	D3
Exchange Arc. EC2	43	F3
Exchange Ct. WC2	55	F3
Exchange Pl. EC2	43	E3
Exchange Sq. EC2	43	E3
Exeter St. WC2	55	F2
Exeter Way SE14	120	A2
Exhibition Clo.	46	A3
W12		
Exhibition Rd. SW7	75	D3
Exmoor St. W10	31	D2
Exmouth Mkt. EC1	40	C1
Exmouth Ms. NW1	22	B5
Exmouth Pl. E8	17	E4
Exon St. SE17	107	E1
Exton St. SE1	56	C5
Eynham Rd. W12	30	A5
Eyre Ct. NW8	18	C2
Eyre St. Hill EC1	40	C2
Ezra St. E2	28	B4

F

Fair St. SE1	83	F1
Faircharm Trd.	121	E1
Est. SE8		
Fairchild Pl. EC2	43	F2
Fairchild St. EC2	43	F2
Fairclough St. E1	61	D1
Fairfax Ms. E16	69	E4
Fairfax Pl. NW6	6	B4
Fairfax Rd. NW6	6	B4
Fairholme Rd. W14	95	F3
Fairholt St. SW7	75	F3
Fairstead Wk. N1	14	A5
Fairthorn Rd. SE7	117	D2
Fakruddin St. E1	45	D2
Falcon Clo. SE1	57	F4
Falcon Way E14	89	F5
Falconberg Ct. W1	39	D5
Falconberg Ms. W1	38	C5
Falkirk St. N1	27	F3
Fallow Ct. SE16	109	D3
Falmouth Rd. SE1	82	B4
Fane St. W14	96	B4
Fann St. EC1	42	A2
Fann St. EC2	42	A2
Fanshaw St. N1	27	E4
Faraday Clo. N7	12	B2
Faraday Rd. W10	31	E3
Fareham St. W1	38	C5
Farm La. SW6	97	D5
Farm Pl. W8	48	C4
Farm St. W1	53	E3
Farmdale Rd.	117	D2
SE10		
Farmer St. W8	48	C4
Farncombe St.	85	D2
SE16		
Farnell Ms. SW5	97	E2
Farnham Pl. SE1	57	F5
Farnham Royal	104	B3
SE11		
Faroe Rd. W14	71	D4
Farrance St. E14	64	C1
Farrell Ho. E1	62	B1
Farrier St. NW1	9	F3
Farrier Wk. SW10	98	A4
Farringdon La. EC1	41	D2
Farringdon Rd. EC1	40	C1
Farringdon St. EC4	41	E5
Farrins Rents SE16	63	E5
Farrow La. SE14	118	B1
Farrow Pl. SE16	87	E3
Farthing All. SE1	84	C2
Farthing Flds. E1	61	F4
Fashion St. E1	44	B4
Fassett Rd. E8	17	D1
Fassett Sq. E8	16	C1
Faulkner St. SE14	118	B3
Faulkner's All. EC1	41	E3
Faunce St. SE17	105	E3
Fawcett St. SW10	98	A5
Fearon St. SE10	116	C2
Feathers Pl. SE10	115	D4
Featherstone St.	42	C1
EC1		
Felix St. E2	29	F2
Fellbrigg St. E1	45	F2
Fellows Ct. E2	28	A3
Fellows Rd. NW3	7	D3
Felltram Way SE7	117	D2
Felstead Gdns.	114	A3
E14		
Felton St. N1	27	D1
Fen Ct. EC3	59	E2
Fen St. E16	68	B2
Fenchurch Ave. EC3	59	E1
Fenchurch Bldgs.	59	F1
EC3		
Fenchurch Pl. EC3	59	F2
Fenchurch St. EC3	59	E2
Fendall St. SE1	83	F4
Fendt Clo. E16	68	B1
Fenelon Pl. W14	96	B1

Goldwing Clo. E16	69	D1
Gomm Rd. SE16	86	A4
Gonson Pl. SE8	113	D5
Gonson St. SE8	113	E5
Goodge Pl. W1	38	B4
Goodge St. W1	38	B4
Goodhart Pl. E14	63	F2
Goodinge Clo. N7	11	E1
Goodman's Stile E1	44	C5
Goodmans Yd. E1	60	A2
Goods Way NW1	23	E2
Goodwin Clo. SE16	84	B4
Goodwins Ct. WC2	55	E2
Goodwood Rd. SE14	119	E2
Gophir La. EC4	58	C2
Gopsall St. N1	27	D1
Gordon Ct. W12	46	A1
Gordon Pl. W8	73	D1
Gordon Sq. WC1	38	C1
Gordon St. WC1	38	C1
Gore St. SW7	74	B3
Gorham Pl. W11	47	E3
Goring St. EC3	43	F5
Gorleston St. W14	71	F5
Gorse Clo. E16	68	C1
Gorsuch Pl. E2	28	A4
Gorsuch St. E2	28	A4
Gosfield St. W1	38	A3
Goslett Yd. WC2	55	D1
Gosset St. E2	28	B5
Gosterwood St. SE8	111	F4
Goswell Rd. EC1	25	E3
Gough Sq. EC4	41	D5
Gough St. WC1	40	B1
Gough Wk. E14	64	C1
Goulston St. E1	44	A5
Govan St. E2	29	D1
Gower Ct. WC1	38	C1
Gower Ms. WC1	39	D4
Gower Pl. WC1	38	B1
Gower St. WC1	38	C2
Gower's Wk. E1	44	C5
Grace Jones Clo. E8	16	C2
Gracechurch St. EC3	59	D2
Grace's All. E1	60	C2
Grafton Cres. NW1	9	E2
Grafton Ms. W1	38	A2
Grafton Pl. NW1	22	C5
Grafton Rd. NW5	9	E1
Grafton St. W1	53	F3

Grafton Way W1	38	A2
Grafton Way WC1	38	B2
Grafton Yd. NW5	9	F2
Graham Rd. E8	16	B1
Graham St. N1	25	F3
Graham Ter. SW1	100	C1
Granary Rd. E1	45	E2
Granary St. NW1	22	C1
Granby Bldgs. SE11	104	A1
Granby St. E2	44	C1
Granby Ter. NW1	22	A3
Grand Ave. EC1	41	F3
Grand Junct. Wf. N1	26	A3
Grand Union Cres. E8	17	D4
Grange, The SE1	84	A3
Grange Ct. E8	16	B3
Grange Ct. WC2	56	B1
Grange Gro. N1	14	A1
Grange Ms. SE10	122	C2
Grange Rd. SE1	83	F4
Grange Wk. SE1	83	F3
Grange Yd. SE1	84	A4
Gransden Ave. E8	17	F4
Grant St. N1	24	C2
Grantbridge St. N1	25	F2
Grantham Pl. W1	53	E5
Granville Ct. N1	15	D5
Granville Pl. W1	52	C1
Granville Sq. WC1	24	B5
Granville St. WC1	24	B5
Grape St. WC2	39	E5
Graphite Sq. SE11	104	A2
Gratton Rd. W14	71	E4
Gravel La. E1	44	A5
Gray St. SE1	81	D2
Grayling Sq. E2	29	D4
Gray's Inn WC1	40	B3
Gray's Inn Pl. WC1	40	B4
Gray's Inn Rd. WC1	23	F4
Gray's Inn Sq. WC1	40	C3
Gray's Yd. W1	37	D5
Great Bell All. EC2	42	C5
Great Castle St. W1	37	F5
Great Cen. St. NW1	36	A3
Great Chapel St. W1	38	C5
Great Ch. La. W6	94	C2
Great College St. SW1	79	E3

Great Cross Ave. SE10	123	E2
Great Cumberland Ms. W1	52	A1
Great Cumberland Pl. W1	36	B5
Great Dover St. SE1	82	C2
Great Eastern St. EC2	27	E5
Great Eastern Wk. EC2	43	E4
Great George St. SW1	79	D2
Great Guildford St. SE1	58	A4
Great James St. WC1	40	A3
Great Marlborough St. W1	54	A1
Great Maze Pond SE1	83	D1
Great New St. EC4	41	D5
Great Newport St. WC2	55	D2
Great Ormond St. WC1	39	F3
Great Percy St. WC1	24	B4
Great Peter St. SW1	78	C4
Great Portland St. W1	37	F3
Great Pulteney St. W1	54	B2
Great Queen St. WC2	55	F1
Great Russell St. WC1	39	D5
Great St. Helens EC3	43	E5
Great St. Thomas Apostle EC4	58	B2
Great Scotland Yd. SW1	55	E5
Great Smith St. SW1	79	D3
Great Suffolk St. SE1	57	F5
Great Sutton St. EC1	41	F2
Great Swan All. EC2	42	C5
Great Titchfield St. W1	38	A3

Guinness Trust Bldgs. SW3	100	A1
Gulland Wk. N1	14	B2
Gulliver St. SE16	88	A3
Gulston Wk. SW3	100	B1
Gun St. E1	44	A4
Gunpowder Sq. EC4	41	D5
Gunter Gro. SW10	98	A5
Gunterstone Rd. W14	95	E1
Gunthorpe St. E1	44	B4
Gunwhale Clo. SE16	63	D5
Gurdon Rd. SE7	117	D3
Guthrie St. SW3	99	E2
Gutter La. EC2	42	B5
Guy St. SE1	83	D1
Gwendwr Rd. W14	95	F2
Gwynne Pl. WC1	24	B5

H

Haarlem Rd. W14	70	C4
Haberdasher Pl. N1	27	D4
Haberdasher St. N1	27	D4
Hackney Gro. E8	17	F2
Hackney Rd. E2	28	A4
Haddo St. SE10	114	A5
Haddonfield SE8	111	D1
Hadley St. NW1	9	E2
Hadrian Est. E2	29	D3
Hadrian St. SE10	115	E3
Haggerston Rd. E8	16	A4
Hague St. E2	29	D5
Hainton Clo. E1	45	F5
Halcomb St. N1	27	E1
Halcrow St. E1	45	F4
Hale St. E14	65	E2
Hales St. SE8	120	C2
Half Moon Ct. EC1	42	A4
Half Moon Cres. N1	24	B2
Half Moon Pas. E1	60	B1
Half Moon St. W1	53	F4
Halford Rd. SW6	96	C5
Haliday Wk. N1	15	D1
Halkin Arc. SW1	76	C3
Halkin Ms. SW1	76	C3
Halkin Pl. SW1	76	C3
Halkin St. SW1	77	D2
Hall Gate NW8	18	B4
Hall Pl. W2	34	C2
Hall Rd. NW8	18	B5

Hall St. EC1	25	F4
Hallam Ms. W1	37	F3
Hallam St. W1	37	F2
Hallfield Est. W2	50	A1
Halliford St. N1	14	B3
Hallsville Rd. E16	68	A1
Halpin Pl. SE17	107	D1
Halsey Ms. SW3	76	A5
Halsey St. SW3	76	A5
Halstead Ct. N1	27	D3
Halstow Rd. SE10	116	C3
Halton Cross St. N1	13	F5
Halton Rd. N1	13	F3
Ham Yd. W1	54	C2
Hamilton Clo. NW8	18	C5
Hamilton Clo. SE16	87	F2
Hamilton Ct. W9	18	A4
Hamilton Gdns. NW8	18	B4
Hamilton Ms. W1	77	E1
Hamilton Pl. W1	53	D5
Hamilton Sq. SE1	83	D1
Hamilton St. SE8	120	C1
Hamilton Ter. NW8	18	A4
Hamlet Way SE1	83	D1
Hammersmith Bri. Rd. W6	94	A3
Hammersmith Bdy. W6	94	B1
Hammersmith Flyover W6	94	A2
Hammersmith Gro. W6	70	A2
Hammersmith Rd. W6	94	C1
Hammersmith Rd. W14	95	D1
Hammett St. EC3	60	A2
Hammond St. NW5	10	A1
Hampden Clo. NW1	23	D3
Hampden Gurney St. W1	52	A1
Hampshire St. NW5	10	C1
Hampstead Rd. NW1	22	A3
Hampton Ct. N1	13	E2
Hampton St. SE1	105	F1
Hampton St. SE17	105	F1
Hanameel St. E16	69	D4
Hanbury Ms. N1	26	B1
Hanbury St. E1	44	B3
Hand Ct. WC1	40	B4
Handa Wk. N1	14	B1

Handel St. WC1	39	E1
Hankey Pl. SE1	83	D2
Hannah Mary Way SE1	109	D1
Hanover Ave. E16	68	C4
Hanover Gdns. SE11	104	C5
Hanover Gate NW1	19	F5
Hanover Pl. WC2	55	F1
Hanover Sq. W1	53	F1
Hanover St. W1	53	F1
Hanover Ter. NW1	19	F5
Hanover Ter. Ms. NW1	19	F5
Hanover Yd. N1	25	F2
Hans Cres. SW1	76	A3
Hans Pl. SW1	76	B3
Hans Rd. SW3	76	A3
Hans St. SW1	76	B4
Hansard Ms. W14	71	D1
Hanson St. W1	38	A3
Hanway Pl. W1	38	C5
Hanway St. W1	38	C5
Harben Rd. NW6	6	B3
Harbet Rd. W2	35	D4
Harbinger Rd. E14	113	E1
Harbour Ex. Sq. E14	89	F2
Harcourt St. W1	35	F4
Harcourt Ter. SW10	97	F3
Harding Clo. SE17	106	A5
Hardinge St. E1	62	B1
Hardman Rd. SE7	117	E2
Hardwick St. EC1	25	D5
Hardwidge St. SE1	83	E1
Hardy Ave. E16	69	D4
Hardy Clo. SE16	87	D2
Hardy Rd. SE3	116	B5
Hare & Billet Rd. SE3	123	D4
Hare Ct. EC4	56	C1
Hare Marsh E2	44	C1
Hare Pl. EC4	57	D1
Hare Row E2	29	F2
Hare Wk. N1	27	F3
Harecourt Rd. N1	14	A1
Harewood Ave. NW1	35	F2
Harewood Pl. W1	53	F1
Harewood Row NW1	35	F3
Harley Gdns. SW10	98	B3
Harley Pl. W1	37	E4
Harley Rd. NW3	7	E4

Harley St. W1	37	E2
Harleyford Rd. SE11	104	A4
Harleyford St. SE11	104	C5
Harmood Gro. NW1	9	E3
Harmood Pl. NW1	9	E3
Harmood St. NW1	9	E2
Harmsworth St. SE17	105	E3
Harold Est. SE1	83	F4
Harold Pl. SE11	104	C3
Harp All. EC4	41	E5
Harp La. EC3	59	E3
Harper Rd. SE1	82	B3
Harpur Ms. WC1	40	A3
Harpur St. WC1	40	A3
Harrap St. E14	66	B2
Harriet Clo. E8	16	C5
Harriet St. SW1	76	B2
Harriet Wk. SW1	76	B2
Harrington Gdns. SW7	97	F1
Harrington Rd. SW7	75	D5
Harrington Sq. NW1	22	A3
Harrington St. NW1	22	A3
Harriott Clo. SE10	116	A1
Harrison St. WC1	23	F5
Harrow La. E14	66	A3
Harrow Pl. E1	43	F5
Harrow Rd. W2	33	D3
Harrow Rd. W9	33	D3
Harrow Rd. W10	31	E1
Harrowby St. W1	35	F5
Hart St. EC3	59	F2
Hartington Rd. E16	69	E1
Hartland Rd. NW1	9	E3
Harton St. SE8	120	C3
Harts La. SE14	119	E3
Hartshorn All. EC3	59	F1
Hartwell St. E8	16	A1
Harvey St. N1	27	D1
Harvington Wk. E8	17	D3
Harwich La. EC2	43	F3
Hasker St. SW3	75	F5
Haslam Clo. N1	13	D3
Hassard St. E2	28	B3
Hassendean Rd. SE3	117	E5
Hastings St. WC1	23	E5
Hat and Mitre Ct. EC1	41	F2
Hatcham Pk. Ms. SE14	119	D3
Hatcham Pk. Rd. SE14	119	D3
Hatcham Rd. SE15	110	A4
Hatcliffe St. SE10	116	A2
Hatfield Clo. SE14	118	C2
Hatfields SE1	57	D4
Hatherley Gro. W2	33	E5
Hatherley St. SW1	102	B1
Hatteraick St. SE16	86	B1
Hatton Gdn. EC1	41	D3
Hatton Ho. E1	61	D2
Hatton Pl. EC1	41	D3
Hatton Row NW8	35	D2
Hatton St. NW8	35	D2
Hatton Wall EC1	40	C3
Haunch of Venison Yd. W1	53	E1
Havannah St. E14	89	D2
Havelock St. N1	11	F5
Haven St. NW1	9	E4
Havering St. E1	62	C1
Haverstock Hill NW3	8	A1
Haverstock St. N1	25	F3
Hawes St. N1	13	F4
Hawke Pl. SE16	87	D1
Hawks Ms. SE10	122	B2
Hawksmoor Ms. E1	61	E2
Hawksmoor St. W6	95	D5
Hawkstone Rd. SE16	86	B5
Hawkwell Wk. N1	14	B5
Hawley Cres. NW1	9	F4
Hawley Ms. NW1	9	E3
Hawley Rd. NW1	9	F3
Hawley St. NW1	9	E4
Hawthorn Wk. W10	31	E1
Hawthorne Clo. N1	15	F1
Hawtrey Rd. NW3	7	E4
Hay Hill W1	53	F3
Hay St. E2	29	D1
Haydens Pl. W11	32	A5
Haydon St. EC3	60	A2
Haydon Wk. E1	60	B2
Hayes Pl. NW1	35	F2
Hayles St. SE11	81	E5
Haymarket SW1	54	C3
Haymarket Arc. SW1	54	C3
Haymerle Rd. SE15	108	C5
Hayne St. EC1	41	F3
Hay's La. SE1	59	E5
Hay's Ms. W1	53	E4
Hayton Clo. E8	16	B2
Hayward's Pl. EC1	41	E2
Hazel Way SE1	84	A5
Hazlewood Cres. W10	31	F2
Hazlitt Ms. W14	71	E4
Hazlitt Rd. W14	71	E4
Head St. E1	62	C1
Headfort Pl. SW1	77	D2
Headlam St. E1	45	F2
Head's Ms. W11	48	C1
Heald St. SE14	120	C3
Healey St. NW1	9	E2
Hearn St. EC2	43	F2
Hearn's Bldgs. SE17	107	D1
Heathcote St. WC1	40	A1
Heather Wk. W10	31	F1
Heathfield St. W11	47	E3
Heathway SE3	124	C2
Hebden Ct. E2	28	A1
Heckford St. E1	63	D2
Heddon St. W1	54	A2
Hedingham Clo. N1	14	A4
Heiron St. SE17	105	F5
Helena Sq. SE16	63	E3
Hellings St. E1	61	D5
Helmet Row EC1	42	B1
Helmsley Pl. E8	17	E4
Helsinki Sq. SE16	87	F3
Hemingford Rd. N1	24	B1
Hemming St. E1	45	D2
Hemp Wk. SE17	83	D5
Hemsworth Ct. N1	27	E2
Hemsworth St. N1	27	E2
Hemus Pl. SW3	99	F3
Henderson Dr. NW8	34	C1
Hendre Rd. SE1	107	F1
Heneage La. EC3	59	F1
Heneage St. E1	44	B3
Henley Dr. SE1	84	B5
Henniker Ms. SW3	98	C4
Henrietta Clo. SE8	113	D4
Henrietta Ms. WC1	39	F1
Henrietta Pl. W1	37	E5
Henrietta St. WC2	55	F2
Henriques St. E1	45	D5
Henry Dickens Ct. W11	47	D3
Henshall St. N1	15	D2
Henshaw St. SE17	82	C5
Henstridge Pl. NW8	19	E1

Herald St. E2	45	F1
Herald's Ct. SE11	105	E1
Herald's Pl. SE11	81	D5
Herbal Hill EC1	41	D2
Herbert Cres. SW1	76	B3
Herbert St. NW5	8	C1
Herbrand St. WC1	39	E1
Hercules Rd. SE1	80	B4
Hercules Twr. SE14	111	F5
Hereford Ms. W2	49	D1
Hereford Pl. SE14	120	A1
Hereford Rd. W2	33	D5
Hereford Sq. SW7	98	B1
Hereford St. E2	16	C5
Hermes Pt. W9	32	C2
Hermes St. N1	24	C3
Hermit St. EC1	25	E4
Hermitage St. W2	34	C4
Hermitage Wall E1	61	D5
Heron Pl. SE16	63	F4
Heron Quay E14	64	C5
Herrick St. SW1	103	D1
Hertford Pl. W1	38	A2
Hertford Rd. N1	15	F5
Hertford St. W1	53	D5
Hertsmere Rd. E14	64	C3
Hervey Rd. SE3	125	F3
Hesketh Pl. W11	47	E3
Hesper Ms. SW5	97	E2
Hesperus Cres. E14	113	E1
Hessel St. E1	61	E1
Heston St. SE14	120	C3
Hevelius Clo. SE10	116	A2
Hewer St. W10	31	D3
Hewett St. EC2	43	F2
Heygate St. SE17	106	A1
Hickin St. E14	90	A3
Hicks St. SE8	111	E2
Hide Pl. SW1	102	C1
Hides St. N7	12	B1
High Bri. SE10	115	D3
High Bri. Wf. SE10	114	C3
High Holborn WC1	39	E5
High Timber St. EC4	58	A2
Highbury Cor. N5	13	E1
Highbury Cres. N5	13	D1
Highbury Gro. N5	13	F1
Highbury Ms. N7	13	D1
Highbury Pl. N5	13	E1
Highbury Sta. Rd. N1	13	D2
Highcombe SE7	117	F4
Highlever Rd. W10	30	A3
Highmore Rd. SE3	123	F1
Highway, The E1	61	D3
Highway, The E14	61	D3
Hildyard Rd. SW6	97	D4
Hilgrove Rd. NW6	6	B4
Hill Fm. Rd. W10	30	B3
Hill Rd. NW8	18	B3
Hill St. W1	53	D4
Hillbeck Clo. SE15	118	A1
Hillery Clo. SE17	107	D1
Hillgate Pl. W8	48	C4
Hillgate St. W8	48	C4
Hilliards Ct. E1	62	A4
Hillingdon St. SE5	105	E5
Hillingdon St. SE17	106	A5
Hillman Dr. W10	30	B2
Hillman St. E8	17	F2
Hills Pl. W1	54	A1
Hillsleigh Rd. W8	48	B4
Hind Ct. EC4	57	D1
Hind Gro. E14	64	C1
Hinde St. W1	37	D5
Hindmarsh Clo. E1	61	D2
Hippodrome Ms. W11	47	E3
Hippodrome Pl. W11	47	E3
Hobart Pl. SW1	77	E3
Hobbs Pl. Est. N1	27	E1
Hobsons Pl. E1	44	C3
Hobury St. SW10	98	B5
Hocker St. E2	28	A5
Hockett Clo. SE8	87	F5
Hodnet Gro. SE16	86	C5
Hofland Rd. W14	71	D3
Hogan Ms. W2	34	C4
Hogarth Ct. EC3	59	F2
Hogarth Pl. SW5	97	E1
Hogarth Rd. SW5	97	E1
Hogshead Pas. E1	61	F3
Holbein Ms. SW1	100	C2
Holbein Pl. SW1	100	C1
Holborn EC1	40	C4
Holborn Circ. EC1	41	D4
Holborn Pl. WC1	40	A4
Holborn Viaduct EC1	41	D4
Holford Pl. WC1	24	B4
Holford St. WC1	24	C4
Holland Gdns. W14	71	F3
Holland Pk. W8	72	A1
Holland Pk. W11	47	F5
Holland Pk. Ave. W11	71	D1
Holland Pk. Gdns. W14	71	E1
Holland Pk. Ms. W11	47	F5
Holland Pk. Rd. W14	72	A4
Holland Pl. W8	73	E1
Holland Rd. W14	71	D1
Holland St. SE1	57	F4
Holland St. W8	73	D1
Holland Vil. Rd. W14	71	E1
Holland Wk. W8	72	C2
Hollen St. W1	38	B5
Holles St. W1	37	F5
Holloway Rd. N7	13	D1
Holly Ms. SW10	98	B3
Holly St. E8	16	B3
Holly St. Est. E8	16	A3
Hollybush Gdns. E2	29	F4
Hollybush Pl. E2	29	F4
Hollydale Rd. SE15	118	A4
Hollymount Clo. SE10	122	A3
Hollywood Ms. SW10	98	A4
Hollywood Rd. SW10	98	A4
Holmefield Ct. NW3	7	F1
Holmes Pl. SW10	98	B4
Holmes Rd. NW5	9	E1
Holmes Ter. SE1	80	C1
Holms St. E2	28	C2
Holmwood Vil. SE7	117	D2
Holsworthy Sq. WC1	40	B2
Holyoak Rd. SE11	81	E5
Holyoake Ct. SE16	87	F1
Holyrood Ms. E16	69	D4
Holyrood St. SE1	59	E5
Holywell Clo. SE3	117	D4
Holywell La. EC2	43	F1
Holywell Row EC2	43	E2
Homefield St. N1	27	E3
Homer Dr. E14	88	C5
Homer Row W1	35	F4
Homer St. W1	35	F4

King Edward Wk. SE1   81 D3

King Edwards Rd. E9   17 F5

King George St. SE10   122 B2

King Henry's Rd. NW3   7 D4

King Henry's Wk. N1   15 E1

King James St. SE1   81 F2

King John Ct. EC2   43 F1

King Sq. EC1   26 A5

King Stairs Clo. SE16   85 F1

King St. EC2   58 B1

King St. SW1   54 B5

King St. W6   94 A1

King St. WC2   55 E2

King William La. SE10   115 E3

King William St. EC4   59 D3

King William Wk. SE10   114 B4

Kingfield St. E14   114 B1

Kingfisher Sq. SE8   112 A4

Kingham Clo. W11   71 E1

Kinghorn St. EC1   42 A4

Kinglake Est. SE17   107 F2

Kinglake St. SE17   107 F3

Kingly Ct. W1   54 B2

Kingly St. W1   54 A2

Kings Arms Ct. E1   44 C4

Kings Arms Yd. EC2   42 C5

Kings Bench St. SE1   81 F1

Kings Bench Wk. EC4   57 D1

Kings College Rd. NW3   7 E3

King's Cross Bri. N1   23 F4

King's Cross Rd. WC1   24 A4

Kings Head Yd. SE1   58 C5

King's Ms. WC1   40 B2

Kings Pl. SE1   82 A2

King's Reach Twr. SE1   57 D4

King's Rd. SW1   99 D4

King's Rd. SW3   99 D4

King's Scholars' Pas. SW1   78 A4

King's Ter. NW1   22 A1

Kingsbridge Rd. W10   30 B5

Kingsbury Rd. N1   15 F1

Kingsbury Ter. N1   15 F1

Kingscote St. EC4   57 E2

Kingsdale Gdns. W11   47 D5

Kingsdown Clo. W10   47 D1

Kingsland NW8   19 F1

Kingsland Grn. E8   15 F1

Kingsland High St. E8   16 A1

Kingsland Pas. E8   15 F1

Kingsland Rd. E2   27 F4

Kingsland Rd. E8   15 F5

Kingsley Ms. E1   61 F3

Kingsley Ms. W8   73 F4

Kingsmill Ter. NW8   19 D2

Kingstown St. NW1   8 C5

Kingsway WC2   40 A5

Kinnerton Pl. N. SW1   76 B2

Kinnerton Pl. S. SW1   76 B2

Kinnerton St. SW1   76 C2

Kinnerton Yd. SW1   76 B2

Kinnoul Rd. W6   95 E4

Kintore Way SE1   84 A5

Kipling Est. SE1   83 D2

Kipling St. SE1   83 D2

Kirby Est. SE16   85 F3

Kirby Gro. SE1   83 E1

Kirby St. EC1   41 D3

Kirkland Wk. E8   16 A2

Kirkman Pl. W1   38 C4

Kirkside Rd. SE3   116 C4

Kirton Gdns. E2   28 B5

Knaresborough Pl. SW5   73 E5

Knighten St. E1   61 D5

Knights Arc. SW1   76 A2

Knights Rd. E16   93 D1

Knights Wk. SE11   105 E1

Knightsbridge SW1   76 B1

Knightsbridge SW7   75 F2

Knightsbridge Grn. SW1   76 A2

Knivet Rd. SW6   96 C5

Knox St. W1   36 A3

Knoyle St. SE14   111 E5

Kossuth St. SE10   115 E2

Kotree Way SE1   109 D1

Kramer Ms. SW5   97 D3

Kynance Ms. SW7   73 F4

Kynance Pl. SW7   74 A4

L

Laburnum Clo. SE15   118 A2

Laburnum Ct. E2   28 A1

Laburnum St. E2   28 A1

Lackington St. EC2   43 D3

Ladbroke Cres. W11   47 F1

Ladbroke Gdns. W11   48 A2

Ladbroke Gro. W10   31 D1

Ladbroke Gro. W11   47 F1

Ladbroke Ms. W11   47 F5

Ladbroke Rd. W11   48 A4

Ladbroke Sq. W11   48 B3

Ladbroke Ter. W11   48 B3

Ladbroke Wk. W11   48 B4

Lafone St. SE1   84 A1

Lagado Ms. SE16   63 D5

Lairs Clo. N7   11 F1

Lakeside Rd. W14   70 C3

Lamb La. E8   17 F4

Lamb St. E1   44 A3

Lamb Wk. SE1   83 E2

Lambert St. N1   12 C4

Lambeth Bri. SE1   79 F5

Lambeth Bri. SW1   79 F5

Lambeth High St. SE1   80 A5

Lambeth Hill EC4   58 A2

Lambeth Palace Rd. SE1   80 A4

Lambeth Rd. SE1   80 C4

Lambeth Rd. SE11   80 A5

Lambeth Wk. SE11   80 B5

Lambolle Pl. NW3   7 F2

Lambolle Rd. NW3   7 E2

Lambourne Pl. SE3   125 E3

Lamb's Bldgs. EC1   42 C2

Lambs Conduit Pas. WC1   40 A3

Lamb's Conduit St. WC1   40 A2

Lambs Ms. N1   25 E1

Lamb's Pas. EC1   42 C3

Lambton Pl. W11   48 B2

Lamerton St. SE8   112 C5

Lamlash St. SE11   81 E5

Lamont Rd. SW10 98 B5
Lamont Rd. Pas. 98 C5
  SW10
Lampern Sq. E2 29 D4
Lampeter Sq. W6 95 E5
Lanark Pl. W9 34 B1
Lanark Rd. W9 18 A5
Lanark Sq. E14 89 F3
Lancashire Ct. W1 53 F2
Lancaster Clo. N1 15 F4
Lancaster Ct. W2 50 B3
Lancaster Dr. E14 66 B5
Lancaster Dr. NW3 7 E2
Lancaster Gate W2 50 B3
Lancaster Gro. NW3 7 D2
Lancaster Ms. W2 50 B2
Lancaster Pl. WC2 56 A2
Lancaster Rd. W11 47 E1
Lancaster St. SE1 81 F2
Lancaster Ter. W2 50 C2
Lancaster Wk. W2 50 B4
Lancefield St. W10 32 A1
Lancelot Pl. SW7 76 A2
Lancer Sq. W8 73 E1
Lancing St. NW1 22 C5
Lancresse Ct. N1 15 E5
Landmann Way 111 D4
  SE14
Landon Pl. SW1 76 A3
Landon Wk. E14 65 F2
Landons Clo. E14 66 B4
Lane, The NW8 18 A3
Lanesborough Pl. 77 D1
  SW1
Lanfrey Pl. W14 96 A3
Langdale Clo. 106 A4
  SE17
Langdale Rd. SE10 122 A2
Langdale St. E1 61 E1
Langdon Way SE1 109 D1
Langford Clo. NW8 18 B2
Langford Ct. NW8 18 B3
Langford Pl. NW8 18 B2
Langham Pl. W1 37 F4
Langham St. W1 37 F4
Langley Ct. WC2 55 E2
Langley La. SW8 103 F4
Langley St. WC2 55 E1
Langthorn Ct. EC2 43 D5
Langton Clo. WC1 40 B1
Langton St. SW10 98 B5
Langton Way SE3 124 B3
Langtry Wk. NW8 6 A5
Lanhill Rd. W9 32 C1

Lansdowne Cres. 47 F2
  W11
Lansdowne Dr. E8 17 D2
Lansdowne Ms. 48 A4
  W11
Lansdowne Pl. SE1 83 D3
Lansdowne Ri. W11 47 F3
Lansdowne Rd. 47 F2
  W11
Lansdowne Row W1 53 F4
Lansdowne Ter. 39 F2
  WC1
Lansdowne Wk. 48 A4
  W11
Lant St. SE1 82 A1
Lanterns Ct. E14 89 D2
Lanvanor Rd. SE15 118 A5
Lapford Clo. W9 32 B1
Larch Clo. SE8 112 B5
Larcom St. SE17 106 B1
Larissa St. SE17 107 D2
Larnach Rd. W6 94 C5
Lassell St. SE10 115 D3
Latimer SE17 107 E3
Latimer Pl. W10 30 B5
Latimer Rd. W10 30 A4
Latona Rd. SE15 108 C5
Latymer Ct. W6 94 C1
Laud St. SE11 104 A2
Launcelot St. SE1 80 C2
Launceston Pl. W8 74 A3
Launch St. E14 90 A3
Laundry La. N1 14 A4
Laundry Rd. W6 95 E5
Laurel St. E8 16 B1
Laurence Pountney 58 C2
  Hill EC4
Laurence Pountney 58 C2
  La. EC4
Laurie Gro. SE14 119 F3
Lausanne Rd. 118 B4
  SE15
Lavender Clo. SW3 99 D5
Lavender Gro. E8 16 B4
Lavender Rd. SE16 63 F4
Laverton Ms. SW5 97 F1
Laverton Pl. SW5 97 F1
Lavina Gro. N1 24 A2
Lavington St. SE1 57 F5
Law St. SE1 83 D3
Lawford Rd. N1 15 E4
Lawford Rd. NW5 10 A2
Lawless St. E14 65 F2
Lawn Ho. Clo. E14 90 A1

Lawn La. SW8 103 F5
Lawrence La. EC2 58 B1
Lawrence Pl. N1 11 F5
Lawrence St. SW3 99 E5
Lawson Est. SE1 82 C4
Laxton Pl. NW1 37 F1
Layard Rd. SE16 85 F5
Layard Sq. SE16 85 F5
Laycock St. N1 13 D2
Laystall St. EC1 40 C2
Layton Rd. N1 25 D2
Laytons Bldgs. SE1 82 C1
Leadenhall Mkt. 59 E1
  EC3
Leadenhall Pl. EC3 59 E1
Leadenhall St. EC3 59 E1
Leake Ct. SE1 80 B1
Leake St. SE1 80 B1
Leamington Rd. 32 B4
  Vil. W11
Leamouth Rd. E14 67 D1
Leander Ct. SE8 120 C4
Leather La. EC1 40 C3
Leathermarket Ct. 83 E2
  SE1
Leathermarket St. 83 E2
  SE1
Lecky St. SW7 98 C2
Ledbury Ms. N. 48 C2
  W11
Ledbury Ms. W. 48 C2
  W11
Ledbury Rd. W11 32 B5
Lee St. E8 16 A5
Leeke St. WC1 24 A4
Leerdam Dr. E14 90 B4
Lees Pl. W1 52 C2
Leeway SE8 112 A2
Legion Clo. N1 13 D2
Leicester Ct. WC2 55 D2
Leicester Pl. WC2 55 D2
Leicester Sq. WC2 55 D3
Leicester St. WC2 55 D2
Leigh Hunt St. SE1 82 A1
Leigh St. WC1 39 E1
Leinster Gdns. W2 50 A1
Leinster Ms. W2 50 A3
Leinster Pl. W2 50 A1
Leinster Sq. W2 49 D1
Leinster Ter. W2 50 A2
Lelitia Clo. E8 28 C1
Leman St. E1 60 B1
Lemmon Rd. SE10 115 E4
Lena Gdns. W6 70 B4

M

May St. W14	96	B3
Mayfair Ms. NW1	8	B4
Mayfair Pl. W1	53	F4
Mayfield Clo. E8	16	A2
Mayfield Rd. E8	16	A4
Mayflower Clo. SE16	87	D5
Mayflower St. SE16	86	A2
Maygood St. N1	24	C2
Mayhill Rd. SE7	117	E5
Maynards Quay E1	62	A3
Mays Ct. WC2	55	E3
Maze Hill SE3	115	E5
Maze Hill SE10	115	E4
McAuley Clo. SE1	80	C3
McCoid Way SE1	82	A2
McCrone Ms. NW3	7	D1
McGregor Rd. W11	32	A4
McLeod's Ms. SW7	73	F5
McMillan St. SE8	113	D5
Mead Row SE1	80	C3
Meadcroft Rd. SE11	105	E5
Meadow Ms. SW8	104	A5
Meadow Rd. SW8	104	A5
Meadow Row SE1	82	A4
Meadowbank NW3	8	A4
Meakin Est. SE1	83	E3
Meard St. W1	54	C1
Mechanics Path SE8	120	C1
Mecklenburgh Pl. WC1	40	A1
Mecklenburgh Sq. WC1	40	A1
Mecklenburgh St. WC1	40	A1
Medburn St. NW1	22	C2
Medway St. SW1	79	D4
Meetinghouse All. E1	61	F4
Melba Way SE13	121	F4
Melbourne Pl. WC2	56	B1
Melbury Ct. W8	72	B3
Melbury Rd. W14	72	A3
Melbury Ter. NW1	35	F2
Melcombe Pl. NW1	36	A3
Melcombe St. NW1	36	B2
Melina Pl. NW8	18	C5
Melior Pl. SE1	83	E1
Melior St. SE1	83	E1
Mellish St. E14	88	C3
Melon Pl. W8	73	D1
Melrose Gdns. W6	70	B3
Melrose Ter. W6	70	B3
Melton Ct. SW7	99	D1
Melton St. NW1	22	B5
Memel Ct. EC1	42	A2
Memel St. EC1	42	A2
Menotti St. E2	45	D1
Mentmore Ter. E8	17	F3
Mepham St. SE1	56	B5
Mercator Pl. E14	113	D2
Mercer St. WC2	55	E1
Merceron St. E1	45	F2
Mercers Clo. SE10	116	A1
Mercers Pl. W6	70	B5
Mercury Way SE14	110	C4
Meredith St. EC1	25	E5
Meridian Gate E14	90	A1
Meridian Pl. E14	90	A1
Meridian Trd. Est. SE7	93	F5
Merlin St. WC1	24	C5
Mermaid Ct. SE1	82	C1
Mermaid Ct. SE16	64	A5
Merrick Sq. SE1	82	C3
Merrington Rd. SW6	97	D4
Merrow St. SE17	106	C3
Merrow Wk. SE17	107	D2
Merton Ri. NW3	7	E3
Methley St. SE11	105	D3
Methwold Rd. W10	30	C3
Mews, The N1	14	B5
Mews Deck E1	61	F3
Mews St. E1	60	C4
Meymott St. SE1	57	E5
Micawber St. N1	26	B4
Michael Faraday Ho. SE17	107	D3
Micklethwaite Rd. SW6	97	D5
Middle Fld. NW8	6	C5
Middle Row W10	31	E2
Middle St. EC1	42	A3
Middle Temple EC4	56	C2
Middle Temple La. EC4	56	C1
Middle Yd. SE1	59	E4
Middlesex Pas. EC1	41	F4
Middlesex St. E1	43	F4
Middleton Bldgs. W1	38	A4
Middleton Dr. SE16	87	D2
Middleton Rd. E8	16	A4
Middleton St. E2	29	E4
Midford Pl. W1	38	B2
Midhope St. WC1	23	F5
Midland Pl. E14	114	A2
Midland Rd. NW1	23	D3
Midship Clo. SE16	63	D5
Midship Pt. E14	88	C2
Milborne Gro. SW10	98	B3
Milcote St. SE1	81	E2
Mildmay Ave. N1	15	D1
Mildmay St. N1	15	D1
Miles Pl. NW1	35	E3
Miles St. SW8	103	E5
Milford La. WC2	56	C2
Milk St. EC2	42	B5
Milk Yd. E1	62	A3
Mill Pl. E14	63	F1
Mill Rd. E16	69	F4
Mill Row N1	27	F1
Mill St. SE1	84	B2
Mill St. W1	54	A2
Mill Yd. E1	60	C2
Millbank SW1	79	E3
Millbank Twr. SW1	103	E1
Millender Wk. SE16	110	B1
Millennium Dr. E14	90	C5
Millennium Pl. E2	29	F3
Millennium Sq. SE1	84	B1
Millennium Way SE10	91	E1
Miller St. NW1	22	A2
Miller Wk. SE1	57	D5
Millers Way W6	70	B2
Millharbour E14	89	E2
Milligan St. E14	64	B3
Millman Ms. WC1	40	A2
Millman St. WC1	40	A2
Millpond Est. SE16	85	E2
Mills Ct. EC2	43	E1
Millstream Rd. SE1	84	A2
Millwall Dock Rd. E14	88	C3
Millwood St. W10	31	E4
Milman's St. SW10	98	C5
Milner Pl. N1	13	D5
Milner Sq. N1	13	D4
Milner St. SW3	76	A5
Milroy Wk. SE1	57	E4
Milson Rd. W14	71	D3
Milton Clo. SE1	108	A1
Milton Ct. EC2	42	C3
Milton Ct. Rd. SE14	111	F5
Milton St. EC2	42	C3

Mullet Gdns. E2	29	D4
Mulready St. NW8	35	E2
Mulvaney Way SE1	83	D2
Mumford Ct. EC2	42	B5
Mund St. W14	96	B3
Munday Rd. E16	68	C2
Munden St. W14	71	E5
Mundy St. N1	27	F4
Munro Ms. W10	31	F3
Munster Sq. NW1	21	F5
Munton Rd. SE17	82	B5
Murdock St. SE15	109	E5
Muriel St. N1	24	B1
Murphy St. SE1	80	C2
Murray Gro. N1	26	B3
Murray Ms. NW1	10	C3
Murray Sq. E16	69	D1
Murray St. NW1	10	C3
Musard Rd. W6	95	F4
Musard Rd. W14	95	F4
Muscal W6	95	E4
Muscovy St. EC3	59	F3
Museum La. SW7	75	D4
Museum St. WC1	39	E4
Musgrove Rd. SE14	119	D4
Mutton Pl. NW1	9	D2
Mycenae Rd. SE3	124	C1
Myddelton Pas. EC1	25	D4
Myddelton Sq. EC1	25	D4
Myddelton St. EC1	25	D5
Myers La. SE14	110	C4
Mylius Clo. SE14	118	B3
Mylne St. EC1	24	C3
Myrdle St. E1	45	D5
Myrtle Wk. N1	27	E3
Myrtleberry Clo. E8	16	A2

N

Nag's Head Ct. EC1	42	B2
Naish Ct. N1	11	F5
Nankin St. E14	65	D1
Nant St. E2	29	F4
Nantes Pas. E1	44	A3
Naoroji St. WC1	24	C5
Napier Ave. E14	113	E2
Napier Clo. SE8	120	B1
Napier Clo. W14	72	A3
Napier Gro. N1	14	B1
Napier Pl. W14	72	A4
Napier Rd. W14	71	F4

Napier Ter. N1	13	E4
Narrow St. E14	63	E2
Nascot St. W12	30	A5
Naseby Clo. NW6	6	B3
Nash Pl. E14	65	E5
Nash St. NW1	21	F4
Nassau St. W1	38	A4
Nathaniel Clo. E1	44	B4
Naval Row E14	66	B2
Navarino Gro. E8	17	D1
Navarino Rd. E8	17	D1
Navarre St. E2	44	A1
Nazrul St. E2	28	A4
Neal St. WC2	55	E1
Neal's Yd. WC2	55	E1
Neate St. SE5	107	E5
Neathouse Pl. SW1	78	A5
Nebraska St. SE1	82	C2
Neckinger SE16	84	B3
Neckinger Est. SE16	84	B3
Neckinger St. SE1	84	B3
Nectarine Way SE13	121	F5
Needham Rd. W11	48	C1
Needleman St. SE16	86	C2
Nella Rd. W6	94	C5
Nelldale Rd. SE16	86	A5
Nelson Gdns. E2	29	D4
Nelson Pas. EC1	26	B5
Nelson Pl. N1	25	F3
Nelson Rd. SE10	114	B5
Nelson Sq. SE1	81	E1
Nelson St. E1	45	E5
Nelson St. E16	68	B2
Nelson Ter. N1	25	F3
Nelson Wk. SE16	63	F5
Neptune St. SE16	86	A3
Nesham St. E1	60	C4
Ness St. SE16	84	C3
Netherhall Gdns. NW3	6	B1
Netherton Gro. SW10	98	B5
Netherwood Pl. W14	70	C3
Netherwood Rd. W14	70	C3
Netley St. NW1	22	A5
Nettleton Rd. SE14	119	D3
Nevada St. SE10	114	B5
Nevern Pl. SW5	97	D1

Nevern Rd. SW5	96	C1
Nevern Sq. SW5	96	C1
Neville Clo. NW1	23	D3
Neville St. SW7	98	C2
Neville Ter. SW7	98	C2
New Bond St. W1	53	E1
New Bri. St. EC4	57	E1
New Broad St. EC2	43	E4
New Burlington Ms. W1	54	A2
New Burlington Pl. W1	54	A2
New Burlington St. W1	54	A2
New Butt La. SE8	121	D2
New Butt La. N. SE8	120	C2
New Cavendish St. W1	37	D4
New Change EC4	58	A1
New Charles St. EC1	25	F4
New College Ms. N1	13	D3
New Compton St. WC2	55	D1
New Ct. EC4 WC2	56	C2
New Coventry St. W1	55	D3
New Crane Pl. E1	62	A4
New Cross Rd. SE14	118	B2
New Fetter La. EC4	41	D5
New Globe Wk. SE1	58	A4
New Goulston St. E1	44	A5
New Inn Bdy. EC2	43	F1
New Inn Pas. WC2	56	B1
New Inn St. EC2	43	F1
New Inn Yd. EC2	43	F1
New Kent Rd. SE1	82	A4
New King St. SE8	112	C4
New London St. EC3	59	F2
New N. Pl. EC2	43	E2
New N. Rd. N1	26	C2
New N. St. WC1	40	A3
New Oxford St. WC1	39	D5
New Pl. Sq. SE16	85	E3
New Quebec St. W1	52	B1
New Ride SW7	75	E1
New River Wk. N1	14	B2

New Rd. E1 45 E4
New Row WC2 55 E2
New Spring Gdns. 103 F3
Wk. SE11
New Sq. WC2 40 B5
New St. EC2 43 F4
New St. Sq. EC4 41 D5
New Turnstile WC1 40 A4
New Union Clo. 90 B3
E14
New Union St. EC2 42 C4
New Wf. Rd. N1 23 F2
Newark St. E1 45 E4
Newburgh St. W1 54 A1
Newburn St. SE11 104 B3
Newbury Ms. NW5 9 D2
Newbury St. EC1 42 A3
Newby Pl. E14 66 A2
Newcastle Clo. EC4 41 E5
Newcastle Pl. W2 35 D4
Newcastle Row EC1 41 D2
Newcombe St. W8 49 D4
Newcomen St. SE1 82 C1
Newcourt St. NW8 19 E3
Newell St. E14 64 A1
Newgate St. EC1 41 F5
Newhams Row SE1 83 F2
Newington Butts 105 F1
SE1
Newington Butts 105 F1
SE11
Newington 81 F4
Causeway SE1
Newington Grn. 14 C1
Rd. N1
Newlands Quay E1 62 A3
Newman Pas. W1 38 B4
Newman St. W1 38 B4
Newman Yd. W1 38 B5
Newman's Ct. EC3 59 D1
Newman's Row 40 B4
WC2
Newnham Ter. SE1 80 C3
Newport Ave. E14 67 D2
Newport Ct. WC2 55 D2
Newport Pl. WC2 55 D2
Newport St. SE11 104 A1
Newton Rd. W2 49 D1
Newton St. WC2 39 F5
Nicholas La. EC4 59 D2
Nicholl St. E2 28 C1
Nicholson St. SE1 57 E5
Nightingale Pl. 98 B4
SW10

Nile St. N1 26 B4
Nile Ter. SE15 108 B3
Nimrod Pas. N1 15 F2
Noble St. EC2 42 A5
Noel Rd. N1 25 F2
Noel St. W1 54 B1
Norburn St. W10 31 E4
Norfolk Cres. W2 35 E5
Norfolk Ho. SE3 115 F4
Norfolk Pl. W2 35 D5
Norfolk Rd. NW8 19 D1
Norfolk Row SE1 80 A5
Norfolk Sq. W2 51 D1
Norfolk Sq. Ms. W2 51 D1
Norfolk Ter. W6 95 E3
Norland Pl. W11 47 F5
Norland Rd. W11 47 D5
Norland Sq. W11 47 F5
Norman Rd. SE10 121 F1
Norman St. EC1 26 A5
Normand Gdns. 95 F4
W14
Normand Ms. W14 95 F4
Normand Rd. W14 96 A4
Normandy Ter. E16 69 E1
Norris St. SW1 54 C3
North Audley St. 52 C1
W1
North Bank NW8 19 E5
North Carriage Dr. 51 E2
W2
North Colonnade 65 D4
E14
North Ct. W1 38 B3
North Cres. WC1 38 C3
North End Cres. 96 A1
W14
North End Ho. W14 95 F1
North End Rd. SW6 96 B5
North End Rd. W14 71 F5
North Flockton St. 84 C1
SE16
North Gower St. 22 B5
NW1
North Ms. WC1 40 B2
North Pole Rd. W10 30 A4
North Ride W2 51 E3
North Rd. N7 11 E1
North Row W1 52 B2
North Tenter St. E1 60 B1
North Ter. SW3 75 E4
North Vil. NW1 10 C2
North Wk. W2 50 A3
North Wf. Rd. W2 34 C4

North Woolwich Rd. 69 D5
E16
Northampton Pk. 14 B1
N1
Northampton Rd. 41 D1
EC1
Northampton Sq. 25 E5
EC1
Northampton St. 14 A3
N1
Northburgh St. EC1 41 F2
Northchurch SE17 107 D2
Northchurch Rd. 14 C3
N1
Northchurch Ter. 15 E4
N1
Northdown St. N1 23 F2
Northey St. E14 63 F2
Northiam St. E9 29 F1
Northington St. 40 B2
WC1
Northport St. N1 27 D1
Northumberland 59 F1
All. EC3
Northumberland 55 E4
Ave. WC2
Northumberland 32 C5
Pl. W2
Northumberland 55 E4
St. WC2
Northwest Pl. N1 25 D2
Northwick Clo. 34 C1
NW8
Northwick Ter. 34 C1
NW8
Norton Folgate E1 43 F3
Norway Gate SE16 87 F3
Norway Pl. E14 64 A1
Norway St. SE10 113 F4
Norwich St. EC4 40 C5
Notting Barn Rd. 30 C2
W10
Notting Hill Gate 48 C4
W11
Nottingdale Sq. 47 E4
W11
Nottingham Ct. 55 E1
WC2
Nottingham Pl. W1 36 C2
Nottingham St. W1 36 C3
Nottingham Ter. 36 C2
NW1
Nugent Ter. NW8 18 B3
Nun Ct. EC2 42 C5

Nursery La. W10	30	A4
Nutford Pl. W1	35	F5
Nutley Ter. NW3	6	B1
Nutmeg La. E14	66	C1
Nuttall St. N1	27	F2
Nynehead St. SE14	119	E1

O

Oak La. E14	64	A2
Oak Tree Rd. NW8	19	D5
Oakden St. SE11	81	D5
Oakey La. SE1	80	C3
Oakfield St. SW10	98	A4
Oakington Rd. W9	33	D1
Oakley Cres. EC1	25	F3
Oakley Gdns. SW3	99	F4
Oakley Pl. SE1	108	A3
Oakley Rd. N1	14	C3
Oakley Sq. NW1	22	B2
Oakley St. SW3	99	E4
Oakley Wk. W6	95	D4
Oakley Yd. E2	44	B1
Oakwood Ct. W14	72	A3
Oakwood La. W14	72	A3
Oakworth Rd. W10	30	B3
Oat La. EC2	42	B5
Observatory Gdns. W8	73	D1
Observatory Ms. E14	90	C5
Occupation Rd. SE17	106	A2
Ocean Wf. E14	88	C2
Ockendon Rd. N1	14	C2
Octagon Arc. EC2	43	E4
Octavius St. SE8	120	C1
Odessa St. SE16	88	A2
Odhams Wk. WC2	55	E1
Offord Rd. N1	12	A3
Offord St. N1	12	B3
Ogle St. W1	38	A3
Olaf St. W11	47	D3
Old Bailey EC4	57	F1
Old Barrack Yd. SW1	76	C2
Old Bellgate Wf. E14	88	C4
Old Bethnal Grn. Rd. E2	29	D4
Old Bond St. W1	54	A3
Old Brewers Yd. WC2	55	E1

Old Broad St. EC2	59	D1
Old Brompton Rd. SW5	97	D3
Old Brompton Rd. SW7	98	B2
Old Bldgs. WC2	40	C5
Old Burlington St. W1	54	A2
Old Castle St. E1	44	A5
Old Cavendish St. W1	37	E5
Old Chelsea Ms. SW3	99	D5
Old Ch. St. SW3	99	D3
Old Compton St. W1	54	C2
Old Ct. Pl. W8	73	E1
Old Dover Rd. SE3	125	D1
Old Fish St. Hill EC4	58	A2
Old Fleet La. EC4	41	E5
Old Gloucester St. WC1	39	F3
Old Jamaica Rd. SE16	84	C3
Old Jewry EC2	58	C1
Old Kent Rd. SE1	83	E5
Old Kent Rd. SE15	109	D4
Old Manor Yd. SW5	97	E1
Old Marylebone Rd. NW1	35	F4
Old Montague St. E1	44	C4
Old Nichol St. E2	44	A1
Old N. St. WC1	40	A3
Old Palace Yd. SW1	79	E3
Old Paradise St. SE11	80	A5
Old Pk. La. W1	53	D5
Old Pye St. SW1	78	C3
Old Quebec St. W1	52	B1
Old Queen St. SW1	79	D2
Old Royal Free Pl. N1	25	D1
Old Royal Free Sq. N1	25	D1
Old Seacoal La. EC4	57	E1
Old Sq. WC2	40	B5
Old St. EC1	42	A2
Old Woolwich Rd. SE10	115	D4
Oldbury Pl. W1	37	D3
Oldfield Gro. SE16	110	C1

Olivers Yd. EC1	43	D1
Olliffe St. E14	90	B4
Olmar St. SE1	108	C4
Olney Rd. SE17	106	A4
Olympia Ms. W2	49	F3
Olympia Way W14	71	F4
O'Meara St. SE1	58	B5
Omega Clo. E14	89	E3
Omega Pl. N1	23	F3
Omega St. SE14	120	B3
Ommaney Rd. SE14	119	E1
Onega Gate SE16	87	E3
Ongar Rd. SW6	96	C4
Onslow Gdns. SW7	98	C2
Onslow Ms. E. SW7	98	C1
Onslow Ms. W. SW7	98	C1
Onslow Sq. SW7	99	D1
Onslow St. EC1	41	D2
Ontario St. SE1	81	F4
Ontario Way E14	64	C3
Opal St. SE11	105	E2
Oppenheim Rd. SE13	122	A5
Oppidans Ms. NW3	8	A4
Oppidans Rd. NW3	8	A4
Orange Ct. E1	61	D5
Orange Pl. SE16	86	B4
Orange St. WC2	55	D3
Orange Yd. W1	55	D1
Oratory La. SW3	99	D2
Orb St. SE17	106	C1
Orchard, The SE3	123	D5
Orchard Clo. W10	31	F3
Orchard Dr. SE3	123	D5
Orchard Hill SE13	121	F5
Orchard Ms. N1	15	D4
Orchard Pl. E14	67	E2
Orchard Sq. W14	96	A3
Orchard St. W1	52	C1
Orchardson St. NW8	34	C2
Orde Hall St. WC1	40	A3
Ordnance Cres. SE10	91	D1
Ordnance Hill NW8	19	D1
Ordnance Ms. NW8	19	D2
Oregano Dr. E14	67	D1
Orient St. SE11	81	E5
Oriental St. E14	65	D2
Orleston Ms. N7	13	D1
Orleston Rd. N7	13	D1
Orlop St. SE10	115	E3
Orme Ct. W2	49	E3

Orme Ct. Ms. W2	49	F3
Orme La. W2	49	E3
Orme Sq. W2	49	E3
Ormiston Rd. SE10	116	C3
Ormond Clo. WC1	39	F3
Ormond Ms. WC1	39	F2
Ormond Yd. SW1	54	B4
Ormonde Gate SW3	100	B3
Ormonde Pl. SW1	100	C1
Ormonde Ter. NW8	20	A1
Ormsby St. E2	28	A3
Ormside St. SE15	110	A5
Oronsay Wk. N1	14	B2
Orsett St. SE11	104	B2
Orsett Ter. W2	33	F5
Orsman Rd. N1	27	E1
Orton St. E1	60	C5
Osbert St. SW1	102	C1
Osborn Clo. E8	16	C5
Osborn St. E1	44	B4
Oscar St. SE8	120	C4
Oseney Cres. NW5	10	B1
Oslo Ct. NW8	19	E3
Oslo Sq. SE16	87	F3
Osman Rd. W6	70	B3
Osnaburgh St. NW1	37	F1
Osnaburgh Ter. NW1	37	F1
Osric Path N1	27	E3
Ossington Bldgs. W1	36	C3
Ossington Clo. W2	49	D3
Ossington St. W2	49	E3
Ossory Rd. SE1	108	C4
Ossulston St. NW1	22	C3
Osten Ms. SW7	73	F4
Oswell Ho. E1	61	F4
Oswin St. SE11	81	F5
Othello Clo. SE11	105	E2
Otto St. SE17	105	E5
Outer Circle NW1	36	C2
Outram Pl. N1	11	F5
Outwich St. EC3	43	F5
Oval, The E2	29	E2
Oval Rd. NW1	9	E5
Oval Way SE11	104	B3
Oversley Ho. W2	33	D3
Overstone Rd. W6	70	A4
Ovex Clo. E14	90	B2
Ovington Gdns. SW3	75	F4
Ovington Ms. SW3	75	F4
Ovington Sq. SW3	75	F4
Ovington St. SW3	75	F4
Owen St. EC1	25	D3
Owen's Ct. EC1	25	E4
Owen's Row EC1	25	E4
Oxendon St. SW1	54	C3
Oxenholme NW1	22	B3
Oxestalls Rd. SE8	111	F2
Oxford Circ. Ave. W1	54	A1
Oxford Ct. EC4	58	C2
Oxford Gdns. W10	46	B1
Oxford Gate W6	71	D5
Oxford Sq. W2	51	F1
Oxford St. W1	52	C1
Oxley Clo. SE1	108	B2
Oyster Row E1	62	B1

P

Pace Pl. E1	61	F1
Packington Sq. N1	26	A1
Packington St. N1	13	F5
Padbury SE17	107	E3
Padbury Ct. E2	28	B5
Paddington Grn. W2	35	D3
Paddington St. W1	36	C3
Page St. SW1	79	D5
Pageant Cres. SE16	63	F4
Pageantmaster Ct. EC4	57	E1
Pages Wk. SE1	83	E5
Paget St. EC1	25	E4
Pagnell St. SE14	120	A1
Pakenham St. WC1	24	B5
Palace Ave. W8	49	F5
Palace Ct. W2	49	E2
Palace Gdns. Ms. W8	49	D4
Palace Gdns. Ter. W8	49	D4
Palace Gate W8	74	A2
Palace Grn. W8	49	E5
Palace Ms. SW1	101	D1
Palace Pl. SW1	78	A3
Palace St. SW1	78	A3
Palissy St. E2	28	A5
Pall Mall SW1	54	B5
Pall Mall E. SW1	55	D4
Pall Mall Pl. SW1	54	B5
Palliser Rd. W14	95	E2
Palmer St. SW1	78	C3
Pancras La. EC4	58	B1
Pancras Rd. NW1	23	E3
Pangbourne Ave. W10	30	B3
Pankhurst Clo. SE14	118	C2
Panton St. SW1	54	C3
Panyer All. EC4	42	A5
Paradise Pas. N7	12	C1
Paradise Row E2	29	F4
Paradise St. SE16	85	F2
Paradise Wk. SW3	100	B4
Paragon, The SE3	124	B5
Paragon Ms. SE1	83	D5
Paragon Pl. SE3	124	B5
Paragon Rd. E9	17	F2
Pardon St. EC1	41	F1
Pardoner St. SE1	83	D3
Parfett St. E1	45	D4
Parfrey St. W6	94	B4
Paris Gdns. SE1	57	E4
Park Clo. SW1	76	A2
Park Clo. W14	72	B3
Park Cres. W1	37	E2
Park Cres. Ms. E. W1	37	F2
Park Cres. Ms. W. W1	37	E2
Park Gdn. Pl. W2	51	D1
Park La. W1	52	B2
Park Pl. E14	64	C4
Park Pl. SW1	54	A5
Park Pl. Vil. W2	34	B3
Park Rd. NW1	19	E4
Park Rd. NW8	19	E4
Park Row SE10	114	C4
Park Sq. E. NW1	37	E1
Park Sq. Ms. NW1	37	E2
Park Sq. W. NW1	37	E1
Park St. SE1	58	A4
Park St. W1	52	C2
Park Village E. NW1	21	E2
Park Village W. NW1	21	E2
Park Vista SE10	115	D5
Park Wk. SE10	122	C2
Park Wk. SW10	98	B4
Park W. W2	51	D1
Park W. Pl. W2	35	F5
Parker Ms. WC2	39	F5
Parker St. WC2	39	F5
Parkers Row SE1	84	B2
Parkfield Rd. SE14	120	A3
Parkfield St. N1	25	D2
Parkhill Rd. NW3	8	A1

Parkholme Rd. E8	16	B1
Parkhurst Ave. E16	69	F4
Parkside Wk. SE10	91	E4
Parkway NW1	21	E1
Parliament Sq. SW1	79	E2
Parliament St. SW1	79	E2
Parmiter St. E2	29	F2
Parr St. N1	26	C2
Parry St. SW8	103	E4
Parsonage St. E14	114	B1
Parson's Ho. W2	34	C2
Pasley Clo. SE17	106	A3
Passing All. EC1	41	E2
Passmore St. SW1	100	C1
Pastor St. SE11	81	F5
Pater St. W8	72	C4
Paternoster Row EC4	58	A1
Paternoster Sq. EC4	41	F5
Paton St. EC1	26	A5
Patriot Sq. E2	29	F3
Patshull Pl. NW5	10	A2
Patshull Rd. NW5	10	A1
Patterdale Rd. SE15	118	A1
Paul Julius Clo. E14	66	C3
Paul St. EC2	43	D2
Paultons Sq. SW3	99	D4
Paultons St. SW3	99	D5
Paveley St. NW8	19	F5
Pavilion Rd. SW1	76	B2
Pavilion St. SW1	76	B4
Paxton Ter. SW1	101	F4
Payne St. SE8	112	B5
Paynes Wk. W6	95	E5
Peabody Ave. SW1	101	E3
Peabody Clo. SE10	121	F3
Peabody Dws. WC1	39	E1
Peabody Est. EC1	42	B2
Peabody Est. SE1	57	D5
Peabody Est. SW3	99	F4
Peabody Est. W6	94	B3
Peabody Est. W10	30	B2
Peabody Sq. N1	13	F5
Peabody Sq. SE1	81	E2
Peabody Trust SE1	58	A5
Peabody Yd. N1	14	A5
Peachum Rd. SE3	116	B4
Peacock St. SE17	105	F1
Peacock Yd. SE17	105	F1
Pear Clo. SE14	119	F2
Pear Pl. SE1	80	C1
Pear Tree Ct. EC1	41	D2
Pear Tree St. EC1	41	F1
Pearl St. E1	61	F4
Pearman St. SE1	81	D3
Pearson St. E2	28	A2
Pearsons Ave. SE14	120	C3
Peartree La. E1	62	B3
Peartree Way SE10	92	C5
Pedlars Wk. N7	11	F1
Pedley St. E1	44	B2
Pedworth Gdns. SE16	110	A1
Peel Pas. W8	48	C5
Peel St. W8	48	C5
Peerless St. EC1	26	C5
Pegasus Pl. SE11	104	C4
Pekin Clo. E14	65	D1
Pekin St. E14	65	D1
Peldon Wk. N1	13	F5
Pelham Cres. SW7	99	E1
Pelham Pl. SW7	75	E5
Pelham St. SW7	75	D5
Pelier St. SE17	106	B4
Pellant Rd. SW6	95	F5
Pelter St. E2	28	A4
Pelton Rd. SE10	115	E2
Pemberton Pl. E8	17	F4
Pemberton Row EC4	41	D5
Pembridge Cres. W11	48	C2
Pembridge Gdns. W2	48	C3
Pembridge Ms. W11	48	C2
Pembridge Pl. W2	49	D2
Pembridge Rd. W11	48	C3
Pembridge Sq. W2	49	D3
Pembridge Vil. W2	49	D3
Pembridge Vil. W11	48	C2
Pembroke Clo. SW1	77	D2
Pembroke Gdns. W8	72	B5
Pembroke Gdns. Clo. W8	72	C4
Pembroke Ms. W8	72	C4
Pembroke Pl. W8	72	C4
Pembroke Rd. W8	72	B5
Pembroke Sq. W8	72	C4
Pembroke St. N1	11	F4
Pembroke Studios W8	72	B4
Pembroke Vil. W8	72	C5
Pembroke Wk. W8	72	C5
Penally Pl. N1	15	D5
Penang St. E1	61	F4
Penarth St. SE15	110	A4
Pencombe Ms. W11	48	B2
Pencraig Way SE15	109	E5
Penfold Pl. NW1	35	E3
Penfold St. NW1	35	D2
Penfold St. NW8	35	D2
Peninsular Pk. Rd. SE7	117	D1
Penn St. N1	27	D1
Pennack Rd. SE15	108	B5
Pennant Ms. W8	73	E5
Pennard Rd. W12	70	A1
Pennington St. E1	61	D3
Pennyfields E14	65	D2
Pennymoor Wk. W9	32	B1
Penpoll Rd. E8	17	E1
Penrose Gro. SE17	106	A3
Penrose Ho. SE17	106	A3
Penrose St. SE17	106	A3
Penry St. SE1	107	F1
Penryn St. NW1	22	C2
Penton Gro. N1	24	C3
Penton Pl. SE17	105	F2
Penton Ri. WC1	24	B4
Penton St. N1	24	C3
Pentonville Rd. N1	24	A3
Penywern Rd. SW5	97	D2
Penzance Pl. W11	47	E4
Penzance St. W11	47	E4
Pepper St. E14	89	E3
Pepper St. SE1	82	A1
Pepys Cres. E16	69	D4
Pepys Rd. SE14	119	D4
Pepys St. EC3	59	F2
Percival St. EC1	41	E1
Percy Circ. WC1	24	B4
Percy Ms. W1	38	C4
Percy Pas. W1	38	B4
Percy St. W1	38	C4
Percy Yd. WC1	24	B4
Peregrine Ho. EC1	25	F4
Perham Rd. W14	95	F3
Perkin's Rents SW1	78	C3
Perkins Sq. SE1	58	B4
Perren St. NW5	9	E1
Perryn Rd. SE16	85	E3
Perrys Pl. W1	38	C5
Peter St. W1	54	C2
Peterboat Clo. SE10	91	F5
Peterchurch Ho. SE15	109	E5

Peters Hill EC4	58 A1	
Peter's La. EC1	41 E3	
Petersham La. SW7	74 A3	
Petersham Ms. SW7	74 A4	
Petersham Pl. SW7	74 A3	
Petley Rd. W6	94 B5	
Peto Pl. NW1	37 F1	
Petticoat Sq. E1	44 A5	
Petty France SW1	78 B3	
Petyt Pl. SW3	99 E5	
Petyward SW3	99 F1	
Peyton Pl. SE10	122 A1	
Phelp St. SE17	106 C4	
Phene St. SW3	99 F4	
Philbeach Gdns. SW5	96 C1	
Philchurch Pl. E1	61 D1	
Phillimore Gdns. W8	72 C2	
Phillimore Gdns. Clo. W8	72 C3	
Phillimore Pl. W8	72 C2	
Phillimore Wk. W8	72 C3	
Phillipp St. N1	27 E1	
Philpot La. EC3	59 E2	
Philpot St. E1	45 F5	
Phipp St. EC2	43 E1	
Phipp's Ms. SW1	77 E4	
Phoenix Clo. E8	16 A5	
Phoenix Pl. WC1	40 B1	
Phoenix Rd. NW1	22 C4	
Phoenix St. WC2	55 D1	
Phoenix Wf. SE10	92 A1	
Physic Pl. SW3	100 A3	
Piccadilly W1	53 F5	
Piccadilly Arc. SW1	54 A4	
Piccadilly Circ. W1	54 C3	
Piccadilly Pl. W1	54 B3	
Pickard St. EC1	25 F4	
Pickering Ms. W2	33 F5	
Pickering Pl. SW1	54 B5	
Pickering St. N1	13 F5	
Pickfords Wf. N1	26 A3	
Pickwick St. SE1	82 A2	
Picton Pl. W1	53 D1	
Pier St. E14	90 B5	
Pierrepoint Row N1	25 E2	
Pigott St. E14	64 C1	
Pilgrim St. EC4	57 E1	
Pilgrimage St. SE1	82 C2	
Pilgrims Ct. SE3	125 D3	
Pimlico Rd. SW1	100 C2	
Pimlico Wk. N1	27 E4	
Pinchin St. E1	61 D2	
Pindar St. EC2	43 E3	
Pindock Ms. W9	33 F2	
Pine St. EC1	40 C1	
Pineapple Ct. SW1	78 A3	
Pinefield Clo. E14	64 C2	
Pinelands Clo. SE3	124 B2	
Pirie St. E16	69 F5	
Pitfield Est. N1	27 E4	
Pitfield St. N1	27 E5	
Pitsea Pl. E1	63 D1	
Pitsea St. E1	63 D1	
Pitt St. W8	73 D1	
Pitt's Head Ms. W1	53 D5	
Plantain Pl. SE1	82 C1	
Platina St. EC2	43 D1	
Platt St. NW1	22 C2	
Playfair St. W6	94 B3	
Playhouse Yd. EC4	57 E1	
Pleasant Pl. N1	13 F4	
Pleasant Row NW1	21 F1	
Plender St. NW1	22 A1	
Plender St. Est. NW1	22 B1	
Plevna St. E14	90 A3	
Pleydell St. EC4	57 D1	
Plimsoll Clo. E14	65 E1	
Plough Ct. EC3	59 D2	
Plough Pl. EC4	41 D5	
Plough St. E1	44 B5	
Plough Way SE16	87 D5	
Plough Yd. EC2	43 F2	
Ploughmans Clo. NW1	10 C5	
Plover Way SE16	87 F3	
Plumbers Row E1	45 D4	
Plumbridge St. SE10	122 A3	
Plumtree Ct. EC4	41 E5	
Plymouth Wf. E14	90 C5	
Plympton Pl. NW8	35 E2	
Plympton St. NW8	35 E2	
Pocock St. SE1	81 E1	
Point Clo. SE10	122 B3	
Point Hill SE10	122 B2	
Point of Thomas Path E1	62 B3	
Pointers Clo. E14	113 E2	
Poland St. W1	38 B5	
Polesworth Ho. W2	33 D3	
Pollard Clo. E16	68 C2	
Pollard Row E2	29 D4	
Pollard St. E2	29 D4	
Pollen St. W1	54 A1	
Pollitt Dr. NW8	35 D1	
Polygon Rd. NW1	22 C3	
Pomell Way E1	44 B5	
Pomeroy St. SE14	118 B2	
Pond Pl. SW3	99 E1	
Pond Rd. SE3	124 B5	
Ponder St. N7	12 A3	
Ponler St. E1	61 E1	
Ponsonby Pl. SW1	103 D2	
Ponsonby Ter. SW1	103 D2	
Pont St. SW1	76 A4	
Pont St. Ms. SW1	76 A4	
Ponton Rd. SW8	103 D5	
Pontypool Pl. SE1	81 E1	
Poole St. N1	26 C1	
Pooles Bldgs. EC1	40 C2	
Poolmans St. SE16	86 C1	
Poonah St. E1	62 B1	
Pope St. SE1	83 F2	
Popham Rd. N1	14 A5	
Popham St. N1	14 A5	
Poplar Bath St. E14	65 F2	
Poplar Business Pk. E14	66 A3	
Poplar Gro. W6	70 B2	
Poplar High St. E14	65 E2	
Poplar Pl. W2	49 E2	
Poppins Ct. EC4	57 E1	
Porchester Gdns. W2	49 F2	
Porchester Gdns. Ms. W2	49 F1	
Porchester Ms. W2	33 F5	
Porchester Pl. W2	51 F1	
Porchester Rd. W2	33 F5	
Porchester Sq. W2	33 F5	
Porchester Ter. W2	50 A2	
Porchester Ter. N. W2	33 F5	
Porlock Rd. W10	31 D2	
Porlock St. SE1	83 D1	
Porten Rd. W14	71 E4	
Porter St. SE1	58 B4	
Porter St. W1	36 B3	
Porters Wk. E1	61 F3	
Porteus Rd. W2	34 B3	
Portgate Clo. W9	32 B1	
Portland Ms. W1	54 B1	
Portland Pl. W1	37 E2	
Portland Rd. W11	47 E3	
Portland Sq. E1	61 E4	
Portland St. SE17	106 C2	
Portland Wk. SE17	107 D4	
Portman Clo. W1	36 B5	
Portman Gate NW1	35 F2	

Portman Ms. S. W1	52	C1
Portman Sq. W1	36	C5
Portman St. W1	52	C1
Portobello Ct. W11	48	B1
Portobello Ms. W11	48	C3
Portobello Rd. W10	31	E3
Portobello Rd. W11	32	A5
Portpool La. EC1	40	C3
Portsea Ms. W2	51	F1
Portsea Pl. W2	51	F1
Portsmouth Ms. E16	69	F4
Portsmouth St. WC2	56	A1
Portsoken St. E1	60	A2
Portugal St. WC2	56	A1
Post Office Ct. EC3	59	D1
Potier St. SE1	83	D4
Pott St. E2	29	F5
Pottery La. W11	47	F3
Pottery St. SE16	85	E2
Poulton Clo. E8	17	E1
Poultry EC2	58	C1
Powis Gdns. W11	32	B5
Powis Ms. W11	32	B5
Powis Pl. WC1	39	F2
Powis Sq. W11	48	B1
Powis Ter. W11	32	B5
Powlett Pl. NW1	9	E2
Pownall Rd. E8	28	C1
Poyser St. E2	29	F3
Praed Ms. W2	35	D5
Praed St. W2	35	D5
Pratt Ms. NW1	22	A1
Pratt St. NW1	22	A1
Pratt Wk. SE11	80	B5
Prebend St. N1	26	A1
Premiere Pl. E14	64	C3
Prescot St. E1	60	B2
Prescott Ho. SE17	105	F5
President Dr. E1	61	E4
President St. EC1	26	A4
Prestage Way E14	66	B2
Preston Clo. SE1	83	E5
Prestons Rd. E14	66	B5
Prestwood St. N1	26	B3
Price's Yd. N1	24	B1
Prideaux Pl. WC1	24	B4
Priest Ct. EC2	42	A5
Primrose Gdns. NW3	7	F1
Primrose Hill EC4	57	D1
Primrose Hill Ct. NW3	8	A4
Primrose Hill Rd. NW3	7	F2
Primrose Hill Studios NW1	8	C5
Primrose Ms. NW1	8	B4
Primrose Ms. SE3	125	E2
Primrose St. EC2	43	E3
Prince Albert Rd. NW1	19	F3
Prince Albert Rd. NW8	19	F3
Prince Charles Rd. SE3	124	A3
Prince Consort Rd. SW7	74	C3
Prince of Wales Gate SW7	75	E1
Prince of Wales Pas. NW1	22	A5
Prince of Wales Rd. NW5	8	C2
Prince of Wales Rd. SE3	124	B4
Prince of Wales Ter. W8	73	F2
Prince St. SE8	112	B4
Princedale Rd. W11	47	F4
Princelet St. E1	44	B3
Prince's Arc. SW1	54	B4
Princes Ct. E1	61	F3
Princes Ct. SE16	88	A4
Princes Gdns. SW7	75	D3
Princes Gate SW7	75	D2
Princes Gate Ct. SW7	75	D2
Princes Gate Ms. SW7	75	D3
Princes Ms. W2	49	E2
Princes Pl. SW1	54	B4
Princes Pl. W11	47	E4
Princes Ri. SE13	122	B5
Princes Riverside Rd. SE16	62	C4
Princes Sq. W2	49	E2
Princes St. EC2	58	C1
Princes St. W1	53	F1
Princes Yd. W11	47	F5
Princess Ms. NW3	7	D1
Princess Rd. NW1	8	C5
Princess St. SE1	81	F4
Princethorpe Ho. W2	33	E3
Princeton St. WC1	40	A4
Printing Ho. Yd. E2	27	F5
Prior Bolton St. N1	13	F2
Prior St. SE10	122	A2
Prioress St. SE1	83	D4
Priory Grn. Est. N1	24	B2
Priory Wk. SW10	98	B3
Pritchard's Rd. E2	29	D1
Priter Rd. SE16	85	D4
Procter St. WC1	40	A4
Prospect Pl. E1	62	A4
Prospect St. SE16	85	F3
Providence Ct. W1	53	D2
Providence Pl. N1	25	E1
Providence Row N1	24	A3
Providence Yd. E2	28	C4
Provost Est. N1	26	C4
Provost Rd. NW3	8	B3
Provost St. N1	26	C3
Prowse Pl. NW1	10	A3
Prudent Pas. EC2	42	C5
Prusom St. E1	61	F4
Pudding La. EC3	59	D3
Puddle Dock EC4	57	F2
Pulteney Ter. N1	24	B1
Puma Ct. E1	44	A3
Pump Ct. EC4	56	C1
Pump La. SE14	118	B1
Pundersons Gdns. E2	29	F4
Purbrook Est. SE1	83	F2
Purbrook St. SE1	83	F3
Purcell St. N1	27	E2
Purchese St. NW1	23	D2
Purley Pl. N1	13	E3

Q

Quadrant Arc. W1	54	B3
Quaker St. E1	44	A2
Quality Ct. WC2	40	C5
Quarterdeck, The E14	88	C2
Quebec Ms. W1	52	B1
Quebec Way SE16	87	D2
Queen Anne Ms. W1	37	F4
Queen Anne St. W1	37	E5
Queen Anne's Gate SW1	78	C2
Queen Anne's Wk. WC1	39	F2

Rawlings St. SW3	76	A5
Rawreth Wk. N1	14	B5
Rawstorne Pl. EC1	25	E4
Rawstorne St. EC1	25	E4
Ray St. EC1	41	D2
Ray St. Bri. EC1	41	D2
Rayleigh Rd. E16	69	F4
Raymond Bldgs. WC1	40	B3
Raymouth Rd. SE16	85	F5
Raynor Pl. N1	14	B4
Reachview Clo. NW1	10	B4
Reading La. E8	17	E2
Reapers Clo. NW1	10	C5
Reardon Path E1	61	F5
Reardon St. E1	61	E4
Reaston St. SE14	118	B1
Record St. SE15	110	A4
Rector St. N1	26	A1
Reculver Rd. SE16	110	C2
Red Anchor Clo. SW3	99	E5
Red Lion Clo. SE17	106	C4
Red Lion Ct. EC4	57	D1
Red Lion Row SE17	106	B4
Red Lion Sq. WC1	40	A4
Red Lion St. WC1	40	A3
Red Lion Yd. W1	53	D4
Red Pl. W1	52	C2
Redan Pl. W2	49	E1
Redan St. W14	71	D3
Redburn St. SW3	100	A4
Redcastle Clo. E1	62	A2
Redchurch St. E2	44	A1
Redcliffe Gdns. SW5	97	F3
Redcliffe Gdns. SW10	97	F3
Redcliffe Ms. SW10	97	F3
Redcliffe Pl. SW10	98	A5
Redcliffe Rd. SW10	98	A3
Redcliffe Sq. SW10	97	F3
Redcliffe St. SW10	97	F4
Redcross Way SE1	82	B1
Reddins Rd. SE15	108	C5
Rede Pl. W2	49	D2
Redesdale St. SW3	99	F4
Redfield La. SW5	73	D5
Redford Wk. N1	13	F5
Redhill St. NW1	21	F4
Redlaw Way SE16	109	D3
Redmead La. E1	60	C5
Redriff Est. SE16	88	A3
Redriff Rd. SE16	87	D4
Redstart Clo. SE14	119	E1
Redvers St. N1	27	F4
Redwood Clo. SE16	63	F5
Reece Ms. SW7	74	C5
Reeds Pl. NW1	10	A3
Reedworth St. SE11	105	D1
Rees St. N1	26	B1
Reeves Ms. W1	52	C3
Regal Clo. E1	45	D3
Regal La. NW1	21	D1
Regan Way N1	27	E3
Regency Pl. SW1	79	D5
Regency St. SW1	79	D5
Regent Pl. W1	54	B2
Regent Sq. WC1	23	F5
Regent St. SW1	54	C3
Regent St. W1	37	F5
Regents Ms. NW8	18	B2
Regent's Pk. NW1	20	A3
Regent's Pk. Est. NW1	22	A5
Regents Pk. Rd. NW1	8	B5
Regents Pk. Ter. NW1	9	E5
Regent's Pl. SE3	124	C5
Regents Row E8	28	B1
Reginald Rd. SE8	121	D2
Reginald Sq. SE8	120	C2
Regnart Bldgs. NW1	38	B1
Relay Rd. W12	46	B3
Relton Ms. SW7	75	F3
Rembrandt Clo. E14	90	C4
Rembrandt Clo. SW1	100	C1
Remington St. N1	25	F3
Remnant St. WC2	40	A5
Rempstone Ms. N1	27	D2
Renforth St. SE16	86	B2
Renfrew Rd. SE11	81	E5
Rennie Est. SE16	109	F1
Rennie St. SE1	57	E4
Rephidim St. SE1	83	D4
Restell Clo. SE3	115	F4
Reston Pl. SW7	74	A2
Reunion Row E1	61	F3
Reveley Sq. SE16	87	F2
Reverdy Rd. SE1	108	C1
Rex Pl. W1	53	D3
Reynolds Pl. SE3	125	F1
Rheidol Ms. N1	26	A2
Rheidol Ter. N1	25	F2
Rhoda St. E2	44	B1
Rhyl St. NW5	9	D1
Ricardo St. E14	65	E1
Rich La. SW5	97	E3
Rich St. E14	64	B2
Richard St. E1	61	E1
Richards Pl. SW3	75	F5
Richardson Clo. E8	16	A5
Richardson's Ms. W1	38	A2
Richbell Pl. WC1	40	A3
Richford St. W6	70	A2
Richmond Ave. N1	12	B5
Richmond Bldgs. W1	54	C1
Richmond Cres. N1	12	B5
Richmond Gro. N1	13	E4
Richmond Ms. W1	54	C1
Richmond Rd. E8	16	A3
Richmond Ter. SW1	79	E1
Richmond Way W12	71	D1
Richmond Way W14	71	D2
Rickett St. SW6	97	D4
Ridgmount Gdns. WC1	38	C3
Ridgmount Pl. WC1	38	C3
Ridgmount St. WC1	38	C3
Riding Ho. St. W1	37	F4
Rifle Pl. SE11	105	D4
Rifle Pl. W11	47	D4
Rigden St. E14	65	E1
Riley Rd. SE1	84	A3
Riley St. SW10	98	C5
Ring, The W2	51	E2
Ring Rd. W12	46	A3
Ringwood Gdns. E14	89	D5
Ripplevale Gro. N1	12	B4
Risborough St. SE1	81	F1
Risdon St. SE16	86	B2
Rising Sun Ct. EC1	41	F4
Risinghill St. N1	24	C2
Rita Rd. SW8	103	F3
Ritchie St. N1	25	D2
Ritson Rd. E8	16	C1
River Barge Clo. E14	90	B2
River Pl. N1	14	A4
River St. EC1	24	C4

Sanford St. SE14 111 E5
Sanford Wk. SE14 111 E5
Sans Wk. EC1 41 D1
Sapphire Rd. SE8 111 F1
Saracen St. E14 65 D1
Saracen's Head Yd. 60 A1
EC3
Sarah St. N1 27 F4
Sardinia St. WC2 56 A1
Sarnesfield Ho. 109 E5
SE15
Satchwell Rd. E2 28 C5
Saunders Clo. E14 64 B3
Saunders Ness Rd. 114 B2
E14
Saunders St. SE11 80 C5
Savage Gdns. EC3 59 F2
Savile Row W1 54 A2
Savoy Bldgs. WC2 56 A3
Savoy Ct. WC2 55 F3
Savoy Hill WC2 56 A3
Savoy Pl. WC2 55 F3
Savoy Row WC2 56 A3
Savoy Steps WC2 56 A3
Savoy St. WC2 56 A3
Savoy Way WC2 56 A3
Sawyer St. SE1 82 A1
Sayes Ct. SE8 112 B4
Sayes Ct. St. SE8 112 B4
Scala St. W1 38 B3
Scampston Ms. 47 D1
W10
Scandrett St. E1 61 E5
Scarba Wk. N1 14 C2
Scarborough St. E1 60 B1
Scarsdale Pl. W8 73 E3
Scarsdale Vil. W8 73 D4
Scawen Rd. SE8 111 E3
Scawfell St. E2 28 B3
Schofield Wk. SE3 125 E1
Schoolhouse La. E1 62 C2
Schooner Clo. E14 90 C4
Schooner Clo. SE16 86 C1
Sclater St. E1 44 A1
Scoresby St. SE1 57 E5
Scotland Pl. SW1 55 E4
Scotswood St. EC1 41 D1
Scott Ellis Gdns. 18 C5
NW8
Scott Lidgett Cres. 84 C2
SE16
Scott Russell Pl. 113 E2
E14
Scott St. E1 45 E2

Scott's Yd. EC4 58 C2
Scouler St. E14 66 C3
Scovell Cres. SE1 82 A2
Scovell Rd. SE1 82 A2
Scriven St. E8 16 B5
Scrubs La. W10 30 A4
Scrutton St. EC2 43 E2
Seabright St. E2 29 E5
Seaford St. WC1 23 F5
Seaforth Pl. SW1 78 B3
Seagrave Rd. SW6 97 D4
Searles Rd. SE1 83 D5
Seaton Clo. SE11 105 E2
Seaton Pl. NW1 38 A1
Sebastian St. EC1 25 F5
Sebbon St. N1 13 F4
Sebright Pas. E2 29 D3
Secker St. SE1 56 C5
Second Ave. W10 31 F1
Sedan Way SE17 107 E2
Sedding St. SW1 76 C5
Seddon St. WC1 24 B5
Sedlescombe Rd. 96 B5
SW6
Sedley Pl. W1 53 E1
Seething La. EC3 59 F2
Sekforde St. EC1 41 E2
Selby St. E1 45 D2
Sellon Ms. SE11 104 B1
Selsdon Way E14 89 F4
Selwood Pl. SW7 98 C2
Selwood Ter. SW7 98 C2
Semley Pl. SW1 101 D1
Senior St. W2 33 E3
Serjeants Inn EC4 57 D1
Serle St. WC2 40 B5
Serpentine Rd. W2 52 A5
Setchell Rd. SE1 84 A5
Setchell Way SE1 84 A5
Seth St. SE16 86 B2
Settles St. E1 45 D4
Severnake Clo. E14 89 D5
Seville Ms. N1 15 E4
Seville St. SW1 76 B2
Sevington St. W9 33 E2
Seward St. EC1 25 F5
Sextant Ave. E14 90 C5
Seymour Ms. W1 36 C5
Seymour Pl. W1 35 F3
Seymour St. W1 52 A1
Seymour St. W2 52 A1
Seymour Wk. SW10 98 A4
Seyssel St. E14 90 B5
Shacklewell St. E2 44 B1

Shad Thames SE1 60 A5
Shadwell Gdns. E1 62 A2
Shadwell Pierhead 62 B3
E1
Shadwell Pl. E1 62 A2
Shaftesbury Ave. 54 C2
W1
Shaftesbury Ave. 54 C3
WC2
Shaftesbury Ms. W8 73 D4
Shaftesbury St. N1 26 B3
Shafto Ms. SW1 76 A4
Shalcomb St. SW10 98 B5
Shalfleet Dr. W10 46 C2
Shand St. SE1 83 F1
Shannon Pl. NW8 19 F2
Shardeloes Rd. 120 A5
SE14
Sharpleshall St. 8 B4
NW1
Sharratt St. SE15 110 B4
Sharsted St. SE17 105 E3
Shavers Pl. SW1 54 C3
Shawfield St. SW3 99 F3
Shearling Way N7 11 F1
Shearsmith Ho. E1 61 D2
Sheen Gro. N1 12 C5
Sheep La. E8 29 E1
Sheffield St. WC2 56 A1
Sheffield Ter. W8 48 C5
Sheldrake Pl. W8 72 C1
Shelton St. WC2 55 E1
Shenfield St. N1 27 F3
Shepherd Mkt. W1 53 E5
Shepherd St. W1 53 E5
Shepherdess Pl. N1 26 B4
Shepherdess Wk. 26 B3
N1
Shepherds Bush 70 B1
Grn. W12
Shepherds Bush 70 A1
Mkt. W12
Shepherds Bush Pl. 70 C1
W12
Shepherds Bush Rd. 70 A2
W6
Shepherds Ct. W12 70 C1
Shepherds Pl. W1 52 C2
Sheppard Dr. SE16 109 E2
Shepperton Rd. N1 14 B5
Sheppey Wk. N1 14 B3
Sheraton St. W1 54 C1
Sherborne La. EC4 58 C2
Sherborne St. N1 14 C5

Stanley Gdns. Ms. W11	48	B2
Stanley Pas. NW1	23	E3
Stanley St. SE8	120	B2
Stanmore Pl. NW1	9	F5
Stanmore St. N1	12	A5
Stannard Ms. E8	16	C1
Stannard Rd. E8	16	C1
Stannary Pl. SE11	105	D3
Stannary St. SE11	105	D4
Stanway St. N1	27	F2
Stanwick Rd. W14	96	A1
Stanworth St. SE1	84	A2
Staple Inn Bldgs. WC1	40	C4
Staple St. SE1	83	D2
Staples Clo. SE16	63	E4
Star Pl. E1	60	B3
Star Rd. W14	96	A4
Star St. W2	35	D5
Star Yd. WC2	40	C5
Starboard Way E14	89	E3
Starcross St. NW1	22	B5
Station App. SE1	80	B2
Station Cres. SE3	116	C3
Station Path E8	17	F1
Staunton St. SE8	112	B4
Stave Yd. Rd. SE16	63	E5
Stead St. SE17	106	C1
Stean St. E8	16	A5
Stebondale St. E14	114	B1
Stedham Pl. WC1	39	E5
Steedman St. SE17	106	A1
Steeles Ms. N. NW3	8	A2
Steeles Ms. S. NW3	8	B2
Steeles Rd. NW3	8	A2
Steel's La. E1	62	B1
Steeple Ct. E1	45	F1
Steeple Wk. N1	14	B5
Steers Way SE16	87	F2
Stephan Clo. E8	17	D5
Stephen Ms. W1	38	C4
Stephen St. W1	38	C4
Stephenson Way NW1	38	B1
Stepney Causeway E1	63	D1
Stepney Way E1	45	E4
Sterling Gdns. SE14	111	E5
Sterling St. SW7	75	F2
Sterndale Rd. W14	70	C4

Sterne St. W12	70	C1
Sterry St. SE1	82	C2
Stevedore St. E1	61	E4
Stevens St. SE1	83	F3
Stevenson Cres. SE16	109	D2
Stew La. EC4	58	A2
Steward St. E1	43	F3
Stewart St. E14	90	B2
Stewart's Gro. SW3	99	E2
Stillington St. SW1	78	B5
Stockholm Rd. SE16	110	B3
Stockholm Way E1	60	C4
Stocks Pl. E14	64	B2
Stockwell St. SE10	114	B5
Stone Bldgs. WC2	40	B4
Stone Hall Gdns. W8	73	E4
Stone Hall Pl. W8	73	E4
Stone Ho. Ct. EC3	43	F5
Stonebridge Common E8	16	A4
Stonecutter St. EC4	41	E5
Stonefield St. N1	13	D5
Stoneleigh Pl. W11	47	D3
Stoneleigh St. W11	47	D3
Stones End St. SE1	82	A2
Stoney La. E1	44	A5
Stoney St. SE1	58	C4
Stoneyard La. E14	65	E3
Stonor Rd. W14	96	A1
Stopford Rd. SE17	105	F3
Store St. WC1	38	C4
Storers Quay E14	114	C1
Storey's Gate SW1	79	D2
Storks Rd. SE16	85	D4
Story St. N1	12	A4
Stoughton Clo. SE11	104	B1
Stourcliffe St. W1	52	A1
Stowage SE8	113	E5
Strafford St. E14	88	C1
Straightsmouth SE10	122	A1
Strand WC2	55	E3
Strand La. WC2	56	B2
Strangways Ter. W14	72	A3
Stranraer Way N1	11	F4
Stratford Ave. W8	73	D4
Stratford Pl. W1	53	E1
Stratford Rd. W8	73	D4

Stratford Vil. NW1	10	B3
Strathearn Pl. W2	51	E2
Stratheden Rd. SE3	124	C3
Strathmore Gdns. W8	49	D4
Strathnairn St. SE1	109	D1
Strathray Gdns. NW3	7	E2
Stratton St. W1	53	F4
Strattondale St. E14	90	A3
Streatham St. WC1	39	E5
Strickland St. SE8	121	D4
Strouts Pl. E2	28	A4
Strutton Grd. SW1	78	C3
Strype St. E1	44	A4
Stuart Twr. W9	18	A5
Stubbs Dr. SE16	109	E2
Stucley Pl. NW1	9	F4
Studd St. N1	13	E5
Studio Pl. SW1	76	B2
Studland SE17	106	C2
Stukeley St. WC2	39	F5
Sturge St. SE1	82	A1
Sturgeon Rd. SE17	106	A3
Sturry St. E14	65	F1
Sturt St. N1	26	B3
Stutfield St. E1	61	D1
Sudeley St. N1	25	F3
Sudrey St. SE1	82	A2
Suffolk La. EC4	58	C2
Suffolk Pl. SW1	55	D4
Suffolk St. SW1	55	D3
Sugar Bakers Ct. EC3	59	F1
Sugar Quay Wk. EC3	59	F3
Sulgrave Gdns. W6	70	B2
Sulgrave Rd. W6	70	B3
Sullivan Rd. SE11	81	D5
Summer St. EC1	40	C2
Sumner Pl. SW7	99	D1
Sumner Pl. Ms. SW7	99	D1
Sumner Rd. SE15	108	B5
Sumner St. SE1	57	F4
Sumpter Clo. NW3	6	B2
Sun Ct. EC3	59	D1
Sun La. SE3	125	F2
Sun Pas. SE16	84	C3
Sun Rd. W14	96	A3
Sun St. EC2	43	D3

Sun St. Pas. EC2	43	E4
Sun Wk. E1	60	B3
Sunbeam Cres. W10	30	B2
Sunderland Ter. W2	33	E5
Sunfields Pl. SE3	125	E1
Sunningdale Gdns. W8	73	D4
Surma Clo. E1	45	E2
Surrendale Pl. W9	33	D2
Surrey Canal Rd. SE14	110	B4
Surrey Canal Rd. SE15	110	B4
Surrey Gro. SE17	107	E3
Surrey Lo. SE1	80	C4
Surrey Quays Rd. SE16	86	C2
Surrey Row SE1	81	E1
Surrey Sq. SE17	107	E2
Surrey St. WC2	56	B2
Surrey Ter. SE17	107	F2
Surrey Water Rd. SE16	63	D5
Susannah St. E14	66	A1
Sussex Gdns. W2	50	C2
Sussex Ms. E. W2	51	D1
Sussex Ms. W. W2	51	D2
Sussex Pl. NW1	20	A5
Sussex Pl. W2	51	D1
Sussex Pl. W6	94	B2
Sussex Sq. W2	51	D2
Sussex St. SW1	101	F3
Sutherland Ave. W9	33	D2
Sutherland Pl. W2	32	C5
Sutherland Row SW1	101	F2
Sutherland Sq. SE17	106	A3
Sutherland St. SW1	101	E2
Sutherland Wk. SE17	106	B3
Sutterton St. N7	12	A2
Sutton Est. SW3	99	F2
Sutton Est. W10	30	A3
Sutton Est., The N1	13	E3
Sutton Row W1	39	D5
Sutton St. E1	62	A2
Sutton Way W10	30	A3
Sutton's Way EC1	42	B2
Swallow Clo. SE14	118	C4
Swallow Pas. W1	53	F1
Swallow Pl. W1	53	F1

Swallow St. W1	54	B3
Swallowfield Rd. SE7	117	F3
Swan Ct. SW3	99	F3
Swan La. EC4	58	C3
Swan Mead SE1	83	E4
Swan Rd. SE16	86	B1
Swan St. SE1	82	B3
Swan Wk. SW3	100	A4
Swan Yd. N1	13	E2
Swanfield St. E2	28	A5
Swanscombe Rd. W11	47	D5
Sweden Gate SE16	87	F5
Swedenborg Gdns. E1	61	E2
Sweeney Cres. SE1	84	B2
Swinbrook Rd. W10	31	F3
Swinton Pl. WC1	24	A4
Swinton St. WC1	24	A4
Swiss Ter. NW6	6	C3
Sybil Phoenix Clo. SE8	111	D2
Sybil Thorndike Ho. N1	14	B1
Sycamore St. EC1	42	A2
Sycamore Wk. W10	31	E1
Sydney Clo. SW3	99	D1
Sydney Ms. SW3	99	D1
Sydney Pl. SW7	99	D1
Sydney St. SW3	99	E2
Sylvester Rd. E8	17	F1
Symes Ms. NW1	22	A2
Symons St. SW3	100	B1

T

Tabard Gdn. Est. SE1	83	D2
Tabard St. SE1	82	C2
Tabernacle St. EC2	43	D2
Tachbrook Est. SW1	103	D3
Tachbrook Ms. SW1	78	A5
Tachbrook St. SW1	102	B1
Tadmor St. W12	46	C5
Taeping St. E14	89	E5
Tailworth St. E1	44	C4
Talacre Rd. NW5	9	D1
Talbot Ct. EC3	59	D2
Talbot Pl. SE3	123	E5
Talbot Rd. W2	32	C5
Talbot Rd. W11	32	A5
Talbot Sq. W2	51	D1

Talbot Wk. W11	47	E1
Talbot Yd. SE1	58	C5
Talgarth Rd. W6	94	B2
Talgarth Rd. W14	95	D2
Tallis Clo. E16	69	E1
Tallis Gro. SE7	117	F4
Tallis St. EC4	57	D2
Tamarind Yd. E1	61	D4
Tamworth St. SW6	96	C4
Tankerton St. WC1	23	F5
Tanner St. SE1	83	F2
Tanners Hill SE8	120	B4
Tanswell Est. SE1	81	D2
Tanswell St. SE1	80	C2
Taplow NW3	7	D4
Taplow St. N1	26	B3
Tapp St. E1	45	E1
Tarbert Wk. E1	62	A2
Tariff Cres. SE8	88	A5
Tarling Rd. E16	68	B1
Tarling St. E1	62	A1
Tarling St. Est. E1	62	A1
Tarn St. SE1	82	A4
Tarragon Clo. SE14	119	E1
Tarrant Pl. W1	36	A4
Tarry La. SE8	87	E5
Tarver Rd. SE17	105	F3
Tarves Way SE10	121	F1
Tasso Rd. W6	95	E4
Tatum St. SE17	107	D1
Taunton Ms. NW1	36	A2
Taunton Pl. NW1	36	A1
Taverners Clo. W11	47	E5
Tavistock Cres. W11	32	A4
Tavistock Pl. WC1	39	E1
Tavistock Rd. W11	32	A4
Tavistock Sq. WC1	39	D1
Tavistock St. WC2	55	F2
Taviton St. WC1	38	C1
Tavy Clo. SE11	105	D2
Tawny Way SE16	87	D5
Tayport Clo. N1	11	F4
Teak Clo. SE16	63	F5
Teale St. E2	29	D2
Tedworth Gdns. SW3	100	A3
Tedworth Sq. SW3	100	A3
Teesdale Clo. E2	29	D3
Teesdale St. E2	29	E3
Telegraph Pl. E14	89	E5
Telegraph St. EC2	42	C5
Telephone Pl. SW6	96	B4
Telford Rd. W10	31	E3

Telford Ter. SW1	102 A4
Telfords Yd. E1	61 D3
Temeraire St. SE16	86 B2
Temple EC4	56 C2
Temple Ave. EC4	57 D2
Temple La. EC4	57 D1
Temple Pl. WC2	56 B2
Temple St. E2	29 E3
Temple W. Ms. SE11	81 E4
Templeton Pl. SW5	97 D1
Tench St. E1	61 E5
Tenda Rd. SE16	109 E1
Tenison Ct. W1	54 A2
Tenison Way SE1	56 B5
Tenniel Clo. W2	50 A2
Tennis St. SE1	82 C1
Tent St. E1	45 E1
Tenter Grd. E1	44 A4
Tenterden St. W1	53 F1
Teredo St. SE16	87 D4
Terling Wk. N1	14 A5
Terminus Pl. SW1	77 F4
Terretts Pl. N1	13 E4
Testerton Wk. W11	47 D2
Tetbury Pl. N1	25 E1
Tetterby Way SE16	109 D3
Thackeray St. W8	73 F2
Thalia Clo. SE10	115 D4
Thame Rd. SE16	87 D1
Thames Circle E14	89 D5
Thames St. SE10	113 F4
Thames Wf. E16	68 A4
Thanet St. WC1	23 E5
Thavies Inn EC1	41 D5
Thaxton Rd. W14	96 B4
Thayer St. W1	37 D4
Theberton St. N1	13 D5
Theed St. SE1	56 C5
Theobald St. SE1	82 C4
Theobald's Rd. WC1	40 A3
Thermopylae Gate E14	113 F1
Theseus Wk. N1	25 F3
Thirleby Rd. SW1	78 B4
Thistle Gro. SW10	98 B2
Thomas Darby Ct. W11	47 E1
Thomas Doyle St. SE1	81 F3
Thomas More St. E1	60 C3
Thomas Pl. W8	73 E4
Thorburn Sq. SE1	108 C1
Thoresby St. N1	26 B4

Thorndike St. SW1	102 C1
Thorney St. SW1	79 E5
Thorngate Rd. W9	33 D1
Thornham St. SE10	113 F5
Thornhaugh Ms. WC1	39 D2
Thornhaugh St. WC1	39 D3
Thornhill Bri. Wf. N1	24 A1
Thornhill Cres. N1	12 B4
Thornhill Gro. N1	12 B4
Thornhill Ho. N1	12 C3
Thornhill Rd. N1	12 C5
Thornhill Sq. N1	12 B4
Thornley Pl. SE10	115 E3
Thornton Pl. W1	36 A3
Thornville St. SE8	120 C4
Thorpe Clo. W10	31 F5
Thrale St. SE1	58 B5
Thrasher Clo. E8	16 A5
Thrawl St. E1	44 B4
Threadneedle St. EC2	59 D1
Three Colt St. E14	64 B1
Three Colts La. E2	45 E1
Three Cups Yd. WC1	40 B4
Three Kings Yd. W1	53 E2
Three Oak La. SE1	84 A1
Threshers Pl. W11	47 E2
Throckmorten Rd. E16	69 F1
Throgmorton Ave. EC2	43 D5
Throgmorton St. EC2	43 D5
Thrush St. SE17	106 A2
Thurland Rd. SE16	84 C3
Thurloe Clo. SW7	75 E5
Thurloe Pl. SW7	75 D5
Thurloe Pl. Ms. SW7	75 D5
Thurloe Sq. SW7	75 E5
Thurloe St. SW7	75 D5
Thurlow St. SE17	107 D2
Thurtle Rd. E2	28 B1
Tibberton Sq. N1	14 A4
Tiber Gdns. N1	23 F1
Tidal Basin Rd. E16	68 B2
Tile Yd. E14	64 B1
Tileyard Rd. N7	11 E3
Tiller Rd. E14	88 C3

Tillett Sq. SE16	87 F2
Tillett Way E2	28 C4
Tillman St. E1	61 F1
Tilloch St. N1	12 A4
Tilney Ct. EC1	42 B1
Tilney Gdns. N1	14 C2
Tilney St. W1	53 D4
Tilton St. SW6	96 A5
Timber Pond Rd. SE16	63 D5
Timber St. EC1	42 A1
Timberland Rd. E1	61 F1
Timbrell Pl. SE16	64 A5
Tinworth St. SE11	103 F2
Tisbury Ct. W1	54 C2
Tisdall Pl. SE17	107 D1
Titchborne Row W2	51 F1
Titchfield Rd. NW8	19 F1
Tite St. SW3	100 A3
Tiverton St. SE1	82 A4
Tivoli Ct. SE16	88 A1
Tobacco Quay E1	61 E3
Tobago St. E14	88 C1
Tobin Clo. NW3	7 F3
Tokenhouse Yd. EC2	42 C5
Tollbridge Clo. W10	31 F1
Tolmers Sq. NW1	38 B1
Tolpuddle St. N1	24 C2
Tom Jenkinson Rd. E16	69 D4
Tom Smith Clo. SE10	115 E4
Tomlinson Clo. E2	28 B5
Tompion St. EC1	25 E5
Tonbridge St. WC1	23 E4
Tonbridge Wk. WC1	23 E4
Took's Ct. EC4	40 C5
Tooley St. SE1	59 D4
Topham St. EC1	40 C1
Topmast Pt. E14	88 C2
Tor Gdns. W8	72 C1
Torbay St. NW1	9 F4
Torquay St. W2	33 E4
Torrens St. EC1	25 D3
Torrington Pl. E1	61 D5
Torrington Pl. WC1	38 B3
Torrington Sq. WC1	39 D2
Tothill St. SW1	78 C2
Tottenham Ct. Rd. W1	38 B2
Tottenham Ms. W1	38 B3
Tottenham Rd. N1	15 E2

U

Vinegar St. E1   61 E4
Vinegar Yd. SE1   83 E1
Vineyard Wk. EC1   40 C1
Violet Hill NW8   18 A3
Violet St. E2   45 F1
Virgil Pl. W1   36 A4
Virgil St. SE1   80 B3
Virginia Rd. E2   28 A5
Virginia St. E1   61 D3
Viscount St. EC1   42 A3
Voss St. E2   29 D5
Vulcan Rd. SE4   120 A5
Vulcan Sq. E14   113 D1
Vulcan Ter. SE4   120 A5
Vulcan Way N7   12 B1
Vyner St. E2   29 F1

W

Wadding St. SE17   106 C1
Wades Pl. E14   65 E2
Wadeson St. E2   29 F2
Wadham Gdns. NW3   7 E4
Wagner St. SE15   118 A1
Waite St. SE15   108 A4
Waithman St. EC4   57 E1
Wakefield Ms. WC1   23 F5
Wakefield St. WC1   23 F5
Wakeham St. N1   14 C2
Wakeling St. E14   63 E1
Wakley St. EC1   25 E4
Walbrook EC4   58 C2
Walburgh St. E1   61 E1
Walcorde Ave. SE17   106 B1
Walcot Sq. SE11   81 D5
Walcott St. SW1   78 B5
Walden St. E1   45 E5
Waldron Ms. SW3   99 D4
Walkers Ct. E8   16 C2
Walkers Ct. W1   54 C2
Wall St. N1   15 D2
Wallace Rd. N1   14 B1
Waller Rd. SE14   118 C4
Wallgrave Rd. SW5   73 E5
Wallingford Ave. W10   30 C4
Wallis All. SE1   82 B2
Walmer Pl. W1   36 A3
Walmer Rd. W10   46 B1
Walmer Rd. W11   47 E2
Walmer St. W1   36 A3
Walney Wk. N1   14 B2
Walnut Clo. SE8   112 B5

Walnut Tree Rd. SE10   115 F3
Walnut Tree Wk. SE11   80 C5
Walpole Ms. NW8   18 C1
Walpole St. SW3   100 A2
Walsham Rd. SE14   118 C5
Walters Ho. SE17   105 E5
Walterton Rd. W9   32 B2
Walton Pl. SW3   76 A3
Walton St. SW3   75 F5
Walworth Pl. SE17   106 B3
Walworth Rd. SE1   106 A1
Walworth Rd. SE17   106 A1
Wandsworth Rd. SW8   103 E4
Wansey St. SE17   106 B1
Wapping Dock St. E1   61 F5
Wapping High St. E1   61 D5
Wapping La. E1   61 F3
Wapping Wall E1   62 A4
Warburton Rd. E8   17 F5
Wardalls Gro. SE14   118 B1
Warden Rd. NW5   9 D1
Wardens Gro. SE1   58 A5
Wardour Ms. W1   54 B1
Wardour St. W1   38 B5
Wardrobe Pl. EC4   57 F1
Wardrobe Ter. EC4   57 F2
Warlock Rd. W9   32 B1
Warndon St. SE16   110 B1
Warneford St. E9   17 F5
Warner Pl. E2   29 D3
Warner St. EC1   40 C2
Warner Yd. EC1   40 C2
Warren Ms. W1   38 A2
Warren St. W1   37 F2
Warrington Cres. W9   34 A2
Warrington Gdns. W9   34 A2
Warrington Pl. E14   66 B4
Warwick Ave. W2   34 B3
Warwick Ave. W9   33 F2
Warwick Ct. WC1   40 B4
Warwick Cres. W2   34 A3
Warwick Est. W2   33 F4
Warwick Gdns. W14   72 B4

Warwick Ho. St. SW1   55 D4
Warwick La. EC4   57 F1
Warwick Pl. W9   34 A3
Warwick Pl. N. SW1   102 A1
Warwick Rd. SW5   97 D2
Warwick Rd. W14   72 B5
Warwick Row SW1   77 F3
Warwick Sq. EC4   41 F5
Warwick Sq. SW1   102 A2
Warwick Sq. Ms. SW1   102 A1
Warwick St. W1   54 B2
Warwick Way SW1   101 F2
Warwick Yd. EC1   42 B2
Warwickshire Path SE8   120 B1
Wat Tyler Rd. SE3   122 B5
Wat Tyler Rd. SE10   122 B5
Water La. NW1   9 F4
Water La. SE14   118 B1
Water St. WC2   56 B2
Watercress Pl. N1   15 F4
Watergate EC4   57 E2
Watergate St. SE8   112 C5
Watergate Wk. WC2   55 F3
Waterhouse Clo. W6   95 D2
Waterhouse Sq. EC1   40 C4
Waterloo Bri. SE1   56 A3
Waterloo Bri. WC2   56 A3
Waterloo Pl. SW1   54 C4
Waterloo Rd. SE1   80 C1
Waterloo Ter. N1   13 E4
Waterman Way E1   61 E4
Watermans Wk. SE16   87 E3
Waterside Clo. SE16   85 D2
Waterside Pl. NW1   9 D5
Waterson St. E2   27 F4
Watkinson Rd. N7   12 A1
Watling Ct. EC4   58 B1
Watling St. EC4   58 A1
Watney Mkt. E1   45 F5
Watney St. E1   61 F1
Watsons Ms. W1   35 F4
Watson's St. SE8   120 C2
Watts St. E1   61 F4
Watts Way SW7   75 D3

Waveney Clo. E1	61 D4	
Waverley Pl. NW8	18 C2	
Waverley Wk. W2	33 D3	
Waverton St. W1	53 E4	
Waxwell Ter. SE1	80 B2	
Wayman Ct. E8	17 E2	
Waynflete Sq. W10	46 C1	
Weald Clo. SE16	109 E2	
Wear Pl. E2	29 E5	
Weaver St. E1	44 C2	
Weavers Ter. SW6	97 D5	
Weavers Way NW1	10 C4	
Webb Rd. SE3	116 B4	
Webb St. SE1	83 E4	
Webber Row SE1	81 D2	
Webber St. SE1	81 E2	
Webster Rd. SE16	85 D4	
Wedgwood Ms. W1	55 D1	
Wedlake St. W10	31 F1	
Weighouse St. W1	53 D1	
Weir's Pas. NW1	23 D4	
Welbeck St. W1	37 D4	
Welbeck Way W1	37 E5	
Well Ct. EC4	58 B1	
Well St. E9	17 F4	
Welland Ms. E1	61 D4	
Welland St. SE10	114 A4	
Wellclose Sq. E1	61 D2	
Wellclose St. E1	61 D3	
Weller St. SE1	82 A1	
Weller's Ct. N1	23 E3	
Wellesley Ct. W9	18 A4	
Wellesley Pl. NW1	22 C5	
Wellesley Ter. N1	26 B4	
Wellington Bldgs. SW1	101 D3	
Wellington Clo. SE14	118 C4	
Wellington Clo. W11	48 C1	
Wellington Ct. NW8	18 C3	
Wellington Gro. SE10	122 C2	
Wellington Pl. NW8	19 D4	
Wellington Rd. NW8	18 C2	
Wellington Row E2	28 B4	
Wellington Sq. SW3	100 A2	
Wellington St. WC2	55 F2	
Wellington Ter. E1	61 E4	
Wells Ms. W1	38 B4	
Wells Ri. NW8	20 A1	
Wells Rd. W12	70 A2	
Wells Sq. WC1	24 A5	
Wells St. W1	38 A4	
Wells Way SE5	107 D4	
Wells Way SW7	74 C3	
Welsford St. SE1	108 C2	
Welshpool Ho. E8	17 D5	
Welshpool St. E8	17 D5	
Wendle Ct. SW8	103 E5	
Wendover SE17	107 E2	
Wenlock Ct. N1	27 D3	
Wenlock Rd. N1	26 A3	
Wenlock St. N1	26 B3	
Wentworth St. E1	44 A5	
Werrington St. NW1	22 B3	
Wesley Ave. E16	69 E4	
Wesley Clo. SE17	105 F1	
Wesley Rd. SE17	105 F1	
Wesley Sq. W11	47 E1	
Wesley St. W1	37 D4	
West Carriage Dr. W2	51 E3	
West Cen. St. WC1	39 E5	
West Cromwell Rd. SW5	96 C1	
West Cromwell Rd. W14	96 A2	
West Cross Route W10	46 C2	
West Cross Route W11	46 C3	
West Eaton Pl. SW1	76 C5	
West Eaton Pl. Ms. SW1	76 C4	
West Gdn. Pl. W2	51 F1	
West Gdns. E1	61 F3	
West Gro. SE10	122 B3	
West Halkin St. SW1	76 C3	
West Harding St. EC4	41 D5	
West India Ave. E14	64 C4	
West India Dock Rd. E14	64 B1	
West Kentish Town Est. NW5	9 D1	
West La. SE16	85 E2	
West Mall W8	49 D4	
West Mersea Clo. E16	69 E5	
West Ms. SW1	102 A1	
West Parkside SE10	91 F2	
West Pier E1	61 E5	
West Poultry Ave. EC1	41 E4	
West Rd. SW3	100 B3	
West Row W10	31 E1	
West Smithfield EC1	41 E4	
West Sq. SE11	81 E4	
West St. E2	29 F3	
West St. WC2	55 D1	
West Tenter St. E1	60 B1	
West Warwick Pl. SW1	102 A1	
Westbourne Bri. W2	34 A4	
Westbourne Cres. W2	50 C2	
Westbourne Cres. Ms. W2	50 C2	
Westbourne Gdns. W2	33 E5	
Westbourne Gro. W2	49 D1	
Westbourne Gro. W11	48 A2	
Westbourne Gro. Ms. W11	48 C1	
Westbourne Gro. Ter. W2	49 E1	
Westbourne Pk. Ms. W2	33 E5	
Westbourne Pk. Pas. W2	33 D4	
Westbourne Pk. Rd. W2	33 D4	
Westbourne Pk. Rd. W11	47 F1	
Westbourne Pk. Vil. W2	33 D4	
Westbourne Rd. N7	12 B1	
Westbourne St. W2	50 C2	
Westbourne Ter. W2	34 A5	
Westbourne Ter. Ms. W2	34 A5	
Westbourne Ter. Rd. W2	34 A4	
Westbrook Rd. SE3	125 E4	
Westcombe Hill SE3	117 D4	

THE
LITTLE,
BROWN
HANDBOOK
BRIEF
VERSION

LB *Brief*

THIRD EDITION

JANE E. AARON

PEARSON
Longman

New York   Boston   San Francisco
London   Toronto   Sydney   Tokyo   Singapore   Madrid
Mexico City   Munich   Paris   Cape Town   Hong Kong   Montreal

Executive Editor:	Lynn M. Huddon
Development Editor:	Carol Hollar-Zwick
Senior Supplements Editor:	Donna Campion
Media Supplements Editor:	Jenna Egan
Executive Marketing Manager:	Megan Galvin-Fak
Production Manager:	Bob Ginsberg
Project Coordination, Text Design, and Electronic Page Makeup:	Nesbitt Graphics, Inc.
Cover Design Manager:	John Callahan
Cover Designer:	Kay Petronio
Background Cover Image:	Courtesy of Shutterstock
Photo Researcher:	Vivette Porges
Manufacturing Buyer:	Roy L. Pickering, Jr.
Printer and Binder:	RR Donnelley & Sons Company/Crawfordsville
Cover Printer:	Phoenix Color Corporation

For permission to use copyrighted material, grateful acknowledgment is made to the copyright holders on pp. 569–70, which are hereby made part of this copyright page.

Library of Congress Cataloging-in-Publication Data

Aaron, Jane E.
  LB : the Little, Brown handbook, brief version / Jane E. Aaron. — 3rd ed.
     p. cm.
  Little Brown brief
  Includes bibliographical references and index.
  ISBN 978-0-205-53059-5
  1. English language—Grammar—Handbooks, manuals, etc. 2. English language—Rhetoric—Handbooks, manuals, etc. I. Title. II. Title: Little Brown brief.
PE1112.A22 2007
808'.042—dc22

                                                                    2006102371

Visit us at www.ablongman.com

ISBN-13: 978-0-205-53059-5
ISBN-10:   0-205-53059-1

1 2 3 4 5 6 7 8 9 10—DOC—10 09 08 07

Preface for Students

LB Brief contains the basic information you'll need for writing in and out of school. Here you can find out how to get ideas, use commas, search the Web, cite sources, write a résumé, and more—all in a convenient, accessible package.

This book is mainly a reference for you to dip into as needs arise. You probably won't read the book all the way through, nor will you use everything it contains: you already know much of the content anyway, whether consciously or not. The trick is to figure out what you *don't* know—taking cues from your own writing experiences and the comments of others—and then to find the answers to your questions in these pages.

Before you begin using this book, you may need to clear your mind of a very common misconception: that writing is only, or even mainly, a matter of correctness. True, any written message will find a more receptive audience if it is correct in grammar, punctuation, and similar matters. But these concerns should come late in the writing process, after you've allowed yourself to discover what you have to say, freeing yourself to make mistakes along the way. As one writer put it, you need to get the clay on the potter's wheel before you can shape it into a bowl, and you need to shape it into a bowl before you can perfect it. So get your clay on the wheel and work with it until it looks like a bowl. Then worry about correctness.

Finding what you need

You have many ways to find what you need in the handbook:

- **Use a directory.** "Frequently Asked Questions" (inside the front cover) provides questions in everyday language that are commonly asked about the book's main topics. "Contents" (inside the back cover) gives a detailed overview of the entire book.
- **Use the glossary.** "Glossary of Usage" (pp. 555–68) clarifies more than 250 words that are often confused or misused.
- **Use the index.** The extensive index lists every topic, term, and problem word or expression mentioned in the book.
- **Use a list.** Two helpful aids fall on the last pages of the book: " CULTURE LANGUAGE Guide" pulls together all the book's material for students using standard American English as a second language or a second dialect. And "Editing Symbols" explains abbreviations often used to mark papers.
- **Use the elements of the page.** As shown on the next page, each page of the handbook tells you what you can find there.

v

The handbook's page elements

Frequently asked question about the chapter topic

Boldfaced word: a term being introduced and defined

Examples, always indented, with color underlining and annotations highlighting sentence elements and revisions

Culture-language connection, a pointer for students using standard American English as a second language or a second dialect

Page tab containing the code of the nearest chapter or section heading (**31**) and its editing symbol (**pn agr**)

Key terms box defining terms used on the page

Web box linking to the handbook's companion Web site (see the facing page)

---

31 Agreement of Pronoun and Antecedent

● Is this the right pronoun?

The right pronoun is the one that matches its antecedent—the word to which it refers—in number, person, and gender. This chapter focuses on agreement in number: singular and plural antecedents and the pronouns that replace them.

Homeowners fret over their tax bills.
antecedent   pronoun

Its constant increases make the tax bill a dreaded document.
pronoun   antecedent

Note Grammar and style checkers cannot help with agreement between pronoun and antecedent because they cannot recognize the intended relation between the two.

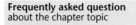 CULTURE ▸ The gender of a pronoun should match its antecedent, not a noun that the pronoun may modify: *Sara Young invited her* [not *his*] *son to join the company's staff.* Also, nouns in English have only neuter gender unless they specifically refer to males or females. Thus nouns such as *book, table, sun,* and *earth* take the pronoun *it.*

pn agr
31

Key terms

	Number	
Person	Singular	Plural
First	*I*	*we*
Second	*you*	*you*
Third	*he, she, it,*	*they,*
	indefinite pronouns,	plural nouns
	singular nouns	
Gender		
Masculine	*he,* nouns naming males	
Feminine	*she,* nouns naming females	
Neuter	*it,* all other nouns	

http://www.ablongman.com/littlebrown ▶
Visit the companion Web site for more help and electronic exercises on pronoun-antecedent agreement.

31d Collective nouns such as *team* take singular or plural pronouns depending on meaning.

Use a singular pronoun with a collective noun when referring to the group as a unit:

The committee voted to disband itself.

When referring to the individual members of the group, use a plural pronoun:

The old group have gone their separate ways.

EXERCISE 31.1
Revising: Pronoun-antecedent agreement

Revise the following sentences so that pronouns and their antecedents agree in person and number. Some items have more than one possible answer. Try to avoid the generic *he* (see p. 287). If you change the subject of a sentence, be sure to change the verb as necessary for agreement. If a sentence is already correct as given, mark the number preceding it. Answers to starred items appear at the end of the book. (You can do this exercise online at *ablongman.com/littlebrown*.)

Section heading, a main convention or topic labeled with the section code **31d:** the chapter number (**31**) and the section letter (**d**)

Exercise providing opportunity for practice (answers to selected exercises appear at the back of the book)

Using the companion Web site

The companion Web site offers many resources to help you use the book and improve your writing. You can use the site on your own (it is not password protected), or your instructor may direct you to portions of it as part of his or her course assignments.

Go to *www.ablongman.com/littlebrown,* and click on *LB Brief.* You'll see further directions to the following:

- Downloadable checklists and other material from the book.
- The book's exercises in electronic format.
- More than a thousand additional electronic exercises.
- Video tutorials that supplement the book's explanations.
- Hundreds of links to other Web sites providing help on the book's topics.
- Sample research papers from various academic disciplines.
- Usage flashcards allowing you to test yourself on tricky words and phrases.

LB Brief provides writers with a reliable, accessible, and affordable reference. Merging the authority of its parent, *The Little, Brown Handbook,* and a concise format, this handbook answers frequently asked questions about the writing process, critical reading, grammar and style, research writing, and more. With its cross-curricular outlook, easy-to-use format, and assumption of little or no experience with writing or handbooks, *LB Brief* helps students of varying interests and skills.

This third edition improves on the handbook's strengths while keeping pace with the rapid changes in writing and its teaching. In the context of the handbook's many functions, the following pages highlight as **New** the significant additions and changes.

A source for examples and exercises

Bringing concepts to earth, *LB Brief* provides examples for students to emulate and exercises for them to practice on.

- **New** Nineteen sample documents, highlighted in the table of contents, illustrate many varieties of college-level writing, including personal narrative, response to reading, critique, argument, research writing using MLA and APA styles, writing about literature with and without secondary sources, essay exams, and public and online writing.

- Hundreds of examples use color underlining to show clearly both the look of errors and the means of correcting them.

- More than 120 exercise sets offer hands-on work with words, sentences, paragraphs, and whole essays—all drawing on content from across the disciplines, all in connected discourse. About half the exercises are answered in the back of the book. Most are available in electronic format on the handbook's companion Web site.

A guide to writing in and out of college

The handbook's Part 2 collects chapters that students can draw on for their college courses and beyond.

- **New** A revised and expanded chapter on academic writing covers audience, purpose, language, and other concerns.

- **New** A chapter on study skills offers practical tips for managing time, reading for comprehension, taking notes, and preparing for and taking essay exams.

- **New** A chapter on public writing discusses the rhetorical con-

siderations for business writing, job applications, e-mail, writing for community work, and composing for the Web.
- Two chapters detail techniques of critical reading and argument.
- Two chapters cover reading and writing about literature (including two sample student papers) and making oral presentations (including *PowerPoint*).

A guide to research writing

LB Brief gives close attention to research writing, mindful of the dramatic changes in the methods and challenges of research.

- The discussion emphasizes using the library as Web gateway, managing information, evaluating and synthesizing sources, integrating sources, and avoiding plagiarism.
- **New** Guidelines and an example explain how to prepare an annotated bibliography.
- **New** Library subscription services receive even greater emphasis. In addition to a detailed, annotated sample search, the text now provides help with choosing databases.
- **New** Web logs are covered as possible sources requiring careful evaluation and documentation.
- **New** Additional discussion of evaluating Web sites includes tips for distinguishing scholarly, personal, and other kinds of sites.
- **New** MLA documentation now includes annotated sample pages from key source types, showing students how to find the bibliographical information needed to cite each type.

A guide to the writing process

The handbook takes a concise, practical approach to assessing the writing situation, generating ideas, writing the thesis statement, revising, and other elements of the writing process.

- Numerous examples, including a student work-in-progress on Internet communication, illustrate every stage.
- **New** A student paper shows techniques for achieving whole-essay unity and coherence.

A guide to visual literacy

The handbook helps students process visual information and use it effectively in their writing.

- **New** An expanded section on using illustrations includes annotated examples.

- **New** An expanded discussion of viewing images critically uses examples to demonstrate identifying and analyzing visual elements.
- **New** A section introduces images as research sources and provides URLs for image banks.

A guide for culturally and linguistically diverse students

At notes labeled ❮ **CULTURE LANGUAGE** ❯, the handbook provides extensive rhetorical and grammatical help for writers whose first language or dialect is not standard American English.

- Fully integrated coverage, instead of a separate section, means that students can find what they need without having to know which problems they do and don't share with native SAE speakers.
- **New** "❮ **CULTURE LANGUAGE** ❯ Guide," just before the back endpapers, orients students with advice on mastering SAE and pulls all the integrated coverage together in one place.

A uniquely accessible reference

LB Brief opens itself to students, featuring not only a convenient spiral binding but also numerous features designed to help students find what they need and then use what they find:

- "Frequently Asked Questions," both on the front endpapers and at the beginning of every chapter, provide students with a common-language portal for reaching the handbook's contents.
- An unusually direct organization arranges topics in ways that students can easily grasp.
- Rules and other headings use minimal terminology, with examples replacing or supplementing terms.
- "Key terms" boxes define secondary terms used on each page and minimize cross-references.
- Nearly fifty checklist and summary boxes highlight key reference information, such as questions about audience, uses of the comma, and indexes to documentation formats.
- **New** Dictionary-style headers in the index make it easy to find entries.

An integrated text and Web site

At the start of every handbook chapter, a Web box links students to the book's companion Web site, a powerful online resource for students and teachers.

- **New** Most of the handbook's exercises can be downloaded and completed electronically or on paper. A cross-reference to the Web site appears in the instruction of each dual-format exercise.

- More than a thousand additional self-study questions, keyed to the handbook, provide immediate feedback for every answer.
- Many of the handbook's checklists can be downloaded for practice, invention, and revision.
- More than thirty video tutorials provide explanations, examples, and tips to help students understand concepts and techniques.
- Hundreds of Web links direct students to helpful sites on the writing process, critical thinking, argument, grammar, research, writing in the disciplines, and more.
- Ten documented student research papers provide examples of writing across the curriculum.
- Usage flashcards allow students to test their knowledge and practice usage.
- The "Instructor Resources" section provides answers to the handbook's exercises, lists and summaries from the book in transparency and *PowerPoint* format, and links to Web sites useful to writing teachers.

Supplements

LB Brief is accompanied by many helpful supplements for both teachers and students, including the following:

- *MyCompLab*, Longman's premier site for college writing students and teachers, provides the best multimedia resources for writing, research, and grammar in one easy-to-use site. Students will find guided assistance through each step of the writing process; interactive tutorials and videos that illustrate key concepts; more than thirty model documents from across the curriculum; *Exchange*, Longman's online peer-review program; the tutorial "Avoiding Plagiarism"; diagnostic grammar tests and thousands of practice questions; and *Research Navigator*™, a database with thousands of magazines and academic journals, the subject-search archive of the *New York Times*, "Link Library," library guides, and more. Visit *www.mycomplab.com* for additional information.
- For students, *Developmental Exercises to Accompany LB Brief*, by Kathryn Riley and Christopher Lam, provides practical activities for developing writers.
- For instructors, separate booklets provide answers to all the exercises in *LB Brief* and *Developmental Exercises to Accompany LB Brief*.

Please contact your local Longman representative for a complete list of all available supplements.

Acknowledgments

This edition of *LB Brief* owes much to the instructors who offered thoughtful and insightful suggestions for improvement. I am grateful to Jeff Andelora, Mesa Community College; Barclay Barrios, Florida Atlantic University; Joyce D. Brotton, Northern Virginia Community College; Patricia Cullinan, Truckee Meadows Community College; Julia McGregor, Inver Hills Community College; Theresa Mohamed, Onondaga Community College; Steve Moore, Arizona Western College; Lisa Moreno, Los Angeles Trade-Technical College; Derek Soles, Drexel University; and Jonnetta Woodard, Robeson Community College.

In responding to the ideas of these thoughtful critics, I had the help of many creative people. Brooke Hessler, Oklahoma City University, was an invaluable consultant on visual literacy and research writing. Caroline Crouse, University of Minnesota, served as a guide through the labyrinth of the contemporary library. Susan Smith Nash, Excelsior College, helped with disabilities issues and new technologies. And Sylvan Barnet, Tufts University, continued to lend his expertise in the chapter "Reading and Writing About Literature," which is adapted from his *Short Guide to Writing About Literature* and *Introduction to Literature* (with William Burto and William E. Cain).

At Longman, Lynn Huddon, assisted by Nicole Solano, captained the project thoughtfully and supportively. During development Carol Hollar-Zwick once again proved a superb idea source, sounding board, and hand holder. And during production Susan McIntyre, Nesbitt Graphics, managed traffic and schedules with customary high standards. My thanks to all these colleagues.

1

The Writing Process

1 The Writing Situation

Many writers find it helpful to break writing tasks into manageable steps. Such steps are part of the **writing process**—the term for all activities, mental and physical, that go into creating what eventually becomes a finished piece of work.

There is no one writing process: no two writers proceed in the same way, and even an individual writer adapts his or her process to the task at hand. Still, most experienced writers pass through certain stages that overlap and circle back on each other:

- **Analyzing the writing situation,** especially considering subject, audience, and purpose (this chapter).
- **Invention and planning:** generating ideas, gathering information, focusing on a central theme, and organizing material (Chapters 2–3).
- **Drafting:** expressing and connecting ideas (Chapter 4).
- **Revising and editing:** rethinking and improving structure, content, style, and presentation (Chapter 5).

As you complete varied assignments and try the many techniques included in this book, you will develop your own writing process.

1a Analyze the writing situation.

Any writing you do for others occurs in a **writing situation** that both limits and clarifies your choices. You are communicating within a particular context, about a particular subject, to a particular audience of readers, for a specific reason. You may need to conduct research. You probably face a length requirement and a deadline. And you may be expected to present your work in a certain format.

Analyzing the elements of the writing situation at the very start of a project can tell you much about how to proceed. (For more information about any of the following elements, refer to the page numbers given.)

Context (pp. 86–173)

- **What is your writing for?** A course in school? Work? Something else? What are the requirements for writing in this context?

---

http://www.ablongman.com/littlebrown ▶

Visit the companion Web site for more help and electronic exercises on the writing situation.

- **Will you present your writing on paper, online, or orally?** What does the presentation method require in preparation time, special skills, and use of technology?
- **How much leeway do you have for this writing?** What does the stated or implied assignment tell you?

Subject (pp. 4–6)

- **What does your writing assignment instruct you to write about?** If you don't have a specific assignment, what do you want to write about?
- **What interests you about the subject?** What do you already have ideas about or want to know more about?
- **What does the assignment require you to do with the subject?**

Audience (pp. 6–8)

- **Who will read your writing?**
- **What do your readers already know and think about your subject?** Do they have any characteristics—such as educational background, experience in your field, or political views—that could influence their reception of your writing?
- **What is your relationship to your readers?** How formal or informal should your writing be?
- **What do you want readers to do or think after they read your writing?**

Purpose (p. 9)

- **What aim does your assignment specify?** For instance, does it ask you to explain something or argue a point?
- **Why are you writing? What do you want your work to accomplish?** What effect do you intend it to have on readers?
- **How can you best achieve your purpose?**

Research (pp. 416–82)

- **What kinds of evidence will best suit your subject, audience, and purpose?** What combination of facts, examples, and expert opinions will support your ideas?
- **Does your assignment require research?** Will you need to consult sources of information or conduct other research, such as interviews, surveys, or experiments?
- **Even if research is not required, what additional information do you need to develop your subject?** How will you obtain it?
- **What style should you use to cite your sources?** (See pp. 477–79 on documenting sources in the academic disciplines.)

Deadline and length

- **When is the assignment due?** How will you complete the work you have to do in the available time?
- **How long should your writing be?** If no length is assigned, what seems appropriate for your topic, audience, and purpose?

Document design

- **What organization and format does the assignment require?** (See p. 71 on formats in academic disciplines and pp. 152–68 on format in public writing.)
- **How might you use margins, headings, and other elements to achieve your purpose?** (See pp. 74–83.)
- **How might you use graphs, photographs, or other illustrations to support ideas and interest readers?** (See pp. 78–82 on using illustrations in writing.)

EXERCISE 1.1
Analyzing a writing situation

The following assignment was made in a survey course in psychology. What does the assignment specify and imply about the elements of the writing situation? Given this assignment, how would you answer the questions on page 3 and above? (You can do this exercise online at *ablongman.com/littlebrown*.)

When is psychotherapy most likely to work? That is, what combinations of client, therapist, and theory tend to achieve good results? In your paper, cite studies supporting your conclusions. Length: 1500 to 1800 words. Post your paper online to me and your discussion group by March 30.

1b   Find an appropriate subject.

A subject for writing has several basic requirements:

- **It should be suitable for the assignment.**
- **It should be neither too general nor too limited** for the length of paper and deadline assigned.
- **It should be something you care about.**

When you receive an assignment, study its wording and its implications about your writing situation to guide your choice of subject:

- **What's wanted from you?** Many writing assignments contain words such as *discuss, describe, analyze, report, interpret, explain, define, argue,* or *evaluate.* These words specify the way you are to approach your subject, what kind of thinking is expected of you, and what your general purpose is. (See p. 9.)

1b

- **For whom are you writing?** Many assignments will specify your readers, but sometimes you will have to figure out for yourself who your audience is and what it expects of you. (For more on analyzing your audience, see pp. 6–8.)
- **What kind of research is required?** Sometimes an assignment specifies the kinds of sources you are expected to consult, and you can use such information to choose your subject. (If you are unsure whether research is required, check with your instructor.)
- **Does the subject need to be narrowed?** To do the subject justice in the length and time required, you'll often need to limit it. (See below.)

Answering these questions about your assignment will help set some boundaries for your choice of subject. Then you can explore your own interests and experiences to narrow the subject so that you can cover it adequately within the space and time assigned. Federal aid to college students could be the subject of a book; the kinds of aid available or why the government should increase aid would be a more appropriate subject for a four-page paper due in a week.

One helpful technique for narrowing a subject is to ask focused questions about it, seeking one that seems appropriate for your assignment and that promises to sustain your interest through the writing process. The following examples illustrate how questioning can scale down broad subjects to specific subjects that are limited and manageable:

Broad subjects	Specific subjects
Communication on the Internet	What are the advantages of online communications?
	How, if at all, should the government regulate Internet content?
	How might the Internet contribute to social and economic equality?
Mrs. Mallard in Kate Chopin's "The Story of an Hour"	What changes does Mrs. Mallard undergo?
	Why does Mrs. Mallard respond as she does to news of her husband's death?
	What does the story's irony contribute to the character of Mrs. Mallard?
Lincoln's weaknesses as President	What was Lincoln's most significant error as commander-in-chief of the Union army?
	Why did Lincoln delay emancipating the slaves?
	Why did Lincoln have difficulties controlling his cabinet?

Use the following guidelines to narrow broad subjects:

1c

- **Ask as many questions about your broad subject as you can think of.** Make a list.
- **For each question that interests you and fits the assignment, roughly sketch out the main ideas.** Consider how many paragraphs or pages of specific facts, examples, and other details you would need to pin those ideas down. This thinking should give you at least a vague idea of how much work you'd have to do and how long the resulting paper might be.
- **Break a too-broad question down further,** repeating the previous steps.

The Internet can also help you limit a general subject. Browsing a directory such as *BUBL LINK* (*bubl.ac.uk/link*), pursue increasingly narrow categories to find a suitably limited topic.

EXERCISE 1.2
Narrowing subjects

Choose three of the following broad subjects and, using the techniques above, narrow each one to at least one specific question that can be answered in a three- to four-page paper.

1. Bilingual education
2. Training of teachers
3. Distribution of music by conventional versus electronic means
4. Dance in America
5. The history of women's suffrage
6. Food additives
7. Immigrants in the United States
8. Space exploration
9. The effect of television on professional sports
10. Child abuse
11. African Americans and civil rights
12. Successes in cancer research
13. Television evangelism
14. Treatment and prevention of AIDS
15. Women writers
16. Campaign finance reform
17. Genetic engineering
18. Trends in popular music
19. Immigration in your community
20. The World Wide Web and popular culture

1c   Consider your audience.

The readers likely to see your work—your **audience**—may influence your choice of subject and your definition of purpose. Your audience will certainly influence what you say about your subject

1c

and how you say it—for instance, how much background information you give and whether you adopt a serious or a friendly tone. Consider, for instance, these two memos written by a student who worked part-time at a small company:

To coworkers

Ever notice how much paper collects in your trash basket every day? Well, most of it can be recycled with little effort, I promise. Basically, all you need to do is set a bag or box near your desk and deposit wastepaper in it. I know, space is cramped in these little cubicles. But what's a little more crowding when the earth's at stake? . . .

Information: how employees could handle recycling; no mention of costs

Role: cheerful, equally harried colleague

Tone: informal, personal (*Ever notice; you; what's; Well; I know, space is cramped*)

To management

In my four months here, I have observed that all of us throw out baskets of potentially recyclable paper every day. Considering the drain on our forest resources and the pressure on landfills that paper causes, we could make a valuable contribution to the environmental movement by helping to recycle the paper we use. At the company where I worked before, the employees separate clean wastepaper from other trash at their desks. The maintenance staff collects trash in two receptacles, and the trash hauler (the same one we use here) makes separate pickups. I do not know what the hauler charges for handling recyclable material. . . .

Information: specific reasons; view of company as a whole; reference to another company; problem of cost

Role: serious, thoughtful, responsible employee

Tone: formal, serious (*Considering the drain; forest resources; valuable contribution;* no *you* or contractions)

For much academic and public writing, readers have definite needs and expectations. (See Chapters 8 and 13, respectively.) Still, in these areas you must make many choices based on audience. In areas where the conventions are vaguer, the choices are even more numerous. The box on the next page contains questions that can help you define and make these choices.

CULTURE LANGUAGE If English is not your native language, you may not be accustomed to appealing to your readers when you write. In some cultures, for instance, readers may accept a writer's statements with little or no questioning. When writing in English, try to reach out to readers by being accurate, fair, interesting, and clear.

EXERCISE 1.3
Analyzing audience

Choosing one of the topics you worked with in Exercise 1.2, use the questions in the box on the next page to determine as much as you can about the probable readers of an essay based on that topic. What does your analysis reveal about the specific information your readers would need? What role would you want to assume, and what tone would best convey your attitude toward your topic?

Questions about audience

Identity and expectations

- **Who _are_ my readers?**
- **What are my readers' expectations for the kind of writing I'm doing?** Do they expect features such as a particular organization and format, distinctive kinds of evidence, or a certain style of documenting sources?
- **What do I want readers to know or do after reading my work?** How should I make that clear to them?
- **What is my relationship to my readers?** How formal or informal will they expect me to be? What role and tone should I assume? What role do I want readers to play?

Characteristics, knowledge, and attitudes

- **What characteristics of readers are relevant for my subject and purpose?** For instance:

  Age and sex
  Occupation: students, professional colleagues, etc.
  Social or economic role: car buyers, potential employers, etc.
  Economic or educational background
  Ethnic background
  Political, religious, or moral beliefs and values
  Hobbies or activities

- **How will the characteristics of readers influence their attitudes toward my subject?**
- **What do readers already know and _not_ know about my topic?** How much do I have to tell them?
- **How should I handle any specialized terms?** Will readers know them? If not, should I define them?
- **What ideas, arguments, or information might surprise, excite, or offend readers?** How should I handle these points?
- **What misconceptions might readers have of my subject and/or my approach to it?** How can I dispel these misconceptions?

Uses and format

- **What will readers do with my writing?** Should I expect them to read every word from the top, to scan for information, or to look for conclusions? Can I help with a summary, headings, illustrations, or other aids? (See pp. 71–83 on document design.)

You can download these questions from _ablongman.com/littlebrown_. Duplicate the list for each writing project, write appropriate answers, and print a copy for reference as you compose.

1d   Define your purpose.

Your **purpose** in writing is your chief reason for communicating something about your subject to a particular audience of readers. Most writing you do will have one of four main purposes. Occasionally, you will *entertain* readers or *express yourself*—your feelings or ideas—to readers. More often you will *explain* something to readers or *persuade* readers to respect and accept, and sometimes even act on, your well-supported opinion. These purposes often overlap in a single essay, but usually one predominates. And the dominant purpose will influence your particular slant on your subject, the details you choose, and even the words you use.

Many writing assignments narrow the purpose by using a signal word, such as the following:

- **Report:** survey, organize, and objectively present the available evidence on the subject.
- **Summarize:** concisely state the main points in a text, argument, theory, or other work.
- **Discuss:** examine the main points, competing views, or implications of the subject.
- **Compare and contrast:** explain the similarities and differences between two subjects. (See also p. 63.)
- **Define:** specify the meaning of a term or a concept—distinctive characteristics, boundaries, and so on. (See also p. 61.)
- **Analyze:** identify the elements of the subject and discuss how they work together. (See also pp. 64–65 and 110.)
- **Interpret:** infer the subject's meaning or implications.
- **Evaluate:** judge the quality or significance of the subject, considering pros and cons. (See also p. 112.)
- **Argue:** take a position on the subject and support your position with evidence. (See also pp. 123–42.)

You can conceive of your purpose more specifically, too, in a way that incorporates your particular topic and the outcome you intend:

To explain how Annie Dillard's "Total Eclipse" builds to its climax so that readers appreciate the author's skill.

To explain the steps in a new office procedure so that staffers will be able to follow it without difficulty.

To persuade readers to support the college administration's plan for more required courses.

To argue against additional regulation of health-maintenance organizations so that readers will perceive the disadvantages for themselves.

EXERCISE 1.4
Finding purpose in assignments

For each of your narrowed topics in Exercise 1.2 (p. 6), suggest a likely purpose (entertainment, self-expression, explanation, persuasion) and try to define a specific purpose as well. Make audience part of your suggestions: what would you want readers to do or think in each case?

2   Invention

How do writers get ideas?

Writers use a host of techniques to discover ideas for their writing projects, from keeping a journal to making lists to reading magazines and books. There are many such **invention** techniques, but they don't all work for every writer. As you read through this chapter, try a few of the invention strategies that appeal to you. If they don't work, try others.

Whichever of the techniques you use, do your work in writing, not just in your head. That way, your ideas will be retrievable, and the very act of writing will lead you to fresh insights.

CULTURE LANGUAGE The discovery process encouraged here rewards rapid writing without a lot of thinking beforehand about what you will write or how. If your first language is not standard American English, you may find it helpful initially to do this exploratory writing in your native language or dialect and then to translate the worthwhile material for use in your drafts. This process can be productive, but it is extra work. You may want to try it at first and gradually move to composing in standard American English.

2a   Keep a journal.

A **journal** is a diary of ideas kept on paper or on a computer. It gives you a place to record your thoughts and can provide ideas for writing. Because you write for yourself, you can work out your ideas without the pressure of an audience "out there" who will evaluate logic or organization or correctness. If you write every day, even just

http://www.ablongman.com/littlebrown ▶

Visit the companion Web site for more help with invention.

for a few minutes, the routine will loosen your writing muscles and improve your confidence.

You can use a journal for varied purposes: perhaps to confide your feelings, explore your responses to movies and other media, practice certain kinds of writing (such as poems or news stories), think critically about what you read, or pursue ideas from your courses. In both examples following, the students planted the seeds for essays they later wrote. Megan Polanyis pondered something she learned from her biology textbook:

> Ecology and economics have the same root—the Greek word for "house."
> Economy = management of the house. Ecology = study of the house. In ecology the house is all of nature, ourselves, other animals, plants, earth, air, the whole environment. Ecology has a lot to do with economy: study the house in order to manage it.

Sara Ling responded to an experience:

> Had an exchange today on the snowboarding forum with a woman who joined the forum a while ago. She says she signed on at first with a screen name that didn't give away her gender, and she didn't tell anyone she was a woman. She was afraid the guys on the forum might shout her down. She waited until she'd established herself as an experienced snowboarder. Then she revealed her gender, and no one reacted badly. She asked me about my experiences, since my screen name says Sara. Had to admit I'd had problems of the what-does-a-girl-know sort. Wish I'd taken her approach.

(Further examples of Ling's writing appear on p. 13 and in the next three chapters.)

CULTURE LANGUAGE A journal can be especially helpful if your first language is not standard American English. You can practice writing to improve your fluency, try out sentence patterns, and experiment with vocabulary words. Equally important, you can experiment with applying what you know from experience to what you read and observe.

2b   Observe your surroundings.

Sometimes you can find a good subject—or gather information about a subject—by looking around you, not in the half-conscious way most of us move from place to place in our daily lives but deliberately, all senses alert. On a bus, for instance, are there certain types of passengers? What seems to be on the driver's mind? To get the most from observation, you should have a tablet and pen or pencil handy for notes and sketches. Back at your desk, study your notes and sketches for oddities or patterns that you'd like to explore further.

2c   Freewrite.

1 • Writing into a subject

Many writers find subjects or discover ideas by **freewriting:** writing without stopping for a certain amount of time (say, ten minutes) or to a certain length (say, one page). The goal of freewriting is to generate ideas and information from *within* yourself by going around the part of your mind that doesn't want to write or can't think of anything to write. You let words themselves suggest other words. *What* you write is not important; that you *keep* writing is. Don't stop, even if that means repeating the same words until new words come. Don't go back to reread, don't censor ideas that seem dumb or repetitious, and above all don't stop to edit: grammar, punctuation, spelling, and the like are irrelevant at this stage.

The physical act of freewriting may give you access to ideas you were unaware of. For example, the following freewriting by a student, Robert Benday, gave him the subject of writing as a disguise:

> Write to write. Seems pretty obvious, also weird. What to gain by writing? never anything before. Writing seems always—always—Getting corrected for trying too hard to please the teacher, getting corrected for not trying hard enuf. Frustration, nail biting, sometimes getting carried away making sentences to tell stories, not even true stories, esp. not true stories, that feels like creating something. Writing just pulls the story out of me. The story lets me be someone else, gives me a disguise.

(A later phase of Benday's writing appears on p. 15.)

If you write on a computer, you can ensure that your freewriting keeps moving forward by turning off your computer's monitor or turning its brightness control all the way down so that the screen is dark. The computer will record what you type but keep it from you and thus prevent you from tinkering with your prose. This **invisible writing** may feel uncomfortable at first, but it can free the mind for very creative results. When you've finished freewriting, simply turn the monitor on or turn up the brightness control to read what you've written, and then save or revise it as appropriate. Later, you may be able to transfer some of your freewriting into your draft.

CULTURE LANGUAGE Invisible writing can be especially helpful if you are uneasy about writing in standard American English and you tend to worry about errors while writing: the blank computer screen leaves you no choice but to explore ideas without regard for their expression. If you choose to write with the monitor on, concentrate on *what* you want to say, not *how* you're saying it.

2 • Focused freewriting

Focused freewriting is more concentrated: you start with your question about your subject and answer it without stopping for, say, fifteen minutes or one full page. As in all freewriting, you push to by-pass mental blocks and self-consciousness, not debating what to say or editing what you've written. With focused freewriting, though, you let the physical act of writing take you into and around your subject.

An example of focused freewriting can be found in the work of Sara Ling, whose journal entry appears on page 11. In a composition course, Ling's instructor had distributed "Welcome to Cyberbia," an essay by M. Kadi about communication on the Internet. The instructor then gave the following assignment:

> **Response to a reading.** M. Kadi's "Welcome to Cyberbia" holds that the Internet will do little to bridge differences among people because its users gravitate toward other users who are like themselves in most respects. More than a decade later, do Kadi's concerns seem valid? Can the Internet serve as a medium for positive change in the way people of diverse backgrounds relate to each other? If so, how? If not, why not? In an essay of 500–700 words, respond to Kadi's essay with a limited and well-supported opinion of your own. The first draft is due Monday, October 30, for class discussion.

On first reading Kadi's essay, Ling had been impressed with its tight logic but had found unconvincing its pessimistic view of the Internet's potential. She reread the essay and realized that some of Kadi's assertions did not correspond to her own Internet experiences. This discovery prompted the following focused freewriting:

> Kadi says we only meet people like ourselves on the Internet, but I've met lots who have very different backgrounds and interests—or "turned out to have" is more like it, since I didn't know anything about them at first. There's the anonymity thing, but Kadi ignores it. You can be anyone or no one. People can get to know me and my ideas without knowing I'm female or Asian American or a student. Then they can find out the facts about me, but the facts will be less likely to get in the way of communication. Communication without set identity, especially physical appearance. This could make for more tolerance of others, of difference.

(We will continue to follow Ling's work in this and the next three chapters.)

2d   Brainstorm.

A method similar to freewriting is **brainstorming**—focusing intently on a subject for a fixed period (say, fifteen minutes), pushing

2e

yourself to list every idea and detail that comes to mind. Like free-writing, brainstorming requires turning off your internal editor so that you keep moving ahead. (The technique of invisible writing on a computer, described on p. 12, can help you move forward.)

Here is an example of brainstorming by a student, Johanna Abrams, on what a summer job can teach:

summer work teaches—

how to look busy while doing nothing
how to avoid the sun in summer
seriously: discipline, budgeting money, value of money

which job? Burger King cashier? baby-sitter? mail-room clerk?
mail room: how to sort mail into boxes: this is learning??
how to survive getting fired—humiliation, outrage
Mrs. King! the mail-room queen as learning experience
the shock of getting fired: what to tell parents, friends?
Mrs. K was so rigid—dumb procedures
initials instead of names on the mail boxes—confusion!
Mrs. K's anger, resentment: the disadvantages of being smarter than your boss
The odd thing about working in an office: a world with its own rules for how to act
what Mr. D said about the pecking order—big chick (Mrs. K) pecks on little chick (me)
a job can beat you down—make you be mean to other people

(A later phase of Abrams's writing process appears on p. 24, and her final essay appears in Exercise 5.2, pp. 46–47.)

Working on a computer makes it fairly easy to edit and shape a brainstorming list into a preliminary outline of your paper. With a few keystrokes, you can delete weak ideas, expand strong ones, and rearrange items. You can also freewrite from the list if you think some ideas are especially promising and deserve more thought.

2e   Cluster.

Like freewriting and brainstorming, **clustering** also draws on free association and rapid, unedited work. But it emphasizes the relations between ideas by combining writing and nonlinear drawing. When clustering, you radiate outward from a center point—your topic. When an idea occurs, you pursue related ideas in a branching structure until they seem exhausted. Then you do the same with other ideas, staying open to connections, continuously branching out or drawing arrows.

The following example of clustering shows how Robert Benday used the technique for ten minutes to expand on the topic of writing as a means of disguise, an idea he arrived at through freewriting (see p. 12).

2f

Clustering

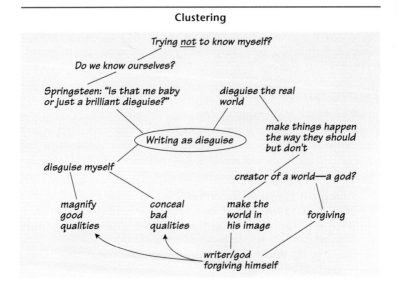

Trying <u>not</u> to know myself?

Do we know ourselves?

Springsteen: "Is that me baby or just a brilliant disguise?"   disguise the real world

make things happen the way they should but don't

Writing as disguise

disguise myself   creator of a world—a god?

magnify good qualities   conceal bad qualities   make the world in his image   forgiving

writer/god forgiving himself

EXERCISE 2.1
Using freewriting, brainstorming, or clustering

If you haven't tried any of them before, experiment with freewriting, brainstorming, or clustering. Continue with one of the topics you se-lected in Exercise 1.2 (p. 6), or begin with a new topic. Write or draw for at least ten minutes without stopping to reread or edit. When you finish, examine what you have written for ideas that could help you develop the topic. What do you think of the technique you tried? Did you have any difficulties with it? Did it help you to loosen up and generate ideas?

2f   Ask questions.

Asking yourself a set of questions about your subject—and writing out the answers—can help you look at the topic objectively and see fresh possibilities in it.

1 • Journalist's questions

A journalist with a story to report poses a set of questions:

Who was involved?
What happened, and what were the results?

2g

When did it happen?
Where did it happen?
Why did it happen?
How did it happen?

These questions can also be useful in probing an essay subject, especially when you are telling a story or examining causes and effects.

2 • Questions about patterns

We think about and understand a vast range of subjects through patterns such as narration, classification, and comparison and contrast. Asking questions based on the patterns can help you view your topic from many angles. Sometimes you may want to develop an entire essay using just one pattern.

How did it happen? (Narration)
How does it look, sound, feel, smell, taste? (Description)
What are examples of it or reasons for it? (Illustration or support)
What is it? What does it encompass, and what does it exclude? (Definition)
What are its parts or characteristics? (Division or analysis)
What groups or categories can it be sorted into? (Classification)
How is it like, or different from, other things? (Comparison and contrast)
Why did it happen? What results did or could it have? (Cause-and-effect analysis)
How do you do it, or how does it work? (Process analysis)

For more on these patterns, including paragraph-length examples, see pages 59–65.

2g   Read.

Many assignments require reading for the purpose of exploring ideas or gathering information. To respond to M. Kadi's essay about the Internet, for instance, Sara Ling had to understand and question Kadi's work. Essays on literary works as well as research papers also demand reading. But even when reading is not required by an assignment, it can help you locate or develop your topic by introducing you to ideas you didn't know and testing or expanding on what you do know.

Say you were writing in favor of amateur athletics, a subject to which you had given a lot of thought. You might be inclined to proceed entirely on your own, drawing on facts, examples, and opinions already in your head. But a little reading might open up more. For instance, an article in *Time* magazine could introduce you to an old rule for amateur status, or a posting to an online newsgroup could suggest a pro-amateurism argument that hadn't occurred to you. (See pp. 424–25 for techniques of library and computer research that you can use to locate sources on a topic.)

People often read passively, absorbing content like sponges, not interacting with it. To read for ideas, you need to be more active, probing text and illustrations with your mind, connecting them and the world you know. Always write while you read so that you can keep notes on content and—just as important—on what the content makes you *think*. See pages 94–97 for specific guidelines on the process of active reading.

Note Whenever you use the information or ideas of others in your writing, you must acknowledge your sources in order to avoid the serious offense of plagiarism. (See p. 470.)

EXERCISE 2.2
Developing a topic
Use at least two of the discovery techniques discussed on the preceding pages to develop one of the topics you worked with in Exercise 1.2 (p. 6).

3   Thesis and Organization

How does writing take shape?

You'll form rough ideas into writing through two main operations: developing a thesis and organizing the ideas and information that support the thesis. Finding your thesis, or main idea, gives you a focus and direction. Organizing your raw material emphasizes your central concerns and helps you clear away unneeded ideas, spot possible gaps, and energize your topic.

http://www.ablongman.com/littlebrown ▶

Visit the companion Web site for more help and an electronic exercise on thesis and organization.

3a   Develop a thesis statement.

3a

Your readers will expect your essay to be focused on a main idea, or **thesis.** In your final draft you may express this idea in a **thesis statement,** often at the end of your introduction. You can think of a thesis statement as both a claim about your subject and a promise you make to readers about how you approach the subject. The rest of your essay supports the claim and thus delivers on the promise.

Your thesis statement may be the answer to the question you posed in narrowing your subject (pp. 4–5), but it probably will not leap fully formed into your head. You may begin with an idea you want to communicate, but you will need to refine that idea to fit the realities of the paper you write. Often you will have to write and rewrite before you come to a conclusion about what you have. Still, try to pin down your thesis when you have a good stock of ideas. Then the thesis can help you start drafting, help keep you focused, and serve as a point of reference when changes inevitably occur.

1 • Functions of the thesis statement

As shown in the box below, the thesis statement serves three crucial functions and one optional one.

The thesis statement

- The thesis statement **narrows your subject** to a single, central idea that you want readers to gain from your essay.
- It **claims something specific and significant** about your subject, a claim that requires support.
- It **conveys your purpose,** your reason for writing.
- It often concisely **previews the arrangement of ideas.**

Here are examples of questions and answering thesis statements. As assertions, the thesis statements each consist of a topic (usually naming the general subject) and a claim about the topic.

Question	Thesis statement
1. What are the advantages of direct distribution of music via the Web?	The music available on the Web gives consumers many more choices than traditional distribution allows. [**Topic:** music available on the Web. **Claim:** gives consumers many more choices.]
2. What steps can prevent juvenile crime?	Juveniles can be diverted from crime by active learning programs, full-time sports, and intervention by mentors and role models.

Question	Thesis statement
	[**Topic**: juveniles. **Claim**: can be diverted from crime in three ways.]
3. Why did Abraham Lincoln delay in emancipating the slaves?	Lincoln delayed emancipating any slaves until 1863 because his primary goal was to restore and preserve the Union, with or without slavery. [**Topic**: Lincoln's delay. **Claim**: was caused by his goal of preserving the Union.]
4. Which college students should be entitled to federal aid?	As an investment in its own economy, the federal government should provide a tuition grant to any college student who qualifies academically. [**Topic**: federal government. **Claim**: should provide a tuition grant to any college student who qualifies academically.]
5. Should the state government play a role in moving consumers to hybrid cars?	Each proposal for the state to encourage purchase of hybrid cars—advertising campaigns, trade-in deals, and tax incentives—needlessly involves government in decisions that consumers are already making on their own. [**Topic**: each of three proposals. **Claim:** needlessly involves government in consumer decisions.]

3a

Notice that statements 2 and 5 clearly predict the organization of the essay that will follow.

CULTURE LANGUAGE In some cultures it is considered unnecessary or impolite for a writer to have an opinion or to state his or her main idea outright. When writing in standard American English for school or work, you can assume that your readers expect a clear and early idea of what you think.

2 • Drafting and revision of the thesis statement

While you are developing your thesis statement, ask the questions below about each attempt.

• **Does the statement make a concise *claim* about your subject?**

Original   Toni Morrison won the Nobel Prize in Literature in 1993.

The original sentence states a fact, not a claim about Morrison's work. The following revision states the significance of the prize:

Revised   Toni Morrison's 1993 Nobel Prize in Literature, the first awarded to an African American woman, affirms both the strength of her vivid prose style and the importance of her subject matter.

- **Is the claim *limited* to a single specific idea?**

Original   Diets are dangerous.

The original sentence is so broad that it seems insupportable. The revision limits the kinds of diets and their effects:

Revised   Fad diets can be dangerous when they deprive the body of essential nutrients or rely on excessive quantities of potentially harmful foods.

The following original sentence is also too general, whereas the revision specifies differences and their significance:

Original   Televised sports are different from live sports.

Revised   Although television cannot transmit all the excitement of being in a crowd during a game, its close-ups and slow-motion replays reveal much about the players and the strategy of the game.

- **Is the statement *unified* so that its parts clearly relate to each other?**

Original   Seat belts can save lives, but carmakers now install air bags.

With two facts linked by *but*, the original sentence moves in two directions, not one. The revision clarifies the relation between the parts and their significance.

Revised   If drivers had used lifesaving seat belts more often, carmakers might not have needed to install air bags.

- **Does the statement at least imply your *purpose*?**

Original   Educators' motives for using the Internet vary widely.

The original sentence conveys no hint of the writer's reason for exploring the subject. In contrast, the revision implies a purpose of arguing against a mainly financial motivation for using the Internet in education:

Revised   Too often, educators' uses of the Internet seem motivated less by teaching and learning than by making or saving money.

EXERCISE 3.1
Evaluating thesis statements
Evaluate the following thesis statements, considering whether each one is sufficiently limited, specific, and unified. Also consider whether each is a claim that implies the essay's purpose. Rewrite the statements as necessary to meet these goals. (You can do this exercise online at *ablongman.com/littlebrown.*)

1. Aggression usually leads to violence, injury, and even death, and we should use it constructively.
2. The religion of Islam is widely misunderstood in the United States.
3. One evening of a radio talk show amply illustrates both the appeal of such shows and their silliness.
4. Good manners make our society work.
5. The poem is about motherhood.
6. Television is useful for children and a mindless escape for adults who do not want to think about their problems.
7. I disliked American history in high school, but I like it in college.
8. Drunken drivers, whose perception and coordination are impaired, should receive mandatory suspensions of their licenses.
9. Business is a good major for many students.
10. The state's lenient divorce laws undermine the institution of marriage, which is fundamental to our culture, and they should certainly be made stricter for couples who have children.

3b Organize your ideas.

Most essays share a basic pattern of introduction (states the subject), body (develops the subject), and conclusion (pulls the essay's ideas together). Introductions and conclusions are discussed on pages 66–69. Within the body, every paragraph develops some aspect of the essay's main idea, or thesis. See pages 41–43 for Sara Ling's essay, with annotations highlighting the body's pattern of support for the thesis statement.

CULTURE LANGUAGE If you are not used to reading and writing American academic prose, its pattern of introduction-body-conclusion and the particular schemes discussed here may seem unfamiliar. For instance, instead of introductions that focus quickly on the topic and thesis, you may be used to openings that establish personal connections with readers or that approach the thesis indirectly. And instead of body paragraphs that first emphasize general points and then support those points with specific evidence, you may be used to general statements without support (because writers can assume that readers will supply the evidence themselves) or to evidence without explanation (because writers can assume that readers will infer the general points). When writing American academic prose, you need to take into account readers' expectations for directness and for the statement and support of general points.

1 • The general and the specific

Organizing material for an essay requires that you distinguish general and specific ideas and see the relations between ideas. **General** and **specific** refer to the number of instances or objects included in a group signified by a word. The following "ladder" illustrates a general-to-specific hierarchy:

Most general
↑ life form
   plant
   rose
↓ Uncle Dan's prize-winning American Beauty rose
Most specific

As you arrange your material, pick out the general ideas and then the specific points that support them. Set aside points that seem irrelevant to your key ideas. On a computer, you can easily experiment with various arrangements of general ideas and supporting information: save the master list, duplicate it, and then use the Cut and Paste functions to move material around or (a little quicker) drag selected text to where you want it.

2 • Schemes for organizing essays

An essay's body paragraphs may be arranged in many ways that are familiar to readers. The choice depends on your subject, purpose, and audience.

- **Spatial:** In describing a person, place, or thing, move through space systematically from a starting point to other features—for instance, top to bottom, near to far, left to right.
- **Chronological:** In recounting a sequence of events, arrange the events as they actually occurred in time, first to last.
- **General to specific:** Begin with an overall discussion of the subject; then fill in details, facts, examples, and other support.
- **Specific to general:** First provide the support; then draw a conclusion from it.
- **Climactic:** Arrange ideas in order of increasing importance to your thesis or increasing interest to the reader.
- **Problem-solution:** First outline a problem that needs solving; then propose a solution.

You can adapt these schemes to the different kinds of writing discussed in Chapters 8–14 of this book. For instance, an argument might take a climactic or a problem-solution approach, building in the key element of a response to probable objections (see pp. 138–39).

3 • Outlines

It's not essential to craft a detailed outline before you begin drafting an essay; in fact, too detailed a plan could prevent you from discovering ideas while you draft. Still, even a rough scheme can show you patterns of general and specific, suggest proportions, and highlight gaps or overlaps in coverage.

There are several different kinds of outlines, some more flexible than others.

Scratch or informal outline

A scratch or informal outline includes key general points in the order they will be covered. It may also suggest specific evidence.

Here is Sara Ling's scratch outline for her essay on Internet communication:

Thesis statement

By lowering the barriers of physical appearance, the unique anonymity of Internet communication could build diversity into community.

Scratch outline

No fear of prejudgment

Physical attributes unknown—age, race, gender, etc.
We won't be shut out because of appearance

Inability to prejudge others

No assumptions based on appearance
Meeting of minds only
Finding shared interests and concerns

A scratch or informal outline may be all you need to begin drafting. Sometimes, though, it may prove too skimpy a guide, and you may want to use it as a preliminary to a more detailed outline. Indeed, Sara Ling used her scratch outline as a base for a detailed formal outline that gave her an even more definite sense of direction (see the next page).

Tree diagram

In a tree diagram, ideas and details branch out in increasing specificity. Unlike more linear outlines, this diagram can be supplemented and extended indefinitely, so it is easy to alter. From her brainstorming about a summer job (p. 14), Johanna Abrams developed the following thesis statement and the tree diagram on the next page.

Thesis statement

Two months working in a large agency taught me that an office's pecking order should be respected.

A tree diagram or other visual map can be especially useful for planning a project for the Web. The diagram can help you lay out the organization of your project and then later can serve as a site map for readers. (See pp. 164–68 for more on Web composition.)

3b

Tree diagram

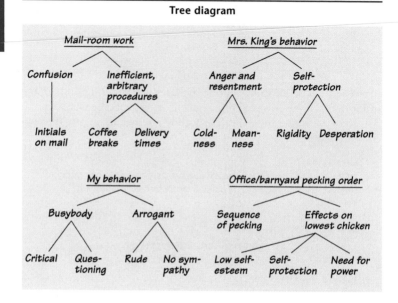

Formal outline

A formal outline not only lays out main ideas and their support but also shows the relative importance of all the essay's elements. On the basis of her scratch outline (previous page), Sara Ling prepared a formal outline for her essay on the Internet:

Thesis statement

By lowering the barriers of physical appearance, the unique anonymity of Internet communication could build diversity into community.

Formal outline

   I. No fear of being prejudged
      A. Unknown physical attributes
         1. Gender
         2. Age
         3. Race
         4. Style
      B. Freer communication
      C. No automatic rejection
  II. Inability to prejudge others
      A. No assumptions based on appearance
         1. Body type
         2. Physical disability
         3. Race

    B. Discovery of shared interests and concerns
       1. Sports and other activities
       2. Family values
       3. Political views
    C. Reduction of physical bias

This example illustrates several principles of outlining that can ensure completeness, balance, and clear relationships:

- **All parts are systematically indented and labeled:** Roman numerals (I, II) for primary divisions; indented capital letters (A, B) for secondary divisions; further indented Arabic numerals (1, 2) for supporting examples. (The next level down would be indented further still and labeled with small letters: a, b.)
- **The outline divides the material into several groups.** A long list of points at the same level should be broken up into groups.
- **Topics of equal generality appear in parallel headings,** with the same indention and numbering or lettering.
- **All subdivided headings break into at least two parts.** A topic cannot logically be divided into only one part.
- **All headings are expressed in parallel grammatical form**—in the example, as phrases using nouns plus modifiers. This is a topic outline; in a sentence outline all headings are expressed as full sentences (see pp. 524–25).

Note Because of its structure, a formal outline can be an excellent tool for analyzing a draft before revising it. See page 31.

4 • Unity and coherence

Two qualities of effective writing relate to organization: unity and coherence. When you perceive that someone's writing "flows well," you are probably appreciating these qualities.

To check an outline or draft for **unity,** ask these questions:

- **Is each section relevant to the main idea (thesis) of the essay?**
- **Within main sections, does each example or detail support the principal idea of that section?**

To check your outline or draft for **coherence,** ask the following questions:

- **Do the ideas follow a clear sequence?**
- **Are the parts of the essay logically connected?**
- **Are the connections clear and smooth?**

The following essay illustrates some ways of achieving unity and coherence (highlighted in the annotations).

A Picture of Hyperactivity

A hyperactive committee member can contribute to efficiency. A hyperactive salesperson can contribute to profits. When children are hyperactive, though, people—even parents—may wish they had never been born. A collage of those who must cope with hyperactivity in children is a picture of frustration, anger, and loss.

The first part of the collage is the doctors. In their terminology, the word hyperactivity has been replaced by ADHD, attention-deficit hyperactivity disorder. They apply the term to children who are abnormally or excessively busy. But doctors do not fully understand the problem and thus differ over how to treat it. Some recommend a special diet, others recommend behavior-modifying drugs, and still others, who do not consider ADHD a medical problem, recommend psychotherapy. The result is a merry-go-round of tests, confusion, and frustration for the children and their parents.

As the mother of an ADHD child, I can say what the disorder means to the parents who form the second part of the collage. It means worry that is deep and enduring. It means despair that is a constant companion. It means a mixture of frustration, guilt, and anger. And finally, since there are times when parents' anger goes out of control and threatens the children, it means self-loathing.

The weight of ADHD, however, does not rest on the doctors and parents. The darkest part of the collage belongs to the children. From early childhood they may be dragged from doctor to doctor, attached to machines, medicated until they feel numb, and tested or discussed by physicians, teachers, neighbors, and strangers on the street. They may be highly intelligent, but they'll still do poorly in school because of their short attention spans. Their playmates dislike them because of their temper and their unwillingness to follow rules. Even their pets mistrust them because of their erratic behavior. As time goes on, the children see their parents more and more in tears and anger, and they know they are the cause.

The collage is complete, and it is dark and somber. ADHD, as applied to children, is a term with uncertain, unattractive, and bitter associations. The picture does have one bright spot, however, for inside every ADHD child is a lovely, trusting, calm person waiting to be recognized.

—Linda Devereaux (student)

See also pages 49–57 on unity and coherence in paragraphs.

4

EXERCISE 3.2
Organizing ideas

The following list of ideas was extracted by a student from freewriting he did for a brief paper on soccer in the United States. Using his thesis statement as a guide, pick out the general ideas and arrange the relevant specific points under them. In some cases you may have to infer general ideas to cover specific points in the list. (You can do this exercise online at *ablongman.com/littlebrown.*)

Thesis statement

Soccer will probably never be the sport in the United States that it is elsewhere because both the potential fans and the potential backers resist it.

List of ideas

Sports seasons are already too crowded for fans.
Soccer rules are confusing to Americans.
A lot of kids play soccer in school, but the game is still "foreign."
Sports money goes where the money is.
Backers are wary of losing money on new ventures.
Fans have limited time to watch.
Fans have limited money to pay for sports.
Backers are concerned with TV contracts.
Previous attempts to start a pro soccer league failed.
TV contracts almost matter more than live audiences.
Failure of the US Football League was costly.
Baseball, football, hockey, and basketball seasons overlap.
Soccer fans couldn't fill huge stadiums.
American soccer fans are too few for TV interest.

4 Drafting

What can I do about writer's block?

Writer's block happens to everyone, even the most experienced writers. To confront it, try to think of drafting as an occasion for exploration. Don't expect to transcribe solid thoughts into polished prose: solidity and polish will come with revision and editing. Instead, let the act of writing help you to find and form your meaning.

http://www.ablongman.com/littlebrown

Visit the companion Web site for more help with drafting.

4b

4a　Start writing.

Beginning a draft often takes courage, even for seasoned professionals. Procrastination may actually help if you let ideas simmer at the same time. At some point, though, you'll have to face the blank paper or computer screen. The following techniques can help you begin:

- **Read over what you've already written**—notes, outlines, and so on—and immediately start your draft with whatever comes to mind.
- **Freewrite** (see p. 12).
- **Write scribbles or type nonsense** until usable words start coming.
- **Pretend you're writing to a friend about your subject.**
- **Describe an image that represents your subject**—a physical object, a facial expression, two people arguing over something, a giant machine gouging the earth for a mine, whatever.
- **Skip the opening and start in the middle.** Or write the conclusion.
- **Write a paragraph.** Explain what you think your essay will be about when you finish it.
- **Start writing the part that you understand best or feel most strongly about.** Using your outline, divide your essay into chunks—say, one for the introduction, another for the first point, and so on. One of these chunks may call out to be written.

4b　Maintain momentum.

Drafting requires momentum: the forward movement opens you to fresh ideas and connections. To keep moving while drafting, try one or more of these techniques:

- **Set aside enough time for yourself.** For a brief essay, a first draft is likely to take at least an hour or two.
- **Work in a quiet place.**
- **Make yourself comfortable.**
- **If you must stop working, write down what you expect to do next.** Then you can pick up where you stopped with minimal disruption.
- **Be as fluid as possible.** Spontaneity will allow your attitudes toward your subject to surface naturally in your sentences.
- **Keep going.** Skip over sticky spots; leave a blank if you can't find the right word; put alternative ideas or phrasings in brack-

ets so that you can consider them later without bogging down. If an idea pops out of nowhere but doesn't seem to fit in, quickly jot it down on a separate sheet, or write it into the draft and bracket or boldface it for later attention.

- **Resist self-criticism.** Don't worry about your style, grammar, spelling, punctuation, and the like. Don't worry about what your readers will think. These are very important matters, but save them for revision.
- **Use your thesis statement and outline.** They can remind you of your planned purpose, organization, and content. However, if your writing leads you in a direction you find more interesting, then follow.

If you write on a word processor, frequently save the text you're drafting—at least every ten to fifteen minutes and every time you leave the computer.

4c   A sample first draft

Sara Ling's first draft on Internet communication appears below. As you read the draft, mark the thesis statement and each key idea developing the thesis. Note places where you think the ideas could be clearer or better supported.

Title?

In "Welcome to Cyberbia," written in 1995, M. Kadi predicts that the Internet will lead to more fragmentation in society because people just seek out others like themselves. But Kadi fails to foresee how the unique anonymity of Internet communication could actually build diversity into community by lowering the barriers of physical appearance.

Anonymity on the Internet. It's one of the best things about technology. Most people who communicate online use an invented screen name to avoid revealing personal details such as age, gender, and ethnic background. No one knows whether you're fat or thin or neat or sloppy. What kind of clothes you wear. (Maybe you're not wearing clothes at all.) People who know you personally don't even know who you are with an invented screen name.

We can make ourselves known without first being prejudged because of our physical attributes. For example, I participate in a snowboarding forum that has mostly men. I didn't realize what I was getting into when I used my full name as my screen name. Before long, I had received unfriendly responses such as "What does a girl know?" and "Why don't you go back to knitting?" I guess I had run into a male prejudice against female snowboarders. However, another woman on the forum had no such problems. At first she signed on with a screen name that did not reveal her gender, and no one responded negatively to her messages. When she had contributed for a while, she earned respect from the other snowboarders. When she revealed that she was a woman at that point, no one responded negatively in the way I had experienced. She posed at first as someone different from who she really was and could make herself heard.

We also cannot prejudge others because of their appearance. Often in face-to-face interaction we assume we know things about people just because of the way they look. Assumptions prevent people from discovering their shared interests and concerns, and this is particularly true where race is concerned. The anonymity of the Internet makes physical barriers irrelevant, and only people's minds meet. Because of this, the Internet could create a world free of physical bias.

Logged on to the Internet we can become more tolerant of others. We can become a community.

> **EXERCISE 4.1**
> **Analyzing a first draft**
> Compare Sara Ling's draft, above, with the previous step in her planning (her formal outline) on pages 24–25. List the places where the act of drafting led Ling to rearrange her information, add or delete material, or explore new ideas. (You can do this exercise online at *ablongman.com/littlebrown*.)

5 Revising and Editing

Why and how should I revise?

Revising is an essential task in creating an effective piece of writing. During revision (literally "re-seeing") you shift your focus outward from yourself and your subject toward your readers, concentrating on what will help them respond as you want. Many writers revise in two stages, first viewing the work as a whole, evaluating and improving its overall meaning and structure, and then

---

http://www.ablongman.com/littlebrown ▶

Visit the companion Web site for more help with revising and editing.

editing sentences for wording, grammar, punctuation, spelling, and so on.

For you as for many writers, overall revision may be more difficult than editing because often you must pull your work apart before you can put it back together and look for sentence-level errors. But knowing that you will edit later also gives you the freedom at first to look beyond the confines of the page or screen to the whole paper.

5a Revise the essay as a whole.

Your first step in revising your writing should be to examine large-scale issues such as whether your purpose and main idea will be clear to readers and whether the draft fully develops the thesis. In revising, you may need to move, combine, or delete whole paragraphs; rethink major points; or flesh out ideas with details or research.

1 • Reading your work critically

To revise your writing, you have to read it critically, and that means you have to create some distance between your draft and yourself. One of the following techniques may help you see your work objectively:

- **Take a break after finishing the draft.** A few hours may be enough; a whole night or day is preferable.
- **Ask someone to read and react to your draft.** If your instructor encourages collaboration among students, by all means take advantage of the opportunity to hear the responses of others. (See pp. 43–45 for more on collaboration.)
- **Type a handwritten draft.** The act of transcription can reveal gaps in content or problems in structure.
- **Outline your draft.** Highlight the main points supporting the thesis, and write these sentences down separately in outline form. Then examine the outline you've made for logical order, gaps, and digressions. A formal outline can be especially illuminating because of its careful structure (see pp. 24–25).
- **Listen to your draft.** Read the draft out loud to yourself or a friend or classmate, record and listen to it, or have someone read the draft to you.
- **Ease the pressure.** Don't try to re-see everything in your draft at once. Use the checklist on the next page, making a separate pass through the draft for each item.

Checklist for whole-essay revision

Purpose

What is the essay's purpose? Does it conform to the assignment?

Thesis

What is the thesis of the essay? Where does it become clear? How well does the paper deliver on the commitment of the thesis?

Structure

What are the main points supporting the thesis? (List them.) How does the arrangement of these points contribute to the paper's purpose?

Development

How well do details, examples, and other evidence support each main point? Where, if at all, might readers find support skimpy or have trouble understanding the content?

Tone

How appropriate is the paper's tone for the purpose, topic, and intended readers? Where is it most and least successful?

Unity

Which, if any, sentences or paragraphs do not contribute to the thesis? Should these digressions be cut, or can they be rewritten to support the thesis?

Coherence

How clearly and smoothly does the paper flow? Where does it seem rough or awkward? Can any transitions be improved?

Title, introduction, conclusion

Does the title reflect the essay's content and purpose? Is it interesting? How well does the introduction engage and focus readers' attention on the thesis of the essay? How effective is the conclusion in providing a sense of completion?

You can download this checklist from *ablongman.com/littlebrown*. Make a copy for each writing project, and insert answers to each question with your ideas for changes.

2 • Revising on a word processor

When you revise on a computer, take a few precautions to avoid losing your work and to keep track of your drafts:

- **Save your work every five to ten minutes.**
- **After doing any major work on a project, create a backup version of the file.**

- **Work on a duplicate of your latest draft.** Then the original will remain intact until you're truly finished with it. On the duplicate you can use your word processor's Track Changes function, which shows changes alongside the original text and allows you to accept or reject alterations later.
- **Save each draft under its own file name.** You may need to consult it for ideas or phrasings.

3 • Writing a title

The revision stage is a good time to consider a title because attempting to sum up your essay in a phrase can focus your attention sharply on your subject, purpose, and audience.

Here are suggestions for titling an essay:

- A *descriptive title* **announces the subject clearly and accurately.** Such a title is almost always appropriate and is usually expected for academic writing. Sara Ling's final title—"The Internet: Fragmentation or Community?"—is an example. Other examples are "Images of Lost Identity in *North by Northwest*"; "An Experiment in Small-Group Dynamics"; "Why Lincoln Delayed Emancipating the Slaves"; "Food Poisoning Involving *E. coli* Bacteria: A Review of the Literature."
- A *suggestive title* **hints at the subject to arouse curiosity.** It is common in popular magazines and may be appropriate for more informal writing. Examples include "Making Peace" (for an essay on the Peace Corps) and "Anyone for Soup?" (for an essay on working in a soup kitchen). For a more suggestive title, Ling might have chosen something like "What We Don't Know Can Help Us" or "Secrets of the Internet." Such a title conveys the writer's attitude and hints at the topic, thereby pulling readers into the essay to learn more. A source for such a title may be a familiar phrase, a fresh image, or a significant expression from the essay itself.
- **A title tells readers how big the topic is.** For Ling's essay, the title "The Internet" or "Anonymity" would have been too broad, whereas "Lose Your Body" or "Discovering Common Ground" would have been too narrow because each deals with only part of the paper's content.
- **A title should not restate the assignment or the thesis statement,** as in "The Trouble with M. Kadi's Picture of the Internet" or "What I Think About Diversity on the Internet."

For more information on essay titles, see pages 403 (capitalizing words in a title), 523 (MLA title format), and 548 (APA title format).

5b   A sample revision

In revising her first draft, Sara Ling had the help of her instructor and several classmates, to whom she showed the draft as part of her assignment. (See pp. 43–45 for more on this kind of collaboration.) Based on the revision checklist, she thought that she wanted to stick with her initial purpose and thesis statement and that they had held up well in the draft. But she also knew without being told that her introduction and conclusion were too hurried, that the movement between paragraphs was too abrupt, that the example of the snowboarding forum went on too long, and that the fourth paragraph was thin: she hadn't supplied enough details to support her ideas and convince her readers.

Ling's readers confirmed her self-evaluation. Several, however, raised points that she had not considered, reflected in these comments by classmates:

Comment 1

Why do you say (par. 2) that most people use invented screen names? I don't, and I know other people who don't either. Do you have evidence of how many people use invented names or why they do?

Comment 2

I would have an easier time agreeing with you about the Internet if you weren't quite so gung-ho. For instance, what about the dangers of the Internet, as when adults prey on children or men prey on women? In par. 3, you don't acknowledge that such things can and do happen. Also, is a bias-free world (par. 4) really such a sure thing? People will still meet in person, after all.

At first Ling was tempted to resist these comments because the writers seemed to object to her ideas. But eventually she understood that the comments showed ways she could make the ideas convincing to more readers. The changes took some time, partly because Ling decided to conduct a survey of students in order to test her assumption about people's use of invented screen names.

The first half of Ling's draft appears below, showing the survey results and other changes explained in annotations. Ling used the Track Changes function on her word processor, so that deletions are crossed out and additions are in color.

Descriptive title names topic and forecasts approach.

The Internet: Fragmentation or Community?

Title?

We hear all sorts of predictions about how the Internet will enrich our lives and promote equality, tolerance, and thus community in our society. But are these promises realistic? In her 1995 essay "Welcome to

Cyberbia," M. Kadi argues that they are not. Instead, she~~In "Welcome to Cyberbia," written in 1995, M. Kadi~~ predicts that the Internet will lead to more fragmentation, not community, ~~in society~~ because users merely ~~people just~~ seek out others ~~like themselves~~ with the same biases, needs, and concerns as their own. The point is an interesting one, ~~B~~but Kadi fails to foresee that ~~how~~ the unique anonymity of Internet communication could actually build diversity into community by lowering the barriers of physical appearance.

Expanded introduction draws readers into Ling's question and summarizes Kadi's essay.

Internet communication can be anonymous on at least two levels. ~~Anonymity on the Internet. It's one of the best things about technology. Most people who communicate online use an invented screen name to avoid revealing personal details such as age, gender, and ethnic background. No one knows~~ The people who communicate with you do not know your age. ~~w~~Whether you're fat or thin or neat or sloppy. What kind of clothes you wear. (Maybe you're not wearing clothes at all.) Or anything else about physical appearance. ~~People who know you personally don't even know who you are with an invented screen name.~~ If you use an invented screen name instead of your real name, readers don't even know whatever your name says about you, such as gender or ethnic background.

New transition relates paragraph to thesis statement and smoothes flow.

Blanket assertion is deleted in favor of survey results added later.

Addition clarifies use of invented screen names.

Internet anonymity seems a popular option, judging by the numbers of invented user names seen in online forums. But I thought it would be a good idea to determine the extent of invented user names as well as the reasons for them, so I surveyed seventy-eight students with two questions: (1) Do you ever write with an invented user name when contributing to chat rooms, newsgroups, blogs, and so on? (2) If yes, why do you use an invented name: to protect your privacy, to avoid revealing personal information, or for some other reason? Fig. 1 shows that most of the students do use invented names online. And most do so to protect their privacy or to avoid revealing personal details.

Largest revision presents results of survey conducted to support use of invented screen names.

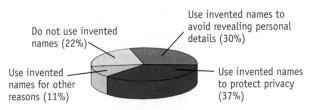

Do not use invented names (22%)

Use invented names to avoid revealing personal details (30%)

Use invented names for other reasons (11%)

Use invented names to protect privacy (37%)

New pie graph presents survey results in an easy-to-read format.

Fig. 1. Use of invented screen names among seventy-eight Internet users.

EXERCISE 5.1
Analyzing a revised draft

Compare Ling's revision with her first draft on pages 29–30. Referring to the discussion of her revision and the annotations on it, can you see the reasons for most of her changes? Where would you suggest further revisions, and why? (You can do this exercise online at *ablongman.com/littlebrown*.)

5c   Edit the revised draft.

After you've revised your essay so that all the content is in place, then turn to the important work of removing any surface problems that could interfere with a reader's understanding or enjoyment of your ideas.

1 • Discovering what needs editing

Try these approaches to spot possible flaws in your work:

- **Take a break.** Even fifteen or twenty minutes can clear your head.
- **Read the draft slowly, and read what you actually see.** Otherwise, you're likely to read what you intended to write but did not.
- **Read as if you are encountering the draft for the first time.** Put yourself in the reader's place.
- **Have a classmate, friend, or relative read your work.** Make sure you understand and consider the reader's suggestions, even if eventually you decide not to take them.
- **Read the draft aloud or, even better, record it.** Listen for awkward rhythms, repetitive sentence patterns, and missing or clumsy transitions.
- **Learn from your own experience.** Keep a record of the problems that others have pointed out in your writing. When editing, check your work against this record.

In your editing, work first for clarity and a smooth movement among sentences and then for correctness. Use the questions in the checklist on the next page to guide your editing, referring to the page numbers in parentheses as needed.

The second paragraph of Sara Ling's edited draft appears on page 38. One change Ling made throughout the essay shows up in this paragraph: she resolved an inconsistency in references to *you, people,* and *we,* settling on a consistent *we.* In addition, Ling corrected several sentence fragments in the middle of the paragraph.

Checklist for editing

Clarity

How well do words and sentences convey their intended meanings? Which if any words and sentences are confusing? Check especially for these:

Exact words (pp. 203–13)
Parallelism (pp. 187–89)
Clear modifiers (pp. 318–24)
Clear reference of pronouns (pp. 301–04)
Complete sentences (pp. 326–30)
Sentences separated correctly (pp. 332–36)

Effectiveness

How well do words and sentences engage and direct readers' attention? Where, if at all, does the writing seem wordy, choppy, or dull? Check especially for these:

Emphasis of main ideas (pp. 176–86)
Smooth and informative transitions (pp. 55–57)
Variety in sentence length and structure (pp. 191–94)
Appropriate words (pp. 196–202)
Concise sentences (pp. 216–21)

Correctness

How little or how much do surface errors interfere with clarity and effectiveness? Check especially for these:

Spelling (pp. 392–96)
Verb forms, especially -s and -ed endings and correct forms of irregular verbs (pp. 250–66)
Verb tenses, especially consistency (pp. 267–73)
Agreement between subjects and verbs, especially when words come between them or the subject is a word like *everyone* (pp. 280–86)
Pronoun forms (pp. 289–95)
Agreement between pronouns and the words they refer to (their antecedents), especially when the antecedent contains *or* or it is *everyone, person,* or a similar word (pp. 296–300)
Sentence fragments (pp. 326–30)
Commas, especially with comma splices (pp. 332–36), with *and* or *but,* with introductory elements, with nonessential elements, and with series (pp. 349–58)
Apostrophes in possessives but not plural nouns (*Dave's/witches*) and in contractions but not possessive personal pronouns (*it's/its*) (pp. 373–77)

You can download this checklist from *ablongman.com/littlebrown*. Make a copy for each writing project, and insert answers along with notes on specific changes to make.

Internet communication can be anonymous on at least two levels. The people we~~you~~ communicate with do not know our~~your~~ age~~.~~, ~~W~~whether we're~~you're~~ fat or thin or neat or sloppy~~.~~, ~~W~~what kind of clothes we~~you~~ wear~~.~~ (~~Maybe you're not~~ if we're wearing clothes at all)~~.~~, ~~O~~or anything else about physical appearance. If we~~you~~ use ~~an~~ invented screen names instead of our~~your~~ real names, readers don't even know whatever our~~your~~ names may reveal or suggest ~~says~~ about us~~you~~, such as gender or ethnic background.

2 • Editing on a word processor

When you work on a word processor, consider these additional approaches to editing:

- **Don't rely on your word processor's spelling or grammar and style checker to find what needs editing.** See the discussion of these checkers below.
- **If possible, work on a double-spaced paper copy.** Most people find it much harder to spot errors on a computer screen than on paper.
- **Use the Find command to locate and correct your common problems**—certain misspellings, overuse of *there is,* wordy phrases such as *the fact that,* and so on.
- **Resist overediting.** The ease of editing on a computer can lead to rewriting sentences over and over, stealing the life from your prose. If your grammar and style checker contributes to the temptation, consider turning it off.
- **Take special care with additions and omissions.** Make sure you haven't omitted needed words or left in unneeded words.

3 • Working with spelling and grammar/style checkers

The spelling checker and grammar and style checker that may come with your word processor can be helpful *if* you work within their limitations. The programs miss many problems and may even flag items that are actually correct. Further, they cannot make important decisions about your writing because they know nothing of your subject, your purpose, and your audience. Always use these tools critically:

- **Read your work yourself to ensure that it's clear and error-free.**
- **Consider a checker's suggestions carefully, weighing each one against your intentions.** If you aren't sure whether to accept a checker's suggestion, consult a dictionary, writing handbook, or other source. Your version may be fine.

Using a spelling checker

Your word processor's spelling checker can be a great ally: it will flag words that are spelled incorrectly and usually suggest alternative spellings that resemble what you've typed. However, this ally also has the potential to undermine you because of its limitations:

- **The checker may flag a word that you've spelled correctly** just because the word does not appear in its dictionary.

- **The checker may suggest incorrect alternatives.** In providing a list of alternative spellings for your word, the checker may highlight the one it considers most likely to be correct. You need to verify that this alternative is actually what you intend. Consult an online or printed dictionary when you aren't sure of the checker's recommendations (see p. 204).

- **Most important, a spelling checker will not flag words that appear in its dictionary but you have misused.** The jingle shown in the screen shot below has circulated widely as a warning about spelling checkers. (See also p. 397 for an exercise on working with a spelling checker.)

Spelling checker

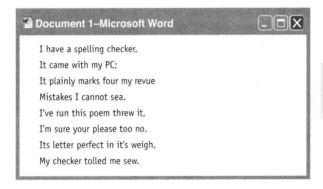

Document 1—Microsoft Word

I have a spelling checker,
It came with my PC;
It plainly marks four my revue
Mistakes I cannot sea.
I've run this poem threw it,
I'm sure your please too no.
Its letter perfect in it's weigh,
My checker tolled me sew.

A spelling checker failed to catch any of the thirteen errors in this jingle. Can you spot them?

You can supplement a spelling checker by maintaining a file of your frequent misspellings and selecting Find under the Edit menu to check for them. But in the end *the only way to rid your papers of spelling errors is to proofread your papers yourself.* See the next page for proofreading tips. And see Chapter 45 for more advice on spelling.

Using a grammar and style checker

Word processors' grammar and style checkers can flag incorrect grammar or punctuation and wordy or awkward sentences.

However, these programs can call your attention only to passages that *may* be faulty. They miss many errors because they are not yet capable of analyzing language in all its complexity. (For instance, they can't accurately distinguish a word's part of speech when there are different possibilities, as *light* can be a noun, a verb, or an adjective.) And they often question passages that don't need editing, such as an appropriate passive verb or a deliberate and emphatic use of repetition.

You can customize a grammar and style checker to suit your needs and habits as a writer. (Select Options under the Tools menu.) Most checkers allow you to specify whether to check grammar only or grammar and style. Some style checkers can be set to the level of writing you intend, such as formal, standard, and informal. (For academic writing choose formal.) You can also instruct the checker to flag specific grammar and style problems that tend to bother you, such as apostrophes in plural nouns, overused passive voice, or a confusion between *its* and *it's*.

5d   Format and proofread the final draft.

After editing your essay, retype or print it one last time. Follow your instructor's directions in formatting your document. Two common formats are discussed and illustrated in this book: Modern Language Association (MLA) on pages 521–24 and American Psychological Association (APA) on pages 547–50. In addition, Chapter 7 treats principles and elements of document design.

Be sure to proofread the final essay several times to spot and correct errors. To increase the accuracy of your proofreading, you may need to experiment with ways to keep yourself from relaxing into the rhythm and the content of your prose. Here are a few tricks, including some used by professional proofreaders:

- **Read printed copy,** even if you will eventually submit the paper electronically. Most people proofread more accurately when reading type on paper than when reading it on a computer screen. (At the same time, don't view the printed copy as necessarily error-free just because it's clean. Clean-looking copy may still harbor errors.)
- **Read the paper aloud,** very slowly, and distinctly pronounce exactly what you see.
- **Place a ruler under each line as you read it.**
- **Read "against copy,"** comparing your final draft one sentence at a time against the edited draft.
- **Ignore content.** To keep the content of your writing from dis-

tracting you while you proofread, read the essay backward, end to beginning, examining each sentence as a separate unit. Or, taking advantage of a word processor, isolate each paragraph from its context by printing it on a separate page. (Of course, reassemble the paragraphs before submitting the paper.)

5e   A sample final draft

Sara Ling's final essay appears below, typed in MLA format except for margins and page numbers. Comments in the margins point out key features of the essay's content.

Sara Ling

Professor Nelson

English 120A

6 November 2006

The Internet:

Fragmentation or Community?

We hear all sorts of predictions about how the Internet will enrich our individual lives and promote communication, tolerance, and thus community in our society. But are these promises realistic? In her 1995 essay "Welcome to Cyberbia," M. Kadi argues that they are not. Instead, she predicts that the Internet will lead to more fragmentation, not community, because users merely seek out others with the same biases, concerns, and needs as their own. The point is an interesting one, but Kadi fails to foresee that the unique anonymity of Internet communication could actually build diversity into community by lowering the barriers of physical appearance.

Internet communication can be anonymous on at least two levels. The people we communicate with do not know our age, whether we're fat or thin or neat or sloppy, what kind of clothes we wear (if we're wearing clothes at all), or anything else about physical appearance. If we use invented screen names instead of our real names, readers don't even know whatever our names may reveal or suggest about us, such as gender or ethnic background.

Internet anonymity seems a popular option, judging by the numbers of invented user names seen in online forums. To determine the extent of invented user names as well as the reasons for them, I surveyed seventy-eight students. I asked two questions: (1) Do you ever write with an

Descriptive title

Introduction

Question to be addressed

Summary of Kadi's essay

Thesis statement

Explanation of Internet's anonymity

Presentation of survey conducted to gauge use of invented screen names

Explanation of survey method

invented user name when contributing to chat rooms, newsgroups, Web logs, and so on? (2) If yes, why do you use an invented name: to protect your privacy, to avoid revealing personal information, or for some other reason? The results are shown in fig. 1. A large majority of the students

Summary of survey results

(seventy-eight percent) do use invented names online. And most of them do so to protect their privacy (thirty-seven percent) or to avoid revealing personal details (thirty percent).

Graph display-ing survey results, with self-explanatory labels and caption

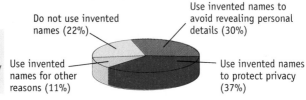

Fig. 1. Use of invented screen names among seventy-eight Internet users.

First main point: We are not prejudged by others.

Users of the Internet clearly value the anonymity it can give them. This anonymity allows users to communicate freely without being pre-judged because of physical attributes. In follow-up interviews, twenty stu-

Examples of first point

dents said that they use invented names to mask personal details because they think the details might work against them in online communication. One said she is able to participate in a physics discussion list without fear of being ignored by the group's professional physicists. Another said he thinks he can contribute more freely to a political forum because no one knows he's African American. I learned the benefits of anonymity myself when I joined a snowboarding forum using my full name and received hostile responses such as "What does a girl know?" and "Why don't you go back to knitting?" I assumed I had run into a male prejudice against fe-male snowboarders. However, another woman on the forum had no such problems when she contributed for a while before revealing her gender.

Qualification of first point

Granted, concealing or altering identities on the Internet can be a problem, as when adults pose as children to seduce or harm them. These well-publicized occurrences say much about the need to monitor children's use of the Internet and to be cautious about meeting Internet corre-

Conclusion of first point

spondents. However, they do not undermine the value of being able to make ourselves heard in situations where normally (in the real world) we would be shut out.

The Internet's anonymity has a flip side, too: just as we cannot be prejudged, so we cannot prejudge others because of their appearance. Often in face-to-face interaction, we assume we know things about people just because of the way they look. Someone with an athletic build must be unintelligent. Someone who is heavy must be uninteresting. Perhaps most significant, someone of another race must have fixed and contrary views about all kinds of issues, from family values to crime to affirmative action. Assumptions like these prevent us from discovering the interests and concerns we share with people who merely look different. But with the anonymity of the Internet, such physical barriers to understanding are irrelevant.

Second main point: We cannot prejudge others

Clarification of second point

Examples of second point

Effects of assumptions

Conclusion of second point

A world without physical bias may be an unreachable ideal. However, the more we communicate with just our minds, the more likely it is that our minds will find common ground and put less emphasis on physical characteristics. Logged on, we can begin to become more accepted and more accepting, more tolerated and more tolerant. We can begin to become a community.

Conclusion, summarizing essay

Work Cited

Kadi, M. "Welcome to Cyberbia." <u>Utne Reader</u> Mar.-Apr. 1995: 57-59.

Work cited in MLA style (see p. 491)

5f Collaborate on revisions.

In many writing courses students work together on writing, most often commenting on each other's work to help with revision. This collaborative writing gives experience in reading written work critically and in reaching others through writing.

Whether you collaborate in person, on paper, or on a computer, you will be more comfortable and helpful and will benefit more from others' comments if you follow a few guidelines:

Commenting on others' writing

- **Be sure you know what the writer is saying.** If necessary, summarize the paper to understand its content. (See pp. 96–97.)
- **Address only your most significant concerns with the work.** Use the revision checklist on page 32 as a guide to what is significant. Unless you have other instructions, ignore mistakes in grammar, punctuation, spelling, and the like. (The temptation to focus on such errors may be especially strong if

the writer is less experienced than you are with standard American English.) Emphasizing mistakes will contribute little to the writer's revision.

- **Remember that you are the reader, not the writer.** Don't edit sentences, add details, or otherwise assume responsibility for the paper.

- **Phrase your comments carefully.** Avoid misunderstandings by making sure comments are both clear and respectful. If you are responding on paper or online, not face to face with the writer, remember that the writer has nothing but your written words to go on. He or she can't ask you for immediate clarification and can't infer your attitudes from gestures, facial expressions, and tone of voice.

- **Be specific.** If something confuses you, say *why*. If you disagree with a conclusion, say *why*.

- **Be supportive as well as honest.** Tell the writer what you like about the paper. Word comments positively: instead of *This paragraph doesn't interest me*, say *You have an interesting detail here that I almost missed.* Question the writer in a way that emphasizes the effect of the work on you, the reader: *This paragraph confuses me because. . . .* And avoid measuring the work against a set of external standards: *This essay is poorly organized. Your thesis statement is inadequate.*

- **While reading, make your comments in writing.** Even if you will be delivering your comments in person later on, the written record will help you recall what you thought.

- **Link comments to specific parts of a paper.** Especially if you are reading the paper on a computer, be clear about what in the paper each comment relates to. You can embed your comments directly into the paper, distinguishing them with highlighting or color. Or you can use a word processor's Comment function, which annotates documents.

Benefiting from comments on your writing

- **Think of your readers as counselors or coaches.** They can help you see the virtues and flaws in your work and sharpen your awareness of readers' needs.

- **Read or listen to comments closely.**

- **Know what the critic is saying.** If you need more information, ask for it, or consult the appropriate section of this handbook.

- **Don't become defensive.** Letting comments offend you will only erect a barrier to improvement in your writing. As one writing teacher advises, "Leave your ego at the door."

- **Revise your work in response to appropriate comments.** You will learn more from the act of revision than from just thinking about changes.

- **Remember that you are the final authority on your work.** You should be open to suggestions, but you are free to decline advice when you think it is inappropriate.
- **Keep track of both the strengths and the weaknesses others identify.** Then in later assignments you can build on your successes and give special attention to problem areas.

⟨ CULTURE LANGUAGE ⟩ In some cultures writers do not expect criticism from readers, or readers do not expect to think critically about what they read. If critical responses are uncommon in your native culture, collaboration may at first be uncomfortable for you. As a writer in English, think of a draft or even a final paper as more an exploration of ideas than the last word on your subject; then you may be more receptive to readers' suggestions. As a reader, allow yourself to approach a text skeptically, and know that your tactful questions and suggestions will usually be considered appropriate.

5g Prepare a writing portfolio.

Your writing teacher may ask you to assemble samples of your writing into a portfolio, or folder, once or more during the course. Such a portfolio gives you a chance to consider all your writing over a period and showcase your best work.

Although the requirements for portfolios vary, most teachers are looking for a range of writing that demonstrates your progress and strengths as a writer. You, in turn, see how you have advanced from one assignment to the next, as you've had time for new knowledge to sink in and time for practice. Teachers often allow students to revise papers before placing them in the portfolio, even if the papers have already been submitted earlier. In that case, every paper in the portfolio can benefit from all your learning.

A portfolio assignment will probably also provide guidelines for what to include and how the portfolio will be evaluated. Be sure you understand the purpose of the portfolio and who will read it. For instance, if your composition teacher will be the only reader and his or her guidelines encourage you to show evidence of progress, you might include a paper that took big risks but never entirely succeeded. In contrast, if a committee of teachers will read your work and the guidelines urge you to demonstrate your competence as a writer, you might include only papers that did succeed.

Unless the guidelines specify otherwise, provide error-free copies of your final drafts, label all your samples with your name, and assemble them all in a folder. Add a cover letter or memo that lists the samples, explains why you've included each one, and evaluates your progress as a writer. The self-evaluation involved should be a learning experience for you and will help your readers assess your development as a writer.

EXERCISE 5.2
Analyzing an essay

Johanna Abrams, a student, was asked to write a narrative essay based on a personal experience that turned out to be a significant event or that represented a turning point—big or small—in her life. Read the essay carefully; then answer the following questions. (You can do this exercise online at *ablongman.com/littlebrown*.)

1. What is Abrams's purpose?
2. Who do you think constitutes Abrams's intended audience? What does the tone reveal about her attitude toward the topic?
3. How well does the thesis statement convey Abrams's purpose and attitude? What claim does the thesis statement make? How specific is the statement? How well does it preview Abrams's ideas and organization?
4. What organization does Abrams use? Is it clear throughout the essay?
5. What details, examples, and reasons does Abrams use to support her ideas? Where is the supporting evidence skimpy?
6. How successful is Abrams in making you care about the topic and her view of it?

Working in the Barnyard

Until two months ago I thought summer jobs occupied time and helped pay the next year's tuition but otherwise provided no useful training. Then I took a temporary job in a large government agency. Two months there taught me the very valuable lesson that the hierarchy of supervisor to employee should be respected.

Last May I was hired by the personnel department of the agency to fill in for vacationing workers in the mail room. I had seven coworkers and a boss, Mrs. King. Our job was to sort the huge morning and afternoon mail shipments into four hundred slots, one for every employee in the agency. Then we delivered the sorted mail out of grocery carts that we wheeled from office to office along assigned corridors, picking up outgoing mail as we went along. Each mail delivery took an entire half-day to sort and deliver.

My trouble began almost as soon as I arrived. Hundreds of pieces of mail were dumped on a shallow table against a wall of mail slots. I was horrified to see that the slots were labeled not with people's names but with their initials—whereas the incoming letters, of course, contained full names. Without thinking, I asked why this was a good idea, only to receive a sharp glance from Mrs. King. So I repeated the question. This time Mrs. King told me not to question what I didn't understand. It was the first of many such exchanges, and I hadn't been on the job a half-hour.

I mastered the initials and the sort and delivery procedures after about a week. But the longer I worked at the job, the more I saw how inefficient all the procedures were, from delivery routes to times for coffee breaks. When I asked Mrs. King about the procedures, however, she always reacted the same way: it was none of my business.

I pestered Mrs. King more and more over the next seven weeks, but my efforts were fruitless, even counterproductive. Mrs. King began calling me snide names. Then she began picking on my work and singling me out for reprimands, even though I did my best and worked faster than most of the others.

Two months after I had started work, the personnel manager called me in and fired me. I objected, of course, calling up all the deficiencies I had seen in Mrs. King and her systems. The manager interrupted to ask if I had ever heard of the barnyard pecking order. As he explained it, the top chicken pecks on the one below it, the second pecks on the third, and so on all the way down the line to the lowliest chicken, whose life is a constant misery. Mrs. King, the manager said, was that lowliest chicken at the bottom of the pecking order in the agency's management. With little education, she had spent her entire adult life building up her small domain, and she had to protect it from everyone, especially the people who worked for her. The arbitrariness of her systems was an assertion of her power, for no one should doubt for a moment that she ruled her roost.

I had a month before school began again to think about my adventure. At first it irritated me that I should be humiliated while Mrs. King continued on as before. But eventually I saw how arrogant, and how unsympathetic, my behavior had been. In my next job, I'll learn the pecking order before I become a crusader, if I do.

—Johanna Abrams (student)

6 Paragraphs

How can paragraphs help me and my readers?

Paragraphs give you a means of developing your essay's central idea (its thesis) step by step, point by point. They help your readers distinguish your ideas and follow your organization, and they give readers a breather from long stretches of text. In the body of an essay, you may use paragraphs for any of these purposes:

- **To introduce and give evidence for a main point supporting the thesis.** See pages 18–20 for a discussion of an essay's thesis.
- **Within a group of paragraphs centering on one main point, to develop a key example or other important evidence.**
- **To shift approach**—for instance, from pros to cons, from problem to solution, from questions to answers.
- **To mark movement in a sequence,** such as from one reason or step to another.

This chapter discusses the three qualities of an effective body paragraph: the topic sentence and unity (next page), coherence (p. 52), and development (p. 58). It describes two special kinds of paragraphs: introductions and conclusions (pp. 66 and 68). And finally it shows how paragraphs can be linked in a unified and coherent essay (p. 69).

CULTURE LANGUAGE Not all cultures share the paragraphing conventions of American academic writing. The conventions are not universal even among users of standard American English: for instance, US newspaper writers compose very short paragraphs that will break up text in narrow columns. In some other languages, writing moves differently from English—not from left to right, but from right to left or down rows from top to bottom. Even in languages that move as English does, writers may not use paragraphs at all. Or they may use paragraphs but not state their central ideas or provide transitional expressions to show readers how sentences relate. If your native language is not English and you have difficulty with paragraphs, don't worry about paragraphing during drafting. Instead, during a separate step of revision, divide your text into parts that develop your main points. Mark those parts with indentions.

http://www.ablongman.com/littlebrown ▶

Visit the companion Web site for more help and electronic exercises on paragraphs.

¶ un

6a

Checklist for revising paragraphs

- **Is the paragraph unified?** Does it focus on one central idea that is either stated in a **topic sentence** or otherwise apparent? (See section 6a, below.)
- **Is the paragraph coherent?** Do the sentences follow a clear sequence? Are the sentences linked as appropriate by parallelism, repetition or restatement, pronouns, consistency, and transitional expressions? (See p. 52.)
- **Is the paragraph developed?** Is the general idea of the paragraph well supported with specific evidence such as details, facts, examples, and reasons? (See p. 58.)

6a   Unify the paragraph around a central idea.

An effective paragraph develops one central idea related to the overall thesis of the paper. Often, the central idea is stated up front in a **topic sentence.** The paragraph is **unified** if the rest of the sentences in the paragraph support the topic sentence, as they do in this example:

> Some people really like chili, apparently, but nobody can agree how the stuff should be made. C. V. Wood, twice winner at Terlingua, uses flank steak, pork chops, chicken, and green chilis. My friend Hughes Rudd of CBS News, who imported five hundred pounds of chili powder into Russia as a condition of accepting employment as Moscow correspondent, favors coarse-ground beef. Isadore Bleckman, the cameraman I must live with on the road, insists upon one-inch cubes of stew beef and puts garlic in his chili, an Illinois affectation. An Indian of my acquaintance, Mr. Fulton Batisse, who eats chili for breakfast when he can, uses buffalo meat and plays an Indian drum while it's cooking. I ask you.
>
> —Charles Kuralt, *Dateline America*

Topic sentence: general statement announcing topic of paragraph

Four specific examples, all providing evidence for general statement

Kuralt's paragraph works because it follows through on its central idea, which is stated in the topic sentence. Each of the next four sentences offers an example of a chili concoction. (In the final sentence Kuralt comments on the examples.)

What if instead Kuralt had written his paragraph as follows? Here the topic of chili preparation is forgotten mid-paragraph, as the sentences digress to describe life in Moscow:

> Some people really like chili, apparently, but nobody can agree how the stuff should be made. }— Topic sentence: general statement
>
> C. V. Wood, twice winner at Terlingua, uses flank steak, pork chops, chicken, and green chilis. My friend Hughes Rudd, who imported five hundred pounds of chili powder into Russia as a condition of accepting employment as Moscow correspondent, favors coarse-ground beef. }— Two examples supporting statement
>
> He had some trouble finding the beef in Moscow, though. He sometimes had to scour all the markets and wait in long lines. For any American used to overstocked supermarkets and department stores, Russia can be quite a shock. }— Digression

Instead of following through on its topic sentence, the paragraph loses its way.

A central idea must always govern a paragraph's content as if it were standing guard at the opening, but in fact paragraphs often do not begin with a topic sentence. You may want to start with a transition from the previous paragraph, not stating the central idea until the second or third sentence. You may want to give the evidence for your idea first and let it build to a topic sentence at the end, as in this example about the Civil War general William Tecumseh Sherman:

> Sherman is considered by some to be the inventor of "total war": the first general in human history to carry the logic of war to its ultimate extreme, the first to scorch the earth, the first to consciously demoralize the hostile civilian population in order to subdue its army, the first to wreck an economy in order to starve its soldiers. He has been called our first "merchant of terror" and seen as the spiritual father of our Vietnam War concepts of "search and destroy," "pacification," "strategic hamlets," and "free-fire zones." }— Information supporting and building to topic sentence
>
> As such, he remains a cardboard figure of our history: a monstrous arch-villain to unreconstructed Southerners, and an embarrassment to Northerners. }— Topic sentence
>
> —Adapted from James Reston, Jr., "You Cannot Refine It"

Even when the central idea falls at the end of the paragraph, it must still govern all of the preceding details.

Sometimes you may not state a paragraph's central idea at all, especially in narrative and descriptive writing in which the point becomes clear in the details. But the point must be clear whether it is stated or not.

EXERCISE 6.1
Revising a paragraph for unity

The following paragraph contains ideas or details that do not support its central idea. Identify the topic sentence in the paragraph, and delete the unrelated material. (You can do this exercise online at *ablongman.com/ littlebrown*.)

In the southern part of the state, some people still live much as they did a century ago. They use coal- or wood-burning stoves for heating and cooking. Their homes do not have electricity or indoor bathrooms or running water. The towns they live in don't receive adequate funding from the state and federal governments, so the schools are poor and in bad shape. Beside most homes there is a garden where fresh vegetables are gathered for canning. Small pastures nearby support livestock, including cattle, pigs, horses, and chickens. Most of the people have cars or trucks, but the vehicles are old and beat-up from traveling on unpaved roads.

EXERCISE 6.2
Writing a unified paragraph

Develop the following topic sentence into a unified paragraph by using the relevant information in the supporting statements. Delete each statement that does not relate directly to the topic, and then rewrite and combine sentences as appropriate. Place the topic sentence in the position that seems most effective to you. (You can do this exercise online at *ablongman.com/littlebrown*.)

Topic sentence
Mozart's accomplishments in music seem remarkable even today.

Supporting information
Wolfgang Amadeus Mozart was born in 1756 in Salzburg, Austria.
He began composing music at the age of five.
He lived most of his life in Salzburg and Vienna.
His first concert tour of Europe was at the age of six.
On his first tour he played harpsichord, organ, and violin.
He published numerous compositions before reaching adolescence.
He married in 1782.
Mozart and his wife were both poor managers of money.
They were plagued by debts.
Mozart composed over six hundred musical compositions.
His most notable works are his operas, symphonies, quartets, and piano concertos.
He died at the age of thirty-five.

EXERCISE 6.3
Turning topic sentences into unified paragraphs

Develop three of the following topic sentences into detailed and unified paragraphs. (You can do this exercise online at *ablongman.com/ littlebrown*.)

1. Men and women are different in at least one important respect.
2. The best Web search engine is [*name*].
3. Fans of _____ music [*country, classical, rock, rap, jazz, or another kind*] come in [*number*] varieties.
4. Professional sports have [*or have not*] been helped by extending the regular season with championship play-offs.
5. Working for good grades can interfere with learning.

6b   Make the paragraph coherent.

When a paragraph is **coherent**, readers can see how it holds together: the sentences seem to flow logically and smoothly into one another. Exactly the opposite happens with this paragraph:

> The ancient Egyptians were masters of preserving dead people's bodies by making mummies of them. Mummies several thousand years old have been discovered nearly intact. The skin, hair, teeth, finger- and toenails, and facial features of the mummies were evident. It is possible to diagnose the diseases they suffered in life, such as smallpox, arthritis, and nutritional deficiencies. The process was remarkably effective. Sometimes apparent were the fatal afflictions of the dead people: a middle-aged king died from a blow on the head, and polio killed a child king. Mummification consisted of removing the internal organs, applying natural preservatives inside and out, and then wrapping the body in layers of bandages.

— Topic sentence

Sentences related to topic sentence but disconnected from each other

The paragraph is hard to read. The sentences lurch instead of gliding from point to point.

The paragraph as it was actually written appears below. It is much clearer because the writer arranged information differently and also built links into his sentences so that they would flow smoothly:

- After stating the central idea in a topic sentence, the writer moves to two more specific explanations and illustrates the second with four sentences of examples.
- (Circled words) repeat or restate key terms or concepts.
- Boxed words link sentences and clarify relationships.
- Underlined phrases are in parallel grammatical form to reflect their parallel content.

> The ancient Egyptians were masters of preserving dead people's bodies by (making mummies) of them. Basically, (mummification) consisted

— Topic sentence

of removing the internal organs, applying natural preservatives inside and out, and then wrapping the body in layers of bandages. And the process was remarkably effective. Indeed, mummies several thousand years old have been discovered nearly intact. Their skin, hair, teeth, finger- and toenails, and facial features are still evident. Their diseases in life, such as smallpox, arthritis, and nutritional deficiencies, are still diagnosable. Even their fatal afflictions are still apparent: a middle-aged king died from a blow on the head; a child king died from polio.

> Explanation 1: what mummification is

> Explanation 2: why the Egyptians were masters

> Specific examples of explanation 2

—Mitchell Rosenbaum (student),
"Lost Arts of the Egyptians"

1 • Paragraph organization

A coherent paragraph organizes information so that readers can easily follow along. These are common paragraph schemes:

- **General to specific:** Sentences downshift from more general statements to more specific ones. (See the paragraph above by Mitchell Rosenbaum.)
- **Climactic:** Sentences increase in drama or interest, ending in a climax. (See the paragraph by Lawrence Mayer on the next page.)
- **Spatial:** Sentences scan a person, place, or object from top to bottom, from side to side, or in some other way that approximates the way people actually look at things. (See the paragraph by Virginia Woolf on p. 60.)
- **Chronological:** Sentences present events as they occurred in time, earlier to later. (See the paragraph by Kathleen LaFrank on p. 56.)

2 • Parallelism

Parallelism helps tie sentences together. In the paragraph on the next page, the underlined parallel structures of *She* and a verb link all sentences after the first one. Parallelism also appears *within* many of the sentences. Aphra Behn (1640–89) was the first English-woman to write professionally.

> **Key term**
>
> **parallelism** The use of similar grammatical structures for similar elements of meaning within or among sentences: *The book caused a stir in the media and aroused debate in Congress.* (See also Chapter 16.)

> In addition to her busy career as a writer, <u>Aphra Behn</u> also <u>found</u> time to briefly marry and spend a little while in debtor's prison. <u>She found</u> time to take up a career as a spy for the English in their war against the Dutch. <u>She made</u> the long and difficult voyage to Suriname [in South America] and became involved in a slave rebellion there. <u>She plunged</u> into political debate at Will's Coffee House and defended <u>her</u> position from the stage of the Drury Lane Theater. <u>She</u> actively <u>argued</u> for women's rights to be educated and to marry whom they pleased, or not at all. <u>She defied</u> the seventeenth-century dictum that ladies must be "modest" and wrote freely about sex.
>
> —Angeline Goreau, "Aphra Behn"

3 • Repetition and restatement

Repeating or restating key words helps make a paragraph coherent and also reminds readers what the topic is. In the following paragraph note the underlined repetition of *sleep* and restatement of *adults:*

> Perhaps the simplest fact about <u>sleep</u> is that individual needs for it vary widely. Most <u>adults sleep</u> between seven and nine hours, but occasionally <u>people</u> turn up who need twelve hours or so, while some <u>rare types</u> can get by on three or four. Rarest of all are those <u>legendary types</u> who require almost no <u>sleep</u> at all; respected researchers have recently studied three <u>such people</u>. One of them—a healthy, happy woman in her seventies—<u>sleeps</u> about an hour every two or three days. The other two are men in early middle age, who get by on a few minutes a night. One of them complains about the daily fifteen minutes or so he's forced to "waste" in <u>sleeping</u>. —Lawrence A. Mayer,
> "The Confounding Enemy of Sleep"

4 • Pronouns

Because pronouns refer to nouns, they can help relate sentences to each other. In the paragraph above by Angeline Goreau, *she* works just this way by substituting for *Aphra Behn* in every sentence after the first.

5 • Consistency

Consistency (or the lack of it) occurs primarily in the tense of verbs and in the person and number of nouns and pronouns. Any inconsistencies not required by meaning will interfere with a reader's ability to follow the development of ideas.

Key term

pronoun A word that refers to and functions as a noun, such as *I, you, he, she, it, we, they: The patient could not raise <u>her</u> arm.* (See p. 225.)

In the following paragraphs, inconsistencies appear in the underlined words:

Shifts in tense

In the Hopi religion, water <u>is</u> the driving force. Since the Hopi <u>lived</u> in the Arizona desert, they <u>needed</u> water urgently for drinking, cooking, and irrigating crops. Their complex beliefs <u>are</u> focused in part on gaining the assistance of supernatural forces in obtaining water. Many of the Hopi kachinas, or spirit essences, <u>were</u> directly concerned with clouds, rain, and snow.

Shifts in number

<u>Kachinas</u> represent spiritually the things and events of the real world, such as cumulus clouds, mischief, cornmeal, and even death. A <u>kachina</u> is not worshiped as a god but regarded as an interested friend. <u>They</u> visit the Hopi from December through July in the form of men who dress in kachina costumes and perform dances and other rituals.

Shifts in person

Unlike the man, the Hopi <u>woman</u> does not keep contact with kachinas through costumes and dancing. Instead, <u>one</u> receives a tihu, or small effigy, of a kachina from the man impersonating the kachina. <u>You</u> are more likely to receive a tihu as a girl approaching marriage, though a child or older woman may receive one, too.

Note A grammar checker cannot help you locate shifts in tense, number, or person among sentences. Shifts are sometimes necessary (as when tenses change to reflect actual differences in time), and even a passage with needless shifts may still consist of sentences that are grammatically correct, as all the sentences are in the preceding examples.

6 • Transitional expressions

Transitional expressions such as *therefore, in contrast,* and *meanwhile* can forge specific connections between sentences. Notice the difference in two versions of the same paragraph:

Medical science has succeeded in identifying the hundreds of viruses that can cause the common

Paragraph is choppy and hard to follow

Key terms

tense The form of a verb that indicates the time of its action, such as present (*I run*), past (*I ran*), or future (*I will run*). (See p. 267.)

number The form of a noun, pronoun, or verb that indicates whether it is singular (one) or plural (more than one): *boy, boys.*

person The form of a pronoun that indicates whether the subject is speaking (first person: *I, we*), spoken to (second person: *you*), or spoken about (third person: *he, she, it, they*). All nouns are in the third person.

cold. It has discovered the most effective means of prevention. One person transmits the cold viruses to another most often by hand. An infected person covers his mouth to cough. He picks up the telephone. His daughter picks up the telephone. She rubs her eyes. She has a cold. It spreads. To avoid colds, people should wash their hands often and keep their hands away from their faces.

Medical science has ⬚thus⬚ succeeded in identifying the hundreds of viruses that can cause the common cold. It has ⬚also⬚ discovered the most effective means of prevention. One person transmits the cold virus to another most often by hand. ⬚For instance,⬚ an infected person covers his mouth to cough. ⬚Then⬚ he picks up the telephone. ⬚Half an hour later,⬚ his daughter picks up the ⬚same⬚ telephone. ⬚Immediately afterward,⬚ she rubs her eyes. ⬚Within a few days,⬚ she, ⬚too,⬚ has a cold. ⬚And thus,⬚ it spreads. To avoid colds, ⬚therefore,⬚ people should wash their hands often and keep their hands away from their faces.
—Kathleen LaFrank (student),
"Colds: Myth and Science"

Transitional expressions (boxed) remove choppiness and spell out relationships

Note that transitional expressions can link paragraphs as well as sentences. In the first sentence of LaFrank's paragraph, the word *thus* signals a connection to an effect discussed in the preceding paragraph. See pages 69–70 for more on such transitions.

The following box lists many transitional expressions by the functions they perform:

Transitional expressions

To add or show sequence
again, also, and, and then, besides, equally important, finally, first, further, furthermore, in addition, in the first place, last, moreover, next, second, still, too

To compare
also, in the same way, likewise, similarly

To contrast
although, and yet, but, but at the same time, despite, even so, even though, for all that, however, in contrast, in spite of, nevertheless,

notwithstanding, on the contrary, on the other hand, regardless, still, though, yet

To give examples or intensify
after all, an illustration of, even, for example, for instance, indeed, in fact, it is true, of course, specifically, that is, to illustrate, truly

To indicate place
above, adjacent to, below, elsewhere, farther on, here, near, nearby, on the other side, opposite to, there, to the east, to the left

To indicate time
after a while, afterward, as long as, as soon as, at last, at length, at that time, before, earlier, formerly, immediately, in the meantime, in the past, lately, later, meanwhile, now, presently, shortly, simultaneously, since, so far, soon, subsequently, then, thereafter, until, until now, when

To repeat, summarize, or conclude
all in all, altogether, as has been said, in brief, in conclusion, in other words, in particular, in short, in simpler terms, in summary, on the whole, that is, therefore, to put it differently, to summarize

To show cause or effect
accordingly, as a result, because, consequently, for this purpose, hence, otherwise, since, then, therefore, thereupon, thus, to this end

Note Draw carefully on this list of transitional expressions because the ones in each group are not interchangeable. For instance, *besides*, *finally*, and *second* may all be used to add information, but each has its own distinct meaning.

CULTURE LANGUAGE If transitional expressions are not common in your native language, you may be tempted to compensate when writing in English by adding them to the beginnings of most sentences. But such explicit transitions aren't needed everywhere, and in fact too many can be intrusive and awkward. When inserting transitional expressions, consider the reader's need for a signal: often the connection from sentence to sentence is already clear from the context or can be made clear by relating the content of sentences more closely (see pp. 179–80). When you do need transitional expressions, try varying their positions in your sentences, as illustrated in LaFrank's paragraph on the facing page.

EXERCISE 6.4
Arranging sentences coherently

After the topic sentence (sentence 1), the sentences in the student paragraph below have been deliberately scrambled to make the paragraph incoherent. Using the topic sentence and other clues as guides, re-arrange the sentences to form a well-organized, coherent unit. (You can do this exercise online at *ablongman.com/littlebrown*.)

We hear complaints about the Postal Service all the time, but we 1
should not forget what it does *right*. The total volume of mail delivered by 2
the Postal Service each year makes up almost half the total delivered mail in
all the world. Its 70,000 employees handle 140 billion pieces of mail each 3
year. And when was the last time they failed to deliver yours? In fact, on 4, 5
any given day the Postal Service delivers almost as much mail as the rest of
the world combined. That huge number means over 2 million pieces per 6
employee and over 560 per man, woman, and child in the country.

EXERCISE 6.5
Analyzing paragraphs for coherence

Study the paragraphs by Hillary Begas (p. 59) and Freeman Dyson (p. 61) for the authors' use of various devices to achieve coherence. Look especially for organization, parallel structures and ideas, repetition and restatement, pronouns, and transitional expressions.

EXERCISE 6.6
Writing a coherent paragraph

Write a coherent paragraph from the following information, combining and rewriting sentences as necessary. First, begin the paragraph with the topic sentence given and arrange the supporting sentences in a climactic order. Then combine and rewrite the supporting sentences, helping the reader see connections by introducing repetition and restatement, paral-lelism, pronouns, consistency, and transitional expressions. (You can do this exercise online at *ablongman.com/littlebrown*.)

Topic sentence
Hypnosis is far superior to drugs for relieving tension.

Supporting information
Hypnosis has none of the dangerous side effects of the drugs that relieve tension.
Tension-relieving drugs can cause weight loss or gain, illness, or even death.
Hypnosis is nonaddicting.
Most of the drugs that relieve tension do foster addiction.
Tension-relieving drugs are expensive.
Hypnosis is inexpensive even for people who have not mastered self-hypnosis.

6c   Develop the central idea.

An effective, well-developed paragraph always provides the spe-cific information that readers need and expect in order to under-stand you and to stay interested in what you say. Paragraph length can be a rough gauge of development: anything much shorter than 75 to 125 words may leave readers with a sense of incompleteness. Take this example:

> Untruths can serve as a kind of social oil when they smooth connections between people. In preventing confrontation and injured feelings, they allow everyone to go on as before.

General statements needing examples to be clear and convincing

This paragraph lacks development, or completeness. It does not provide enough information for us to evaluate or even care about the writer's assertions. To improve the paragraph, the writer needs to support the general statements with specific examples, as in this revision:

> Untruths can serve as a kind of social oil when they smooth connections between people. Assuring a worried friend that his haircut is flattering, claiming an appointment to avoid an aunt's dinner invitation, pretending interest in an acquaintance's children—these lies may protect the liar, but they also protect the person lied to. In preventing confrontation and injured feelings, the lies allow everyone to go on as before.
> —Joan Lar (student), "The Truth of Lies"

Examples specifying kinds of lies and consequences

To develop or shape a paragraph's central idea, one or more of the following patterns may help. (These patterns may also be used to develop entire essays. See p. 16.)

1 • Narration

Narration retells a significant sequence of events, usually in the order of their occurrence (that is, chronologically). A narrator is concerned not just with the sequence of events but also with their consequence, their importance to the whole.

> Jill's story is typical for "recruits" to religious cults. She was very lonely in college and appreciated the attention of the nice young men and women who lived in a house near campus. They persuaded her to share their meals and then to move in with them. Between intense bombardments of "love," they deprived her of sleep and sometimes threatened to throw her out. Jill became increasingly confused and dependent, losing touch with any reality besides the one in the group. She dropped out of school and refused to see or communicate with her family. Before long she, too, was preying on lonely college students.
> —Hillary Begas (student), "The Love Bombers"

Important events in chronological order

2 • Description

Description details the sensory qualities of a person, scene, thing, or feeling, using concrete and specific words to convey a dominant mood, to illustrate an idea, or to achieve some other purpose. In the following paragraph, almost every word helps to create a picture in the reader's mind:

> The sun struck straight upon the house, making the white walls glare between the dark windows. Their panes, woven thickly with green branches, held circles of impenetrable darkness. Sharp-edged wedges of light lay upon the window-sill and showed inside the room plates with blue rings, cups with curved handles, the bulge of a great bowl, the criss-cross pattern in the rug, and the formidable corners and lines of cabinets and bookcases. Behind their conglomeration hung a zone of shadow in which might be a further shape to be disencumbered of shadow or still denser depths of darkness.
>
> —Virginia Woolf, *The Waves*

Specific record of sensory details

3 • Illustration or support

An idea may be developed with several specific examples, like those used by Charles Kuralt on page 49 and by Joan Lar on the previous page. Or it may be developed with a single extended example, as in this paragraph:

> The language problem that I was attacking loomed larger and larger as I began to learn more. When I would describe in English certain concepts and objects enmeshed in Korean emotion and imagination, I became slowly aware of nuances, of differences between two languages even in simple expression. The remark "Kim entered the house" seems to be simple enough, yet, unless a reader has a clear visual image of a Korean house, his understanding of the sentence is not complete. When a Korean says he is "in the house," he may be in his courtyard, or on his porch, or in his small room! If I wanted to give a specific picture of entering the house in the Western sense, I had to say "room" instead of house—sometimes. I say "sometimes" because many Koreans entertain their guests on their porches and still are considered to be hospitable, and in the Korean sense, going into the "room" may be a more intimate act than it would be in the English sense. Such problems!
>
> —Kim Yong Ik, "A Book-Writing Venture"

Topic sentence (assertion to be illustrated)

Single detailed example

Sometimes you can develop a paragraph by providing your reasons for stating a general idea. For instance:

> There are three reasons, quite apart from scientific considerations, that mankind needs to travel in space. | Topic sentence
>
> The first reason is the need for garbage disposal: we need to transfer industrial processes into space, so that the earth may remain a green and pleasant place for our grandchildren to live in. The second reason is the need to escape material impoverishment: the resources of this planet are finite, and we shall not forgo forever the abundant solar energy and minerals and living space that are spread out all around us. The third reason is our spiritual need for an open frontier: the ultimate purpose of space travel is to bring to humanity not only scientific discoveries and an occasional spectacular show on television but a real expansion of our spirit. | Three reasons arranged in order of increasing drama and importance
>
> —Freeman Dyson, "Disturbing the Universe"

4 • Definition

Defining a complicated, abstract, or controversial term often requires extended explanation. The following definition of the word *quality* comes from an essay asserting that "quality in product and effort has become a vanishing element of current civilization." Notice how the writer pins down her meaning by offering examples and by setting up contrasts with nonquality:

> In the hope of possibly reducing the hail of censure which is certain to greet this essay (I am thinking of going to Alaska or possibly Patagonia in the week it is published), let me say that quality, as I understand it, means investment of the best skill and effort possible to produce the finest and most admirable result possible. | General definition
>
> Its presence or absence in some degree characterizes every man-made object, service, skilled or unskilled labor—laying bricks, painting a picture, ironing shirts, practicing medicine, shoemaking, scholarship, writing a book. You do it well or you do it half-well. | Activities in which quality may figure
>
> Materials are sound and durable or they are sleazy; method is painstaking or whatever is easiest. Quality is achieving or reaching for the highest standard as against being satisfied with the sloppy or fraudulent. It is honesty of purpose as against catering to cheap or sensational sentiment. It does not allow compromise with the second-rate. | Contrast between quality and nonquality
>
> —Barbara Tuchman, "The Decline of Quality"

¶ dev

6c

5 • Division or analysis

With division or analysis, you separate something into its elements to understand it better—for instance, you might divide a newspaper into its sections, such as national news, regional news, life-style, and so on. As in the paragraph below, you may also interpret the meaning and significance of the elements you identify.

> The surface realism of the soap opera conjures up an illusion of "liveness." The domestic settings and easygoing rhythms encourage the viewer to believe that the drama, however ridiculous, is simply an extension of daily life. The conversation is so slow that some have called it "radio with pictures." (Advertisers have always assumed that busy housewives would listen, rather than watch.) Conversation is casual and colloquial, as though one were eavesdropping on neighbors. There is plenty of time to "read" the character's face; close-ups establish intimacy. The sets are comfortably familiar: well-lit interiors of living rooms, restaurants, offices, and hospitals. Daytime soaps have little of the glamour of their prime-time relations. The viewer easily imagines that the conversation is taking place in real time.
>
> —Ruth Rosen, "Search for Yesterday"

Topic and focus: how "liveness" seems an extension of daily life

Elements:
Slow conversation

Casual conversation

Intimate close-ups
Familiar sets

Absence of glamour

Appearance of real time

Analysis is a key skill in critical reading. See page 110.

6 • Classification

When you sort many items into groups, you classify the items to see their relations more clearly. The following paragraph identifies three groups, or classes, of parents:

> In my experience, the parents who hire daytime sitters for their school-age children tend to fall into one of three groups. The first group includes parents who work and want someone to be at home when the children return from school. These parents are looking for an extension of themselves, someone who will give the care they would give if they were at home. The second group includes parents who may be home all day themselves but are too disorganized or too frazzled by their children's demands to handle child care alone. They are looking for an organizer and helpmate. The third and final group includes parents who do not want to be bothered by their children, whether they are

Topic sentence

Three groups:
Alike in one way (all hire sitters)
No overlap in groups (each has a different attitude)

Classes arranged in order of increasing drama

home all day or not. Unlike the parents in the first two groups, who care for their children whenever and however they can, these parents are looking for a permanent substitute for themselves.
—Nancy Whittle (student), "Modern Parenting"

7 • Comparison and contrast

Comparison and contrast may be used separately or together to develop an idea. The following paragraph illustrates one of two common ways of organizing a comparison and contrast: **subject by subject,** first one subject and then the other.

Consider the differences also in the behavior of rock and classical music audiences. At a rock concert, the audience members yell, whistle, sing along, and stamp their feet. They may even stand during the entire performance. The better the music, the more active they'll be. At a classical concert, in contrast, the better the performance, the more *still* the audience is. Members of the classical audience are so highly disciplined that they refrain from even clearing their throats or coughing. No matter what effect the powerful music has on their intellects and feelings, they sit on their hands.   —Tony Nahm (student), "Rock and Roll Is Here to Stay"

> Subjects: rock and classical audiences
>
> Rock audience
>
> Classical audience

The next paragraph illustrates the other common organization: **point by point,** with the two subjects discussed side by side and matched feature for feature:

The first electronic computer, ENIAC, went into operation just over fifty years ago, yet the differences between it and today's personal computer are enormous. ENIAC was enormous itself, consisting of forty panels, each two feet wide and four feet deep. Today's notebook PC or Macintosh, by contrast, can fit on one's lap. ENIAC had to be configured by hand, with its programmers taking up to two days to reset switches and cables. Today, the average user can change programs in an instant. And for all its size and inconvenience, ENIAC was also slow. In its time, its operating speed of 100,000 pulses per second seemed amazingly fast. However, today's notebook can operate at more than 1 billion pulses per second.   —Shirley Kajiwara (student), "The Computers We Deserve"

> Subjects: ENIAC and personal computer
>
> Size: ENIAC, personal computer
>
> Ease of programming: ENIAC, personal computer
>
> Speed: ENIAC, personal computer

8 • Cause-and-effect analysis

When you use analysis to explain why something happened or what did or may happen, then you are determining causes or effects. In the following paragraph the author looks at the cause of an effect—Japanese collectivism:

> This *shinkansen* or "bullet train" speeds across the rural areas of Japan giving a quick view of cluster after cluster of farmhouses surrounded by rice paddies. This particular pattern did not develop purely by chance, but as a consequence of the technology peculiar to the growing of rice, the staple of the Japanese diet. The growing of rice requires the construction and maintenance of an irrigation system, something that takes many hands to build. More importantly, the planting and the harvesting of rice can only be done efficiently with the cooperation of twenty or more people. The "bottom line" is that a single family working alone cannot produce enough rice to survive, but a dozen families working together can produce a surplus. Thus the Japanese have had to develop the capacity to work together in harmony, no matter what the forces of disagreement or social disintegration, in order to survive.
> —William Ouchi, *Theory Z*

Effect: pattern of Japanese farming

Causes: Japanese dependence on rice, which requires collective effort

Effect: working in harmony

9 • Process analysis

When you analyze how to do something or how something works, you explain a process. The following example identifies the process, describes the equipment needed, and details the steps in the process:

> As a car owner, you waste money when you pay a mechanic to change the engine oil. The job is not difficult, even if you know little about cars. All you need is a wrench to remove the drain plug, a large, flat pan to collect the draining oil, plastic bottles to dispose of the used oil, and fresh oil. First, warm up the car's engine so that the oil will flow more easily. When the engine is warm, shut it off and remove its oil-filler cap (the owner's manual shows where this cap is). Then locate the drain plug under the engine (again consulting the owner's manual for its location) and place the flat pan under the plug. Remove the plug with the wrench, letting the oil flow into the pan. When the oil stops flowing, replace the plug and, at the

Process: changing the oil

Equipment needed

Steps in process

engine's filler hole, add the amount and kind of fresh oil specified by the owner's manual. Pour the used oil into the plastic bottles and take it to a waste-oil collector, which any garage mechanic can recommend.   —Anthony Andres (student), "Do-It-Yourself Car Care"

EXERCISE 6.7
Analyzing and revising skimpy paragraphs

The following paragraphs are not well developed. Rewrite one into a well-developed paragraph, supplying your own concrete details or examples to support general statements. (You can do this exercise online at *ablongman.com/littlebrown*.)

1. One big difference between successful and unsuccessful teachers is the quality of communication. A successful teacher is sensitive to students' needs and excited by the course subject. In contrast, an unsuccessful teacher seems uninterested in students and bored by the subject.

2. Gestures are one of our most important means of communication. We use them instead of speech. We use them to supplement the words we speak. And we use them to communicate some feelings or meanings that words cannot adequately express.

EXERCISE 6.8
Writing with the patterns of development

Write at least three focused, coherent, and well-developed paragraphs, each one developed with a different pattern. Draw on the topics here or choose your own topics.

1. **Narration:** an experience of public speaking, a disappointment, leaving home, waking up
2. **Description:** your room, a crowded or deserted place, a food, an intimidating person
3. **Illustration or support:** study habits, having a headache, the best sports event, usefulness (or uselessness) of a self-help book
4. **Definition:** humor, an adult, fear, authority
5. **Division or analysis:** a television news show, a barn, a Web site, a piece of music
6. **Classification:** factions in a campus controversy, styles of playing poker, types of Web sites, kinds of teachers
7. **Comparison and contrast:** surfing the Web and watching TV, AM and FM radio announcers, high school and college football, movies on TV and in a theater
8. **Cause-and-effect analysis:** connection between tension and anger, causes of failing a course, connection between credit cards and debt, causes of a serious accident
9. **Process analysis:** preparing for a job interview, setting up a Web log, protecting your home from burglars, making a jump shot

¶

6d

6d   Write introductory and concluding paragraphs.

Introductory paragraphs set up your essay, piquing readers' interest in your topic. Concluding paragraphs finish your essay, giving readers a sense of completion.

1 • Introductions

An introduction draws readers from their world into your world:

- It focuses readers' attention on the topic and arouses their curiosity about what you have to say.
- It specifies your subject and implies your attitude.
- Often it includes your thesis statement (see p. 18).
- It is concise and sincere.

To focus readers' attention, you have a number of options:

Some strategies for introductions

- Ask a question.
- Relate an incident.
- Use a vivid quotation.
- Offer a surprising statistic or other fact.
- State an opinion related to your thesis.
- Provide background.
- Create a visual image that represents your subject.
- Make a historical comparison or contrast.
- Outline a problem or dilemma.
- Define a word central to your subject.
- In some business or technical writing, summarize your paper.

CULTURE LANGUAGE ⟩   These options for an introduction may not be what you are used to if your native language is not English. In other cultures, readers may seek familiarity or reassurance from an author's introduction, or they may prefer an indirect approach to the subject. In academic and business English, however, writers and readers prefer originality and concise, direct expression.

Effective openings

A very common introduction opens with a statement of the essay's general subject, clarifies or limits the subject in one or more sentences, and then asserts the point of the essay in the thesis statement. Here are two examples:

> Can your home or office computer make you sterile? Can it strike you blind or dumb? The ⎤ Subject related to reader's experience

answer is, probably not. Nevertheless, reports of side effects relating to computer use should be examined, especially in the area of birth defects, eye complaints, and postural difficulties. — Clarification of subject: bridge to thesis statement

Although little conclusive evidence exists to establish a causal link between computer use and problems of this sort, the circumstantial evidence can be disturbing. — Thesis statement

          —Thomas Hartmann, "How Dangerous Is Your Computer?"

The Declaration of Independence is so widely regarded as a statement of American ideals that its origins in practical politics tend to be forgotten. — Statement about subject

Thomas Jefferson's draft was intensely debated and then revised in the Continental Congress. Jefferson was disappointed with the result. — Clarification of subject: bridge to thesis statement

However, a close reading of both the historical context and the revisions themselves indicates that the Congress improved the document for its intended purpose. — Thesis statement

          —Ann Weiss (student), "The Editing of the Declaration of Independence"

In much business writing, it's more important to tell readers immediately what your point is than to try to engage them. This introduction to a brief memo quickly outlines a problem and (in the thesis statement) suggests a way to solve it:

Starting next month, staff vacations will leave our department short-handed. We need to hire two or perhaps three temporary keyboarders to maintain our schedules for the month. — Thesis statement

Additional examples of effective introductions appear in complete writing samples on pages 26, 41, 46, 120, 139, 149, and 151.

Introduction *don'ts*

When writing and revising your introduction, avoid approaches that are likely to bore readers or make them question your sincerity or control:

- **A vague generality or truth.** Don't extend your reach too wide with a line such as *Throughout human history . . .* or *In today's world. . . .* You may have needed a warm-up paragraph to start drafting, but your readers can do without it.
- **A flat announcement.** Don't start with *The purpose of this essay is . . . , In this essay I will . . . ,* or any similar presentation of your intention or topic.

¶
6d

- **A reference to the essay's title.** Don't refer to the title of the essay in the first sentence—for example, *This is a big problem* or *This book is about the history of the guitar.*
- *According to Webster. . . .* Don't start by citing a dictionary definition. A definition can be an effective springboard to an essay, but this kind of lead-in has become dull with overuse.
- **An apology.** Don't fault your opinion or your knowledge with *I'm not sure if I'm right, but I think . . . , I don't know much about this, but . . .* , or similar lines.

2 • Conclusions

Your conclusion finishes off your essay and tells readers where you think you have brought them. It answers the question "So what?"

Effective conclusions

Usually set off in its own paragraph, the conclusion may consist of a single sentence or a group of sentences. It may take one or more of the following approaches:

Some strategies for conclusions

- Recommend a course of action.
- Summarize the paper.
- Echo the approach of the introduction.
- Restate your thesis and reflect on its implications.
- Strike a note of hope or despair.
- Give a symbolic or powerful fact or other detail.
- Give an especially compelling example.
- Create a visual image that represents your subject.
- Use a quotation.

The following paragraph concludes an essay on the Declaration of Independence (the introduction appears on the previous page):

The Declaration of Independence has come to be a statement of this nation's political philosophy, but that was not its purpose in 1776. Jefferson's passionate expression had to bow to the goals of the Congress as a whole to forge unity among the colonies and to win the support of foreign nations.

Echo of introduction: contrast between past and present

Restatement and elaboration of thesis

—Ann Weiss (student), "The Editing of the Declaration of Independence"

In the next paragraph the author concludes an essay on environmental protection with a call for action:

Until we get the answers [about the effects of pollutants], I think we had better keep on building power plants and growing food with the help of fertilizers and such insect-controlling chemicals as we now have. The risks are well known, thanks to the environmentalists. If they had not created a widespread public awareness of the ecological crisis, we wouldn't stand a chance. — Summary and opinion

But such awareness by itself is not enough. Flaming manifestos and prophecies of doom are no longer much help, and a search for scapegoats can only make matters worse. The time for sensations and manifestos is about over. Now we need rigorous analysis, united effort and very hard work. — Call for action

—Peter F. Drucker,
"How Best to Protect the Environment"

Conclusions to avoid

Several kinds of conclusions rarely work well:

- **A repeat of the introduction.** Don't simply replay your introduction. The conclusion should capture what the paragraphs of the body have added to the introduction.

- **A new direction.** Don't introduce a subject different from the one your essay has been about.

- **A sweeping generalization.** Don't conclude more than you reasonably can from the evidence you have presented. If your essay is about your frustrating experience trying to clear a parking ticket, you cannot reasonably conclude that *all* local police forces are too tied up in red tape to serve the people.

- **An apology.** Don't cast doubt on your essay. Don't say, *Even though I'm no expert* or *This may not be convincing, but I believe it's true* or anything similar. Rather, to win your readers' confidence, display confidence.

EXERCISE 6.9
Analyzing an introduction and conclusion

Analyze the introductory and concluding paragraphs in the first and final drafts of the student essay on pages 29–30 and 41–43. What is wrong with the first-draft paragraphs? Why are the final-draft paragraphs better? Could they be improved still further?

6e   Link paragraphs within an essay.

Though you may draft paragraphs or groups of paragraphs almost as mini-essays, you will eventually need to stitch them

¶
6e

together into a logical, larger whole. The techniques for linking paragraphs mirror those for linking sentences within paragraphs:

- **Make sure each paragraph contributes to your thesis.**
- **Arrange the paragraphs in a clear, logical order.** See pages 21–25 for advice on organization.
- **Create links between paragraphs.** Use repetition and restatement to stress and connect key terms, and use transitional expressions and transitional sentences to indicate sequence, direction, contrast, and other relationships.

The essay "A Picture of Hyperactivity" on page 26 illustrates the first two of these techniques. The following passages from the essay illustrate the third technique, with circled repetitions and restatements, boxed transitional expressions, and transitional sentences noted in annotations.

Introduction establishing subject and stating thesis	A hyperactive committee member can contribute to efficiency. A hyperactive salesperson can contribute to profits. When children are hyperactive, though, people—even parents—may wish they had never been born. A
Thesis statement	collage of those who must cope with hyperactivity in children is a picture of frustration, anger, and loss.
Transitional topic sentence relating to thesis statement	The first part of the collage is the doctors. In their terminology, the word hyperactivity has been replaced by ADHD, attention-deficit hyperactivity disorder. They apply the term to children who are abnormally or excessively busy. . . .
Transitional topic sentence relating to thesis statement	As the mother of an ADHD child, I can say what the disorder means to the parents who form the second part of the collage. . . .
Transitional sentence	The weight of ADHD, however, does not rest on the
Topic sentence relating to thesis statement	doctors and parents. The darkest part of the collage belongs to the children. . . .
Transitional sentence into conclusion, restating thesis statement	The collage is complete, and it is dark and somber. ADHD, as applied to children is a term with uncertain, unattractive, and bitter associations. The picture does have one bright spot, however, for inside every ADHD child is a lovely, trusting, calm person waiting to be recognized.

7 Document Design

What makes documents clear and attractive?

Page margins, paragraph breaks, headings, illustrations, and other elements of design can clarify and further the purpose of a document. An appropriate, clear, and pleasing design will not transform poor writing, but it will make strong writing even more effective.

This chapter looks at the principles and elements of design that can help you effectively present various academic documents. See Chapter 13 for tips on designing business documents and Web pages.

7a Format academic papers appropriately for each discipline.

Many academic disciplines prefer specific formats for students' papers. This book details two such formats:

- MLA, used in English, foreign languages, and other humanities (pp. 521–24).
- APA, used in the social sciences and some natural and applied sciences (pp. 574–50).

Other academic formats can be found in the style guides listed on pages 478–79.

The design guidelines in this chapter extend the range of elements and options covered by most academic styles. Your instructors may want you to adhere strictly to a particular style or may allow some latitude in design. Ask them for their preferences.

7b Work with the principles of document design.

Most of the principles of design respond to the ways we read. White space, for instance, relieves our eyes and helps to lead us through a document. Groupings or lists help to show relationships. Type sizes, images, and color add variety and help to emphasize important elements.

http://www.ablongman.com/littlebrown ▶

Visit the companion Web site for more help with document design.

The sample documents on these two pages illustrate quite different ways of presenting a report for a marketing course. Even at a glance, the second document is easier to scan and read. It uses white space, groups similar elements, uses bullets and fonts for emphasis, and integrates the chart more successfully.

As you design your own documents, think about your purpose, the expectations of your readers, and how readers will move through your document. Also consider the following general principles, noting that they overlap and support one another:

- **Conduct readers through the document.** Establish **flow,** a pattern for the eye to follow, with headings, lists, and other elements.

Original design

Runs title and subtitle together. Does not distinguish title from text.

Crowds the page with minimal margins.

Downplays paragraph breaks with small indentions.

Buries statistics in a paragraph. Obscures relationships with non-parallel wording.

Does not introduce the figure, leaving readers to infer its meaning and purpose.

Overemphasizes the figure with large size and excessive white space.

Presents the figure undynamically, flat on.

Does not caption the figure to explain what it shows, offering only a figure number and a partial text explanation.

Ready or Not, Here They Come: College Students and the Internet

College life once meant classrooms of students listening to teachers or groups of students talking over lunch in the union. But the reality today is more complex: students interact with their peers and professors by computer as much as face to face. As these students graduate and enter the workforce, all of society will be affected by their experience.

According to the Pew Internet Research Center (2005), today's college students are practiced computer and Internet users. The Pew Center reports that 20 percent of students in college today started using computers between ages five and eight. By age eighteen all students were using computers. Almost all college students, 86 percent, rely on the Internet, with 66 percent of students using more than one e-mail address. Computer ownership among this group is also very high: 85 percent have purchased or have been given at least one computer.

Students are eager to tap into the Internet's benefits and convenience.

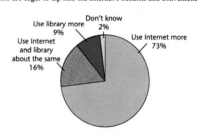

Figure 1

The Internet has eclipsed the library as the site of college students' research, as shown in Figure 1 from the Pew Report. In fact, a mere 9 percent of students

- **Use white space to ease crowding and focus readers' attention.** Provide ample margins, and give breathing room to headings, lists, and other elements. Even the space indicating new paragraphs (indentions or blank lines) gives readers a break and reassures them that ideas are divided into manageable chunks.
- **Group information to show relationships.** Use headings (like those in this chapter) and lists (like the one you're reading) to convey the similarities and differences among parts of a document.
- **Emphasize important elements.** Establish hierarchies of information with type fonts and sizes, headings, indentions, color,

des

7b

Revised design

Ready or Not, Here They Come
College Students and the Internet

College life once meant classrooms of students listening to teachers or groups of students talking over lunch in the union. But the reality today is more complex: students interact with their peers and professors by computer as much as face to face. As these students graduate and enter the workforce, all of society will be affected by their experience.

According to the Pew Internet Research Center (2005), today's college students are practiced computer users and Internet users.

- They started young: 20 percent were using computers between ages five and eight, and all were using them by age eighteen.
- They rely on the Internet: 86 percent have used the network, and 66 percent use more than one e-mail address.
- They own computers: 85 percent have purchased or have been given at least one computer.

Students are eager to tap into the Internet's benefits and convenience. Figure 1, from the Pew Report, shows that the Internet has eclipsed the library as the site of college students' research.

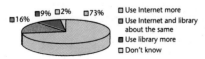

■9% □2%   □73%   □ Use Internet more
■16%   ■ Use Internet and library
                              about the same
                           ■ Use library more
                           □ Don't know

Figure 1. College students' use of the Internet and the library for research

Distinguishes title from subtitle and both from text.

Provides adequate margins.

Emphasizes paragraph breaks with white space.

Groups statistics in a bulleted list set off with white space. Uses parallel wording for parallel information.

Introduces the figure to indicate its meaning and purpose.

Reduces white space around the figure.

Presents the figure to emphasize the most significant segment.

Captions the figure so that it can be read independently from the text.

boxes, and white space. In this book, for example, the importance of headings is clear from their size and color and from the presence or absence of decorative devices, such as the rule above 7c below.

- **Standardize to create and fulfill expectations.** Help direct readers through a document by, for instance, using the same size and color for all headings at the same level of importance. Standardizing also reduces clutter, making it easier for readers to determine the significance of the parts.

7c Use the elements of design appropriately for your content and purpose.

Applying the preceding design principles involves margins, text, lists, headings, color, and illustrations. You won't use all these elements for every project, however, and in many academic writing situations you will be required to follow a prescribed format. If you are addressing readers who have vision disabilities, consider the additional guidelines on pages 83–84.

Note Your word processor may provide wizards or templates for many kinds of documents, such as letters, memos, reports, agendas, résumés, and brochures. **Wizards** guide you through setting up and writing complicated documents. **Templates** are preset forms to which you add your own text, headings, and other elements. Wizards and templates can be helpful, but not if they lead you to create cookie-cutter documents no matter what the writing situation. Always keep in mind that a document should be appropriate for your subject, audience, and purpose.

1 • Margins

Margins at the top, bottom, and sides of a page help to prevent the page from overwhelming readers with unpleasant crowding. Most academic and business documents use a minimum one-inch margin on all sides.

2 • Text

A document must be readable. You can make text readable by attending to line spacing, type fonts and sizes, highlighting, word spacing, and line breaks.

Line spacing

Most academic documents are double-spaced, with an initial indention for paragraphs. Single-spaced exceptions may include documents written for business courses (see Chapter 13) and papers submitted on the Web (see p. 82).

Type fonts and sizes

The readability of text also derives from the type fonts (or faces) and their sizes. For academic and business documents, choose a type size of 10 or 12 points, as in these samples:

```
10-point Courier        10-point Times New Roman
12-point Courier        12-point Times New Roman
```

These fonts and the one you're reading have **serifs**—the small lines that finish the letters. Serif fonts are suitable for formal writing and are often easier to read on paper. **Sans serif** fonts (*sans* means "without" in French) include the one below, found on many word processors:

10-point Arial   **12-point Arial**

Sans serif fonts can be easier to read on a computer screen and are clearer on paper for readers with some vision disabilities (see p. 83).

Your word processor probably offers many decorative fonts as well:

10-point Corvallis Sans   10-point Tekton
10-POINT STENCIL   10-point Park Avenue

Avoid decorative fonts in academic writing, where letter forms should be conventional and regular. Decorative fonts do have their uses in publicity documents and Web pages (see Chapter 13).

Note The point size of a type font is often an unreliable guide to its actual size, as the preceding decorative fonts illustrate: all the samples are 10 points, but they vary considerably. Before you use a font, print out a sample to be sure it is the size you want.

Highlighting

Within a document's text, underlined, *italic*, **boldface,** or even color type can emphasize key words or sentences. Underlining is rarest these days, though it remains called for in MLA style. (See Chapter 56.) Academic writing sometimes uses boldface to give strong emphasis—for instance, to a term being defined—and sometimes uses color for headings and illustrations. (See pp. 77–78 for more on color in document design.)

No matter what your writing situation, use highlighting selectively to complement your meaning, not merely to decorate your

work. Many readers consider type embellishments to be distracting.

Word spacing

In most writing situations, follow these guidelines for spacing
within and between words:

- **Leave one space between words.**
- **Leave one space after all punctuation, with these exceptions:**

Dash (two hyphens or the so-called em-dash on a computer)	book--its	book—its
Hyphen	one-half	
Apostrophe within a word	book's	
Two or more adjacent marks	book.")	
Opening quotation mark, parenthesis, or bracket	("book	[book

- **Leave one space before and after an ellipsis mark.** In the
  examples below, ellipsis marks indicate omissions within a
  sentence and at the end of a sentence. See pages 386–87 for additional examples.

  book . . . in   book. . . . The

Line breaks

Your word processor will generally insert appropriate breaks between lines of continuous text: it will not, for instance, automatically
begin a line with a comma or period, and it will not end a line with
an opening parenthesis or bracket. However, you will have to prevent it from breaking a two-hyphen dash or a three-dot ellipsis mark
by spacing to push the beginning of each mark to the next line.

When you instruct it to do so (usually under the Tools menu),
your word processor will also automatically hyphenate words to
prevent very short lines. If you must decide yourself where to break
words, follow the guidelines on page 399.

3 • Lists

Lists give visual reinforcement to the relations between like
items—for example, the steps in a process or the elements of a proposal. A list is easier to read than a paragraph and adds white space
to the page.

When wording a list, work for parallelism among items—for instance, all complete sentences or all phrases (see also p. 189). Set
the list with space above and below and with numbering or bullets
(centered dots or other devices, used in the following list about

headings). On most word processors you can format a numbered or bulleted list automatically using the Format menu.

4 • Headings

Headings are signposts: they direct the reader's attention by focusing the eye on a document's most significant content. Most academic documents use headings functionally, to divide text, orient readers, and create emphasis. A short paper may not need headings at all. For longer papers, follow these guidelines:

- **Use one, two, or three levels of headings** depending on the needs of your material and the length of your document. Some level of heading every two or so pages will help keep readers on track.
- **Create an outline of your document** to plan where headings should go. Use the first level of heading for the main points (and sections) of your document. Use a second and perhaps a third level of heading to mark subsections of supporting information.
- **Keep headings as short as possible** while making them specific about the material that follows.
- **Word headings consistently**—for instance, all questions (*What Is the Scientific Method?*), all phrases with *-ing* words (*Understanding the Scientific Method*), or all phrases with nouns (*The Scientific Method*).
- **Indicate the relative importance of headings** with type size, positioning, and highlighting, such as capital letters, underlining, or boldface.

First-Level Heading

Second-Level Heading

Third-Level Heading

Generally, you can use the same type font and size for headings as for the text.

- **Double- or triple-space around headings.**
- **Don't break a page immediately after a heading.** Push the heading to the next page.

Note Document format in psychology and some other social sciences requires a particular treatment of headings. See page 549.

5 • Color

With a color printer, many word processors can produce documents that use color for bullets, headings, borders, boxes, illustrations, and other elements. Ask your instructor whether color is appropriate in your documents. If you do use it, follow these guidelines:

- **Employ color to clarify and highlight your content.** Too much color or too many colors on a page will distract rather than focus readers' attention.
- **Make sure that color type is readable.** For text, where type is likely to be relatively small, use only dark colors. For headings, lighter colors may be readable if the type is large and boldfaced.
- **Stick to the same color for all headings at the same level**—for instance, red for main headings, black for secondary headings.
- **Use color for bullets, lines, and other nontext elements.** But use no more than a few colors to keep pages clean.
- **Use color to distinguish the parts of illustrations**—the segments of charts, the lines of graphs, and the parts of diagrams. Use only as many colors as you need to make your illustrations clear.

See also page 84 on the use of color for readers who have vision disabilities.

EXERCISE 7.1
Redesigning a paper

Save a duplicate copy of a recent paper or one you are currently working on. Then format the duplicate using appropriate elements of design, such as type fonts, lists, and headings. (For a new paper, be sure your instructor will accept your new design.) When you have finished the redesign, share the work with your instructor.

7d   Use illustrations appropriately for the writing situation.

Illustrations can often make a point for you more efficiently than words can. Tables present data. Figures (such as graphs and charts) usually recast data in visual form. Diagrams, drawings, photographs, and other images can explain processes, represent what something looks like, or add emphasis.

In most academic writing, illustrations directly reinforce and amplify the text. Follow these guidelines:

- **Focus on a purpose for each illustration**—a reason for including it and a point you want it to make. Otherwise, readers may find it irrelevant or confusing.
- **Provide a source note for someone else's independent material**—whether data or an entire illustration (see p. 474). Each discipline has a slightly different style for such source notes: those in the illustrations on the next several pages reflect MLA style for English and some other humanities.

- **Number figures, photographs, and other images together:** Figure 1, Figure 2, and so on.
- **Number and label tables separately:** Table 1, Table 2, and so on.
- **Refer to each illustration in your text**—for instance, "See fig. 2." Place the text reference at the point(s) in the text where readers will benefit by consulting the illustration.
- **Determine the placement of illustrations.** The social sciences and some other disciplines require each illustration to fall on a page by itself immediately after the text reference to it (see p. 550). You may want to follow this rule in other situations as well if you have a large number of illustrations. Otherwise, you can place them on your text pages just after their references.

1 • Tables

Tables usually present raw data, making complex information accessible to readers. The data may show how variables relate to one another, how two or more groups contrast, or how variables change over time. The following table emphasizes the last two functions.

Table

Table 1
Percentage of Young Adults Living at Home, 1960-2000

	1960	1970	1980	1990	2000
Males					
Age 18-24	52	54	54	58	57
Age 25-34	9	9	10	15	13
Females					
Age 18-24	35	41	43	48	47
Age 25-34	7	7	7	8	8

Source: Data from United States, Dept. of Commerce, Census Bureau, Census 2000 Summary Tables, 1 July 2005 <http:www.census.gov/servlet/QTTTable?_ts=30543101060>.

A self-explanatory title falls above the table.

Self-explanatory headings label horizontal rows and vertical columns.

The layout of rows and columns is clear: headings align with their data, and numbers align vertically down columns.

2 • Figures

Figures represent data or show concepts visually. They include charts, graphs, diagrams, and photographs.

Pie charts

Pie charts show the relations among the parts of a whole. The whole totals 100 percent, and each pie slice is proportional in size to its share of the whole. Use a pie chart when shares, not the underlying data, are your focus.

Pie chart

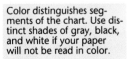

Color distinguishes segments of the chart. Use distinct shades of gray, black, and white if your paper will not be read in color.

Segment percentages total 100.

Every segment is clearly labeled. You can also use a key, as in the chart on p. 73.

Self-explanatory caption falls below the chart.

Married (59.5%)   Never married (23.9%)

Divorced (9.9%)

Widowed (6.7%)

Fig. 1. Marital status in 2005 of adults aged eighteen and over. Data from United States, Dept. of Commerce, Census Bureau, Statistical Abstract of the United States, 2005-06 (Washington, GPO, 2006) no. 30.

Bar charts

Bar charts compare groups or time periods on a measure such as quantity or frequency. Use a bar chart when relative size is your focus.

Bar chart

Vertical scale shows and clearly labels the values being measured. Zero point clarifies values.

Horizontal scale shows and clearly labels the groups being compared.

Self-explanatory caption falls below the chart.

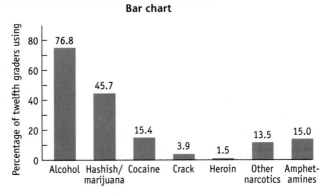

Fig. 2. Lifetime prevalence of use of alcohol, compared with other drugs, among twelfth graders in 2005. Data from Monitoring the Future: A Continuing Study of American Youth, U of Michigan, 19 Dec. 2005, 10 Oct. 2006 <http://www.monitoringthefuture.org/05data/pr05t1.pdf>.

Line graphs

Line graphs show change over time in one or more subjects. They compare many points of data economically and visually.

Line graph

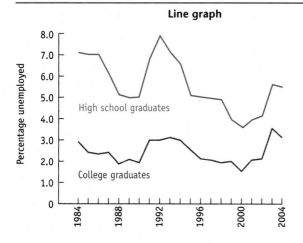

Vertical scale shows and clearly labels the values being measured. Zero point clarifies values.

Color and labels distinguish the subjects being compared. Use dotted and dashed black lines if your paper will not be read in color.

Horizontal scale shows and clearly labels the range of dates.

Fig. 3. Unemployment rates of high school graduates and college graduates, 1984-2004. Data from Antony Davies, The Economics of College Tuition, 3 Mar. 2005, 26 June 2006 <http://www.mercatus.org/capitalhill/php?id=420>.

Self-explanatory caption falls below the graph.

Diagrams

Diagrams show concepts visually, such as the structure of an organization, the way something works or looks, or the relations among subjects. Often, diagrams show what can't be described economically in words.

Diagram

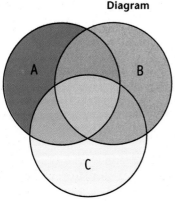

Diagram makes concept comprehensible.

Fig. 4. A Venn diagram, showing all possible relations among individuals or groups A, B, and C. From "Venn Diagram," Wikipedia, 29 Dec. 2006. 8 Jan. 2007 <http://en.wikipedia.org/wiki/Venn_diagram>.

Self-explanatory caption falls below the diagram.

Photographs and other images

Sometimes you may focus an entire paper on analyzing an image such as a photograph, painting, or advertisement. But most commonly you'll use images to add substance to ideas or to enliven them. You might clarify a psychology paper with a photograph from a key experiment, add information to an analysis of a novel with a drawing of the author, or illustrate one side of an argument with a cartoon. Images grab readers' attention, so use them carefully to explain, reinforce, or enhance your writing. Generally avoid using **clip art,** or decorative icons and drawings that may reinforce a theme but do not add substance.

Photograph

Photograph shows subject more economically and dramatically than words could.

Self-explanatory caption falls below the image.

Fig. 5. View of Saturn from the Cassini spacecraft, showing the planet and its rings. From United States, National Atmospheric and Space Administration, Jet Propulsion Laboratory, Cassini-Huygens: Mission to Saturn and Titan, 24 Feb. 2005, 26 Apr. 2006 <http://saturn.jpl.nasa.gov/multimedia/images/image-details.cfm?imageID=1398>.

Note When using an image prepared by someone else—for instance, a photograph downloaded from the Web—you must verify that the source permits reproduction of the image before you use it. In most documents but especially academic papers, you must also fully cite the source of any borrowed image. See pages 476–77 on copyright issues with Internet sources.

7e   Consider design when submitting papers on the Web.

Some instructors may ask you to post your papers to a Web site or Web log. Most of the preceding design guidelines apply to online papers as well except that the text is often single-spaced for better readability on screen. The illustration below shows the opening screen of a student's project for a composition course, with annotations highlighting its design elements.

Paper submitted on the Web

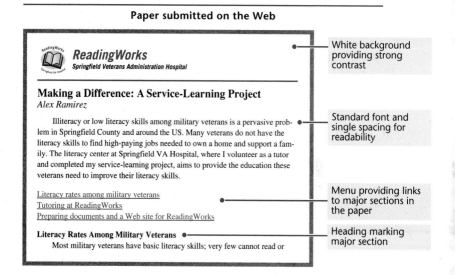

You can usually compose an online paper on your word processor and then use the Save As HTML function to translate the paper into a Web page. (HTML is the most common Web language.) After translating a paper, your word processor should allow you to modify some of the elements on the page, or you can open the translated document in an HTML editor. For more on Web composition, see pages 164–68.

7f Consider readers with disabilities.

Your audience may include readers who have low vision, problems with color perception, or difficulties processing visual information. If so, consider adapting your design to meet these readers' needs. Here are a few pointers:

- **Use large type fonts.** Most guidelines call for 14 points or larger.
- **Use standard type fonts.** Many people with low vision find it easier to read sans serif fonts such as Arial than serif fonts (see p. 75). Avoid decorative fonts with unusual flourishes, even in headings.

- Avoid words in all-capital letters.
- **Avoid relying on color alone to distinguish elements.** Label elements, and distinguish them by position or size.
- **Use red and green selectively.** To readers who are red-green colorblind, these colors will appear in shades of gray, yellow, or blue.
- **Use contrasting colors.** To make colors distinct, choose them from opposite sides of the color spectrum—violet and yellow, for instance, or orange and blue.
- **Use only light colors for tints behind type.** Make the type itself black or a very dark color.

2

Writing in and out of College

8 Academic Writing

When you write in college, you work within a community of teachers and students who have specific aims and expectations. The basic aim of this community—whether in English, psychology, biology, or some other discipline—is to contribute to and build knowledge through questioning, research, and communication. This broad aim, the discipline's specific concerns, and the kind of paper you're writing will shape your choice of subject, conception of audience, definition of purpose, choice of structure and content, and even choice of language.

8a Acquire academic habits.

As an academic writer, you participate in a discipline community first by studying a subject, acquiring its vocabulary, and learning to express yourself in its ways. As you gain experience and knowledge, you begin to contribute to the community by asking questions and communicating your answers. In any discipline, making the transition to academic writing will be easier if you practice the strategies outlined in the following box.

Tips for becoming an academic writer

- **Study the syllabus for each course.** This outline lays out the instructor's expectations as well as the course topics, assignments, and deadlines.
- **Do the assigned reading.** You'll gain experience with the discipline's terms and ideas, and you'll become familiar with the kinds of writing expected of you.
- **Attend and participate in class.** Make class attendance a priority, whether or not the instructor checks the roll. Listen carefully, take notes (see p. 93 for tips), ask questions, and join in discussions.
- **Ask questions.** Instructors, advisers, tutors, other students—all can help you.
- **Understand the writing situation posed by each assignment.** Knowing your audience, purpose, options for subjects, and other elements of the situation will help you meet the assignment's expectations. (See pp. 4–5 on analyzing assignments.)

---

http://www.ablongman.com/littlebrown ▶

Visit the companion Web site for more help with academic writing.

8b   Analyze the audience.

Some of your writing assignments may specify an identifiable group of readers—for instance, fellow students, the city council, or the editors of a newspaper. Such readers' needs and expectations vary widely; the discussion on pages 6–8 can help you discover what they might be. Many assignments will specify or assume an educated audience or an academic audience. This more general group of readers looks for writing that is clear, balanced, well organized, and well reasoned, among other qualities discussed on the next two pages. Still other assignments will specify or assume an audience of experts on your subject, readers who look in addition for writing that meets the subject's requirements for claims and evidence, organization, language, format, and other qualities.

Of course, much of your academic writing will have only one reader besides you: the instructor of the course for which you are writing. Instructors fill two main roles as readers:

- **They represent the audience you are addressing.** They may actually be members of the audience, as when you address academic readers or subject experts. Or they may imagine themselves as members of your audience—reading, for instance, as if they sat on the city council. In either case, they're interested in how effectively you write for the audience.
- **They serve as coaches,** guiding you toward achieving the goals of the course and, more broadly, toward the academic aims of building and communicating knowledge.

Like everyone else, instructors have preferences and peeves, but you'll waste time and energy trying to anticipate them. Do attend to written and spoken directions for assignments, of course. But otherwise view your instructors as representatives of the community you are writing for. Their responses will be guided by the community's aims and expectations and by a desire to teach you about them.

8c   Determine your purpose.

For most academic writing, your general purpose will be mainly explanatory or mainly argumentative. That is, you will aim to clarify your subject so that readers understand it as you do, or you will aim to gain readers' agreement with a debatable idea about the subject. (See p. 9 for more on general purposes and pp. 123–42 for more on argument.)

Your specific purpose—including your subject and how you hope readers will respond—depends on the kind of writing you're doing. In a biology lab report, for instance, you want your readers to understand why you conducted your study, how you conducted it, what the results were, and what their significance is. Not coincidentally, these topics correspond to the major sections of a biology lab report. In following the standard format, you both help to define your purpose and begin to meet the discipline's (and thus your instructor's) expectations.

8d

Your specific purpose will be more complex as well. You take a course to learn about a subject and the ways experts think about it. Your writing, in return, contributes to the discipline through the knowledge you uncover and the lens of your perspective. At the same time, as a student you want to demonstrate your competence with research, evidence, format, and other requirements of the discipline.

8d   Choose the structure and content.

Many academic writing assignments will at least imply how you should organize your paper and even how you should develop your ideas. Like the biology lab report mentioned above, the type of paper required will break into discrete parts, each with its own requirements for content.

No matter what type of paper an assignment specifies, the broad academic aims of building and exchanging knowledge determine features that are common across disciplines. Follow these general guidelines for your academic writing, supplementing them as indicated with others elsewhere in this book:

- **Develop a central idea or claim, called a** *thesis*. Everything in the paper should relate clearly to this claim. For more on the thesis, see pages 18–20.
- **State the thesis,** usually near the beginning of the paper.
- **Support the thesis with evidence,** drawn usually from research and sometimes from your own experience. The kinds of evidence will depend on the discipline you're writing in and the type of paper you're doing.
- **Interact with sources.** Do not merely summarize sources but evaluate and synthesize them from your own perspective. For more on using sources, see pages 447–58.
- **Acknowledge sources fully,** using the documentation style appropriate to the discipline. For lists of disciplines' style guides, see pages 478–79. For documentation guidelines and samples, see Chapters 56 (MLA) and 57 (APA).

- **Balance your presentation.** Discuss evidence and opposing views fairly, and take a serious and impartial approach.
- **Organize clearly within the framework of the type of writing you're doing.** Develop your ideas as simply and directly as your purpose and content allow. Clearly relate sentences, paragraphs, and sections so that readers always know where they are in the paper's development.

CULTURE LANGUAGE These features are far from universal. In other cultures, for instance, academic writers may be indirect or may not have to acknowledge well-known sources. Recognizing such differences between practices in your native culture and in the United States can help you adapt to US academic writing.

8e

8e   Use academic language.

American academic writing relies on a dialect called standard American English. The dialect is also used in business, the professions, government, the media, and other sites of social and economic power where people of diverse backgrounds must communicate with one another. It is "standard" not because it is better than other forms of English, but because it is accepted as the common language, much as the dollar bill is accepted as the common currency.

Standard American English varies a lot, from the formal English of a President's State of the Union address through the middle formality of this handbook to the informal chitchat between anchors on morning TV. Even in academic writing, standard American English allows much room for the writer's own tone and voice, as these passages on the same topic show:

More formal

Using the technique of "color engineering," manufacturers and advertisers can heighten the interest of consumers in a product by adding color that does not contribute to the utility of the product but appeals more to emotions. In one example from the 1920s, manufacturers of fountain pens, which had previously been made of hard black rubber, dramatically increased sales simply by producing the pens in bright colors.	Two complicated sentences, one explaining the technique and one giving the example
	Drawn-out phrasing, such as *interest of consumers* instead of *consumers' interest*
	Formal vocabulary, such as *heighten, contribute,* and *utility*

Less formal

A touch of "color engineering" can sharpen the emotional appeal of a product or its ad. New color can boost sales even when the color serves	Four sentences, two each for explaining the technique and giving the example

no use. In the 1920s, for example, fountain-pen makers introduced brightly colored pens along with the familiar ones of hard black rubber. Sales shot up.

> More informal phrasing, such as *Sales shot up*

> More informal vocabulary, such as *touch, boost,* and *ad*

As different as they are, both examples illustrate several common features of academic language:

- **It follows the conventions of standard American English for grammar and usage.** These conventions are described in guides to the dialect, such as this handbook.

- **It uses a standard vocabulary,** not one that only some groups understand, such as slang, an ethnic or regional dialect, or another language. (See pp. 196–98 for more on specialized vocabularies.)

- **It creates some distance between writer and reader with the third person (*he, she, it, they*).** The first person (*I, we*) is sometimes appropriate to express personal opinions or invite readers to think along, but not with a strongly explanatory purpose (*I discovered that "color engineering" can heighten . . .*). The second person (*you*) is appropriate only in addressing readers directly (as in this handbook), and even then it may seem condescending or too chummy (*You should know that "color engineering" can heighten . . .*).

- **It is authoritative and neutral.** In the preceding examples, the writers express themselves confidently, not timidly (as in *One possible example of color engineering that might be considered in this case is . . .*). They also refrain from hostility (*Advertisers will stop at nothing to achieve their goals*) and enthusiasm (*Color engineering is genius at work*).

At first, the diverse demands of academic writing may leave you groping for an appropriate voice. In an effort to sound fresh and confident, you may write too casually:

Too casual

"Color engineering" is a great way to get at consumers' feelings. . . . When the guys jazzed up the color, sales shot through the roof.

In an effort to sound "academic," you may produce wordy and awkward sentences:

Wordy and awkward

The emotions of consumers can be made more engaged by the technique known as "color engineering." . . . A very large increase in the sales of fountain pens was achieved by the manufacturers of the pens as a result of this color enhancement technique. [The passive voice in this example, such as *increase . . . was achieved* instead of *the manufacturers achieved,* adds to its wordiness and indirection. See pp. 277–79 for more on voice.]

A cure for writing too informally or too stiffly is to read academic writing so that the language and style become familiar and to edit your writing (see pp. 36–37).

CULTURE LANGUAGE If your first language is not English or is an English dialect besides standard American, you know well the power of communicating with others who share your language. Learning to write standard American English in no way requires you to abandon your first language. Like most multilingual people, you are probably already adept at switching between languages as the situation demands—speaking one way with your relatives, say, and another way with an employer. As you practice academic writing, you'll develop the same flexibility with it.

8e

EXERCISE 8.1
Using academic language
Revise the following paragraph to make the language more academic while keeping the factual information the same. Possible revisions of starred sentences appear at the back of the book. (You can do this exercise online at *ablongman.com/littlebrown.*)

　*If you buy into the stereotype of girls chatting away on their cell phones, you should think again. *One of the major wireless companies surveyed 1021 cell phone owners for a period of five years and—surprise!—reported that guys talk on cell phones more than girls do. In fact, guys were way ahead of girls, using an average of 571 minutes a month compared to 424 for girls. That's 35 percent more time on the phone! The survey also asked about conversations on home phones, and while girls still beat the field, the guys are catching up.

EXERCISE 8.2
Considering your academic writing
Look back at a paper you wrote for a course in high school or college. To what extent does it share the features of academic writing discussed in this chapter? How does it differ?

EXERCISE 8.3
Considering your native language or dialect　**CULTURE LANGUAGE**
What main similarities and differences do you notice between writing in your native language or dialect and writing for US college courses? Consider especially content, structure, and the expression of ideas. Which differences do you think are easiest to bridge? Which are most difficult? Why?

9 Studying Effectively and Taking Exams

How can I improve my study and exam-taking skills?

Academic success depends on active, involved learning. You'll get maximum benefit from studying if you manage your time, listen and take notes in class, read for comprehension, prepare well for exams, and use effective strategies for taking exams.

9a Manage your time.

Planning and pacing your schoolwork and other activities will help you study more efficiently with less stress.

1 • Scheduling your time

To organize your time, use a calendar that divides each day into waking hours. Block out your activities that occur regularly and at specific times, such as commuting, attending classes, and working. Then fill in the other activities (such as exercise, eating, and studying) that do not necessarily occur at fixed times. Be sure to leave time for relaxing: an unrealistic schedule that assigns all available time to studying will quickly prove too difficult to live by.

2 • Organizing your workload

Use the syllabuses for your courses to estimate the amount of weekly study time required for each course. Generally, plan on two hours of studying for each hour in class—that is, about six hours for a typical course. Block out study periods using these guidelines:

- **Schedule study time close to class time.** You'll study more productively if you review notes, read assigned material, or work on projects shortly after each class period.
- **Pace assignments.** Plan to start early and work regularly on projects requiring extensive time, such as research papers, so that you will not be overwhelmed near the deadline. (See pp. 416–17 for advice on scheduling research projects.)
- **Adjust the weekly plan as needed to accommodate changes in your workload.** Before each week begins, examine its schedule to be sure you've built in enough time to study for an exam, finish a paper, or meet other deadlines and commitments.

http://www.ablongman.com/littlebrown ▶

Visit the companion Web site for more help with study skills and taking exams.

3 • **Using study time well**

When you sit down to study, use your time efficiently:

- **Set realistic study goals.** Divide your study sessions into small chunks, each with a short-term goal, such as previewing a textbook chapter or drafting three paragraphs of a paper. Plan breaks, too, so that you can clear your mind, stretch, and refocus on your goals.
- **Tackle difficult homework first.** Resist any urge to put off demanding jobs, such as working on papers, reading textbooks, or doing math problems. Save easy tasks for when you're less alert.
- **Evaluate how you use your study time.** At the end of each week, ask yourself whether you were as productive as you needed to be. If not, what changes can you make to accomplish your goals for the coming week?

9b   **Listen and take notes in class.**

When you begin each class, push aside other concerns so that you can focus and listen. Either on paper or on a computer, record what you hear as completely as possible while sorting out the main ideas from the secondary and supporting ones. (See the box below.) Such active note taking will help you understand the instructor's approach to the course and provide you with complete material for later study.

Tips for taking class notes

- **Use your own words.** You will understand and retain the material better if you rephrase it. But use the speaker's words if necessary to catch everything.
- **Leave space in your notes if you miss something.** Ask someone for the missing information as soon as possible after the class.
- **Include any reading content mentioned by your instructor.** Use the notes to integrate all the components of the course—your instructor's views, your own thoughts, and the assigned reading, even if you've already read it.
- **Review your notes shortly after class.** Reinforce your new knowledge when it is fresh by underlining key words and ideas, adding headings and comments in the margins, converting your notes to questions, or outlining the lecture based on your notes.

9c Read for comprehension.

The assigned reading you do for college courses—such as textbooks, journal articles, and works of literature—requires a greater focus on understanding and retention than does the reading you do for entertainment or for practical information. The process outlined below may seem time consuming, but with practice you'll become efficient at it.

Note The following process stresses ways of understanding what you read. In critical reading, covered in the next chapter, you extend this process to analyze and evaluate what you read and see.

1 • Writing while reading

Reading for comprehension is an *active* process. Students often believe they are reading actively when they roll a highlighter over the important ideas in a text, but truly engaged reading requires more than that. If you take notes while reading, you "translate" the work into your own words and reconstruct it for yourself.

The substance of your reading notes will change as you preview, read, and summarize. At first, you may jot quick, short notes in the margins, on separate pages, or on a computer. (Use the last two for material you don't own or are reading online.) As you delve into the work, the notes should become more detailed, restating important points, asking questions, connecting ideas. (See p. 108 for an example of a text annotated in this way by a student.) For some reading, you may want to keep a reading journal that records both what the work says and what you think about it.

2 • Previewing

For most course reading, you should **skim** before reading word for word. Skimming gives you an overview of the material: its length and difficulty, organization, and principal ideas.

- **Gauge length and level.** Is the material brief and straightforward enough to read in one sitting, or do you need more time?
- **Examine the title and introduction.** The title and first couple of paragraphs will give you a sense of the topic, the author's approach, and the main ideas. As you read them, ask yourself what you already know about the subject so that you can integrate new information with old.

- **Move from heading to heading.** Viewing the headings as headlines or as the levels of an outline will give you a feeling for which ideas the author sees as primary and which subordinate.
- **Note highlighted words.** You will likely need to learn the meanings of terms in **bold,** *italic,* or color.
- **Slow down for pictures, diagrams, tables, graphs, and other illustrations.** They often contain concentrated information.
- **Read the summary or conclusion.** These paragraphs often recap the main ideas.
- **Think over what you've skimmed.** Try to recall the central idea, or thesis, and the sequence of ideas.

9c

3 • Reading

After previewing a text, you can settle into it to learn what it has to say.

First reading

The first time through new material, read as steadily and smoothly as possible, trying to get the gist of what the author is saying.

- **Read in a place where you can concentrate.** Choose a quiet environment away from distractions such as music or talking.
- **Give yourself time.** Rushing yourself or worrying about something else you have to do will prevent you from grasping what you read.
- **Try to enjoy the work.** Seek connections between it and what you already know. Appreciate new information, interesting relationships, forceful writing, humor, good examples.
- **Make notes sparingly during this first reading.** Mark major stumbling blocks—such as a paragraph you don't understand—so that you can try to resolve them before rereading.

CULTURE LANGUAGE If English is not your first language and you come across unfamiliar words, don't stop and look up every one. You will lose more in concentration than you will gain in understanding. Instead, try to guess the meanings of unfamiliar words from their contexts, circle them, and look them up later.

Rereading

After the first reading, plan on at least one other. This time read *slowly.* Your main concern should be to grasp the content and how it is constructed. That means rereading a paragraph if you didn't get the point or using a dictionary to look up words you don't know.

Use your pen, pencil, or keyboard freely to highlight and distill the text:

- **Distinguish main ideas from supporting ideas.** Look for the central idea, or thesis, for the main idea of each paragraph or section, and for the evidence supporting ideas.
- **Learn key terms.** Understand both their meanings and their applications.
- **Discern the connections among ideas.** Be sure you see why the author moves from point A to point B to point C and how those points relate to support the central idea. It often helps to outline the text or summarize it (see below).
- **Add your own comments.** In the margins or separately, note links to other readings or to class discussions, questions to explore further, possible topics for your writing, points you find especially strong or weak. (This last category will occupy much of your time when you are expected to read critically. See pp. 105–12.)

4 • Summarizing

A good way to master the content of a text is to **summarize** it: reduce it to its main points, in your own words.

Writing a summary

- **Understand the meaning.** Look up words or concepts you don't know so that you understand the author's sentences and how they relate to one another.
- **Understand the organization.** Work through the text to identify its sections—single paragraphs or groups of paragraphs focused on a single topic. To understand how parts of a work relate to one another, try drawing a tree diagram or creating an outline (pp. 23–25).
- **Distill each section.** Write a one- or two-sentence summary of each section you identify. Focus on the main point of the section, omitting examples, facts, and other supporting evidence.
- **State the main idea.** Write a sentence or two capturing the author's central idea.
- **Support the main idea.** Write a full paragraph (or more, if needed) that begins with the central idea and supports it with the sentences that summarize sections of the work. The paragraph should concisely and accurately state the thrust of the entire work.
- *Use your own words.* By writing, you re-create the meaning of the work in a way that makes sense for you.

Summarizing even a passage of text can be tricky. Below is one attempt to summarize the following material from an introductory biology textbook.

Original text

As astronomers study newly discovered planets orbiting distant stars, they hope to find evidence of water on these far-off celestial bodies, for water is the substance that makes possible life as we know it here on Earth. All organisms familiar to us are made mostly of water and live in an environment dominated by water. They require water more than any other substance. Human beings, for example, can survive for quite a few weeks without food, but only a week or so without water. Molecules of water participate in many chemical reactions necessary to sustain life. Most cells are surrounded by water, and cells themselves are about 70–95% water. Three-quarters of Earth's surface is submerged in water. Although most of this water is in liquid form, water is also present on Earth as ice and vapor. Water is the only common substance to exist in the natural environment in all three physical states of matter: solid, liquid, and gas.

—Neil A. Campbell and Jane B. Reece, *Biology*

9d

Draft summary

Astronomers look for water in outer space because life depends on it. It is the most common substance on Earth and in living cells, and it can be a liquid, a solid (ice), or a gas (vapor).

This summary accurately restates ideas in the original, but it does not pare the passage to its essence. The work of astronomers and the three physical states of water add color and texture to the original, but they are asides to the key concept that water sustains life because of its role in life. The following revision narrows the summary to this concept:

Revised summary

Water is the most essential support for life, the dominant substance on Earth and in living cells and a component of life-sustaining chemical processes.

Note Do not count on the AutoSummarize function on your word processor for summarizing texts that you may have copied onto your computer. The summaries are rarely accurate, and you will not gain the experience of interacting with the texts on your own.

9d   Prepare for exams.

Studying for an exam involves three main steps, each requiring about a third of the preparation time: reviewing the material, organizing summaries of the material, and testing yourself. Your main goals are to strengthen your understanding of the subject, making both its ideas and its details more memorable, and to increase the flexibility of your new knowledge so that you can apply it in new contexts.

The procedure outlined here works for any exam, no matter how much time you have, what material you're studying, or what kind of test you'll be taking. Because an essay exam requires a distinctive approach during the exam itself, it receives special attention on pages 99–104.

9d

Note Cramming for an exam is about the least effective way of preparing for one. It takes longer to learn under stress, and the learning is shallower, more difficult to apply, and more quickly forgotten. Information learned under stress is even harder to apply in stressful situations, such as taking an exam. And the lack of sleep that usually accompanies cramming makes a good performance even more unlikely. If you must cram for a test, face the fact that you can't learn everything. Spend your time reviewing main concepts and facts.

1 • Reviewing and memorizing the material

Divide your class notes and reading assignments into manageable units. Reread the material, recite or write out the main ideas and selected supporting ideas and examples, and then skim for an overview. Proceed in this way through all the units of the course, returning to earlier ones as needed to refresh your memory or to relate ideas.

During this stage you should be memorizing what you don't already know by heart. Try these strategies for strengthening your memory:

- **Link new and known information.** For instance, to remember a sequence of four dates in twentieth-century African history, link the dates to simultaneous and more familiar events in the United States.
- **Create groups of ideas or facts that make sense to you.** For instance, memorize French vocabulary words in related groups, such as words for parts of the body or parts of a house. Keep the groups small: research has shown that we can easily memorize about seven items at a time but have trouble with more.
- **Create narratives and visual images.** You may recall a story or a picture more easily than words. For instance, to remember how the economic laws of supply and demand affect the market for rental housing, you could tie the principles to a narrative about the aftermath of the 1906 San Francisco earthquake,

when half the population was suddenly homeless. Or you could visualize a person who has dollar signs for eyes and is converting a spare room into a high-priced rental unit, as many did after the earthquake to meet the new demand for housing.

- Use *mnemonic devices,* or tricks for remembering. Say the history dates you want to remember are separated by five years, then four, then nine. By memorizing the first date and recalling 5 + 4 = 9, you'll have command of all four dates.

2 • Organizing summaries of the material

Allow time to reorganize the material in your own way, creating categories that will help you apply the information in various contexts. For instance, in studying for a biology exam, work to understand a process, such as how a plant develops or how photosynthesis occurs. Or in studying for an American government test, explain the structures of the local, state, and federal levels of government. Other useful categories include advantages/disadvantages and causes/effects. Such analytical thinking will improve your mastery of the course material and may even prepare you directly for specific essay questions.

3 • Testing yourself

Convert each heading in your lecture notes and course reading into a question. Answer in writing, going back to the course material to fill in what you don't yet know. Be sure you can define and explain all key terms. For subjects that require solving problems (such as mathematics, statistics, or physics), work out a difficult problem for every type on which you will be tested. For all subjects, focus on the main themes and questions of the course. In a psychology course, for example, be certain you understand principal theories and their implications. In a literature course, test your knowledge of literary movements and genres or the relations among specific works.

When you are satisfied with your preparation, stop studying and get a good night's sleep.

4 • Taking essay exams

In writing an essay for an examination, you summarize or analyze a topic, usually in several paragraphs or more and usually within a time limit. An essay question not only tests your knowledge of a subject (as short-answer and objective questions do) but also tests your ability to think critically about what you have learned.

9d

Planning your time and your answer

When you first receive an exam, take a few minutes to get your bearings and plan an approach. The time spent will not be wasted.

- **Read the exam all the way through at least once.** Don't start answering any questions until you've seen them all.
- **Weigh the questions.** Determine which questions seem most important, which ones are going to be most difficult for you, and approximately how much time you'll need for each question. (Your instructor may help by assigning a point value to each question as a guide to its importance or by suggesting an amount of time for you to spend on each question.)

Planning continues when you turn to an individual essay question. Resist the temptation to rush right into an answer without some planning: a few minutes can save you time later and help you produce a stronger essay.

- **Read the question at least twice.** You will be more likely to stick to the question and answer it fully.
- **Examine the words in the question and consider their implications.** Look especially for words such as *describe, define, explain, summarize, analyze, evaluate,* and *interpret,* each of which requires a different kind of response. Here, for example, is an essay question whose key term is *explain:*

Question

Given humans' natural and historical curiosity about themselves, why did a scientific discipline of anthropology not arise until the 20th century? Explain, citing specific details.

Consult discussions of such terms on pages 6 and 59–65.

- **Make a brief outline of the main ideas you want to cover.** Use the back of the exam sheet or booklet for scratch paper. In the following brief outline, a student planned her answer to the anthropology question above.

Outline

1. Unscientific motivations behind 19th-c anthro.

   Imperialist/colonialist govts.
   Practical goals
   Nonobjective and unscientific (Herodotus, Cushing)

2. 19th-c ethnocentricity (vs. cultural relativism)

3. 19th-c anthro. = object collecting

   20th-c shift from museum to univ.
   Anthro. becomes acad. disc. and professional (Boas, Malinowski)

- **Write a thesis statement for your essay that responds directly to the question and represents your view of the topic.** (If you are unsure of how to write a thesis statement, see pp. 18–20.) Include key phrases that you can expand with supporting evidence for your view. The thesis statement for the anthropology exam concisely previews a three-part answer to the question:

9d

Thesis statement

Anthropology did not emerge as a scientific discipline until the 20th century because of the practical and political motivations behind 19th-century ethnographic studies, the ethnocentric bias of Western researchers, and a conception of culture that was strictly material.

Starting the essay

An essay exam does not require a smooth and inviting opening. Instead, begin by stating your thesis immediately and giving an overview of the rest of your essay. Such a capsule version of your answer tells your reader (and grader) generally how much command you have and also how you plan to develop your answer. It also gets you off to a good start.

The opening statement should address the question directly and exactly, as it does in the successful essay answer beginning on the next page. In contrast, the opening of the unsuccessful essay (p. 103) restates the question but does not answer it, nor does the opening provide any sense of the writer's thesis.

Developing the essay

Develop your essay as you would develop any piece of sound academic writing:

- **Observe the methods, terms, or other special requirements of the discipline in which you are writing.**
- **Support your thesis statement with solid generalizations,** each one perhaps the topic sentence of a paragraph.
- **Support each generalization with specific, relevant evidence.**

If you observe a few *don't*s as well, your essay will have more substance:

- **Avoid filling out the essay by repeating yourself.**
- **Avoid other kinds of wordiness that pad and confuse,** whether intentionally or not. (See pp. 216–20.)
- **Avoid resorting to purely subjective feelings.** Keep focused on analysis or whatever is asked of you. (It may help to abolish the word *I* from the essay.)

The following essays illustrate a successful and an unsuccessful answer to the sample essay question on page 100 about anthropology. Both answers were written in the allotted time of forty minutes. Marginal comments on each essay highlight their effective and ineffective elements.

Successful essay answer

Introduction stating thesis	Anthropology did not emerge as a scientific discipline until the 20th century because of the practical and political motivations behind 19th-century ethnographic studies, the ethnocentric bias of Western researchers, and a conception of culture that was strictly material.
Direct answer to question and preview of three-part response	
First main point: practical aims	Before the 20th century, ethnographic studies were almost always used for practical goals. The study of human culture can be traced back at least as far as Herodotus's investigations of the Mediterranean peoples. Herodotus was like many pre-20th-century "anthropologists" in that he was employed by a government that needed information about its neighbors, just as the colonial nations in the 19th century needed information about their newly conquered subjects. The early politically motivated ethnographic studies that the colonial nations sponsored tended to be isolated projects, and they aimed less to advance general knowledge than to solve a specific problem. Frank Hamilton Cushing, who was employed by the American government to study the Zuni tribe of New Mexico, and who is considered one of the pioneers of anthropology, didn't even publish his findings. The political and practical aims of anthropologists and the nature of their research prevented their work from being a scholarly discipline in its own right.
Example	
Example	
Second main point: ethnocentricity	Anthropologists of the 19th century also fell short of the standards of objectivity needed for truly scientific study. This partly had to do with anthropologists' close connection to imperialist governments. But even independent researchers were hampered by the prevailing assumption that Western cultures were inherently superior. While the modern anthropologist believes that a culture must be studied in terms of its own values, early ethnographers were ethnocentric: they judged "primitive" cultures by their own "civilized" values. "Primitive" peoples were seen as uninteresting in their own right. The reasons to study them, ultimately, were to satisfy curiosity, to exploit them, or to prove their inferiority. There was even some debate as to whether so-called savage peoples were human.
Third main point (with transition *Finally*): focus on objects	Finally, the 19th century tended to conceive of culture in narrow, material terms, often reducing it to a collection of artifacts. When not working for a government, early ethnographers usually worked for a museum. The enormous collections of exotica still found in many museums today are the legacy of this 19th-century object-oriented conception of anthropology, which ignored the myths, symbols, and rituals the objects related to. It was only when the museum tradition was broadened to include all aspects of a culture

that anthropology could come into existence as a scientific discipline. When anthropologists like Franz Boas and Bronislaw Malinowski began to publish their findings for others to read and criticize and began to move from the museum to the university, the discipline gained stature and momentum.

Examples

In brief, anthropology required a whole series of ideological shifts to become modern. Once it broke free of its purely practical bent, the cultural prejudices of its practitioners, and the narrow conception that limited it to a collection of objects, anthropology could grow into a science.

Conclusion, restating thesis supported by essay

Unsuccessful essay answer

The discipline of anthropology, the study of humans and their cultures, actually began in the early 20th century and was strengthened by the Darwinian revolution, but the discipline did not begin to take shape until people like Franz Boas and Alfred Kroeber began doing scientific research among nonindustrialized cultures. (Boas, who was born in Germany but emigrated to the US, is the father of the idea of historical particularism.)

Introduction, not answering question

No thesis statement or sense of direction

Irrelevant information

Since the dawn of time, humans have always had a natural curiosity about themselves. Art and literature have always reflected this need to understand human emotions, thought, and behavior. Anthropology is yet another reflection of this need. Anthropologists have a different way of looking at human societies than artists or writers. Whereas the latter paint an individualistic, impressionistic portrait of the world they see, anthropologists study cultures systematically, scientifically. They are thus closer to biologists. They are social scientists, with the emphasis on both words.

Cliché added to language of question without answering question

Wheel spinning, positioning contemporary anthropology as a scientific discipline

Another reason why anthropology did not develop until the 20th century is that people in the past did not travel very much. The expansion of the automobile and the airplane has played a major role in the expansion of the discipline.

Not Another reason but the first reason given

Assertion without support

Cushing's important work among the Zuni Indians in New Mexico is a good example of the transition between 19th-century and 20th-century approaches to anthropology. Cushing was one of the first to develop the method of participant observation. Instead of merely coming in as an outsider, taking notes, and leaving, Cushing actually lived among the Zuni, dressing like them and following their customs. In this way, he was able to build a relationship of trust with his informants, learning much more than someone who would have been seen as an outsider.

Next three paragraphs: discussion of pioneers showing familiarity with their work but not answering question

Franz Boas, as mentioned earlier, was another anthropology pioneer. A German immigrant, Boas proposed the idea of historical particularism as a response to the prevailing theory of cultural evolution. Cultural evolution is the idea that cultures gradually evolve toward higher levels of efficiency and complexity. Historical particularism is the idea that every culture is unique and develops differently. Boas developed his theory to counter those who

Padding with repetition

Irrelevant information

believed in cultural evolution. Working with the Kwakiutl Indians, he was also one of the first anthropologists to use a native assistant to help him gain access to the culture under study.

    A third pioneer in anthropology was Malinowski, who developed a theory of functionalism—that culture responds to biological, psychological, and other needs. Malinowski's work is extremely important and still influential today.

Vague assertion without support

Irrelevant and empty conclusion

    Anthropologists have made great contributions to society over the course of the past century. One can only hope that they will continue the great strides they have made, building on the past to contribute to a bright new future.

Rereading the essay

The time limit on an essay examination does not allow for the careful rethinking and revision you would give an essay or research paper. You need to write clearly and concisely the first time. But try to leave yourself a few minutes after finishing the entire exam for rereading the essay (or essays) and doing touch-ups.

- **Correct mistakes:** illegible passages, misspellings, grammatical errors, and accidental omissions.
- **Verify that your thesis is accurate**—that it is, in fact, what you ended up writing about.
- **Ensure that you have supported all your generalizations.** Cross out irrelevant ideas and details, and add any information that now seems important. (Write on another page, if necessary, keying each addition to the page on which it belongs.)

10 Critical Reading and Writing

Why and how should I think critically when I read and write?

Throughout college and beyond, you will be expected to think, read, and write critically—that is, to question, test, and build on what others say and what you yourself think. In daily life, critical thinking helps you figure out why things happen to you or what

http://www.ablongman.com/littlebrown ▶

Visit the companion Web site for more help and an electronic exercise on critical reading and writing.

your experiences mean. In school and at work, critical thinking sharpens your ability to learn and to perform. It helps you understand which ideas are useful, fair, and wise—and which are not.

Note Critical thinking plays a large role in research writing. See pages 447–56 on evaluating print and online sources and pages 457–58 on synthesizing sources.

crit

10a

10a   Read texts critically.

In college and work, much of your critical thinking will focus on written texts (a short story, a journal article, a Web log) or on visual objects (a photograph, a chart, a film). Like all subjects worthy of critical consideration, such works operate on at least three levels: (1) what the creator actually says or shows, (2) what the creator does not say or show but builds into the work (intentionally or not), and (3) what you think. Discovering the first of these levels— reading for comprehension—is discussed in the preceding chapter as part of study skills (see pp. 94–97). This chapter builds on the earlier material to help you discover the other two levels.

CULTURE LANGUAGE The idea of reading critically may require you to make some adjustments if readers in your native culture tend to seek understanding or agreement more than engagement from what they read. Readers of English use texts for all kinds of reasons, including pleasure, reinforcement, and information. But they also read skeptically, critically, to see the author's motives, test their own ideas, and arrive at new knowledge.

1 • Previewing the material

When you're reading a work of literature, such as a short story or a poem, it's often best just to plunge right in. But for critical reading of other works, it's worthwhile to skim before reading word for word, forming expectations and even some preliminary questions. The preview will make your reading more informed and fruitful.

- **What is the work's subject and structure?** Following the steps outlined on pages 94–95, gauge the length and level, read the title and introduction for clues to the topic and main ideas, read the headings, note highlighted words (defined terms), examine illustrations, and read the summary or conclusion.
- **What are the facts of publication?** Does the date of publication suggest currency or datedness? Does the publisher or publication specialize in a particular kind of material—scholarly articles, say, or popular books? For a Web document, who or what sponsors the site: an individual? a nonprofit organization? an academic institution? a corporation? a government body?

• **What do you know about the author?** Does a biography tell you about the author's publications, interests, biases, and reputation in the field? For an online source, which may be posted by an unfamiliar or anonymous author, what can you gather about the author from his or her words? If possible, trace unfamiliar authors to learn more about them.

• **What is your preliminary response?** What do you already know about the author's topic? What questions do you have about either the topic or the author's approach to it? What biases of your own might influence your reception of the work— for instance, curiosity, boredom, or an outlook similar or opposed to the author's?

EXERCISE 10.1
Previewing an essay

Reprinted below is an essay by Thomas Sowell, an economist, newspaper columnist, and author of many books on economics, politics, and education. Preview the essay using the preceding guidelines, and then read it once or twice, until you think you understand what the author is saying. Note your questions and reactions in writing.

Student Loans

The first lesson of economics is scarcity: There is never enough of anything to fully satisfy all those who want it. 1

The first lesson of politics is to disregard the first lesson of economics. When politicians discover some group that is being vocal about not having as much as they want, the "solution" is to give them more. Where do politicians get this "more"? They rob Peter to pay Paul. 2

After a while, of course, they discover that Peter doesn't have enough. Bursting with compassion, politicians rush to the rescue. Needless to say, they do not admit that robbing Peter to pay Paul was a dumb idea in the first place. On the contrary, they now rob Tom, Dick, and Harry to help Peter. 3

The latest chapter in this long-running saga is that politicians have now suddenly discovered that many college students graduate heavily in debt. To politicians it follows, as the night follows the day, that the government should come to their rescue with the taxpayers' money. 4

How big is this crushing burden of college students' debt that we hear so much about from politicians and media deep thinkers? For those students who graduate from public colleges owing money, the debt averages a little under $7000. For those who graduate from private colleges owing money, the average debt is a little under $9000. 5

Buying a very modestly priced automobile involves more debt than that. And a car loan has to be paid off faster than the ten years that college graduates get to repay their student loans. Moreover, you have to keep buying cars every several years, while one college education lasts a lifetime. 6

College graduates of course earn higher incomes than other peo- 7
ple. Why, then, should we panic at the thought that they have to repay
loans for the education which gave them their opportunities? Even graduates with relatively modest incomes pay less than 10 percent of their
annual salary on the first loan the first year—with declining percentages
in future years, as their pay increases.

Political hysteria and media hype may focus on the low-income stu- 8
dent with a huge debt. That is where you get your heart-rending stories—
even if they are not all that typical. In reality, the soaring student loans of
the past decade have resulted from allowing high-income people to borrow under government programs.

crit
10a

Before 1978, college loans were available through government pro- 9
grams only to students whose family income was below some cut-off
level. That cut-off level was about double the national average income,
but at least it kept out the Rockefellers and the Vanderbilts. But, in an era
of "compassion," Congress took off even those limits.

That opened the floodgates. No matter how rich you were, it still 10
paid to borrow money through the government at low interest rates.
The money you had set aside for your children's education could be in-
vested somewhere else, at higher interest rates. Then, when the student
loan became due, parents could pay it off with the money they had set
aside—pocketing the difference in interest rates.

To politicians and the media, however, the rapidly growing loans 11
showed what a great "need" there was. The fact that many students
welshed when time came to repay their loans showed how "crushing"
their burden of debt must be. In reality, those who welsh typically
have smaller loans, but have dropped out of college before finishing.
People who are irresponsible in one way are often irresponsible in other
ways.

No small amount of the deterioration of college standards has been 12
due to the increasingly easy availability of college to people who are not
very serious about getting an education. College is not a bad place to
hang out for a few years, if you have nothing better to do, and if someone else is paying for it. Its costs are staggering, but the taxpayers carry
much of that burden, not only for state universities and city colleges, but
also to an increasing extent even for "private" institutions.

Numerous government subsidies and loan programs make it possible 13
for many people to use vast amounts of society's resources at low cost to
themselves. Whether in money terms or in real terms, federal aid to higher
education has increased several hundred percent since 1970. That has enabled colleges to raise their tuition by leaps and bounds and enabled professors to be paid more and more for doing less and less teaching.

Naturally all these beneficiaries are going to create hype and hyste- 14
ria to keep more of the taxpayers' money coming in. But we would be
fools to keep on writing blank checks for them.

When you weigh the cost of things, in economics that's called 15
"trade-offs." In politics, it's called "mean-spirited." Apparently, if we just
took a different attitude, scarcity would go away.

—Thomas Sowell

2 • Reading

Reading is itself more than a one-step process. You want to understand the first level on which the text operates—what the author actually says—and begin to form your impressions.

A procedure for this stage appears in the preceding chapter (pp. 95–96). To recap: Read once through fairly smoothly, trying to appreciate the work and keeping notes to a minimum. Then read again more carefully, this time making detailed notes, to grasp the ideas and their connections and to pose questions. In the following example, a student, Charlene Robinson, annotates the first four paragraphs of "Student Loans":

The first lesson of economics is scarcity: There is never enough of anything to fully satisfy all those who want it.	*basic contradiction between economics and politics*
The first lesson of politics is to disregard the first lesson of economics. When politicians discover some group that is being vocal about not having as much as they want, the "solution" is to give them more. Where do politicians get this "more"? <u>They rob Peter to pay Paul.</u>	← *biblical reference?*
After a while, <u>of course</u>, they discover that Peter doesn't have enough. <u>Bursting with compassion</u>, politicians <u>rush to the rescue</u>. <u>Needless to say</u>, they do not admit that robbing Peter to pay Paul was a <u>dumb idea</u> in the first place. On the contrary, they now rob Tom, Dick, and Harry to help Peter.	*ironic and dismissive language*
The latest chapter in this <u>long-running saga</u> is that politicians have now <u>suddenly discovered</u> that many college students graduate heavily in debt. To politicians it follows, as the night follows the day, that the government should come to their rescue with the taxpayers' money.	*politicians = fools? or irresponsible?*

After reading the text, Robinson wrote about it in the journal she kept on her computer. She divided the journal into two columns, one each for the text and her responses. Here is the portion pertaining to the paragraphs above:

Text	**Responses**
Economics teaches lessons (1), and politics (politicians) and economics are at odds.	Is economics truer or more reliable than politics? More scientific?
Politicians don't accept econ. limits—always trying to satisfy "vocal" voters by giving them more of what they want (2).	Politicians do spend a lot of our money. Is that what they're elected to do, or do they go too far?
"Robbing Peter to pay Paul" (2)— from the Bible (the Apostles)?	

Politicians support student-loan program with taxpayer refunds bec. of "vocal" voters (2-4): another ex. of not accepting econ. limits.	I support the loan program, too. Are politicians being irresponsible when they do? (Dismissive language underlined on copy.)

You should try to answer the questions about meaning that you raise in your annotations and your journal, and that may take another reading or some digging in other sources, such as dictionaries and encyclopedias. Recording in your journal what you think the author means will help you build an understanding of the text, and a focused attempt to summarize will help even more (see below). Such efforts will resolve any confusion you feel, or they will give you the confidence to say that your confusion is the fault of the author, not the reader.

crit

10a

EXERCISE 10.2
Reading

Read Sowell's essay on pages 106–07 at least twice, until you think you understand what the author is saying. Either on these pages or separately, note your questions and reactions in writing, as student writer Charlene Robinson did for the first four paragraphs. Look up any words you don't know, and try to answer your questions. You might want to discuss the essay with your classmates as well.

---

3 • Summarizing

Summarizing a text—distilling it to its essential ideas, in your own words—is an important step for comprehending it and is discussed in detail in the previous chapter (pp. 96–97). Here, we'll look at how Charlene Robinson summarized paragraphs 1–4 of Thomas Sowell's "Student Loans." She first drafted this sentence:

Draft summary
As much as politicians would like to satisfy voters by giving them everything they ask for, the government cannot afford a student loan program.

Reading the sentence and Sowell's paragraphs, Robinson saw that this draft misread the text by asserting that the government cannot afford student loans. She realized that Sowell's point is more complicated than that and rewrote her summary:

Revised summary
As their support of the government's student loan program illustrates, politicians ignore the economic reality that using resources to benefit one group (students in debt) involves taking the resources from another group (taxpayers).

Note Using your own words when writing a summary not only helps you understand the meaning but also constitutes the first step in avoiding plagiarism. The second step is to cite the source when you use it in something written for others. See pages 470–77.

crit

10a

> **EXERCISE 10.3**
> **Summarizing**
> Start where the preceding summary of Thomas Sowell's essay ends (at paragraph 5) to summarize the entire essay. Your summary, in your own words, should not exceed one paragraph. (For additional exercises in summarizing, see pp. 464–65.)

4 • Developing a critical response

Once you've grasped the content of what you're reading—what the author says—then you can turn to understanding what the author does not say outright but suggests or implies or even lets slip. At this stage you are concerned with the purpose or intention of the author and with how he or she carries it out.

Critical thinking and reading consist of four overlapping operations: analyzing, interpreting, synthesizing, and (often) evaluating.

Analyzing

Analysis is the separation of something into its parts or elements, the better to understand it. To see these elements in what you are reading, begin with a question that reflects your purpose in analyzing the text: why you're curious about it or what you're trying to make out of it. This question will serve as a kind of lens that highlights some features and not others.

Analyzing Thomas Sowell's "Student Loans" (pp. 106–07), you might ask one of these questions:

Questions for analysis	Elements
What is Sowell's attitude toward politicians?	References to politicians: content, words, tone
How does Sowell support assertions about the loan program's costs?	Support: evidence, such as statistics and examples

Interpreting

Identifying the elements of something is of course only the beginning: you also need to interpret the meaning or significance of the elements and of the whole. Interpretation usually requires you to infer the author's **assumptions**—that is, opinions or beliefs about what is or what could or should be. (*Infer* means to draw a conclusion based on evidence.)

Assumptions are pervasive: we all adhere to certain values, beliefs, and opinions. But assumptions are not always stated outright. Speakers and writers may judge that their audience already understands and accepts their assumptions; they may not even be aware of their assumptions; or they may deliberately refrain from stating their assumptions for fear that the audience will disagree. That is why your job as a critical thinker is to interpret what the assumptions are.

Thomas Sowell's "Student Loans" is based on certain assumptions, some obvious, some not so obvious. If you were analyzing Sowell's attitude toward politicians, as suggested earlier, you would focus on his statements about them. Sowell says that they "disregard the first lesson of economics" (paragraph 2), which implies that they ignore important principles (knowing that Sowell is an economist himself makes this a reasonable assumption on your part). Sowell also says that politicians "rob Peter to pay Paul," are "[b]ursting with compassion," "do not admit . . . a dumb idea," are characters in a "long-running saga," and arrive at the solution of spending taxes "as the night follows the day"—that is, inevitably (paragraphs 2–4). From these statements and others, you can infer the following:

> Sowell assumes that politicians become compassionate when a cause is loud and popular, not necessarily just, and they act irresponsibly by trying to solve the problem with other people's (taxpayers') money.

Synthesizing

If you stopped at analysis and interpretation, critical thinking and reading might leave you with a pile of elements and possible meanings but no vision of the whole. With **synthesis** you make connections among parts *or* among wholes. You create a new whole by drawing conclusions about relationships and implications.

The statement below about Thomas Sowell's essay "Student Loans" connects his assumptions about politicians to a larger idea also implied by the essay:

> Sowell's view that politicians are irresponsible with taxpayers' money reflects his overall opinion that the laws of economics, not politics, should drive government.

Synthesis may involve working within the text, as in the preceding example, or it may take you outside the text to the surroundings. (This emphasis is important in research writing, as discussed on pp. 457–58.) The following questions can help you investigate the context of a work:

- **How does the work compare with works by others?** For instance, how have other writers responded to Sowell's views on student loans?
- **How does the work fit into the context of other works by the same author or group?** How do Sowell's views on student loans typify, or not, the author's other writing on political and economic issues?
- **What cultural, economic, or political forces influence the work?** What other examples might Sowell have given to illustrate his view that economics, not politics, should determine government spending?
- **What historical forces influence the work?** How has the indebtedness of college students changed over the past four decades?

Evaluating

Critical reading and writing often end at synthesis: you form and explain your understanding of what the work says and doesn't say. If you are also expected to **evaluate** the work, however, you will go further to judge its quality and significance. You may be evaluating a source you've discovered in research (see pp. 447–56), or you may be completing an assignment to state and defend a judgment, a statement such as *Thomas Sowell does not summon the evidence to support his case*. You can read Charlene Robinson's critical analysis of Thomas Sowell's "Student Loans" on pages 120–22.

Evaluation takes a certain amount of confidence. You may think that you lack the expertise to cast judgment on another's work, especially if the work is difficult or the author well known. True, the more informed you are, the better a critical reader you are. But conscientious reading and analysis will give you the internal authority to judge a work *as it stands* and *as it seems to you*, against your own unique bundle of experiences, observations, and attitudes.

> **EXERCISE 10.4**
> **Reading on essay critically**
> Reread Thomas Sowell's "Student Loans" (pp. 106–07) to form your own critical response to it. Focus on any elements suggested by your questions about the text: possibilities are assumptions, evidence, organization, use of language, tone, vision of education or students. Be sure to write while reading and thinking; your notes will help your analysis and enhance your creativity, and they will be essential for writing about the selection.

10b   View images critically.

Every day we are bombarded with images—pictures on billboards, commercials on television, graphs and charts in newspapers and textbooks, to name just a few examples. Most images slide by without our noticing them, or so we think. But images, sometimes even more than text, can influence us covertly. Their creators have purposes, some worthy, some not, and understanding those purposes requires critical reading. The method parallels that in the previous section for reading text critically: preview, read for comprehension, analyze, interpret, synthesize, and (often) evaluate.

1 • Previewing an image

Your first step in exploring an image is to form initial impressions of the work's origin and purpose and to note distinctive features. This previewing process is like the one for previewing a text (pp. 105–06):

- **What do you see?** What is most striking about the image? What is its subject? What is the gist of any text or symbols? What is the overall effect of the image?
- **What are the facts of publication?** Where did you first see the image? Do you think the image was created especially for that location or for others as well? What can you tell about when the image was created?
- **What do you know about the person or group that created the image?** For instance, was the creator an artist, scholar, news organization, or corporation? What seems to have been the creator's purpose?
- **What is your preliminary response?** What about the image interests, confuses, or disturbs you? Are the form, style, and subject familiar or unfamiliar? How might your knowledge, experiences, and values influence your reception of the image?

If possible, print a copy of the image or scan it into your reading journal, and write comments in the image margins or separately.

2 • Reading an image

Reading an image requires the same level of concentration as reading a text. Try to answer the following questions about the image. If some answers aren't clear at this point, skip the question until later.

- **What is the purpose of the image?** Is it mainly explanatory, conveying information, or is it argumentative, trying to convince readers of something or persuade them to act? What information or point of view does it seem intended to get across?
- **Who is the intended audience for the image?** What does the source of the image, including its publication facts, tell about the image creator's expectations for readers' knowledge, interests,

and attitudes? What do the features of the image itself add to your impression?

- **What do any words or symbols add to the image?** Whether located on the image or outside it (such as in a caption), do words or symbols add information, focus your attention, or alter your impression of the image?

- **What people, places, things, or action does the image show?** Does the image tell a story? Do its characters or other features tap into your knowledge, or are they unfamiliar?
- **What is the form of the image?** Is it a photograph, advertisement, painting, graph, diagram, cartoon, or something else? How do its content and apparent purpose and audience relate to its form?

The illustration below shows the notes that a student, John Latner, made on an advertisement for *Time* magazine.

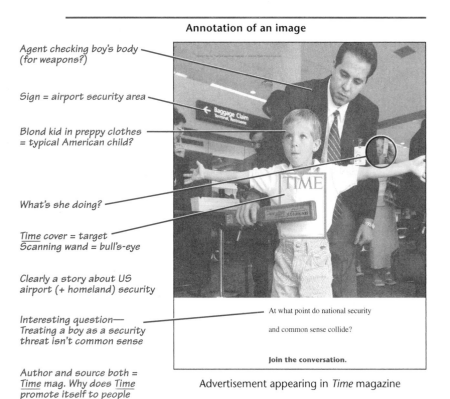

Annotation of an image

Agent checking boy's body (for weapons?)

Sign = airport security area

Blond kid in preppy clothes = typical American child?

What's she doing?

Time cover = target
Scanning wand = bull's-eye

Clearly a story about US airport (+ homeland) security

Interesting question—
Treating a boy as a security threat isn't common sense

Author and source both = *Time* mag. Why does *Time* promote itself to people who are already reading it?

At what point do national security and common sense collide?

Join the conversation.

Advertisement appearing in *Time* magazine

3 • Analyzing an image

Elements for analysis

As when analyzing a written work, you analyze an image by identifying its elements. The image elements you might consider appear in the box below. Keep in mind that an image is a visual *composition* whose every element likely reflects a deliberate effort to communicate. Still, few images include all the elements, and you can narrow the list further by posing a question about the image you are reading, as illustrated on the next page.

Elements of images

- **Emphasis:** Most images pull your eyes to certain features: a graph line moving sharply upward, a provocative figure, bright color, thick lines, and so on. The cropping of a photograph or the date range in a chart will also reflect what the image creator considers important.

- **Narration:** Most images tell stories, whether in a sequence (a TV commercial or a graph showing changes over time) or at a single moment (a photograph, a painting, or a pie chart). Sometimes dialog or a title or caption contributes to the story.

- **Point of view:** The image creator influences responses by taking account of both the viewer's physical relation to the image subject—for instance, whether it is seen head-on or from above—and the viewer's assumed attitude toward the subject.

- **Arrangement:** Patterns among colors or forms, figures in the foreground and background, and elements that are juxtaposed or set apart contribute to the image's meaning and effect.

- **Color:** An image's colors can direct the viewer's attention and convey the creator's attitude toward the subject. Color may also suggest a mood, an era, a cultural connection, or another frame for viewing the image.

- **Characterization:** The figures and objects in an image have certain qualities—sympathetic or not, desirable or not, and so on. Their characteristics reflect the roles they play in the image's story.

- **Context:** The source of an image or the background in an image affects its meaning, whether it is a graph from a scholarly journal or a photo of a car on a sunny beach.

- **Tension:** Images often communicate a problem or seize attention with features that seem wrong, such as misspelled or misaligned words, distorted figures, or controversial relations between characters.

- **Allusions:** An **allusion** is a reference to something the audience is likely to recognize and respond to. Examples include a cultural symbol such as a dollar sign, a mythological figure such as a unicorn, or a familiar movie character such as Darth Vader from *Star Wars*.

Question for analysis

You can focus your analysis of elements by framing your main interest in the image as a question. John Latner posed this question about the *Time* advertisement: *Does the ad challenge readers to view airport security differently, or does it just reinforce common perceptions?* The question led Latner to focus on certain elements of the ad and to ignore others. Here is an entry from his reading journal:

crit

10b

Image elements	Responses
Emphasis	The ad foregrounds the boy (especially his eyes looking upward), the security agent, and the <u>Time</u> cover around a scanner like a target around a bull's-eye.
Point of view	We identify with the boy—so innocent and uncomfortable—and we're positioned at his eye level. The security agent almost hovers over us, too.
Narration	The collision point of the caption ("At what point do national security and common sense collide?") seems to be the bull's-eye—treating a boy as a security threat. The ad's commonsense opinion seems to be that airport security procedures are flawed, unfair. But the caption's question mark and "Join the conversation" imply that there may be other views, too.
Allusions	The familiar <u>Time</u> cover and the security checkpoint stand out. Also, is there Christian symbolism in the boy's outstretched arms, open hands, and upward gaze—like Christ on the cross?
Characterization	The boy is the unlikely terrorist, maybe even a victim. He is the stereotyped all-American kid, blond, blue-eyed, wholesome. The security agent is the boy's "interrogator"—serious, dark, menacing.
Tension	The security agent hovering over the boy is disturbing. So are their actions and the busy scene behind them—bound to evoke a negative response from anyone who's experienced air travel in recent years.

Sample image for analysis

The following image gives you a chance to analyze elements of a Web page. Try to answer the questions in the annotations.

Elements of a Web page

Narration: What story is being told by the Web page as a whole and by the chart? Who is telling the story, and why?

Arrangement: How are the bars in the chart organized? What does their arrangement contribute to the story?

Point of view: What can you tell about the intended audience? What is the audience's interest in the story?

Context: How do the CNN source and the page's banner and titles affect the story being told by the chart?

crit

10b

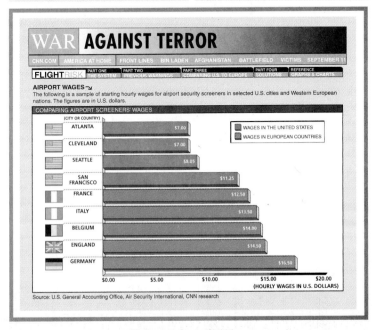

Web page from *CNN.com*

4 • Interpreting an image

The strategies for interpreting an image parallel those for interpreting a written text (pp. 110–11). In this process you look more deeply at the elements, considering them in relation to the image creator's likely assumptions and intentions. You aim to draw reasonable inferences about the image creator's assumptions to explain *why* the image looks as it does. Consider this inference about the *Time* advertisement on page 114:

The creators of the *Time* ad assume that the magazine's readers are concerned about both national security and the treatment of air travelers.

This statement is supported by the ad's text and photograph: the caption specifically mentions national security, and the photograph clearly emphasizes the experience of air travelers.

5 • Synthesizing ideas about an image

As discussed on pages 111–12, with synthesis you take analysis and interpretation a step further to consider how a work's elements and underlying assumptions relate and what the overall message is. You may also expand your synthesis to view the whole image in a larger context: How does the work fit into the context of other works? What cultural, economic, political, or historical forces influence the work?

Placing an image in its context often requires research. For instance, to learn more about the assumptions underlying the *Time* advertisement, John Latner investigated data on the backgrounds and perceptions of the magazine's readers. And to understand the marketing strategies at work in the image, he consulted a book on advertising campaigns that, like the *Time* ad, promote products to people who already use them. The following ideas resulted from his synthesis:

Social and political context

The visual emphasis on the boy plays to two views often held by travelers and Time's readers: airport searches needlessly inconvenience people who are very unlikely to be terrorists, and the better alternative may be profiling, treating people differently based on physical characteristics such as skin and hair color.

"Common sense"

The ad implies certain understandings of readers' "common sense" about national security and airport security: security is a serious issue, many airport procedures are unreasonably broad based and time consuming, and profiling might be used to focus on people who look like terrorists. The ad doesn't challenge these perceptions, but with "Join the conversation" it does suggest that the problem is open to interpretation.

Marketing context

The provocative photograph seems to promise an unconventional perspective on the subject, but the ad mostly reinforces the views assumed to be held by readers. Time's strategy reflects marketing studies: people are more likely to purchase a product that reflects their own opinions and values, even when they're acquiring the product to broaden their understanding.

6 • Evaluating an image

If your critical reading moves on to evaluation, you'll form judgments about the quality and significance of the image: Is the message of the image accurate and fair, or is it distorted and biased? Can you support, refute, or extend the message? Does the image achieve its apparent purpose, and is the purpose worthwhile? How does the image affect you?

You can read John Latner's evaluation of the *Time* advertisement at *ablongman.com/littlebrown*.

crit

10c

EXERCISE 10.5
Viewing an image critically

Review the list of visual elements on page 115 and then take another close look at the *Time* advertisement on page 114. Using the guidelines on the preceding pages, draw your own conclusions about the ad. Write while reading and thinking to help yourself concentrate and develop ideas. A writing suggestion based on this activity appears in Exercise 10.10, page 122.

EXERCISE 10.6
Viewing an image critically

Examine the CNN Web page (p. 117) in more detail. Using the guidelines on the preceding pages, read the image methodically and critically. Write down your ideas. A writing suggestion based on this activity appears in Exercise 10.11, page 122.

EXERCISE 10.7
Viewing an image critically

Look in a magazine or book for an image that interests you. Or search the wide array of images at the Corbis photograph collection (*pro.corbis .com*) or the *WebMuseum* (*ibiblio.org/wm*). Using the approach given on the preceding pages, "read" the image methodically and critically, writing down your responses. A writing suggestion based on this activity appears in Exercise 10.12, page 123.

10c   Write critically.

Critical writing (often called *critique*) builds on the skills of critical reading. It involves shaping your analysis, interpretation, synthesis, and perhaps evaluation of the work into an essay that states and supports an idea (or thesis) about the work. Critical writing is *not* summarizing, or merely reporting what the author says. You may write a summary to clarify the author's meaning for yourself (pp. 96–97), and you may briefly summarize a work in your own larger piece of writing. But in writing critically you must go further.

In the following essay, the student Charlene Robinson writes critically about Thomas Sowell's "Student Loans," the essay appearing on pages 106–07. Robinson received the following assignment:

Form your own critical response to one of the readings assigned so far this term. Then write your response into a well-structured critique of the reading. Feel free to agree or disagree with the author, but do not assume that your readers see the same things in the reading or share your views; be sure to offer evidence of the author's ideas in the form of direct quotations, summaries, and paraphrases. Document any borrowings from the author using the style of the Modern Language Association (MLA). The length should be 500–700 words.

In responding to Sowell's essay, Robinson used a process of critical reading like the one outlined in this chapter, making notes not only on what Sowell says but also on her own questions and ideas. She then focused and organized her ideas, developing her own thesis about Sowell's text, and drafted and revised until she believed she had supported her thesis.

Robinson does not assume that her readers see the same things in Sowell's essay or share her views, so she offers evidence of Sowell's ideas in the form of direct quotations, summaries, and paraphrases (restatements in her own words). (See pp. 460–64 for more on these techniques.) Robinson then documents these borrowings from Sowell using the style of the Modern Language Association (MLA): the numbers in parentheses are page numbers in the book containing Sowell's essay, listed at the end as a "work cited." (See Chapter 56 for more on MLA style.)

Weighing the Costs

Introduction

Summary of Sowell's essay

In his essay "Student Loans," the economist Thomas Sowell challenges the US government's student-loan program for several reasons: a scarce resource (taxpayers' money) goes to many undeserving students, a high number of recipients fail to repay their loans, and the easy availability of money has led to both lower academic standards and higher college tuitions. Sowell wants his readers to "weigh the costs of things" (133) in order to see, as he does, that the loan program should not receive so much government funding. But does he provide the evidence of cost and other problems to lead the reader to agree with him? The answer is no, because hard evidence is less common than debatable and unsupported assumptions about students, scarcity, and the value of education.

Robinson's critical question

Thesis statement

First main point

Sowell's portrait of student-loan recipients is questionable. It is based on averages, some statistical and some not, but averages are often deceptive. For example, Sowell cites college graduates' low average debt of $7000 to $9000 (131) without acknowledging the fact that many students' debts are much higher or giving the full range of statistics. Similarly,

Evidence for first point: paraphrases and quotations from Sowell's text

Sowell dismisses "heart-rending stories" of "the low-income student with a huge debt" as "not at all typical" (132), yet he invents his own exaggerated version of the typical loan recipient: an affluent slacker ("Rockefellers" and "Vanderbilts") for whom college is a "place to hang out for a few years" sponging off the government, while his or her parents clear a profit from making use of the loan program (132). Although such students (and parents) may well exist, are they really typical? Sowell does not offer any data one way or the other—for instance, how many loan recipients come from each income group, what percentage of loan funds go to each group, how many loan recipients receive significant help from their parents, and how many receive none.

Evidence for first point: Sowell's omissions

Another set of assumptions in the essay has to do with "scarcity": "There is never enough of anything to fully satisfy all those who want it," Sowell says (131). This statement appeals to readers' common sense, but does the "lesson" of scarcity necessarily apply to the student-loan program? Sowell omits many important figures needed to prove that the nation's resources are too scarce to support the program, such as the total cost of the program, its percentage of the total education budget and the total federal budget, and its cost compared to the cost of defense, Medicare, and other expensive programs. Moreover, Sowell does not mention the interest paid by loan recipients, even though the interest must offset some of the costs of running the program and covering unpaid loans.

Transition to second main point

Second main point

Evidence for second point: Sowell's omissions

The most fundamental and most debatable assumption underlying Sowell's essay is that higher education is a kind of commodity that not everyone is entitled to. In order to diminish the importance of graduates' average debt from education loans, Sowell claims that a car loan will probably be higher (131). This comparison between education and an automobile implies that the two are somehow equal as products and that an affordable higher education is no more a right than a new car is. Sowell also condemns the "irresponsible" students who drop out of school and "the increasingly easy availability of college to people who are not very serious about getting an education" (132). But he overlooks the value of encouraging education, including education of those who don't finish college or who aren't scholars. For many in the United States, education has a greater value than that of a mere commodity like a car. And even from an economic perspective such as Sowell's, the cost to society of an uneducated public needs to be taken into account.

Third main point

Evidence for third point: paraphrases and quotations from Sowell's text

Conclusion, beginning with acknowledgment of Sowell's concerns	Sowell writes with conviction, and his concerns are valid: high taxes, waste, unfairness, declining educational standards, obtrusive government. However, the essay's flaws make it unlikely that Sowell could convince readers who do not already agree with him. He does not support his
Summary of three main points	portrait of the typical loan recipient, he fails to demonstrate a lack of resources for the loan program, and he neglects the special nature of
Return to theme of introduction: weighing costs	education compared to other services and products. Sowell may have the evidence to back up his assumptions, but by omitting it he himself does not truly weigh the costs of the loan program.

Work Cited

Reference to complete source (in MLA style)	Sowell, Thomas. "Student Loans." <u>Is Reality Optional? and Other Essays.</u> Stanford: Hoover, 1993. 131-33.

—Charlene Robinson (student)

EXERCISE 10.8
Responding to critical writing

Read Charlene Robinson's essay carefully. Do you think the author's critique is accurate and fair? Is it perceptive? Does the author provide enough evidence to convince you of her points? Does she miss anything you would have mentioned? Write your responses to the essay in a brief critique of your own. (You can do this exercise online at *ablongman.com/littlebrown.*)

EXERCISE 10.9
Writing critically about a text

Write an essay based on your own critical reading of Thomas Sowell's "Student Loans" (Exercise 10.4, p. 112). Your critique may be entirely different from Charlene Robinson's, or you may develop some of the same points. If there are similarities, they should be expressed and supported in your own way, in the context of your own critical perspective.

EXERCISE 10.10
Writing critically about an image

Write an essay based on your own critical reading of the *Time* advertisement (Exercise 10.5, p. 119). Your responses may be entirely different from John Latner's, or you may develop some of the same points. If there are similarities, they should be expressed and supported in your own way, in the context of your own critical perspective.

EXERCISE 10.11
Writing critically about an image

Write an essay based on your critical reading of the CNN Web page (Exercise 10.6, p. 119).

EXERCISE 10.12
Writing critically about an image
Write an essay based on your critical response to an image (Exercise 10.7, p. 119). Be sure to use specific descriptions of the image to support your ideas about it.

11 Writing Arguments

How do I make a case for an idea?

Making a case for an idea involves opening readers' minds to your opinion, changing readers' own opinions, or moving readers to action. The method is called **argument:** forming and stating an opinion about a debatable issue, gathering and providing support for your idea, organizing logically, expressing yourself reasonably, and acknowledging views different from your own.

 CULTURE / LANGUAGE The ways of conceiving and writing arguments described here may be initially uncomfortable to you if your native culture approaches such writing differently. In some cultures, for example, a writer is expected to begin indirectly, to avoid asserting his or her opinion outright, to rely for evidence on appeals to tradition, or to establish a compromise rather than argue a position. In American academic and business settings, writers aim for a well-articulated opinion, evidence gathered from many sources, and a direct and concise argument for the opinion.

11a   Use the elements of argument.

In one common view, an argument has four main elements: a subject, claims, evidence, and assumptions. (The last three are adapted from the work of the British philosopher Stephen Toulmin.)

1 • The subject

An argument starts with a subject and often with an opinion about the subject as well—that is, an idea that makes you want to write about the subject. For instance, you might think that your

http://www.ablongman.com/littlebrown

Visit the companion Web site for more help and electronic exercises on argument.

school should do more for energy conservation or that the school's chemistry laboratory is a disgrace. (If you don't have a subject or you aren't sure what you think about it, try some of the invention techniques discussed on pages 10–17.)

Your initial opinion should meet several requirements:

- **It can be disputed:** reasonable people can disagree over it.
- **It *will* be disputed:** it is controversial.
- **It is narrow enough to argue in the space and time available.**

On the flip side of these requirements, some subjects will not work as the starting place of argument because they concern indisputable facts, such as the functions of the human liver; personal preferences or beliefs, such as a moral commitment to vegetarianism; or ideas that few would disagree with, such as the virtues of a secure home.

EXERCISE 11.1
Testing argument subjects

Analyze each subject below to determine whether it is appropriate for argument. Explain your reasoning in each case. (You can do this exercise online at *ablongman.com/littlebrown*.)

1. Granting of athletic scholarships
2. Care of automobile tires
3. Censoring the Web sites of hate groups
4. History of the town park
5. Housing for the homeless
6. Billboards in urban residential areas or in rural areas
7. Animal testing for cosmetics research
8. Cats versus dogs as pets
9. Ten steps in recycling wastepaper
10. Benefits of being a parent

2 • Claims

Claims are statements that require support. In an argument you develop your subject into a central claim or **thesis**, asserted outright as the **thesis statement** (p. 18). This central claim is what the argument is about.

A thesis statement is always an **opinion**—that is, a judgment based on facts and arguable on the basis of facts. It may be one of the following:

- **A claim about past or present reality:**

  In both its space and its equipment, the college's chemistry laboratory is outdated.

Academic cheating increases with students' economic insecurity.

- **A claim of value:**

    The new room fees are unjustified given the condition of the dormitories.

    Computer music pirates undermine the system that encourages the very creation of music.

- **A recommendation for a course of action,** often a solution to a perceived problem:

    The college's outdated chemistry laboratory should be replaced incrementally over the next five years.

    Schools and businesses can help to resolve the region's traffic congestion by implementing car pools and rewarding participants.

The backbone of an argument consists of specific claims that support the thesis statement. These may also be statements of opinion, or they may fall in two other categories:

- **Statements of** *fact,* including facts that are generally known or are verifiable (such as the cost of tuition at your school) and those that can be inferred from verifiable facts (such as the monetary value of a college education).
- **Statements of** *belief,* or convictions based on personal faith or values, such as *The primary goal of government should be to provide equality of opportunity for all.* Although seemingly arguable, a statement of belief is not based on facts and so cannot be contested on the basis of facts.

> **EXERCISE 11.2**
> **Conceiving a thesis statement**
> Narrow each arguable subject in Exercise 11.1 to a specific opinion, and draft a tentative thesis statement for each. Or choose five arguable subjects and opinions of your own, and draft a thesis statement for each one. One thesis statement should interest you enough to develop it into a complete argument in later exercises.

3 • Evidence

You show the validity of your claims by supporting them with **evidence.** The evidence to support the claim opposite about the outdated chemistry lab might include the present lab's age, an inventory of facilities and equipment, and the testimony of chemistry professors.

There are several kinds of evidence:

- **Facts,** statements whose truth can be verified or inferred: *Poland is slightly smaller than New Mexico.*
- **Statistics,** facts expressed as numbers: *Of those polled, 22 percent prefer a flat tax.*
- **Examples,** specific instances of the point being made: *Many groups, such as the elderly and the disabled, would benefit from this policy.*
- **Expert opinions,** the judgments formed by authorities on the basis of their own examination of the facts: *Affirmative action is necessary to right past injustices, a point argued by Howard Glickstein, a past director of the US Commission on Civil Rights.*
- **Appeals to readers' beliefs or needs,** statements that ask readers to accept a claim in part because it states something they already accept as true without evidence: *The shabby, antiquated chemistry lab shames the school, making it seem a second-rate institution.*

arg
11a

Evidence must be reliable to be convincing. Ask these questions about your evidence:

- **Is it accurate**—trustworthy, exact, and undistorted?
- **Is it relevant**—authoritative, pertinent, and current?
- **Is it representative**—true to its context, neither under- nor overrepresenting any element of the sample it's drawn from?
- **Is it adequate**—plentiful and specific?

> **EXERCISE 11.3**
> Using evidence
>
> Gather and develop evidence for the thesis statement you chose to develop in Exercise 11.2. You may want to begin drafting your argument at this point, testing your evidence as you support your claim.

4 • Assumptions

An **assumption** is an opinion, a principle, or a belief that ties evidence to claims: the assumption explains why a particular piece of evidence is relevant to a particular claim. For instance:

> **Claim:** The college's chemistry laboratory is outdated.
> **Evidence** (in part): The testimony of chemistry professors.
> **Assumption:** Chemistry professors are the most capable of evaluating the present lab's quality.

Assumptions are not flaws in arguments but necessities: we all acquire beliefs and opinions that shape our views of the world.

Interpreting a work's assumptions is a significant part of critical reading (see pp. 110–11), and discovering your own assumptions is a significant part of argumentative critical writing. If your readers do not share your assumptions or if they perceive that you are not forthright about your biases, they will be less receptive to your argument. (See the following discussion of reasonableness.)

11b   Write reasonably.

To establish common ground between you and your readers, your argument must be reasonable. Readers expect logical thinking, appropriate appeals, fairness toward the opposition, and, combining all of these, writing that is free of fallacies.

1 • Logical thinking

The thesis of your argument is a conclusion you reach by reasoning about evidence. Two processes of reasoning, induction and deduction, are familiar to you even if you aren't familiar with their names.

Induction

When you're about to buy a used car, you consult friends, relatives, and consumer guides before deciding what kind of car to buy. Using **induction,** or **inductive reasoning,** you make specific observations about cars (your evidence) and you induce, or infer, a **generalization** that Car X is most reliable. The generalization is a claim supported by your observations.

You might also use inductive reasoning in a term paper on print advertising:

Evidence: Advertisements in newspapers and magazines.
Evidence: Comments by advertisers and publishers.
Evidence: Data on the effectiveness of advertising.
Generalization or claim: Print is the most cost-effective medium for advertising.

This reasoning builds from the evidence to the claim, with the assumptions connecting evidence to claim. (See the diagram on the next page.) In this way, inductive reasoning creates new knowledge from what is already known.

When you reason inductively, you connect your evidence to your generalization by assuming that what is true in one set of circumstances (the ads you look at) is true in a similar set of circumstances (other ads). The more evidence you accumulate, the more

Inductive reasoning

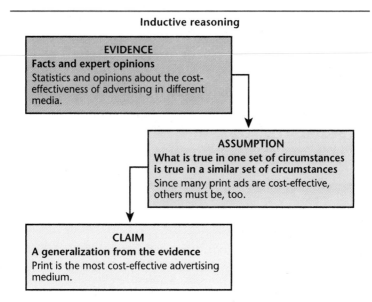

EVIDENCE
Facts and expert opinions
Statistics and opinions about the cost-effectiveness of advertising in different media.

ASSUMPTION
What is true in one set of circumstances is true in a similar set of circumstances
Since many print ads are cost-effective, others must be, too.

CLAIM
A generalization from the evidence
Print is the most cost-effective advertising medium.

probable it is that your generalization is true. Note, however, that absolute certainty is not possible. At some point you must *assume* that your evidence justifies your generalization, for yourself and your readers. Most errors in inductive reasoning involve oversimplifying either the evidence or the generalization. See pages 133–37 on fallacies.

Deduction

You use **deduction**, or **deductive reasoning**, when you proceed from your generalization that Car X is the most reliable used car to your own specific circumstances (you want to buy a used car) to the conclusion that you should buy a Car X. In deduction your assumption is a generalization, principle, or belief that you think is true. You apply it to the evidence (new information) in order to arrive at your claim (the conclusion you draw). The diagram on the facing page corresponds to the one above for induction, picking up the example of print advertising.

The conventional way of displaying a deductive argument is in a **syllogism.** If you want the school administration to postpone new room fees for one dormitory, your deductive argument might be expressed in the following syllogism:

Deductive reasoning

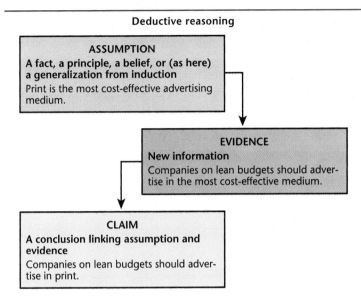

ASSUMPTION
**A fact, a principle, a belief, or (as here)
a generalization from induction**
Print is the most cost-effective advertising
medium.

EVIDENCE
New information
Companies on lean budgets should advertise in the most cost-effective medium.

CLAIM
**A conclusion linking assumption and
evidence**
Companies on lean budgets should advertise in print.

Premise: The administration should not raise fees on dorm rooms in poor condition. [A generalization or belief that you assume to be true.]
Premise: The rooms in Polk Hall are in poor condition. [New information: a specific case of the first premise.]
Conclusion: The administration should not raise fees on the rooms in Polk Hall. [Your claim.]

As long as the premises of a syllogism are true, the conclusion derives logically and certainly from them.

The force of deductive reasoning depends on the reliability of the premises and the care taken to apply them in drawing conclusions. The reasoning process is **valid** if the premises lead logically to the conclusion. It is **true** if the premises are believable. Sometimes the reasoning is true but *not* valid:

Premise: The administration should not raise fees on dorm rooms in bad condition.
Premise: Polk Hall is a dormitory.
Conclusion: The administration should not raise fees on the rooms in Polk Hall.

Both premises may be true, but the first does not *necessarily* apply to the second, so the conclusion is invalid. Sometimes, too, the reasoning is valid but *not* true:

> **Premise:** All college administrations are indifferent to students' needs.
> **Premise:** The administration of Valley College is a college administration.
> **Premise:** The administration of Valley College is indifferent to students' needs.

This syllogism is valid but useless: the first premise is an untrue assumption, so the entire argument is untrue. Invalid and untrue syllogisms underlie many of the logical fallacies discussed on pages 133–37.

A particular hazard of deductive reasoning is the **unstated premise:** the basic assumption linking evidence and conclusion is not stated but implied. Here the unstated premise is believable and the argument is reasonable:

> Ms. Stein has worked with drug addicts for fifteen years, so she knows a great deal about their problems. [Unstated premise: Anyone who has worked fifteen years with drug addicts knows about their problems.]

But when the unstated premise is wrong or unfounded, the argument is false. For example:

> Since Jane Lightbow is a senator, she must receive money illegally from lobbyists. [Unstated premise: All senators receive money illegally from lobbyists.]

2 • Appeals

Rational and emotional appeals

In most arguments you will combine **rational appeals** to readers' capacities for logical reasoning with **emotional appeals** to readers' beliefs and feelings. In the following example, the second sentence makes a rational appeal (to the logic of financial gain), and the third sentence makes an emotional appeal (to the sense of fairness and open-mindedness):

> Advertising should show more physically challenged people. The millions of Americans with disabilities have considerable buying power, yet so far advertisers have made little or no attempt to tap that power. Furthermore, by keeping the physically challenged out of the mainstream depicted in ads, advertisers encourage widespread prejudice against disability, prejudice that frightens and demeans those who hold it.

For an emotional appeal to be successful, it must be appropriate for the audience and the argument:

- It must not misjudge readers' actual feelings.
- It must not raise emotional issues that are irrelevant to the claims and the evidence. See page 135 for a discussion of

specific inappropriate appeals, such as bandwagon and ad hominem.

Ethical appeal

A third kind of approach to readers, the **ethical appeal,** is the sense you give of being a competent, fair person who is worth heeding. A rational appeal and an appropriate emotional appeal contribute to your ethical appeal, and so does your acknowledging opposing views (see below). An argument that is concisely written and correct in grammar, spelling, and other matters will underscore your competence. In addition, a sincere and even tone will assure readers that you are balanced and want to reason with them.

arg

11b

A sincere and even tone need not exclude language with emotional appeal—words such as *frightens* and *demeans* at the end of the example about advertising on the facing page. But avoid certain forms of expression that will mark you as unfair:

- **Insulting words** such as *idiotic* or *fascist.*
- **Biased language** such as *fags* or *broads.* (See pp. 199–201.)
- **Sarcasm**—for instance, using the phrase *What a brilliant idea* to indicate contempt for the idea and its originator.
- **Exclamation points**! They'll make you sound shrill!

3 • Acknowledgment of opposing views

A good test of your fairness in argument is how you handle possible objections. Assuming your thesis is indeed arguable, then others can marshal their own evidence to support a different view or views. You need to determine what these other views are and what evidence supports them. Then, in your argument, you need to take these views on, refute those you can, grant the validity of others, and demonstrate why, despite their validity, the opposing views are less compelling than your own. (See the sample essay on pp. 139–42 for examples.)

Before you draft your essay, list for yourself all the opposing views you can think of. You'll find them in your research, by talking to friends, and by critically thinking about your own ideas. You can also look for a range of views in a discussion group dealing with your subject. (The archive at *groups.yahoo.com* is a place to start.)

To deal with opposing views, figure out which views you can refute (do more research if necessary), and prepare to concede those views you can't refute. It's not a mark of weakness or failure to admit that the opposition has a point or two. Indeed, by showing yourself to be honest and fair, you strengthen your ethical appeal and thus your entire argument.

EXERCISE 11.4
Reasoning inductively

Study the facts below and then evaluate each of the numbered conclusions. Which of the generalizations are reasonable given the evidence, and which are not? Why? Answers to starred items appear at the back of the book. (You can do this exercise online at *ablongman.com/littlebrown*.)

In 2005–06 each American household viewed an average of 50 hours and 12 minutes of television, DVDs, or videos weekly.

Each individual viewed an average of 30 hours and 23 minutes per week.

Those viewing the most television per week (43 hours and 6 minutes) were women over age 55.

Those viewing the least television per week (19 hours and 17 minutes) were children ages 6 to 11.

Households earning under $30,000 a year watched an average of 53 hours and 19 minutes a week.

Households earning more than $60,000 a year watched an average of 48 hours and 7 minutes a week.

*1. Households with incomes under $30,000 tend to watch more television than average.
*2. Women watch more television than men.

3. Nonaffluent people watch less television than affluent people.
4. Women over age 55 tend to watch more television than average.
5. Children watch less television than critics generally assume.

EXERCISE 11.5
Reasoning deductively

Convert each of the following statements into a syllogism. (You may have to state unstated assumptions.) Use the syllogism to evaluate both the validity and the truth of the statement. Answers to starred items appear at the back of the book. (You can do this exercise online at *ablongman.com/littlebrown*.)

Example:

DiSantis is a banker, so he does not care about the poor.

Premise: Bankers do not care about the poor.
Premise: DiSantis is a banker.
Conclusion: Therefore, DiSantis does not care about the poor.

The statement is untrue because the first premise is untrue.

*1. The mayor opposed pollution controls when he was president of a manufacturing company, so he may not support new controls or vigorously enforce existing ones.
*2. Information on corporate Web sites is unreliable because the sites are sponsored by for-profit entities.

3. Schroeder is a good artist because she trained at Parsons, like many other good artists.
4. Wealthy athletes who use their resources to help others deserve our particular appreciation.
5. Jimson is clearly a sexist because she has hired only one woman.

EXERCISE 11.6
Identifying appeals

Identify each passage below as primarily a rational appeal or primarily an emotional appeal. Which passages make a strong ethical appeal as well? Answers to starred items appear at the back of the book. (You can do this exercise online at *ablongman.com/littlebrown*.)

*1. Web surfing may contribute to the global tendency toward breadth rather than depth of knowledge. Using those most essential of skills—pointing and clicking—our brightest minds may now never even hear of, much less read, the works of Aristotle, Shakespeare, and Darwin.
*2. Thus the data collected by these researchers indicate that a mandatory sentence for illegal possession of handguns may lead to reduction in handgun purchases.

3. Most broadcasters worry that further government regulation of television programming could breed censorship—certainly, an undesirable outcome. Yet most broadcasters also accept that children's television is a fair target for regulation.
4. Anyone who cherishes life in all its diversity could not help being appalled by the mistreatment of laboratory animals. The so-called scientists who run the labs are misguided.
5. Many experts in constitutional law have warned that the rule violates the right to free speech. Yet other experts have viewed the rule, however regretfully, as necessary for the good of the community as a whole.

EXERCISE 11.7
Reaching your readers

Continuing your argument-in-progress from Exercise 11.3 (p. 126), analyze whether your claims are rational or emotional and whether the mix is appropriate for your audience and argument. Analyze your ethical appeal, too, considering whether it can be strengthened. Then make a list of possible opposing views. Think freely at first, not stopping to censor views that seem far-fetched or irrational. When your list is complete, decide which views must be taken seriously and why, and develop a response to each.

4 • Fallacies

Fallacies—errors in argument—either evade the issue of the argument or treat the argument as if it were much simpler than it is.

Evasions

An effective argument squarely faces the central issue or question it addresses. An ineffective argument may dodge the issue in one of the following ways:

- **Begging the question:** treating an opinion that is open to question as if it were already proved or disproved. In essence, the writer begs readers to accept his or her claim from the start.

  The college library's expenses should be reduced by cutting subscriptions to useless periodicals. [Begged questions: Are some of the library's periodicals useless? Useless to whom?]

  The fact is that political financing is too corrupt to be reformed. [Begged questions: How corrupt is political financing? Does corruption, even if extensive, put the system beyond reform?]

- **Non sequitur** (Latin: "It does not follow"): linking two or more ideas that are not necessarily connected.

  She uses a wheelchair, so she must be unhappy. [The second clause does not follow from the first.]

  Kathleen Newsome has my vote for mayor because she has the best-run campaign organization. [Shouldn't one's vote be based on the candidate's qualities, not the campaign's organization?]

- **Red herring:** introducing an irrelevant issue intended to distract readers from the relevant issues. (A red herring is a kind of fish that might be used to distract a dog from a scent.)

  A campus speech code is essential to protect students, who already have enough problems coping with rising tuition. [Tuition costs and speech codes are different subjects. What protections do students need that a speech code will provide?]

  Instead of developing a campus speech code that will infringe on students' First Amendment rights, administrators should be figuring out how to prevent another tuition increase. [Again, tuition costs and speech codes are different subjects. How would the code infringe on rights?]

- **False authority:** citing as an expert someone whose expertise is doubtful or nonexistent.

  Jason Bing, a recognized expert in corporate finance, maintains that pharmaceutical companies do not test their products thoroughly enough. [Bing's expertise in corporate finance bears no apparent relation to the testing of pharmaceuticals.]

  According to Helen Liebowitz, the Food and Drug Administration has approved sixty dangerous drugs in the last two years alone. [Who is Helen Liebowitz? On what authority does she make this claim?]

- **Appeal to readers' fear or pity:** substituting emotions for reasoning.

  By electing Susan Clark to the city council, you will prevent the city's economic collapse. [Trades on people's fears. Can Clark singlehandedly prevent economic collapse? Is collapse even likely?]

  She should not have to pay taxes, because she is an aged widow with no friends or relatives. [Appeals to people's pity. Should age and loneliness, rather than income, determine a person's tax obligation?]

- **Snob appeal:** inviting readers to accept an assertion in order to be identified with others they admire.

  Tiger Woods has an account at Big City Bank, and so should you. [A celebrity's endorsement of course does not automatically guarantee the worth of a product, a service, an idea, or anything else.]

- **Bandwagon:** inviting readers to accept a claim because everyone else does.

  As everyone knows, marijuana use leads to heroin addiction. [What is the evidence?]

- **Ad populum** (Latin: "to the people"): asking readers to accept a conclusion based on shared values or even prejudices and nothing else.

  Any truly patriotic American will support the President's action. [But why is the action worth taking?]

- **Ad hominem** (Latin: "to the man"): attacking the qualities of the people holding an opposing view rather than the substance of the view itself.

  One of the scientists has been treated for emotional problems, so his pessimism about nuclear waste merits no attention. [Do the scientist's previous emotional problems invalidate his current views?]

Oversimplifications

In a vain attempt to create something neatly convincing, an ineffective argument may conceal or ignore complexities in one of the following ways:

- **Hasty generalization:** making a claim on the basis of inadequate evidence.

  It is disturbing that several of the youths who shot up schools were users of violent video games. Obviously, these games can breed violence, and they should be banned. [A few cases do not establish the relation between the games and violent behavior. Most youths who play violent video games do not behave violently.]

From the way it handled this complaint, we can assume that the consumer protection office has little intention of protecting consumers. [One experience with the office does not demonstrate its intention or overall performance.]

- **Sweeping generalization:** making an insupportable statement. Many sweeping generalizations are **absolute statements** involving words such as *all, always, never,* and *no one* that allow no exceptions. Others are **stereotypes,** conventional and oversimplified characterizations of a group of people:

People who live in cities are unfriendly.
Californians are fad-crazy.
Women are emotional.
Men can't express their feelings.

(See also pp. 199–201 on sexist and other biased language.)

- **Reductive fallacy:** oversimplifying (reducing) the relation between causes and effects.

Poverty causes crime. [If so, then why do people who are not poor commit crimes? And why aren't all poor people criminals?]

The better a school's athletic facilities are, the worse its academic programs are. [The sentence assumes a direct cause-and-effect link between athletics and scholarship.]

- **Post hoc fallacy** (from Latin *post hoc, ergo propter hoc,* meaning "after this, therefore because of this"): assuming that because *A* preceded *B,* then *A* must have caused *B.*

In the two months since he took office, Mayor Holcomb has allowed crime in the city to increase 12 percent. [The increase in crime is probably attributable to conditions existing before Holcomb took office.]

The town council erred in permitting the adult bookstore to open, for shortly afterward two women were assaulted. [It cannot be assumed without evidence that the women's assailants visited or were influenced by the bookstore.]

- **Either/or fallacy:** assuming that a complicated question has only two answers—one good and one bad, both good, or both bad.

City police officers are either brutal or corrupt. [Most city police officers are neither.]

Either we permit mandatory drug testing in the workplace or productivity will continue to decline. [Productivity is not necessarily dependent on drug testing.]

- **False analogy:** assuming that because two things are alike in one respect, they are *necessarily* alike in other respects as well. Analogy can be useful in argument when the similarities are reasonable. For instance, the "war on drugs" equates a battle against a foe with a program to eradicate (or at least reduce) sales and use of illegal drugs: both involve an enemy, a desired goal, officials in uniform, and other features. But the following passage takes this analogy to a false extreme:

arg
11b

> To win the war on drugs, we must wage more of a military-style operation. Prisoners of war are locked up without the benefit of a trial by jury, and drug dealers should be, too. Soldiers shoot their enemy on sight, and officials who encounter big drug operators should be allowed to shoot them, too. Military traitors may be executed, and corrupt law enforcers could be, too.

EXERCISE 11.8
Identifying and revising fallacies

Identify at least one fallacy illustrated by each of the following sentences. Then revise the sentence to make it more reasonable. Possible answers to starred items appear at the back of the book. (You can do this exercise online at *ablongman.com/littlebrown*.)

*1. A successful marriage demands a maturity that no one under twenty-five possesses.
*2. Students' persistent complaints about the grading system prove that it is unfair.
*3. The United States got involved in World War II because the Japanese bombed Pearl Harbor.
*4. People watch television because they are too lazy to talk or read or because they want mindless escape from their lives.
*5. Racial tension is bound to occur when people with different backgrounds are forced to live side by side.

6. Emerging nations should not be allowed to use nuclear technology for creating energy because eventually they will use it to wage war.
7. Mountain climbing has more lasting effects than many people think: my cousin blacked out three times after he climbed Pikes Peak.
8. Failing to promote democracy throughout the Middle East will lose the region forever to American influence.
9. She admits to being an atheist, so how could she be a good philosophy teacher?
10. Teenagers are too young to be encouraged to use contraceptives.

EXERCISE 11.9
Analyzing advertisements

Leaf through a magazine or watch commercial television for half an hour, looking for advertisements that attempt to sell a product not on the basis of its worth but by snob appeal, flattery, or other inappropriate appeals to emotions. Be prepared to discuss the advertisers' techniques.

> EXERCISE 11.10
> Identifying fallacies online
>
> At *groups.yahoo.com,* find a conversation about drug testing in the work-place, environmental pollution, violence in the media, or any other de-batable subject that interests you. Read through the arguments, listing any fallacious statements as well as the types of fallacies they illustrate. Keep in mind that a given statement may illustrate more than a single type.

11c Organize your argument effectively.

All arguments include the same parts:

- **The *introduction* establishes the significance of the subject and provides background.** The introduction generally includes the thesis statement, but the statement may come later if you think readers will have difficulty accepting it before they see at least some support. (See pp. 66–68 for more on introductions.)
- **The *body* states and develops the claims supporting the thesis,** with each claim taking one or more paragraphs. See below.
- **The *response to opposing views* details and addresses those views,** either demonstrating your argument's greater strengths or conceding the opponents' points. See below.
- **The *conclusion* completes the argument,** restating the thesis, summarizing the supporting claims, and making a final appeal to readers. (See pp. 68–69 for more on conclusions.)

The structure of the body and the response to opposing views depends on your subject, purpose, audience, and form of reasoning. Here are several possible arrangements:

The traditional scheme	The problem-solution scheme
Claim 1 and evidence	The problem: claims and evidence
Claim 2 and evidence	The solution: claims and evidence
Claim X and evidence	Response to opposing views
Response to opposing views	

Variations on the traditional scheme

Use a variation if you believe your readers will reject your argument with-out an early or intermittent response to opposing views.

Response to opposing views	Claim 1 and evidence
Claim 1 and evidence	Response to opposing views
Claim 2 and evidence	Claim 2 and evidence
Claim X and evidence	Response to opposing views
	Claim X and evidence
	Response to opposing views

EXERCISE 11.11
Organizing your argument

Continuing from Exercise 11.7 (p. 133), develop a structure for your argument. Consider especially how you will introduce it, how you will arrange your claims, where you will place your responses to opposing views, and how you will conclude.

11d   A sample argument

Craig Holbrook, a student, wrote an argument in response to the following assignment:

Select an issue that can be argued, that you care about, and that you know something about through experience, reading, Web surfing, and so on. As you plan and draft your argument, keep the following in mind:

Narrow and shape your subject into a specific thesis statement.

Gather and use evidence to support your claim.

Be aware of assumptions you are making.

Present your claims and evidence reasonably, attempting to establish common ground with your readers.

Acknowledge and try to refute opposing views.

Organize your argument paper straightforwardly and appropriately for your purpose.

The paper should be 900–1200 words in length.

Holbrook's response to this assignment illustrates the principles discussed in this chapter. Note especially the structure, the relation of claims and supporting evidence, the kinds of appeals the author makes, and the ways he addresses opposing views.

TV Can Be Good for You

Television wastes time, pollutes minds, destroys brain cells, and turns some viewers into murderers. Thus runs the prevailing talk about the medium, supported by serious research as well as simple belief. But television has at least one strong virtue, too, which helps to explain its endurance as a cultural force. It provides replacement voices that ease loneliness, spark healthful laughter, and even educate young children.

Most people who have lived alone understand the curse of silence, when the only sound is the buzz of unhappiness or anxiety inside one's own head. Although people of all ages who live alone can experience intense loneliness, the elderly are especially

Introduction

Identification of prevailing view

Disagreement with prevailing view

Thesis statement making three claims for television

Background for claim 1: effects of loneliness

vulnerable to solitude. For example, they may suffer increased confusion or depression when left alone for long periods but then rebound when they have steady companionship (Bondevik and Skogstad 329-30).

A study of elderly men and women in New Zealand found that television can actually serve as a companion by assuming "the role of social contact with the wider world," reducing "feelings of isolation and loneliness because it directs viewers' attention away from themselves" ("Television Programming"). Thus television's replacement voices can provide comfort because they distract from a focus on being alone.

The absence of real voices can be most damaging when it means a lack of laughter. Here, too, research shows that television can have a positive effect on health. Laughter is one of the most powerful calming forces available to human beings, proven in many studies to reduce heart rate, lower blood pressure, and ease other stress-related ailments (Burroughs, Mahoney, and Lippman 172; Griffiths 18). Television offers plenty of laughter: the recent listings for a single Friday night included more than twenty comedy programs running on the networks and on basic cable.

A study reported in a health magazine found that laughter inspired by television and video is as healthful as the laughter generated by live comedy. Volunteers laughing at a video comedy routine "showed significant improvements in several immune functions, such as natural killer-cell activity" (Laliberte 78). Further, the effects of the comedy were so profound that "merely anticipating watching a funny video improved mood, depression, and anger as much as two days beforehand" (Laliberte 79). Even for people with plenty of companionship, television's replacement voices can have healthful effects by causing laughter.

Television also provides information about the world. This service can be helpful to everyone but especially to children, whose natural curiosity can exhaust the knowledge and patience of their parents and caretakers. While the TV may be baby-sitting children, it can also enrich them. For example, educational programs such as those on the Discovery Channel, the Disney Channel, and PBS offer a steady stream of information at various cognitive levels. Even

---

Marginal annotations:

Evidence for effects of loneliness

Evidence for effects of television on loneliness

Statement of claim 1

Background for claim 2: effects of laughter

Evidence for effects of laughter

Evidence for comedy on television

Evidence for effects of laughter in response to television

Statement of claim 2

Background for claim 3: educational effects

Evidence for educational programming on television

many cartoons, which are generally dismissed as mindless or worse, familiarize children with the material of literature, including strong characters enacting classic narratives.

Two researchers studying children and television found that TV is a source of creative and psychological instruction, inspiring children "to play imaginatively and develop confidence and skills" (Colman and Colman 9). Instead of passively watching, children "interact with the programs and videos" and "sometimes include the fictional characters in reality's play time" (Colman and Colman 8). Thus television's voices both inform young viewers and encourage exchange.

Evidence for educational effects of television on children

Statement of claim 3

The value of these replacement voices should not be oversold. For one thing, almost everyone agrees that too much TV does no one any good and may cause much harm. Many studies show that excessive TV watching increases violent behavior, especially in children, and can cause, rather than ease, other antisocial behaviors (Reeks 114; Walsh 34). In addition, human beings require the give and take of actual interaction. Steven Pinker, an expert in children's language acquisition, warns that children cannot develop language properly by watching television. They need to interact with actual speakers who respond directly to their needs (282). Replacement voices are not real voices and in the end can do only limited good.

Anticipation of objection: harm of television

Anticipation of objection: need for actual interaction

Qualification of claims in response to objections

But even limited good is something, especially for those who are lonely or neglected. Television is not an entirely positive force, but neither is it an entirely negative one. Its voices stand by to provide company, laughter, and information whenever they're needed.

Conclusion

Works Cited

Bondevik, Margareth, and Anders Skogstad. "The Oldest Old, ADL, Social Network, and Loneliness." Western Journal of Nursing Research 20.3 (1998): 325-43.

Burroughs, W. Jeffrey, Diana L. Mahoney, and Louis G. Lippman. "Attributes of Health-Promoting Laughter: Cross-Generational Comparison." Journal of Psychology 136.2 (2004): 171-81.

Colman, Robyn, and Adrian Colman. "Inspirational Television." Youth Studies in Australia 21.3 (2003): 8-10.

Griffiths, Joan. "The Mirthful Brain." Omni Aug. 1996: 18-19.

Laliberte, Richard W. "The Benefits of Laughter." Shape Sept. 2003: 78-79.

Pinker, Steven. The Language Instinct: How the Mind Creates Language. New York: Harper, 1994.

Reeks, Anne. "Kids and TV: A Guide." Parenting Apr. 2005: 110-15.

"Television Programming for Older People: Summary Research Report." NZ on Air. 25 July 2004. 15 Oct. 2005 <http://www.nzonair.gov.nz/media/oldpeoplesreport.pdf>.

Walsh, Teri. "Too Much TV Linked to Depression." Prevention Feb. 2001: 34-36.

—Craig Holbrook (student)

12 Reading and Writing About Literature

By Sylvan Barnet

What's involved in analyzing a story, poem, or other literary work?

Writers of literature—stories, novels, poems, and plays—are concerned with presenting human experience concretely, with giving a sense of the feel of life rather than telling about it. Reading and writing about literature thus require extremely close attention to the feel of the words. For instance, the word *woods* in Robert Frost's "Stopping by Woods on a Snowy Evening" has a rural, folksy quality that *forest* doesn't have, and many such small distinctions contribute to the poem's effect.

When you read literature, you interpret distinctions like these, forming an idea of the work. When you write about literature, you state your idea as your thesis, and you support the thesis with evidence from the work. (See pp. 18–20 for more on thesis statements.)

Note Writing about literature is not merely summarizing literature. Your thesis is a claim about the meaning or effect of the literary work, not a statement of its plot. And your paper is a demonstration of your thesis, not a retelling of the work's changes or events.

http://www.ablongman.com/littlebrown ▶

Visit the companion Web site for more help with reading and writing about literature.

12a Write while reading literature.

You will become more engaged in reading literature if you write while you read. If you own the book you're reading, don't hesitate to underline or highlight passages that especially interest you. Don't hesitate to annotate the margins, indicating your pleasures, displeasures, and uncertainties with remarks such as *Nice detail* or *Do we need this long description?* or *Not believable.* If you don't own the book, make these notes on separate sheets or on your computer.

An effective way to interact with a text is to keep a **reading journal.** A journal is not a diary in which you record your doings; instead, it is a place to develop and store your reflections on what you read, such as an answer to a question you may have posed in the margin of the text or a response to something said in class. You may, for instance, want to reflect on why your opinion is so different from that of another student. You may even make an entry in the form of a letter to the author or from one character to another. (See p. 10 for more on journal keeping.)

12b

12b Read literature critically.

Reading literature critically involves interacting with a text, not in order to make negative judgments but in order to understand the work and evaluate its significance or quality. Such interaction is not passive, like scanning a newspaper or watching television. Instead, it is a process of engagement, of diving into the words themselves.

1 • Meaning in literature

In analyzing any literary work, you face right off the question of *meaning.* Readers disagree all the time over the meanings of works of literature, partly because literature *shows* rather than *tells:* it gives concrete images of imagined human experiences, but it usually does not say how we ought to understand the images. Further, readers bring different experiences to their reading and thus understand images differently. In writing about literature, then, we can offer only our *interpretation* of the meaning rather than *the* meaning. Still, most people agree that there are limits to interpretation: it must be supported by evidence that a reasonable person finds at least plausible if not totally convincing.

2 • Questions for literary analysis

One reason interpretations of meaning differ is that readers approach literary works differently, focusing on certain elements and interpreting those elements distinctively. For instance, some critics look at a literary work mainly as an artifact of the particular time and culture in which it was created, while other critics stress the work's effect on its readers.

This chapter emphasizes so-called formalist criticism, which sees a literary work primarily as something to be understood in itself. This critical framework engages the reader immediately in the work of literature, without requiring extensive historical or cultural background, and it introduces the conventional elements of literature that all critical approaches discuss, even though they view the elements differently. The list below poses questions for each element that can help you think constructively and imaginatively about what you read.

12b

- *Plot:* **the relationships and patterns of events.** Even a poem has a plot—for instance, a change in mood from grief to resignation.

  What actions happen?
  What conflicts occur?
  How do the events connect to each other and to the whole?

- *Characters:* **the people the author creates,** including the narrator of a story or the speaker of a poem.

  Who are the principal people in the work?
  How do they interact?
  What do their actions, words, and thoughts reveal about their personalities and the personalities of others?
  Do the characters stay the same, or do they change? Why?

- *Point of view:* **the perspective or attitude of the speaker in a poem or the voice who tells a story.** The point of view may be **first person** (a participant, using *I*) or **third person** (an outsider, using *he, she, it, they*). A first-person narrator may be a major or a minor character in the narrative and may be **reliable** or **unreliable** (unable to report events wholly or accurately). A third-person narrator may be **omniscient** (knows what goes on in all characters' minds), **limited** (knows what goes on in the mind of only one or two characters), or **objective** (knows only what is external to the characters).

  Who is the narrator (or the speaker of a poem)?
  How does the narrator's point of view affect the narrative?

- *Tone:* **the narrator's or speaker's attitude,** perceived through the words (for instance, joyful, bitter, or confident).

  What tone (or tones) do you hear? If there is a change, how do you account for it?

Is there an ironic contrast between the narrator's tone (for instance, confidence) and what you take to be the author's attitude (for instance, pity for human overconfidence)?

- *Imagery:* **word pictures or details involving the senses of sight, sound, touch, smell, taste.**

  What images does the writer use? What senses do they draw on?
  What patterns are evident in the images (for instance, religious or commercial images)?
  What is the significance of the imagery?

- *Symbolism:* **concrete things standing for larger and more abstract ideas.** For instance, the American flag may symbolize freedom, or a dead flower may symbolize mortality.

  What symbols does the author use? What do they seem to signify?
  How does the symbolism relate to the theme of the work?

- *Setting:* **the place where the action happens.**

  What does the locale contribute to the work?
  Are scene shifts significant?

- *Form:* **the shape or structure of the work.**

  What *is* the form? (For example, a story might divide sharply in the middle, moving from happiness to sorrow.)
  What parts of the work does the form emphasize, and why?

- *Theme:* **the central idea, a conception of human experience suggested by the work as a whole.** Theme is neither plot (what happens) nor subject (such as youth or marriage). Rather it is what the author says with that plot about that subject.

  Can you state the theme in a sentence? For instance, you might state the following about Kate Chopin's "The Story of an Hour" (p. 147): *Happiness depends partly on freedom.*
  Do certain words, passages of dialog or description, or situations seem to represent the theme most clearly?
  How do the work's elements combine to develop the theme?

- *Appeal:* **the degree to which the work pleases you.**

  What do you especially like or dislike about the work? Why?
  Do you think your responses are unique, or would they be common to most readers? Why?

12c   Two literary works and sample papers

Pages 147–52 reprint two works of literature (a short story and a poem) along with a student paper on each work. In the student papers, each author develops a thesis about the work, supporting this main idea with quotations, paraphrases, and summaries from the work being discussed, a primary source. In the second paper (p. 151), the author also draws sparingly on secondary sources (other critics' views), which further support his own views.

Note the following features of the students' papers:

- **The writers do not merely summarize the literary works they write about.** Occasionally, they briefly summarize to make their meaning clear, but their essays consist mostly of their own analysis.
- **Each writer uses many quotations from the literary work.** The quotations provide evidence for the writer's ideas and let readers hear the voice of the work.
- **Both writers integrate quotations smoothly into their own sentences.** See pages 465–69.
- **The writers use the present tense of verbs** (*Chopin shows*; *Mrs. Mallard dies*) to describe both the author's work and the action in the work.

For the format of a literature paper, consult several other sections of this handbook:

- **Use MLA document format** for treatment of margins, quotations, and other elements (pp. 521–24).
- **Cite sources in MLA style:** parenthetical text citations and a list of works cited (pp. 481–520).
- **Indicate any editing of quotations.** Use ellipsis marks (. . .) to indicate deletions from quotations (pp. 481–520). Use brackets to indicate additions to or changes in quotations (p. 388).

⌐ Key terms ─────────────────────────────────

quotation An exact repetition of an author's words, placed in quotation marks. (See also pp. 379, 463–64.)

paraphrase A restatement of an author's words, closely following the author's line of thought but using different words and sentence structures. (See also pp. 461–62.)

summary A condensation of an extended passage into a sentence or more. (See also pp. 96–97, 460–61.)

primary source A firsthand account: for instance, a historical document, a work of literature, or your own observations. (See also p. 421.)

secondary source A report on or analysis of other sources, often primary ones: for instance, a historian's account of a battle or a critic's view of a poem. (See also p. 421.)

1 • A short story and an essay about it

Short story

Kate Chopin

The Story of an Hour

Knowing that Mrs. Mallard was afflicted with a heart trouble, great care was taken to break to her as gently as possible the news of her husband's death.

It was her sister Josephine who told her, in broken sentences, veiled hints that revealed in half concealing. Her husband's friend Richards was there, too, near her. It was he who had been in the news-paper office when intelligence of the railroad disaster was received, with Brently Mallard's name leading the list of "killed." He had only taken the time to assure himself of its truth by a second telegram, and had hastened to forestall any less careful, less tender friend in bearing the sad message.

She did not hear the story as many women have heard the same, with a paralyzed inability to accept its significance. She wept at once with sudden, wild abandonment, in her sister's arms. When the storm of grief had spent itself she went away to her room alone. She would have no one follow her.

There stood, facing the open window, a comfortable, roomy arm-chair. Into this she sank, pressed down by a physical exhaustion that haunted her body and seemed to reach into her soul.

She could see in the open square before her house the tops of trees that were all aquiver with the new spring life. The delicious breath of rain was in the air. In the street below a peddler was crying his wares. The notes of a distant song which some one was singing reached her faintly, and countless sparrows were twittering in the eaves.

There were patches of blue sky showing here and there through the clouds that had met and piled one above the other in the west facing her window.

She sat with her head thrown back upon the cushion of the chair quite motionless, except when a sob came up into her throat and shook her, as a child who has cried itself to sleep continues to sob in its dreams.

She was young, with a fair, calm face, whose lines bespoke repres-sion and even a certain strength. But now there was a dull stare in her eyes, whose gaze was fixed away off yonder on one of those patches of blue sky. It was not a glance of reflection, but rather indicated a suspen-sion of intelligent thought.

There was something coming to her and she was waiting for it, fearfully. What was it? She did not know; it was too subtle and elusive to name. But she felt it creeping out of the sky, reaching toward her through the sounds, the scents, the color that filled the air.

Now her bosom rose and fell tumultuously. She was beginning to recognize this thing that was approaching to possess her, and she was striving to beat it back with her will—as powerless as her two white slender hands would have been.

When she abandoned herself a little whispered word escaped her slightly parted lips. She said it over and over under her breath: "Free, free, free!" The vacant stare and the look of terror that had followed it went from her eyes. They stayed keen and bright. Her pulses beat fast, and the coursing blood warmed and relaxed every inch of her body.

She did not stop to ask if it were not a monstrous joy that held her. A clear and exalted perception enabled her to dismiss the suggestion as trivial.

She knew that she would weep again when she saw the kind, tender hands folded in death; the face that had never looked save with love upon her, fixed and gray and dead. But she saw beyond that bitter moment a long procession of years to come that would belong to her absolutely. And she opened and spread her arms out to them in welcome.

There would be no one to live for her during those coming years; she would live for herself. There would be no powerful will bending her in the blind persistence with which men and women believe they have a right to impose a private will upon a fellow creature. A kind intention or a cruel intention made the act seem no less a crime as she looked upon it in that brief moment of illumination.

And yet she had loved him—sometimes. Often she had not. What did it matter! What could love, the unsolved mystery, count for in face of this possession of self-assertion which she suddenly recognized as the strongest impulse of her being.

"Free! Body and soul free!" she kept whispering.

Josephine was kneeling before the closed door with her lips to the keyhole, imploring for admission. "Louise, open the door! I beg; open the door—you will make yourself ill. What are you doing, Louise? For heaven's sake open the door."

"Go away. I am not making myself ill." No; she was drinking in the very elixir of life through that open window.

Her fancy was running riot along those days ahead of her. Spring days, and summer days, and all sorts of days that would be her own. She breathed a quick prayer that life might be long. It was only yesterday she had thought with a shudder that life might be long.

She arose at length and opened the door to her sister's importunities. There was a feverish triumph in her eyes, and she carried herself unwittingly like a goddess of Victory. She clasped her sister's waist and together they descended the stairs. Richards stood waiting for them at the bottom.

Some one was opening the front door with a latchkey. It was Brently Mallard who entered, a little travel-stained, composedly carrying his grip-sack and umbrella. He had been far from the scene of accident, and did not even know there had been one. He stood amazed at Josephine's piercing cry; at Richards' quick motion to screen him from the view of his wife.

But Richards was too late.

When the doctors came they said she had died of heart disease—of joy that kills.

An essay on fiction (no secondary sources)

Note The parenthetical citations in the following essay refer to page numbers in the source cited at the end of the essay.

Janet Vong

Mr. Romano

English 102

20 November 2006

Ironies of Life in Kate Chopin's

"The Story of an Hour"

Kate Chopin's "The Story of an Hour"—which takes only a few minutes to read—has an ironic ending: Mrs. Mallard dies just when she is beginning to live. On first reading, the ending seems almost too ironic for belief. On rereading the story, however, one sees that the ending is believable partly because it is consistent with other ironies in the story.

Irony appears at the very start of the story. Because Mrs. Mallard's friends and her sister assume, mistakenly, that she was deeply in love with her husband, Brently Mallard, they take great care to tell her gently of his death. They mean well, and in fact they do well, bringing her an hour of life, an hour of joyous freedom, but it is ironic that they think their news is sad. True, Mrs. Mallard at first expresses grief when she hears the news, but soon (unknown to her friends) she finds joy in it. So Richards's "sad message" (23), though sad in Richards's eyes, is in fact a happy message.

Among the small but significant ironic details is the statement near the end of the story that when Mallard enters the house, Richards tries to conceal him from Mrs. Mallard, but Richards is "too late" (24). Almost at the start of the story, in the second paragraph, Richards has "hastened" (23) to bring his sad news. But if Richards had arrived "too late" at the start, Brently Mallard would have arrived at home first, and Mrs. Mallard's life would not end an hour later but would simply go on as before. Yet another irony at the end of the story is the diagnosis of the doctors. They say she died of "heart disease—of joy that kills" (24). In one sense they are right: Mrs. Mallard has for the last hour experienced a great joy. But of course the doctors totally misunderstand the joy that kills her. It is not joy at seeing her husband alive, but her realization that the great joy she experienced during the last hour is over.

All of these ironic details add richness to the story, but the central irony resides not in the well-intentioned but ironic actions of Richards, or in the unconsciously ironic words of the doctors, but in Mrs. Mallard's own life. She "sometimes" (24) loved her husband, but in a way she has been dead, a body subjected to her husband's will. Now, his apparent death brings her new life. Appropriately, this new life comes to her at the season of the year when "the tops of trees . . . were all aquiver with the new spring life" (24). But, ironically, her new life will last only an hour. She is "Free, free, free" (24), but only until her husband walks through the doorway. She looks forward to "summer days" (24), but she will not see even the end of this spring day. If her years of marriage were ironic, bringing her a sort of living death instead of joy, her new life is ironic too, not only because it grows out of her moment of grief for her supposedly dead husband, but also because her vision of "a long procession of years" (24) is cut short within an hour on a spring day.

[New page.]

Work Cited

Chopin, Kate. "The Story of an Hour." An Introduction to Literature: Fiction, Poetry, and Drama. Ed. Sylvan Barnet, William Burto, and William E. Cain. 13th ed. New York: Longman, 2004. 23-24.

2 • A poem and an essay about it

Poem

Gwendolyn Brooks

The Bean Eaters

They eat beans mostly, this old yellow pair.
Dinner is a casual affair.
Plain chipware on a plain and creaking wood,
Tin flatware.

Two who are Mostly Good.   5
Two who have lived their day,
But keep on putting on their clothes
And putting things away.

And remembering . . .
Remembering, with twinklings and twinges,   10
As they lean over the beans in their rented back room that
    is full of beads and receipts and dolls and cloths,
    tobacco crumbs, vases and fringes.

An essay on poetry (with secondary sources)

Note The parenthetical citations in the following essay refer either to lines of Brooks's poem or to pages in the secondary sources cited at the end of the essay. We know which is which from the context and from the word *line* in the first citation in the second paragraph.

Kenneth Scheff

Professor MacGregor

English 101A

7 December 2006

Marking Time Versus Enduring in

Gwendolyn Brooks's "The Bean Eaters"

Gwendolyn Brooks's poem "The Bean Eaters" runs only eleven lines. It is
written in plain language about very plain people. Yet its meaning is ambiguous. One
critic, George E. Kent, says the old couple who eat beans "have had their day and
exist now as time-markers" (141). However, another reader, D. H. Melhem, perceives
not so much time marking as "endurance" in the old couple (123). Is this poem a
despairing picture of old age or a more positive portrait?

"The Bean Eaters" describes an "old yellow pair" who "eat beans mostly" (line 1)
off "Plain chipware" (3) with "Tin flatware" (4) in "their rented back room" (11).
Clearly, they are poor. They live alone, not with friends or relatives—children or
grandchildren are not mentioned—but with memories and a few possessions (9–11).
They are "Mostly Good" (5), words Brooks capitalizes at the end of a line, perhaps to
stress the old people's adherence to traditional values as well as their lack of
saintliness. They are unexceptional.

The isolated routine of the couple's life is something Brooks draws attention to
with a separate stanza:

> Two who are Mostly Good.
>
> Two who have lived their day,
>
> But keep on putting on their clothes
>
> And putting things away. (5-8)

Brooks emphasizes how isolated the couple is by repeating "Two who." Then she
emphasizes how routine their life is by repeating "putting."

A pessimistic reading of this poem seems justified. The critic Harry B. Shaw
reads the lines just quoted as perhaps despairing: "they are putting things away as if
winding down an operation and readying for withdrawal from activity" (80). However,
Shaw observes, the word <u>But</u> also indicates that the couple resist slipping away, that
they intend to hold on (80). This dual meaning is at the heart of Brooks's poem: the
old people live a meager existence, yes, but their will, their self-control, and their
connection with another person—their essential humanity—are unharmed.

The truly positive nature of the poem is revealed in the last stanza. In Brooks's
words, the old couple remembers with some "twinges" perhaps, but also with
"twinklings" (10), a cheerful image. As Melhem says, these people are "strong in
mutual affection and shared memories" (123). And the final line, which is much

12c

longer than all the rest and which catalogs the evidence of the couple's long life together, is almost musically affirmative: "As they lean over the beans in their rented back room that is full of beads and receipts and dolls and cloths, tobacco crumbs, vases and fringes" (11).

What these people have is not much, but it is something.

[New page.]

Works Cited

Brooks, Gwendolyn. "The Bean Eaters." An Introduction to Literature: Fiction, Poetry, and Drama. Ed. Sylvan Barnet, William Burto, and William E. Cain. 13th ed. New York: Longman, 2004. 807.

Kent, George E. A Life of Gwendolyn Brooks. Lexington: UP of Kentucky, 1990.

Melhem, D. H. Gwendolyn Brooks: Poetry and the Heroic Voice. Lexington: UP of Kentucky, 1987.

Shaw, Harry B. Gwendolyn Brooks. Twayne's United States Authors Ser. 395. Boston: Twayne, 1980.

13   Public Writing

How can I communicate effectively in business letters, Web pages, and other writing outside of school?

Writing to members of the public outside of school resembles academic writing in many ways. It usually involves the same basic writing process, discussed on pages 2–45: assessing the writing situation, developing what you want to say, freely working out your meaning in a draft, and editing and revising so that your writing will achieve your purpose with readers. It often involves research, as discussed on pages 416–79. And it involves the standards of conciseness, appropriate and exact language, and correct grammar and usage discussed in Chapters 15–50.

But public writing has its own conventions, too, depending on what you're writing and why. This chapter covers several types of public writing: business letters and résumés (opposite), memos (p. 158),

http://www.ablongman.com/littlebrown ▶

Visit the companion Web site for more help with all kinds of public writing.

e-mail (p. 158), newsletters and brochures for community work (p. 161), and Web sites (p. 164).

CULTURE & LANGUAGE Public writing in the United States, especially business writing, favors efficiency and may seem abrupt or impolite compared with such writing in your native culture. For instance, a business letter elsewhere may be expected to begin with polite questions about the addressee or with compliments for the addressee's company, whereas US business letters are expected to get right to the point.

13a   Use established formats for business letters and résumés.

When you write for business, you are addressing busy people who want to see quickly why you are writing and how they should respond to you. Follow these general guidelines:

- **State your purpose right at the start.**
- **Be straightforward, clear, concise, objective, and courteous.**
- **Observe conventions of grammar and usage,** which make your writing clear and impress your reader with your care.

1 • Business letter format

For any business letter, use either unlined white paper measuring 8½″ × 11″ or what is called letterhead stationery with your address printed at the top of the sheet. Type the letter single-spaced (with double spacing between elements) on only one side of a sheet.

A common business-letter form is illustrated on the next page:

- The *return-address heading* gives your address and the date. Do not include your name. If you are using stationery with a printed heading, you need only give the date.
- The *inside address* shows the name, title, and complete address of the person you are writing to.
- The *salutation* greets the addressee. Whenever possible, address your letter to a specific person. (Call the company or department to ask whom to address.) If you can't find a person's name, then use a job title (*Dear Human Resources Manager, Dear Customer Service Manager*) or use a general salutation (*Dear Smythe Shoes*). Use *Ms.* as the title for a woman when she has no other title, when you don't know how she prefers to be addressed, or when you know that she prefers *Ms.*
- The *body* contains the substance. Instead of indenting the first line of each paragraph, insert an extra line of space between paragraphs.

13a

Business letter (job application)

Minimum 1"

Double-space →

3712 Swiss Avenue
Dallas, TX 75204 ⎤——— Return-address heading
March 2, 2007 ⎦

Raymond Chipault
Human Resources Manager
Dallas News ⎤——— Inside address
Communications Center
Dallas, TX 75222 ⎦

Double-space

Dear Mr. Chipault: ⎤——————— Salutation

In response to your posting in the English Department of Southern Methodist University, I am applying for the summer job of part-time editorial
assistant for the *Dallas News*.

Double-space

I am now enrolled at Southern Methodist University as a sophomore, with a
dual major in English literature and journalism. My courses so far have included news reporting, copy editing, and electronic publishing. I worked a
1" ← summer as a copy aide for my hometown newspaper, and for two years I → 1"
have edited and written sports stories and features for the university newspaper. My feature articles cover subjects as diverse as campus elections,
parking regulations, visiting professors, and speech codes.

Double-space

As the enclosed résumé and writing samples indicate, my education and
knowledge of newspaper work prepare me for the opening you have.

Double-space

Body

I am available for an interview at your convenience and would be happy to
show more samples of my writing. Please e-mail me at ianirv@mail.smu
.edu or call me at 214-744-3816.

Sincerely, ⎤——————— Close

Quadruple-space

Ian M. Irvine ⎤
——————— Signature
Ian M. Irvine ⎦

Enc.

Minimum 1"

- The *close* should reflect the level of formality in the salutation: *Respectfully, Cordially, Yours truly,* and *Sincerely* are more
  formal closes; *Regards* and *Best wishes* are less formal.
- The *signature* has two parts: your name typed four lines below
  the close, and your handwritten signature in the space between.
  Give your name as you sign checks and other documents.

- **Include any additional information below the signature,** such as *Enc.* (indicating an enclosure with the letter) or *cc: Margaret Zusky* (indicating that a copy is being sent to the person named).

Use an envelope that will accommodate the letter once it is folded horizontally in thirds. The envelope should show your name and address in the upper left corner and the addressee's name, title, and address in the center. For easy machine reading, the United States Postal Service recommends all capital letters and no punctuation (spaces separate the elements on a line), as in this address:

\
13a

RAYMOND CHIPAULT
HUMAN RESOURCES MANAGER
DALLAS NEWS
COMMUNICATIONS CENTER
DALLAS TX 75222-0188

2 • Job-application letter

The sample on the facing page illustrates the key features of a job-application letter:

- **Interpret your résumé for the particular job.** Don't detail your entire résumé, reciting your job history. Instead, highlight and reshape only the relevant parts.
- **Announce at the outset what job you seek and how you heard about it.**
- **Include any special reason you have for applying,** such as a specific career goal.
- **Summarize your qualifications for this particular job,** including relevant facts about education and employment history and emphasizing notable accomplishments. Mention that additional information appears in an accompanying résumé.
- **Describe your availability.** At the end of the letter, mention that you are free for an interview at the convenience of the addressee, or specify when you will be available (for instance, when your current job or classes leave you free, or when you could travel to the employer's city).

3 • Résumé

The résumé that accompanies your letter of application should provide information in table format so that a potential employer can quickly evaluate your qualifications. The résumé should include your name and address, your career objective, your education and employment history, any special skills you have or awards you've received, and information about how to obtain your references. All the information should fit on one uncrowded page unless your education and experience are extensive. See the sample below for writing and formatting guidelines for a résumé that you submit in print.

Résumé (print)

Name and contact information	**Ian M. Irvine**	3712 Swiss Avenue Dallas, TX 75204 214-744-3816 ianirv@mail.smu.edu

Career objective stated simply and clearly

Position desired   Part-time editorial assistant.

Education before work experience for most college students

Education   *Southern Methodist University*, 2005 to present.
Current standing: sophomore.
Major: English literature and journalism.
Journalism courses: news reporting, copy editing, electronic publishing, communication arts, broadcast journalism.

Standard, consistent type font

Abilene (Texas) Senior High School, 2001-05.
Graduated with academic, college-preparatory degree.

Headings marking sections, set off with space and highlighting

Employment history   2005 to present. Reporter, *Daily Campus*, student newspaper of Southern Methodist University.
Write regular coverage of baseball, track, and soccer teams. Write feature stories on campus policies and events. Edit sports news, campus listings, features.

Conventional use of capital letters: yes for proper nouns and after periods; no for job titles, course names, department names, and so on

Summer 2006. Copy aide, *Abilene Reporter-News*.
Assisted reporters with copy routing and research.

Summer 2005. Painter, Longhorn Painters, Abilene.
Prepared and painted exteriors and interiors of houses.

Special skills   Fluent in Spanish.
Proficient in Internet research and word processing.

References   Available on request:

Placement Office
Southern Methodist University
Dallas, TX 75275

Some employers may ask for an electronic version of your résumé so that they can add it to a computerized database of applicants. The employers may scan your printed résumé to convert it to an electronic file, which they can then store in an appropriate database, or they may request that you embed your résumé in an e-mail message. To produce a scannable or electronic résumé, follow the guidelines on the next page and consult the sample below.

Résumé (scannable or electronic)

Ian M. Irvine
3712 Swiss Avenue
Dallas, TX 75204
214-744-3816

KEYWORDS: Editor, editorial assistant, publishing, electronic publishing.

OBJECTIVE
Part-time editorial assistant.

EDUCATION
Southern Methodist University, 2005 to present.
Major: English literature and journalism.
Journalism courses: news reporting, copy editing, electronic publishing, communication arts, broadcast journalism.

Abilene (Texas) Senior High School, 2001-05.
Academic, college preparatory degree.

EMPLOYMENT HISTORY
Reporter, Daily Campus, Southern Methodist University, 2005 to present.
Writer of articles for student newspaper on sports teams, campus policies, and local events. Editor of sports news, campus listings, and features.

Copy aide, Abilene Reporter-News, Abilene, summer 2006.
Assistant to reporters, routing copy and doing research.

Painter, Longhorn Painters, Abilene, summer 2005.
Preparation and painting of exteriors and interiors of houses.

SPECIAL SKILLS
Fluent in Spanish.
Proficient in Internet research and word processing.

REFERENCES
Available on request:
Placement Office
Southern Methodist University
Dallas, TX 75275

Accurate keywords, allowing the employer to place the résumé into an appropriate database

Simple design, avoiding unusual type, italics, multiple columns, decorative lines, and images

Standard font easily read by scanners

Every line aligning at left margin

- **Keep the design simple for accurate scanning or electronic transmittal.** Avoid images, unusual type, more than one column, vertical or horizontal lines, italics, and underlining.
- **Use concise, specific words to describe your skills and experience.** The employer's computer may use keywords (often nouns) to identify the résumés of suitable job candidates, and you want to ensure that your résumé includes the appropriate keywords. Name your specific skills—for example, the computer programs you can operate—and write concretely with words like *manager* (not *person with responsibility for*) and *reporter* (not *staff member who reports*). Look for likely keywords in the employer's description of the job you seek.

13b Write focused memos.

Business memorandums (memos, for short) address people within the same organization. Most memos deal briefly with a specific topic, such as an answer to a question or an evaluation.

Both the form and the structure of a memo are designed to get to the point and dispose of it quickly (see the sample on the facing page). State your reason for writing in the first sentence. Devote the first paragraph to a concise presentation of your answer, conclusion, or evaluation. In the rest of the memo explain your reasoning or evidence. Use headings or lists as appropriate to highlight key information.

13c Write effective electronic mail.

E-mail has a wide range of uses, from corresponding with relatives and friends to collaborating with classmates to presenting a business proposal. Sometimes, as when e-mailing a friend or a classmate, you can write quickly and casually, not worrying much about how the message reads. But when e-mailing people you don't know well and want to impress, you should apply the same care as you would to a business letter. That is, consider your audience and purpose in choosing both content and tone, focus on a central idea, organize effectively, and write concisely, clearly, and accurately. A crafted message like the one on page 160 is more likely to achieve the intended purpose.

Effective e-mail abides by some rules of behavior and simple courtesies. You won't always see others observing this **netiquette,** or

Business memo

Bigelow Wax Company

TO: Aileen Rosen, Director of Sales
FROM: Patricia Phillips, Territory 12   *PP*
DATE: March 17, 2007
SUBJECT: 2006 sales of Quick Wax in Territory 12

Since it was introduced in January 2006, Quick Wax has been unsuccessful in Territory 12 and has not affected the sales of our Easy Shine. Discussions with customers and my own analysis of Quick Wax suggest three reasons for its failure to compete with our product.

1. Quick Wax has not received the promotion necessary for a new product. Advertising—primarily on radio—has been sporadic and has not developed a clear, consistent image for the product. In addition, the Quick Wax sales representative in Territory 12 is new and inexperienced; he is not known to customers, and his sales pitch (which I once overheard) is weak. As far as I can tell, his efforts are not supported by phone calls or mailings from his home office.

2. When Quick Wax does make it to the store shelves, buyers do not choose it over our product. Though priced competitively with our product, Quick Wax is poorly packaged. The container seems smaller than ours, though in fact it holds the same eight ounces. The lettering on the Quick Wax package (red on blue) is difficult to read, in contrast to the white-on-green lettering on the Easy Shine package.

3. Our special purchase offers and my increased efforts to serve existing customers have had the intended effect of keeping customers satisfied with our product and reducing their inclination to stock something new.

Copies: L. Mendes, Director of Marketing
      J. MacGregor, Customer Service Manager

Heading: company's name, addressee's name, writer's name and initials, date, and subject description

Body: single-spaced with double spacing between paragraphs; paragraphs not indented

People receiving copies

Internet etiquette, but you will see that those who do observe it receive the more thoughtful and considerate replies.

Addressing messages

- **Avoid spamming.** With a few keystrokes, you can broadcast a message to many recipients at once—all the students in a course,

E-mail message

Consider who needs to read your message as you address it.

Send copies to others who are involved in or affected by your message.

Use the *Subject* line to describe accurately the content of the message.

Attach relevant files.

Adjust the content and tone to the intended audience.

Use short paragraphs with space between them.

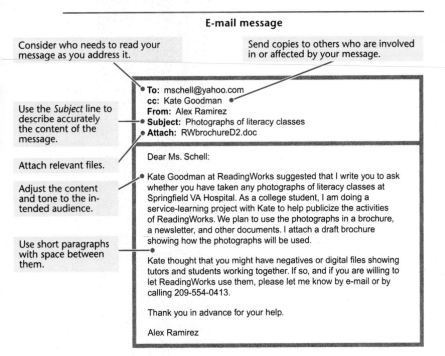

To: mschell@yahoo.com
cc: Kate Goodman
From: Alex Ramirez
Subject: Photographs of literacy classes
Attach: RWbrochureD2.doc

Dear Ms. Schell:

Kate Goodman at ReadingWorks suggested that I write you to ask whether you have taken any photographs of literacy classes at Springfield VA Hospital. As a college student, I am doing a service-learning project with Kate to help publicize the activities of ReadingWorks. We plan to use the photographs in a brochure, a newsletter, and other documents. I attach a draft brochure showing how the photographs will be used.

Kate thought that you might have negatives or digital files showing tutors and students working together. If so, and if you are willing to let ReadingWorks use them, please let me know by e-mail or by calling 209-554-0413.

Thank you in advance for your help.

Alex Ramirez

say, or all the participants in a discussion group. Occasionally you may indeed have a worthwhile idea or important information that everyone on the list will want to know. But flooding whole lists with irrelevant messages—called **spamming**—is rude and irritating.

- **Avoid sending frivolous messages to all the members of a group.** Instead of dashing off "I agree" and distributing the two-word message widely, put some time into composing a thoughtful response and send it only to those who will be interested.

Composing messages

- **Use names.** In the body of your message, address your reader(s) by name if possible and sign off with your own name and information on how to contact you. Your own name is especially important if your e-mail address does not spell it out.
- **Pay careful attention to tone.** Refrain from **flaming,** or attacking, correspondents. Don't use all-capital letters, which SHOUT. And use irony or sarcasm only cautiously: in the absence of facial expressions, they can lead to misunderstandings. To

indicate irony and emotions, you can use **emoticons,** such as the smiley :-). These sideways faces made up of punctuation can easily be overused, though, and should not substitute for thoughtfully worded opinions.

- **Avoid saying anything in e-mail that you would not say in a printed document such as a letter or memo.** E-mail can usually be retrieved from the server, and in business and academic settings it may well be retrieved in disputes over contracts, grades, and other matters.

Reading and responding to messages

- **Be a forgiving reader.** Avoid nitpicking over spelling or other surface errors. And because attitudes are sometimes difficult to convey, give authors an initial benefit of the doubt: a writer who at first seems hostile may simply have tried too hard to be concise; a writer who at first seems unserious may simply have failed at injecting humor into a worthwhile message.
- **Remember that the messages you receive represent individuals.** Don't say anything that you wouldn't say face to face.
- **Use quoted material from earlier messages critically.** Most e-mail programs can copy the original message into your response, setting off the quoted material with a vertical line or some other device. By weaving your replies into the quoted material, you can respond to the author point by point, as you would in conversation. However, delete from the original anything you are not responding to so that your recipient can focus on what you have to say without wading through his or her own words.
- **Forward messages only with permission.** You may want to send a message you've received to someone else, but do so only if you know that the author of the message won't mind.
- **Avoid participating in flame "wars,"** overheated dialogs that contribute little or no information or understanding. If a war breaks out in a discussion, ignore it: don't rush to defend someone who is being attacked, and don't respond even if you are under attack yourself.

13d Create effective documents when writing for community work.

At some point in your life, you're likely to volunteer for a community organization such as a soup kitchen, a daycare center, or a literacy program. Many college courses involve service learning, in which you do such volunteer work, write about the experience for your course, and write *for* the organization you're helping.

The writing you do for a community group may range from flyers to grant proposals. The newsletter and brochure shown on these two pages were prepared for ReadingWorks, a literacy program. Two guidelines in particular can help you prepare effective projects:

- **Craft each document for its purpose and audience.** You are trying to achieve a specific aim with your readers, and the approach and tone you use will influence their responses. If, for

13d

Newsletter

Annotations (left column)

Multicolumn format allowing room for headings, articles, and other elements on a single page

Two-column heading emphasizing the main article

Elements helping readers skim for highlights: spacing, varied font sizes, lines, and a bulleted list

Color focusing readers' attention on banner, headlines, and table of contents

Lively but uncluttered overall appearance

Box in the first column highlighting table of contents

ReadingWorks

Springfield Veterans Administration Hospital   **SUMMER 2006**

From the director

Can you help? With more and more learners in the ReadingWorks program, we need more and more tutors. You may know people who would be interested in participating in the program, if only they knew about it.

Those of you who have been tutoring VA patients in reading and writing know both the great need you fulfill and the great benefits you bring to the students. New tutors need no special skills—we'll provide the training—only patience and an interest in helping others.

We've scheduled an orientation meeting for Friday, September 12, at 6:30 PM. Please come and bring a friend who is willing to contribute a couple of hours a week to our work.

Thanks,
Kate Goodman

FIRST ANNUAL AWARDS DINNER

A festive night for students and tutors

The first annual ReadingWorks Awards Dinner on May 25th was a great success. Springfield's own Golden Fork provided tasty food and Amber Allen supplied lively music. The students decorated Suite 42 on the theme of books and reading. In all, 127 people attended.

The highlight of the night was the awards ceremony. Nine students, recommended by their tutors, received certificates recognizing their efforts and special accomplishments in learning to read and write:

Ramon Berva
Edward Byar
David Dunbar
Tony Garnier
Chris Guigni
Akili Haynes
Josh Livingston
Alex Obeld
B. J. Resnansky

In addition, nine tutors received certificates commemorating five years of service to ReadingWorks:

Anita Crumpton
Felix Cruz-Rivera
Bette Elgen
Kayleah Bortoluzzi
Harriotte Henderson
Ben Obiso
Meggie Puente
Max Smith
Sara Villante

Congratulations to all!

PTSD: New Guidelines

Most of us are working with veterans who have been diagnosed with post-traumatic stress disorder. Because this disorder is often complicated by alcoholism, depression, anxiety, and other problems, the National Center for PTSD has issued some guidelines for helping PTSD patients in ways that reduce their stress.

- The hospital must know your tutoring schedule, and you need to sign in and out before and after each tutoring session.

- To protect patients' privacy, meet them only in designated visiting and tutoring areas, never in their rooms.

- Treat patients with dignity and respect, even when (as sometimes happens) they grow frustrated and angry. Seek help from a nurse or orderly if you need it.

Brochure

Do you know a veteran who needs help with reading and writing?

Do you need to improve your reading and writing skills to get a job?

ReadingWorks can make a difference. We organize volunteers to help military veterans achieve literacy and to prepare them for life-long learning.

For more information about our services, call Kate Goodman at 209-556-1212 or visit www.readingworks.org.

ReadingWorks
Springfield VA Hospital
111 South Springdale Drive
Springfield, MI 45078

ReadingWorks
Springfield VA Hospital

Helping
military
veterans
achieve
literacy

13d

Panel 2: The right page when the cover is opened, the first one readers see, containing key information

Panel 6: The back, usually including the return address and space for a mailing label and postage

Panel 1: The cover, drawing readers' attention to the group's name, purpose, and affiliation

---

ReadingWorks
Springfield VA Hospital

OUR MISSION
- We provide workshops and formal lessons for veterans wishing to develop their reading and writing skills
- We train volunteers to tutor veterans one on one.
- We maintain outreach programs to provide access to literacy training for all veterans.
- We create literacy resources and share them with others who promote literacy for veterans.

OUR SERVICES
One-on-one tutoring
One to three hours a week with a trained volunteer tutor.

Workshops and classes
Small-group meetings centered on reading and writing, computer skills, and English as a second language.

Library
Books and other resources for students at various literacy levels.

Computer lab
Five computers with high-speed Internet access and a full range of software.

OUR TUTORS
The goodwill and generosity of our volunteer tutors allows us to reach out to those who have served our country.

If you or someone you know can join our team, contact Kate Goodman at 209-556-1212.

Hours
12:00 to 8:00, Mon., Wed.
9:00 to 5:00, Tues., Thurs., Fri.

Eligibility
Any veteran of the US military is eligible for our services.

How to reach us
Springfield VA Hospital
Room 172, first floor
111 South Springdale Drive
Springfield, MI 45078
209-556-1212
www.readingworks.org

Panel 3: The left page when the cover is opened, reinforcing the message of panel 2

Varied type, color, and photographs, adding visual interest and focusing readers' attention

Panels 4 and 5: The inside panels, containing contact information and other details

example, you are writing letters to local businesses to raise funds for a homeless shelter, bring to mind the person or people who will read your letter. How can you best persuade those readers to donate money?

- **Expect to work with others.** Much public writing is the work of more than one person. Even if you draft the document on your own, others will review the content, tone, and design. Such collaboration is rewarding, but it sometimes requires patience and goodwill. See pages 43–45 for advice on collaborating.

See also pages 153–55 and 158 on letters and memos and pages 171–72 on *PowerPoint* presentations.

13e   Create effective Web compositions.

When you are submitting a paper over the Web, you can often just save the document in a different format. (See p. 82.) But when you are creating a Web site from scratch, you may have to think in a different way. The diagrams on the next page show a key distinction between traditional printed documents and Web sites. Most traditional documents are meant to be read in sequence from start to finish. In contrast, most Web sites are intended to be examined in whatever order readers choose as they follow links to pages within the site and to other sites. A Web site thus requires careful planning of the links between pages and thoughtful cues to orient readers.

Note If you anticipate that some of your readers may have visual, hearing, or reading disabilities, you'll need to consider their needs while designing Web sites. Some of these considerations are covered under document design on pages 83–84, and others are fundamental to any effective Web design, as discussed in this section. In addition, avoid any content that relies exclusively on images or sound, instead supplementing such elements with text descriptions, and try to provide key concepts both as text and as images and sound. For more on Web design for readers with disabilities, visit the World Wide Web Consortium at *w3.org/tr/wai-webcontent* or the American Council for the Blind at *acb.org/accessible-formats.html*.

1 • Using HTML

Most Web pages are created using hypertext markup language, or HTML, and an HTML editor. The HTML editing program inserts command codes into your document that achieve the effects you want when the material appears on the Web.

From the user's point of view, most HTML editors work much as word processors do, with similar options for sizing, formatting,

13e

13e

Traditional print document

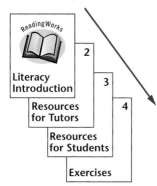

Web site

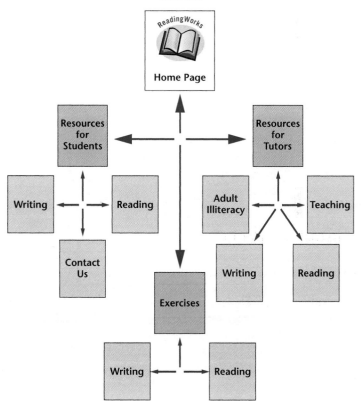

and highlighting copy and with a display that shows what you will see in the final version. Indeed, you can compose a Web page without bothering at all about the behind-the-scenes HTML coding. As you gain experience with Web building, however, you may want to create more sophisticated pages by editing the codes themselves.

There are many HTML editors on the market. *FrontPage, GoLive,* and *Dreamweaver* are three of the most popular. The Web site for this book (*ablongman.com/littlebrown*) provides links to free or low-cost HTML editors.

13e

2 • Building structure and content

Organize your site so that it efficiently arranges your content and orients readers:

- **Sketch possible site plans before getting started.** (See the previous page for an example.) Your aim is to develop a sense of the major components of your project and to create a logical space for each component.
- **Consider how menus on the site's pages can provide overviews of the organization as well as direct access to the pages.** The Web page below includes a menu on the left.
- **Treat the first few sentences of any page as a get-acquainted space for you and your readers.** On the Web page below, the

Web page

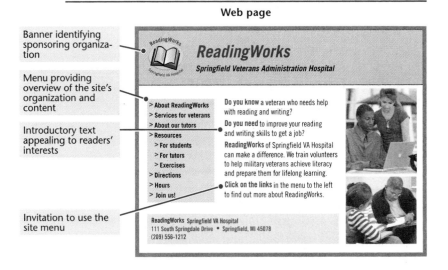

Banner identifying sponsoring organization

Menu providing overview of the site's organization and content

Introductory text appealing to readers' interests

Invitation to use the site menu

ReadingWorks
Springfield Veterans Administration Hospital

> About ReadingWorks
> Services for veterans
> About our tutors
> Resources
> For students
> For tutors
> Exercises
> Directions
> Hours
> Join us!

Do you know a veteran who needs help with reading and writing?

Do you need to improve your reading and writing skills to get a job?

ReadingWorks of Springfield VA Hospital can make a difference. We train volunteers to help military veterans achieve literacy and prepare them for lifelong learning.

Click on the links in the menu to the left to find out more about ReadingWorks.

ReadingWorks Springfield VA Hospital
111 South Springdale Drive • Springfield, MI 45078
(209) 556-1212

text hooks readers with questions and then orients them with general information.

- **Distill your text so that it includes only essential information.** Concise prose is essential in any writing situation, of course. But Web readers expect to scan text quickly and, in any event, have difficulty following long text passages on a computer screen.

3 • Achieving flow

Beginning Web authors sometimes start at the top of the page and then add element upon element until information proceeds down the screen much as it would in a printed document. However, by thinking about how information will flow on the screen, you can take better advantage of the Web's visual nature. Follow these guidelines:

- **Standardize elements of your design to create expectations in readers and to fulfill those expectations.** For instance, develop a uniform style for the main headings of pages, for headings within pages, and for menus.
- **Make scanning easy for readers.** Focus readers on crucial text by adding space around it. Add headings to break up text and to highlight content. Use lists to reinforce the parallel importance of items. (See pp. 76–77 for a discussion of headings and lists.)

4 • Using menus

A Web site of more than a few pages requires a menu on every page that lists the features of the site, giving its plan at a glance. By clicking on any item in the menu, readers can go directly to a page that interests them.

You can embed a menu at the top, side, or bottom of a page. Menus at the top or side are best on short pages because they will not scroll off the screen as readers move down the page. On longer pages, menus at the bottom prevent readers from reaching a dead end, a point where they can't easily move forward or backward. You can also use a combination of menus.

5 • Using images, video, and sound

Most Web readers expect at least some enhancement of text with multimedia elements—images, video, and sound.

Note See pages 476–77 on observing copyright restrictions with images, video, and sound.

Images

To use photographs, charts, and other images effectively, follow these guidelines:

- **Use visual elements for a purpose.** They should supplement text, highlight important features, and direct the flow of information. Don't use them as mere decoration.
- **Make the size of your files a central concern** so that readers don't have to wait forever for your site to download. If you are using photographs or other images, try to keep the file size below thirty kilobytes (30k).
- **Compose descriptions of images that relate them to your text.** Don't ask the elements to convey your meaning by themselves.
- **Provide alternative descriptions of images** for readers with disabilities or readers whose Web browsers can't display the images.

Video and sound

Video and sound files can provide information that is simply unavailable in printed documents. For instance, as part of a film review you might show and analyze a short clip from the film. Or as part of a project on a controversial issue you might provide links to sound files containing political speeches.

Video and sound files can be difficult to work with and can be slow to download at the reader's end. Make sure they're worth the time: they should provide essential information and should be well integrated with the rest of your composition.

Sources of multimedia elements

You can use your own multimedia elements or obtain them from other sources:

- **Create your own graphs, diagrams, and other illustrations using a graphics program.** Any graphics program requires learning and practice to be used efficiently but can produce professional-looking illustrations.
- **Incorporate your own artwork, photographs, video clips, and sound recordings.** You may be able to find the needed equipment and software at your campus computer lab.
- **Obtain icons, video, and other multimedia elements from other electronic sources.** Be sure that you have enough space on your hard drive or a disk to hold the file.

14 Making Oral Presentations

How can I speak effectively to a group?

Oral presentation is partly writing, involving the same consideration of subject, audience, and purpose. Yet speechmaking and writing also differ, notably in that a listener cannot stop to rehear a section the way a reader can reread. Effective speakers use organization, voice, body language, and other techniques to help their audience listen.

14a

14a Consider purpose and audience.

The most important step in developing an oral presentation is to identify your purpose: what do you want your audience to know or do as a result of your speech? In school and work settings, you're likely to be speaking for the same reasons that you write: to explain something to listeners or to persuade listeners to accept your opinion or take an action. See page 9 for more on these purposes.

Adapting to your audience is a critical task in public speaking as well as in writing. You'll want to consider the questions about audience on page 8. But a listening audience requires additional considerations as well:

- **Why is your audience assembled?** Listeners who are required to attend may be more difficult to interest and motivate than listeners who attend because they want to hear you and your ideas.
- **How large is your audience?** With a small group you can be informal. If you are speaking to a hundred or more people, you may need a public address system, a lectern, special lighting, and audiovisual equipment.
- **Where will you speak?** Your approach should match the setting—more casual for a small classroom, more formal for an auditorium.
- **How long are you scheduled to speak?** Whatever your time limit, stick to it. Audiences lose patience when speeches run longer than expected.

http://www.ablongman.com/littlebrown ▶
Visit the companion Web site for more help
with oral presentations and *PowerPoint*.

14b Organize the presentation.

Give your oral presentation a recognizable shape so that listeners can see how ideas and details relate to each other.

The introduction

The beginning of an oral presentation should try to accomplish three goals:

- **Gain the audience's attention and interest.** Begin with a question, an unusual example or statistic, or a short, relevant story.
- **Put yourself in the speech.** Demonstrate your expertise, experience, or concern to gain the interest and trust of your audience.
- **Introduce and preview your topic and purpose.** By the time your introduction is over, listeners should know what your subject is and the direction you'll take to develop your ideas.

Your introduction should prepare your audience for your main points but not give them away. Think of it as a sneak preview of your speech, not the place for an apology such as *I wish I'd had more time to prepare . . .* or a dull statement such as *My speech is about. . . .*

Supporting material

Just as you do when writing, you should use facts, statistics, examples, and expert opinions to support the main points of your oral presentation. In addition, you can make your points more memorable with vivid description, well-chosen quotations, true or fictional stories, and analogies.

The conclusion

You want your conclusion to be clear, of course, but you also want it to be memorable. Remind listeners of how your topic and main idea connect to their needs and interests. If your speech was motivational, tap an emotion that matches your message. If your speech was informational, give some tips on how to remember important details.

14c Deliver the presentation.

Methods of delivery

You can deliver an oral presentation in several ways:

- **Impromptu, without preparation:** Make a presentation without planning what you will say. Impromptu speaking requires confidence and excellent general preparation.

- **Extemporaneously:** Prepare notes to glance at but not read from. This method allows you to look and sound natural while ensuring that you don't forget anything.
- **Speaking from a text:** Read aloud from a written presentation. You won't lose your way, but you may lose your audience. Avoid reading for an entire presentation.
- **Speaking from memory:** Deliver a prepared presentation without notes. You can look at your audience every minute, but the stress of retrieving the next words may make you seem tense and unresponsive.

14c

Vocal delivery

The sound of your voice will influence how listeners receive you. Rehearse your presentation several times until you are confident that you are speaking loudly, slowly, and clearly enough for your audience to understand you.

Physical delivery

You are more than your spoken words when you make an oral presentation. If you are able, stand up to deliver your presentation, moving your body toward one side of the room and the other, stepping out from behind any lectern or desk, and gesturing as appropriate. Above all, make eye contact with your audience as you speak. Looking directly in your listeners' eyes conveys your honesty, your confidence, and your control of the material.

Visual aids

You can supplement an oral presentation with visual aids such as posters, models, slides, or videos.

- **Use visual aids to underscore your points.** Short lists of key ideas, illustrations such as graphs or photographs, or objects such as models can make your presentation more interesting and memorable. But use visual aids judiciously: a battery of illustrations or objects will bury your message rather than amplify it.
- **Coordinate visual aids with your message.** Time each visual to reinforce a point you're making. Tell listeners what they're looking at. Give them enough viewing time so they don't mind turning their attention back to you.
- **Show visual aids only while they're needed.** To regain your audience's attention, remove or turn off any aid as soon as you have finished with it.

Many speakers use *PowerPoint* or other software to present visual aids. Preparing screens of brief points supported by data, images, or video, you can use such software to help listeners follow your main points. To use *PowerPoint* or other software effectively, follow the guidelines on the previous page and also the following:

14c

- **Don't put your whole presentation on screen.** Select key points, and distill them to as few words as possible. Think of the slides as quick, easy-to-remember summaries.
- **Use a simple design.** Avoid turning your presentation into a show about the software's many capabilities.
- **Use a consistent design.** For optimal flow through the presentation, each slide should be formatted similarly.
- **Add only relevant illustrations.** Avoid loading the presentation with mere decoration.

PowerPoint **slides**

First slide, introducing the project and presentation

Simple, consistent slide design focusing viewers' attention on information, not *PowerPoint* features

Making a Difference?

A Service-Learning Project at ReadingWorks

Springfield Veterans
Administration Hospital

Jessica Cho
Nathan Hall
Alex Ramirez

FALL 2006

Later slide, using brief, bulleted points to be explained by the speaker

Photographs reinforcing the project's activities

Semester goals

- Tutor military veterans
- Research adult literacy
- Keep a journal
- Collaborate on documents for ReadingWorks
- Report experiences and findings

Practice

Take time to rehearse your presentation out loud, with the notes you will be using. Gauge your performance by making an audio- or videotape of yourself or by practicing in front of a mirror. Practicing out loud will also tell you if your presentation is running too long or too short.

If you plan to use visual aids, you'll need to practice with them, too. Your goal is to eliminate hitches (upside-down slides, missing charts) and to weave the visuals seamlessly into your presentation.

14c

Stage fright

Many people report that speaking in front of an audience is their number-one fear. Even many experienced and polished speakers have some anxiety about delivering an oral presentation, but they use this nervous energy to their advantage, letting it propel them into working hard on each presentation. Several techniques can help you reduce anxiety:

- **Use simple relaxation exercises.** Deep breathing or tensing and relaxing your stomach muscles can ease some of the physical symptoms of speech anxiety—stomachache, rapid heartbeat, and shaky hands, legs, and voice.
- **Think positively.** Instead of worrying about the mistakes you might make, concentrate on how well you've prepared and practiced your presentation and how significant your ideas are.
- **Don't avoid opportunities to speak in public.** Practice and experience build speaking skills and offer the best insurance for success.

3

Clarity and Style

15 Emphasis

How can my sentences stress the meanings I intend?

To write exactly what you mean, edit to emphasize the main ideas in your sentences. You can gain emphasis by attending to your subjects and verbs (below), using sentence beginnings and endings (p. 179), coordinating equally important ideas (p. 181), and subordinating less important ideas (p. 184). In addition, emphatic writing is concise writing, the subject of Chapter 20.

Note Many grammar and style checkers can spot some problems with emphasis, such as nouns made from verbs, passive voice, wordy phrases, and long sentences that may also be flabby and unemphatic. However, the checkers cannot help you identify the important ideas in your sentences or tell you whether those ideas receive appropriate emphasis for your meaning.

emph

15a

15a Use subjects and verbs for key actors and actions.

The heart of every sentence is its subject, which usually names the actor, and its predicate verb, which usually specifies the subject's action: *Children* [subject] *grow* [verb]. When these elements do not identify the key actor and action in the sentence, readers must find that information elsewhere and the sentence may be wordy and unemphatic.

In the next sentences, the subjects and verbs are underlined.

Unemphatic   The <u>intention</u> of the company <u>was</u> to expand its workforce. A <u>proposal</u> <u>was</u> also <u>made</u> to diversify the backgrounds and abilities of employees.

These sentences are unemphatic because their key ideas do not appear in their subjects and verbs. Revised as shown on the facing page, the sentences are not only clearer but more concise.

Key terms

subject Who or what a sentence is about: *Birds fly.* (See p. 232.)

predicate The part of a sentence containing a verb that asserts something about the subject: *Birds <u>fly</u>.* (See p. 232.)

---

http://www.ablongman.com/littlebrown ▶

Visit the companion Web site for more help and electronic exercises on emphasis.

Revised   The <u>company</u> <u>intended</u> to expand its workforce. <u>It</u> also <u>proposed</u> to diversify the backgrounds and abilities of employees.

The constructions discussed below and on the next page usually drain meaning from a sentence's subject and verb.

Nouns made from verbs

Nouns made from verbs can obscure the key actions of sentences and add words. These nouns include *intention* (from *intend*), *proposal* (from *propose*), *decision* (from *decide*), *expectation* (from *expect*), *persistence* (from *persist*), *argument* (from *argue*), and *inclusion* (from *include*).

emph

15a

Unemphatic After the company made a <u>decision</u> to hire more workers with disabilities, its next step was the <u>construction</u> of wheelchair ramps and other facilities.

Revised   After the company <u>decided</u> to hire more workers with disabilities, it next <u>constructed</u> wheelchair ramps and other facilities.

Weak verbs

Weak verbs, such as *made* and *was* in the unemphatic sentence above, tend to stall sentences just where they should be moving and often bury key actions:

Unemphatic The company <u>is</u> now the leader among businesses in complying with the 1990 disabilities act. Its officers <u>make</u> frequent speeches on the act to business groups.

Revised   The company now <u>leads</u> other businesses in complying with the 1990 disabilities act. Its officers frequently <u>speak</u> on the act to business groups.

Forms of *be, have,* and *make* are often weak, but don't try to eliminate every use of them: *be* and *have* are essential as helping verbs (<u>*is* going</u>, <u>*has* written</u>); *be* links subjects and words describing them (<u>*Planes* *are* noisy</u>); and *have* and *make* have independent meanings (among them "possess" and "force," respectively). But do consider replacing forms of *be, have,* and *make* when one of the words after the verb could be made into a strong verb itself, as in the following examples.

┌─ **Key terms** ───

noun A word that names a person, thing, quality, place, or idea: *student, desk, happiness, city, democracy.* (See p. 225.)

helping verb A verb used with another verb to convey time, obligation, and other meanings: <u>*was* drilling</u>, <u>*would have been*</u> drilling. (See p. 227.)

Unemphatic	Emphatic
was influential	influenced
have a preference	prefer
had the appearance	appeared, seemed
made a claim	claimed

Passive voice

Verbs in the passive voice state actions received by, not performed by, their subjects. Thus the passive de-emphasizes the true actor of the sentence, sometimes omitting it entirely. Generally, prefer the active voice, in which the subject performs the action. (See also pp. 277–78 for help with editing the passive voice.)

emph

15a

Unemphatic   The 1990 <u>law</u> <u>is seen</u> by most businesses as fair, but the <u>costs</u> of complying <u>have</u> sometimes <u>been exaggerated</u>.

Revised   Most <u>businesses</u> <u>see</u> the 1990 law as fair, but some <u>opponents</u> <u>have exaggerated</u> the costs of complying.

EXERCISE 15.1
Revising: Emphasis of subjects and verbs

Rewrite the following sentences so that their subjects and verbs identify their key actors and actions. Answers to starred items appear at the end of the book. (You can do this exercise online at *ablongman.com/littlebrown*.)

Example:

The issue of students making a competition over grades is a reason why their focus on learning may be lost.

<u>Students</u> who compete over grades <u>may lose</u> their focus on learning.

*1. The work of many heroes was crucial in helping to emancipate the slaves.

*2. The contribution of Harriet Tubman, an escaped slave herself, included the guidance of hundreds of other slaves to freedom on the Underground Railroad.

3. A return to slavery was risked by Tubman or possibly death.

4. During the Civil War she was also a carrier of information from the South to the North.

5. After the war, needy former slaves were helped by Tubman's raising of money.

Key terms

passive voice   The verb form when the subject names the *receiver* of the verb's action: *The house <u>was destroyed</u> by the tornado.*

active voice   The verb form when the subject names the *performer* of the verb's action: *The tornado <u>destroyed</u> the house.*

15b   Use sentence beginnings and endings.

Readers automatically seek a writer's principal meaning in the main clause of a sentence—essentially, in the subject that names the actor and the predicate verb that usually specifies the action (see p. 176). Thus you can help readers understand your intended meaning by controlling the information in your subjects and the relation of the main clause to any modifiers attached to it.

Old and new information

Generally, readers expect the beginning of a sentence to contain information that they already know or that you have already introduced. They then look to the ending for new information. In the unemphatic passage below, the second and third sentences both begin with new topics, while the old topics appear at the ends of the sentences. The pattern of the passage is A→B. C→B. D→A.

<table>
<tr><td>Unemphatic</td><td>Education almost means controversy these days, with rising costs and constant complaints about its inadequacies. But the value of schooling should not be obscured by the controversy. The single best means of economic advancement, despite its shortcomings, remains education.</td></tr>
</table>

In the more emphatic revision below, old information begins each sentence and new information ends the sentence. The passage follows the pattern A→B. B→C. A→D.

<table>
<tr><td>Revised</td><td>Education almost means controversy these days, with rising costs and constant complaints about its inadequacies. But the controversy should not obscure the value of schooling. Education remains, despite its shortcomings, the single best means of economic advancement.</td></tr>
</table>

Key terms

main clause A word group that can stand alone as a sentence, containing a subject and a predicate and not beginning with a subordinating word: *The books were expensive.* (See p. 244.)

modifier A word or word group that describes another word or word group—for example, *sweet candy, running in the park.* (See pp. 228 and 306.)

Cumulative and periodic sentences

You can call attention to information by placing it first or last in a sentence, reserving the middle for incidentals:

Unemphatic	Education remains the single best means of economic advancement, despite its shortcomings. [Emphasizes shortcomings.]
Revised	Despite its shortcomings, education remains the single best means of economic advancement. [Emphasizes advancement more than shortcomings.]
Revised	Education remains, despite its shortcomings, the single best means of economic advancement. [Deemphasizes shortcomings.]

emph

15b

A sentence that begins with the main clause and then adds modifiers is called **cumulative** because it accumulates information as it proceeds:

Cumulative	Education has no equal in opening minds, instilling values, and creating opportunities.
Cumulative	Most of the Great American Desert is made up of bare rock, rugged cliffs, mesas, canyons, mountains, separated from one another by broad flat basins covered with sun-baked mud and alkali, supporting a sparse and measured growth of sagebrush or creosote or saltbush, depending on location and elevation. —Edward Abbey

The opposite kind of sentence, called **periodic**, saves the main clause until just before the end (the period) of the sentence. Everything before the main clause points toward it:

Periodic	In opening minds, instilling values, and creating opportunities, education has no equal.
Periodic	With people from all over the world—Korean grocers, Jamaican cricket players, Vietnamese fishers, Haitian cabdrivers—the American mosaic is continually changing.

The periodic sentence creates suspense by reserving important information for the end. But readers should already have an idea of the sentence's subject—because it appeared in the preceding sentence—so that they know what the opening modifiers describe.

EXERCISE 15.2
Sentence combining: Beginnings and endings

Locate the main idea in each group of sentences below. Then combine each group into a single sentence that emphasizes that idea by placing it at the beginning or the end. For sentences 2–5, determine the position of the main idea by considering its relation to the previous sentences: if the main idea picks up a topic that's already been introduced, place it at the beginning; if it adds new information, place it at the end. Possible answers to starred items appear at the end of the book. (You can do this exercise online at *ablongman.com/littlebrown*.)

Example:

The storm blew roofs off buildings. It caused extensive damage. It knocked down many trees. It severed power lines.

Main idea at beginning: The storm caused extensive damage, blowing roofs off buildings, knocking down many trees, and severing power lines.

Main idea at end: Blowing roofs off buildings, knocking down many trees, and severing power lines, the storm caused extensive damage.

coord

15c

*1. Pat Taylor strode into the room. The room was packed. He greeted students called "Taylor's Kids." He nodded to their parents and teachers.
*2. This was a wealthy Louisiana oilman. He had promised his "Kids" free college educations. He was determined to make higher education available to all qualified but disadvantaged students.
  3. The students welcomed Taylor. Their voices joined in singing. They sang "You Are the Wind Beneath My Wings." Their faces beamed with hope. Their eyes flashed with self-confidence.
  4. The students had thought a college education was beyond their dreams. It seemed too costly. It seemed too demanding.
  5. Taylor had to ease the costs and the demands of getting to college. He created a bold plan. The plan consisted of scholarships, tutoring, and counseling.

15c Use coordination to relate equal ideas.

Use **coordination** to show that two or more elements in a sentence are equally important in meaning and thus to clarify the relation between them:

- **Link two main clauses with a comma and a coordinating conjunction,** such as *and* or *but.*

Independence Hall in Philadelphia is now restored, but fifty years ago it was in bad shape.

- **Link two main clauses with a semicolon alone or with a semicolon and a conjunctive adverb,** such as *however.*

The building was standing; however, it suffered from decay.

- **Within clauses, link words and phrases with a coordinating conjunction,** such as *and* or *or.*

equally
← important →
The people and officials of the nation were indifferent to Indepen-

← equally important →
dence Hall or took it for granted.

- **Link main clauses, words, or phrases with a correlative conjunction,** such as *not only . . . but also*.

← equally important →
People not only took the building for granted but also neglected it.

For the punctuation of coordinate elements, see pages 349 (comma and coordinating conjunction), 363 (coordinating conjunction alone), and 366–67 (semicolon alone or with a conjunctive adverb).

coord

15c

Note Grammar and style checkers may spot some errors in punctuating coordinated elements, and they can flag long sentences that may contain excessive coordination. But otherwise they provide little help with coordination because they cannot recognize the relations among ideas in sentences.

1 • Coordinating to smooth sentences

Coordination shows the equality between elements, as illustrated above. At the same time as it clarifies meaning, it can also help smooth choppy sentences like these:

Choppy sentences: We should not rely so heavily on oil. Coal and uranium are also overused. We have a substantial energy resource in the moving waters of our rivers. Smaller streams add to the total volume of water. The resource renews itself. Coal and oil are irreplaceable. Uranium is also irreplaceable. The cost of water does not increase much over time. The costs of coal, oil, and uranium rise dramatically.

The following revision groups coal, oil, and uranium and clearly opposes them to water (the connecting words are underlined):

Ideas coordinated: We should not rely so heavily on coal, oil, and uranium, for we have a substantial energy resource in the moving

---

┌─ Key terms ────────────────────────────────

coordinating conjunctions *And, but, or, nor,* and sometimes *for, so, yet.* (See p. 231.)

conjunctive adverbs Modifiers that describe the relation of the ideas in two clauses, such as *hence, however, indeed,* and *thus.* (See p. 335.)

correlative conjunctions Pairs of connecting words, such as *both . . . and, either . . . or, not only . . . but also.* (See p. 231.)

waters of our rivers and streams. Coal, oil, and uranium are irreplaceable and thus subject to dramatic cost increases; water, however, is self-renewing and more stable in cost.

2 • Coordinating effectively

Use coordination only to express the *equality* of ideas or details. A string of coordinated elements—especially main clauses—implies that all points are equally important:

Excessive coordination	The weeks leading up to the resignation of President Nixon were eventful, and the Supreme Court and the Congress closed in on him, and the Senate Judiciary Committee voted to begin impeachment proceedings, and finally the President resigned on August 9, 1974.

coord

15c

Such a passage needs editing to stress the important points (underlined below) and to de-emphasize the less important information:

Revised	The weeks leading up to the resignation of President Nixon were eventful, as the Supreme Court and the Congress closed in on him and the Senate Judiciary Committee voted to begin impeachment proceedings. Finally, the President resigned on August 9, 1974.

Even within a single sentence, coordination should express a logical equality between ideas:

Faulty	John Stuart Mill was a nineteenth-century utilitarian, and he believed that actions should be judged by their usefulness or by the happiness they cause. [The two clauses are not separate and equal: the second expands on the first by explaining what a utilitarian such as Mill believed.]
Revised	John Stuart Mill, a nineteenth-century utilitarian, believed that actions should be judged by their usefulness or by the happiness they cause.

EXERCISE 15.3
Revising: Excessive or faulty coordination
Revise the following sentences to eliminate excessive or faulty coordination by adding or subordinating information or by forming more than one sentence. Each item has more than one answer. Possible answers to starred items appear at the end of the book. (You can do this exercise online at *ablongman.com/littlebrown*.)

Example:

My dog barks, and I have to move out of my apartment.

Because my dog's barking disturbs my neighbors, I have to move out of my apartment.

*1. Often soldiers admired their commanding officers, and they gave them nicknames, and these names frequently contained the word *old,* but not all of the commanders were old.

*2. General Thomas "Stonewall" Jackson was also called "Old Jack," and he was not yet forty years old.

3. Another Southern general in the Civil War was called "Old Pete," and his full name was James Longstreet.

4. The Union general Henry W. Halleck had a reputation as a good military strategist, and he was an expert on the work of a French military authority, Henri Jomini, and Halleck was called "Old Brains."

5. General William Henry Harrison won the Battle of Tippecanoe, and he received the nickname "Old Tippecanoe," and he used the name in his presidential campaign slogan, "Tippecanoe and Tyler, Too," and he won the election in 1840, but he died of pneumonia a month after taking office.

sub
15d

15d   Use subordination to emphasize ideas.

Use **subordination** to indicate that some elements in a sentence are less important than others for your meaning. Usually, the main idea appears in the main clause, and supporting details appear in subordinate structures:

- Use a subordinate clause beginning with *although, because, if, until, who (whom), that, which,* or another subordinating word:

                                    more important
  ___ less important (subordinate clause) ___ ___(main clause)___
  Although production costs have declined, they are still high.

              less important
      _____(subordinate clause)_____
  Costs, which include labor and facilities, are difficult to control.
      _____more important (main clause)_____

- Use a phrase:

  less important   more important
  _____(phrase)_____   _____(main clause)_____
  Despite some decline, production costs are still high.

      ___less important (phrase)___
  Costs, including labor and facilities, are difficult to control.
      _____more important (main clause)_____

Key terms

subordinate clause A word group that contains a subject and a predicate, begins with a subordinating word such as *because* or *who,* and is not a question: *Words can do damage when they hurt feelings.* (See p. 244.)

phrase A word group that lacks a subject or predicate or both: *Words can do damage by hurting feelings.* (See p. 241.)

- **Use a single word:**

<u>Declining</u> costs have not matched prices.
<u>Labor</u> costs are difficult to control.

For punctuating subordinate elements, see pages 351–52 (comma with introductory elements) and 353–57 (commas with interrupting elements).

Note Grammar and style checkers may spot some errors in punctuating subordinated elements, and they can flag long sentences that may contain excessive subordination. But otherwise they provide little help with subordination because they cannot recognize the relations among ideas in sentences.

sub
15d

1 • Subordinating to distinguish important ideas

A string of main clauses can make everything in a passage seem equally important:

String of main clauses	Computer prices have dropped, and production costs have dropped more slowly, and computer manufacturers have struggled, for their profits have been shrinking.

Emphasis comes from keeping the important information in the main clause (underlined) and subordinating less important details:

Revised	Because production costs have dropped more slowly than prices, <u>computer manufacturers have struggled with shrinking profits.</u>

2 • Subordinating effectively

Subordinate only the less important information in a sentence.

Faulty	Ms. Angelo was a first-year teacher, although she was a better instructor than others with years of experience.

The sentence above suggests that Angelo's inexperience is the main idea, whereas the writer intended to stress her skill *despite* her inexperience. Subordinating the inexperience and elevating the skill to the main clause (underlined) gives appropriate emphasis:

Revised	Although Ms. Angelo was a first-year teacher, <u>she was a better instructor than others with years of experience.</u>

Subordination loses its power to organize and emphasize when too much loosely related detail crowds into one long sentence:

Overloaded	The boats that were moored at the dock when the hurricane, which was one of the worst in three decades, struck were ripped from their moorings, because the owners had not been adequately prepared, since the

weather service had predicted that the storm would blow
out to sea, as storms do at this time of year.

The revision stresses important information in the main clauses
(underlined):

Revised   Struck by one of the worst hurricanes in three decades, the
boats at the dock were ripped from their moorings. The
owners were unprepared because the weather service had
said that hurricanes at this time of year blow out to sea.

EXERCISE 15.4
Revising: Faulty or excessive subordination

Revise the following sentences to eliminate faulty or excessive subordination and to achieve appropriate emphasis. Possible answers to starred
items appear at the end of the book. (You can do this exercise online at
ablongman.com/littlebrown.)

Example:

Terrified to return home, he had driven his mother's car into a
cornfield.

Having driven his mother's car into a cornfield, he was terrified to
return home.

*1. Genaro González is a successful writer, which means that his stories
and novels have been published to critical acclaim.
*2. He loves to write, although he has also earned a doctorate in
psychology.
3. His first story, which reflects his growing consciousness of his Aztec
heritage and place in the world, is titled "Un Hijo del Sol."
4. González, who writes equally well in English and Spanish, received a
large fellowship that enabled him to take a leave of absence from
the University of Texas–Pan American, where he teaches psychology, so that he could write without worrying about an income.
5. González wrote the first version of "Un Hijo del Sol" while he was a
sophomore at Pan American, which is in the Rio Grande valley of
southern Texas, which González calls "el Valle" in the story.

EXERCISE 15.5
Revising: Coordination and subordination

The following paragraph consists entirely of simple sentences. Use coordination and subordination to combine sentences in the way you think
most effective to emphasize main ideas. Possible answers to starred sentences appear at the end of the book. (You can do this exercise online at
ablongman.com/littlebrown.)

*Sir Walter Raleigh personified the Elizabethan Age. *That was the
period of Elizabeth I's rule of England. *The period occurred in the last
half of the sixteenth century. *Raleigh was a courtier and poet. *He was
also an explorer and entrepreneur. *Supposedly, he gained Queen

Elizabeth's favor. *He did this by throwing his cloak beneath her feet at the right moment. *She was just about to step over a puddle. There is no evidence for this story. It does illustrate Raleigh's dramatic and dynamic personality. His energy drew others to him. He was one of Elizabeth's favorites. She supported him. She also dispensed favors to him. However, he lost his queen's goodwill. Without her permission he seduced one of her maids of honor. He eventually married the maid of honor. Elizabeth died. Then her successor imprisoned Raleigh in the Tower of London. Her successor was James I. The king falsely charged Raleigh with treason. Raleigh was released after thirteen years. He was arrested again two years later on the old treason charges. At the age of sixty-six he was beheaded.

//
16a

16   Parallelism

How can I make connections plain within sentences?

When ideas within sentences have the same function and importance, you can show their connection using parallelism, or parallel structure, as shown in the following example:

The air is dirtied by <u>factories belching smoke</u> and <u>cars spewing exhaust</u>.

With **parallelism**, you use the same grammatical forms to express equally important ideas. In the example above, the two underlined phrases have the same function and importance (two sources of air pollution), so they also have the same grammatical construction.

Note A grammar and style checker cannot recognize faulty parallelism because it cannot recognize the relations among ideas.

16a   Use parallelism with *and, but, or, nor, yet.*

The coordinating conjunctions *and, but, or, nor,* and *yet* always signal a need for parallelism, as shown in the following examples.

┌─ **Key term** ───
│ **coordinating conjunctions** Words that connect elements of the same
│ kind and importance: *and, but, or, nor,* and sometimes *for, so, yet.* (See
│ p. 231.)
└───

http://www.ablongman.com/littlebrown

Visit the companion Web site for more help and electronic exercises on parallelism.

The industrial base was <u>shifting</u> and <u>shrinking</u>. [Parallel words.]

Politicians rarely <u>acknowledged the problem</u> or <u>proposed alternatives.</u> [Parallel phrases.]

Industrial workers were understandably disturbed <u>that they were losing</u> <u>their jobs</u> and <u>that no one seemed to care.</u> [Parallel clauses.]

When sentence elements linked by coordinating conjunctions are not parallel in structure, the sentence is awkward and distracting:

Nonparallel	The reasons steel companies kept losing money were <u>that</u> <u>their plants were inefficient</u>, <u>high labor costs</u>, and <u>foreign</u> <u>competition was increasing.</u>
Revised	The reasons steel companies kept losing money were <u>in-</u> <u>efficient plants</u>, <u>high labor costs</u>, and <u>increasing foreign</u> <u>competition.</u>
Nonparallel	Success was difficult even for efficient companies because <u>of the shift away from all manufacturing in the United</u> <u>States</u> and <u>the fact that steel production was shifting to-</u> <u>ward emerging nations.</u>
Revised	Success was difficult even for efficient companies be- cause <u>of the shift away from all manufacturing in the</u> <u>United States</u> and <u>toward steel production in emerging</u> <u>nations.</u>

// 16b

All the words required by idiom or grammar must be stated in compound constructions (see also p. 214):

Faulty	Given training, workers can acquire the <u>skills</u> and <u>interest</u> in other jobs. [Idiom dictates different prepositions with *skills* and *interest*.]
Revised	Given training, workers can acquire the skills <u>for</u> and inter- est <u>in</u> other jobs.

16b Use parallelism with *both . . . and, not . . . but,* or another correlative conjunction.

Correlative conjunctions stress equality and balance between elements. Parallelism confirms the equality.

Key term

correlative conjunctions Pairs of words that connect elements of the same kind and importance, such as *both . . . and, either . . . or, neither . . . nor, not . . . but, not only . . . but also.* (See p. 231.)

It is not <u>a tax bill</u> but <u>a tax relief bill</u>, providing relief not <u>for the needy</u> but <u>for the greedy</u>.   —Franklin Delano Roosevelt

With correlative conjunctions, the element after the second connector must match the element after the first connector:

Nonparallel	Huck Finn learns not only <u>that human beings have an enormous capacity for folly</u> but also <u>enormous dignity</u>. [The first element includes *that human beings have;* the second element does not.]
Revised	Huck Finn learns <u>that human beings have</u> not only <u>an enormous capacity for folly</u> but also <u>enormous dignity</u>. [Repositioning *that human beings have* makes the two elements parallel.]

16c   Use parallelism in comparisons.

Parallelism confirms the likeness or difference between two elements being compared using *than* or *as*.

Nonparallel	Huck Finn proves less <u>a bad boy</u> than <u>to be an independent spirit</u>. In the end he is every bit as determined <u>in rejecting help</u> as he is <u>to leave</u> for "the territory."
Revised	Huck Finn proves less a bad boy than <u>an independent spirit</u>. In the end he is every bit as determined <u>to reject help</u> as he is to leave for "the territory."

(See also pp. 309–10 on making comparisons logical.)

16d   Use parallelism with lists, headings, and outlines.

The items in a list or outline are coordinate and should be parallel. Parallelism is essential in the headings that divide a paper into sections (see p. 77) and in a formal topic outline (see pp. 24–25).

Nonparallel	Revised
Changes in Renaissance England	Changes in Renaissance England
1. Extension of trade routes	1. Extension of trade routes
2. Merchant class became more powerful	2. <u>Increased power</u> of the merchant class
3. The death of feudalism	3. <u>Death</u> of feudalism
4. Upsurging of the arts	4. <u>Upsurge</u> of the arts
5. Religious quarrels began	5. <u>Rise</u> of religious quarrels

//
16d

EXERCISE 16.1
Revising: Parallelism

Revise the following sentences to create parallelism wherever it is required for grammar and coherence. Add or delete words or rephrase as necessary. Answers to starred items appear at the end of the book. (You can do this exercise online at *ablongman.com/littlebrown.*)

Example:

After emptying her bag, searching the apartment, and she called the library, Jennifer realized she had lost the book.

After emptying her bag, searching the apartment, and <u>calling</u> the library, Jennifer realized she had lost the book.

//
16d

*1. The ancient Greeks celebrated four athletic contests: the Olympic Games at Olympia, the Isthmian Games were held near Corinth, at Delphi the Pythian Games, and the Nemean Games were sponsored by the people of Cleonae.

*2. Each day the games consisted of either athletic events or holding ceremonies and sacrifices to the gods.

*3. In the years between the games, competitors were taught wrestling, javelin throwing, and how to box.

*4. Competitors participated in running sprints, spectacular chariot and horse races, and running long distances while wearing full armor.

*5. The purpose of such events was developing physical strength, demonstrating skill and endurance, and to sharpen the skills needed for war.

6. Events were held for both men and for boys.

7. At the Olympic Games the spectators cheered their favorites to victory, attended sacrifices to the gods, and they feasted on the meat not burned in offerings.

8. The athletes competed less to achieve great wealth than for gaining honor both for themselves and their cities.

9. Of course, exceptional athletes received financial support from patrons, poems and statues by admiring artists, and they even got lavish living quarters from their sponsoring cities.

10. With the medal counts and flag ceremonies, today's Olympians sometimes seem to be proving their countries' superiority more than to demonstrate individual talent.

EXERCISE 16.2
Sentence combining: Parallelism

Combine each of the following groups of sentences into one concise sentence that uses parallel structure for parallel elements. You will have to add, delete, change, and rearrange words. Each item has more than one possible answer. Answers to starred items appear at the end of the book. (You can do this exercise online at *ablongman.com/littlebrown.*)

Example:

The new process works smoothly. It is efficient, too.
The new process works smoothly and <u>efficiently</u>.

*1. People can develop post-traumatic stress disorder (PTSD). They develop it after experiencing a dangerous situation. They will also have felt fear for their survival.

*2. The disorder can be triggered by a wide variety of events. Combat is a typical cause. Similarly, natural disasters can result in PTSD. Some people experience PTSD after a hostage situation.

3. PTSD can occur immediately after the stressful incident. Or it may not appear until many years later.

4. Sometimes people with PTSD will act irrationally. Moreover, they often become angry.

5. Other symptoms include dreaming that one is reliving the experience. They include hallucinating that one is back in the terrifying place. In another symptom one imagines that strangers are actually one's former torturers.

var
17a

17 Variety and Details

What makes sentences interesting?

Writing that is interesting as well as clear has at least two features: the sentences vary in length and structure, and they are well textured with details.

Note Some grammar and style checkers will flag long sentences, and you can check for appropriate variety in a series of such sentences. But generally these programs cannot help you see where variety may be needed because they cannot recognize the relative importance and complexity of your ideas. Nor can they suggest where you should add details.

17a Vary sentence length.

In most contemporary writing, sentences tend to vary from about ten to about forty words, with an average of between fifteen and twenty-five words. If your sentences are all at one extreme or the other, your readers may have difficulty focusing on main ideas and seeing the relations among them.

http://www.ablongman.com/littlebrown ▶

Visit the companion Web site for more help and an electronic exercise on variety and details.

- **Long sentences.** If most of your sentences contain thirty-five words or more, your main ideas may not stand out from the details that support them. Break some of the long sentences into shorter, simpler ones.
- **Short sentences.** If most of your sentences contain fewer than ten or fifteen words, all your ideas may seem equally important and the links between them may not be clear. Try combining them with coordination (p. 181) and subordination (p. 184) to show relationships and stress main ideas over supporting information.

var
17b

17b Vary sentence structure.

A passage will be monotonous if all its sentences follow the same pattern, like soldiers marching in a parade. To vary structure, try subordination, sentence combining, varying sentence beginnings, and varying word order.

1 • Subordination

A string of main clauses in simple or compound sentences can be especially plodding:

Monotonous   The moon is now drifting away from the earth. It moves away at the rate of about one inch a year. This movement is lengthening our days. They increase a thousandth of a second every century. Forty-seven of our present days will someday make up a month. We might eventually lose the moon altogether. Such great planetary movement rightly concerns astronomers, but it need not worry us. It will take 50 million years.

Enliven such writing—and make the main ideas stand out—by expressing the less important information in subordinate clauses and phrases. In the following revision, underlining indicates subordinate structures that used to be main clauses.

┌─ **Key terms** ─────────────────────────────────

main clause A word group that contains a subject and a predicate and does not begin with a subordinating word: *Tourism is an industry. It brings in over $2 billion a year.* (See p. 244.)

subordinate clause A word group that contains a subject and a predicate, begins with a subordinating word such as *because* or *who,* and is not a question: *Tourism is an industry that brings in over $2 billion a year.* (See p. 244.)

phrase A word group that lacks a subject or a predicate or both: *Tourism is an industry valued at over $2 billion a year.* (See p. 241.)

Revised   The moon is now drifting away from the earth <u>about one inch a year</u>. <u>At a thousandth of a second every century</u>, this movement is lengthening our days. Forty-seven of our present days will someday make up a month, <u>if we don't eventually lose the moon altogether</u>. Such great planetary movement rightly concerns astronomers, but it need not worry us. It will take 50 million years.

2 • Sentence combining

As the preceding example shows, subordinating to achieve variety often involves combining short, choppy sentences into longer units that link related information and stress main ideas. Here is another example of such sentence combining:

Monotonous   Astronomy may seem a remote science. It may seem to have little to do with people's daily lives. Many astronomers find otherwise. They see their science as soothing. It gives perspective to everyday routines and problems.

Combining five sentences into one, the revision is both clearer and easier to read. Underlining highlights the changes:

Revised   Astronomy may seem a remote science <u>having</u> little to do with people's daily lives, <u>but</u> many astronomers <u>find their science soothing</u> <u>because</u> it gives perspective to everyday routines and problems.

3 • Varying sentence beginnings

An English sentence often begins with its subject, which generally captures old information from a preceding sentence (see p. 179):

The defendant's <u>lawyer</u> was determined to break the prosecution's witness. <u>He</u> relentlessly cross-examined the stubborn witness for a week.

However, an unbroken sequence of sentences beginning with the subject quickly becomes monotonous:

Monotonous   The defendant's lawyer was determined to break the prosecution's witness. He relentlessly cross-examined the witness for a week. The witness had expected to be dismissed within an hour and was visibly irritated. She did not cooperate. She was reprimanded by the judge.

Beginning some of these sentences with other expressions improves readability and clarity:

Revised   The defendant's lawyer was determined to break the prosecution's witness. <u>For a week</u> he relentlessly cross-examined the witness. <u>Expecting to be dismissed within an hour</u>, the witness was visibly irritated. She did not cooperate. Indeed, she was reprimanded by the judge.

The underlined expressions represent the most common choices for varying sentence beginnings:

- **Adverb modifiers,** such as *For a week* (modifies the verb *cross-examined*).
- **Adjective modifiers,** such as *Expecting to be dismissed within an hour* (modifies *witness*).
- **Transitional expressions,** such as *Indeed*. (See pp. 56–57 for a list.)

CULTURE LANGUAGE In standard American English, placing certain adverb modifiers at the beginning of a sentence requires you to change the normal subject-verb order as well. The most common of these modifiers are negatives, including *seldom, rarely, in no case, not since*, and *not until*.

17c

| | verb |
| adverb   subject | phrase |

Faulty   Seldom a witness has held the stand so long.

| | helping | main |
| adverb | verb   subject | verb |

Revised   Seldom has a witness held the stand so long.

4 • Varying word order

Occasionally, you can vary a sentence and emphasize it at the same time by inverting the usual order of parts:

A dozen witnesses testified for the prosecution, and the defense attorney barely questioned eleven of them. The twelfth, however, he grilled. [Normal word order: *He grilled the twelfth, however.*]

Inverted sentences used without need are artificial. Use them only when emphasis demands.

17c   Add details.

Relevant details such as facts and examples create the texture and life that keep readers awake and help them grasp your meaning. Notice the difference in the following two examples.

> ┌ **Key terms** ──────────────────────────────
>
> **adverb** A word or word group that describes a verb, an adjective, another adverb, or a whole sentence: *dressed sharply, clearly unhappy, soaring from the mountain*. (See p. 228.)
>
> **adjective** A word or word group that describes a noun or pronoun: *sweet smile, certain someone*. (See p. 228.)

Flat   Constructed after World War II, Levittown, New York, consisted of thousands of houses in two basic styles. Over the
decades, residents have altered the houses so dramatically
that the original styles are often unrecognizable.

Detailed   Constructed <u>on potato fields</u> after World War II, Levittown,
New York, consisted of <u>more than seventeen thousand</u>
houses in <u>Cape Cod and ranch</u> styles. Over the decades, residents have <u>added expansive front porches, punched dormer
windows through roofs, converted garages to sun porches,
and otherwise</u> altered the houses so dramatically that the
original styles are often unrecognizable.

EXERCISE 17.1
Revising: Variety

The following paragraph consists entirely of simple sentences that begin
with their subjects. Use the techniques discussed in this chapter to vary
the sentences. Delete, add, change, and rearrange words to make the
paragraph more readable and to make important ideas stand out clearly.
Answers to starred sentences appear at the end of the book. (You can do
this exercise online at *ablongman.com/littlebrown*.)

*The Italian volcano Vesuvius had been dormant for many years.
*It then exploded on August 24 in the year AD 79. *The ash, pumice,
and mud from the volcano buried two busy towns. *Herculaneum is
one. *The more famous is Pompeii. Both towns lay undiscovered for
many centuries. Herculaneum and Pompeii were discovered in 1709 and
1748, respectively. The excavation of Pompeii was the more systematic.
It was the occasion for initiating modern methods of conservation and
restoration. Herculaneum was simply looted of its more valuable finds. It
was then left to disintegrate. Pompeii appears much as it did before the
eruption. A luxurious house opens onto a lush central garden. An election poster decorates a wall. A dining table is set for breakfast.

18

18 Appropriate and Exact Words

Is this the right word?

The choice of the "right" word depends partly on whether the
word is appropriate for your writing situation (next page) and
partly on whether it expresses your meaning exactly (p. 203).

http://www.ablongman.com/littlebrown ▶

Visit the companion Web site for more help
and electronic exercises on appropriate and
exact words.

18a   Choose appropriate words.

Appropriate words suit your writing situation—your subject, purpose, and audience. In most college and career writing you should rely on what's called **standard American English,** the dialect of English normally expected and used in schools, businesses, government, and the communications media. (For more on its role in academic writing, see pp. 89–91.)

The vocabulary of standard American English is huge, allowing expression of an infinite range of ideas and feelings; but it does exclude words that only some groups of people use, understand, or find inoffensive. Some of these more limited vocabularies should be avoided altogether; others should be used cautiously and in relevant situations, as when aiming for a special effect with an audience you know will appreciate it. Whenever you doubt a word's status, consult a dictionary (see p. 204).

Note Many grammar and style checkers can be set to flag potentially inappropriate words, such as nonstandard language, slang, colloquialisms, and gender-specific terms (*manmade, mailman*). However, the checker can flag only words listed in its dictionary of questionable words. For example, a checker flagged *businessman* as potentially sexist in *A successful businessman puts clients first,* but the checker did not flag *his* in *A successful businessperson listens to his clients.* If you use a checker to review your language, you'll need to determine whether a flagged word is or is not appropriate for your writing situation.

1 • Nonstandard dialect   CULTURE LANGUAGE

Like many countries, the United States includes scores of regional, social, or ethnic groups with their own distinct **dialects,** or versions of English. Standard American English is one of those dialects, and so are Black English, Appalachian English, Creole, and the English of coastal Maine. All the dialects of English share many features, but each also has its own vocabulary, pronunciation, and grammar.

If you speak a dialect of English besides standard American English, be careful about using your dialect in situations where standard English is the norm, such as in academic or business writing. Dialects are not wrong in themselves, but forms imported from one dialect into another may still be perceived as unclear or incorrect. When you know standard English is expected in your writing, edit to eliminate expressions in your dialect that you know (or have been told) differ from standard English. These expressions may include *theirselves, hisn, them books,* and others labeled "nonstandard" by a dictionary. They may also include verb forms, as discussed on pages 255–61. For help identifying and editing nonstandard language, see the "◣ CULTURE ▪ LANGUAGE ▪ Guide" just before the back endpapers of this book.

Your participation in the community of standard American English does not require you to abandon your own dialect. You may want to use it in writing you do for yourself, such as journals, notes, and drafts, which should be composed as freely as possible. You may want to quote it in an academic paper, as when analyzing or reporting conversation in dialect. And, of course, you will want to use it with others who speak it.

appr

18a

2 • Slang

Slang is the language used by a group, such as musicians or computer programmers, to reflect common experiences and to make technical references efficient. The following example is from an essay on the slang of "skaters" (skateboarders):

> Curtis slashed ultra-punk crunchers on his longboard, while the Rube-man flailed his usual Gumbyness on tweaked frontsides and lofty fakie ollies.
>
> —Miles Orkin, "Mucho Slingage by the Pool"

Among those who understand it, slang may be vivid and forceful. It often occurs in dialog, and an occasional slang expression can enliven an informal essay. But most slang is too flippant and imprecise for effective communication, and it is generally inappropriate for college or business writing. Notice the gain in seriousness and precision achieved in the following revision:

Slang   Many students start out <u>pretty together</u> but then <u>get weird</u>.
Revised   Many students start out <u>with clear goals</u> but then <u>lose their direction</u>.

3 • Colloquial language

Colloquial language is the everyday spoken language, including expressions such as *get together, go crazy,* and *do the dirty work.*

When you write informally, colloquial language may be appropriate to achieve the casual, relaxed effect of conversation. An occasional colloquial word dropped into otherwise more formal writing can also help you achieve a desired emphasis. But most colloquial language is not precise enough for college or career writing. In such writing you should generally avoid any words and expressions labeled "informal" or "colloquial" in your dictionary.

Colloquial	According to a Native American myth, the Great Creator <u>had a dog hanging around with him</u> when he created the earth.
Revised	According to a Native American myth, the Great Creator <u>was accompanied by a dog</u> when he created the earth.

4 • Technical words

All disciplines and professions rely on specialized language that allows the members to communicate precisely and efficiently with each other. Chemists, for instance, have their *phosphatides,* and literary critics have their *motifs* and *subtexts.* Without explanation technical words are meaningless to nonspecialists. When you are writing for nonspecialists, avoid unnecessary technical terms and carefully define terms you must use.

appr
18a

5 • Indirect and pretentious writing

Small, plain, and direct words are almost always preferable to big, showy, or evasive words. Take special care to avoid euphemisms, double-talk, and pretentious writing.

A **euphemism** is a presumably inoffensive word that a writer or speaker substitutes for a word deemed potentially offensive or too blunt, such as *passed away* for *died, misspeak* for *lie,* or *remains* for *corpse.* Use euphemisms only when you know that blunt, truthful words would needlessly hurt or offend members of your audience.

A kind of euphemism that deliberately evades the truth is **double-talk** (also called **doublespeak** or **weasel words**): language intended to confuse or to be misunderstood. Today double-talk is unfortunately common in politics and advertising—the *revenue enhancement* that is really a tax, the *peace-keeping function* that is really war making, the *biodegradable* bags that last decades. Double-talk has no place in honest writing.

Euphemism and sometimes double-talk seem to keep company with **pretentious writing,** fancy language that is more elaborate than its subject requires. Choose your words for their exactness and economy. The big, ornate word may be tempting, but pass it up. Your readers will be grateful.

Pretentious	To perpetuate our endeavor of providing funds for our elderly citizens as we do at the present moment, we will face the exigency of enhanced contributions from all our citizens.
Revised	We cannot continue to fund Social Security and Medicare for the elderly unless we raise taxes.

6 • Sexist and other biased language

Even when we do not mean it to, our language can reflect and perpetuate hurtful prejudices toward groups of people. Such biased language can be obvious—words such as *nigger, honky, mick, kike, fag, dyke,* and *broad.* But it can also be subtle, generalizing about groups in ways that may be familiar but that are also inaccurate or unfair.

Biased language reflects poorly on the user, not on the person or persons whom it mischaracterizes or insults. Unbiased language does not submit to false generalizations. It treats people respectfully as individuals and labels groups as they wish to be labeled.

Stereotypes of race, ethnicity, religion, age, and other characteristics

appr
18a

A **stereotype** is a generalization based on poor evidence, a kind of formula for understanding and judging people simply because of their membership in a group:

Men are uncommunicative.
Women are emotional.
Liberals want to raise taxes.
Conservatives are affluent.

At best, stereotypes betray a noncritical writer, one who is not thinking beyond notions received from others. In your writing, be alert for statements that characterize whole groups of people.

Stereotype	Elderly drivers should have their licenses limited to daytime driving only. [Asserts that all elderly people are poor night drivers.]
Revised	Drivers with impaired night vision should have their licenses limited to daytime driving only.

Some stereotypes have become part of the language, but they are still potentially offensive:

Stereotype	The administrators <u>are too blind</u> to see the need for a new gymnasium. [Equates vision disability and lack of understanding.]
Revised	The administrators <u>do not understand</u> the need for a new gymnasium.

Sexist language

Among the most subtle and persistent biased language is that expressing narrow ideas about men's and women's roles, position, and value in society. Like other stereotypes, this **sexist language** can wound or irritate readers, and it indicates the writer's thoughtlessness or unfairness. The box below suggests some ways of eliminating sexist language.

appr

18a

Eliminating sexist language

- **Avoid demeaning and patronizing language:**

  Sexist   Dr. Keith Kim and Lydia Hawkins coauthored the article.

  Revised   Dr. Keith Kim and Dr. Lydia Hawkins coauthored the article.

  Revised   Keith Kim and Lydia Hawkins coauthored the article.

  Sexist   Ladies are entering almost every occupation formerly filled by men.

  Revised   Women are entering almost every occupation formerly filled by men.

- **Avoid occupational or social stereotypes:**

  Sexist   The considerate doctor commends a nurse when she provides his patients with good care.

  Revised   The considerate doctor commends a nurse who provides good care for patients.

  Sexist   The grocery shopper should save her coupons.

  Revised   Grocery shoppers should save their coupons.

- **Avoid referring needlessly to gender:**

  Sexist   Marie Curie, a woman chemist, discovered radium.

  Revised   Marie Curie, a chemist, discovered radium.

  Sexist   The patients were tended by a male nurse.

  Revised   The patients were tended by a nurse.

- **Avoid using *man* or words containing *man* to refer to all human beings.** Here are a few alternatives:

businessman	businessperson
chairman	chair, chairperson
congressman	representative in Congress, legislator
craftsman	craftsperson, artisan
layman	layperson
mankind	humankind, humanity, human beings, humans
manmade	handmade, manufactured, synthetic, artificial
manpower	personnel, human resources
policeman	police officer
salesman	salesperson, sales representative

  Sexist   Man has not reached the limits of social justice.

  Revised   Humankind [or Humanity] has not reached the limits of social justice.

| Sexist | The furniture consists of <u>manmade</u> materials. |
| Revised | The furniture consists of <u>synthetic</u> materials. |

● **Avoid the generic** *he,* **the male pronoun used to refer to both genders.** (See also pp. 298–99.)

Sexist	The newborn <u>child</u> explores <u>his</u> world.
Revised	Newborn <u>children</u> explore <u>their</u> world. [Use the plural for the pronoun and the word it refers to.]
Revised	The newborn <u>child</u> explores <u>the</u> world. [Avoid the pronoun altogether.]
Revised	The newborn <u>child</u> explores <u>his or her</u> world. [Substitute male and female pronouns.]

Use the last option sparingly—only once in a group of sentences and only to stress the singular individual.

appr

18a

CULTURE LANGUAGE Forms of address vary widely from culture to culture. In some cultures, for instance, one shows respect by referring to all older women as if they were married, using the equivalent of *Mrs.* Usage in the United States is changing toward making no assumptions about marital status, rank, or other characteristics—for instance, addressing a woman as *Ms.* unless she is known to prefer *Mrs.* or *Miss.*

Appropriate labels

We often need to label groups: *swimmers, politicians, mothers, Christians, Westerners, students.* But labels can be shorthand stereotypes, slighting the person labeled and ignoring the preferences of the group members themselves. Although sometimes dismissed as "political correctness," showing sensitivity about labels hurts no one and helps gain your readers' trust and respect.

● **Avoid labels that (intentionally or not) disparage the person or group you refer to.** A person with emotional problems is not a *mental patient.* A person with cancer is not a *cancer victim.* A person using a wheelchair is not *wheelchair-bound.*

● **Use names for racial, ethnic, and other groups that reflect the preferences of each group's members,** or at least many of them. Examples of current preferences include *African American* or *black, latino/latina* (for Americans and American immigrants of Spanish-speaking descent), and *disabled* (rather than *handicapped*). But labels change often. To learn how a group's members wish to be labeled, ask them directly, attend to usage in reputable periodicals, or check a recent dictionary.

A helpful reference is *Guidelines for Bias-Free Writing*, by Marilyn Schwartz and the Task Force on Bias-Free Language of the Association of American University Presses.

appr
18a

EXERCISE 18.1
Revising: Appropriate words

Rewrite the following sentences as needed for standard American English, focusing on inappropriate slang, technical or pretentious language, and biased language. Consult a dictionary to determine whether particular words are appropriate and to find suitable substitutes. Answers to starred items appear at the end of the book. (You can do this exercise online at *ablongman.com/littlebrown*.)

Example:

If negotiators get hyper during contract discussions, they may mess up chances for a settlement.

If negotiators <u>become excited or upset</u> during contract discussions, they may <u>harm</u> chances for a settlement.

*1. Acquired immune deficiency syndrome (AIDS) is a major deal all over the world.

*2. The disease gets around primarily by sexual intercourse, exchange of bodily fluids, shared needles, and blood transfusions.

*3. Those who think the disease is limited to homos, druggies, and foreigners are quite mistaken.

*4. Stats suggest that in the United States one in every five hundred college kids carries the HIV virus that causes AIDS.

*5. A person with HIV or full-blown AIDS does not deserve to be subjected to exclusionary behavior or callousness on the part of his fellow citizens. Instead, he has the necessity for all the compassion, medical care, and financial assistance due those who are in the extremity of illness.

6. An HIV or AIDS victim often sees a team of doctors or a single doctor with a specialized practice.

7. The doctor may help his patients by obtaining social services for them as well as by providing medical care.

8. The HIV or AIDS sufferer who loses his job may need public assistance.

9. For someone who is very ill, a home-care nurse may be necessary. She can administer medications and make the sick person as comfortable as possible.

10. Some people with HIV or AIDS have insurance, but others lack the dough for premiums.

EXERCISE 18.2
Revising: Sexist language

Revise the following sentences to eliminate sexist language. If you change a singular noun or pronoun to plural, be sure to make any needed changes in verbs or other pronouns. Answers to starred items appear at the end of the book. (You can do this exercise online at *ablongman.com/littlebrown*.)

Example:

The career placement officer at most colleges and universities spends part of his time advising students how to write successful résumés.

<u>Career placement officers</u> at most colleges and universities <u>spend</u> part of <u>their</u> time advising students how to write successful résumés.

*1. When a person applies for a job, he should represent himself with the best possible résumé.
*2. A person applying for a job as a mailman should appear to be honest and responsible.
*3. A girl applying for a position as an in-home nurse should also represent herself as honest and responsible.
*4. Of course, she should also have a background of capable nursing.
*5. The businessman who is scanning a stack of résumés will, of necessity, read them all quickly.

6. The person who wants his résumé to stand out will make sure it highlights his best points.
7. The Web designer will highlight his experience with computers.
8. Volunteer work may be appropriate, too, such as being chairman of a student organization.
9. If the student has been secretary for a campus organization, she could include that volunteer experience in her résumé.
10. If everyone writing a résumé would keep in mind the man who will be reading it, the applicant might know better what he should include and how he should format that information.

18b   Choose exact words.

To write clearly and effectively, you will want to find the words that fit your meaning exactly and convey your attitude precisely.

Note A grammar and style checker can provide some help with inexact language. For instance, you can set it to flag commonly confused words (such as *continuous/continual*), misused prepositions in idioms (such as *accuse for* instead of *accuse of*), and clichés. But a checker can't help you at all with appropriate connotation, excessive abstraction, or other problems discussed in this section.

1 • Word meanings and synonyms

For writing exactly, a dictionary is essential and a thesaurus can be helpful.

Desk dictionaries

A desk dictionary defines about 150,000 to 200,000 words and provides pronunciation, grammatical functions, history, and other information. Here is a sample from *Merriam-Webster's Collegiate Dictionary:*

Dictionary entry for *reckon*

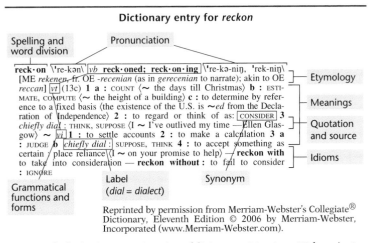

exact
18b

Reprinted by permission from Merriam-Webster's Collegiate® Dictionary, Eleventh Edition © 2006 by Merriam-Webster, Incorporated (www.Merriam-Webster.com).

Good desk dictionaries, in addition to *Merriam-Webster's*, include the *American Heritage College Dictionary,* the *Random House Webster's College Dictionary,* and *Webster's New World Dictionary.* Most of these are available in both print and electronic form (CD-ROM or online). In addition, several Web sites provide online dictionaries or links to online dictionaries. For links, visit *ablongman .com/littlebrown.*

CULTURE LANGUAGE If English is not your native language, you probably should have a dictionary prepared especially for students using English as a second language (ESL). Such a dictionary contains special information on prepositions, count versus noncount nouns, and many other matters. Reliable ESL dictionaries include *CO-BUILD English Language Dictionary, Longman Dictionary of Contemporary English,* and *Oxford Advanced Learner's Dictionary.*

Thesauruses

To find a word with the exact shade of meaning you intend, you may want to consult a thesaurus, or book of **synonyms**—words with approximately the same meaning. A reference such as *Roget's International Thesaurus* lists most imaginable synonyms for thousands of words. The word *news,* for instance, has half a page of synonyms, including *tidings, dispatch, gossip,* and *journalism.*

Since a thesaurus aims to open up possibilities, its lists of synonyms include approximate as well as precise matches. The thesaurus does not define synonyms or distinguish among them, however, so you need a dictionary to discover exact meanings. In general, don't use a word from a thesaurus—even one you like the sound of—until you are sure of its appropriateness for your meaning.

Note For links to online thesauruses, visit *ablongman.com/ littlebrown.* Your word processor may also include a thesaurus, making it easy to look up synonyms and insert the chosen word into your text. But still you should consult a dictionary unless you are certain of the word's meaning and appropriateness.

2 • The right word for your meaning

All words have one or more basic meanings (called **denotations**)—the meanings listed in the dictionary, without reference to emotional associations. If readers are to understand you, you must use words according to their established meanings.

- Consult a dictionary whenever you are unsure of a word's meaning.
- Distinguish between similar-sounding words that have widely different denotations:

Inexact Older people often suffer <u>infirmaries</u> [places for the sick].
Exact Older people often suffer <u>infirmities</u> [disabilities].

Some words, called **homonyms,** sound exactly alike but differ in meaning: for example, *principal/principle* or *rain/reign/rein.* (See pp. 393–94 for a list of commonly confused homonyms.)

- Distinguish between words with related but distinct meanings:

Inexact Television commercials <u>continuously</u> [unceasingly] interrupt programming.
Exact Television commercials <u>continually</u> [regularly] interrupt programming.

In addition to their emotion-free meanings, many words also carry associations with specific feelings. These **connotations** can shape readers' responses and are thus a powerful tool for writers. The following word pairs have related denotations but very different connotations:

pride: sense of self-worth
vanity: excessive regard for oneself

firm: steady, unchanging, unyielding
stubborn: unreasonable, bullheaded

lasting: long-lived, enduring
endless: without limit, eternal

enthusiasm: excitement
mania: excessive interest or desire

A dictionary can help you track down words with the exact connotations you want. Besides providing meanings, your dictionary may also list and distinguish synonyms to guide your choices. A thesaurus can also help if you use it carefully, as discussed on pages 204–05.

exact

18b

EXERCISE 18.3
Using a dictionary

Look up five of the following words in a dictionary. For each word, write down (*a*) the division into syllables, (*b*) the pronunciation, (*c*) the grammatical functions and forms, (*d*) the etymology, (*e*) each meaning, and (*f*) any special uses indicated by labels. Finally, use the word in two sentences of your own.

1. depreciation   5. assassin   8. steal
2. secretary   6. astrology   9. plain (*adjective*)
3. grammar   7. toxic   10. ceremony
4. manifest

EXERCISE 18.4
Revising: Denotation

Revise any underlined word below that is used incorrectly. Consult a dictionary if you are uncertain of a word's precise meaning. Answers to starred items appear at the end of the book. (You can do this exercise online at *ablongman.com/littlebrown*.)

Example:

Sam and Dave are going to Bermuda and Hauppage, respectfully, for spring vacation.

Sam and Dave are going to Bermuda and Hauppage, respectively, for spring vacation.

*1. Maxine Hong Kingston was rewarded many prizes for her first two books, *The Woman Warrior* and *China Men.*
*2. Kingston sites her mother's tales about ancestors and ancient Chinese customs as the sources of these memoirs.
*3. Two of Kingston's progeny, her great-grandfathers, are focal points of *China Men.*
*4. Both men led rebellions against suppressive employers: a sugarcane farmer and a railroad-construction engineer.

*5. In her childhood Kingston was greatly effected by her mother's tale about a pregnant aunt who was ostracized by villagers.

6. The aunt gained avengeance by drowning herself in the village's water supply.

7. Kingston decided to make her nameless relative infamous by giving her immortality in *The Woman Warrior*.

8. Kingston's novel *Tripmaster Monkey* has been called the premier novel about the 1960s.

9. Her characters embody the principles that led to her own protest against the Vietnam War.

10. Kingston's innovative books infer her opposition to racism and sexism both in the China of the past and in the United States of the present.

EXERCISE 18.5
Considering the connotations of words

Fill in the blank in each sentence below with the most appropriate word from the list in parentheses. Consult a dictionary to be sure of your choice. Answers to starred items appear at the end of the book. (You can do this exercise online at *ablongman.com/littlebrown*.)

Example:

Channel 5 _____ Oshu the winner before the polls closed. (*advertised, declared, broadcast, promulgated*)

Channel 5 declared Oshu the winner before the polls closed.

*1. AIDS is a serious health _____. (*problem, worry, difficulty, plight*)
*2. Once the virus has entered the blood system, it _____ T-cells. (*murders, destroys, slaughters, executes*)

3. The _____ of T-cells is to combat infections. (*ambition, function, aim, goal*)

4. Without enough T-cells, the body is nearly _____ against infections. (*defenseless, hopeless, desperate*)

5. To prevent exposure to the disease, one should be especially _____ in sexual relationships. (*chary, circumspect, cautious, calculating*)

3 • Concrete and specific words

Clear, exact writing balances abstract and general words, which outline ideas and objects, with concrete and specific words, which sharpen and solidify.

- **Abstract words** name ideas: *beauty, inflation, management, culture, liberal.* **Concrete words** name qualities and things we can know by our five senses of sight, hearing, touch, taste, and smell: *sleek, humming, musty, teapot, brick.*

- **General words** name classes or groups of things, such as *buildings, weather,* or *birds,* and include all the varieties of the class. **Specific words** limit a general class, such as *buildings,* by naming one of its varieties, such as *skyscraper* or *my house on Emerald Street.*

Abstract and general words are useful in the broad statements that set the course for your writing:

The wild horse in America has a romantic history.

Relations between the sexes today are more relaxed than they were in the past.

exact

18b

But such statements need development with concrete and specific detail. Detail can turn a vague sentence into an exact one:

Vague   The size of his hands made his smallness real. [How big were his hands? How small was he?]

Exact   Not until I saw his delicate, doll-like hands did I realize that he stood a full head shorter than most other men.

Note If you write on a computer, you can use its Find function to help you find and revise abstract and general words that you tend to overuse. Examples of such words include *nice, interesting, things, very, good, a lot, a little,* and *some.*

EXERCISE 18.6
Revising: Concrete and specific words
Make the following paragraph vivid by expanding the sentences with appropriate details of your own choosing. Substitute concrete and specific words for the abstract and general ones that are underlined. (You can do this exercise online at *ablongman.com/littlebrown*.)

I remember clearly how awful I felt the first time I attended Mrs. Murphy's second-grade class. I had recently moved from a small town in Missouri to a crowded suburb of Chicago. My new school looked big from the outside and seemed dark inside as I walked down the long corridor toward the classroom. The class was noisy as I neared the door; but when I entered, everyone became quiet and looked at me. I felt uncomfortable and wanted a place to hide. However, in a loud voice Mrs. Murphy directed me to the front of the room to introduce myself.

---

4 • Idioms

Idioms are expressions in any language that do not fit the rules for meaning or grammar—for instance, *put up with, plug away at, make off with.*

Idiomatic combinations of verbs or adjectives and prepositions can be confusing for both native and nonnative speakers of English. A number of these pairings are listed below. (More appear on pp. 265–66.)

Idioms with prepositions

abide by a rule
abide in a place or state

according to
accords with

accuse of a crime

accustomed to

adapt from a source
adapt to a situation

afraid of

agree on a plan
agree to a proposal
agree with a person

angry with

aware of

based on

capable of

certain of

charge for a purchase
charge with a crime

concur in an opinion
concur with a person

contend for a principle
contend with a person

dependent on

differ about or over a question
differ from in some quality
differ with a person

disappointed by or in a person
disappointed in or with a thing

familiar with

identical with or to

impatient at her conduct
impatient for a raise
impatient of restraint
impatient with a person

independent of

infer from

inferior to

involved in a task
involved with a person

oblivious of or to one's surroundings
oblivious of something forgotten

occupied by a person
occupied in study
occupied with a thing

opposed to

part from a person
part with a possession

prior to

proud of

related to

rewarded by the judge
rewarded for something done
rewarded with a gift

similar to

superior to

wait at a place
wait for a train, a person
wait in a room
wait on a customer

exact
18b

CULTURE
LANGUAGE   If you are learning standard American English, you are justified in stumbling over its prepositions: their meanings

can shift depending on context, and they have many idiomatic uses. In mastering English prepositions, you probably can't avoid memorization. But you can help yourself by memorizing related groups, such as *at/in/on* and *for/since*.

At, in, or *on* in expressions of time

- Use *at* before actual clock time: *at* 8:30.
- Use *in* before a month, year, century, or period: *in April, in 2007, in the twenty-first century, in the next month.*
- Use *on* before a day or date: *on Tuesday, on August 3, on Labor Day.*

At, in, or *on* in expressions of place

- Use *at* before a specific place or address: *at the school, at 511 Iris Street.*
- Use *in* before a place with limits or before a city, state, country, or continent: *in the house, in a box, in Oklahoma City, in China, in Asia.*
- Use *on* to mean "supported by" or "touching the surface of": *on the table, on Iris Street, on page 150.*

For or *since* in expressions of time

- Use *for* before a period of time: *for an hour, for two years.*
- Use *since* before a specific point in time: *since 1999, since Friday.*

A dictionary of English as a second language is the best source for the meanings of prepositions; see the suggestions on page 204.

EXERCISE 18.7
Using prepositions in idioms

In the sentences below, insert the preposition that correctly completes each idiom. Consult the box on the previous page or a dictionary as needed. Answers to starred items appear at the end of the book. (You can do this exercise online at *ablongman.com/littlebrown.*)

Example:

I disagree _____ many feminists who say women should not be homemakers.

I disagree <u>with</u> many feminists who say women should not be homemakers.

*1. As Mark and Lana waited _____ the justice of the peace, they seemed oblivious _____ the other people in the lobby.

*2. But Mark inferred _____ Lana's glance at a handsome man that she was no longer occupied _____ him alone.

exact
18b

3. Angry _____ Lana, Mark charged her _____ not loving him enough to get married.
4. Impatient _____ Mark's childish behavior, Lana disagreed _____ his interpretation of her glance.
5. They decided that if they could differ so violently _____ a minor incident, they should part _____ each other.

EXERCISE 18.8
Using prepositions in idioms ⟨ **CULTURE** ⟩ LANGUAGE

Complete the following sentences by filling in the blanks with the appropriate prepositions from this list: *at, by, for, from, in, of, on, to, with*. Answers to starred items appear at the end of the book. (You can do this exercise online at *ablongman.com/littlebrown*.)

Example:

The most recent amendment to the US Constitution, ratified _____ May 18, 1992, was first proposed _____ 1789.

The most recent amendment to the US Constitution, ratified <u>on</u> May 18, 1992, was first proposed <u>in</u> 1789.

*1. The Eighteenth Amendment _____ the Constitution _____ the United States was ratified _____ 1919.

*2. It prohibited the "manufacture, sale, or transportation _____ intoxicating liquors."

3. It was adopted _____ response _____ a nationwide crusade _____ temperance groups.

4. The amendment did not prevent Americans _____ drinking, and the sale _____ alcoholic beverages was taken over _____ organized crime.

5. Wide-scale smuggling and bootlegging came _____ the demand _____ liquor.

exact
18b

5 • Figurative language

Figurative language (or a **figure of speech**) departs from the literal meanings of words, usually by comparing very different ideas or objects:

Literal   As I try to write, I can think of nothing to say.
Figurative   As I try to write, <u>my mind is a slab of black slate.</u>

Imaginatively and carefully used, figurative language can capture meaning more precisely and feelingly than literal language. Here is a figure of speech at work in technical writing (paraphrasing the physicist Edward Andrade):

The molecules in a liquid move continuously like couples on an over-crowded dance floor, jostling each other.

The two most common figures of speech are the simile and the metaphor. Both compare two things of different classes, often one abstract and the other concrete. A **simile** makes the comparison explicit and usually begins with *like* or *as:*

> Whenever we grow, we tend to feel it, as a young seed must feel the weight and inertia of the earth when it seeks to break out of its shell on its way to becoming a plant.   —Alice Walker

A **metaphor** claims that the two things are identical, omitting such words as *like* and *as:*

> A school is a hopper into which children are heaved while they are young and tender; therein they are pressed into certain standard shapes and covered from head to heels with official rubber stamps.
> —H. L. Mencken

Successful figurative language is fresh and unstrained, calling attention not to itself but to the writer's meaning. Be wary of mixed metaphors, which combine two or more incompatible figures:

Mixed	Various thorny problems that we try to sweep under the rug continue to bob up all the same.
Improved	Various thorny problems that we try to weed out continue to thrive all the same.

EXERCISE 18.9
Using figurative language

Invent appropriate similes or metaphors of your own to describe each scene or quality below, and use the figure in a sentence. (You can do this exercise online at *ablongman.com/littlebrown.*)

Example:

The attraction of a lake on a hot day
The small waves like fingers beckoned us irresistibly.

1. The sound of a kindergarten classroom
2. People waiting in line to buy tickets to a rock concert
3. The politeness of strangers meeting for the first time
4. A streetlight seen through dense fog
5. The effect of watching television for ten hours straight

6 • Trite expressions

Trite expressions, or **clichés,** are phrases so old and so often repeated that they have become stale. They include the following:

add insult to injury	crushing blow
better late than never	easier said than done

face the music	pride and joy
few and far between	ripe old age
green with envy	rude awakening
hard as a rock	sadder but wiser
heavy as lead	shoulder the burden
hit the nail on the head	shoulder to cry on
hour of need	sneaking suspicion
ladder of success	stand in awe
moving experience	thin as a rail
needle in a haystack	tried and true
point with pride	wise as an owl

To edit clichés, listen to your writing for any expressions that you have heard or used before. You can also supplement your efforts with a style checker, which may include a cliché detector. When you find a cliché, substitute fresh words of your own or restate the idea in plain language.

exact
18b

EXERCISE 18.10
Revising: Trite expressions

Revise the following sentences to eliminate trite expressions. Answers to starred items appear at the end of the book. (You can do this exercise online at *ablongman.com/littlebrown*.)

Example:

The basketball team had almost seized victory, but it faced the test of truth in the last quarter of the game.

The basketball team <u>seemed about to win</u>, but the <u>real test</u> came in the last quarter of the game.

*1. The disastrous consequences of the war have shaken the small nation to its roots.

*2. Prices for food have shot sky high, and citizens have sneaking suspicions that others are making a killing on the black market.

*3. Medical supplies are so few and far between that even civilians who are as sick as dogs cannot get treatment.

*4. With most men fighting or injured or killed, women have had to bite the bullet and bear the men's burden in farming and manufacturing.

*5. Last but not least, the war's heavy drain on the nation's pocketbook has left the economy in shambles.

6. Our reliance on foreign oil to support our driving habit has hit record highs in recent years.

7. Gas-guzzling sport-utility vehicles are responsible for part of the increase.

8. In the near future, we may have to bite the bullet and make use of public transportation or drive more fuel-efficient cars.

9. Both solutions are easier said than done.

10. But it stands to reason that we cannot go on using the world's oil reserves at such a rapid rate.

19 Completeness

Are all needed words in place?

Sometimes, omitting even a little word like *of* or *in* can make a sentence unclear. In editing, check your sentences to be sure you've included all the words they need. For additional help with complete sentences, see Chapter 35 on sentence fragments.

Note Grammar and style checkers will not flag most kinds of incomplete sentences discussed in this section.

19a Write complete compounds.

You may omit words from a compound construction when the omission will not confuse readers:

> Environmentalists have hopes for alternative fuels and [for] public transportation.
>
> Some cars will run on electricity and some [will run] on ethanol.

Such omissions are possible only when the words omitted are common to all the parts of a compound construction. When the parts differ in any way, all words must be included in all parts.

> One new hybrid car <u>gets</u> eighty miles per gallon; some old cars <u>get</u> as little as five miles per <u>gallon</u>. [One verb is singular, the other plural.]
>
> Environmentalists believe <u>in</u> and work <u>for</u> fuel conservation. [Idiom requires different prepositions with *believe* and *work*.]

> **Key term**
>
> **compound construction** Two or more elements (words, phrases, clauses) that are equal in importance and that function as a unit: *Rain fell, and streams overflowed* (clauses); *dogs and cats* (words).

http://www.ablongman.com/littlebrown ▶

Visit the companion Web site for more help and an electronic exercise on complete sentences.

19b   Add needed words.

In haste or carelessness, do not omit small words that are needed for clarity:

Incomplete	Regular payroll deductions are a type painless savings. You hardly notice missing amounts, and after period of years the contributions can add a large total.
Revised	Regular payroll deductions are a type of painless savings. You hardly notice the missing amounts, and after a period of years the contributions can add up to a large total.

Attentive proofreading is the only insurance against this kind of omission. *Proofread all your papers carefully.* See pages 40–41 for suggestions.

inc

19b

⟨ CULTURE LANGUAGE ⟩ If your native language is not English, you may have difficulty knowing when to use the English articles *a, an,* and *the.* For guidelines on using articles, see pages 312–15.

EXERCISE 19.1
Revising: Completeness

Add words to the following sentences so that the sentences are complete and clear. Possible answers to starred items appear at the end of the book. (You can do this exercise online at *ablongman.com/littlebrown.*)

Example:

Our house is closer to the courthouse than the subway stop.
Our house is closer to the courthouse than it is to the subway stop.
Our house is closer to the courthouse than the subway stop is.

*1. The first ice cream, eaten China in about 2000 BC, was lumpier than modern ice cream.
*2. The Chinese made their ice cream of milk, spices, and overcooked rice and packed in snow to solidify.

 3. In the fourteenth century ice milk and fruit ices appeared in Italy and the tables of the wealthy.
 4. At her wedding in 1533 to the king of France, Catherine de Médicis offered several flavors fruit ices.
 5. Modern sherbets resemble her ices; modern ice cream her soft dessert of thick, sweetened cream.

20 Conciseness

Have I deleted all unneeded words?

Unnecessary words pad your sentences without adding to your meaning, and they can make your writing unclear. You want to make every word count. Bear in mind, however, that writing concisely is not the same as writing briefly: detail and originality should not be cut with needless words. Rather, the length of the expression should be appropriate to the thought.

You may find yourself writing wordily when you are unsure of your subject or when your thoughts are tangled. It's fine, even necessary, to stumble and grope while drafting. But straighten out your ideas and aim for conciseness during revision and editing.

con
20

Ways to achieve conciseness

Wordy (87 words)

The highly pressured <u>nature</u> of critical-care nursing is <u>due to the fact that</u> the patients have life-threatening illnesses. Critical-care nurses must have possession of steady nerves to care for patients who are critically ill and very sick. The nurses must also have possession of interpersonal skills. They must also have medical skills. It is considered by most health-care professionals that these nurses are essential if there is to be improvement of patients who are now in critical care from that status to the status of intermediate care.

- Focus on subject and verb, and cut or shorten empty words and phrases.
- Avoid nouns made from verbs.
- Cut unneeded repetition.
- Combine sentences.
- Change passive voice to active voice.
- Eliminate *there is* constructions.
- Cut unneeded repetition, and reduce clauses and phrases.

Concise (37 words)

Critical-care nursing is highly pressured because the patients have life-threatening illnesses. Critical-care nurses must possess steady nerves and interpersonal and medical skills. Most health-care professionals consider these nurses essential if patients are to improve to intermediate care.

---

http://www.ablongman.com/littlebrown ▶

Visit the companion Web site for more help and electronic exercises on writing concisely.

Note Any grammar and style checker will identify at least some wordy structures, such as repeated words, weak verbs, passive voice, and *there is* and *it is* constructions. No checker can identify all wordy structures, however, nor can it tell you whether the structure is appropriate for your ideas.

 CULTURE ↘ Wordiness is not a problem of incorrect grammar. LANGUAGE
A sentence may be perfectly grammatical but still contain unneeded words that interfere with the clarity and force of your idea.

20a Focus on the subject and verb.

Using the subjects and verbs of your sentences for the key actors and actions will reduce words and emphasize important ideas. (See pp. 176–78 for more on this topic.)

con

20a

Wordy	The reason why most of the country shifts to daylight savings time is that winter days are much shorter than summer days.
Concise	Most of the country shifts to daylight savings time because winter days are much shorter than summer days.

Focusing on subjects and verbs will also help you avoid several other causes of wordiness discussed further on pages 176–78:

Nouns made from verbs

Wordy	The occurrence of the winter solstice, the shortest day of the year, is an event taking place about December 22.
Concise	The winter solstice, the shortest day of the year, occurs about December 22.

Weak verbs

Wordy	The earth's axis has a tilt as the planet is in orbit around the sun so that the northern and southern hemispheres are alternately in alignment toward the sun.
Concise	The earth's axis tilts as the planet orbits around the sun so that the northern and southern hemispheres alternately align toward the sun.

Passive voice

Wordy	During its winter the northern hemisphere is tilted farthest away from the sun, so the nights are made longer and the days are made shorter.

┌ **Key term** ─────────────────────────────────

passive voice The verb form when the subject names the *receiver* of the verb's action: *The house was destroyed by the tornado.* (See p. 277.)

Concise   During its winter the northern hemisphere tilts away from the sun, making the nights longer and the days shorter.

See also pages 277–78 on changing the passive voice to the active voice, as in the example above.

20b   Cut empty words.

Empty words walk in place, gaining little or nothing in meaning. Many of them can be cut entirely. The following are just a few examples.

all things considered	in a manner of speaking
as far as I'm concerned	in my opinion
for all intents and purposes	last but not least
for the most part	more or less

Other empty words can also be cut, usually along with some of the words around them:

area	element	kind	situation
aspect	factor	manner	thing
case	field	nature	type

Still others can be reduced from several words to a single word:

For	Substitute
at all times	always
at the present time	now, yet
because of the fact that	because
by virtue of the fact that	because
due to the fact that	because
for the purpose of	for
in order to	to
in the event that	if
in the final analysis	finally

Cutting or reducing such words and phrases will make your writing move faster and work harder:

Wordy   As far as I am concerned, because of the fact that a situation of discrimination continues to exist in the field of medicine,

---

Key term

active voice   The verb form when the subject names the *performer* of the verb's action: *The tornado destroyed the house.* (See p. 277.)

women have not <u>at the present time</u> achieved equality with
men.

Concise   Because of continuing discrimination in medicine, women
have not yet achieved equality with men.

20c Cut unneeded repetition.

Deliberate repetition and restatement can make writing more
coherent by linking sentences (see p. 54). But unnecessary repetition weakens sentences:

Wordy   Many unskilled workers <u>without training in a particular job</u> are
unemployed <u>and do not have any work</u>.

Concise   Many unskilled workers are unemployed.

con
20d

Be especially alert to phrases that say the same thing twice. In
the examples below, the unneeded words are underlined:

circle <u>around</u>	important [<u>basic</u>] essentials
consensus <u>of opinion</u>	puzzling <u>in nature</u>
cooperate <u>together</u>	repeat <u>again</u>
final comp<u>letion</u>	return <u>again</u>
<u>frank and</u> honest exchange	square [<u>round</u>] in shape
the future <u>to come</u>	<u>surrounding</u> circumstances

CULTURE LANGUAGE The preceding phrases are redundant because the
main word already implies the underlined word or words. A dictionary will tell you what meanings a word implies. *Assassinate,* for
instance, means "murder someone well known," so the following
sentence is redundant: *Julius Caesar was <u>assassinated and killed</u> in
44 BC.*

20d Tighten clauses and phrases.

Modifiers can be expanded or contracted depending on the emphasis you want to achieve. (Generally, the longer a construction,
the more emphasis it has.) When editing your sentences, consider
whether any modifiers can be reduced without loss of emphasis or
clarity.

> ┌─ **Key term** ─────────────────────────────
> **modifier** A word or word group that limits or qualifies another word:
> *slippery* road. (See p. 306.)

Wordy	The Channel Tunnel, <u>which runs between Britain and France,</u> bores through <u>a bed of solid chalk that is twenty-three miles across</u>.
Concise	The Channel Tunnel <u>between Britain and France</u> bores through <u>twenty-three miles of solid chalk</u>.

20e   Cut *there is* or *it is* constructions.

You can postpone the sentence subject with the words *there is* (*there are, there was, there were*) and *it is* (*it was*): *There is* a good reason to vote. *It is* your vote that counts. These **expletive constructions** can be useful to emphasize the subject (as when introducing it for the first time) or to indicate a change in direction. But often they just add words and weaken sentences:

Wordy	<u>There were delays and cost overruns that</u> plagued construction of the Channel Tunnel. <u>It is the expectation of investors</u> to earn profits at last, now that <u>there are trains passing daily</u> through the tunnel.
Concise	<u>Delays and cost overruns</u> plagued construction of the Channel Tunnel. <u>Investors expect</u> to earn profits at last, now that <u>trains pass daily</u> through the tunnel.

CULTURE LANGUAGE When you must use an expletive construction, be careful to include *there* or *it*. Only commands and some questions can begin with verbs.

20f   Combine sentences.

Often the information in two or more sentences can be combined into one tight sentence:

Wordy	An unexpected problem with the Channel Tunnel is stowaways. The stowaways are mostly illegal immigrants. They are trying to smuggle themselves into England. They cling to train roofs and undercarriages.
Concise	An unexpected problem with the Channel Tunnel is stowaways, <u>mostly</u> illegal immigrants <u>who</u> are trying to smuggle themselves into England <u>by clinging</u> to train roofs and undercarriages.

(See also p. 193 on combining sentences to achieve variety.)

20g   Avoid jargon.

Jargon can refer to the special vocabulary of any discipline or profession (see p. 198). But it has also come to describe vague, in-

con
20g

flated language that is overcomplicated, even incomprehensible. When it comes from government or business, we call it **bureaucratese.**

Jargon	The necessity for individuals to become separate entities in their own right may impel children to engage in open rebelliousness against parental authority or against sibling influence, with resultant bewilderment of those being rebelled against.
Translation	Children's natural desire to become themselves may make them rebel against bewildered parents or siblings.

EXERCISE 20.1
Revising: Writing concisely

con

20g

Make the following sentences more concise. Combine sentences when doing so reduces wordiness. Answers to starred items appear at the end of the book. (You can do this exercise online at *ablongman.com/ littlebrown.*)

> *Example:*
>
> It is thought by some people that there is gain from exercise only when it involves pain.
>
> <u>Some people think</u> that <u>gain comes</u> from exercise only <u>with</u> pain.

*1. If sore muscles after exercising are a problem for you, there are some measures that can be taken by you to ease the discomfort.
 *2. First, the immediate application of cold will help to reduce inflammation.
*3. Blood vessels are constricted by cold. Blood is kept away from the injured muscles.
*4. It is advisable to avoid heat for the first day.
*5. The application of heat within the first twenty-four hours can cause an increase in muscle soreness and stiffness.

6. There are two ways the application of cold can be made: you can take a cold shower or use an ice pack.
7. Inflammation of muscles can also be reduced with aspirin, ibuprofen, or another anti-inflammatory medication.
8. There is the idea that muscle soreness can be worsened by power lifting.
9. While healing is occurring, you need to take it easy.
10. A day or two after overdoing exercise, it is advisable for you to get some light exercise and gentle massage.

EXERCISE 20.2
Revising: Conciseness

Make the following paragraph as concise as possible. Be merciless. Answers to starred sentences appear at the end of the book. (You can do this exercise online at *ablongman.com/littlebrown.*)

*At the end of a lengthy line of reasoning, he came to the conclusion that the situation with carcinogens [cancer-causing substances] should be regarded as similar to the situation with the automobile. *Instead of giving in to an irrational fear of cancer, we should consider all aspects of the problem in a balanced and dispassionate frame of mind, making a total of the benefits received from potential carcinogens (plastics, pesticides, and other similar products) and measuring said total against the damage done by such products. This is the nature of most discussions about the automobile. Instead of responding irrationally to the visual, aural, and air pollution caused by automobiles, we have decided to live with them (while simultaneously working to improve on them) for the benefits brought to society as a whole.

con
20

4

Sentence Parts and Patterns

Basic Grammar

How are sentences constructed?

Every language constructs sentences by arranging the words of the language into patterns and sometimes by altering the words as well. The **grammar** of a language describes how it works, and understanding the grammar of English can help you create clear and accurate sentences. This section explains the kinds of words in sentences (Chapter 21) and how to build basic sentences (22), expand them (23), and classify them (24).

Note Grammar and style checkers can both offer assistance and cause problems as you compose sentences. Look for the cautions and tips for using such checkers in this and the next two parts of this book. For more information about grammar and style checkers, see pages 38–40.

21 Parts of Speech

What are the kinds of words, and how do they work?

All English words fall into eight groups, or **parts of speech,** such as nouns, verbs, adjectives, and adverbs. A word's part of speech determines its form and its position in a sentence. The same word may even serve as different parts of speech in different sentences, as these examples show:

> The government sent <u>aid</u> to the city. [*Aid* is a noun.]
> Governments <u>aid</u> citizens. [*Aid* is a verb.]

The *function* of a word in a sentence always determines its part of speech in that sentence.

---

http://www.ablongman.com/littlebrown ▶

Visit the companion Web site for more help and an electronic exercise on the parts of speech.

21a   Learn to recognize nouns.

Nouns name. They may name a person (*Rosie O'Donnell, Jesse Jackson, astronaut*), a thing (*chair, book, Mt. Rainier*), a quality (*pain, mystery, simplicity*), a place (*city, Washington, ocean, Red Sea*), or an idea (*reality, peace, success*).

The forms of nouns depend partly on where they fit in certain groups. As the examples indicate, the same noun may appear in more than one group.

- **Common nouns** name general classes of things and do not begin with capital letters: *earthquake, citizen, earth, fortitude, army.*
- **Proper nouns** name specific people, places, and things and begin with capital letters: *Helen Hunt, Washington Monument, El Paso, US Congress.*
- **Count nouns** name things considered countable in English. Most add -*s* or -*es* to distinguish between singular (one) and plural (more than one): *citizen, citizens; city, cities.* Some count nouns form irregular plurals: *woman, women; child, children.*
- **Noncount nouns** name things that aren't considered countable in English (*earth, sugar*), or they name qualities (*chaos, fortitude*). Noncount nouns do not form plurals.
- **Collective nouns** are singular in form but name groups: *army, family, herd, US Congress.*

In addition, most nouns form the **possessive** by adding -'*s* to show ownership (*Nadia's books, citizen's rights*), source (*Auden's poems*), and some other relationships.

gram
21b

21b   Learn to recognize pronouns.

Most **pronouns** substitute for nouns and function in sentences as nouns do: *Susanne Ling enlisted in the Navy when she graduated.*

Pronouns fall into several subclasses depending on their form or function:

- **Personal pronouns** refer to a specific individual or to individuals: *I, you, he, she, it, we,* and *they.*
- **Indefinite pronouns,** such as *everybody* and *some,* do not substitute for any specific nouns, though they function as nouns (*Everybody speaks*).
- **Relative pronouns**—*who, whoever, which, that*—relate groups of words to nouns or other pronouns (*The book that won is a novel*).

- **Interrogative pronouns,** such as *who, which,* and *what,* introduce questions (<u>*Who*</u> *will contribute?*).
- **Demonstrative pronouns,** including *this, that,* and *such,* identify or point to nouns (<u>*This*</u> *is the problem*).
- **Intensive pronouns**—a personal pronoun plus *-self* or *-selves* (*himself, ourselves*)—emphasize a noun or other pronoun (*He* <u>*himself*</u> *asked that question*).
- **Reflexive pronouns** have the same form as intensive pronouns but indicate that the sentence subject also receives the action of the verb (*They injured* <u>*themselves*</u>).

The personal pronouns *I, he, she, we,* and *they* and the relative pronouns *who* and *whoever* change form depending on their function in the sentence. (See Chapter 30.)

---

gram

21c

21c   Learn to recognize verbs.

Verbs express an action (*bring, change, grow, consider*), an occurrence (*become, happen, occur*), or a state of being (*be, seem, remain*).

1 • Forms of verbs

Verbs have five distinctive forms. If the form can change as described here, the word is a verb:

- The **plain form** is the dictionary form of the verb. When the subject is a plural noun or the pronoun *I, we, you,* or *they,* the plain form indicates action that occurs in the present, occurs habitually, or is generally true.

   A few artists <u>live</u> in town today.
   They <u>hold</u> classes downtown.

- The **-s form** ends in *-s* or *-es.* When the subject is a singular noun, a pronoun such as *everyone,* or the personal pronoun *he, she,* or *it,* the *-s* form indicates action that occurs in the present, occurs habitually, or is generally true.

   The artist <u>lives</u> in town today.
   She <u>holds</u> classes downtown.

- The **past-tense form** indicates that the action of the verb occurred before now. It usually adds *-d* or *-ed* to the plain form, although most irregular verbs create it in different ways (see pp. 250–53).

   Many artists <u>lived</u> in town before this year.
   They <u>held</u> classes downtown. [Irregular verb.]

- The **past participle** is usually the same as the past-tense form, except in most irregular verbs. It combines with forms of *have* or *be* (*has climbed, was created*), or by itself it modifies nouns and pronouns (*the sliced apples*).

Artists have lived in town for decades.
They have held classes downtown. [Irregular verb.]

- The **present participle** adds *-ing* to the verb's plain form. It combines with forms of *be* (*is buying*), modifies nouns and pronouns (*the boiling water*), or functions as a noun (*Running exhausts me*).

A few artists are living in town today.
They are holding classes downtown.

The verb *be* has eight forms rather than the five forms of most other verbs:

Plain form	be		
Present participle	being		
Past participle	been		
	I	*he, she, it*	*we, you, they*
Present tense	am	is	are
Past tense	was	was	were

gram
21c

2 • Helping verbs

Some verb forms combine with **helping verbs** to indicate time, possibility, obligation, necessity, and other kinds of meaning: *can run, was sleeping, had been working.* In these **verb phrases** *run, sleeping,* and *working* are **main verbs**—they carry the principal meaning.

	Verb phrase	
	Helping	*Main*
Artists	can	train others to draw.
The techniques	have	changed little.

These are the most common helping verbs:

be able to	had better	must	used to
be supposed to	have to	ought to	will
can	may	shall	would
could	might	should	

Forms of *be:* be, am, is, are, was, were, been, being
Forms of *have:* have, has, had, having
Forms of *do:* do, does, did

See pages 256–61 for more on helping verbs.

EXERCISE 21.1
Identifying nouns, pronouns, and verbs

Identify the words that function as nouns, pronouns, and verbs in the following sentences, using the initials *N, P,* or *V.* Answers to starred items appear at the end of the book. (You can do this exercise online at *ablongman.com/littlebrown.*)

Example:

```
            N   V              N    P V                      N
The gingko tree has another name: it is the maidenhair tree.
```

*1. Ancestors of the gingko tree, a relic from the age of the dinosaurs, lived 175 to 200 million years ago.

*2. The tree sometimes grows to over a hundred feet in height.

*3. It has fan-shaped leaves about three inches wide.

*4. A deciduous tree, the gingko loses its leaves in the fall after they turn bright yellow.

*5. The gingko tree is esteemed in the United States and Europe as an ornamental tree.

6. Because the gingko shows tolerance for smoke, low temperatures, and low rainfall, it appears in many cities.

7. A shortcoming, however, is the foul odor of its fruit.

8. The fruit of the gingko looks something like a plum.

9. Inside the fruit lies a large white seed that some Asians value as a food.

10. Because only the female gingko bears fruit, the male is more common as an ornamental tree.

21d Learn to recognize adjectives and adverbs.

Adjectives describe or modify nouns and pronouns. They specify which one, what quality, or how many.

old	city	generous	one	two	pears
adjective	noun	adjective	pronoun	adjective	noun

Adverbs describe or modify verbs, adjectives, other adverbs, and whole groups of words. They specify when, where, how, and to what extent.

nearly	destroyed	too	quickly
adverb	verb	adverb	adverb

very	generous	Unfortunately,	taxes will rise.
adverb	adjective	adverb	word group

An *-ly* ending often signals an adverb, but not always: *friendly* is an adjective; *never* is an adverb. The only way to tell whether a word is an adjective or an adverb is to determine what it modifies.

Adjectives and adverbs appear in three forms: **positive** (*green, angrily*), **comparative** (*greener, more angrily*), and **superlative** (*greenest, most angrily*).

See Chapter 33 for more on adjectives and adverbs.

EXERCISE 21.2
Identifying adjectives and adverbs

Identify the adjectives (*ADJ*) and adverbs (*ADV*) in the following sentences. Mark *a, an,* and *the* as adjectives. Answers to starred items appear at the end of the book. (You can do this exercise online at *ablongman.com/littlebrown*.)

Example:

ADV
Stress can hit people when they least expect it.

*1. You can reduce stress by making a few simple changes.
*2. Get up fifteen minutes earlier than you ordinarily do.
*3. Eat a healthy breakfast, and eat it slowly so that you enjoy it.
*4. Do your unpleasant tasks early in the day.
*5. Every day, do at least one thing you really enjoy.
  6. If waiting in lines is stressful for you, carry a book or magazine when you know you'll have to wait.
  7. Make promises sparingly and keep them faithfully.
  8. Plan ahead to prevent stressful situations.
  9. For example, carry spare keys so you won't be locked out of your car or house.
 10. See a doctor and a dentist regularly.

gram
21e

21e Learn to recognize connecting words: Prepositions and conjunctions.

Connecting words are mostly small words that link parts of sentences. They never change form.

1 • Prepositions

Prepositions form nouns or pronouns (plus any modifiers) into word groups called **prepositional phrases**: <u>*about*</u> *love,* <u>*down*</u> *the stairs*. These phrases usually serve as modifiers in sentences, as in *The plants trailed <u>down the stairs</u>.* (See also p. 241.) A list of prepositions appears on the next page.

 CULTURE LANGUAGE The meanings and uses of English prepositions can be difficult to master. See pages 208–10 for a discussion of prepositions in idioms. See pages 264–66 for uses of prepositions in two-word verbs such as *look after* or *look up*.

Common prepositions

about	before	except for	of	throughout
above	behind	excepting	off	till
according to	below	for	on	to
across	beneath	from	onto	toward
after	beside	in	on top of	under
against	between	in addition to	out	underneath
along	beyond	inside	out of	unlike
along with	by	inside of	outside	until
among	concerning	in spite of	over	up
around	despite	instead of	past	upon
as	down	into	regarding	up to
aside from	due to	like	round	with
at	during	near	since	within
because of	except	next to	through	without

2 • Subordinating conjunctions

Subordinating conjunctions form sentences into word groups called **subordinate clauses,** such as *when the meeting ended.* These clauses serve as parts of sentences: *Everyone was relieved when the meeting ended.* (See p. 244 for more on subordinate clauses.)

Common subordinating conjunctions

after	even if	rather than	until
although	even though	since	when
as	if	so that	whenever
as if	if only	than	where
as long as	in order that	that	whereas
as though	now that	though	wherever
because	once	till	whether
before	provided	unless	while

CULTURE LANGUAGE Subordinating conjunctions convey meaning without help from other function words, such as the coordinating conjunctions *and, but, for,* or *so:*

Faulty   Even though the parents are illiterate, but their children may read well. [*Even though* and *but* have the same meaning, so both are not needed.]

Revised   Even though the parents are illiterate, their children may read well.

3 • Coordinating and correlative conjunctions

Coordinating and correlative conjunctions connect words or word groups of the same kind, such as nouns, adjectives, or sentences.

Coordinating conjunctions consist of a single word:

Coordinating conjunctions

and	nor	for	yet
but	or	so	

Biofeedback <u>or</u> simple relaxation can relieve headaches.
Relaxation works well, <u>and</u> it is inexpensive.

Correlative conjunctions are combinations of coordinating conjunctions and other words:

Common correlative conjunctions

both . . . and	neither . . . nor
not only . . . but also	whether . . . or
not . . . but	as . . . as
either . . . or	

<u>Both</u> biofeedback <u>and</u> relaxation can relieve headaches.

The headache sufferer learns <u>not only</u> to recognize the causes of headaches <u>but also</u> to control those causes.

EXERCISE 21.3
Adding connecting words

Fill each blank in the following sentences with the appropriate connecting word: a preposition, a subordinating conjunction, or a coordinating conjunction. Consult the lists on these two pages if you need help. Answers to starred items appear at the end of the book. (You can do this exercise online at *ablongman.com/littlebrown.*)

> *Example:*
>
> A Trojan priest warned, "Beware _____ Greeks bearing gifts." (*preposition*)
>
> A Trojan priest warned, "Beware <u>of</u> Greeks bearing gifts."

*1. Just about everyone has heard the story _____ the Trojan Horse. (*preposition*)
*2. This incident happened at the city of Troy _____ was planned by the Greeks. (*coordinating conjunction*)

*3. The Greeks built a huge wooden horse; _____ it was a hollow space big enough to hold many men. (*preposition*)

*4. At night, they rolled the horse to the gate of Troy _____ left it there before sailing their ships out to sea. (*coordinating conjunction*)

*5. _____ the morning, the Trojans were surprised to see the enormous horse. (*preposition*)

6. _____ they were amazed when they saw that the Greeks were gone. (*coordinating conjunction*)

7. _____ they were curious to examine this gift from the Greeks, they dragged the horse into the city and left it outside the temple. (*subordinating conjunction*)

8. In the middle of the night, the hidden Greeks emerged _____ the horse and began setting fires all over town. (*preposition*)

9. _____ the Trojan soldiers awoke and came out of their houses, the Greeks killed them one by one. (*subordinating conjunction*)

10. By the next morning, the Trojan men were dead _____ the women were slaves to the Greeks. (*coordinating conjunction*)

21f   Learn to recognize interjections.

Interjections express feeling or command attention. They are rarely used in academic or business writing.

<u>Oh</u>, the meeting went fine.
They won seven thousand dollars! <u>Wow!</u>

22   The Sentence

What makes a sentence a sentence?

The essential elements of any sentence are the subject and the predicate. Usually naming an actor and an action, the subject and predicate together form a complete thought.

22a   Learn to recognize subjects and predicates.

Most sentences make statements. First the **subject** names something; then the **predicate** makes an assertion about the subject or describes an action by the subject.

http://www.ablongman.com/littlebrown ▶

Visit the companion Web site for more help and electronic exercises on the sentence.

Subject   Predicate

Art   thrives.

The **simple subject** consists of one or more nouns or pronouns, whereas the **complete subject** also includes any modifiers. The **simple predicate** consists of one or more verbs, whereas the **complete predicate** adds any words needed to complete the meaning of the verb plus any modifiers.

Sometimes, as in the short example *Art thrives,* the simple and complete subject and predicate are the same. More often, they are different:

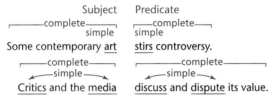

Subject   Predicate

———complete———   ———complete———
          simple   simple

Some contemporary <u>art</u>   <u>stirs</u> controversy.

———complete———   ———complete———
——simple——   ——simple——

<u>Critics</u> and the <u>media</u>   <u>discuss</u> and <u>dispute</u> its value.

In the second example, the simple subject and simple predicate are both **compound:** in each, two words joined by a coordinating conjunction (*and*) serve the same function.

gram

22a

Tests to find subjects and predicates

The tests below use the following example:

Art that makes it into museums has often survived controversy.

Identify the subject.

- **Ask *who* or *what* is acting or being described in the sentence.**

  Complete subject   art that makes it into museums

- **Isolate the simple subject by deleting modifiers**—words or word groups that don't name the actor of the sentence but give information about it. In the example, the word group *that makes it into museums* does not name the actor but modifies it.

  Simple subject   art

Identify the predicate.

- **Ask what the sentence asserts about the subject:** what is its action, or what state is it in? In the example, the assertion about *art* is that it *has often survived controversy.*

  Complete predicate   has often survived controversy

(continued)

Tests to find subjects and predicates
(continued)

- **Isolate the verb, the simple predicate, by changing the time of the subject's action.** The simple predicate is the word or words that change as a result.

Example	Art . . . has often survived controversy.
Present	Art . . . often <u>survives</u> controversy.
Future	Art . . . often <u>will survive</u> controversy.
Simple predicate	has survived

Note If a sentence contains a word group such as *that makes it into established museums* or *because viewers finally agree about its quality,* you may be tempted to mark the subject and verb in the word group as the subject and verb of the sentence. But these word groups are subordinate clauses, made into modifiers by the words they begin with: *that* and *because*. See pages 244–46 for more on subordinate clauses.

gram 22a

CULTURE LANGUAGE The subject of an English sentence may be a noun (*art*) or a pronoun that refers to the noun (*it*), but not both. (See pp. 242–43.)

Faulty	Some <u>art it</u> stirs controversy.
Revised	Some <u>art</u> stirs controversy.

EXERCISE 22.1
Identifying subjects and predicates

In the following sentences, insert a line between the complete subject and the complete predicate. Underline each simple subject once and each simple predicate twice. Answers to starred items appear at the end of the book. (You can do this exercise online at *ablongman.com/ littlebrown.*)

Example:

The <u>pony</u>, the light <u>horse</u>, and the draft <u>horse</u> | <u><u>are</u></u> the three main types of domestic horses.

*1. The horse has a long history of serving humanity but today is mainly a show and sport animal.
*2. A member of the genus *Equus,* the domestic horse is related to the wild Przewalski's horse, the ass, and the zebra.
*3. The domestic horse and its relatives are all plains-dwelling herd animals.
*4. An average-sized adult horse may require twenty-six pounds or more of pasture feed or hay per day.

*5. Racehorses require grain for part of their forage.

6. Oddly, the modern horse evolved in North America and then became extinct here after spreading to other parts of the world.

7. It was reintroduced here by the Spaniards, profoundly affecting the culture of Native Americans.

8. The North American animals called wild horses are actually descended from escaped domesticated horses that reproduced in the wild.

9. According to records, horses were hunted and domesticated as early as four to five thousand years ago.

10. The earliest ancestor of the modern horse may have been eohippus, approximately 55 million years ago.

22b   Learn the basic predicate patterns.

English sentences usually follow one of five patterns, each differing in the complete predicate (the verb and any words following it).

⚑ CULTURE LANGUAGE Word order in English sentences may not correspond to word order in the sentences of your native language or dialect. English, for instance, strongly prefers subject first, then verb, then any other words, whereas some other languages prefer the verb first.

gram
22b

Pattern 1: The earth trembled.

In the simplest pattern the predicate consists only of an **intransitive verb,** a verb that does not require a following word to complete its meaning.

Subject	Predicate
	Intransitive verb
The earth	trembled.
The hospital	may close.

Pattern 2: The earthquake destroyed the city.

In pattern 2 the verb is followed by a **direct object,** a noun or pronoun that identifies who or what receives the action of the verb. A verb that requires a direct object to complete its meaning is called **transitive.**

Subject	Predicate	
	Transitive verb	*Direct object*
The earthquake	destroyed	the city.
Education	opens	doors.

CULTURE LANGUAGE Only transitive verbs can be used in the passive voice: *The city was destroyed*. Your dictionary will indicate whether a verb is transitive or intransitive. For some verbs (*begin, learn, read, write,* and others), it will indicate both uses.

Pattern 3: The result was chaos.

In pattern 3 the verb is followed by a **subject complement,** a word that renames or describes the subject. A verb in this pattern is called a **linking verb** because it links its subject to the description following. The linking verbs include *be, seem, appear, become, grow, remain, stay, prove, feel, look, smell, sound,* and *taste.* Subject complements are usually nouns or adjectives.

Subject	Predicate	
	Linking verb	*Subject complement*
The result	was	chaos.
The man	became	an accountant.

Pattern 4: The government sent the city aid.

In pattern 4 the verb is followed by a direct object and an **indirect object,** a word identifying to or for whom the action of the verb is performed. The direct object and indirect object refer to different things, people, or places.

Subject	Predicate		
	Transitive verb	*Indirect object*	*Direct object*
The government	sent	the city	aid.
One company	offered	its employees	bonuses.

A number of verbs can take indirect objects, including *allow, bring, buy, deny, find, get, give, leave, make, offer, pay, read, sell, send, show, teach,* and *write.*

CULTURE LANGUAGE Some verbs are never followed by an indirect object—*admit, announce, demonstrate, explain, introduce, mention, prove, recommend, say,* and some others. However, the direct objects of these verbs may be followed by *to* or *for* and a noun or pronoun that specifies to or for whom the action was done: *The manual explains the new procedure to workers*. *A video demonstrates the procedure for us*.

Key term

passive voice The verb form when the subject names the receiver of the verb's action: *Bad weather was predicted*. (See pp. 277–78.)

Pattern 5: The citizens considered the earthquake a disaster.

In pattern 5 the verb is followed by a direct object and an **object complement**, a word that renames or describes the direct object. Object complements may be nouns or adjectives.

Subject	Predicate		
	Transitive verb	*Direct object*	*Object complement*
The citizens	considered	the earthquake	a disaster.
Success	makes	some people	nervous.

EXERCISE 22.2
Identifying sentence parts

In the following sentences identify the subject (S) and verb (V) as well as any direct objects (DO), indirect objects (IO), subject complements (SC), or object complements (OC). Answers to starred items appear at the end of the book. (You can do this exercise online at *ablongman.com/ littlebrown.*)

> *Example:*
>   S   V   V   DO
> Crime statistics can cause surprise.

*1. The number of serious crimes in the United States decreased.
*2. A decline in serious crimes occurred each year.
*3. The Crime Index measures serious crime.
*4. The FBI invented the index.
*5. The four serious violent crimes are murder, robbery, forcible rape, and aggravated assault.
 6. Auto theft, burglary, arson, and larceny-theft are the four serious crimes against property.
 7. The Crime Index gives the FBI a measure of crime.
 8. The index shows trends in crimes and criminals.
 9. The nation's largest cities showed the largest decline in crime.
10. Their crime-fighting success made some cities models for others.

gram
22c

22c Learn alternative sentence patterns.

Most English sentences first name the actor in the subject and then assert something about the actor in the predicate. But four kinds of sentences alter this basic pattern.

1 • Questions

The following are the most common ways of forming questions from statements. Remember to end a question with a question mark (p. 347).

- Move the verb or a part of it to the beginning of the question. These questions may be answered yes or no. The verb may be a form of *be*:

The rate <u>is</u> high.	<u>Is</u> the rate high?

Or the verb may consist of a helping verb and a main verb. Then move the helping verb—or the first helping verb if there's more than one—to the front of the question:

Rates <u>can</u> rise.	<u>Can</u> rates rise?
Rates <u>have</u> been rising.	<u>Have</u> rates been rising?

- If the verb consists of only one word and is not a form of *be*, start the question with a form of *do* and use the plain form of the verb. These questions can also be answered yes or no.

Interest rates <u>rose</u>.	<u>Did</u> interest rates <u>rise</u>?

gram
22c

- Add a question word—*how, what, who, when, where, which, why*—to the beginning of a yes-or-no question. Such a question requires an explanatory answer.

Did rates rise today?	<u>Why</u> did rates rise today?
Is the rate high?	<u>Why</u> is the rate high?

- Add *who, what,* or *which* to the beginning of a question as the subject. Then the subject-verb order remains the same as in a statement:

Something is the answer.	<u>What</u> is the answer?
Someone can answer.	<u>Who</u> can answer?

2 • Commands

Construct a command simply by deleting the subject of the sentence, *you:*

Think of options.	Eat your spinach.
Watch the news.	Leave me alone.

Key terms

helping verb A verb such as *can, may, be, have,* or *do* that forms a verb phrase with another verb to show time, permission, and other meanings. (See p. 227.)

main verb The verb that carries the principal meaning in a verb phrase: *has <u>walked</u>, could be <u>happening</u>.* (See p. 227.)

plain form The dictionary form of the verb: *You <u>forget</u>.* (See p. 226.)

3 • Passive sentences

In the basic subject-predicate pattern, the subject performs the action of the verb. The verb is in the **active voice:**

active
subject verb   object
Kyong wrote the paper.

In the **passive voice,** the subject *receives* the action of the verb:

passive
subject   verb
The paper was written by Kyong.

In the passive voice, the object of the active verb (*paper*) becomes the subject of the passive verb.

Passive verbs always consist of a form of *be* plus the past participle of the main verb (*paper was written, absences were excused*). The actual actor (the person or thing performing the action of the verb) may be expressed in a phrase (as in the example above: *by Kyong*) or may be omitted entirely if it is unknown or unimportant: *The house was flooded.*

For more on the formation and uses of the passive voice, see pages 277–78.

gram
22c

4 • Sentences with postponed subjects

Two kinds of sentences state the subject after the predicate. In one, the normal word order reverses for emphasis:

The cause of the problem lies here. [Normal order.]
Here lies the cause of the problem. [Reversed order.]

The second kind of sentence starts with *there* or *it* and postpones the subject:

verb   subject
There will be eighteen people at the meeting. [Normal order: *Eighteen people will be at the meeting.*]

verb   subject
It was surprising that Marinetti was nominated. [Normal order: *That Marinetti was nominated was surprising.*]

The words *there* and *it* in such sentences are **expletives.** Their only function is to postpone the sentence subject. Expletive sentences do have their uses (see p. 220), but they are often just wordy.

CULTURE
LANGUAGE   When you use an expletive construction, be careful to include *there* or *it*. Only commands and some questions can begin with verbs (see the facing page).

Faulty	No one predicted the nomination. Were no polls showing Marinetti ahead.
Revised	No one predicted the nomination. There were no polls show- ing Marinetti ahead.

EXERCISE 22.3
Rewriting passives and expletives

Rewrite each passive sentence below as active, and rewrite each exple- tive construction to restore normal subject-predicate order. Answers to the starred items appear at the end of the book. (You can do this exer- cise online at *ablongman.com/littlebrown*.) For additional exercises with the passive voice and with expletives, see pages 178, 221, and 279.

> *Example:*
>
> All the trees in the park were planted by the city.
> The city planted all the trees in the park.

*1. The screenplay for *Monster's Ball* was cowritten by Milo Addica and Will Rokos.

*2. The film was directed by Marc Foster.

3. There was only one performance in the movie that received an Academy Award.

4. It was Halle Berry who won the award for best actress.

5. Berry was congratulated by the press for being the first African American to win the award.

gram

23

23 Phrases and Subordinate Clauses

How do word groups work within sentences?

Word groups within sentences serve as modifiers (adjectives or adverbs) or as nouns. Most word groups are one of the following:

- A **phrase,** which lacks either a subject or a predicate or both: *fearing an accident; in a panic.*

- A **subordinate clause,** which contains a subject and a predicate (like a sentence) but begins with a subordinating word: *when prices rise; whoever laughs.*

---

http://www.ablongman.com/littlebrown ▶

Visit the companion Web site for more help and electronic exercises on phrases and subordinate clauses.

Because they function as parts of speech (adjectives, adverbs, or nouns), phrases and subordinate clauses cannot stand alone as complete sentences (see Chapter 35 on sentence fragments).

23a   Learn to recognize phrases.

1 • Prepositional phrases

A **prepositional phrase** consists of a preposition plus a noun, pronoun, or word group serving as a noun, called the **object of the preposition.** Prepositions include *about, at, by, for, to, under,* and *with.* A fuller list appears on page 230.

Preposition	Object
of	spaghetti
on	the surface
with	great satisfaction
upon	entering the room
from	where you are standing

Prepositional phrases usually function as adjectives or adverbs, adding details and making sentences more interesting for readers. An adjective phrase usually falls immediately after the word it modifies, but an adverb phrase need not.

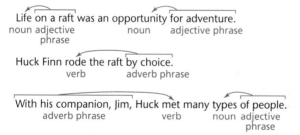

Life on a raft was an opportunity for adventure.
noun adjective   noun   adjective phrase
        phrase

Huck Finn rode the raft by choice.
          verb   adverb phrase

With his companion, Jim, Huck met many types of people.
    adverb phrase   verb   noun adjective
                                                    phrase

2 • Verbal phrases

Certain forms of verbs, called **verbals,** can serve as modifiers or nouns. Often these verbals appear with their own modifiers and objects in **verbal phrases.**

Key terms ─────────────────────────────

subject The part of a word group that names who or what performs the action: *The moon rises* (main clause); *the moon rising* (phrase). (See p. 232.)

predicate The part of a word group containing a verb that asserts something about the subject: *On some days the moon rises* (main clause) *before the sun sets* (subordinate clause). (See p. 232.)

---

gram
23a

Note Verbals cannot serve alone as predicates in sentences. *The sun rises over the dump* is a sentence; *The sun rising over the dump* is a sentence fragment. (See p. 326.)

Participial phrases

Present participles (ending in *-ing*), **past participles** (usually ending in *-d* or *-ed*), and phrases made from them serve as adjectives. They usually fall just before or after the word they modify.

Strolling shoppers fill the malls.
adjective   noun

They make selections determined by personal taste.
          noun   adjective phrase

Note With irregular verbs, the past participle may have a different ending—for instance, *hidden funds*. (See p. 250.)

CULTURE LANGUAGE For verbs expressing feeling, the present and past participles have different meanings: *It was a boring lecture. The bored students slept.* (See p. 311.)

gram
23a

Gerund phrases

A **gerund** is the *-ing* form of a verb when it serves as a noun. Gerunds and gerund phrases replace nouns and can do whatever nouns can do.

sentence
subject
Shopping satisfies personal needs.
  noun

                    object of
                  preposition
Malls are good at creating such needs.
                    noun phrase

Infinitive phrases

An **infinitive** is the plain form of a verb plus *to: to hide*. Infinitives and infinitive phrases serve as adjectives, adverbs, or nouns. A noun or noun phrase replaces a noun:

          sentence
        subject   subject complement
To design a mall is to create an artificial environment.
    noun phrase   noun phrase

An adverb or adverb phrase modifies a verb, adjective, other adverb, or entire word group and may fall near or away from the word it modifies:

To achieve this goal, designers emphasize the familiar.
  adverb phrase   verb

Malls are designed to make shoppers feel safe.
    verb   adverb phrase

An adjective or adjective phrase modifies a noun or pronoun and usually falls immediately after the word it modifies:

The environment supports the impulse to shop.
                     noun   adjective

CULTURE LANGUAGE Infinitives and gerunds may follow some verbs and not others and may differ in meaning after a verb: *The singer stopped to sing. The singer stopped singing.* (See pp. 262–64.)

3 • Absolute phrases

An **absolute phrase** consists of a noun or pronoun and a participle, plus any modifiers. It modifies the rest of its sentence and may fall in more than one place in the sentence.

Their own place established, many ethnic groups are making way for
          absolute phrase
new arrivals.

gram
23a

Unlike a participial phrase (opposite), an absolute phrase always contains a noun that serves as its subject:

Learning English, many immigrants discover American culture.
  participial phrase

Immigrants having learned English, their opportunities widen.
      absolute phrase

4 • Appositive phrases

An **appositive** is usually a noun that renames another noun. An appositive phrase includes modifiers as well. Both appositives and appositive phrases usually fall immediately after the nouns they rename.

Bizen ware, a dark stoneware, is produced in Japan.
  noun   appositive phrase

Appositives and appositive phrases sometimes begin with *that is, such as, for example,* or *in other words.*

Bizen ware is used in the Japanese tea ceremony, that is, the Zen Bud-
                          noun   appositive phrase
dhist observance that links meditation and art.

EXERCISE 23.1
Identifying phrases

In each sentence below, identify every verbal, appositive, and verbal, appositive, prepositional, and absolute phrase. All but one sentence include two or more such words or phrases. Answers to starred items appear at the end of the book. (You can do this exercise online at *ablongman.com/ littlebrown.*)

> *Example:*
>   ⌐── participial phrase ───┐
> Modern English contains words borrowed from many sources.
>   ⌐prepositional phrase⌐

*1. Because of its many synonyms, or words with similar meanings, English can make it difficult to choose the exact word.

*2. Borrowing words from other languages such as French and Latin, English acquired an unusual number of synonyms.

*3. Having so many choices, how does a writer decide between *motherly* and *maternal* or among *womanly, feminine,* and *female?*

*4. Some people prefer longer and more ornate words to avoid the flatness of short words.

*5. During the Renaissance a heated debate occurred between the Latinists, favoring Latin words, and the Saxonists, preferring native Anglo-Saxon words.

6. Students in writing classes are often told to choose the shorter word, generally an Anglo-Saxon derivative.

7. Better advice, wrote William Hazlitt, is the principle of choosing "the best word in common use."

8. Keeping this principle in mind, a writer would choose either *womanly,* the Anglo-Saxon word, or *feminine,* a French derivative, according to meaning and situation.

9. Synonyms rarely have exactly the same meaning, usage having defined differences.

10. The Old English word *handbook,* for example, has a slightly different meaning from the French derivative *manual,* a close synonym.

gram
23b

23b   Learn to recognize subordinate clauses.

A **clause** is any group of words that contains both a subject and a predicate. There are two kinds of clauses, and the distinction between them is important:

- A **main clause** makes a complete statement and can stand alone as a sentence: *The sky darkened.*
- A **subordinate clause** is just like a main clause *except* that it begins with a subordinating word: <u>*when*</u> *the sky darkened;* <u>*whoever calls.*</u> The subordinating word reduces the clause from a complete statement to a single part of speech: an adjective, adverb, or noun.

Note A subordinate clause punctuated as a sentence is a sentence fragment. (See pp. 326–29.)

Adjective clauses

An **adjective clause** modifies a noun or pronoun. It usually begins with the relative pronoun *who, whom, whose, which,* or *that* but may also begin with *where, when,* or *why.* The clause ordinarily falls immediately after the word it modifies.

Parents who cannot read may have bad memories of school.
noun   adjective clause

Children whom the schools fail sometimes have illiterate parents.
noun   adjective clause

One school, which is open year-round, helps parents learn to read.
noun   adjective clause

The school is in a city where the illiteracy rate is high.
noun   adjective clause

gram

23b

In the first three examples, the relative pronouns *who, whom,* and *which* refer to the nouns modified by the clause (*Parents, Children, school*). The relative pronoun serves as the subject of its clause (*who cannot read, which is open year-round*) or as an object (*whom the schools fail*). In the last example, *where* substitutes for *in which* (*a city in which the illiteracy rate is high*).

See pages 353–55 for advice on punctuating adjective clauses.

Adverb clauses

An **adverb clause** modifies a verb, an adjective, another adverb, or a whole word group. It always begins with a subordinating conjunction, such as *after, although, because, even though, how, if, until, when,* or *while.* (See p. 230 for a fuller list.) The clause may fall in more than one place in its sentence (but see p. 319 for limitations).

The school began teaching parents when adult illiteracy gained national attention.
verb   adverb clause

At first the program was not as successful as its founders had hoped.
adjective   adverb clause

Because it was directed at people who could not read, advertising had
adverb clause   main clause
to be inventive.

Noun clauses

A **noun clause** replaces a noun in a sentence and serves as a subject, object, or complement. It begins with *that, what, whatever, who, whom, whoever, whomever, when, where, whether, why,* or *how.*

┌─────── sentence subject ───────┐
Whether the program would succeed depended on door-to-door adver-
                  noun clause

tising.

                          ┌─────── object of verb ───────┐
Teachers explained in person how the program would work.
                                   noun clause

┌─────── sentence subject ───────┐
Whoever seemed slightly interested was invited to an open meeting.
         noun clause

                          ┌─── object of preposition ───┐
A few parents were anxious about what their children would think.
                                   noun clause

                       ┌─────── subject complement ───────┐
The children's needs were what the parents asked most about.
                                noun clause

gram
23b

EXERCISE 23.2
Identifying clauses

Underline the subordinate clauses in the following sentences and identify each one as adjective (ADJ), adverb (ADV), or noun (N) by determining how it functions in its sentence. Answers to starred items appear at
the end of the book. (You can do this exercise online at *ablongman.com/
littlebrown.*)

> *Example:*
>   N
> Whoever follows the Koran refers to God as *Allah,* the Arabic word
> for his name.

*1. The Prophet Muhammad, who was the founder of Islam, was born
    about 570 CE in the city of Mecca.
*2. He grew up in the care of his grandfather and an uncle because
    both of his parents had died.
*3. His family was part of a powerful Arab tribe that lived in western Arabia.
*4. When he was about forty years old, he had a vision in a cave outside
    Mecca.

┌─ **Key terms** ──

object A noun, pronoun, or word group that receives the action of or is
influenced by a transitive verb, a verbal, or a preposition. An object may
be a *direct object,* an *indirect object,* or an *object of a preposition.* (See
pp. 235–36 and 241.)

complement A word or word group that completes the sense of a subject, an object, or a verb. (See pp. 236 and 237.)

*5. He believed that God had selected him to be the prophet of a true religion for the Arab people.

6. Throughout his life he continued to have revelations, which have been written in the Koran.

7. The Koran is the sacred book of Muslims, who as adherents of Islam view Muhammad as God's messenger.

8. When he no longer had the support of the clans of Mecca, Muhammad and his followers moved to Medina.

9. There they established an organized Muslim community that sometimes clashed with the Meccans and with Jewish clans.

10. Throughout his life Muhammad continued as the religious, political, and military leader of Islam as it spread in Asia and Africa.

24 Sentence Types

How can classifying sentences help me construct them?

Understanding the ways of structuring sentences can be helpful for managing the flow and emphasis of information. One useful classification identifies four sentence types: simple, compound, complex, and compound-complex.

24a Learn to recognize simple sentences.

A **simple sentence** consists of a single main clause and no subordinate clause:

┌─────── main clause ────────┐
Last summer was unusually hot.

┌─────────────────────── main clause ───────────────────────┐
The summer made many farmers leave the area for good or reduced them to bare existence.

24b Learn to recognize compound sentences.

A **compound sentence** consists of two or more main clauses and no subordinate clause.

http://www.ablongman.com/littlebrown ▶

Visit the companion Web site for more help and an electronic exercise on sentence types.

┌─main clause─┐   ┌──── main clause ─────┐
Last July was hot, but August was even hotter.

┌──────── main clause ────────┐   ┌────────main clause──────┐
The hot sun scorched the earth, and the lack of rain killed many crops.

24c Learn to recognize complex sentences.

A **complex sentence** consists of one main clause and one or more subordinate clauses:

┌─main clause─┐ ┌─────────subordinate clause──────────┐
Rain finally came, although many had left the area by then.

┌──────────────main clause──────────────┐ ┌subordinate clause─┐
Those who remained were able to start anew because the govern-
                 subordinate clause

ment came to their aid.

---

gram

24d

24d Learn to recognize compound-complex sentences.

A **compound-complex sentence** has the characteristics of both the compound sentence (two or more main clauses) and the complex sentence (at least one subordinate clause):

┌──────────subordinate clause───────────┐ ┌────────main clause────────┐
Even though government aid finally came, many people had already
┌──────────────────────────┐ ┌──────── main clause ────────┐
been reduced to poverty; and others had been forced to move.

> **EXERCISE 24.1**
> **Identifying sentence structures**
> Mark the main clauses and subordinate clauses in the following sentences. Then identify each sentence as simple, compound, complex, or compound-complex. Answers to starred items appear at the end of the book. (You can do this exercise online at *ablongman.com/littlebrown*.)
>
> > *Example:*
> > ┌──────────main clause──────────┐
> > The human voice is produced in the larynx, a section of the throat
> >
> > ┌──────────subordinate clause──────────┐
> > that has two bands called vocal chords. [Complex.]
>
> *1. Our world has many sounds, but they all have one thing in common.
> *2. The one thing that all sounds share is that they are produced by vibrations.
> *3. The vibrations make the air move in waves, and these sound waves travel to the ear.
> *4. When sound waves enter the ear, the brain has to interpret them.

*5. Sound waves can also travel through other material, such as water and even the solid earth.

6. Some sounds are pleasant, and others, which we call noise, are not.
7. Most noises are produced by irregular vibrations at irregular intervals; an example is the barking of a dog.
8. Sounds have frequency and pitch.
9. When an object vibrates rapidly, it produces high-frequency, high-pitched sounds.
10. People can hear sounds over a wide range of frequencies; dogs and cats can hear sounds with higher frequencies.

gram
24d

Verbs

How and why do verbs change?

Verbs change in many ways to indicate differences in time, subject, and other aspects of sentences. The following chapters explain and solve the most common problems with verbs' forms (Chapter 25), tenses (26), mood (27), voice (28), and agreement with their subjects (29).

25 Verb Forms

What's wrong with *throwed* and *have went*?

Throwed and *have went* are forms of the verbs *throw* and *go* that are considered incorrect in standard American English. (The standard forms are *threw* or *thrown* and *have gone*.) Errors like these in verb forms can frustrate or confuse readers who expect standard English.

This chapter focuses on the verb forms most likely to cause difficulty: irregular verbs (below), *-s* and *-ed* endings (p. 255), helping verbs (p. 256), verbs followed by *-ing* or *to* words (p. 262), and two-word verbs (p. 264).

25a Use the correct forms of *sing/sang/sung* and other irregular verbs.

Most verbs are **regular:** they form their past tense and past participle by adding *-d* or *-ed* to the plain form:

Plain form	Past tense	Past participle
live	lived	lived
act	acted	acted

About two hundred English verbs are **irregular:** they form their past tense and past participle in some irregular way. Check a dic-

http://www.ablongman.com/littlebrown ▶

Visit the companion Web site for more help
and electronic exercises on verb forms.

tionary under the verb's plain form if you have any doubt about its other forms. If the verb is irregular, the dictionary will list the plain form, the past tense, and the past participle in that order (*go, went, gone*). If the dictionary gives only two forms (as in *think, thought*), then the past tense and the past participle are the same.

Common irregular verbs

Plain form	Past tense	Past participle
arise	arose	arisen
be	was, were	been
become	became	become
begin	began	begun
bend	bent	bent
bite	bit	bitten, bit
blow	blew	blown
break	broke	broken
bring	brought	brought
build	built	built
burst	burst	burst
buy	bought	bought
catch	caught	caught
choose	chose	chosen
come	came	come
cut	cut	cut
dig	dug	dug
dive	dived, dove	dived
do	did	done
draw	drew	drawn
dream	dreamed, dreamt	dreamed, dreamt
drink	drank	drunk
drive	drove	driven
eat	ate	eaten
fall	fell	fallen
find	found	found
fly	flew	flown

(continued)

vb

25a

> **Key terms**
>
> **plain form** The dictionary form of the verb: *I* _walk_. *You* _forget_. (See p. 226.)
>
> **past-tense form** The verb form indicating action that occurred in the past: *I* _walked_. *You* _forgot_. (See p. 226.)
>
> **past participle** The verb form used with *have, has,* or *had: I have* _walked_. It may also serve as a modifier: *This is a* _forgotten_ *book.* (See p. 227.)

Common irregular verbs

(continued)

Plain form	Past tense	Past participle
forget	forgot	forgotten, forgot
freeze	froze	frozen
get	got	got, gotten
give	gave	given
go	went	gone
grow	grew	grown
hang (suspend)	hung	hung
hang (execute)	hanged	hanged
have	had	had
hear	heard	heard
hide	hid	hidden
hold	held	held
hurt	hurt	hurt
keep	kept	kept
know	knew	known
lay	laid	laid
lead	led	led
leave	left	left
let	let	let
lie	lay	lain
lose	lost	lost
pay	paid	paid
ride	rode	ridden
ring	rang	rung
rise	rose	risen
run	ran	run
say	said	said
see	saw	seen
set	set	set
shake	shook	shaken
shrink	shrank, shrunk	shrunk, shrunken
sing	sang, sung	sung
sink	sank, sunk	sunk
sit	sat	sat
sleep	slept	slept
speak	spoke	spoken
stand	stood	stood
steal	stole	stolen
swim	swam	swum
swing	swung	swung
take	took	taken
throw	threw	thrown
wear	wore	worn
write	wrote	written

CULTURE / LANGUAGE Some English dialects use distinctive verb forms that differ from those of standard American English: for instance, *drug* for *dragged, growed* for *grew, come* for *came,* or *went* for *gone.* In situations requiring standard American English, use the forms in the preceding list or in a dictionary.

Note A grammar and style checker may flag incorrect forms of irregular verbs, but it may also fail to do so. For example, a checker flagged *The runner stealed second base* (*stole* is correct) but not *The runner had steal second base* (*stolen* is correct). When in doubt about the forms of irregular verbs, refer to the preceding list or consult a dictionary.

EXERCISE 25.1
Using irregular verbs

For each irregular verb in brackets, supply either the past tense or the past participle, as appropriate, and identify the form you used. Answers to starred items appear at the end of the book. (You can do this exercise online at *ablongman.com/littlebrown.*)

vb

25a

> *Example:*
> Though we had [hide] the cash box, it was [steal].
> Though we had hidden the cash box, it was stolen. [Two past participles.]

*1. The world population has [grow] by two-thirds of a billion people in less than a decade.
*2. Recently it [break] the 6 billion mark.
*3. Experts have [draw] pictures of a crowded future.
*4. They predict that the world population may have [slide] up to as much as 10 billion by the year 2050.
*5. Though the food supply [rise] in the last decade, the share to each person [fall].
6. At the same time the water supply, which had actually [become] healthier in the twentieth century, [sink] in size and quality.
7. The number of species on earth [shrink] by 20 percent.
8. Changes in land use [run] nomads and subsistence farmers off the land.
9. Yet all has not been [lose].
10. Recently human beings have [begin] to heed these and other problems and to explore how technology can be [drive] to help the earth and all its populations.
11. Some new techniques for waste processing have [prove] effective.
12. Crop management has [take] some pressure off lands with poor soil, allowing their owners to produce food.
13. Genetic engineering could replenish food supplies that have [shrink].
14. Population control has [find] adherents all over the world.
15. Many endangered species have been [give] room to thrive.

25b Distinguish between *sit* and *set, lie* and *lay,* and *rise* and *raise.*

The forms of *sit* and *set, lie* and *lay,* and *rise* and *raise* are easy to confuse.

Plain form	Past tense	Past participle
sit	sat	sat
set	set	set
lie	lay	lain
lay	laid	laid
rise	rose	risen
raise	raised	raised

In each of these confusing pairs, one verb is intransitive (it does not take an object) and one is transitive (it does take an object). (See p. 235 for more on this distinction.)

vb

25b

Intransitive

The patients lie in their beds. [*Lie* means "recline" and takes no object.]

Visitors sit with them. [*Sit* means "be seated" or "be located" and takes no object.]

Patients' temperatures rise. [*Rise* means "increase" or "get up" and takes no object.]

Transitive

Orderlies lay the dinner trays on tables. [*Lay* means "place" and takes an object, here *trays.*]

Orderlies set the trays down. [*Set* means "place" and takes an object, here *trays.*]

Nursing aides raise the shades. [*Raise* means "lift" or "bring up" and takes an object, here *shades.*]

> **EXERCISE 25.2**
> **Distinguishing between *sit/set, lie/lay, rise/raise***
>
> Choose the correct verb from the pair given in brackets. Then supply the past tense or past participle, as appropriate. Answers to starred items appear at the end of the book. (You can do this exercise online at *ablongman.com/littlebrown.*)
>
> *Example:*
>
> After I washed all the windows, I [lie, lay] down the squeegee and then I [sit, set] the table.
>
> After I washed all the windows, I laid down the squeegee and then I set the table.

* 1. Yesterday afternoon the child [lie, lay] down for a nap.
* 2. The child has been [rise, raise] by her grandparents.
3. Most days her grandfather has [sit, set] with her, reading her stories.
4. She has [rise, raise] at dawn most mornings.
5. Her toys were [lie, lay] on the floor.

25c   Use the *-s* and *-ed* forms of the verb when they are required.   CULTURE LANGUAGE

Speakers of some English dialects and nonnative speakers of English sometimes omit the *-s* and *-ed* verb endings when they are required in standard American English.

Note A grammar and style checker will flag many omitted *-s* and *-ed* endings from verbs, as in *he ask* and *was ask*. But it will miss many omissions, too.

1 • Required *-s* ending

vb

25c

Use the *-s* form of a verb when *both* of these situations hold:

• **The subject is a singular noun** (*boy*), **an indefinite pronoun** (*everyone*), **or** *he, she,* **or** *it*. These subjects are **third person,** used when someone or something is being spoken about.
• **The verb's action occurs in the present.**

The letter <u>asks</u> [not <u>ask</u>] for a quick response.
Delay <u>costs</u> [not <u>cost</u>] money.

Be especially careful with the *-s* forms of *be* (*is*), *have* (*has*), and *do* (*does, doesn't*). These forms should always be used to indicate present time with third-person singular subjects.

The company <u>is</u> [not <u>be</u>] late in responding.
It <u>has</u> [not <u>have</u>] problems.
It <u>doesn't</u> [not <u>don't</u>] have the needed data.
The contract <u>does</u> [not <u>do</u>] depend on the response.

In addition, *be* has an *-s* form in the past tense with *I* and third-person singular subjects:

The company <u>was</u> [not <u>were</u>] in trouble before.

I, you, and plural subjects do *not* take the *-s* form of verbs:

I <u>am</u> [not <u>is</u>] a student.
You <u>are</u> [not <u>is</u>] also a student.
They <u>are</u> [not <u>is</u>] students, too.

2 • Required -ed or -d ending

The -ed or -d verb form is required in *any* of these situations:

- **The verb's action occurred in the past:**

The company asked [not ask] for more time.

- **The verb form functions as a modifier:**

The data concerned [not concern] should be retrievable.

- **The verb form combines with a form of *be* or *have*:**

The company is supposed [not suppose] to be the best.
It has developed [not develop] an excellent reputation.

Watch especially for a needed -ed or -d ending when it isn't pronounced clearly in speech, as in *asked, discussed, mixed, supposed, walked,* and *used.*

---

vb

25d

EXERCISE 25.3
Using -s and -ed verb endings ◖ CULTURE LANGUAGE ◗

Supply the correct form of each verb in brackets. Be careful to include -s and -ed (or -d) endings where they are needed for standard English. Answers to starred items appear at the end of the book. (You can do this exercise online at *ablongman.com/littlebrown.*)

Example:

Unfortunately, the roof on our new house already [leak].
Unfortunately, the roof on our new house already leaks.

*1. A teacher sometimes [ask] too much of a student.
*2. In high school I was once [punish] for being sick.
*3. I had [miss] a week of school because of a serious case of the flu.
*4. I [realize] that I would fail a test unless I had a chance to make up the class work.
*5. I [discuss] the problem with the teacher.
 6. He said I was [suppose] to make up the work while I was sick.
 7. At that I [walk] out of the class.
 8. I [receive] a failing grade then, but it did not change my attitude.
 9. I [work] harder in the courses that have more understanding teachers.
10. Today I still balk when a teacher [make] unreasonable demands or [expect] miracles.

25d Use helping verbs with main verbs appropriately. ◖ CULTURE LANGUAGE ◗

Helping verbs combine with main verbs in verb phrases: *The line should have been cut. Who was calling?*

Note Grammar and style checkers often spot omitted helping verbs and incorrect main verbs with helping verbs, but sometimes they do not. A checker flagged *Many been fortunate, She working,* and *Her ideas are grow more complex* but overlooked other errors, such as *The conference will be occurred.*

1 • Required helping verbs

Standard American English requires helping verbs in certain situations:

- **The main verb ends in *-ing*:**

  Researchers <u>are</u> conducting fieldwork all over the world. [Not <u>Researchers conducting</u>. . . .]

- **The main verb is *been* or *be*:**

  Many <u>have</u> been fortunate in their discoveries. [Not <u>Many been</u>. . . .]
  Some <u>could</u> be real-life Indiana Joneses. [Not <u>Some be</u>. . . .]

- **The main verb is a past participle,** such as *talked, begun,* or *thrown*:

  Their discoveries <u>were</u> covered in newspapers and magazines. [Not <u>Their discoveries covered</u>. . . .]
  The researchers <u>have</u> given interviews on TV. [Not <u>The researchers given</u>. . . .]

vb

25d

The omission of a helping verb may create an incomplete sentence, or **sentence fragment,** because a present participle (*conducting*), an irregular past participle (*been*), or the infinitive *be* cannot stand alone as the only verb in a sentence (see pp. 327–28). To work as sentence verbs, these verb forms need helping verbs.

2 • Combination of helping verb + main verb

Helping verbs and main verbs combine into verb phrases in specific ways.

┌ Key terms ────────────────────────────────

helping verb A verb such as *can, may, be, have,* or *do* that forms a verb phrase with another verb to show time, permission, and other meanings. (See p. 227.)

main verb The verb that carries the principal meaning in a verb phrase: *has <u>walked</u>, could be <u>happening</u>.* (See p. 227.)

verb phrase A helping verb plus a main verb: *will be singing, would speak.* (See p. 227.)

Note The main verb in a verb phrase (the one carrying the main meaning) does not change to show a change in subject or time: *she has* <u>*sung*</u>, *you had* <u>*sung*</u>. Only the helping verb may change.

Form of *be* + present participle

The progressive tenses indicate action in progress. Create them with *be, am, is, are, was, were,* or *been* followed by the main verb's present participle, as in the following example.

She <u>is working</u> on a new book.

Be and *been* require additional helping verbs to form the progressive tenses:

can	might	should ⎫		have ⎫	
could	must	will ⎬ *be* working		has ⎬ <u>*been*</u> working	
may	shall	would ⎭		had ⎭	

When forming the progressive tenses, be sure to use the *-ing* form of the main verb:

Faulty   Her ideas are <u>grow</u> more complex. She is <u>developed</u> a new approach to ethics.

Revised   Her ideas are <u>growing</u> more complex. She is <u>developing</u> a new approach to ethics.

Form of *be* + past participle

The passive voice of the verb indicates that the subject *receives* the action of the verb. Create the passive voice with *be, am, is, are, was, were, being,* or *been* followed by the past participle of a transitive verb:

Her latest book <u>was completed</u> in four months.

Key terms

present participle The *-ing* form of the verb: *flying, writing.* (See p. 227.)

progressive tenses Verb tenses expressing action in progress—for instance, *I am flying* (present progressive), *I was flying* (past progressive), *I will be flying* (future progressive). (See pp. 269–70.)

past participle The *-d* or *-ed* form of a regular verb: *hedged, walked.* Most irregular verbs have distinctive past participles: *eaten, swum.* (See p. 227.)

passive voice The verb form when the subject names the receiver of the verb's action: *An essay* <u>*was written*</u> *by every student.* (See p. 227.)

transitive verb A verb that requires an object to complete its meaning: *Every student* <u>*completed*</u> *an essay* (*essay* is the object of *completed*). (See p. 235.)

Be, being, and *been* require additional helping verbs to form the passive voice:

have			am	was		
has	} been completed		is	were	} being completed	
had			are			

will be completed

Be sure to use the main verb's past participle for the passive voice:

Faulty   Her next book will be publish soon.
Revised Her next book will be published soon.

Note Only transitive verbs may form the passive voice:

Faulty   A philosophy conference will be occurred in the same week.
         [*Occur* is not a transitive verb.]
Revised A philosophy conference will occur in the same week.

See pages 277–78 for advice on when to use and when to avoid the passive voice.

vb
25d

Forms of *have*

Four forms of *have* serve as helping verbs: *have, has, had, having.* One of these forms plus the main verb's past participle creates one of the perfect tenses, those expressing action completed before another specific time or action:

Some students have complained about the laboratory.
Others had complained before.

Will and other helping verbs sometimes accompany forms of *have* in the perfect tenses:

Several more students will have complained by the end of the week.

Forms of *do*

Do, does, and *did* have three uses as helping verbs, always with the plain form of the main verb:

- **To pose a question:** *How did the trial end?*
- **To emphasize the main verb:** *It did end eventually.*

Key term
perfect tenses Verb tenses expressing an action completed before another specific time or action: *We have eaten* (present perfect), *We had eaten* (past perfect), *We will have eaten* (future perfect). (See p. 269.)

- To negate the main verb, along with *not* or *never*: *The judge did not withdraw*.

Be sure to use the main verb's plain form with any form of *do:*

| Faulty | The judge did <u>remained</u> in court. |
| Revised | The judge did <u>remain</u> in court. |

Modals

The modal helping verbs include *can, could, may,* and *might,* along with several two- and three-word combinations, such as *have to, be able to, be supposed to,* and *had better*. (See p. 227 for a list of modals.)

Modals convey various meanings, with these being most common:

- **Ability:** *can, could, be able to*

  The equipment <u>can detect</u> small vibrations. [Present.]
  The equipment <u>could detect</u> small vibrations. [Past.]
  The equipment <u>is able to detect</u> small vibrations. [Present. Past: *was able to*. Future: *will be able to.*]

- **Possibility:** *could, may, might, could/may/might have* + past participle

  The equipment <u>could fail</u>. [Present.]
  The equipment <u>may fail</u>. [Present and future.]
  The equipment <u>might fail</u>. [Present and future.]
  The equipment <u>may have failed</u>. [Past.]

- **Necessity or obligation:** *must, have to, be supposed to*

  The lab <u>must purchase</u> a backup. [Present or future.]
  The lab <u>has to purchase</u> a backup. [Present or future. Past: *had to.*]
  The lab <u>will have to purchase</u> a backup. [Future.]
  The lab <u>is supposed to purchase</u> a backup. [Present. Past: *was supposed to.*]

- **Permission:** *may, can, could*

  The lab <u>may spend</u> the money. [Present or future.]
  The lab <u>can spend</u> the money. [Present or future.]
  The lab <u>could spend</u> the money. [Present or future, more tentative.]
  The lab <u>could have spent</u> the money. [Past.]

- **Intention:** *will, shall, would*

  The lab <u>will spend</u> the money. [Future.]

Shall we <u>offer</u> advice? [Future. Use *shall* for questions requesting opinion or consent.]

We <u>would have offered</u> advice. [Past.]

● **Request:** *could, can, would*

<u>Could</u> [or <u>can</u> or <u>would</u>] you please <u>obtain</u> a bid? [Present or future.]

● **Advisability:** *should, had better, ought to, should have* + past participle

You <u>should obtain</u> three bids. [Present or future.]
You <u>had better obtain</u> three bids. [Present or future.]
You <u>ought to obtain</u> three bids. [Present or future.]
You <u>should have obtained</u> three bids. [Past.]

● **Past habit:** *would, used to*

In years past we <u>would obtain</u> five bids.
We <u>used to obtain</u> five bids.

vb
25d

EXERCISE 25.4
Using helping verbs CULTURE LANGUAGE

Add helping verbs to the following sentences where they are needed for standard American English. Answers to starred items appear at the end of the book. (You can do this exercise online at *ablongman.com/littlebrown.*)

  Example:
  The school be opened to shelter storm victims.
  The school <u>will</u> be opened to shelter storm victims.

*1. Each year thousands of new readers been discovering Agatha Christie's mysteries.
*2. The books written by a prim woman who had worked as a nurse during World War I.
  3. Christie never expected that her play *The Mousetrap* be performed for decades.
  4. During her life Christie always complaining about movie versions of her stories.
  5. Readers of her stories been delighted to be baffled by her.

EXERCISE 25.5
Revising: Helping verbs plus main verbs CULTURE LANGUAGE

Revise the following sentences so that helping verbs and main verbs are used correctly. If a sentence is correct as given, mark the number preceding it. Answers to starred items appear at the end of the book. (You can do this exercise online at *ablongman.com/littlebrown.*)

Example:

The college testing service has test as many as five hundred students at one time.

The college testing service has <u>tested</u> as many as five hundred students at one time.

*1. A report from the Bureau of the Census has confirm a widening gap between rich and poor.

*2. As suspected, the percentage of people below the poverty level did increased over the last decade.

3. More than 17 percent of the population is make 5 percent of all the income.

4. About 1 percent of the population will keeping an average of $500,000 apiece after taxes.

5. The other 99 percent all together will retain about $300,000.

25e Use a gerund or an infinitive after a verb as appropriate. ◖ CULTURE LANGUAGE ◗

Gerunds and infinitives may follow certain verbs but not others. And sometimes the use of a gerund or infinitive with the same verb changes the meaning of the verb.

Note A grammar and style checker will spot some but not all errors in matching gerunds or infinitives with verbs. For example, a checker flagged *I adore to shop* but not *I practice to swim* or *I promise helping out*. Use the lists given here and a dictionary of English as a second language to determine whether an infinitive or a gerund is appropriate. (See p. 204 for a list of ESL dictionaries.)

1 • Either gerund or infinitive

A gerund or an infinitive may come after the following verbs with no significant difference in meaning:

begin	continue	intend	prefer
can't bear	hate	like	start
can't stand	hesitate	love	

The pump began <u>working</u>. The pump began <u>to work</u>.

Key terms

gerund The *-ing* form of the verb used as a noun: <u>Smoking</u> is unhealthful. (See p. 242.)

infinitive The plain form of the verb usually preceded by *to: to smoke.* An infinitive may serve as an adjective, adverb, or noun. (See p. 242.)

2 • Meaning change with gerund or infinitive

With four verbs, a gerund has quite a different meaning from an infinitive:

forget   stop
remember   try

The engineer stopped eating. [He no longer ate.]
The engineer stopped to eat. [He stopped in order to eat.]

3 • Gerund, not infinitive

Do not use an infinitive after these verbs:

admit	discuss	mind	recollect
adore	dislike	miss	resent
appreciate	enjoy	postpone	resist
avoid	escape	practice	risk
consider	finish	put off	suggest
deny	imagine	quit	tolerate
detest	keep	recall	understand

Faulty   He finished to eat lunch.
Revised   He finished eating lunch.

vb

25e

4 • Infinitive, not gerund

Do not use a gerund after these verbs:

agree	claim	manage	promise
appear	consent	mean	refuse
arrange	decide	offer	say
ask	expect	plan	wait
assent	have	prepare	want
beg	hope	pretend	wish

Faulty   He decided checking the pump.
Revised   He decided to check the pump.

5 • Noun or pronoun + infinitive

Some verbs may be followed by an infinitive alone or by a noun or pronoun and an infinitive. The presence of a noun or pronoun changes the meaning.

ask	dare	need	wish
beg	expect	promise	would like
choose	help	want	

He expected to watch.
He expected his workers to watch.

Some verbs *must* be followed by a noun or pronoun before an infinitive:

admonish	encourage	oblige	require
advise	forbid	order	teach
allow	force	permit	tell
cause	hire	persuade	train
challenge	instruct	remind	urge
command	invite	request	warn
convince			

He instructed <u>his workers</u> <u>to watch</u>.

Do not use *to* before the infinitive when it follows one of the next verbs and a noun or pronoun:

feel	make ("force")
have	see
hear	watch
let	

He let his workers <u>learn</u> by observation.

vb

25f

EXERCISE 25.6
Revising: Verbs plus gerunds or infinitives 🌐 **CULTURE LANGUAGE**

Revise the following sentences so that gerunds or infinitives are used correctly with verbs. Mark the number preceding any sentence that is already correct. Answers to starred items appear at the end of the book. (You can do this exercise online at *ablongman.com/littlebrown*.)

> *Example:*
>
> A politician cannot avoid to alienate some voters.
> A politician cannot avoid <u>alienating</u> some voters.

*1. A program called HELP Wanted tries to encourage citizens take action on behalf of American competitiveness.
*2. Officials working on this program hope improving education for work.

3. American businesses find that their workers need learning to read.
4. In the next ten years the United States expects facing a shortage of 350,000 scientists.
5. HELP Wanted suggests creating a media campaign.

25f Use the appropriate particles with two-word verbs. 🌐 CULTURE LANGUAGE

Standard American English includes some verbs that consist of two words: the verb itself and a **particle**, a preposition or adverb that affects the meaning of the verb. For example:

Look up the answer. [Research the answer.]
Look over the answer. [Examine the answer.]

The meanings of these two-word verbs are often quite different from the meanings of the individual words that make them up. (There are some three-word verbs, too, such as *look out for, put up with,* and *run out of.*)

A dictionary of English as a second language will define two-word verbs for you and say whether the verbs may be separated in a sentence, as explained below. (See p. 204 for a list of ESL dictionaries.) A grammar and style checker will recognize few if any misuses of two-word verbs.

Note Many two-word verbs are more common in speech than in more formal academic or public writing. For formal writing, consider using *research* instead of *look up, examine* or *inspect* instead of *look over.*

1 • Inseparable two-word verbs

Verbs and particles that may not be separated by any other words include the following:

catch on	go over	play around	stay away
come across	grow up	run into	stay up
get along	keep on	run out of	take care of
give in	look into	speak up	turn up at

Faulty   Children grow quickly up.
Revised   Children grow up quickly.

2 • Separable two-word verbs

Most two-word verbs that take direct objects may be separated by the object.

Parents help out their children.
Parents help their children out.

If the direct object is a pronoun, the pronoun *must* separate the verb from the particle.

Key terms

preposition A word such as *about, for,* or *to* that takes a noun or pronoun as its object: *at the house, in the woods.* (See p. 230 for a list of prepositions.)

adverb A word that modifies a verb (*went down*), adjective (*very pretty*), another adverb (*too sweetly*), or a whole word group (*Eventually, the fire died*). (See p. 228.)

Faulty	Parents <u>help out</u> them.
Revised	Parents <u>help</u> them <u>out</u>.

The separable two-word verbs include the following:

bring up	give back	make up	throw out
call off	hand in	point out	try on
call up	hand out	put away	try out
drop off	help out	put back	turn down
fill out	leave out	put off	turn on
fill up	look over	take out	turn up
give away	look up	take over	wrap up

EXERCISE 25.7
Revising: Verbs plus particles   **CULTURE LANGUAGE**

The two- and three-word verbs in the sentences below are underlined. Some are correct as given, and some are not because they should or should not be separated by other words. Revise the verbs and other words that are incorrect. Consult the preceding lists or an ESL dictionary if necessary to determine which verbs are separable. Answers to starred items appear at the end of the book. (You can do this exercise online at *ablongman.com/littlebrown.*)

Example:

Hollywood producers never seem to <u>come up with</u> entirely new plots, but they also never <u>run</u> new ways <u>out of</u> to present old ones.

Hollywood producers never seem to come up with [correct] entirely new plots, but they also never <u>run out of new ways</u> to present old ones.

*1. American movies treat everything from <u>going out with</u> someone to <u>making up</u> an ethnic identity, but few people <u>look</u> their significance <u>into</u>.

*2. While some viewers <u>stay away from</u> topical films, others <u>turn</u> at the theater <u>up</u> simply because a movie has sparked debate.

3. Some movies attracted rowdy spectators, and the theaters had to <u>throw out</u> them.

4. Filmmakers have always been eager to <u>point</u> their influence <u>out</u> to the public.

5. Everyone agrees that filmmakers will <u>keep</u> creating controversy <u>on</u>, if only because it can <u>fill up</u> theaters.

26 Verb Tenses

How do *walked* and *had walked* differ?

Walked and *had walked* illustrate different **tenses** of the verb *to walk*. That is, they show the action of the verb to be occurring at different times, one (*had walked*) before the other (*walked*) and both before the present. The box on the next page illustrates the tense forms for a regular verb. (Irregular verbs have some different forms. See pp. 251–52.)

Note Grammar and style checkers can provide little help with incorrect verb tenses and tense sequences because correctness usually depends on meaning.

CULTURE LANGUAGE In standard American English, a verb conveys time and sequence through its form. In some other languages and English dialects, various markers besides verb form may indicate the time of a verb. For instance, in African American dialect *I be attending class on Friday* means that the speaker attends class every Friday. To a speaker of standard American English, however, the sentence may be unclear: last Friday? this Friday? every Friday? The intended meaning must be indicated by verb tense. *I <u>attended</u> class on Friday. I <u>will attend</u> class on Friday. I <u>attend</u> class on Friday.*

26a Observe the special uses of the present tense (*sing*).

The present tense has several distinctive uses.

Action occurring now

She <u>understands</u> the problem.
We <u>define</u> the problem differently.

Habitual or recurring action

Banks regularly <u>undergo</u> audits.
The audits <u>monitor</u> the banks' activities.

A general truth

The mills of the gods <u>grind</u> slowly.
The earth <u>is</u> round.

Discussion of literature, film, and so on

Huckleberry Finn <u>has</u> adventures we all envy.

> http://www.ablongman.com/littlebrown ▶
>
> Visit the companion Web site for more help and electronic exercises on verb tenses.

Tenses of a regular verb (active voice)

Present Action that is occurring now, occurs habitually, or is generally true

Simple present Plain form or *-s* form

I walk.
You/we/they walk.
He/she/it walks.

Present progressive *Am, is,* or *are* plus *-ing* form

I am walking.
You/we/they are walking.
He/she/it is walking.

Past Action that occurred before now

Simple past Past-tense form (*-d* or *-ed*)

I/he/she/it walked.
You/we/they walked.

Past progressive *Was* or *were* plus *-ing* form

I/he/she/it was walking.
You/we/they were walking.

Future Action that will occur in the future

Simple future Plain form plus *will*

I/you/he/she/it/we/they will walk.

Future progressive *Will be* plus *-ing* form

I/you/he/she/it/we/they will be walking.

Present perfect Action that began in the past and is linked to the present

Present perfect *Have* or *has* plus past participle (*-d* or *-ed*)

I/you/we/they have walked.
He/she/it has walked.

Present perfect progressive *Have been* or *has been* plus *-ing* form

I/you/we/they have been walking.
He/she/it has been walking.

Past perfect Action that was completed before another past action

Past perfect *Had* plus past participle (*-d* or *-ed*)

I/you/he/she/it/we/they had walked.

Past perfect progressive *Had been* plus *-ing* form

I/you/he/she/it/we/they had been walking.

Future perfect Action that will be completed before another future action

Future perfect *Will have* plus past participle (*-d* or *-ed*)

I/you/he/she/it/we/they will have walked.

Future perfect progressive *Will have been* plus *-ing* form

I/you/he/she/it/we/they will have been walking.

In that article the author <u>examines</u> several causes of crime.

Future time
Next week we <u>draft</u> a new budget.
Funding <u>ends</u> in less than a year.

The present tense shows future time with expressions like those in the examples above: *next week, in less than a year.*

26b Observe the uses of the perfect tenses (*have/had/will have sung*).

The **perfect tenses** consist of a form of *have* plus the verb's past participle (*closed, hidden*). They indicate an action that is completed before another specific time or action. The present perfect tense also indicates action that is begun in the past and continued into the present.

present perfect
The dancer <u>has performed</u> here only once. [The action is completed at the time of the statement.]

present perfect
Critics <u>have written</u> about the performance ever since. [The action began in the past and continues now.]

past perfect
The dancer <u>had trained</u> in Asia before his performance. [The action was completed before another past action.]

future perfect
He <u>will have danced</u> here again by the end of the year. [The action begins now or in the future and will be completed by a specific time in the future.]

CULTURE LANGUAGE With the present perfect tense, the words *since* and *for* are followed by different information. After *since,* give a specific point in time: *The play has run <u>since 1999</u>.* After *for,* give a span of time: *It could run <u>for decades</u>.*

26c Observe the uses of the progressive tenses (*is/was/will be singing*). **CULTURE LANGUAGE**

The **progressive tenses** indicate continuing (therefore progressive) action. They consist of a form of *be* plus the verb's *-ing* form (present participle). (The words *be* and *been* must be combined with other helping verbs. See p. 258.)

t
26c

present progressive
The economy is improving.

past progressive
Last year the economy was stagnating.

future progressive
Economists will be watching for signs of growth.

present perfect progressive
The government has been expecting an upturn.

past perfect progressive
Various indicators had been suggesting improvement.

future perfect progressive
By the end of this year, investors will have been watching interest rates nervously for nearly a decade.

Note Verbs that express unchanging states (especially mental states) rather than physical actions do not usually appear in the progressive tenses. These verbs include *adore, appear, believe, belong, care, hate, have, hear, know, like, love, mean, need, own, prefer, remember, see, sound, taste, think, understand,* and *want.*

Faulty	She is wanting to study ethics.
Revised	She wants to study ethics.

t seq

26d

26d Keep tenses consistent.

Within a sentence, the tenses of verbs and verb forms need not be identical as long as they reflect actual changes in time: *Ramon will graduate from college thirty years after his father arrived in America.* But needless shifts in tense will confuse or distract readers:

Inconsistent	Immediately after Booth shot Lincoln, Major Rathbone threw himself upon the assassin. But Booth pulls a knife and plunges it into the major's arm.
Revised	Immediately after Booth shot Lincoln, Major Rathbone threw himself upon the assassin. But Booth pulled a knife and plunged it into the major's arm.
Inconsistent	The main character in the novel suffers psychologically because he has a clubfoot, but he eventually triumphed over his disability.
Revised	The main character in the novel suffers psychologically because he has a clubfoot, but he eventually triumphs over his disability. [Use the present tense when discussing the content of literature, film, and so on.]

EXERCISE 26.1
Revising: Consistent past tense

In the paragraph below, change the tenses of the verbs as needed to maintain consistent simple past tense. Answers to the starred sentences appear at the end of the book. (You can do this exercise online at *ablongman.com/littlebrown*.)

*The 1960 presidential race between Richard Nixon and John F. Kennedy was the first to feature a televised debate. *Despite his extensive political experience, Nixon perspires heavily and looks haggard and uneasy in front of the camera. *By contrast, Kennedy was projecting cool poise and providing crisp answers that made him seem fit for the office of President. The public responded positively to Kennedy's image. His poll ratings shoot up immediately, while Nixon's take a corresponding drop. Kennedy won the election by a close 118,564 votes.

EXERCISE 26.2
Revising: Consistent present tense

In the paragraph below, change the tenses of the verbs as needed to maintain consistent simple present tense. Answers to the starred sentences appear at the end of the book. (You can do this exercise online at *ablongman.com/littlebrown*.)

*E. B. White's famous children's novel *Charlotte's Web* is a wonderful story of friendship and loyalty. *Charlotte, the wise and motherly spider, decided to save her friend Wilbur, the young and childlike pig, from being butchered by his owner. *She made a plan to weave words into her web that described Wilbur. She first weaves "Some Pig" and later presented "Terrific," "Radiant," and "Humble." Her plan succeeded beautifully. She fools the humans into believing that Wilbur was a pig unlike any other, and Wilbur lived.

26e Use the appropriate sequence of verb tenses.

The **sequence of tenses** is the relation between the verb tense in a main clause and the verb tense in a subordinate clause. The tenses often differ to reflect differences in relative time, as in the following sentence:

Ramon's father <u>arrived</u> in the United States thirty years ago, after he <u>had married</u>, and now Ramon <u>has decided</u> that he <u>will return</u> to his father's homeland.

English tense sequence can be tricky for native speakers and especially challenging for nonnative speakers. The main difficulties are discussed on the following pages.

1 • Past or past perfect tense in main clause

When the verb in the main clause is in the past or past perfect tense, the verb in the subordinate clause must also be past or past perfect:

main clause: subordinate clause:
past   past

The researchers <u>discovered</u> that people <u>varied</u> widely in their knowledge of public events.

main clause: subordinate clause:
past   past perfect

The variation <u>occurred</u> because respondents <u>had been born</u> in different decades.

main clause: subordinate clause:
past perfect   past

None of them <u>had been born</u> when Eisenhower <u>was</u> President.

Exception Always use the present tense for a general truth, such as *The earth is round:*

main clause: subordinate clause:
past   present

Most <u>understood</u> that popular Presidents <u>are</u> not necessarily good Presidents.

2 • Conditional sentences

A **conditional sentence** states a factual relation between cause and effect, makes a prediction, or speculates about what might happen. Such a sentence usually consists of a subordinate clause beginning with *if, when,* or *unless* and a main clause stating the result. The three kinds of conditional sentences use distinctive verbs.

Factual relation

For statements asserting that something always or usually happens whenever something else happens, use the present tense in both clauses:

subordinate clause: main clause:
present   present

When a voter <u>casts</u> a ballot, he or she <u>has</u> complete privacy.

Key terms

main clause A word group that contains a subject and a predicate and does not begin with a subordinating word: *Books are valuable.* (See p. 244.)

subordinate clause A word group that contains a subject and a predicate, begins with a subordinating word such as *because* or *who,* and is not a question: *Books are valuable <u>when they enlighten</u>.* (See p. 244.)

---

t seq

26e

If the linked events occurred in the past, use the past tense in both clauses:

subordinate clause: main clause:
    past   past
When voters <u>registered</u> in some states, they <u>had</u> to pay a poll tax.

Prediction

For a prediction, generally use the present tense in the subordinate clause and the future tense in the main clause:

subordinate clause: main clause:
    present   future
Unless citizens <u>regain</u> faith in politics, they <u>will</u> not <u>vote</u>.

Sometimes the verb in the main clause consists of *may, can, should,* or *might* plus the verb's plain form: *If citizens <u>regain</u> faith, they <u>may vote</u>.*

Speculation

Speculations are mainly of two kinds, each with its own verb pattern. For events that are possible in the present but unlikely, use the past tense in the subordinate clause and *would, could,* or *might* plus the verb's plain form in the main clause:

subordinate clause: main clause:
    past   *would* + verb
If voters <u>had</u> more confidence, they <u>would vote</u> more often.

Use *were* instead of *was* when the subject is *I, he, she, it,* or a singular noun. (See pp. 275–76 for more on this distinctive verb form.)

subordinate clause: main clause:
    past   *would* + verb
If the voter <u>were</u> more confident, he or she <u>would vote</u> more often.

For events that are impossible now, that are contrary to fact, use the same forms as above (including the distinctive *were* when applicable):

subordinate clause: main clause:
    past   *might* + verb
If Lincoln <u>were</u> alive, he <u>might inspire</u> confidence.

For events that were impossible in the past, use the past perfect tense in the subordinate clause and *would, could,* or *might* plus the present perfect tense in the main clause:

subordinate clause: main clause:
    past perfect   *might* + present perfect
If Lincoln <u>had lived</u> past the Civil War, he <u>might have helped</u> stabilize the country.

t seq

26e

EXERCISE 26.3

Adjusting tense sequence: Past or past perfect tense

The tenses in each sentence below are in correct sequence. Change the tense of one verb as instructed. Then change the tenses of other verbs as needed to restore correct sequence. Some items have more than one possible answer. Answers to starred items appear at the end of the book. (You can do this exercise online at *ablongman.com/littlebrown.*)

Example:

Delgado will call when he reaches his destination. (*Change will call to called.*)

Delgado called when he reached [or had reached] his destination.

*1. Diaries that Adolf Hitler is supposed to have written have surfaced in Germany. (*Change have surfaced to had surfaced.*)

*2. Many people believe that the diaries are authentic because a well-known historian has declared them so. (*Change believe to believed.*)

3. However, the historian's evaluation has been questioned by other authorities, who call the diaries forgeries. (*Change has been questioned to was questioned.*)

4. They claim, among other things, that the paper is not old enough to have been used by Hitler. (*Change claim to claimed.*)

5. Eventually, the doubters will win the debate because they have the best evidence. (*Change will win to won.*)

EXERCISE 26.4

Revising: Tense sequence with conditional sentences

Supply the appropriate tense for each verb in brackets below. Answers to starred items appear at the end of the book. (You can do this exercise online at *ablongman.com/littlebrown.*)

Example:

If Babe Ruth or Jim Thorpe [be] athletes today, they [remind] us that even sports heroes must contend with a harsh reality.

If Babe Ruth or Jim Thorpe were athletes today, they might [or could or would] remind us that even sports heroes must contend with a harsh reality.

*1. When an athlete [turn] professional, he or she commits to a grueling regimen of mental and physical training.

*2. If athletes [be] less committed, they [disappoint] teammates, fans, and themselves.

*3. If professional athletes [be] very lucky, they may play until age forty.

*4. Unless an athlete achieves celebrity status, he or she [have] few employment choices after retirement.

*5. If professional sports [be] less risky, athletes [have] longer careers and more choices after retirement.

6. If you think you [be] exposed to the flu in the winter, you [get] a flu shot.
7. If you are allergic to eggs, you [have] an allergic reaction to the flu shot.
8. If you get the flu after having a flu shot, your illness [be] milder.
9. If you had had a flu shot last year, you [avoid] the illness.
10. If you [be] not so afraid of shots, you [will] get a flu shot every year.

27   Verb Mood

When is it right to say *he were?*

The odd-sounding construction *he were* illustrates a particular **mood** of the verb *is*, a particular attitude on the writer's or speaker's part toward what he or she is saying. In the sentence *I wish he were going,* the *were* reinforces the writer's expression of a desire.

English verbs express three possible moods. The **indicative mood** states a fact or opinion or asks a question: *The theater needs help. Can you help the theater?* The **imperative mood** expresses a command or gives a direction, and it omits the subject of the sentence, *you: Help the theater*. The more complicated **subjunctive mood** expresses wishes, suggestions, and other attitudes, using *he were* and other distinctive verb forms described below.

Note A grammar and style checker may spot some simple errors in the subjunctive mood, but it may miss others. For example, a checker flagged *I wish I was home* (should be *were home*) but not *If I had a hammer, I will hammer in the morning* (should be *would hammer*).

27a   Use the subjunctive verb forms appropriately, as in *I wish I were.*

The subjunctive mood expresses a suggestion, requirement, or desire, or it states a condition that is contrary to fact (that is, imaginary or hypothetical).

- **Verbs such as *ask, insist, urge, require, recommend,* and *suggest* indicate request or requirement.** They often precede a

http://www.ablongman.com/littlebrown

Visit the companion Web site for more help and an electronic exercise on verb mood.

subordinate clause beginning with *that* and containing the substance of the request or requirement. For all subjects, the verb in the *that* clause is the plain form:

> plain form
> Rules require that every donation be mailed.

- **Contrary-to-fact clauses state imaginary or hypothetical conditions and usually begin with *if* or *unless* or follow *wish*.** For present contrary-to-fact clauses, use the verb's past-tense form (for *be,* use the past-tense form *were*):

> past   past
> If the theater were in better shape and had more money, its future would be assured.

> past
> I wish I were able to donate money.

For past contrary-to-fact clauses, use the verb's past perfect form (*had* + past participle):

> past perfect
> The theater would be better funded if it had been better managed last year.

Note Do not use the helping verb *would* or *could* in a contrary-to-fact clause beginning with *if:*

Not	Many people would have helped if they would have known.
But	Many people would have helped if they had known.

See also page 273 for more on verb tenses in contrary-to-fact sentences like these.

27b   Keep mood consistent.

Shifts in mood within a sentence or among related sentences can be confusing. Such shifts occur most frequently in directions.

Inconsistent	Cook the mixture slowly, and you should stir it until the sugar is dissolved. [Mood shifts from imperative to indicative.]
Revised	Cook the mixture slowly, and stir it until the sugar is dissolved. [Consistently imperative.]

EXERCISE 27.1
Revising: Subjunctive mood

Revise the following sentences with appropriate subjunctive verb forms. Answers to starred items appear at the end of the book. (You can do this exercise online at *ablongman.com/littlebrown*.)

vb
27b

Example:

I would help the old man if I was able to reach him.
I would help the old man if I <u>were</u> able to reach him.

*1. If John Hawkins would have known of all the dangerous side effects of smoking tobacco, would he have introduced the dried plant to England in 1565?

*2. Hawkins noted that if a Florida Indian man was to travel for several days, he would have smoked tobacco to satisfy his hunger and thirst.

3. Early tobacco growers feared that their product would not gain acceptance unless it was perceived as healthful.

4. To prevent fires, in 1646 the General Court of Massachusetts passed a law requiring that colonists smoked tobacco only if they were five miles from any town.

5. To prevent decadence, in 1647 Connecticut passed a law mandating that one's smoking of tobacco was limited to once a day in one's own home.

pass
28

28 Verb Voice

Which is better: *The book was written by her* or *She wrote the book?*

Generally, you should prefer the **active voice** of *She wrote the book,* in which the subject (*She*) performs the action of the verb (*wrote*). In the **passive voice** of *The book was written by her,* the subject (*book*) receives the action of the verb (*was written*) and the actual actor appears in a trailing phrase (*by her*). (Naming the actual actor is optional in the passive voice.) The passive voice does have its uses (see the next page), but the active voice is usually more direct and concise.

CULTURE LANGUAGE A passive verb always consists of a form of *be* plus the past participle of the main verb: *rents <u>are controlled</u>, people <u>were inspired</u>.* Other helping verbs must also be used with the words *<u>be, being,</u>* and *been: rents <u>have been controlled</u>, people <u>would have been inspired</u>.* Only a transitive verb (one that takes an object) may be used in the passive voice. (See pp. 235, 259.)

---

http://www.ablongman.com/littlebrown

Visit the companion Web site for more help and electronic exercises on verb voice.

Active and passive voice

Active voice   The subject acts.

Passive voice   The subject is acted upon.

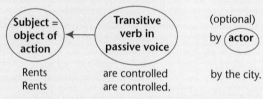

28a   Prefer the active voice. Use the passive voice when the actor is unknown or unimportant.

The active voice is usually clearer, more concise, and more forthright than the passive voice.

Weak passive   The Internet is used by many scholars, and its expansion to the general public has been criticized by some.

Strong active   Many scholars use the Internet, and some have criticized its expansion to the general public.

The passive voice is useful in two situations: when the actor is unknown and when the actor is unimportant or less important than the object of the action.

The Internet was established in 1969 by the US Department of Defense. The network has now been extended internationally to governments, universities, corporations, and private individuals. [In the first sentence the writer wishes to stress the Internet rather than the Department of Defense. In the second sentence the actor is too complicated to name.]

After the solution had been cooled to 10°C, the acid was added. [The person who cooled and added, perhaps the writer, is less important than the facts that the solution was cooled and acid was added. Passive sentences are common in scientific writing.]

Note Most grammar and style checkers can be set to spot the passive voice. But they will also flag appropriate uses of the passive voice (such as when the actor is unknown).

28b   Keep voice consistent.

Shifts in voice that involve shifts in subject are usually unnecessary and confusing.

Inconsistent   Internet newsgroups cover an enormous range of topics
               for discussion. Forums for meeting people with like inter-
               ests are provided in these groups.

Revised   Internet newsgroups cover an enormous range of topics
               for discussion and provide forums for meeting people
               with like interests.

A shift in voice is appropriate when it helps focus the reader's
attention on a single subject, as in *The candidate campaigned vigorously and was nominated on the first ballot.*

EXERCISE 28.1
Revising: Using the active voice

Rewrite each of the following passive sentences into the active voice,
adding a subject as necessary. Possible answers to starred items appear
at the end of the book. (You can do this exercise online at *ablongman.com/
littlebrown.*)

pass

28b

> *Example:*
>
> Contaminants are removed from water by treatment plants.
> Treatment plants remove contaminants from water.

*1. Water quality is determined by many factors.
*2. Suspended and dissolved substances are contained in all natural wa-
     ters.
*3. The amounts of the substances are controlled by the environment.
*4. Some dissolved substances are produced by pesticides.
*5. Sediment is deposited in water by fields, livestock feedlots, and
     other sources.

  6. The bottom life of streams and lakes is affected by sediment.
  7. Light penetration is reduced by sediment, and bottom-dwelling or-
     ganisms may be smothered.
  8. The quality of water in city systems is measured frequently.
  9. If legal levels are exceeded by pollutants, the citizens must be noti-
     fied by city officials.
 10. The chlorine taste of water is disliked by many people.

EXERCISE 28.2
Converting between active and passive voices

To practice using the two voices of the verb, convert the verbs in the following sentences from active to passive or from passive to active. (In
converting from passive to active, you may need to add a subject.)
Which version of the sentence seems more effective and why? Answers

to starred items appear at the end of the book. (You can do this exercise online at *ablongman.com/littlebrown*.)

Example:

The aspiring actor was discovered in a nightclub.
A talent <u>scout</u> <u>discovered</u> the actor in a nightclub.

*1. When the Eiffel Tower was built in 1889, it was thought by the French to be ugly.
*2. At the time, many people still resisted industrial technology.

3. The tower's naked steel construction typified this technology.
4. Beautiful ornament was expected to grace fine buildings.
5. Further, a structure without solid walls could not even be called a building.

**vb agr
29**

29   Agreement of Subject and Verb

Does the verb of this sentence match the subject?

A verb and its subject should match, or **agree**, in number and person: a singular subject takes a singular verb, and a plural subject takes a plural verb, as in the examples below:

<u>Daniel Inouye</u> <u>was</u> the first Japanese American in Congress.
   subject   verb

More <u>Japanese Americans</u> <u>live</u> in Hawaii and California than elsewhere.
     subject   verb

Most problems of subject-verb agreement arise when endings are omitted from subjects or verbs or when the relation between

---

Key terms

	Number	
Person	**Singular**	**Plural**
First	I eat.	We eat.
Second	You eat.	You eat.
Third	He/she/it eats.	They eat.
	The bird eats.	Birds eat.

---

http://www.ablongman.com/littlebrown ▶

Visit the companion Web site for more help and electronic exercises on subject-verb agreement.

sentence parts is uncertain. This chapter covers these tricky situations.

Note A grammar and style checker will catch many simple errors in subject-verb agreement, such as *Addie and John is late*, and some more complicated errors, such as *Is Margaret and Tom going with us?* (should be *are* in both cases). But a checker failed to flag *The old group has gone their separate ways* (should be *have*) and offered a wrong correction for *The old group have gone their separate ways*, which is already correct.

29a The *-s* and *-es* endings work differently for nouns and verbs.

An *-s* or *-es* ending does opposite things to nouns and verbs: it usually makes a noun *plural*, but it always makes a present-tense verb *singular*. Thus a singular-noun subject will not end in *-s*, but its verb will. A plural-noun subject will end in *-s*, but its verb will not. Between them, subject and verb use only one *-s* ending.

vb agr

29a

Singular subject	Plural subject
The boy plays.	The boys play.
The bird soars.	The birds soar.

The only exceptions to these rules involve the nouns that form irregular plurals, such as *child/children*, *woman/women*. The irregular plural still requires a plural verb: *The children play*. *The women read*.

❝ **CULTURE** ❞ If your first language or dialect is not standard American English, subject-verb agreement may be problematic, especially for the following reasons:

- **Some English dialects follow different rules for subject-verb agreement,** such as omitting the *-s* ending for singular verbs or using the *-s* ending for plural verbs.

Nonstandard	The voter resist change.
Standard	The voter resists change.
Standard	The voters resist change.

The verb *be* changes spelling for singular and plural in both present and past tense. (See also p. 227.)

Nonstandard	Taxes is high. They was raised just last year.
Standard	Taxes are high. They were raised just last year.

Have also has a distinctive *-s* form, *has*:

| Nonstandard | The new tax have little chance of passing. |
| Standard | The new tax has little chance of passing. |

- **Some other languages change all parts of verb phrases to match their subjects.** In English verb phrases, however, only the helping verbs *be, have,* and *do* change for different subjects. The modal helping verbs—*can, may, should, will,* and others— do not change:

| Nonstandard | The tax mays pass next year. |
| Standard | The tax may pass next year. |

The main verb in a verb phrase also does not change for different subjects:

| Nonstandard | The tax may passes next year. |
| Standard | The tax may pass next year. |

vb agr

29c

29b Subject and verb should agree even when other words come between them.

The catalog of course requirements often baffles [not baffle] students.

The requirements stated in the catalog are [not is] unclear.

Note Phrases beginning with *as well as, together with, along with,* and *in addition to* do not change the number of the subject:

The president, as well as the deans, has [not have] agreed to revise the catalog.

29c Subjects joined by *and* usually take plural verbs.

Frost and Roethke were contemporaries.

Key terms

verb phrase A combination of helping verb and main verb: *will be singing, has opened, would run.* (See p. 227.)

helping verb A verb such as *be, have,* and *can* that combines with another verb to show time, permission, and other meanings: *will be singing, has opened, would run.* (See p. 227.)

main verb The verb that carries the principal meaning in a verb phrase: *will be singing, has opened, would run.* (See p. 227.)

Exceptions When the parts of the subject form a single idea or refer to a single person or thing, they take a singular verb:

Avocado and bean sprouts is a California sandwich.

When a compound subject is preceded by the adjective *each* or *every*, the verb is usually singular:

Each man, woman, and child has a right to be heard.

29d When parts of a subject are joined by *or* or *nor*, the verb agrees with the nearer part.

Either the painter or the carpenter knows the cost.

The cabinets or the bookcases are too costly.

When one part of the subject is singular and the other plural, avoid awkwardness by placing the plural part closer to the verb so that the verb is plural:

vb agr

29e

Awkward   Neither the owners nor the contractor agrees.

Revised   Neither the contractor nor the owners agree.

29e With *everyone* and other indefinite pronouns, use a singular or plural verb as appropriate.

Most indefinite pronouns are singular in meaning (they refer to a single unspecified person or thing), and they take a singular verb:

Something smells.   Neither is right.

None of them has any money.

> ### Key term
>
> **indefinite pronoun** A pronoun that does not refer to a specific person or thing:
>
> | *Singular* | | | *Singular or plural* | *Plural* |
> |---|---|---|---|---|
> | anybody | everyone | no one | all | both |
> | anyone | everything | nothing | any | few |
> | anything | much | one | more | many |
> | each | neither | somebody | most | several |
> | either | nobody | someone | some | |
> | everybody | none | something | | |

The plural indefinite pronouns refer to more than one unspecified thing, and they take a plural verb:

Both are correct.   Several were invited.

The other indefinite pronouns take a singular or a plural verb depending on whether the word they refer to is singular or plural:

All of the money is reserved for emergencies.

All of the funds are reserved for emergencies.

CULTURE LANGUAGE See page 316 for the distinction between *few* ("not many") and *a few* ("some").

29f Collective nouns such as *team* take singular or plural verbs depending on meaning.

vb agr
29f

Use a singular verb with a collective noun when the group acts as a unit:

The group agrees that action is necessary.

But when the group's members act separately, not together, use a plural verb:

The old group have gone their separate ways.

The collective noun *number* may be singular or plural. Preceded by *a*, it is plural; preceded by *the*, it is singular:

A number of people are in debt.

The number of people in debt is very large.

CULTURE LANGUAGE Some noncount nouns (nouns that don't form plurals) are collective nouns because they name groups: for instance, *furniture, clothing, mail.* These noncount nouns usually take singular verbs: *Mail arrives daily.* But some of these nouns take plural verbs, including *clergy, military, people, police,* and any collective noun that comes from an adjective, such as *the poor, the rich, the*

Key term

collective noun A noun with singular form that names a group of individuals or things—for instance, *army, audience, committee, crowd, family, group, team.*

young, the elderly. If you mean one representative of the group, use a singular noun such as *police officer* or *poor person.*

29g   *Who, which,* and *that* take verbs that agree with their antecedents.

When used as subjects, *who, which,* and *that* refer to another word in the sentence, called the **antecedent.** The verb agrees with the antecedent.

Mayor Garber ought to listen to the people who <u>work</u> for her.

Bardini is the only aide who <u>has</u> her ear.

Agreement problems often occur with *who, which,* or *that* when the sentence includes *one of the* or *the only one of the:*

Bardini is one of the aides who <u>work</u> unpaid. [Of the aides who work unpaid, Bardini is one.]

Bardini is the only one of the aides who <u>knows</u> the community. [Of the aides, only one, Bardini, knows the community.]

CULTURE LANGUAGE   In phrases beginning with *one of the,* be sure the noun is plural: *Bardini is one of the <u>aides</u>* [not <u>aide</u>] *who work unpaid.*

29h   *News* and other singular nouns ending in -*s* take singular verbs.

Singular nouns ending in -*s* include *athletics, economics, linguistics, mathematics, measles, mumps, news, physics, politics,* and *statistics,* as well as place names such as *Athens, Wales,* and *United States.*

After so long a wait, the news <u>has</u> to be good.

Statistics <u>is</u> required of psychology majors.

A few of these words also take plural verbs, but only when they describe individual items rather than whole bodies of activity or knowledge: *The statistics <u>prove</u> him wrong.*

Measurements and figures ending in -*s* may also be singular when the quantity they refer to is a unit.

Three years <u>is</u> a long time to wait.

vb agr

29h

Three-fourths of the library <u>consists</u> of reference books.

29i The verb agrees with the subject even when the normal word order is inverted.

Inverted subject-verb order occurs mainly in questions and in constructions beginning with *there* or *it* and a form of *be*.

<u>Is</u> voting a right or a privilege?

<u>Are</u> a right and a privilege the same thing?

There <u>are</u> differences between them.

29j *Is, are,* and other linking verbs agree with their subjects, not subject complements.

Make a linking verb agree with its subject, usually the first element in the sentence, not with the noun or pronoun serving as a subject complement.

The child's sole support <u>is</u> her court-appointed guardians.

Her court-appointed guardians <u>are</u> the child's sole support.

29k Use singular verbs with titles and with words being defined.

Hakada Associates <u>is</u> a new firm.

Dream Days <u>remains</u> a favorite book.

Folks <u>is</u> a down-home word for *people*.

┌ **Key terms** ─────────────────────────

linking verb A verb that connects or equates the subject and subject complement: for example, *seem, become,* and forms of *be*. (See p. 236.)

subject complement A word that describes or renames the subject: *They became <u>chemists</u>.* (See p. 236.)

EXERCISE 29.1
Revising: Subject-verb agreement

Revise the verbs in the following sentences as needed to make subjects and verbs agree in number. If the sentence is already correct as given, mark the number preceding it. Answers to starred items appear at the end of the book. (You can do this exercise online at *ablongman.com/littlebrown.*)

> *Example:*
> Each of the job applicants type sixty words per minute.
> Each of the job applicants <u>types</u> sixty words per minute.

*1. Weinstein & Associates are a consulting firm that try to make businesspeople laugh.

*2. Statistics from recent research suggests that humor relieves stress.

*3. Reduced stress in businesses in turn reduce illness and absenteeism.

*4. Reduced stress can also reduce friction within an employee group, which then work together more productively.

*5. In special conferences held by one consultant, each of the participants practice making others laugh.

6. "Isn't there enough laughs within you to spread the wealth?" the consultant asks his students.

7. The consultant quotes Casey Stengel's rule that the best way to keep your management job is to separate the underlings who hate you from the ones who have not decided how they feel.

8. Such self-deprecating comments in public is uncommon among business managers, the consultant says.

9. Each of the managers in a typical firm take the work much too seriously.

10. The humorous boss often feels like the only one of the managers who have other things in mind besides profits.

11. One consultant to many companies suggest cultivating office humor with practical jokes such as a rubber fish in the water cooler.

12. When a manager or employees regularly posts cartoons on the bulletin board, office spirit usually picks up.

13. When someone who has seemed too easily distracted is entrusted with updating the cartoons, his or her concentration often improves.

14. In the face of levity, the former sourpuss becomes one of those who hides bad temper.

15. Every one of the consultants caution, however, that humor has no place in life-affecting corporate situations such as employee layoffs.

EXERCISE 29.2
Adjusting for subject-verb agreement

Rewrite the following paragraphs to change the underlined words from plural to singular. (You will sometimes need to add *a* or *the* for the singular, as in the example below.) Then change verbs as necessary so that they agree with their new subjects. Answers to the first paragraph appear at the end of the book. (You can do this exercise online at *ablongman .com/littlebrown.*)

Example:

Siberian tigers are an endangered subspecies.
The Siberian tiger is an endangered subspecies.

  *Siberian tigers are the largest living cats in the world, much bigger than their relative the Bengal tiger. *They grow to a length of nine to twelve feet, including their tails, and to a height of about three and a half feet. *They can weigh over six hundred pounds. *These carnivorous hunters live in northern China and Korea as well as in Siberia. *During the long winter of this Arctic climate, the yellowish striped coats get a little lighter in order to blend with the snow-covered landscape. *The coats also grow quite thick, since the tigers have to withstand temperatures as low as −50°F.

  Siberian tigers sometimes have to travel great distances to find food. They need about twenty pounds of food a day because of their size and the cold climate, but when they have fresh food they may eat as much as a hundred pounds at one time. They hunt mainly deer, boars, and even bears, plus smaller prey such as fish and rabbits. They pounce on their prey and grab them by the back of the neck. Animals that are not killed immediately are thrown to the ground and suffocated with a bite to the throat. Then the tigers feast.

Pronouns

How can I use words such as *he, it,* and *you* clearly?

Pronouns—words such as *she* and *who* that refer to nouns—merit special care because all their meaning comes from the other words they refer to. To show their function in a sentence and their relation to other words, pronouns may change form (for instance, *I, me*), person (*you, she*), number (*I, we*), and gender (*he, she*). This section discusses changing pronoun case (below), matching pronouns and the words they refer to (Chapter 31), and making sure pronouns refer clearly to their nouns (Chapter 32).

30 Pronoun Case

Is it *she and I* or *her and me?* Is it *who* or *whom?*

Choosing the right **case** of a pronoun—the right form, such as *she* or *her*—requires understanding how the pronoun functions in its sentence.

- The **subjective case** indicates that the pronoun is a subject or subject complement.
- The **objective case** indicates that the pronoun is an object of a verb or preposition.

> **Key terms**
>
> **subject** Who or what a sentence is about: *Biologists often study animals. They often work in laboratories.* (See p. 232.)
>
> **subject complement** A word that renames or describes the sentence subject: *Biologists are scientists. The best biologists are she and Scoggins.* (See p. 236.)
>
> **object of verb** The receiver of the verb's action (**direct object**): *Many biologists study animals. The animals teach them.* Or the person or thing the action is performed for (**indirect object**): *Some biologists give animals homes. The animals give them pleasure.* (See pp. 235–36.)

http://www.ablongman.com/littlebrown ▶

Visit the companion Web site for more help and electronic exercises on pronoun case.

- The **possessive case** indicates that the pronoun owns or is the source of a noun in the sentence.

Subjective	Objective	Possessive
I	me	my, mine
you	you	your, yours
he	him	his
she	her	her, hers
it	it	its
we	us	our, ours
you	you	your, yours
they	them	their, theirs
who	whom	whose
whoever	whomever	—

Note Grammar and style checkers may flag some problems with pronoun case, but they will also miss a lot. For instance, one checker spotted the error in *We asked* <u>*whom*</u> *would come* (should be <u>*who*</u> *would come*), but it overlooked *We dreaded* <u>*them*</u> *coming* (should be <u>*their*</u> *coming*).

CULTURE LANGUAGE In standard American English, *-self* pronouns do not change form to show function. Their only forms are *myself, yourself, himself, herself, itself, ourselves, yourselves, themselves.* Avoid nonstandard forms such as *hisself, ourself,* and *theirselves.*

case 30a

30a Distinguish between compound subjects and compound objects: *she and I* vs. *her and me.*

Compound subjects or objects—those consisting of two or more nouns or pronouns—have the same case forms as they would if one noun or pronoun stood alone:

> compound
> subject
> <u>She and Novick</u> discussed the proposal.

> compound
> object
> The proposal disappointed <u>her and him.</u>

If you are in doubt about the correct form, try the test opposite.

Key term

object of preposition The word linked by *with, for,* or another preposition to the rest of the sentence: *Many biologists work in a* <u>*laboratory*</u>*. For* <u>*them*</u> *the lab often provides a second home.* (See p. 241.)

A test for case forms in compound constructions

- **Identify a compound construction** (one connected by *and, but, or, nor*):

  [He, Him] and [I, me] won the prize.
  The prize went to [he, him] and [I, me].

- **Write a separate sentence for each part of the compound:**

  [He, Him] won the prize. [I, Me] won the prize.
  The prize went to [he, him]. The prize went to [I, me].

- **Choose the pronouns that sound correct:**

  <u>He</u> won the prize. <u>I</u> won the prize. [Subjective.]
  The prize went to <u>him</u>. The prize went to <u>me</u>. [Objective.]

- **Put the separate sentences back together:**

  <u>He and I</u> won the prize.
  The prize went to <u>him and me</u>.

case

30b

30b   Use the subjective case for subject complements:
It was she.

After a linking verb, a pronoun renaming the subject (a subject complement) should be in the subjective case:

subject
complement

The ones who care most are <u>she and Novick</u>.

subject
complement
It was <u>they</u> whom the mayor appointed.

If this construction sounds stilted to you, use the more natural order: *She and Novick are the ones who care most. The mayor appointed them.*

┌─ **Key term** ─────────────────────────────

linking verb A verb, such as a form of *be*, that connects a subject and a word that renames or describes the subject (subject complement): *They <u>are</u> biologists.* (See p. 236.)

EXERCISE 30.1
Choosing between subjective and objective pronouns

From the pairs in brackets, select the appropriate subjective or objective pronoun(s) for each of the following sentences. Answers to starred items appear at the end of the book. (You can do this exercise online at *ablongman.com/littlebrown*.)

Example:

"Between you and [I, me]," the seller said, "this deal is a steal."
"Between you and <u>me</u>," the seller said, "this deal is a steal."

*1. Jody and [<u>I</u>, me] had been hunting for jobs.
*2. The best employees at our old company were [she, her] and [I, me], so [we, us] expected to find jobs quickly.

3. Between [she, her] and [I, me] the job search had lasted two months, and still it had barely begun.
4. Slowly, [she, her] and [I, me] stopped sharing leads.
5. It was obvious that Jody and [I, me] could not be as friendly as [we, us] had been.

case

30c

30c The use of *who* vs. *whom* depends on the pronoun's function in its clause.

1 • Questions

At the beginning of a question use *who* for a subject and *whom* for an object:

subject —↴
<u>Who</u> wrote the policy?

object ↙———
<u>Whom</u> does it affect?

To find the correct case of *who* in a question, follow the steps below:

* **Pose the question:**

  [Who, Whom] makes that decision?
  [Who, Whom] does one ask?

* **Answer the question, using a personal pronoun.** Choose the pronoun that sounds correct, and note its case:

  [She, Her] makes that decision. <u>She</u> makes that decision. [Subjective.]
  One asks [she, her]. One asks <u>her</u>. [Objective.]

* **Use the same case (*who* or *whom*) in the question:**

  <u>Who</u> makes that decision? [Subjective.]
  <u>Whom</u> does one ask? [Objective.]

2 • Subordinate clauses

In subordinate clauses use *who* and *whoever* for all subjects, *whom* and *whomever* for all objects.

subject ⟍
Give old clothes to <u>whoever</u> needs them.

object ⟵————————
I don't know <u>whom</u> the mayor appointed.

To determine which form to use, try the test below:

- **Locate the subordinate clause:**

  Few people know [<u>who, whom</u>] <u>they should ask</u>.
  They are unsure [<u>who, whom</u>] <u>makes the decision</u>.

- **Rewrite the subordinate clause as a separate sentence, substituting a personal pronoun for *who, whom*.** Choose the pronoun that sounds correct, and note its case:

  They should ask [<u>she, her</u>]. They should ask <u>her</u>. [Objective.]
  [<u>She, her</u>] usually makes the decision. <u>She</u> usually makes the decision. [Subjective.]

- **Use the same case (*who* or *whom*) in the subordinate clause:**

  Few people know <u>whom</u> they should ask. [Objective.]
  They are unsure <u>who</u> makes the decision. [Subjective.]

case

30c

Note Don't let expressions such as *I think* and *she says* mislead you into using *whom* rather than *who* for the subject of a clause.

subject————⟍
He is the one <u>who</u> I think is best qualified.

To choose between *who* and *whom* in such constructions, delete the interrupting phrase so that you can see the true relation between parts: *He is the one <u>who</u> is best qualified.*

> **EXERCISE 30.2**
> **Choosing between *who* and *whom***
>
> From the pairs in brackets, select the appropriate form of the pronoun in each of the following sentences. Answers to starred items appear at the

┌─ **Key term** ───
subordinate clause A word group that contains a subject and a predicate and also begins with a subordinating word, such as *who, whom,* or *because.* (See p. 244.)
└──

end of the book. (You can do this exercise online at *ablongman.com/ littlebrown.*)

> *Example:*
>
> My mother asked me [who, whom] I was meeting.
> My mother asked me <u>whom</u> I was meeting.

*1. The school administrators suspended Jurgen, [<u>who, whom</u>] they suspected of setting the fire.

*2. Jurgen had been complaining to other custodians, [<u>who, whom</u>] reported him.

*3. He constantly complained of unfair treatment from [<u>whoever, whomever</u>] happened to be passing in the halls, including pupils.

*4. "[<u>Who, Whom</u>] here has heard Mr. Jurgen's complaints?" the police asked.

*5. "[<u>Who, Whom</u>] did he complain most about?"

6. His coworkers agreed that Jurgen seemed less upset with the staff or students, most of [<u>who, whom</u>] he did not even know, than with the building itself.

7. "He took out his aggression on the building," claimed one coworker [<u>who, whom</u>] often witnessed Jurgen's behavior.

8. "He cursed and kicked the walls and [<u>whoever, whomever</u>] he saw nearby."

9. The coworker thought that Jurgen might have imagined people [<u>who, whom</u>] instructed him to behave the way he did.

10. "He's someone [<u>who, whom</u>] other people can't get next to," said the coworker.

case

30d

30d   Use the appropriate case in other constructions.

1 • *We* or *us* with a noun

The choice of *we* or *us* before a noun depends on the use of the noun:

```
                              object of
                              preposition
Freezing weather is welcomed by us skaters.
   subject
We skaters welcome freezing weather.
```

2 • Pronoun in an appositive

In an appositive the case of a pronoun depends on the function of the word the appositive describes or identifies.

> **Key term**
>
> **appositive** A noun or noun substitute that renames another noun immediately before it. (See p. 243.)

appositive
identifies object

The class elected two representatives, DeShawn and <u>me</u>.

appositive
identifies subject

Two representatives, DeShawn and <u>I</u>, were elected.

3 • Pronoun after *than* or *as*

When a pronoun follows *than* or *as* in a comparison, the case of the pronoun indicates what words may have been omitted. A subjective pronoun must be the subject of the omitted verb:

subject

Some critics like Glass more than <u>he</u> [does].

An objective pronoun must be the object of the omitted verb:

object

Some critics like Glass more than [they like] <u>him</u>.

4 • Subject and object of infinitive

Both the object *and* the subject of an infinitive are in the objective case:

case

30d

subject
of infinitive

The school asked <u>him</u> to speak.

object
of infinitive

Students chose to invite <u>him</u>.

5 • Case before a gerund

Ordinarily, use the possessive form of a pronoun or noun immediately before a gerund:

The coach disapproved of <u>their</u> lifting weights.

The <u>coach's</u> disapproving was a surprise.

EXERCISE 30.3
Revising: Pronoun case

Revise all inappropriate case forms in the sentences below. If a sentence is already correct as given, mark the number preceding it. Answers to

---

Key terms

infinitive The plain form of the verb plus *to: to run.* (See p. 242.)

gerund The *-ing* form of a verb used as a noun: *Running is fun.* (See p. 242.)

starred items appear at the end of the book. (You can do this exercise online at *ablongman.com/littlebrown*.)

Example:

Convincing we veterans to vote yes will be difficult.

Convincing <u>us</u> veterans to vote yes will be difficult.

*1. Written four thousand years ago, *The Epic of Gilgamesh* tells of a bored king who his people thought was too harsh.

*2. Gilgamesh found a source of entertainment when he met Enkidu, a wild man who had lived with the animals in the mountains.

*3. Immediately, him and Gilgamesh wrestled to see whom was more powerful.

*4. After hours of struggle, Enkidu admitted that Gilgamesh was stronger than he.

*5. The friendship of the two strong men was sealed by them fighting.

6. Gilgamesh said, "Between you and I, mighty deeds will be accomplished, and our fame will be everlasting."

7. Among their glorious acts, Enkidu and him defeated a giant bull, Humbaba, and cut down the bull's cedar forests.

8. Their bringing back cedar logs to Gilgamesh's treeless land won great praise from the people.

9. When Enkidu died, Gilgamesh mourned his death, realizing that no one had been a better friend than him.

10. When Gilgamesh himself died many years later, his people raised a monument praising Enkidu and he for their friendship and their mighty deeds of courage.

pn agr
31

31 Agreement of Pronoun and Antecedent

Is this the right pronoun?

The right pronoun is the one that matches its **antecedent**—the word to which it refers—in number, person, and gender. This chapter focuses on agreement in number: singular and plural antecedents and the pronouns that replace them.

<u>Homeowners</u> fret over <u>their</u> tax bills.
 antecedent   pronoun

http://www.ablongman.com/littlebrown ▶

Visit the companion Web site for more help and electronic exercises on pronoun-antecedent agreement.

Its constant increases make the tax bill a dreaded document.
pronoun   antecedent

Note Grammar and style checkers cannot help with agreement between pronoun and antecedent because they cannot recognize the intended relation between the two.

CULTURE LANGUAGE   The gender of a pronoun should match its antecedent, not a noun that the pronoun may modify: *Sara Young invited her* [not *his*] *son to join the company's staff.* Also, nouns in English have only neuter gender unless they specifically refer to males or females. Thus nouns such as *book, table, sun,* and *earth* take the pronoun *it.*

31a   Antecedents joined by *and* usually take plural pronouns.

Mr. Bartos and I cannot settle our dispute.

The dean and my adviser have offered their help.

Exceptions When the compound antecedent refers to a single idea, person, or thing, then the pronoun is singular:

My friend and adviser offered her help.

When the compound antecedent follows *each* or *every*, the pronoun is singular:

Every girl and woman took her seat.

pn agr
31a

Key terms		
	Number	
Person	**Singular**	**Plural**
First	*I*	*we*
Second	*you*	*you*
Third	*he, she, it,*	*they,*
	indefinite pronouns,	plural nouns
	singular nouns	
Gender		
Masculine	*he,* nouns naming males	
Feminine	*she,* nouns naming females	
Neuter	*it,* all other nouns	

31b When parts of an antecedent are joined by *or* or *nor*, the pronoun agrees with the nearer part.

Tenants or owners must present <u>their</u> grievances.

Either the tenant or the owner will have <u>her</u> way.

When one subject is plural and the other singular, the sentence will be awkward unless you put the plural subject second.

Awkward   Neither the tenants nor the owner has yet made <u>her</u> case.
Revised   Neither the owner nor the tenants have yet made <u>their</u> case.

31c With *everyone, person,* and other indefinite words, use a singular or plural pronoun as appropriate.

Indefinite words—indefinite pronouns and generic nouns—do not refer to any specific person or thing. Most indefinite pronouns and all generic nouns are singular in meaning. When they serve as antecedents of pronouns, the pronouns should be singular.

Everyone on the women's team now has <u>her</u> own locker.
indefinite
pronoun

Every person on the women's team now has <u>her</u> own locker.
generic
noun

Five indefinite pronouns—*all, any, more, most, some*—may be singular or plural in meaning depending on what they refer to:

Key terms

indefinite pronoun A noun that does not refer to a specific person or thing:

			Singular or plural	Plural
Singular				
anybody	everyone	no one	all	both
anyone	everything	nothing	any	few
anything	much	one	more	many
each	neither	somebody	most	several
either	nobody	someone	some	
everybody	none	something		

generic noun A singular noun such as *person, individual,* or *student* when it refers to a typical member of a group, not to a particular individual: *The <u>individual</u> has rights.*

Few women athletes had changing spaces, so most had to change in their rooms.

Most of the changing space was dismal, its color a drab olive green.

Four indefinite pronouns—*both, few, many, several*—are always plural in meaning:

Few realize how <u>their</u> athletic facilities have changed.

Most agreement problems arise with the singular indefinite words. We often use these words to mean something like "many" or "all" rather than "one" and then refer to them with plural pronouns, as in *Everyone has <u>their</u> own locker* or *A person can padlock <u>their</u> locker.* Often, too, we mean indefinite words to include both masculine and feminine genders and thus resort to *they* instead of the generic *he*—the masculine pronoun referring to both genders, as in *Everyone deserves <u>his</u> privacy.* (For more on the generic *he,* which many readers view as sexist, see p. 201.)

Although some experts accept *they, them,* and *their* with singular indefinite words, most do not, and many teachers and employers regard the plural as incorrect. To be safe, work for agreement between singular indefinite words and the pronouns that refer to them. You have several options:

pn agr
31c

Ways to correct agreement with indefinite words

- **Change the indefinite word to a plural, and use a plural pronoun to match:**

  Faulty   Every athlete deserves <u>their</u> privacy.
  Revised   <u>Athletes</u> deserve their privacy.

- **Rewrite the sentence to omit the pronoun:**

  Faulty   Everyone is entitled to <u>their</u> own locker.
  Revised   Everyone is entitled to <u>a</u> locker.

- **Use *he or she* (*him or her, his or her*) to refer to the indefinite word:**

  Faulty   Now everyone has <u>their</u> private space.
  Revised   Now everyone has <u>his or her</u> private space.

  However, used more than once in several sentences, *he or she* quickly becomes awkward. (Many readers do not accept the alternative *he/she.*) In most cases, using the plural or omitting the pronoun will not only correct agreement problems but also create more readable sentences.

31d Collective nouns such as *team* take singular or plural pronouns depending on meaning.

Use a singular pronoun with a collective noun when referring to the group as a unit:

The committee voted to disband <u>itself</u>.

When referring to the individual members of the group, use a plural pronoun:

The old group have gone <u>their</u> separate ways.

CULTURE LANGUAGE In standard American English, collective nouns that are noncount nouns (they don't form plurals) usually take singular pronouns: *The mail sits in <u>its</u> own basket.* A few noncount nouns take plural pronouns, including *clergy, military, police, the rich,* and *the poor: The police support <u>their</u> unions.*

pn agr

31d

EXERCISE 31.1
Revising: Pronoun-antecedent agreement

Revise the following sentences so that pronouns and their antecedents agree in person and number. Some items have more than one possible answer. Try to avoid the generic *he* (see p. 299). If you change the subject of a sentence, be sure to change the verb as necessary for agreement. If a sentence is already correct as given, mark the number preceding it. Answers to starred items appear at the end of the book. (You can do this exercise online at *ablongman.com/littlebrown.*)

Example:

Each of the Boudreaus' children brought their laundry home at Thanksgiving.

<u>All</u> of the Boudreaus' children brought their laundry home at Thanksgiving. *Or:* Each of the Boudreaus' children brought <u>laundry</u> home at Thanksgiving. *Or:* Each of the Boudreaus' children brought <u>his or her</u> laundry home at Thanksgiving.

*1. Each girl raised in a Mexican American family in the Rio Grande Valley of Texas hopes that one day they will be given a *quinceañera* party for their fifteenth birthday.

*2. Such celebrations are very expensive because it entails a religious service followed by a huge party.

Key term

collective noun A noun with singular form that names a group of individuals or things—for instance, *army, audience, committee, crowd, family, group, team.*

*3. A girl's immediate family, unless they are wealthy, cannot afford the party by themselves.

*4. The parents will ask each close friend or relative if they can help with the preparations.

*5. Surrounded by her family and attended by her friends and their escorts, the *quinceañera* is introduced as a young woman eligible for Mexican American society.

6. Almost any child will quickly astound observers with their capabilities.

7. Despite their extensive research and experience, neither child psychologists nor parents have yet figured out how children become who they are.

8. Of course, the family has a tremendous influence on the development of a child in their midst.

9. Each member of the immediate family exerts their own unique pull on the child.

10. Other relatives, teachers, and friends also can affect the child's view of the world and of themselves.

11. The workings of genetics also strongly influence the child, but it may never be fully understood.

12. The psychology community cannot agree in its views of whether nurture or nature is more important in a child's development.

13. Another debated issue is whether the child's emotional development or their intellectual development is more central.

14. Just about everyone has their strong opinion on these issues, often backed up by evidence.

15. Neither the popular press nor scholarly journals devote much of their space to the wholeness of the child.

32 Reference of Pronoun to Antecedent

Is it clear what this pronoun refers to?

A pronoun should refer clearly to its **antecedent,** the noun or nouns it refers to. Otherwise, readers will have difficulty grasping the pronoun's meaning. In editing your writing, make sure that each pronoun refers to an obvious, close, and specific antecedent.

Note Grammar and style checkers are not sophisticated enough to recognize unclear pronoun reference. For instance, a checker did not flag any of the confusing examples on the next page.

http://www.ablongman.com/littlebrown

Visit the companion Web site for more help and electronic exercises on pronoun reference.

⟨ CULTURE ⟩ In standard American English, a pronoun needs a clear antecedent nearby, but don't use both a pronoun and its antecedent as the subject of the same clause: *Jim* [not *Jim he*] *told Mark to go alone.* (See also pp. 342–43.)

32a   Make a pronoun refer clearly to one antecedent.

When either of two nouns can be a pronoun's antecedent, the reference will not be clear.

Confusing	Emily Dickinson is sometimes compared with Jane Austen, but she was quite different.

Revise such a sentence in one of two ways:

- **Replace the pronoun with the appropriate noun.**

Clear	Emily Dickinson is sometimes compared with Jane Austen, but Dickinson [or Austen] was quite different.

- **Avoid repetition by rewriting the sentence.** If you use the pronoun, make sure it has only one possible antecedent.

Clear	Despite occasional comparison, Emily Dickinson and Jane Austen were quite different.
Clear	Though sometimes compared with her, Emily Dickinson was quite different from Jane Austen.

32b   Place a pronoun close enough to its antecedent to ensure clarity.

A clause beginning with *who, which,* or *that* should generally fall immediately after the word to which it refers:

Confusing	Jody found a dress in the attic that her aunt had worn.
Clear	In the attic Jody found a dress that her aunt had worn.

32c   Make a pronoun refer to a specific antecedent, not an implied one.

A pronoun should refer to a specific noun or other pronoun. A reader can only guess at the meaning of a pronoun when its antecedent is implied by the context, not stated outright.

1 ● Vague *this, that, which,* or *it*

This, that, which, or *it* should refer to a specific noun, not to a whole word group expressing an idea or situation.

Confusing	The faculty agreed on changing the requirements, but it took time.
Clear	The faculty agreed on changing the requirements, but the agreement took time.
Clear	The faculty agreed on changing the requirements, but the change took time.
Confusing	The British knew little of the American countryside, and they had no experience with the colonists' guerrilla tactics. This gave the colonists an advantage.
Clear	The British knew little of the American countryside, and they had no experience with the colonists' guerrilla tactics. This ignorance and inexperience gave the colonists an advantage.

ref

32d

2 ● Implied nouns

A noun may be implied in some other word or phrase, such as an adjective (*happiness* implied in *happy*), a verb (*driver* implied in *drive*), or a possessive (*mother* implied in *mother's*). But a pronoun cannot refer clearly to an implied noun, only to a specific, stated one.

Confusing	Cohen's report brought her a lawsuit.
Clear	Cohen was sued over her report.
Confusing	Her reports on psychological development generally go unnoticed outside it.
Clear	Her reports on psychological development generally go unnoticed outside the field.

32d   Use *it* and *they* to refer to definite antecedents.

It and *they* should have definite noun antecedents. Rewrite the sentence if the antecedent is missing.

Confusing	In Chapter 4 of this book it describes the early flights of the Wright brothers.

Clear	Chapter 4 of this book describes the early flights of the Wright brothers.
Confusing	Even in TV reality shows, they present a false picture of life.
Clear	Even TV reality shows present a false picture of life.

32e Use *you* only to mean "you, the reader."

In all but very formal writing, *you* is acceptable when the meaning is clearly "you, the reader." But the context must be appropriate for such a meaning:

| Inappropriate | In the fourteenth century you had to struggle simply to survive. |
| Revised | In the fourteenth century one [or a person] had to struggle simply to survive. |

ref

32f

Writers sometimes drift into *you* because *one, a person,* or a similar indefinite word can be difficult to sustain. Sentence after sentence, the indefinite word may sound stuffy, and it requires *he* or *he or she* for pronoun-antecedent agreement (see pp. 298–99). To avoid these problems, try using plural nouns and pronouns:

| Original | In the fourteenth century one had to struggle simply to survive. |
| Revised | In the fourteenth century people had to struggle simply to survive. |

32f Keep pronouns consistent.

Within a sentence or a group of related sentences, pronouns should be consistent. Partly, consistency comes from making pronouns and their antecedents agree (see Chapter 31). In addition, the pronouns within a passage should match each other.

| Inconsistent | One finds when reading that your concentration improves with practice, so that I now comprehend more in less time. |
| Revised | I find when reading that my concentration improves with practice, so that I now comprehend more in less time. |

EXERCISE 32.1
Revising: Pronoun reference

Many of the pronouns in the following sentences do not refer to specific, appropriate antecedents. Revise the sentences as necessary to make them clear. Answers to starred items appear at the end of the book. (You can do this exercise online at *ablongman.com/littlebrown*.)

> *Example:*
>
> In Grand Teton National Park they have moose, elk, and trumpeter swans.
>
> <u>Moose, elk, and trumpeter swans live</u> in Grand Teton National Park.

*1. "Life begins at forty" is a cliché many people live by, and this may or may not be true.

*2. Living successfully or not depends on one's definition of it.

*3. When she was forty, Pearl Buck's novel *The Good Earth* won the Pulitzer Prize.

*4. Buck was raised in a missionary family in China, and she wrote about it in her novels.

*5. In *The Good Earth* you have to struggle, but fortitude is rewarded.

6. Buck received much critical praise and earned over $7 million, but she was very modest about it.

7. Pearl Buck donated most of her earnings to a foundation for Asian American children that proves her generosity.

8. In the *Book of Romance* it reserves a chapter for the story of Elizabeth Barrett, who at forty married Robert Browning against her father's wishes.

9. In the 1840s they did not normally defy their fathers, but Elizabeth was too much in love to obey.

10. She left a poetic record of her love for Robert, and readers still enjoy reading them.

ref

32

EXERCISE 32.2
Revising: Pronoun reference

Revise the following paragraph so that each pronoun refers clearly to a single specific and appropriate antecedent. Answers to starred sentences appear at the end of the book. (You can do this exercise online at *ablongman.com/littlebrown*.)

*In Charlotte Brontë's *Jane Eyre*, she is a shy young woman that takes a job as governess. *Her employer is a rude, brooding man named Rochester. *He lives in a mysterious mansion on the English moors, which contributes an eerie quality to Jane's experience. *Eerier still are the fires, strange noises, and other unexplained happenings in the house; but Rochester refuses to discuss this. Eventually, they fall in love. On the day they are to be married, however, she learns that he has a wife hidden in the house. She is hopelessly insane and violent and must be guarded at all times, which explains his strange behavior. Heartbroken, Jane leaves the moors, and many years pass before they are reunited.

Modifiers

What do modifiers do?

Modifiers describe or limit other words in a sentence. They are adjectives, adverbs, or word groups serving as adjectives or adverbs. This section shows you how to identify and solve problems in the forms of modifiers (Chapter 33) and in their relation to the rest of the sentence (Chapter 34).

33 Adjectives and Adverbs

Should I use *bad* or *badly*?

Choosing between *bad* and *badly* means choosing whether to use an adjective (*bad*) or an adverb (*badly*). The choice depends on how the word functions in its sentence. An **adjective** modifies nouns (*bad weather*) and pronouns (*bad one*). An **adverb** modifies verbs (*The fans behaved badly*), adjectives (*badly wrong*), other adverbs (*not badly*), and whole word groups (*Otherwise, the room was empty*).

Note Grammar and style checkers will spot some but not all problems with misused adjectives and adverbs. For instance, a checker flagged *Some children suffer bad* and *Chang was the most wisest person in town* and *Jenny did not feel nothing*. But it did not flag *Educating children good is everyone's focus*.

CULTURE LANGUAGE In standard American English, an adjective does not change along with the noun it modifies to show plural number: *white* [not *whites*] *shoes*, *square* [not *squares*] *spaces*, *better* [not *betters*] *chances*. Only nouns form plurals.

33a Use adjectives only to modify nouns and pronouns.

Using adjectives instead of adverbs to modify verbs, adverbs, or other adjectives is nonstandard.

| Nonstandard | Educating children good is everyone's focus. |
| Standard | Educating children well is everyone's focus. |

| Nonstandard | Some children suffer bad. |
| Standard | Some children suffer badly. |

⟨ CULTURE ⟩ **⟨ LANGUAGE ⟩** To negate a verb or an adjective, use the adverb *not:*

They are not learning.   They are not stupid.

To negate a noun, use the adjective *no:*

No child should fail to read.

EXERCISE 33.1
Revising: Adjectives and adverbs

Revise the sentences below to use adjectives and adverbs appropriately. If any sentence is already correct as given, mark the number preceding it. Answers to starred items appear at the end of the book. (You can do this exercise online at *ablongman.com/littlebrown*.)

> *Example:*
> The announcer warned that traffic was moving very slow.
> The announcer warned that traffic was moving very slowly.

*1. The eighteenth-century essayist Samuel Johnson fared bad in his early life.

*2. Johnson's family was poor, his hearing was bad, and he received little education.

*3. After failing as a schoolmaster, Johnson moved to London, where he did good.

*4. Johnson was taken serious as a critic and dictionary maker.

*5. Johnson was real surprised when he received a pension from King George III.

6. Thinking about his meeting with the king, Johnson felt proudly.

7. Johnson was relieved that he had not behaved badly in the presence of the king.

8. If he had been more diligent, Johnson might have made money quicker.

9. After living cheap for over twenty years, Johnson finally had enough money from the pension to eat and dress good.

10. With the pension, Johnson could spend time writing and live stylish.

---

ad

33b

33b **Use an adjective after a linking verb to modify the subject. Use an adverb to modify a verb.**

Some verbs may or may not be linking verbs, depending on their meaning in the sentence. When the word after the verb modifies the subject, the verb is linking and the word should be an adjective: *He looked happy. The milk turned sour.* When the word modifies the verb, however, it should be an adverb: *He looked carefully. The car turned suddenly.*

Two word pairs are especially tricky. One is *bad* and *badly:*

The weather grew bad.
linking adjective
verb

She felt bad.
linking adjective
verb

Flowers grow badly in such soil.
verb adverb

The other tricky pair is *good* and *well. Good* serves only as an adjective. *Well* may serve as an adverb with a host of meanings or as an adjective meaning only "fit" or "healthy."

Decker trained well.
verb   adverb

She felt well.
linking adjective
verb

Her health was good.
linking adjective
verb

ad

33c

33c   Use the comparative and superlative forms of adjectives and adverbs appropriately.

Adjectives and adverbs can show degrees of quality or amount with the endings *-er* and *-est* or with the words *more* and *most* or *less* and *least.* Most modifiers have three forms:

Positive The basic form listed in the dictionary	Comparative A greater or lesser degree of the quality	Superlative The greatest or least degree of the quality
Adjectives		
red	redder	reddest
awful	more/less awful	most/least awful
Adverbs		
soon	sooner	soonest
quickly	more/less quickly	most/least quickly

If sound alone does not tell you whether to use *-er/-est* or *more/most,* consult a dictionary. If the endings can be used, the dictionary will list them. Otherwise, use *more* or *most.*

Key term

linking verb A verb that connects a subject and a word that describes the subject: *They are golfers.* Linking verbs are forms of *be,* the verbs of our five senses (*look, sound, smell, feel, taste*), and *appear, seem, become, grow, turn, prove, remain, stay.* (See p. 236.)

1 • Irregular adjectives and adverbs

The irregular modifiers change the spelling of their positive form to show comparative and superlative degrees.

Positive	Comparative	Superlative
Adjectives		
good	better	best
bad	worse	worst
little	littler, less	littlest, least
many ⎫		
some ⎬	more	most
much ⎭		
Adverbs		
well	better	best
badly	worse	worst

2 • Double comparisons

A double comparative or double superlative combines the *-er* or *-est* ending with the word *more* or *most*. It is redundant.

Chang was the <u>wisest</u> [not <u>most wisest</u>] person in town.
He was <u>smarter</u> [not <u>more smarter</u>] than anyone else.

3 • Logical comparisons

Absolute modifiers

Some adjectives and adverbs cannot logically be compared—for instance, *perfect, unique, dead, impossible, infinite.* These absolute words can be preceded by adverbs like *nearly* or *almost* that mean "approaching," but they cannot logically be modified by *more* or *most* (as in *most perfect*).

Not	He was the <u>most unique</u> teacher we had.
But	He was a <u>unique</u> teacher.

Completeness

To be logical, a comparison must also be complete in the following ways:

- **The comparison must state a relation fully enough for clarity.**

Unclear	Carmakers worry about their industry more than environmentalists.
Clear	Carmakers worry about their industry more than environmentalists <u>do</u>.
Clear	Carmakers worry about their industry more than <u>they worry about</u> environmentalists.

- **The items being compared should in fact be comparable.**

Illogical	The cost of an electric car is greater than a gasoline-powered car. [Illogically compares a cost and a car.]
Revised	The cost of an electric car is greater than the cost of [or that of] a gasoline-powered car.

See also page 189 on parallelism with comparisons.

Any vs. *any other*

Use *any other* when comparing something with others in the same group. Use *any* when comparing something with others in a different group.

Illogical	Los Angeles is larger than any city in California. [Since Los Angeles is itself a city in California, the sentence seems to say that Los Angeles is larger than itself.]
Revised	Los Angeles is larger than any other city in California.
Illogical	Los Angeles is larger than any other city in Canada. [The cities in Canada constitute a group to which Los Angeles does not belong.]
Revised	Los Angeles is larger than any city in Canada.

ad
33d

33d Watch for double negatives.

A **double negative** is a nonstandard construction in which two negative words such as *no, not, none, barely, hardly,* or *scarcely* cancel each other out. Some double negatives are intentional: for instance, *She was not unhappy* indicates with understatement that she was indeed happy. But most double negatives say the opposite of what is intended: *Jenny did not feel nothing* asserts that Jenny felt other than nothing, or something. For the opposite meaning, one of the negatives must be eliminated (*She felt nothing*) or one of them must be changed to a positive (*She did not feel anything*).

Faulty	The IRS cannot hardly audit all tax returns. None of its audits never touch many cheaters.
Revised	The IRS cannot audit all tax returns. Its audits never touch many cheaters.

EXERCISE 33.2
Revising: Double negatives

Identify and revise the double negatives in the following sentences. Each error may have more than one correct revision. If a sentence is already correct as given, mark the number preceding it. Answers to starred items appear at the end of the book. (You can do this exercise online at *ablongman.com/littlebrown*.)

*1. Interest in books about the founding of the United States is not hardly consistent among Americans: it seems to vary with the national mood.

*2. Americans show barely any interest in books about the founders when things are going well in the United States.

3. However, when Americans can't hardly agree on major issues, sales of books about the Revolutionary War era increase.

4. During such periods, one cannot go to no bookstore without seeing several new volumes about John Adams, Thomas Jefferson, and other founders.

5. When Americans feel they don't have nothing in common, their increased interest in the early leaders may reflect a desire for unity.

33e Distinguish between present and past participles as adjectives. ⟨ CULTURE LANGUAGE ⟩

Both present participles and past participles may serve as adjectives: *a burning building, a burned building*. As in the examples, the two participles usually differ in the time they indicate.

But some present and past participles—those derived from verbs expressing feeling—can have altogether different meanings. The present participle modifies something that causes the feeling: *That was a frightening storm* (the storm frightens). The past participle modifies something that experiences the feeling: *They quieted the frightened horses* (the horses feel fright).

The following participles are among those likely to be confused:

amazing/amazed	fascinating/fascinated
amusing/amused	frightening/frightened
annoying/annoyed	frustrating/frustrated
astonishing/astonished	interesting/interested
boring/bored	pleasing/pleased
confusing/confused	satisfying/satisfied
depressing/depressed	shocking/shocked
embarrassing/embarrassed	surprising/surprised
exciting/excited	tiring/tired
exhausting/exhausted	worrying/worried

Key terms

present participle The *-ing* form of a verb: *flying, writing*. (See p. 227.)

past participle The *-d* or *-ed* form of a regular verb: *slipped, walked*. Most irregular verbs have distinctive past participles, such as *eaten* or *swum*. (See p. 227.)

312   Adjectives and adverbs

EXERCISE 33.3
Revising: Present and past participles 🔲 CULTURE LANGUAGE

Revise the adjectives in the following sentences as needed to distinguish between present and past participles. If a sentence is already correct as given, mark the number preceding it. Answers to starred items appear at the end of the book. (You can do this exercise online at *ablongman.com/ littlebrown.*)

Example:

The subject was embarrassed to many people.
The subject was <u>embarrassing</u> to many people.

*1. Several critics found Alice Walker's *The Color Purple* to be a fascinated book.

*2. One confused critic wished that Walker had deleted the scenes set in Africa.

3. Another critic argued that although the book contained many depressed episodes, the overall effect was excited.

4. Since other readers found the book annoyed, this critic pointed out its many surprising qualities.

5. In the end most critics agreed that the book was a satisfied novel about the struggles of an African American woman.

det

33f

33f   Use *a, an, the,* and other determiners appropriately. 🔲 CULTURE LANGUAGE

Determiners are special kinds of adjectives that mark nouns because they always precede nouns. Some common determiners are *a, an,* and *the* (called **articles**) and *my, their, whose, this, these, those, one, some,* and *any.*

Native speakers of standard American English can rely on their intuition when using determiners, but speakers of other languages and dialects often have difficulty with them. In standard American English, the use of determiners depends on the context they appear in and the kind of noun they precede:

• A *proper noun* names a particular person, place, or thing and begins with a capital letter: *February, Joe Allen, Red River.* Most proper nouns are not preceded by determiners.

• A *count noun* names something that is countable in English and can form a plural: *girl/girls, apple/apples, child/children.* A singular count noun is always preceded by a determiner; a plural count noun sometimes is.

• A *noncount noun* names something not usually considered countable in English, and so it does not form a plural. A noncount noun is sometimes preceded by a determiner. Here is a sample of noncount nouns, sorted into groups by meaning:

Abstractions: confidence, democracy, education, equality, evidence, health, information, intelligence, knowledge, luxury, peace, pollution, research, success, supervision, truth, wealth, work

Food and drink: bread, candy, cereal, flour, meat, milk, salt, water, wine

Emotions: anger, courage, happiness, hate, joy, love, respect, satisfaction

Natural events and substances: air, blood, dirt, gasoline, gold, hair, heat, ice, oil, oxygen, rain, silver, smoke, weather, wood

Groups: clergy, clothing, equipment, furniture, garbage, jewelry, junk, legislation, machinery, mail, military, money, police, vocabulary

Fields of study: accounting, architecture, biology, business, chemistry, engineering, literature, psychology, science

A dictionary of English as a second language will tell you whether a noun is a count noun, a noncount noun, or both. (See p. 204 for recommended dictionaries.)

Note Many nouns are sometimes count nouns and sometimes noncount nouns:

The library has a room for readers. [*Room* is a count noun meaning "walled area."]

The library has room for reading. [*Room* is a noncount noun meaning "space."]

Partly because the same noun may fall into different groups, grammar and style checkers are unreliable guides to missing or misused articles and other determiners. For instance, a checker flagged the omitted *a* before *Scientist* in *Scientist developed new processes;* it did not flag the omitted *a* before *new* in *A scientist developed new process;* and it mistakenly flagged the correctly omitted article *the* before *Vegetation* in *Vegetation suffers from drought.*

1 • *A, an,* and *the*

With singular count nouns

A or *an* precedes a singular count noun when the reader does not already know its identity, usually because you have not mentioned it before:

A scientist in our chemistry department developed a process to strengthen metals. [*Scientist* and *process* are being introduced for the first time.]

The precedes a singular count noun that has a specific identity for the reader, for one of the following reasons:

det
33f

- **You have mentioned the noun before:**

  A scientist in our chemistry department developed a process to strengthen metals. The scientist patented the process. [*Scientist* and *process* were identified in the preceding sentence.]

- **You identify the noun immediately before or after you state it:**

  The most productive laboratory is the research center in the chemistry department. [*Most productive* identifies *laboratory*. *In the chemistry department* identifies *research center*. And *chemistry department* is a shared facility—see below.]

- **The noun names something unique—the only one in existence:**

  The sun rises in the east. [*Sun* and *east* are unique.]

- **The noun names an institution or facility that is shared by the community of readers:**

  Many men and women aspire to the presidency. [*Presidency* is a shared institution.]

  The fax machine has changed business communication. [*Fax machine* is a shared facility.]

The is not used before a singular noun that names a general category:

Wordsworth's poetry shows his love of nature [not the nature].
General Sherman said that war is hell. [*War* names a general category.]
The war in Croatia left many dead. [*War* names a specific war.]

With plural count nouns

A or *an* never precedes a plural noun. *The* does not precede a plural noun that names a general category. *The* does precede a plural noun that names specific representatives of a category.

Men and women are different. [*Men* and *women* name general categories.]

The women formed a team. [*Women* refers to specific people.]

With noncount nouns

A or *an* never precedes a noncount noun. *The* does precede a noncount noun that names specific representatives of a general category.

Vegetation suffers from drought. [*Vegetation* names a general category.]

The vegetation in the park withered or died. [*Vegetation* refers to specific plants.]

With proper nouns

A or *an* never precedes a proper noun. *The* generally does not precede proper nouns.

Garcia lives in Boulder.

There are exceptions, however. For instance, we generally use *the* before plural proper nouns (*the Murphys, the Boston Celtics*) and before the names of groups and organizations (*the Department of Justice, the Sierra Club*), ships (*the Lusitania*), oceans (*the Pacific*), mountain ranges (*the Alps*), regions (*the Middle East*), rivers (*the Mississippi*), and some countries (*the United States, the Netherlands*).

2 • Other determiners

The uses of English determiners besides articles also depend on context and kind of noun. The following determiners may be used as indicated with singular count nouns, plural count nouns, or noncount nouns.

det

33f

With any kind of noun (singular count, plural count, noncount)
my, our, your, his, her, its, their, possessive nouns (*boy's, boys'*)
whose, which(ever), what(ever)
some, any, the other
no

Their account is overdrawn. [Singular count.]
Their funds are low. [Plural count.]
Their money is running out. [Noncount.]

Only with singular nouns (count and noncount)
this, that

This account has some money. [Count.]
That information may help. [Noncount.]

Only with noncount nouns and plural count nouns
most, enough, other, such, all, all of the, a lot of

Most funds are committed. [Plural count.]
Most money is needed elsewhere. [Noncount.]

Only with singular count nouns
one, every, each, either, neither, another

One car must be sold. [Singular count.]

Only with plural count nouns
these, those
both, many, few, a few, fewer, fewest, several
two, three, and so forth

Two cars are unnecessary. [Plural count.]

Note *Few* means "not many" or "not enough." *A few* means "some" or "a small but sufficient quantity."

Few committee members came to the meeting.
A few members can keep the committee going.

Do not use *much* with a plural count noun.

Many [not much] members want to help.

Only with noncount nouns
much, more, little, a little, less, least, a large amount of

Less luxury is in order. [Noncount.]

Note *Little* means "not many" or "not enough." *A little* means "some" or "a small but sufficient quantity."

Little time remains before the conference.
The members need a little help from their colleagues.

det

33f Do not use *many* with a noncount noun.

Much [not many] work remains.

EXERCISE 33.4
Revising: Articles   CULTURE LANGUAGE

For each blank, indicate whether *a, an, the,* or no article should be inserted. Answers to starred sentences appear at the end of the book. (You can do this exercise online at *ablongman.com/littlebrown*.)

Example:

On our bicycle trip across _____ country, we carried _____ map and plenty of _____ food and _____ water.

On our bicycle trip across the country, we carried a map and plenty of food and water.

*From _____ native American Indians who migrated from _____ Asia 20,000 years ago to _____ new arrivals who now come by _____ planes, _____ United States is _____ nation of foreigners. *It is _____ country of immigrants who are all living under _____ single flag.

*Back in _____ seventeenth and eighteenth centuries, at least 75 percent of the population came from _____ England. *However, between 1820 and 1975 more than 38 million immigrants came to this country from elsewhere in _____ Europe. Many children of _____ immigrants were self-conscious and denied their heritage; many even refused to learn _____ native language of their parents and grandparents. They tried to "Americanize" themselves. The so-called Melting

Pot theory of _____ social change stressed _____ importance of blending everyone together into _____ kind of stew. Each nationality would contribute its own flavor, but _____ final stew would be something called "American."

This Melting Pot theory was never completely successful. In the last half of the twentieth century, _____ ethnic revival changed _____ metaphor. Many people now see _____ American society as _____ mosaic. Americans are once again proud of their heritage, and _____ ethnic differences make _____ mosaic colorful and interesting.

EXERCISE 33.5
Revising: Adjectives and adverbs

Revise the sentences below to correct errors in the use of adjectives and adverbs. If a sentence is already correct as given, mark the number preceding it. Answers to starred items appear at the end of the book. (You can do this exercise online at *ablongman.com/littlebrown*.)

Example:

Sports fans always feel happily when their team wins.
Sports fans always feel <u>happy</u> when their team wins.

*1. Americans often argue about which professional sport is better: basketball, football, or baseball.
*2. Basketball fans contend that their sport offers more action because the players are constant running and shooting.
*3. Because it is played indoors in relative small arenas, basketball allows fans to be more closer to the action than the other sports do.
*4. Football fanatics say they don't hardly stop yelling once the game begins.
*5. They cheer when their team executes a real complicated play good.
  6. They roar more louder when the defense stops the opponents in a goal-line stand.
  7. They yell loudest when a fullback crashes in for a score.
  8. In contrast, the supporters of baseball believe that it might be the most perfect sport.
  9. It combines the one-on-one duel of pitcher and batter struggling valiant with the tight teamwork of double and triple plays.
 10. Because the game is played slow and careful, fans can analyze and discuss the manager's strategy.

ad

33

Where can a modifier go in a sentence? When does a modifier dangle?

A modifier needs to relate clearly to the word it describes, and that need limits its possible positions in a sentence. A **misplaced modifier** does not relate to the intended word (see below). A **dangling modifier** does not relate sensibly to anything in the sentence (see p. 323).

Note Grammar and style checkers do not recognize many problems with modifiers. For instance, a checker failed to flag the misplaced modifiers in *Gasoline high prices affect usually car sales* or the dangling modifier in *The vandalism was visible passing the building.*

34a   Reposition misplaced modifiers.

A misplaced modifier falls in the wrong place in a sentence. It is usually awkward or confusing. It may even be unintentionally funny.

1 • Clear placement

Readers tend to link a modifier to the nearest word it could modify. Any other placement can link the modifier to the wrong word.

Confusing   He served steak to the men on paper plates.

Clear   He served the men steak on paper plates.

Confusing   According to the police, many dogs are killed by automobiles and trucks roaming unleashed.

Clear   According to the police, many dogs roaming unleashed are killed by automobiles and trucks.

2 • *Only* and other limiting modifiers

Limiting modifiers include *almost, even, exactly, hardly, just, merely, nearly, only, scarcely,* and *simply.* For clarity, place such a modifier immediately before the word or word group you intend it to limit.

Unclear   The archaeologist <u>only</u> found the skull on her last dig.

Clear   The archaeologist found <u>only</u> the skull on her last dig.

Clear   The archaeologist found the skull <u>only</u> on her last dig.

3 • Adverbs with grammatical units

Adverbs can often move around in sentences, but some will be awkward if they interrupt certain grammatical units:

• **A long adverb stops the flow from subject to verb:**

Awkward   subject ————— adverb ——————— verb
           Kuwait, after the Gulf War ended in 1991, began returning to normal.

Revised   ————— adverb ——————— subject verb
           After the Gulf War ended in 1991, Kuwait began returning to normal.

• **Any adverb is awkward between a verb and its direct object:**

Awkward   ——verb——adverb object
           The war had damaged <u>badly</u> many of Kuwait's oil fields.

Revised   ——verb—— object
           The war had <u>badly</u> damaged many of Kuwait's oil fields.
           adverb

• **A *split infinitive*—an adverb placed between *to* and the verb— annoys many readers:**

Awkward   ʏinfinitiveʏ
           The weather service expected temperatures to <u>not</u> rise.

Revised   infinitive
           The weather service expected temperatures <u>not</u> to rise.

┌Key terms────────────────────────────────

adverb A word or word group that describes a verb, adjective, other adverb, or whole word group, specifying how, when, where, or to what extent: *quickly see, solid like a boulder.*

direct object The receiver of the verb's action: *The car hit a tree.* (See p. 235.)

infinitive A verb form consisting of *to* plus the verb's plain (or dictionary) form: *to produce, to enjoy.* (See p. 242.)

mm
34a

A split infinitive may sometimes be natural and preferable, though it may still bother some readers.

infinitive
Several US industries expect to <u>more than</u> triple their use of robots.

Here the split infinitive is more economical than the alternatives, such as *Several US industries expect to increase their use of robots by more than three times.*

- **A long adverb is usually awkward inside a verb phrase:**

	helping verb ┌──── adverb ────┐ main verb

Awkward   The spacecraft *Ulysses* will after traveling near the sun report on the sun's energy fields.

┌──── adverb ────┐   verb phrase
Revised   After traveling near the sun, the spacecraft *Ulysses* will report on the sun's energy fields.

CULTURE / LANGUAGE   In a question, place a one-word adverb after the first helping verb and subject:

helping   rest of
verb   subject adverb verb phrase
Will spacecraft <u>ever</u> be able to leave the solar system?

4 • Other adverb positions   **CULTURE / LANGUAGE**

A few adverbs are subject to special conventions for placement:

- **Adverbs of frequency** include *always, never, often, rarely, seldom, sometimes,* and *usually.* They generally appear at the beginning of a sentence, before a one-word verb, or after the helping verb in a verb phrase:

helping   main
verb   adverb   verb
Robots have <u>sometimes</u> put humans out of work.

adverb   verb phrase
<u>Sometimes</u> robots have put humans out of work.

Adverbs of frequency always follow the verb *be:*

verb adverb
Robots are <u>often</u> helpful to workers.

- **Adverbs of degree** include *absolutely, almost, certainly, com-*

mm
34a

┌─ **Key term** ─────────────────────────────────

verb phrase A verb consisting of a helping verb and a main verb that carries the principal meaning: *will have begun, can see.* (See p. 227.)

└──

pletely, definitely, especially, extremely, hardly, and *only.* They fall just before the word modified (an adjective, another adverb, sometimes a verb):

adverb   adjective
Robots have been <u>especially</u> useful in making cars.

- **Adverbs of manner** include *badly, beautifully, openly, sweetly, tightly, well,* and others that describe how something is done. They usually fall after the verb:

verb   adverb
Robots work <u>smoothly</u> on assembly lines.

- **The adverb** *not* changes position depending on what it modifies. When it modifies a verb, place it after the helping verb (or the first helping verb if more than one):

helping   main
verb   verb
Robots do <u>not</u> think.

mm
34a

When *not* modifies another adverb or an adjective, place it before the other modifier:

adjective
Robots are <u>not</u> sleek machines.

5 • Order of adjectives CULTURE LANGUAGE

English follows distinctive rules for arranging two or three adjectives before a noun. (A string of more than three adjectives before a noun is rare.) The adjectives follow this order:

Determiner	Opinion	Size or shape	Color	Origin	Material	Noun used as adjective	Noun
many						state	**laws**
	lovely		green	Thai			**birds**
a		square			wooden		**table**
all						business	**reports**
the			blue		litmus		**paper**

Key term

adjective A word that describes a noun or pronoun, specifying which one, what quality, or how many: <u>good</u> one, <u>three</u> cars. (See p. 228.)

See page 358 on punctuating adjectives before a noun.

EXERCISE 34.1
Revising: Misplaced modifiers

Revise the following sentences so that modifiers clearly and appropriately describe the intended words. Answers to starred items appear at the end of the book. (You can do this exercise online at *ablongman.com/ littlebrown.*)

> *Example:*
>
> Although at first I feared the sensation of flight, I came to enjoy flying over time.
>
> Although at first I feared the sensation of flight, <u>over time</u> I came to enjoy flying.

*1. People dominate in our society who are right-handed.
*2. Hand tools, machines, and doors even are designed for right-handed people.
*3. However, nearly 15 percent may be left-handed of the population.
*4. Children often when they begin school prefer one hand or the other.
*5. Parents and teachers should not try to deliberately change a child's preference for the left hand.

6. Women have contributed much to American culture of great value.
7. For example, Elizabeth Pinckney during the colonial era introduced indigo, the source of a valuable blue dye.
8. Emma Willard founded the Troy Female Seminary, the first institution to provide a college-level education for women in 1821.
9. Mary Lyon founded Mount Holyoke Female Seminary as the first true women's college with directors and a campus who would sustain the college even after Lyon's death.
10. *Una* was the first US newspaper, which was founded by Pauline Wright Davis in 1853, that was dedicated to gaining women's rights.
11. Mitchell's Comet was discovered in 1847, which was named for Maria Mitchell.
12. Mitchell was the first American woman astronomer who lived from 1818 to 1889.
13. She was a member at Vassar College of the first faculty.
14. She was when elected to the American Academy of Arts and Sciences in 1848 the first woman to join the prestigious organization.
15. Mitchell said that she was persistent rather than especially capable when asked about her many accomplishments.

EXERCISE 34.2
Arranging adjectives 🔊 **CULTURE** **LANGUAGE**

For each of the following sentences, arrange the adjectives given in parentheses as needed for appropriate order in English, and place them in the sentence. Answers to starred items appear at the end of the book. (You can do this exercise online at *ablongman.com/littlebrown.*)

mm
34a

Example:

Programs for computer graphics perform _____ chores. (*drafting, many, tedious*)

Programs for computer graphics perform <u>many tedious drafting</u> chores.

*1. _____ specialist developed image controls. (*computer, a, Chinese, young*)

*2. _____ engineer assisted the specialist. (*a or an, American, skeptical*)

*3. _____ researchers are carrying out further study. (*several, university*)

*4. The controls depend on _____ object connected by wires to the computer. (*T-shaped, hand-sized, a*)

*5. The image allows a biochemist to walk into _____ display of a molecule. (*holographic, gigantic, a*)

6. Using _____ gestures, the biochemist can rotate and change the entire image. (*simple, hand*)

7. _____ games also depend on computer graphics. (*computer, all, video*)

8. Even _____ games operate this way. (*sophisticated, simulation, flight*)

9. One game is played with _____ racquets. (*rectangular, thin, two*)

10. In the early years of computers, scientists made _____ drawings to simulate motion. (*crude, some, animated*)

dm
34b

34b Relate dangling modifiers to their sentences.

A **dangling modifier** does not sensibly modify anything in its sentence.

Dangling   Passing the building, the vandalism became visible.

Dangling modifiers usually introduce sentences, contain a verb form, and imply but do not name a subject. In the example above, the implied subject is the someone or something passing the building. Readers assume that this implied subject is the same as the subject of the sentence (*vandalism* in the example), but vandalism does not pass buildings. The modifier "dangles" because it does not connect sensibly to the rest of the sentence. Here is another example:

Dangling   Although intact, graffiti covered every inch of the walls and windows. [The walls and windows, not the graffiti, were intact.]

To revise a dangling modifier, you have to rewrite the sentence. (Revising just by moving the modifier will leave it dangling: *The*

Identifying and revising dangling modifiers

- **Find a subject.** If the modifier lacks a subject of its own (e.g., *when in diapers*), identify what it describes.
- **Connect the subject and modifier.** Verify that what the modifier describes is in fact the subject of the main clause. If it is not, the modifier is probably dangling:

  ┌—modifier——┐   subject
  Dangling   When in diapers, my mother remarried.

- **Revise as needed.** Revise a dangling modifier (*a*) by recasting it with a subject of its own or (*b*) by changing the subject of the main clause:

  Revision *a*   When I was in diapers, my mother remarried.
  Revision *b*   When in diapers, I attended my mother's second wedding.

---

dm

34b

vandalism became visible passing the building.) Choose a revision method depending on what you want to emphasize in the sentence:

- **Rewrite the dangling modifier as a complete clause with its own stated subject and verb.** Readers can accept that the new subject and the sentence subject are different.

  Dangling   Passing the building, the vandalism became visible.

  Revised   As we passed the building, the vandalism became visible.

- **Change the subject of the sentence to a word the modifier properly describes.**

  Dangling   Trying to understand the causes, vandalism has been extensively studied.

  Revised   Trying to understand the causes, researchers have extensively studied vandalism.

EXERCISE 34.3
Revising: Dangling modifiers

Revise the following sentences to eliminate any dangling modifiers. Each item has more than one possible answer. If a sentence is already correct as given, mark the number preceding it. Answers to starred items appear at the end of the book. (You can do this exercise online at *ablongman.com/littlebrown*.)

Example:

Driving north, the vegetation became more sparse.

Driving north, <u>we noticed that</u> the vegetation became more sparse. *Or:* <u>As we drove north</u>, the vegetation became more sparse.

*1. After accomplishing many deeds of valor, Andrew Jackson's fame led to his election to the presidency in 1828 and 1832.

*2. At the age of fourteen, both of Jackson's parents died.

*3. To aid the American Revolution, service as a mounted courier was Jackson's choice.

*4. After being struck with a saber by a British officer, Jackson's craggy face bore a scar.

*5. Though not well educated, a successful career as a lawyer and judge proved Jackson's ability.

6. Winning many military battles, the American public believed in Jackson's leadership.

7. Earning the nicknames "Old Hickory" and "Sharp Knife," the War of 1812 established Jackson's military prowess.

8. Losing only six dead and ten wounded, the triumph of the Battle of New Orleans burnished Jackson's reputation.

9. After putting down raiding parties from Florida, Jackson's victories helped pressure Spain to cede that territory.

10. While briefly governor of Florida, the US presidency became Jackson's goal.

dm
34b

Sentence Faults

When is a sentence not a sentence?

Readers have definite (if unconscious) expectations for how sentences should be constructed. If a word group is punctuated as a sentence but does not meet these expectations, readers will likely be confused or annoyed. Such word groups may lack needed elements, include too many elements, or contain elements that do not fit together.

35   Sentence Fragments

How can I tell if my sentences are complete?

A complete sentence meets three requirements: it has a subject, the subject has a predicate, and it is not merely a subordinate clause (a word group beginning with *because, who,* or a similar word). A **sentence fragment,** in contrast, is a word group that looks like a whole sentence with an initial capital letter and a final period or other end punctuation. Although writers occasionally use fragments deliberately and effectively (see p. 330), readers perceive most fragments as serious errors. To prevent sentence fragments, first test each word group punctuated as a sentence to be sure it is complete (next three pages) and then revise as needed (pp. 329–30).

Note A grammar and style checker can spot many but not all sentence fragments, and it may flag sentences that are actually complete, such as *Continue reading.*

35a   Test your sentences for completeness.

A word group punctuated as a sentence should pass *all three* of the following tests. If it does not, it is a fragment and needs revision.

---

http://www.ablongman.com/littlebrown ▶

Visit the companion Web site for more help and electronic exercises on sentence fragments.

Complete sentence versus sentence fragment

A complete sentence or main clause

1. contains a subject and a predicate (*The wind blows*)
2. and is not a subordinate clause (beginning with a word such as *because* or *who*).

A sentence fragment

1. lacks a predicate (*The wind blowing*),
2. or lacks a subject (*And blows*),
3. or is a subordinate clause not attached to a complete sentence (*Because the wind blows*).

Test 1: Find the predicate.

Look for a verb that can serve as the predicate of a sentence. Some fragments lack any verb at all:

Fragment	Uncountable numbers of sites on the Web.
Revised	Uncountable numbers of sites make up the Web.

Other fragments may include a verb form but not a **finite verb**—one that changes form as indicated below. A verbal does not change and cannot serve as a predicate without the aid of a helping verb.

	Finite verbs in complete sentences	Verbals in sentence fragments
Singular	The network grows.	The network growing.
Plural	Networks grow.	Networks growing.
Present	The network grows.	⎫
Past	The network grew.	⎬ The network growing.
Future	The network will grow.	⎭

Key terms

predicate The part of a sentence containing a verb that asserts something about the subject: *Ducks swim*. (See p. 232.)

verbal A verb form that can serve as a noun, a modifier, or a part of a predicate, but not alone as the only verb of a sentence: *drawing, to draw, drawn*. (See p. 241.)

helping verb A verb such as *is, were, have, might,* and *could* that combines with various verb forms to indicate time and other kinds of meaning: for instance, *were drawing, might draw*. (See p. 227.)

Fragment	The network <u>taking</u> a primary role in communication and commerce.
Revised	The network <u>is taking</u> a primary role in communication and commerce.

CULTURE LANGUAGE Some languages allow forms of *be* to be omitted as helping verbs or linking verbs, but English requires stating forms of *be:*

Fragments	The network growing rapidly. It much larger than once anticipated.
Revised	The network <u>is</u> growing rapidly. It <u>is</u> much larger than once anticipated.

Test 2: Find the subject.

The subject of the sentence will usually come before the predicate. If there is no subject, the word group is probably a fragment:

Fragment	And has enormous popular appeal.
Revised	And <u>the Web</u> has enormous popular appeal.

frag

35a

In one kind of complete sentence, a command, the subject *you* is understood: [*You*] *Experiment with the Web.*

CULTURE LANGUAGE Some languages allow the omission of the sentence subject, especially when it is a pronoun. But in English, except in commands, the subject is stated:

Fragment	Web commerce is expanding dramatically. <u>Is threatening traditional stores.</u>
Revised	Web commerce is expanding dramatically. <u>It</u> is threatening traditional stores.

Test 3: Make sure the clause is not subordinate.

A subordinate clause usually begins with a subordinating word, such as one of those in the following list.

Key terms

linking verb A verb that connects a subject and a word that describes the subject: *They <u>are</u> golfers.* Linking verbs are forms of *be*, the verbs of our five senses (*look, sound, smell, feel, taste*), and *appear, seem, become, grow, turn, prove, remain, stay.* (See p. 236.)

subject The part of a sentence that names who or what performs the action or makes the assertion of the predicate: *<u>Ducks</u> swim.* (See p. 232.)

subordinate clause A word group that contains a subject and a predicate, begins with a subordinating word such as *because* or *who,* and is not a question: *Ducks can swim <u>when they are young</u>.* A subordinate clause may serve as a modifier or as a noun. (See p. 244.)

Subordinating conjunctions

			Relative pronouns
after	provided	until	that
although	since	when	which
as	so that	whenever	who/whom
because	than	where	whoever/whomever
even if	that	whereas	
even though	though	whether	
if	till	while	
once	unless		

Subordinate clauses serve as parts of sentences (nouns or modifiers), not as whole sentences:

Fragment	When the government devised the Internet.
Revised	The government devised the Internet.
Revised	When the government devised the Internet, <u>no expansive computer network existed</u>.
Fragment	The reason that the government devised the Internet. [This fragment is a noun (*reason*) plus its modifier (*that . . . Internet*).]
Revised	The reason that the government devised the Internet <u>was to provide secure links among departments and defense contractors</u>.

Note Questions beginning with *how, what, when, where, which, who, whom, whose,* and *why* are not sentence fragments: *Who was responsible? When did it happen?*

frag
35b

35b   Revise sentence fragments.

Correct sentence fragments in one of two ways depending on the importance of the information in the fragment and thus how much you want to stress it:

- **Rewrite the fragment as a complete sentence.** The information in the fragment will then have the same importance as that in other complete sentences.

Fragment	A major improvement of the Internet occurred with the Web. <u>Which allows users to move easily between sites</u>.
Revised	A major improvement of the Internet occurred with the Web. <u>It</u> allows users to move easily between sites.
Fragment	The Web is a boon to researchers. <u>A vast and accessible library</u>.
Revised	The Web is a boon to researchers. <u>It forms</u> a vast and accessible library.

- **Combine the fragment with the appropriate main clause.** The information in the fragment will then be subordinated to that in the main clause.

Fragment	The Web is easy to use. <u>Loaded with links and graphics.</u>
Revised	The Web⌒loaded with links and graphics⌒is easy to use.
Fragment	With the links, users can move to other Web sites. <u>That they want to consult.</u>
Revised	With the links, users can move to other Web sites⌒that they want to consult.

35c   Be aware of the acceptable uses of incomplete sentences.

A few word groups lacking the usual subject-predicate combination are incomplete sentences, but they are not fragments because they conform to the expectations of most readers. They include exclamations (*Oh no!*); questions and answers (*Where next? To Kansas.*); and commands (*Move along. Shut the window.*).

Experienced writers sometimes use sentence fragments when they want to achieve a special effect. Such fragments appear more in informal than in formal writing. Unless you are experienced and thoroughly secure in your own writing, however, you should avoid all fragments and concentrate on writing clear, well-formed sentences.

frag

35c

> **EXERCISE 35.1**
> **Revising: Sentence fragments**
>
> Correct any sentence fragment below either by combining it with a complete sentence or by making it a complete sentence. If an item contains no sentence fragment, mark the number preceding it. Answers to starred items appear at the end of the book. (You can do this exercise online at *ablongman.com/littlebrown*.)
>
> *Example:*
>
> Jujitsu is good for self-protection. Because it enables one to overcome an opponent without the use of weapons.
>
> Jujitsu is good for self-protection⌒because it enables one to overcome an opponent without the use of weapons. *Or:* Jujitsu is good for self-protection. <u>It</u> enables one to overcome an opponent without the use of weapons.
>
> *1. Human beings who perfume themselves. They are not much different from other animals.
>
> *2. Animals as varied as insects and dogs release pheromones. Chemicals that signal other animals.
>
> *3. Human beings have a diminished sense of smell. And do not consciously detect most of their own species' pheromones.

*4. The human substitute for pheromones may be perfumes. Most common in ancient times were musk and other fragrances derived from animal oils.

*5. Some sources say that people began using perfume to cover up the smell of burning flesh. During sacrifices to the gods.

6. Perfumes became religious offerings in their own right. Being expensive to make, they were highly prized.

7. The earliest historical documents from the Middle East record the use of fragrances. Not only in religious ceremonies but on the body.

8. In the nineteenth century, chemists began synthesizing perfume oils. Which previously could be made only from natural sources.

9. The most popular animal oil for perfume today is musk. Although some people dislike its heavy, sweet odor.

10. Synthetic musk oil would help conserve a certain species of deer. Whose gland is the source of musk.

EXERCISE 35.2
Revising: Sentence fragments

Revise the following paragraphs to eliminate sentence fragments by combining them with main clauses or rewriting them as main clauses. Answers to the first paragraph appear at the end of the book. (You can do this exercise online at *ablongman.com/littlebrown.*)

frag

35

Example:

Gymnosperms, the most advanced of nonflowering plants. They thrive in diverse environments.

Gymnosperms, the most advanced of nonflowering plants ⌒ thrive in diverse environments. *Or:* Gymnosperms are the most advanced of nonflowering plants. They thrive in diverse environments.

*People generally avoid eating mushrooms except those they buy in stores. *But in fact many varieties of mushrooms are edible. *Mushrooms are members of a large group of vegetation called nonflowering plants. *Including algae, mosses, ferns, and coniferous trees. *Even the giant redwoods of California. *Most of the nonflowering plants prefer moist environments. *Such as forest floors, fallen timber, and still water. *Mushrooms, for example. *They prefer moist, shady soil. *Algae grow in water.

Most mushrooms, both edible and inedible, are members of a class called basidium fungi. A term referring to their method of reproduction. The basidia produce spores. Which can develop into mushrooms. This classification including the prized meadow mushroom, cultivated commercially, and the amanitas. The amanita group contains both edible and poisonous species. Another familiar group of mushrooms, the puffballs. They are easily identified by their round shape. Their spores are contained under a thick skin. Which eventually ruptures to release the spores. The famous morels are in still another group. These pitted, spongy mushrooms called sac fungi because the spores develop in sacs.

Anyone interested in mushrooms as food should heed the US Public Health Service warning. Not to eat any wild mushrooms unless their identity and edibility are established without a doubt.

36 Comma Splices and Fused Sentences

Should a new sentence begin here?

The kernel of a sentence is the main clause consisting of a subject and its predicate. To know that one main clause is ending and another is beginning, readers expect one of these signals:

- **A period,** creating two separate sentences:

  The ship was huge⊙ Its mast stood eighty feet high.

- **A comma and a coordinating conjunction,** linking two clauses in one sentence:

  The ship was huge⊚ <u>and</u> its mast stood eighty feet high.

- **A semicolon,** separating two clauses within one sentence:

  The ship was huge⊚ its mast stood eighty feet high.

cs/fs
36

Readers may be confused if two main clauses run together in a sentence *without* the second or third signal. The result may be a **comma splice,** in which the clauses are joined (or spliced) *only* with a comma:

Comma splice

The ship was huge, its mast stood eighty feet high.

Or the result may be a **fused sentence** (or **run-on sentence**), in which no punctuation or conjunction appears between the clauses:

Fused sentence

The ship was huge its mast stood eighty feet high.

The usual repairs for comma splices and fused sentences are shown in the box opposite and discussed on the following pages.

Note Grammar and style checkers can detect many comma splices, but they will miss most fused sentences. For example, a

---

Key terms

main clause A word group that contains a subject and a predicate and does not begin with a subordinating word: *A dictionary is essential.*

coordinating conjunction *And, but, or, nor, for, so, yet.* (See p. 231.)

---

http://www.ablongman.com/littlebrown ▶

Visit the companion Web site for more help and electronic exercises on comma splices and fused sentences.

Punctuation of two or more main clauses

The following steps can help you identify and revise comma splices and fused sentences.

1. Underline the main clauses in your draft.

<u>Sailors trained on the ship</u>. <u>They learned about wind and sails</u>. <u>Trainees who took the course ranged from high school students to Navy officers</u>. <u>The ship was built in 1910</u>, <u>it had sailed ever since</u>. In almost a century, <u>it had circled the globe forty times</u>. <u>It burned in 2001</u> <u>its cabins and decks were destroyed</u>.

2. Are consecutive main clauses separated by periods?

If **yes,** OK.

If **no,** go to question 3.

Comma splice   The ship was built in 1910, it had sailed ever since.

Fused sentence   It burned in 2001 its cabins and decks were destroyed.

3. Are consecutive main clauses linked by a comma?

If **yes,** go to question 4.

Comma splice   The ship was built in 1910, it had sailed ever since.

If **no,** go to question 5.

Fused sentence   It burned in 2001 its cabins and decks were destroyed.

4. Does a coordinating conjunction follow the comma between main clauses?

If **yes,** OK.
If **no,** add a coordinating conjunction: *and, but, or, nor, for, so, yet.*

Revised   The ship was built in 1910, and it had sailed ever since.

5. Are consecutive main clauses separated by a semicolon?

If **yes,** OK.
If **no,** add a semicolon.

Revised   It burned in 2001; its cabins and decks were destroyed.

As an alternative to these revision methods, you can also subordinate one clause to another:

Revised   When it burned in 2001, its cabins and decks were destroyed.

checker flagged *Money is tight, we need to spend carefully* but not *Money is tight we need to spend carefully.* A checker may also question sentences that are actually correct, such as *Money being tighter now than before, we need to spend carefully.*

CULTURE LANGUAGE   In standard American English, a sentence may not include more than one main clause unless the clauses are separated by a comma and a coordinating conjunction or by a semicolon. If your native language does not have such a rule or has accustomed you to writing long sentences, you may need to edit your English writing especially for comma splices and fused sentences.

36a   Separate main clauses not joined by *and, but,* or another coordinating conjunction.

cs/fs
36a

If your readers point out comma splices or fused sentences in your writing, you're not creating enough separation between main clauses in your sentences. Use one of the following methods to repair the problem.

Separate sentences

Make the clauses into separate sentences when the ideas expressed are only loosely related:

Comma splice	Chemistry has contributed much to our understanding of foods, many foods such as wheat and beans can be produced in the laboratory.
Revised	Chemistry has contributed much to our understanding of foods⊙ Many foods such as wheat and beans can be produced in the laboratory.

CULTURE LANGUAGE   Making separate sentences may be the best option if you are used to writing very long sentences in your native language but often write comma splices in English.

Coordinating conjunction

Insert a coordinating conjunction in a comma splice when the ideas in the main clauses are closely related and are equally important:

Comma splice	Some laboratory-grown foods taste good, they are nutritious.
Revised	Some laboratory-grown foods taste good, <u>and</u> they are nutritious.

In a fused sentence insert a comma and a coordinating conjunction:

| Fused sentence | Chemists have made much progress they still have a way to go. |
| Revised | Chemists have made much progress⌢ but they still have a way to go. |

Semicolon

Insert a semicolon between clauses if the relation between the ideas is very close and obvious without a conjunction:

| Comma splice | Good taste is rare in laboratory-grown vegetables, they are usually bland. |
| Revised | Good taste is rare in laboratory-grown vegetables⌢ they are usually bland. |

Subordination

Subordinate one clause to the other when one idea is less important than the other:

| Comma splice | The vitamins are adequate, the flavor is deficient. |
| Revised | Even though the vitamins are adequate, the flavor is deficient. |

cs/fs
36b

36b Separate main clauses related by *however, for example,* and so on.

Two groups of words that are not conjunctions describe how one main clause relates to another: **conjunctive adverbs** and other **transitional expressions.** (See pp. 56–57 for a longer list.)

Common conjunctive adverbs and transitional expressions

accordingly	for instance	in the meantime	otherwise
anyway	further	in the past	similarly
as a result	furthermore	likewise	so far
at last	hence	meanwhile	still
at length	however	moreover	that is
besides	incidentally	namely	then
certainly	in contrast	nevertheless	thereafter
consequently	indeed	nonetheless	therefore
even so	in fact	now	thus
finally	in other words	of course	to this end
for all that	in short	on the contrary	undoubtedly
for example	instead	on the whole	until now

When two main clauses are related by a conjunctive adverb or another transitional expression, they must be separated by a period or by a semicolon. The adverb or expression is also generally set off by a comma or commas.

Comma splice	Most Americans refuse to give up unhealthful habits, consequently our medical costs are higher than those of many other countries.
Revised	Most Americans refuse to give up unhealthful habits. Consequently, our medical costs are higher than those of many other countries.
Revised	Most Americans refuse to give up unhealthful habits; consequently, our medical costs are higher than those of many other countries.

Conjunctive adverbs and transitional expressions are different from coordinating conjunctions (*and, but,* and so on) and subordinating conjunctions (*although, because,* and so on):

cs/fs

36b

- **Unlike conjunctions, conjunctive adverbs and transitional expressions do not join two clauses into a grammatical unit.** They merely describe the way two clauses relate in meaning.

- **Unlike conjunctions, conjunctive adverbs and transitional expressions can be moved within a clause.** No matter where in the clause an adverb or expression falls, though, the clause must be separated from another main clause by a period or semicolon:

Most Americans refuse to give up unhealthful habits; our medical costs, consequently, are higher than those of many other countries.

EXERCISE 36.1
Sentence combining to avoid comma splices and fused sentences

Using the method suggested in parentheses, combine each of the following pairs of sentences into one sentence without creating a comma splice or a fused sentence. Answers to starred items appear at the end of the book. (You can do this exercise online at *ablongman.com/ littlebrown.*)

Example:

The sun sank lower in the sky. The colors gradually faded.
(*Subordinate one clause to the other.*)

As the sun sank lower in the sky, the colors gradually faded.

*1. Some people think that dinosaurs were the first living vertebrates. Fossils of turtles go back 40 million years further. (*Supply a comma and coordinating conjunction.*)

*2. Most other reptiles exist mainly in tropical regions. Turtles inhabit a variety of environments worldwide. (*Subordinate one clause to the other.*)

*3. Turtles do not have teeth. Their jaws are covered with a sharp, horny sheath. (*Supply a semicolon.*)

*4. Turtles cannot expand their lungs to breathe air. They make adjustments in how space is used within the shell. (*Supply a semicolon and a conjunctive adverb or transitional expression.*)

*5. Some turtles can get oxygen from water. They don't need to breathe air. (*Supply a semicolon and a conjunctive adverb or transitional expression.*)

6. The exact origin of paper money is unknown. It has not survived as coins, shells, and other durable objects have. (*Subordinate one clause to the other.*)

7. Scholars disagree over where paper money originated. Many believe it was first used in Europe. (*Subordinate one clause to the other.*)

8. Perhaps goldsmiths were also bankers. Thus they held the gold of their wealthy customers. (*Supply a semicolon.*)

9. The goldsmiths probably gave customers receipts for their gold. These receipts were then used in trade. (*Supply a comma and coordinating conjunction.*)

10. The goldsmiths were something like modern-day bankers. Their receipts were something like modern-day money. (*Supply a semicolon.*)

11. The goldsmiths became even more like modern-day bankers. They began issuing receipts for more gold than they actually held in their vaults. (*Subordinate one clause to the other.*)

12. Today's bankers owe more to their customers than they actually have in reserve. They keep enough assets on hand to meet reasonable withdrawals. (*Supply a semicolon and a conjunctive adverb or transitional expression.*)

13. In economic crises, bank customers sometimes fear the loss of their money. Consequently, they demand their deposits. (*Supply a semicolon.*)

14. Depositors' demands may exceed a bank's reserves. The bank may collapse. (*Supply a comma and coordinating conjunction.*)

15. The government now regulates banks to protect depositors. Bank failures are less frequent than they once were. (*Supply a semicolon and a conjunctive adverb or transitional expression.*)

cs/fs

36

EXERCISE 36.2
Revising: Comma splices and fused sentences

Correct each of the following comma splices or fused sentences in two of the following ways: (1) make separate sentences of the main clauses; (2) insert an appropriate coordinating conjunction or both a comma and a coordinating conjunction between the main clauses; (3) insert a semicolon and a conjunctive adverb or transitional expression between the main clauses; (4) subordinate one clause to another. If an item contains no comma splice or fused sentence, mark the number preceding it. Answers to starred items appear at the end of the book. (You can do this exercise online at *ablongman.com/littlebrown.*)

Example:

Carolyn still had a headache, she could not get the child-proof cap off the aspirin bottle.

Carolyn still had a headache○because she could not get the child-proof cap off the aspirin bottle. (*Subordination.*)

Carolyn still had a headache, for she could not get the child-proof cap off the aspirin bottle. (*Coordinating conjunction.*)

*1. Money has a long history, it goes back at least as far as the earliest records.

*2. Many of the earliest records concern financial transactions, indeed, early history must often be inferred from commercial activity.

*3. Every known society has had a system of money, though the objects serving as money have varied widely.

*4. Sometimes the objects have had real value, in modern times their value has been more abstract.

*5. Cattle, fermented beverages, and rare shells have served as money each one had actual value for the society.

6. As money, these objects acquired additional value they represented other goods.

7. Today money may be made of worthless paper, it may even consist of a bit of data in a computer's memory.

8. We think of money as valuable only our common faith in it makes it valuable.

9. That faith is sometimes fragile, consequently, currencies themselves are fragile.

10. Economic crises often shake the belief in money, indeed, such weakened faith helped cause the Great Depression of the 1930s.

11. Throughout history money and religion were closely linked, there was little distinction between government and religion.

12. The head of state and the religious leader were often the same person so that all power rested in one ruler.

13. These powerful leaders decided what objects would serve as money, their backing encouraged public faith in the money.

14. Coins were minted of precious metals the religious overtones of money were then strengthened.

15. People already believed the precious metals to be divine, their use in money intensified its allure.

EXERCISE 36.3
Revising: Comma splices and fused sentences

Revise each comma splice and fused sentence in the following paragraphs using the technique that seems most appropriate for the meaning. Answers to the first paragraph appear at the end of the book. (You can do this exercise online at *ablongman.com/littlebrown*.)

*What many call the first genocide of modern times occurred during World War I, the Armenians were deported from their homes in Anatolia, Turkey. *The Turkish government assumed that the Armenians were sympathetic to Russia, with whom the Turks were at war. *Many Armenians died because of the hardships of the journey, many were massacred. *The death toll was estimated at between 600,000 and 1 million.

Many of the deported Armenians migrated to Russia, in 1918 they established the Republic of Armenia, they continued to be attacked by Turkey, in 1920 they became the Soviet Republic of Armenia rather than surrender to the Turks. Like other Soviet republics, Armenia became independent in 1991, about 3.4 million Armenians live there now.

The Armenians have a long history of conquest by others. As a people, they formed a centralized state in the seventh century BC then they were ruled by the Persian empire until it was conquered by Alexander the Great. Greek and Roman rule followed, internal clan leadership marked by disunity and strife was next. In AD 640 the country was invaded by the Arabs in the eleventh century it was conquered by the Byzantines and then by the Turks, under whose control it remained.

Conflict for the Armenians continues Armenia has territorial disputes with its neighbor Azerbaijan, where many Armenians have settled.

mixed

37

37 Mixed Sentences

How can I untangle sentences?

Tangled sentences often come from **mixed constructions:** the sentences contain parts that do not fit together in either grammar or meaning. Usually the misfit lies in the subject and predicate, so most repairs focus on these essential elements.

Note Grammar and style checkers may recognize a simple mixed construction such as *reason is because,* but they will fail to flag most mixed sentences.

http://www.ablongman.com/littlebrown ▶

Visit the companion Web site for more help and an electronic exercise on mixed sentences.

37a Match subjects and predicates in meaning.

In a sentence with mixed meaning, the subject is said to do or be something illogical. Such a mixture is sometimes called **faulty predication** because the predicate conflicts with the subject.

1 • Illogical equation with *be*

When a form of *be* connects a subject and a word that describes the subject (a complement), the subject and complement must be logically related:

Mixed   A compromise between the city and the country would be the ideal place to live.

Revised   A community that offered the best qualities of both city and country would be the ideal place to live.

2 • *Is when, is where*

Definitions require nouns on both sides of *be*. Clauses that define and begin with *when* or *where* are common in speech but should be avoided in writing.

Mixed   An examination is when you are tested on what you know.

Revised   An examination is a test of what you know.

3 • *Reason is because*

The commonly heard construction *reason is because* is redundant since *because* means "for the reason that":

Mixed   The reason the temple requests donations is because the school needs expansion.

Revised   The reason the temple requests donations is that the school needs expansion.

Revised   The temple requests donations because the school needs expansion.

Key terms

subject The part of a sentence that names who or what performs the action or makes the assertion of the predicate: *Geese fly*. (See p. 232.)

predicate The part of a sentence containing a verb that asserts something about the subject: *Geese fly*. (See p. 232.)

4 • Other mixed meanings

Faulty predications are not confined to sentences with *be:*

Mixed   The use of emission controls was created to reduce air pollution.

Revised   Emission controls were created to reduce air pollution.

37b Untangle sentences that are mixed in grammar.

Many mixed sentences start with one grammatical plan or construction but end with a different one:

Mixed   By paying more attention to impressions than facts leads us to misjudge others.

This mixed sentence makes a prepositional phrase work as the subject of *leads,* but prepositional phrases function as modifiers, not as nouns, and thus not as sentence subjects.

Revised   By paying more attention to impressions than facts, we misjudge others.

Mixed sentences are especially likely on a computer when you connect parts of two sentences or rewrite half a sentence but not the other half. Mixed sentences may also occur when you don't make the subject and verb of a sentence carry the principal meaning. (See p. 176.) Here is another example:

Mixed   The fact that someone may be considered guilty just for associating with someone guilty.

Revised   The fact is that someone may be considered guilty just for associating with someone guilty.

EXERCISE 37.1
Revising: Mixed sentences

Revise the following sentences so that their parts fit together both in grammar and in meaning. Each item has more than one possible answer. If a sentence is already correct as given, mark the number preceding it. Answers to starred items appear at the end of the book. (You can do this exercise online at *ablongman.com/littlebrown.*)

Example:

When they found out how expensive pianos are is why they were discouraged.

When they found out how expensive pianos are, <u>they</u> were discouraged. *Or:* They were discouraged <u>because</u> they found out how expensive pianos are.

*1. A hurricane is when the winds in a tropical depression rotate counterclockwise at more than seventy-four miles per hour.

*2. Because hurricanes can destroy so many lives and so much property is why people fear them.

*3. Through high winds, storm surge, floods, and tornadoes is how hurricanes have killed thousands of people.

*4. Storm surge is where the hurricane's winds whip up a tide that spills over seawalls and deluges coastal islands.

*5. The winds themselves are also destructive, uprooting trees and smashing buildings.

6. Many scientists observe that hurricanes in recent years they have become more ferocious and destructive.

7. However, in the last half-century, with improved communication systems and weather satellites have made hurricanes less deadly.

8. The reason is because people have more time to escape.

9. The emphasis on evacuation is in fact the best way for people to avoid a hurricane's force.

10. Simply boarding up a house's windows will not protect a family from wind, water surges, and flying debris.

37c State parts of clauses, such as subjects, only once. CULTURE LANGUAGE

In some languages other than English, certain parts of sentences may be repeated. These include the subject in any kind of clause or an object or adverb in an adjective clause. In English, however, these parts are stated only once in a clause.

1 • Repetition of subject

You may be tempted to restate a subject as a pronoun before the verb. But the subject needs stating only once in its clause:

Faulty   The <u>liquid it</u> reached a temperature of 180°F.
Revised   The <u>liquid</u> reached a temperature of 180°F.

> **Key term**
>
> **clause** A group of words containing both a subject and a predicate. (See p. 244.)

Faulty   <u>Gases</u> in the liquid <u>they</u> escaped.

Revised   <u>Gases</u> in the liquid escaped.

2 • Repetition in an adjective clause

Adjective clauses begin with *who, whom, whose, which, that, where,* and *when* (see also p. 245). The beginning word replaces another word: the subject (*He is the person <u>who</u> called*), an object of a verb or preposition (*He is the person <u>whom</u> I mentioned*), or a preposition and pronoun (*He knows the office <u>where</u> [<u>in which</u>] the conference will occur*).

Do not state the word being replaced in an adjective clause:

Faulty   The technician <u>whom</u> the test depended on <u>her</u> was burned. [*Whom* should replace *her*.]

Revised   The technician <u>whom</u> the test depended on was burned.

Adjective clauses beginning with *where* or *when* do not need an adverb such as *there* or *then*:

Faulty   Gases escaped at a moment <u>when</u> the technician was unprepared <u>then</u>.

Revised   Gases escaped at a moment <u>when</u> the technician was unprepared.

Note *Whom, which,* and similar words are sometimes omitted but are still understood by the reader. Thus the word being replaced should not be stated:

Faulty   Accidents rarely happen to technicians the lab has trained <u>them</u>. [*Whom* is understood: . . . *technicians <u>whom</u> the lab has trained.*]

Revised   Accidents rarely happen to technicians the lab has trained.

EXERCISE 37.2
Revising: Repeated subjects and other parts ✦ CULTURE ✦ LANGUAGE ✦

Revise the following sentences to eliminate any unneeded words. If a sentence is already correct as given, mark the number preceding it. Answers to starred items appear at the end of the book. (You can do this exercise online at *ablongman.com/littlebrown.*)

Example:

Scientists they use special instruments for measuring the age of artifacts.

Scientists <u>use</u> special instruments for measuring the age of artifacts.

*1. Archaeologists and other scientists they can often determine the age of their discoveries by means of radiocarbon dating.

mixed

37c

*2. This technique it can be used on any material that once was living.

*3. This technique is based on the fact that all living organisms they contain carbon.

*4. The most common isotope is carbon 12, which it contains six protons and six neutrons.

*5. A few carbon atoms are classified as the isotope carbon 14, where the nucleus consists of six protons and eight neutrons there.

6. Because of the extra neutrons, the carbon 14 atom it is unstable and radioactive.

7. What is significant about the carbon 14 atom is its half-life of 5700 years.

8. Scientists they measure the proportion of carbon 14 to carbon 12 and estimate the age of the specimen.

9. This kind of dating is most accurate when a specimen is between 500 and 50,000 years old then.

10. With younger specimens too little carbon 14 has decayed, and with older ones too little is left that the scientists can measure it.

mixed
37c

5

Punctuation

What punctuation goes at the end of a sentence?

End a sentence with one of three punctuation marks: a period (.), a question mark (?), or an exclamation point (!).

Note A grammar and style checker may flag missing question marks after direct questions or incorrect combinations of marks (such as a question mark and a period at the end of a sentence), but it cannot do much else.

38a Use a period after most sentences and in many abbreviations.

1 • Statements, mild commands, and indirect questions

Statement

The airline went bankrupt⊙   It no longer flies⊙

Mild command

Think of the possibilities⊙   Please consider others⊙

Indirect question

An **indirect question** reports what someone asked but not in the exact form or words of the original question:

The judge asked why I had been driving with my lights off⊙
No one asked how we got home⊙

CULTURE LANGUAGE In standard American English, an indirect question uses the wording and subject-verb order of a statement: *The reporter asked why the bank failed* [not *why did the bank fail*].

Note A period always falls inside a closing quotation mark: *She said, "The play will close tonight⊡."* (See also p. 381.)

2 • Abbreviations

Use periods with abbreviations that consist of or end in small letters. Otherwise, omit periods from abbreviations.

Dr.	Mr., Mrs.	e.g.	Feb.	ft.
St.	Ms.	i.e.	p.	a.m., p.m.
PhD	BC, AD	USA	IBM	JFK
BA	AM, PM	US	USMC	AIDS

http://www.ablongman.com/littlebrown ▶

Visit the companion Web site for more help and an electronic exercise on end punctuation.

Note When an abbreviation falls at the end of a sentence, use only one period: *My first class is at 8 a.m.*

38b   Use a question mark after a direct question and sometimes to indicate doubt.

1 • Direct questions

Who will follow her?
What is the difference between these two people?

After indirect questions, use a period: *We wondered who would follow her.* (See the facing page.)

Questions in a series are each followed by a question mark:

The officer asked how many times the suspect had been arrested. Three times? Four times? More than that?

Note A question mark falls inside or outside a closing quotation mark depending on whether it is part of a quoted question or part of the larger sentence. (See also pp. 381–82.)

He asked, "Who will go?" [Question mark part of the quoted question.]
Did he say, "I will go"? [Question mark part of the larger sentence, a question.]

2 • Doubt

A question mark within parentheses can indicate doubt about a number or date.

The Greek philosopher Socrates was born in 470 (?) BC and died in 399 BC. [Socrates's birthdate is not known for sure.]

Use sentence structure and words, not a question mark, to express sarcasm or irony.

Not   Stern's friendliness (?) bothered Crane.
But   Stern's insincerity bothered Crane.

. ? !
38c

38c   Use an exclamation point after an emphatic statement, interjection, or command.

No! We must not lose this election!
Come here immediately!

┌─ **Key term** ─────────────────────────────
interjection A word that expresses feeling or commands attention, either alone or within a sentence: *Oh! Hey! Wow!* (See p. 232.)

Follow mild interjections and commands with commas or periods, as appropriate: *Oh⊙ call whenever you can⊙*

Use exclamation points sparingly, even in informal writing. Overused, they'll fail to impress readers, and they may make you sound overemphatic.

Note An exclamation point falls inside or outside a closing quotation mark depending on whether it is part of the quotation or part of the larger sentence. (See also pp. 381–82.)

EXERCISE 38.1
Revising: End punctuation

Insert appropriate end punctuation (periods, question marks, or exclamation points) where needed in the following paragraph. Answers to the starred lines appear at the end of the book. (You can do this exercise online at *ablongman.com/littlebrown*.)

     * When visitors first arrive in Hawaii, they often encounter an unex-
* pected language barrier Standard English is the language of business
* and government, but many of the people speak Pidgin English Instead
* of an excited "Aloha" the visitors may be greeted with an excited Pid-
* gin "Howzit" or asked if they know "how fo' find one good hotel"
Many Hawaiians question whether Pidgin will hold children back because it prevents communication with *haoles,* or Caucasians, who run businesses Yet many others feel that Pidgin is a last defense of ethnic diversity on the islands To those who want to make standard English the official language of the state, these Hawaiians may respond, "Just 'cause I speak Pidgin no mean I dumb" They may ask, "Why you no listen" or, in standard English, "Why don't you listen"

∧
,
39

39 The Comma

What do commas do (and not do)?

The most common punctuation mark within sentences, commas do mainly the following:

- **Separate main clauses linked by** *and, but,* **and other coordinating conjunctions** (facing page).

http://www.ablongman.com/littlebrown ▶

Visit the companion Web site for more help and electronic exercises on the comma.

- Set off most introductory elements (p. 351).
- Set off nonessential elements (p. 353).
- Separate items in a series (p. 358).
- Separate coordinate adjectives (p. 358).
- Separate parts of dates, addresses, place names, and long numbers (p. 360).
- Separate signal phrases and quotations (p. 361).

Commas can be easy to misuse. For guidance on when *not* to use a comma, see page 362.

Note Grammar and style checkers will ignore many comma errors. For example, a checker failed to catch the missing commas in *We cooked lasagna spinach and apple pie* and the misused commas in *The trip was short but, the weather was perfect* and *The travelers were tempted by, the many shops*.

39a   Use a comma before *and, but,* or another coordinating conjunction linking main clauses.

When a coordinating conjunction links words or phrases, do not use a comma: *Dugain plays⟡ and sings Irish⟡ and English folk songs.* However, *do* use a comma when a coordinating conjunction joins main clauses.

> Caffeine can keep coffee drinkers alert⟡ and it may elevate their mood.
>
> Caffeine was once thought to be safe⟡ but now researchers warn of harmful effects.
>
> Coffee drinkers may suffer sleeplessness⟡ for the drug acts as a stimulant to the nervous system.

Note The comma goes *before,* not after, the coordinating conjunction: *Caffeine increases heart rate⟡ and⟡it* [not *and, it*] *constricts blood vessels.*

Exception Some writers omit the comma between main clauses that are very short and closely related in meaning: *Caffeine helps but it also hurts.* If you are in doubt about whether to use the comma in such a sentence, use it. It will always be correct.

⌐ **Key terms** ─────────────────────

coordinating conjunctions *And, but, or, nor,* and sometimes *for, so, yet.* (See p. 231.)

main clause A word group that contains a subject and a predicate and does not begin with a subordinating word: *Water freezes at temperatures below 32°F.* (See p. 244.)

∧
,
39a

Main uses of the comma

* **Separate main clauses linked by a coordinating conjunction** (previous page).

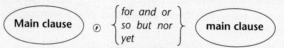

The building is finished‸ but it has no tenants.

* **Set off most introductory elements** (p. 351).

Unfortunately‸ the only tenant pulled out.

* **Set off nonessential elements** (p. 353).

The empty building symbolizes a weak local economy‸ which affects everyone.

The primary cause‸ the decline of local industry‸ is not news.

* **Separate items in a series** (p. 358).

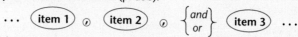

The city needs healthier businesses‸ new schools‸ and improved housing.

* **Separate coordinate adjectives** (p. 358).

A tall‸ sleek skyscraper is not needed.

Other uses of the comma:

Separate parts of dates, addresses, long numbers (p. 360).
Separate quotations and signal phrases (p. 361).

See also page 362 for when *not* to use the comma.

39a

EXERCISE 39.1
Punctuating linked main clauses

Insert a comma before each coordinating conjunction that links main clauses in the following sentences. If a sentence is already correct as given, mark the number preceding it. Answers to starred items appear at the end of the book. (You can do this exercise online at *ablongman.com/ littlebrown*.)

Example:

I would have attended the concert and the reception but I had to baby-sit for my niece.

I would have attended the concert and the reception⊙ but I had to baby-sit for my niece.

*1. Parents once automatically gave their children the father's last name but some no longer do.
*2. Parents were once legally required to give their children the father's last name but these laws have been contested in court.
*3. Parents may now give their children any last name they choose and the arguments for choosing the mother's last name are often strong and convincing.
*4. Parents who choose the mother's last name may do so because they believe that the mother's importance should be recognized or because the mother's name is easier to pronounce.
*5. The child's last name may be just the mother's or it may link the mother's and the father's with a hyphen.

6. Sometimes the first and third children will have the mother's last name and the second child will have the father's.
7. Occasionally, the mother and father combine parts of their names and a new last name is formed.
8. Critics sometimes point out that unusual names confuse others and can create difficulties for children.
9. Children with last names different from their fathers' may feel embarrassed or have identity problems since most children in the United States still bear their fathers' names.
10. Hyphenated names are awkward and difficult to pass on so some observers think they will die out in a generation or two.

39b

39b Use a comma to set off most introductory elements.

An **introductory element** begins a sentence and modifies a word or words in the main clause that follows. It is usually followed by a comma.

Subordinate clause

Even when identical twins are raised apart⌒ they grow up very like each other.

Verbal or verbal phrase

Explaining the similarity⌒ some researchers claim that one's genes are one's destiny.

Concerned⌒ other researchers deny the claim.

Prepositional phrase

In a debate that has lasted centuries⌒ scientists use identical twins to argue for or against genetic destiny.

Transitional expression

Of course⌒ scientists can now look directly at the genes themselves to answer questions.

You may omit the comma after a short subordinate clause or prepositional phrase if its omission does not create confusion: *When snow falls⌒the city collapses. By the year 2000⌒the world population had topped 6 billion.* But the comma is never wrong.

Note Take care to distinguish *-ing* words used as modifiers from *-ing* words used as subjects. The former almost always take a comma; the latter never do.

```
  ┌──────modifier────────┐   subject   verb
Studying identical twins⌒ geneticists learn about inheritance.

  ┌────── subject ────────┐   verb
Studying identical twins⌒ helps geneticists learn about inheritance.
```

┌─**Key terms**─────────────────────────────────

subordinate clause A word group that contains a subject and a predicate, begins with a subordinating word such as *because* or *who*, and is not a question: *When water freezes, crystals form.* (See p. 244.)

verbal A verb form used as an adjective, adverb, or noun. A verbal plus any object or modifier is a **verbal phrase**: *frozen water, ready to freeze, rapid freezing.* (See p. 241.)

prepositional phrase A word group consisting of a preposition, such as *for* or *in*, followed by a noun or pronoun plus any modifiers: *in a jar, with a spoon.* (See p. 241.)

transitional expression A word or phrase that shows the relationship between sentences: *for example, however, in fact, of course, in contrast.* (See p. 55.)

EXERCISE 39.2
Punctuating introductory elements

In the following sentences, insert commas where needed after introductory elements. If a sentence is already correct as given, mark the number preceding it. Answers to starred items appear at the end of the book. (You can do this exercise online at *ablongman.com/littlebrown.*)

Example:

After the new library opened the old one became a student union.
After the new library opened‸ the old one became a student union.

*1. Veering sharply to the right a large flock of birds neatly avoids a high wall.

*2. Moving in a fluid mass is typical of flocks of birds and schools of fish.

*3. With the help of complex computer simulations zoologists are learning more about this movement.

*4. Because it is sudden and apparently well coordinated the movement of flocks and schools has seemed to be directed by a leader.

*5. Almost incredibly the group could behave with more intelligence than any individual seemed to possess.

6. However new studies have discovered that flocks and schools are leaderless.

7. As it turns out evading danger is really an individual response.

8. When each bird or fish senses a predator it follows individual rules for fleeing.

9. To keep from colliding with its neighbors each bird or fish uses other rules for dodging.

10. Multiplied over hundreds of individuals these responses look as if they have been choreographed.

39c   Use a comma or commas to set off nonessential elements.

Commas around part of a sentence often signal that the element is not essential to the meaning. This **nonessential element** may modify or rename the word it refers to, but it does not limit the word to a particular individual or group. The meaning of the word would still be clear if the element were deleted:

Nonessential element

The company‸ which is located in Oklahoma‸ has an excellent reputation.

(Because it does not restrict meaning, a nonessential element is also called a **nonrestrictive element**.)

^
,
39c

In contrast, an **essential** (or **restrictive**) **element** *does* limit the word it refers to: the element cannot be omitted without leaving the meaning too general. Because it is essential, such an element is *not* set off with commas.

Essential element

The company rewards employees⌒who work hard.

Omitting the underlined words would distort the meaning: the company doesn't necessarily reward *all* employees, only the hardworking ones.

The same element in the same sentence may be essential or nonessential depending on your meaning and the context:

Essential

Not all the bands were equally well received, however. The band⌒ playing old music⌒held the audience's attention. The other groups created much less excitement. [*Playing old music* distinguishes a particular band from all possible bands, so the information is essential.]

Nonessential

A new band called Fats made its debut on Saturday night. The band⌒ playing old music⌒ held the audience's attention. If this performance is typical, the group has a bright future. [*Playing old music* adds information about a band already named and thus already familiar to readers, so the phrase is nonessential.]

^
/
39c

A test for nonessential and essential elements

1. **Identify the element:**

   Hai Nguyen who emigrated from Vietnam lives in Denver.
   Those who emigrated with him live elsewhere.

2. **Remove the element.** Does the fundamental meaning of the sentence change?

   Hai Nguyen lives in Denver. **No.**
   Those live elsewhere. **Yes.** [Who are *Those*?]

3. **If *no*,** the element is *nonessential* and *should* be set off with punctuation:

   Hai Nguyen⌒ who emigrated from Vietnam⌒ lives in Denver.

   If *yes*, the element is *essential* and should *not* be set off with punctuation:

   Those⌒who emigrated with him⌒live elsewhere.

Note When a nonessential element falls in the middle of a sentence, be sure to set it off with a pair of commas, one *before* and one *after* the element.

1 • Nonessential phrases and clauses

Most nonessential phrases and subordinate clauses function as adjectives to modify nouns or pronouns. In each of the following examples, the underlined words could be omitted with no loss of clarity:

> Elizabeth Blackwell was the first woman to graduate from an American medical school, in 1849. [Phrase.]
>
> She was a medical pioneer, helping to found the first medical college for women. [Phrase.]
>
> She taught at the school, which was affiliated with the New York Infirmary. [Clause.]
>
> Blackwell, who published books and papers on medicine, practiced pediatrics and gynecology. [Clause.]

Note Use *that* only in an essential clause, never in a nonessential clause: . . . *school, which* [not *that*] *was affiliated.* . . . Many writers reserve *which* for nonessential clauses.

2 • Nonessential appositives

Appositives may also be essential or nonessential, depending on meaning and context. A nonessential appositive merely adds information about the word it refers to:

> Toni Morrison's fifth novel, *Beloved*, won the Pulitzer Prize in 1988. [The word *fifth* identifies the novel, so the book's title simply adds a detail.]

In contrast, an essential appositive limits or defines the word it refers to:

> Morrison's novel *The Bluest Eye* is about an African American girl who longs for blue eyes. [Morrison has written more than one novel, so the title is essential to identify the intended one.]

∧
,
39c

Key terms

phrase A word group lacking a subject or a verb or both: *in Duluth, carrying water.* (See p. 241.)

subordinate clause A word group that contains a subject and a predicate, begins with a subordinating word such as *who* or *although*, and is not a question: *Samson, who won a gold medal, coaches in Utah.* (See p. 244.)

appositive A noun that renames another noun immediately before it: *His wife, Kyra Sedgwick, is also an actor.* (See p. 243.)

3 • Other nonessential elements

Like nonessential modifiers or appositives, many other elements contribute to texture, tone, or overall clarity but are not essential to the meaning. Unlike nonessential modifiers or appositives, these other nonessential elements generally do not refer to any specific word in the sentence.

Note Use a pair of commas—one before, one after—when any of these elements falls in the middle of a sentence.

Absolute phrases

Household recycling having succeeded‸ the city now wants to extend the program to businesses.

Many businesses‸ their profits already squeezed‸ resist recycling.

Parenthetical and transitional expressions

Generally, set off parenthetical and transitional expressions with commas:

The world's most celebrated holiday is‸ perhaps surprisingly‸ New Year's Day. [Parenthetical expression.]

Interestingly‸ Americans have relatively few holidays. [Parenthetical expression.]

American workers‸ for example‸ receive fewer holidays than European workers do. [Transitional expression.]

(Dashes and parentheses may also set off parenthetical expressions. See pp. 384–85.)

When a transitional expression links main clauses, precede it with a semicolon and follow it with a comma (see p. 366):

European workers often have long paid vacations‸ indeed‸ they may receive a full month after just a few years with a company.

Note The conjunctions *and* and *but*, sometimes used as transitional expressions, are not followed by commas (see p. 363). Nor

^
,
39c

Key terms

absolute phrase A phrase modifying a whole main clause and consisting of a participle and its subject: *Their homework completed, the children watched TV.* (See p. 243.)

parenthetical expression An explanatory or supplemental word or phrase, such as *all things considered, to be frank,* or a brief example or fact. (See p. 385.)

transitional expression A word or phrase that shows the relationship between sentences: *for example, however, in fact.* (See p. 55.)

are commas required after some transitional expressions that we read without pauses, such as *also, hence, next, now,* and *thus.* A few transitional expressions, notably *therefore* and *instead,* do not need commas when they fall inside or at the ends of clauses.

American workers◡thus◡put in more work days. But◡the days themselves may be shorter.

Phrases of contrast
The substance◠not the style◠is important.
Substance◠unlike style◠cannot be faked.

Tag questions
Jones should be allowed to vote◠shouldn't he?
They don't stop to consider others◠do they?

Yes and *no*
Yes◠the editorial did have a point.
No◠that can never be.

Words of direct address
Cody◠please bring me the newspaper.
With all due respect◠sir◠I will not.

Mild interjections
Well◠you will never know who did it.
Oh◠they forgot all about the baby.

∧
,
39c

EXERCISE 39.3
Punctuating essential and nonessential elements
Insert commas in the following sentences to set off nonessential elements, and delete any commas that incorrectly set off essential elements. If a sentence is already correct as given, mark the number preceding it. Answers to starred items appear at the end of the book. (You can do this exercise online at *ablongman.com/littlebrown.*)

Example:

Elizabeth Blackwell who attended medical school in the 1840s was the first American woman to earn a medical degree.

Elizabeth Blackwell◠who attended medical school in the 1840s◠was the first American woman to earn a medical degree.

⌐ Key terms ───────────────────────────────

tag question A question at the end of a statement, consisting of a pronoun, a helping verb, and sometimes *not: It isn't wet, is it?*

interjection A word that expresses feeling or commands attention: *Oh, must we?*

*1. Italians insist that Marco Polo the thirteenth-century explorer did not import pasta from China.
*2. Pasta which consists of flour and water and often egg existed in Italy long before Marco Polo left for his travels.
*3. A historian who studied pasta says that it originated in the Middle East in the fifth century.
*4. Most Italians dispute this account although their evidence is shaky.
*5. Wherever it originated, the Italians are now the undisputed masters, in making and cooking pasta.
6. Marcella Hazan, who has written several books on Italian cooking, insists that homemade and hand-rolled pasta is the best.
7. Most cooks buy dried pasta lacking the time to make their own.
8. The finest pasta is made from semolina, a flour from hard durum wheat.
9. Pasta manufacturers choose hard durum wheat, because it makes firmer cooked pasta than common wheat does.
10. Pasta, made from common wheat, gets soggy in boiling water.

39d Use commas between items in a series.

A **series** consists of three or more items of equal importance. The items may be words, phrases, or clauses.

Anna Spingle married at the age of seventeen had three children by twenty-one and divorced at twenty-two.
She worked as a cook a baby-sitter and a crossing guard.

Some writers omit the comma before the coordinating conjunction in a series (*Breakfast consisted of coffee, eggs and kippers*). But the final comma is never wrong, and it always helps the reader see the last two items as separate.

39e Use commas between two or more adjectives that equally modify the same word.

Adjectives that equally modify the same word—**coordinate adjectives**—may be separated either by *and* or by a comma.

Spingle's scratched and dented car is old, but it gets her to work.
She has dreams of a sleek shiny car.

Adjectives are not coordinate—and should not be separated by commas—when the one nearer the noun is more closely related to the noun in meaning.

Spingle's children work at various odd jobs.
They all expect to go to a nearby community college.

Tests for commas with adjectives

1. **Identify the adjectives:**

   She was a <u>faithful sincere</u> friend.
   They are <u>dedicated medical</u> students.

2. **Can the adjectives be reversed without changing meaning?**

   She was a <u>sincere faithful</u> friend. *Yes.*
   They are <u>medical dedicated</u> students. *No.*

3. **Can the word *and* be inserted between the adjectives without changing meaning?**

   She was a <u>faithful and sincere</u> friend. *Yes.*
   They are <u>dedicated and medical</u> students. *No.*

4. **If *yes* to both questions, the adjectives *should* be separated by a comma:**

   She was a <u>faithful, sincere friend</u>.

5. **If *no* to both questions, the adjectives should *not* be separated by a comma:**

   They are <u>dedicated medical</u> students.

^
ʹ
39e

EXERCISE 39.4
Punctuating series and coordinate adjectives

Insert commas in the following sentences to separate coordinate adjectives or elements in a series. If a sentence is already correct as given, mark the number preceding it. Answers to starred items appear at the end of the book. (You can do this exercise online at *ablongman.com/ littlebrown.*)

Example:

Although quiet by day, the club became a noisy smoky dive at night.

Although quiet by day, the club became a noisy, smoky dive at night.

*1. Shoes with high heels were originally designed to protect feet from mud garbage and animal waste in the streets.

*2. The first known high heels worn strictly for fashion appeared in the sixteenth century.

*3. The heels were worn by men and made of colorful silk fabrics soft suedes or smooth leathers.

*4. High-heeled shoes became popular when the short powerful King Louis XIV of France began wearing them.

*5. Louis's influence was so strong that men and women of the court priests and cardinals and even household servants wore high heels.

6. Eventually only wealthy fashionable French women wore high heels.

7. In the seventeenth and eighteenth centuries, French culture represented the one true standard of elegance and refinement.

8. High-heeled shoes for women spread to other courts of Europe among the Europeans of North America and to almost all social classes.

9. Now high heels are common, though depending on the fashion they range from short squat thick heels to tall skinny spikes.

10. A New York boutique recently showed a pair of purple satin pumps with tiny jeweled bows and four-inch stiletto heels.

39f Use commas in dates, addresses, place names, and long numbers.

When they appear within sentences, elements punctuated with a comma also end with a comma, as in the following examples.

Dates

July 4, 1776, is the date the Declaration was signed.

The bombing of Pearl Harbor on Sunday, December 7, 1941, prompted American entry into World War II.

Do not use commas between the parts of a date in inverted order (*15 December 1992*) or in dates consisting of a month or season and a year (*December 1941*).

Addresses and place names

Use the address 220 Cornell Road, Woodside, California 94062, for all correspondence.

Columbus, Ohio, is the location of Ohio State University.

Do not use a comma between a state name and a zip code.

Long numbers

Use the comma to separate the figures in long numbers into groups of three, counting from the right. With numbers of four digits, the comma is optional.

The new assembly plant cost $7,525,000.
A kilometer is 3,281 feet [*or* 3281 feet].

CULTURE LANGUAGE Usage in standard American English differs from that in some other languages, which use a period, not a comma, to separate the figures in long numbers.

^
,
39f

39g   Use commas with quotations according to standard practice.

The words *she said, he writes,* and so on identify the source of a quotation. These **signal phrases** should be separated from the quotation by punctuation, usually a comma or commas.

> Eleanor Roosevelt said, "You must do the thing you think you cannot do."
>
> "Knowledge is power," wrote Francis Bacon.
>
> "The shore has a dual nature," observes Rachel Carson, "changing with the swing of the tides." [The signal phrase interrupts the quotation at a comma and thus ends with a comma.]

Exceptions   When a signal phrase interrupts a quotation between main clauses, follow the signal phrase with a semicolon or a period. The choice depends on the punctuation of the original.

> Not   "That part of my life was over," she wrote, "his words had sealed it shut."
>
> But   "That part of my life was over," she wrote. "His words had sealed it shut." [*She wrote* interrupts the quotation at a period.]
>
> Or   "That part of my life was over," she wrote; "his words had sealed it shut." [*She wrote* interrupts the quotation at a semicolon.]

Do not use a comma when a signal phrase follows a quotation ending in an exclamation point or a question mark:

> "Claude!" Mrs. Harrison called.
>
> "Why must I come home?" he asked.

Do not use a comma with a quotation that is integrated into your sentence structure, including one introduced by *that:*

> James Baldwin insists that "one must never, in one's life, accept . . . injustices as commonplace."
>
> Baldwin thought that the violence of a riot "had been devised as a corrective" to his own violence.

Do not use a comma with a quoted title unless it is a nonessential appositive.

Key term

nonessential appositive A word or words that rename an immediately preceding noun but do not limit or define the noun: *The author's first story, "Biloxi," won a prize.* (See p. 355.)

^
,

39g

The Beatles recorded◯"She Loves You◌"in the early 1960s.
The Beatles' first huge US hit◌ "She Loves You◌" appeared in 1963.

See Exercise 43.1, page 382, for practice with punctuating quotations.

39h   Delete commas where they are not required.

Commas can make sentences choppy and even confusing if they are used more often than needed. The most common spots for misused commas are discussed below.

1 • Not between subject and verb, verb and object, or preposition and object

Not   The returning <u>soldiers, received</u> a warm welcome. [Separated subject and verb.]

But   The returning <u>soldiers◯received</u> a warm welcome.

Not   They had <u>chosen, to fight</u> for their country <u>despite, the risks</u>. [Separated verb *chosen* and its object; separated preposition *despite* and its object.]

But   They had <u>chosen◯to fight</u> for their country <u>despite◯the risks</u>.

2 • Not in most compound constructions

Compound constructions consisting of two elements almost never require a comma. The only exception is the sentence consisting of two main clauses linked by a coordinating conjunction: *The computer failed◌ but employees kept working* (see p. 349).

Not   ┌──────── compound subject ──────────┐
       <u>Banks, and other financial institutions</u> have helped older people
       ┌── compound object of preposition ──┐
       with <u>money management, and investment</u>.

But   <u>Banks◯and other financial institutions</u> have helped older people
       with <u>money management◯and investment</u>.

Not   ┌──────────── compound predicate ────────────┐
       One bank <u>created</u> special accounts for older people, and held
       compound object of verb
       <u>classes, and workshops</u>.

┌─Key term──
│ **compound construction** Two or more words, phrases, or clauses connected by a coordinating conjunction, usually *and, but, or, nor: man and woman, old or young, leaking oil and spewing steam*.
└──

no ⌃
,
39h

But One bank <u>created</u> special accounts for older people⌒and held classes⌒and workshops.

3 • Not after a conjunction

Not Parents of adolescents notice increased conflict at puberty, <u>and,</u> they complain of bickering.

But Parents of adolescents notice increased conflict at puberty, and⌒they complain of bickering.

Not <u>Although,</u> other primates leave the family at adolescence, humans do not.

But Although⌒other primates leave the family at adolescence, humans do not.

4 • Not around essential elements

Not Hawthorne's work, *The Scarlet Letter,* was the first major American novel. [The title is essential to distinguish the novel from the rest of Hawthorne's work.]

But Hawthorne's work⌒*The Scarlet Letter*⌒was the first major American novel.

Not The symbols<u>, that Hawthorne uses,</u> have influenced other novelists. [The clause identifies which symbols were influential.]

But The symbols⌒<u>that Hawthorne uses</u>⌒have influenced other novelists.

5 • Not around a series

no ^,

39h

Commas separate the items *within* a series (p. 358) but do not separate the series from the rest of the sentence.

Not The skills of<u>, hunting, herding, and agriculture,</u> sustained the Native Americans.

But The skills of⌒<u>hunting, herding, and agriculture</u>⌒sustained the Native Americans.

6 • Not before an indirect quotation

Not The report <u>concluded, that</u> dieting could be more dangerous than overeating.

But The report <u>concluded⌒that</u> dieting could be more dangerous than overeating.

⌐ **Key terms**

conjunction A connecting word such as a **coordinating conjunction** (*and, but, or,* and so on) or a **subordinating conjunction** (*although, because, when,* and so on). (See pp. 230–31.)

essential element Limits the word it refers to and thus can't be omitted without leaving the meaning too general. (See p. 354.)

EXERCISE 39.5
Revising: Needless and misused commas

Revise the following sentences to eliminate needless or misused commas. If a sentence is already correct as given, mark the number preceding it. Answers to starred items appear at the end of the book. (You can do this exercise online at *ablongman.com/littlebrown.*)

Example:

Aquifers can be recharged by rainfall, but, the process is slow.
Aquifers can be recharged by rainfall, but⌒the process is slow.

*1. An important source of water, is underground aquifers.
*2. Underground aquifers are deep, and sometimes broad layers of water, that are trapped between layers of rock.
*3. Porous rock, or sediment holds the water.
*4. Deep wells drilled through the top layers of solid rock, produce a flow of water.
*5. Such wells are sometimes called, artesian wells.
  6. One of the largest aquifers in North America, the Ogallala aquifer, is named after the Ogallala Indian tribe, which once lived in the region and hunted buffalo there.
  7. The Ogallala aquifer underlies a region from western Texas through northern Nebraska, and has a huge capacity of fresh water, that is contained in a layer of sand and gravel.
  8. But, the water in the Ogallala is being removed at a rate faster than it is being replaced.
  9. Water is pumped from the aquifer for many purposes, such as, drinking and other household use, industrial use, and, agricultural use.
 10. The great plains area above the Ogallala, often lacks enough rainfall for the crops, that are grown there.
 11. As a consequence, the crops in the great plains are watered by irrigation systems, that pump water from the Ogallala, and distribute it from half-mile-long sprinkler arms.
 12. Scientists estimate that, at the present consumption rate the Ogallala will be depleted in forty years.
 13. Water table levels are receding from six inches to three feet a year, the amount depending on location.
 14. Some areas are experiencing water shortages already, and the pumping continues.
 15. Without federal regulation and conservation, the Ogallala will one day, be depleted.

no⌃,
39h °

EXERCISE 39.6
Revising: Commas

Insert commas in the following paragraphs wherever they are needed, and eliminate any misused or needless commas. Answers to the first paragraph appear at the end of the book. (You can do this exercise online at *ablongman.com/littlebrown.*)

*Ellis Island New York reopened for business in 1990 but now the customers are tourists not immigrants. *This spot which lies in New York Harbor was the first American soil seen, or touched by many of the nation's immigrants. *Though other places also served as ports of entry for foreigners none has the symbolic power of, Ellis Island. *Between its opening in 1892 and its closing in 1954, over 20 million people about two-thirds of all immigrants were detained there before taking up their new lives in the United States. *Ellis Island processed over 2000 newcomers a day when immigration was at its peak between 1900 and 1920.

As the end of a long voyage and the introduction to the New World Ellis Island must have left something to be desired. The "huddled masses" as the Statue of Liberty calls them indeed were huddled. New arrivals were herded about kept standing in lines for hours or days yelled at and abused. Assigned numbers they submitted their bodies to the pokings and proddings of the silent nurses and doctors, who were charged with ferreting out the slightest sign, of sickness disability or insanity. That test having been passed the immigrants faced interrogation by an official through an interpreter. Those, with names deemed inconveniently long or difficult to pronounce, often found themselves permanently labeled with abbreviations, of their names, or with the names, of their hometowns. But, millions survived the examination humiliation and confusion, to take the last short boat ride to New York City. For many of them and especially for their descendants Ellis Island eventually became not a nightmare but the place where a new life began.

40   The Semicolon

When is a semicolon needed?

Use a semicolon (;) to separate equal and balanced sentence elements—usually main clauses (next page) and occasionally items in a series (p. 368).

Note A grammar and style checker can spot a few errors in the use of semicolons. For example, a checker suggested using a semicolon after *perfect* in *The set was perfect, the director had planned every detail*, thus correcting a comma splice. But it missed the incorrect semicolon in *The set was perfect; deserted streets, dark houses, and gloomy mist* (a colon would be correct; see p. 370).

http://www.ablongman.com/littlebrown ▶

Visit the companion Web site for more help and an electronic exercise on the semicolon.

40a Use a semicolon between main clauses not joined by *and*, *but*, or another coordinating conjunction.

When no coordinating conjunction links two main clauses, the clauses should be separated by a semicolon.

> A new ulcer drug arrived on the market with a mixed reputation(;) doctors find that the drug works but worry about its side effects.

> The side effects are not minor(;) some leave the patient quite uncomfortable or even ill.

Note This rule prevents the errors known as comma splice and fused sentence. (See pp. 332–36.)

40b Use a semicolon between main clauses related by *however*, *for example*, and so on.

When a conjunctive adverb or another transitional expression relates two main clauses in a single sentence, the clauses should be separated with a semicolon:

> An American immigrant, Levi Strauss, invented blue jeans in the 1860s(;) eventually, his product clothed working men throughout the West.

The position of the semicolon between main clauses never changes, but the conjunctive adverb or transitional expression may move around within the second clause. Wherever the adverb or expression falls, it is usually set off with a comma or commas.

Key terms

main clause A word group that contains a subject and a predicate and does not begin with a subordinating word: *Parks help cities breathe.*

coordinating conjunctions *And, but, or, nor*, and sometimes *for, so, yet.*

conjunctive adverb A modifier that describes the relation of the ideas in two clauses, such as *anyway, besides, consequently, finally, furthermore, hence, however, indeed, instead, meanwhile, moreover, namely, otherwise, still, then, therefore, thus.* (See p. 335.)

transitional expression A word or phrase that shows the relationship between ideas. Transitional expressions include conjunctive adverbs as well as *as a result, at last, even so, for example, in contrast, in fact, in other words, in the meantime, of course, on the whole, until now*, and many other words and phrases. (See p. 55.)

;
40b

Blue jeans have become fashionable all over the world; however, the American originators still wear more jeans than anyone else.

Blue jeans have become fashionable all over the world; the American originators, however, still wear more jeans than anyone else.

Blue jeans have become fashionable all over the world; the American originators still wear more jeans than anyone else, however.

Note This rule prevents the errors known as comma splice and fused sentence. (See pp. 332–36.)

EXERCISE 40.1
Sentence combining: Related main clauses

Combine each set of three sentences below into one sentence containing only two main clauses. As indicated in parentheses, connect the clauses with a semicolon alone or with a semicolon plus a conjunctive adverb or transitional expression followed by a comma. You will have to add, delete, change, and rearrange words. Each item has more than one possible answer. Answers to starred items appear at the end of the book. (You can do this exercise online at *ablongman.com/littlebrown.*)

Example:

The Albanians censored their news. We got little news from them. And what we got was unreliable. (*Therefore and semicolon.*)

The Albanians censored their news; therefore, the little news we got from them was unreliable.

* 1. Electronic instruments are prevalent in jazz. They are also prevalent in rock music. They are less common in classical music. (*However and semicolon.*)
* 2. Jazz and rock change rapidly. They nourish experimentation. They nourish improvisation. (*Semicolon alone.*)
* 3. The notes and instrumentation of traditional classical music were established by a composer. The composer was writing decades or centuries ago. Such music does not change. (*Therefore and semicolon.*)
* 4. Contemporary classical music not only can draw on tradition. It can also respond to innovations. These are innovations such as jazz rhythms and electronic sounds. (*Semicolon alone.*)
* 5. Much contemporary electronic music is more than just one type of music. It is more than just jazz, rock, or classical. It is a fusion of all three. (*Semicolon alone.*)
  6. Most music computers are too expensive for the average consumer. Digital keyboard instruments can be inexpensive. They are widely available. (*However and semicolon.*)
  7. Inside the keyboard is a small computer. The computer controls a sound synthesizer. The instrument can both process and produce music. (*Consequently and semicolon.*)

;
40b

8. The person playing the keyboard presses keys or manipulates other controls. The computer and synthesizer convert these signals. The signals are converted into vibrations and sounds. (*Semicolon alone.*)

9. The inexpensive keyboards can perform only a few functions. To the novice computer musician, the range is exciting. The range includes drum rhythms and simulated instruments. (*Still and semicolon.*)

10. Would-be musicians can orchestrate whole songs. They start from just the melody lines. They need never again play "Chopsticks." (*Semicolon alone.*)

40c   Use semicolons between main clauses or series items containing commas.

Normally, commas separate main clauses linked by coordinating conjunctions (*and, but, or, nor*) and separate items in a series. But when the clauses or series items contain commas, a semicolon between them makes the sentence easier to read.

> Lewis and Clark led the men of their party with consummate skill, inspiring and encouraging them, doctoring and caring for them⊙ and they kept voluminous journals.   —Page Smith

> The custody case involved Amy Dalton, the child⊙ Ellen and Mark Dalton, the parents⊙ and Ruth and Hal Blum, the grandparents.

40d   Delete or replace unneeded semicolons.

Semicolons are often misused in certain constructions that call for other punctuation or no punctuation.

1 • Not between a main clause and subordinate clause or phrase

The semicolon does not separate unequal parts, such as main clauses and subordinate clauses or phrases.

> Not   Pygmies are in danger of extinction; because of encroaching development.

> But   Pygmies are in danger of extinction○because of encroaching development.

> Not   According to African authorities; only about 35,000 Pygmies exist today.

> But   According to African authorities⊙only about 35,000 Pygmies exist today.

2 • Not before a series or explanation

Colons and dashes, not semicolons, introduce series, explanations, and so forth. (See pp. 370 and 384.)

Not	Teachers have heard all sorts of reasons why students do poorly; psychological problems, family illness, too much work, too little time.
But	Teachers have heard all sorts of reasons why students do poorly: psychological problems, family illness, too much work, too little time.

EXERCISE 40.2
Revising: Semicolons

Insert semicolons in the following paragraph wherever they are needed. Eliminate any misused or needless semicolons, substituting other punctuation as appropriate. Answers to starred sentences appear at the end of the book. (You can do this exercise online at *ablongman.com/ littlebrown.*)

*The set, sounds, and actors in the movie captured the essence of horror films. *The set was ideal; dark, deserted streets, trees dipping their branches over the sidewalks, mist hugging the ground and creeping up to meet the trees, looming shadows of unlighted, turreted houses. *The sounds, too, were appropriate, especially terrifying was the hard, hollow sound of footsteps echoing throughout the film. But the best feature of the movie was its actors; all of them tall, pale, and thin to the point of emaciation. With one exception, they were dressed uniformly in gray and had gray hair. The exception was an actress who dressed only in black; as if to set off her pale yellow, nearly white, long hair; the only color in the film. The glinting black eyes of another actor stole almost every scene, indeed, they were the source of the film's mischief.

41

41   The Colon

What does a colon do?

The colon (:) is mainly a mark of introduction: it signals that the words following it will explain or amplify. It also has several conventional uses, such as in expressions of time.

http://www.ablongman.com/littlebrown ▶

Visit the companion Web site for more help and an electronic exercise on the colon.

Note Most grammar and style checkers cannot recognize missing or misused colons and instead simply ignore them.

41a Use a colon to introduce a concluding explanation, series, appositive, or long or formal quotation.

As an introducer, a colon is always preceded by a complete main clause. It may or may not be followed by a main clause. This is one way the colon differs from the semicolon, which generally separates main clauses only. (See p. 366.)

Explanation

Soul food has a deceptively simple definition⊙ the ethnic cooking of African Americans.

Sometimes a concluding explanation is preceded by *the following* or *as follows* and a colon:

A more precise definition might be the following⊙ soul food draws on ingredients, cooking methods, and dishes that originated in Africa, were brought to the New World by slaves, and were modified in the Caribbean and the American South.

Note A complete sentence *after* a colon may begin with a capital letter or a small letter. Just be consistent throughout an essay.

Series

At least three soul food dishes are familiar to most Americans⊙ fried chicken, barbecued spareribs, and sweet potatoes.

Appositive

Soul food has one disadvantage⊙ fat.

Namely, that is, and other expressions that introduce appositives *follow* the colon: *Soul food has one disadvantage⊙ namely, fat.*

Long or formal quotation

One soul food chef has a solution⊙ "Soul food doesn't have to be greasy to taste good. Instead of using ham hocks to flavor beans, I use smoked turkey wings. The soulful, smoky taste remains, but without all the fat of pork."

Key terms

main clause A word group that contains a subject and a predicate and does not begin with a subordinating word: *Soul food is varied.* (See p. 244.)

appositive A noun or noun substitute that renames another noun immediately before it: *my brother, Jack.* (See p. 243.)

:
41a

When a complete sentence introduces a quotation, as in the preceding example, a colon generally ends the sentence.

41b Use a colon after the salutation of a business letter, between a title and subtitle, and between divisions of time.

Salutation of business letter
Dear Ms. Burak⊙

Title and subtitle
Charles Dickens⊙ *An Introduction to His Novels*

Time
12⊙26 AM   6⊙00 PM

41c Delete or replace unneeded colons.

Use the colon only at the end of a main clause, not in the following situations.

- **Delete a colon after a verb:**

  Not   The best-known soul food dishes <u>are</u>: fried chicken and barbecued spareribs.

  But   The best-known soul food dishes <u>are</u>◯fried chicken and barbecued spareribs.

- **Delete a colon after a preposition:**

  Not   Soul food recipes can be found <u>in</u>: mainstream cookbooks as well as specialized references.

  But   Soul food recipes can be found <u>in</u>◯mainstream cookbooks as well as specialized references.

- **Delete a colon after *such as* or *including*:**

  Not   Many Americans have not tasted delicacies <u>such as</u>: chitlins and black-eyed peas.

  But   Many Americans have not tasted delicacies <u>such as</u>◯chitlins and black-eyed peas.

41c

┌ **Key term** ─────────────────────────────────
preposition *In, on, outside*, or another word that takes a noun or pronoun as its object: *in the house.* (See p. 229.)

EXERCISE 41.1
Revising: Colons and semicolons

In the following sentences, use colons or semicolons where they are needed, and delete or replace them where they are incorrect. If a sentence is already correct as given, mark the number preceding it. Answers to starred items appear at the end of the book. (You can do this exercise online at *ablongman.com/littlebrown*.)

Example:

Mix the ingredients as follows sift the flour and salt together, add the milk, and slowly beat in the egg yolk.

Mix the ingredients as follows⊙ sift the flour and salt together, add the milk, and slowly beat in the egg yolk.

*1. Sunlight is made up of three kinds of radiation; visible rays; infrared rays, which we cannot see; and ultraviolet rays, which are also invisible.

*2. Especially in the ultraviolet range; sunlight is harmful to the eyes.

*3. Ultraviolet rays can damage the retina: furthermore, they can cause cataracts on the lens.

*4. Infrared rays are the longest; measuring 700 nanometers and longer, while ultraviolet rays are the shortest; measuring 400 nanometers and shorter.

*5. The lens protects the eye by: absorbing much of the ultraviolet radiation and thus protecting the retina.

6. By protecting the retina, however, the lens becomes a victim; growing cloudy and blocking vision.

7. The best way to protect your eyes is: to wear hats that shade the face and sunglasses that screen out the ultraviolet rays.

8. Many sunglass lenses have been designed as ultraviolet screens; many others are extremely ineffective.

9. If sunglass lenses do not screen out ultraviolet rays and if people can see your eyes through them, they will not protect your eyes and you will be at risk for cataracts later in life.

10. People who spend much time outside in the sun; really owe it to themselves to buy a pair of sunglasses that will shield their eyes.

:
41

42 The Apostrophe

Where do apostrophes go (and not go)?

The apostrophe (') appears as part of a word to indicate posses-sion (below), the omission of one or more letters (p. 377), and sometimes plural number (p. 377).

Apostrophes are easy to misuse. For safety's sake, check your drafts to be sure that all words ending in -s neither omit needed apostrophes nor add unneeded ones.

Note Grammar and style checkers have mixed results in rec-ognizing apostrophe errors. For instance, most flag missing apos-trophes in contractions (as in *isnt*), but many cannot distinguish between *its* and *it's, their* and *they're, your* and *you're, whose* and *who's*. The checkers can identify some apostrophe errors in posses-sives but will overlook others and may flag correct plurals. Instead of relying on your checker, try using your word processor's Search or Find function to hunt for all words you have ended in -s. Then check them to ensure that apostrophes are used correctly.

42a Use the apostrophe and sometimes -s to form possessive nouns and indefinite pronouns.

A noun or indefinite pronoun shows possession with an apos-trophe and, usually, an -s: *the dog's hair, everyone's hope*. Remember that the apostrophe or apostrophe-plus-*s* is an *addition*. Before this addition, always spell the name of the owner or owners without dropping or adding letters.

✓

42a

1 • **Singular words: Add -'s.**

Bill Boughton's skillful card tricks amaze children.
Anyone's eyes would widen.
Most tricks will pique an adult's curiosity, too.

The -'s ending for singular words pertains also to singular words ending in -s, as the next examples show.

> ┌ **Key term** ───────────────────────────────
> **indefinite pronoun** A pronoun that does not refer to a specific person or thing, such as *anyone, no one,* or *something.* (See p. 283.)

http://www.ablongman.com/littlebrown

Visit the companion Web site for more help and electronic exercises on the apostrophe.

Uses and misuses of the apostrophe

Uses of the apostrophe

- **Use an apostrophe to form the possessives of nouns and indefinite pronouns** (previous page).

Singular	Plural
Ms. Park's	the Parks'
lawyer's	lawyers'
everyone's	two weeks'

- **Use an apostrophe to form contractions** (p. 377).

it's a girl	shouldn't
you're	won't

- **The apostrophe is optional for plurals of abbreviations, dates, and words or characters named as words** (p. 377).

MAs or MA's	Cs or C's
1960s or 1960's	ifs or if's

Misuses of the apostrophe

42a

- **Do not use an apostrophe plus -s to form the possessives of plural nouns** (p. 375). Instead, use an apostrophe alone after the -s that forms the plural.

Not	But
the Kim's car	the Kims' car
boy's fathers	boys' fathers
babie's care	babies' care

- **Do not use an apostrophe to form plurals of nouns** (p. 376).

Not	But
book's are	books are
the Freed's	the Freeds

- **Do not use an apostrophe with verbs ending in -s** (p. 376).

Not	But
swim's	swims

- **Do not use an apostrophe to form the possessives of personal pronouns** (pp. 376–77).

Not	But
it's toes	its toes
your's	yours

Henry James*'s* novels reward the patient reader.
The business*'s* customers filed suit.

Exception An apostrophe alone may be added to a singular word ending in -s if another s would make the word difficult to say:

Moses*'* mother concealed him in the bulrushes.
Joan Rivers*'* jokes offend many people.

However, the added -s is never wrong (*Moses's, Rivers's*).

2 • **Plural words ending in -s: Add -' only.**

Workers*'* incomes have fallen slightly over the past year.
Many students benefit from several years*'* work after high school.
The Jameses*'* talents are extraordinary.

Note the difference in the possessives of singular and plural words ending in -s. The singular form usually takes -s: *James's*. The plural takes only the apostrophe: *Jameses'*.

3 • **Plural words not ending in -s: Add -'s.**

Children*'s* educations are at stake.
We need to attract the media*'s* attention.

4 • **Compound words: Add -'s only to the last word.**

The brother-in-law*'s* business failed.
Taxes are always somebody else*'s* fault.

5 • **Two or more owners: Add -'s depending on possession.**

Individual possession
Zimbale*'s* and Mason*'s* comedy techniques are similar. [Each comedian has his own technique.]

Joint possession
The child recovered despite her mother and father*'s* neglect. [The mother and father were jointly neglectful.]

42a

EXERCISE 42.1
Forming possessives

Form the possessive of each word or word group in brackets. Answers to starred items appear at the end of the book. (You can do this exercise online at *ablongman.com/littlebrown.*)

Example:
The [men] blood pressures were higher than the [women].
The men*'s* blood pressures were higher than the women*'s*.

*1. In the myths of the ancient Greeks, the [goddesses] roles vary widely.
*2. [Demeter] responsibility is the fruitfulness of the earth.
*3. [Athena] role is to guard the city of Athens.
*4. [Artemis] function is to care for wild animals and small children.
*5. [Athena and Artemis] father, Zeus, is the king of the gods.
6. Even a single [goddess] responsibilities are often varied.
7. Over several [centuries] time, Athena changes from a [mariner] goddess to the patron of crafts.
8. Athena is also concerned with fertility and with [children] well-being, since the strength of Athens depended on a large and healthy population.
9. Athena often changes into [birds] forms.
10. In [Homer] *Odyssey* she assumes a [sea eagle] form.
11. In ancient Athens the myths of Athena were part of [everyone] knowledge and life.
12. A cherished myth tells how Athena fights to retain possession of her [people] land when the god Poseidon wants it.
13. [Athena and Poseidon] skills are different, and each promises a special gift to the Athenians.
14. At the [contest] conclusion, Poseidon has given water and Athena has given an olive tree, for sustenance.
15. The other gods decide that the [Athenians] lives depend more on Athena than on Poseidon.

42b   Delete or replace any apostrophe in a plural noun, a singular verb, or a possessive personal pronoun.

1 • Plural nouns

The plurals of nouns are generally formed by adding -*s* or -*es*: *boys, families, Joneses*. Don't add an apostrophe to form the plural:

Not   The Jones' controlled the firm's until 2003.
But   The Joneses controlled the firms until 2003.

2 • Singular verbs

Verbs ending in -*s never* take an apostrophe:

Not   The subway break's down less often now.
But   The subway breaks down less often now.

3 • Possessives of personal pronouns

His, hers, its, ours, yours, theirs, and *whose* are possessive forms of *he, she, it, we, you, they,* and *who.* They do not take apostrophes:

Not   The house is her's. It's roof leaks.

But   The house is hers. Its roof leaks.

Don't confuse possessive pronouns with contractions. See the examples below.

42c   Use the apostrophe to form contractions.

A **contraction** replaces one or more letters, numbers, or words with an apostrophe, as in the following examples:

it is	it's	cannot	can't
they are	they're	does not	doesn't
you are	you're	were not	weren't
who is	who's	class of 2009	class of '09

Note Don't confuse contractions with personal pronouns:

Contractions	Personal pronouns
It's a book.	Its cover is green.
They're coming.	Their car broke down.
You're right.	Your idea is good.
Who's coming?	Whose party is it?

42d   Increasingly, the apostrophe does not mark plurals of abbreviations, dates, and words and characters named as words.

42d

You'll sometimes see apostrophes used to form the plurals of abbreviations (*BA's*), dates (*1900's*), and words or characters named as words (*but's*). However, most current style guides recommend against the apostrophe in these cases.

BAs   PhDs

1990s   2000s

The sentence has too many *buts* [or buts].

Two *3s* [or 3s] end the zip code.

Note Underline or italicize a word or character named as a word (see p. 406), but not the added -*s*.

EXERCISE 42.2
Revising: Apostrophes

In the following paragraph, correct any mistakes in the use of apostrophes or any confusion between contractions and possessive personal pronouns. Answers to starred sentences appear at the end of the book. (You can do this exercise online at *ablongman.com/littlebrown*.)

*Landlocked Chad is among the worlds most troubled countries. *The people's of Chad are poor: they're average per capita income equals $1000 per year. *Just over 30 percent of Chads population is literate, and every five hundred people must share only two teacher's. The natural resources of the nation have never been plentiful, and now, as it's slowly being absorbed into the growing Sahara Desert, even water is scarce. Chads political conflicts go back to the nineteenth century, when the French colonized the land by brutally subduing it's people. The rule of the French—who's inept government of the colony did nothing to ease tensions among racial, tribal, and religious group's—ended with independence in 1960. But since then the Chadians experience has been one of civil war and oppression, and their also threatened with invasions from they're neighbors.

43   Quotation Marks

How do quotation marks work?

" "
43

Quotation marks—either double (" ") or single (' ')—mainly enclose direct quotations from speech or writing, enclose certain titles, and highlight words used in a special sense. These are the uses covered in this chapter, along with placing quotation marks before or after other punctuation marks. Additional issues with quotations are discussed elsewhere in this book:

- Punctuating *she said* and other signal phrases with quotations (p. 361).
- Altering quotations using the ellipsis mark or brackets (pp. 385–87).
- Quoting sources versus paraphrasing or summarizing them (pp. 460–64).
- Integrating quotations into your text (pp. 465–69).
- Avoiding plagiarism when quoting (pp. 470–77).
- Formatting long prose quotations and poetry quotations in MLA style or in APA style (pp. 523–24 and 550).

http://www.ablongman.com/littlebrown   ▶

Visit the companion Web site for more help and an electronic exercise on quotation marks.

Note Always use quotation marks in pairs, one at the beginning of a quotation and one at the end. Some grammar and style checkers will help you use quotation marks in pairs by flagging a lone mark. Most checkers can also be set to ignore other punctuation with quotations or to look for punctuation inside or outside quotation marks, but they may not detect errors when punctuation should actually fall outside quotation marks.

43a Use double quotation marks to enclose direct quotations.

A **direct quotation** reports what someone said or wrote, in the exact words of the original:

> "Life," said the psychoanalyst Karen Horney, "remains a very efficient therapist."

Do not use quotation marks with an **indirect quotation,** which reports what someone said or wrote but not in the exact words.

> The psychoanalyst Karen Horney claimed that life is a good therapist.

When quoting dialog, begin a new paragraph for each speaker.

> "What shall I call you? Your name?" Andrews whispered rapidly, as with a high squeak the latch of the door rose.
> "Elizabeth," she said. "Elizabeth."
> —Graham Greene, *The Man Within*

" "

43b

When you quote a single speaker for more than one paragraph, put quotation marks at the beginning of each paragraph but at the end of only the last paragraph.

43b Use single quotation marks to enclose a quotation within a quotation.

> "In formulating any philosophy," Woody Allen writes, "the first consideration must always be: What can we know? Descartes hinted at the problem when he wrote, 'My mind can never know my body, although it has become quite friendly with my leg.'"

Notice that two different quotation marks appear at the end of the sentence—one single (to finish the interior quotation) and one double (to finish the main quotation).

43c   Put quotation marks around the titles of works that are parts of other works.

Use quotation marks to enclose the titles of works that are published or released within larger works. (See the box below.) Use single quotation marks for a quotation within a quoted title, as in the article title and essay title in the box. And enclose all punctuation in the title within the quotation marks, as in the article title.

Titles to be enclosed in quotation marks

Other titles should be underlined or italicized. (See pp. 405–06.)

Song
"The Star-Spangled Banner"

Short story
"The Gift of the Magi"

Short poem
"Mending Wall"

Article in a periodical
"Does 'Scaring' Work?"

Essay
"Joey: A 'Mechanical Boy'"

Page or document on a Web site
"Readers' Page" (on the site Friends of Prufrock)

Episode of a television or radio program
"The Mexican Connection" (on Sixty Minutes)

Subdivision of a book
"The Mast Head" (Chapter 35 of Moby-Dick)

Note Some academic disciplines do not require quotation marks for titles within source citations. See page 536 on the style of the American Psychological Association (APA).

43d   Quotation marks may enclose words being used in a special sense.

On movie sets movable "wild walls" make a one-walled room seem four-walled on film.

Note Use underlining or italics for words you are defining. (See p. 406.)

43e   Delete quotation marks where they are not required.

Title of your paper
Not   "The Death Wish in One Poem by Robert Frost"

But   The Death Wish in One Poem by Robert Frost
Or   The Death Wish in "Stopping by Woods on a Snowy Evening"

Common nickname
Not   As President, "Jimmy" Carter preferred to use his nickname.
But   As President, Jimmy Carter preferred to use his nickname.

Slang or trite expression

Quotation marks will not excuse slang or a trite expression that is inappropriate to your writing. If slang is appropriate, use it without quotation marks.

Not   We should support the President in his "hour of need" rather than "wimp out on him."

But   We should give the President the support he needs rather than turn away like cowards.

43f Place other punctuation marks inside or outside quotation marks according to standard practice.

1 • Commas and periods: Inside quotation marks

Swift uses irony in his essay "A Modest Proposal."

Many first-time readers are shocked to see infants described as "delicious."

"'A Modest Proposal,'" wrote one critic, "is so outrageous that it cannot be believed."

Exception When a parenthetical source citation immediately follows a quotation, place any period or comma *after* the citation:

One critic calls the essay "outrageous" (Olms 26).

Partly because of "the cool calculation of its delivery" (Olms 27), Swift's satire still chills a modern reader.

2 • Colons and semicolons: Outside quotation marks

A few years ago the slogan in elementary education was "learning by playing"; now educators are concerned with teaching basic skills.

We all know the meaning of "basic skills": reading, writing, and arithmetic.

3 • Dashes, question marks, and exclamation points: Inside quotation marks only if part of the quotation

When a dash, question mark, or exclamation point is part of the quotation, place it *inside* quotation marks. Don't use any other punctuation, such as a period or comma:

" "
43f

"But must you—" Marcia hesitated, afraid of the answer.

"Go away!" I yelled.

Did you say, "Who is she?" [When both your sentence and the quotation would end in a question mark or exclamation point, use only the mark in the quotation.]

When a dash, question mark, or exclamation point applies only to the larger sentence, not to the quotation, place it *outside* quotation marks—again, with no other punctuation:

One evocative line in English poetry—"After many a summer dies the swan"—comes from Alfred, Lord Tennyson.

Who said, "Now cracks a noble heart"?

The woman called me "stupid"!

EXERCISE 43.1
Revising: Quotation marks

Insert quotation marks as needed in the following paragraph. Answers to starred sentences appear at the end of the book. (You can do this exercise online at *ablongman.com/littlebrown*.)

*In one class we talked about a passage from I Have a Dream, the speech delivered by Martin Luther King, Jr., on the steps of the Lincoln Memorial on August 28, 1963:

> *When the architects of our republic wrote the magnificent words of the Constitution and the Declaration of Independence, they were signing a promissory note to which every American was to fall heir. *This note was a promise that all men would be guaranteed the unalienable rights of life, liberty, and the pursuit of happiness.

*What did Dr. King mean by this statement? the teacher asked. *Perhaps we should define promissory note first. Then she explained that a person who signs such a note agrees to pay a specific sum of money on a particular date or on demand by the holder of the note. One student suggested, Maybe Dr. King meant that the writers of the Constitution and Declaration promised that all people in America should be equal. He and over 200,000 people had gathered in Washington, DC, added another student. Maybe their purpose was to demand payment, to demand those rights for African Americans. The whole discussion was an eye-opener for those of us (including me) who had never considered that those documents make promises that we should expect our country to fulfill.

" "
43f

44 Other Marks

How do writers use the dash, parentheses, the ellipsis mark, brackets, and the slash?

Each of these punctuation marks has distinctive uses:

- **The dash (—) sets off interruptions** (below).
- **Parentheses (()) enclose some nonessential information and labels for lists within sentences** (p. 384).
- **The ellipsis mark (. . .) indicates an omission from a quotation** (p. 385).
- **Brackets ([ ]) mainly indicate changes in quotations** (p. 388).
- **The slash (/) separates options, lines of poetry, and the parts of electronic addresses** (p. 388).

Note Many grammar and style checkers will flag a lone parenthesis or bracket so that you can match it with another parenthesis or bracket. But most checkers cannot recognize other misuses of the marks covered here and instead simply ignore the marks.

44a Use the dash or dashes to indicate shifts and to set off some sentence elements.

The **dash** is mainly a mark of interruption: it signals a shift, insertion, or break. Form a dash with two hyphens (--), or use the character called an em dash on your word processor. Do not add extra space around or between the hyphens or around the em dash.

Note When an interrupting element starting with a dash falls in the middle of a sentence, be sure to add the closing dash to signal the end of the interruption. See the first example below.

1 • Shifts and hesitations

The novel⬛if one can call it that⬛appeared in 2006.

If the book had a plot⬛but a plot would be conventional.

"I was worried you might think I had stayed away because I was influenced by⬛" He stopped and lowered his eyes.

Astonished, Howe said, "Influenced by what?"

"Well, by⬛" Blackburn hesitated and for an answer pointed to the table. —Lionel Trilling

http://www.ablongman.com/littlebrown ▶

Visit the companion Web site for more help and electronic exercises on the punctuation marks discussed in this chapter.

44a

2 • Nonessential elements

Dashes may be used instead of commas to set off and emphasize modifiers, parenthetical expressions, and other nonessential elements:

Though they are close together⬛separated by only a few blocks⬛the two neighborhoods could be in different countries.

Dashes are especially useful when a nonessential element contains punctuation of its own:

The qualities Monet painted⬛sunlight, rich shadows, deep colors⬛ abounded near the rivers and gardens he used as subjects.

3 • Introductory series and concluding series and explanations

Shortness of breath, skin discoloration or the sudden appearance of moles, persistent indigestion, the presence of small lumps⬛all these may signify cancer. [Introductory series.]

The patient undergoes a battery of tests⬛CAT scan, bronchoscopy, perhaps even biopsy. [Concluding series.]

Many patients are disturbed by the CAT scan⬛by the need to keep still for long periods in an exceedingly small space. [Concluding explanation.]

A colon could be used instead of a dash in the last two examples. The dash is more informal.

4 • Overuse

Too many dashes can make writing jumpy or breathy:

Not   In all his life—eighty-seven years—my great-grandfather never allowed his picture to be taken—not even once. He claimed the "black box"—the camera—would steal his soul.

But   In all his eighty-seven years, my great-grandfather did not allow his picture to be taken even once. He claimed the "black box"— the camera—would steal his soul.

( )
44b

44b   Use parentheses to enclose parenthetical expressions and labels for lists within sentences.

Note Parentheses *always* come in pairs, one before and one after the punctuated material.

┌─**Key term**───

nonessential element Gives added information but does not limit the word it refers to. (See p. 353.)

1 • Parenthetical expressions

Parenthetical expressions include explanations, facts, digressions, and examples that may be helpful or interesting but are not essential to meaning. Parentheses de-emphasize parenthetical expressions. (Commas emphasize them more and dashes still more.)

> The population of Philadelphia (now about 1.5 million) has declined since 1950.

Note Don't put a comma before a parenthetical expression enclosed in parentheses. Punctuation after the parenthetical expression should be placed outside the closing parenthesis.

> Not Philadelphia's population compares with Houston's, (just over 1.6 million.)
>
> But Philadelphia's population compares with Houston's (just over 1.6 million).

When it falls between other complete sentences, a complete sentence enclosed in parentheses begins with a capital letter and ends with a period.

> In general, coaches will tell you that scouts are just guys who can't coach. (But then, so are brain surgeons.)   —Roy Blount

2 • Labels for lists within sentences

> Outside the Middle East, the countries with the largest oil reserves are (1) Venezuela (63 billion barrels), (2) Russia (57 billion barrels), and (3) Mexico (51 billion barrels).

44c

When you set a list off from your text, do not enclose such labels in parentheses.

44c   Use the ellipsis mark to indicate omissions from quotations.

The **ellipsis mark,** consisting of three spaced periods (. . .), generally indicates an omission from a quotation. The following examples quote from or refer to this passage about environmentalism:

Original quotation

"At the heart of the environmentalist world view is the conviction that human physical and spiritual health depends on sustaining the planet in a relatively unaltered state. Earth is our home in the full, genetic sense, where humanity and its ancestors existed for all the millions of years of their evolution. Natural ecosystems—forests, coral reefs, marine blue waters—maintain the world exactly as we would wish it to be maintained. When we debase the global environment and extinguish the variety of

life, we are dismantling a support system that is too complex to understand, let alone replace, in the foreseeable future."

—Edward O. Wilson, "Is Humanity Suicidal?"

1. Omission of the middle of a sentence

Wilson writes, "Natural ecosystems . . . maintain the world exactly as we
would wish it to be maintained."

2. Omission of the end of a sentence, without source citation

Wilson writes, "Earth is our home . . . ." [The sentence period, closed up
to the last word, precedes the ellipsis mark.]

3. Omission of the end of a sentence, with source citation

Wilson writes, "Earth is our home . . ." (27). [The sentence period follows the source citation.]

4. Omission of parts of two or more sentences

Wilson writes, "At the heart of the environmentalist world view is the
conviction that human physical and spiritual health depends on sustaining the planet . . . where humanity and its ancestors existed for all the
millions of years of their evolution."

5. Omission of one or more sentences

As Wilson puts it, "At the heart of the environmentalist world view is the
conviction that human physical and spiritual health depends on sustaining the planet in a relatively unaltered state. . . . When we debase the
global environment and extinguish the variety of life, we are dismantling
a support system that is too complex to understand, let alone replace, in
the foreseeable future."

. . .
44c

6. Omission from the middle of a sentence through the end of another sentence

"Earth is our home . . . . When we debase the global environment and
extinguish the variety of life, we are dismantling a support system that is
too complex to understand, let alone replace, in the foreseeable future."

7. Omission of the beginning of a sentence, leaving a complete sentence

a. Bracketed capital letter

"[H]uman physical and spiritual health," Wilson writes, "depends on
sustaining the planet in a relatively unaltered state." [No ellipsis mark is
needed because the brackets around the H indicate that the letter was
not capitalized originally and thus that the beginning of the sentence
has been omitted.]

b. Small letter

According to Wilson, "human physical and spiritual health depends on
sustaining the planet in a relatively unaltered state." [No ellipsis mark is
needed because the small h indicates that the beginning of the sentence
has been omitted.]

c. Capital letter from the original

Hami comments, "⟨...⟩Wilson argues eloquently for the environmentalist world view." [An ellipsis mark *is* needed because the quoted part of the sentence begins with a capital letter and it is not clear that the beginning of the original sentence has been omitted.]

8. Use of a word or phrase

Wilson describes the earth as "our home." [No ellipsis mark needed.]

Note these features of the examples:

- **Use an ellipsis mark when it is not otherwise clear that you have left out material from the source,** as when you omit one or more sentences (examples 5 and 6) or when the words you quote form a complete sentence that is different in the original (examples 1–4 and 7c).

- **You don't need an ellipsis mark when it is obvious that you have omitted something,** such as when capitalization indicates omission (examples 7a and 7b) or when a phrase clearly comes from a larger sentence (example 8).

- **Place an ellipsis mark after a sentence period** *except* **when a parenthetical source citation follows the quotation,** as in example 3. Then the sentence period falls after the citation.

If you omit one or more lines of poetry or paragraphs of prose from a quotation, use a separate line of ellipsis marks across the full width of the quotation to show the omission:

In "Song: Love Armed" from 1676, Aphra Behn contrasts two lovers'
experiences of a romance:

> Love in fantastic triumph sate,
>
>   Whilst bleeding hearts around him flowed,
>
> . . . .
>
> But my poor heart alone is harmed,
>
>   Whilst thine the victor is, and free. (lines 1-2, 15-16)

(See pp. 523–24 for the format of displayed quotations like this one.)

EXERCISE 44.1
Using ellipsis marks

Use ellipsis marks and any other needed punctuation to follow the numbered instructions for quoting from the following paragraph. The answer to the starred item appears at the end of the book. (You can do this exercise online at *ablongman.com/littlebrown*.)

Women in the sixteenth and seventeenth centuries were educated in the home and, in some cases, in boarding schools. Men were edu-

44c

cated at home, in grammar schools, and at the universities. The universities were closed to female students. For women, "learning the Bible," as Elizabeth Joceline puts it, was an impetus to learning to read. To be able to read the Bible in the vernacular was a liberating experience that freed the reader from hearing only the set passages read in the church and interpreted by the church. A Protestant woman was expected to read the scriptures daily, to meditate on them, and to memorize portions of them. In addition, a woman was expected to instruct her entire household in "learning the Bible" by holding instructional and devotional times each day for all household members, including the servants.

—Charlotte F. Otten, *English Women's Voices, 1540–1700*

*1. Quote the fifth sentence, but omit everything from *that freed the reader* to the end.

2. Quote the fifth sentence, but omit the words *was a liberating experience that.*

3. Quote the first and sixth sentences.

44d   Use brackets to indicate changes in quotations.

Brackets have specialized uses in mathematical equations, but their main use for all kinds of writing is to indicate that you have altered a quotation to explain, clarify, or correct it.

"That Texaco station [just outside Chicago] is one of the busiest in the nation," said a company spokesperson.

The word *sic* (Latin for "in this manner") in brackets indicates that an error in the quotation appeared in the original and was not made by you. Do not underline or italicize *sic* in brackets.

According to the newspaper report, "The car slammed thru [sic] the railing and into oncoming traffic."

Do not use *sic* to make fun of a writer or to note errors in a passage that is clearly nonstandard.

44e   Use the slash between options, between lines of poetry run into the text, and in electronic addresses.

Option
Some teachers oppose pass/fail courses.

Poetry
Many readers have sensed a reluctant turn away from death in Frost's lines "The woods are lovely, dark and deep, / But I have promises to keep" (13–14).

When separating lines of poetry in this way, leave a space before and after the slash. (See pp. 523–24 for more on quoting poetry.)

Electronic address
http://www.stanford.edu/depts/spc/spc.html

EXERCISE 44.2
Revising: Dashes, parentheses, ellipsis marks, brackets, slashes

Insert dashes, parentheses, ellipsis marks, brackets, or slashes as needed in the following paragraph. In some cases, two or more different marks could be correct. Answers to starred sentences appear at the end of the book. (You can do this exercise online at *ablongman.com/littlebrown*.)

*"Let all the learned say what they can, 'Tis ready money makes the man." *These two lines of poetry by the Englishman William Somerville 1645–1742 may apply to a current American economic problem. *Non-American investors with "ready money" pour some of it as much as $1.3 trillion in recent years into the United States. *Stocks and bonds, savings deposits, service companies, factories, artworks, political campaigns the investments of foreigners are varied and grow more numerous every day. Proponents of foreign investment argue that it revives industry, strengthens the economy, creates jobs more than 3 million, they say, and encourages free trade among nations. Opponents caution that the risks associated with heavy foreign investment namely decreased profits at home and increased political influence from outside may ultimately weaken the economy. On both sides, it seems, "the learned say, 'Tis ready money makes the man or country." The question is, whose money theirs or ours?

/
44e

6

Spelling and Mechanics

45 Spelling

You can train yourself to spell better by following this chapter's tips for pinpointing and fixing your spelling problems. But you can improve your spelling instantly by adopting three habits:

- **Carefully proofread all of your writing.**
- **Cultivate a healthy suspicion of your spellings.**
- **Check a dictionary** *every time* **you doubt a spelling.**

Note A spelling checker can help you find and track spelling errors in your papers. But its usefulness is limited, mainly because it can't spot the confusion of words with similar spellings, such as *their/they're/there* and *principal/principle*. See pages 38–39 for more on spelling checkers.

45a Anticipate typical spelling problems.

Misspellings often result from misleading pronunciation, different forms of the same word, and the confusion of British and American spellings.

1 • Pronunciation

In English, pronunciation of words is an unreliable guide to their spelling. Pronunciation is especially misleading with **homonyms,** words that are pronounced the same but spelled differently. Some homonyms and near-homonyms appear in the box below.

sp
45a

Words commonly confused

accept (to receive)
except (other than)

affect (to have an influence on)
effect (result)

all ready (prepared)
already (by this time)

allusion (an indirect reference)
illusion (an erroneous belief or
  perception)

ascent (a movement up)
assent (agreement)

bare (unclothed)
bear (to carry, or an animal)

---

http://www.ablongman.com/littlebrown

Visit the companion Web site for more help
and an electronic exercise on spelling.

board (a plane of wood)
bored (uninterested)

brake (to stop)
break (to smash)

buy (to purchase)
by (next to)

cite (to quote an authority)
sight (the ability to see)
site (a place)

desert (to abandon)
dessert (after-dinner course)

discreet (reserved, respectful)
discrete (individual, distinct)

elicit (to draw out)
illicit (illegal or immoral)

eminent (prominent, respected)
imminent (about to occur)

fair (average, or lovely)
fare (a fee for transportation)

forth (forward)
fourth (after *third*)

hear (to perceive by ear)
here (in this place)

heard (past tense of *hear*)
herd (a group of animals)

hole (an opening)
whole (complete)

its (possessive of *it*)
it's (contraction of *it is* or *it has*)

know (to be certain)
no (the opposite of *yes*)

lessen (to reduce)
lesson (something learned)

meat (flesh)
meet (encounter)

passed (past tense of *pass*)
past (after, or a time gone by)

patience (forbearance)
patients (persons under medical care)

peace (the absence of war)
piece (a portion of something)

plain (clear)
plane (a carpenter's tool, or an airborne vehicle)

presence (the state of being at hand)
presents (gifts)

principal (most important, or the head of a school)
principle (a basic truth or law)

raise (to lift up)
raze (to tear down)

rain (precipitation)
reign (to rule)
rein (a strap for an animal)

right (correct)
rite (a religious ceremony)
write (to make letters)

road (a surface for driving)
rode (past tense of *ride*)

scene (where an action occurs)
seen (past participle of *see*)

stationary (unmoving)
stationery (writing paper)

their (possessive of *they*)
there (opposite of *here*)
they're (contraction of *they are*)

to (toward)
too (also)
two (following *one*)

waist (the middle of the body)
waste (discarded material)

weak (not strong)
week (Sunday through Saturday)

weather (climate)
whether (*if*, or introducing a choice)

which (one of a group)
witch (a sorcerer)

who's (contraction of *who is* or *who has*)
whose (possessive of *who*)

your (possessive of *you*)
you're (contraction of *you are*)

sp
45a

2 • Different forms of the same word

Spellings often differ for the same word's noun and verb forms or noun and adjective forms: for example, *advice* (noun) and *advise* (verb); *height* (noun) and *high* (adjective). Similar changes occur in the parts of some irregular verbs (*know, knew, known*) and the plurals of irregular nouns (*man, men*).

3 • American vs. British spellings **CULTURE LANGUAGE**

If you learned English outside the United States, you may be accustomed to British rather than American spellings. Here are the chief differences:

American	British
color, humor	colour, humour
theater, center	theatre, centre
canceled, traveled	cancelled, travelled
judgment	judgement
realize, civilize	realise, civilise
connection	connexion

Your dictionary may list both spellings, but it will specially mark the British one with *chiefly Brit* or a similar label.

45b Follow spelling rules.

1 • *ie* vs. *ei*

To distinguish between *ie* and *ei*, use the familiar jingle:

I before *e*, except after *c*, or when pronounced "ay" as in *neighbor* and *weigh*.

i before *e*	believe	thief	hygiene
ei after *c*	ceiling	conceive	perceive
ei sounded as "ay"	sleigh	eight	beige

Exceptions For some exceptions, remember this sentence:

The weird foreigner neither seizes leisure nor forfeits height.

2 • Final *e*

When adding an ending to a word with a final *e*, drop the *e* if the ending begins with a vowel:

advise + able = advisable   surprise + ing = surprising

Keep the *e* if the ending begins with a consonant:

care + ful = care̲ful   like + ly = like̲ly

Exceptions Retain the *e* after a soft *c* or *g*, to keep the sound of the consonant soft rather than hard: *courageous, changeable.* And drop the *e* before a consonant when the *e* is preceded by another vowel: *argue + ment = argu̲ment, true + ly = truly.*

3 • Final *y*

When adding an ending to a word with a final *y*, change the *y* to *i* if it follows a consonant:

beauty, beautie̲s   worry, worrie̲d   supply, supplie̲s

But keep the *y* if it follows a vowel, if it ends a proper name, or if the ending is *-ing:*

day, day̲s   Minsky, Minsky̲s   cry, cry̲ing

4 • Final consonants

When adding an ending to a one-syllable word ending in a consonant, double the final consonant when it follows a single vowel. Otherwise, don't double the consonant.

slap, slapp̲ing   park, park̲ing   pair, pair̲ed

In words of more than one syllable, double the final consonant when it follows a single vowel *and* ends a stressed syllable once the new ending is added. Otherwise, don't double the consonant.

refer, referr̲ing   refer, refer̲ence   relent, relent̲ed

5 • Prefixes

When adding a prefix, do not drop a letter from or add a letter to the original word:

u̲nnecessary   d̲isappoint   m̲isspell

6 • Plurals

Most nouns form plurals by adding *s* to the singular form. Add *es* for the plural of nouns ending in *s, sh, ch,* or *x.*

boy, boy̲s   kiss, kisse̲s   church, churche̲s

Nouns ending in *o* preceded by a vowel usually form the plural with *s.* Those ending in *o* preceded by a consonant usually form the plural with *es.*

sp
45b

ratio, ratios   hero, heroes

Some very common nouns form irregular plurals.

child, children   woman, women   mouse, mice

Some English nouns that were originally Italian, Greek, Latin, or French form the plural according to their original language:

analysis, analyses   criterion, criteria   piano, pianos
basis, bases   datum, data   thesis, theses
crisis, crises   medium, media

A few such nouns may form irregular *or* regular plurals: for instance, *index, indices, indexes*; *curriculum, curricula, curriculums*. The regular plural is more contemporary.

With compound nouns, add *s* to the main word of the compound. Sometimes this main word is not the last word.

city-states   fathers-in-law   passersby

◖CULTURE LANGUAGE◗ Noncount nouns do not form plurals, either regularly (with an added *s*) or irregularly. Examples of noncount nouns are *equipment, intelligence,* and *wealth.* See pages 312–13.

EXERCISE 45.1
Using correct spellings

Select the correct spelling from the choices in brackets, referring as needed to the list of words on pages 392–93, the preceding rules, or a dictionary. Answers to starred items appear at the end of the book. (You can do this exercise online at *ablongman.com/littlebrown*.)

Example:

The boat [passed, past] us so fast that we rocked violently in [its, it's] wake.

The boat passed us so fast that we rocked violently in its wake.

*1. Science [affects, effects] many [important, importent] aspects of our lives.
*2. Many people have a [pore, poor] understanding of the [role, roll] of scientific breakthroughs in [their, they're] health.
*3. Many people [beleive, believe] that [docters, doctors] are more [responsable, responsible] for [improvements, improvments] in health care than scientists are.
*4. But scientists in the [labratory, laboratory] have made crucial steps in the search for [knowlege, knowledge] about human health and [medecine, medicine].
*5. For example, one scientist [who's, whose] discoveries have [affected, effected] many people is Ulf Von Euler.

6. In the 1950s Von Euler's discovery of certain hormones [lead, led] to the invention of the birth control pill.

7. Von Euler's work was used by John Rock, who [developed, developed] the first birth control pill and influenced family [planing, planning].

8. Von Euler also discovered the [principal, principle] neurotransmitter that controls the heartbeat.

9. Another scientist, Hans Selye, showed what [affect, effect] stress can have on the body.

10. His findings have [lead, led] to methods of [baring, bearing] stress.

EXERCISE 45.2
Working with a spelling checker

Try your computer's spelling checker on the following paragraph. Type the paragraph or download it from *ablongman.com/littlebrown*, and run it through your spelling checker. Then proofread it to correct the errors missed by the checker. (Hint: There are fourteen errors in all.) Answers to the starred sentences appear at the end of the book.

*The whether effects all of us, though it's affects are different for different people. *Some people love a fare day with warm temperatures and sunshine. *They revel in spending a hole day outside without the threat of rein. Other people prefer dark, rainy daze. They relish the opportunity to slow down and here they're inner thoughts. Most people agree, however, that to much of one kind of whether—reign, sun, snow, or clouds—makes them board.

46 The Hyphen

hyph
46a

Where do hyphens go?

Hyphens belong in some compound words and with some prefixes and suffixes. They also divide words at the ends of lines.

46a Use the hyphen in some compound words.

1 • Compound adjectives

When two or more words serve together as a single modifier before a noun, a hyphen forms the modifying words clearly into a unit.

http://www.ablongman.com/littlebrown ▶

Visit the companion Web site for more help and an electronic exercise on the hyphen.

She is a well⊙known actor.
Some Spanish⊖speaking students work as translators.

When such a compound adjective follows the noun, the hyphen is unnecessary.

The actor is well○known.
Many students are Spanish◯speaking.

The hyphen is also unnecessary in a compound modifier containing an -*ly* adverb, even before the noun: *clearly⊙defined terms.*

When part of a compound adjective appears only once in two or more parallel compound adjectives, hyphens indicate which words the reader should mentally join with the missing part.

School-age children should have eight⊖ or nine⊖o'clock bedtimes.

2 • Fractions and compound numbers

Hyphens join the numerator and denominator of fractions: *one⊖half, three⊖fourths.* Hyphens also join the parts of the whole numbers *twenty⊙one* to *ninety⊙nine.*

3 • Prefixes and suffixes

Do not use hyphens with prefixes except as follows:

- **With the prefixes** *self-,* *all-,* **and** *ex-:* *self⊖control, all⊖inclusive, ex⊖student.*
- **With a prefix before a capitalized word:** *un⊖American.*
- **With a capital letter before a word:** *T⊖shirt.*
- **To prevent misreading:** *de⊖emphasize, re⊖create a story.*

The only suffix that regularly requires a hyphen is *-elect,* as in *president⊖elect.*

***

46b   Use the hyphen to divide words at the ends of lines.

You can avoid very short lines in your documents by dividing some words between the end of one line and the beginning of the next. You can set a word processor to divide words automatically at

---

┌─ **Key term** ──────────────────────────────

compound word A word expressing a combination of ideas, such as *cross-reference* or *crossroad.*

appropriate breaks (in the Tools menu, select Language and then Hyphenation). To divide words manually, follow these guidelines:

- **Divide words only between syllables**—for instance, *win-dows,* not *wi-ndows.* Check a dictionary for correct syllable breaks.
- **Never divide a one-syllable word.**
- **Leave at least two letters on the first line and three on the second line.** If a word cannot be divided to follow this rule (for instance, *a-bus-er*), don't divide it.

If you must break an electronic address—for instance, in a source citation—do so only after a slash or before a period. Do not hyphenate, because readers may perceive any added hyphen as part of the address.

Not   http://www.library.miami.edu/staff/lmc/soc-
      race.html

But   http://www.library.miami.edu/staff/lmc/
      socrace.html

Or   http://www.library.miami.edu/staff/lmc/socrace
      .html

EXERCISE 46.1
Using hyphens

Insert hyphens wherever they are needed, and delete them where they are not needed. If a sentence is already correct as given, mark the number preceding it. Answers to starred items appear at the end of the book. (You can do this exercise online at *ablongman.com/littlebrown*.)

Example:

Elephants have twelve inch long teeth, but they have only four of them.

Elephants have twelve⊖inch⊖long teeth, but they have only four of them.

*1. The African elephant is well known for its size.
*2. Both male and female African elephants can grow to a ten-foot height.
*3. The non African elephants of south central Asia are somewhat smaller.
*4. A fourteen or fifteen year old elephant has reached sexual maturity.
*5. The elephant life span is about sixty five or seventy years.

6. A newborn elephant calf weighs two to three hundred pounds.
7. It stands about thirty three inches high.
8. A two hundred pound, thirty three inch baby is quite a big baby.
9. Unfortunately, elephants are often killed for their ivory tusks, and partly as a result they are an increasingly-endangered species.
10. African governments have made tusk and ivory selling illegal.

hyph
46b

47 Capital Letters

Although mostly straightforward, the rules for capital letters can sometimes be tricky: it's *South* for a specific geographical region (*I am from the South*) but *south* for a direction (*Birds fly south*).

The conventions described in this chapter and a desk dictionary can help you decide whether to capitalize a particular word in most writing. Consult the style guides listed on pages 478–79 for the requirements of particular disciplines.

Note A grammar and style checker will flag overused capital letters and missing capitals at the beginnings of sentences. It will also spot missing capitals at the beginnings of proper nouns and adjectives—*if* the nouns and adjectives are in the checker's dictionary. For example, a checker caught *christianity* and *europe* but not *china* (for the country) or *Stephen king*.

CULTURE LANGUAGE Conventions of capitalization vary from language to language. English, for instance, is the only language to capitalize the first-person singular pronoun (*I*), and its practice of capitalizing proper nouns but not most common nouns also distinguishes it from some other languages.

47a Capitalize the first word of every sentence.

> Every writer should own a good dictionary.

cap

47a

When quoting other writers, you should reproduce the capital letters beginning their sentences or indicate that you have altered the source's capitalization. Whenever possible, integrate the quotation into your own sentence so that its capitalization coincides with yours:

> "Psychotherapists often overlook the benefits of self-deception," the author argues.

> The author argues that "the benefits of self-deception" are not always recognized by psychotherapists. [Do not capitalize a phrase quoted from inside a sentence.]

If you need to alter the capitalization in the source, indicate the change with brackets.

---

http://www.ablongman.com/littlebrown ▶

Visit the companion Web site for more help and an electronic exercise on capital letters.

"[T]he benefits of self-deception" are not always recognized by psychotherapists, the author argues.

The author argues that "[p]sychotherapists often overlook the benefits of self-deception."

Note Capitalization of questions in a series is optional. Both of the following examples are correct:

Is the population a hundred? Two hundred? More?
Is the population a hundred? two hundred? more?

Also optional is capitalization of the first word in a complete sentence after a colon.

47b   Capitalize proper nouns, proper adjectives, and words used as essential parts of proper nouns.

1 • Proper nouns and proper adjectives

Proper nouns name specific persons, places, and things: *Shakespeare, China, World War I*. **Proper adjectives** are formed from some proper nouns: *Shakespearean, Chinese*. Capitalize all proper nouns and proper adjectives but not the articles (*a, an, the*) that precede them.

Proper nouns and adjectives to be capitalized

Specific persons and things

Stephen King   Boulder Dam
Napoleon Bonaparte   the Empire State Building

Specific places and geographical regions

New York City   the Mediterranean Sea
China   the Northeast, the South
But: northeast of the city, going south

Days of the week, months, holidays

Monday   Yom Kippur
May   Christmas

Government offices or departments and institutions

House of Representatives   Polk Municipal Court
Department of Defense   Northeast High School

Political, social, athletic, and other organizations and associations and their members

Democratic Party, Democrats   League of Women Voters
Sierra Club   Boston Celtics
B'nai B'rith   Chicago Symphony Orchestra
(continued)

cap

47b

Proper nouns and adjectives to be capitalized
(continued)

Races, nationalities, and their languages

Native American	Germans
African American	Swahili
Caucasian	Italian

But: blacks, whites

Religions, their followers, and terms for the sacred

Christianity, Christians	God
Catholicism, Catholics	Allah
Judaism, Orthodox Jews	the Bible [*but* biblical]
Islam, Muslims	the Koran, the Qur'an

Historical events, documents, periods, movements

the Vietnam War	the Renaissance
the Constitution	the Romantic Movement

2 • Common nouns used as essential parts of proper nouns

Capitalize the common nouns *street, avenue, park, river, ocean, lake, company, college, county,* and *memorial* when they are part of proper nouns naming specific places or institutions:

Main Street	Ford Motor Company
Central Park	Madison College
Mississippi River	George Washington Memorial

cap

47b

3 • Compass directions

Capitalize compass directions only when they name a specific region instead of a general direction:

Students from the West often melt in eastern humidity.

4 • Relationships

Capitalize the names of relationships only when they precede or replace proper names:

Our aunt scolded us for disrespecting Father and Uncle Jake.

5 • Titles with persons' names

Before a person's name, capitalize his or her title. After or apart from the name, do not capitalize the title.

Professor Otto Osborne	Otto Osborne, a professor
Doctor Jane Covington	Jane Covington, a doctor
Governor Ella Moore	Ella Moore, the governor

Note Many writers capitalize a title denoting very high rank even when it follows a name or is used alone: *Ronald Reagan, past President of the United States.*

47c   Capitalize most words in titles and subtitles of works.

Within your text, capitalize all the words in a title *except* the following: articles (*a, an, the*); *to* in infinitives; and connecting words (prepositions and conjunctions) of fewer than five letters. Capitalize even these short words when they are the first or last word in a title or when they fall after a colon or semicolon.

"Courtship Through the Ages"	*Management: A New Theory*
A Diamond Is Forever	"Once More to the Lake"
"Knowing Whom to Ask"	*An End to Live For*
Learning from Las Vegas	*File Under Architecture*

Note The style guides of the academic disciplines have their own rules for capitals in titles. For instance, MLA style for English and some other humanities capitalizes all subordinating conjunctions but no prepositions. In addition, APA style for the social sciences capitalizes only the first word and proper names in book and article titles within source citations (see p. 536).

47d   Use capitals according to convention in online communication.

cap
47d

Online messages written in all-capital letters or with no capital letters are difficult to read. Further, messages in all-capital letters may be taken as rude (see also p. 160). Use capital letters according to rules 47a–47c in all your online communication.

EXERCISE 47.1
Revising: Capitals
Edit the following sentences to correct errors in capitalization. Consult a dictionary if you are in doubt. If a sentence is already correct as given, mark the number preceding it. Answers to starred items appear at the end of the book. (You can do this exercise online at *ablongman.com/ littlebrown.*)

Example:

The first book on the reading list is mark twain's *a connecticut yankee in king arthur's court.*

The first book on the reading list is Mark Twain's *A Connecticut Yankee in King Arthur's Court.*

*1. San Antonio, texas, is a thriving city in the southwest.

*2. The city has always offered much to tourists interested in the roots of spanish settlement in the new world.

*3. The alamo is one of five Catholic Missions built by Priests to convert native americans and to maintain spain's claims in the area.

*4. But the alamo is more famous for being the site of an 1836 battle that helped to create the republic of Texas.

*5. Many of the nearby Streets, such as Crockett street, are named for men who died in that Battle.

6. The Hemisfair plaza and the San Antonio river link tourist and convention facilities.

7. Restaurants, Hotels, and shops line the River. the haunting melodies of "Una paloma blanca" and "malagueña" lure passing tourists into Casa rio and other mexican restaurants.

8. The university of Texas at San Antonio has expanded, and a Medical Center lies in the Northwest part of the city.

9. Sea World, on the west side of San Antonio, entertains grandparents, fathers and mothers, and children with the antics of dolphins and seals.

10. The City has attracted high-tech industry, creating a corridor between san antonio and austin.

---

48 Underlining or Italics

Is it <u>Hamlet</u> or *Hamlet* or "Hamlet"?

As a work that appears independently—a play—*Hamlet* should be italicized or underlined, depending on the preference of your instructor or the discipline you're writing in. (Quotation marks are used for shorter works; see p. 380.) This chapter provides general guidelines for using underlining or italics.

---

http://www.ablongman.com/littlebrown ▶

Visit the companion Web site for more help and an electronic exercise on underlining or italics.

Note Grammar and style checkers cannot recognize problems with underlining or italics. Check your work yourself to ensure that you have used highlighting appropriately.

48a Use underlining or italics consistently and appropriately for your writing situation.

Italic type is now used almost universally in academic and public writing. Still, some academic style guides, notably the *MLA Handbook,* continue to prefer underlining, especially in source citations. The other style discussed in this book, APA, calls for italics. Ask your instructor for his or her preference. (Underlining is used for the examples in this chapter because it is easier to see than italics.)

Depending on your instructor's preferences, use either italics or underlining consistently throughout a document. For instance, if you are writing an English paper and following MLA style for underlining in source citations, use underlining in the body of your paper as well.

48b Underline or italicize the titles of works that appear independently.

Within your text underline or italicize the titles of works, such as books and periodicals, that are published, released, or produced separately from other works. (See the box below.) Use quotation marks for all other titles.

und
48b

Titles to be underlined or italicized

Other titles should be placed in quotation marks (see p. 380).

Books	Computer software
War and Peace	Microsoft Internet Explorer
And the Band Played On	Acrobat Reader
Plays	**Pamphlets**
Hamlet	The Truth About Alcoholism
The Phantom of the Opera	
	Long musical works
Web sites	Tchaikovsky's Swan Lake
Friends of Prufrock	*But:* Symphony in C
Google	*(continued)*

Titles to be underlined or italicized
(continued)

Television and radio programs	**Published speeches**
The Shadow	Lincoln's Gettysburg Address
NBC Sports Hour	
	Movies and videos
Long poems	Schindler's List
Beowulf	How to Relax
Paradise Lost	
	Works of visual art
Periodicals	Michelangelo's David
Time	the Mona Lisa
Philadelphia Inquirer	

Exceptions Legal documents, the Bible, the Koran, and their parts are generally not underlined or italicized:

Not   We studied the Book of Revelation in the Bible.

But   We studied the Book of Revelation in the Bible.

48c Underline or italicize the names of ships, aircraft, spacecraft, and trains.

Challenger	Orient Express	Queen Elizabeth 2
Apollo XI	Montrealer	Spirit of St. Louis

48d Underline or italicize foreign words that are not part of the English language.

Underline or italicize a foreign expression that has not been absorbed into English. A dictionary will say whether a word is still considered foreign to English.

The scientific name for the brown trout is Salmo trutta. [The Latin scientific names for plants and animals are always underlined or italicized.]

The Latin De gustibus non est disputandum translates roughly as "There's no accounting for taste."

48e Underline or italicize words or characters named as words.

Use underlining or italics to indicate that you are citing a character or word as a word rather than using it for its meaning. Words you are defining fall under this convention.

und

48e

The word <u>syzygy</u> refers to a straight line formed by three celestial bodies, as in the alignment of the earth, sun, and moon.

Some people say <u>th</u>, as in <u>thought</u>, with a faint <u>s</u> or <u>f</u> sound.

48f   Occasionally, underlining or italics may be used for emphasis.

Underlining or italics can stress an important word or phrase, especially in reporting how someone said something. But use such emphasis very rarely, or your writing may seem overemotional.

48g   In online communication, use alternatives for underlining or italics.

Electronic mail and other forms of online communication sometimes do not allow conventional highlighting such as underlining or italics for the purposes described in this chapter. (On Web sites, for instance, underlining indicates a link to another site.)

To distinguish book titles and other elements that usually require underlining or italics, type an underscore before and after the element: *Measurements coincide with those in _Joule's Handbook_.* You can also emphasize words with asterisks before and after: *I *will not* be able to attend.*

Don't use all-capital letters for emphasis; they yell too loudly. (See also p. 160.)

EXERCISE 48.1
Revising: Underlining or italics

Underline or italicize words and phrases as needed in the following sentences, or delete underlining from any words or phrases that are underlined unnecessarily. Note that some highlighting is correct as given. Answers to starred sentences appear at the end of the book. (You can do this exercise online at *ablongman.com/littlebrown*.)

Example:
Of Hitchcock's movies, Psycho is the scariest.
Of Hitchcock's movies, <u>Psycho</u> is the scariest.

*1. Of the many Vietnam veterans who are writers, Oliver Stone is perhaps the most famous for writing and directing the films Platoon and Born on the Fourth of July.

*2. Tim O'Brien has written short stories for Esquire, GQ, and Massachusetts Review.

*3. Going After Cacciato is O'Brien's dreamlike novel about the horrors of combat.

und

48g

*4. The word Vietnam is technically two words (<u>Viet</u> and <u>Nam</u>), but most American writers spell it as <u>one</u> word.

*5. American writers use words or phrases borrowed from Vietnamese, such as di di mau ("go quickly") or dinky dau ("crazy").

6. Philip Caputo's <u>gripping</u> account of his service in Vietnam appears in the book A Rumor of War.

7. Caputo's book was made into a television movie, also titled <u>A Rumor of War</u>.

8. David Rabe's plays—including The Basic Training of Pavlo Hummel, Streamers, and Sticks and Bones—depict the effects of the war <u>not only</u> on the soldiers <u>but</u> on their families.

9. Called the <u>poet laureate of the Vietnam war</u>, Steve Mason has published two collections of poems: Johnny's Song and Warrior for Peace.

10. The Washington Post published <u>rave</u> reviews of Veteran's Day, an autobiography by Rod Kane.

49 Abbreviations

Is it *in.* or *inch?* Is it *dr.* or *doctor?*

ab
49

In academic writing, appropriate abbreviations depend partly on the discipline: *in.* might be a suitable abbreviation in the text of a technical document, but not in a nontechnical document. Appropriate abbreviations also depend on context: *dr.* is okay before a noun (*Dr. Jones*) but not otherwise (*The <u>doctor</u> is in*).

The guidelines in this chapter pertain to the text of a nontechnical document. Consult one of the style guides listed on pages 478–79 for the requirements of the discipline you are writing in.

Usage varies, but writers increasingly omit periods from abbreviations of two or more words written in all-capital letters: *US, BA, USMC.* See page 346 on punctuating abbreviations.

Note A grammar and style checker may flag some abbreviations, such as *ft.* (for *foot*) and *st.* (for *street*). A spelling checker will flag abbreviations it does not recognize. But neither checker can judge whether an abbreviation is appropriate for your writing situation.

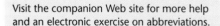

http://www.ablongman.com/littlebrown ▶

Visit the companion Web site for more help and an electronic exercise on abbreviations.

49a **Use standard abbreviations for titles immediately before and after proper names.**

Before the name	After the name
Dr. Michael Hsu	Michael Hsu, MD
Mr., Mrs., Ms., Hon.,	DDS, DVM, PhD,
St., Rev., Msgr., Gen.	EdD, OSB, SJ, Sr., Jr.

Do not use abbreviations such as *Rev., Hon., Prof., Rep., Sen., Dr.,* and *St.* (for *Saint*) unless they appear before a proper name.

49b **Familiar abbreviations and acronyms are acceptable in most writing.**

An **acronym** is an abbreviation that spells a pronounceable word, such as WHO, NATO, and AIDS. These and other abbreviations using initials are acceptable in most writing as long as they are familiar to readers.

Institutions	LSU, UCLA, TCU
Organizations	CIA, FBI, YMCA, AFL-CIO
Corporations	IBM, CBS, ITT
People	JFK, LBJ, FDR
Countries	US, USA

Note If a name or term (such as *operating room*) appears often in a piece of writing, then its abbreviation (*OR*) can cut down on extra words. Spell out the full term at its first appearance, indicate its abbreviation in parentheses, and then use the abbreviation.

ab
49d

49c **Use *BC, BCE, AD, CE, AM, PM, no.,* and *$* only with specific dates and numbers.**

44 BC	44 BCE	11:26 AM (*or* a.m.)	no. 36 (*or* No. 36)
AD 1492	1492 CE	8:05 PM (*or* p.m.)	$7.41

BC ("before Christ"), BCE ("before the common era"), and CE ("common era") always follow a date. In contrast, AD (*anno Domini,* Latin for "in the year of the Lord") precedes a date.

49d **Generally reserve Latin abbreviations for source citations and comments in parentheses.**

i.e.	*id est:*	that is
cf.	*confer:*	compare

e.g.	*exempli gratia:* for example
et al.	*et alii:* and others
etc.	*et cetera:* and so forth
NB	*nota bene:* note well

He said he would be gone a fortnight (i.e., two weeks).
Bloom et al., editors, *Anthology of Light Verse*
Trees, too, are susceptible to disease (e.g., Dutch elm disease).

Some writers avoid these abbreviations in formal writing, even within parentheses.

49e Use *Inc., Bros., Co.,* or & (for *and*) only in official names of business firms.

Not The Santini <u>bros.</u> operate a large moving firm in New York City <u>&</u> environs.

But The Santini <u>brothers</u> operate a large moving firm in New York City <u>and</u> environs.

Or Santini <u>Bros.</u> is a large moving firm in New York City <u>and</u> environs.

49f Generally spell out units of measurement and names of places, calendar designations, people, and courses.

In most academic, general, and business writing, the types of words listed below should always be spelled out. (In source citations and technical writing, however, the first three categories are more often abbreviated.)

ab
49f

Units of measurement
The dog is thirty <u>inches</u> [not <u>in.</u>] high.

Geographical names
The publisher is in <u>Massachusetts</u> [not <u>Mass.</u> or <u>MA</u>].

Names of days, months, and holidays
The truce was signed on <u>Tuesday</u> [not <u>Tues.</u>], <u>April</u> [not <u>Apr.</u>] 16.

Names of people
<u>Robert</u> [not <u>Robt.</u>] Frost writes accessible poems.

Courses of instruction
I'm majoring in <u>political science</u> [not <u>poli. sci.</u>].

EXERCISE 49.1
Revising: Abbreviations

Revise the following sentences as needed to correct inappropriate use of abbreviations for nontechnical writing. If a sentence is already correct as given, mark the number preceding it. Answers to starred items appear at the end of the book. (You can do this exercise online at *ablongman.com/ littlebrown*.)

Example:

One prof. lectured for five hrs.
One <u>professor</u> lectured for five <u>hours</u>.

*1. In an issue of *Science* magazine, Dr. Virgil L. Sharpton discusses a theory that could help explain the extinction of dinosaurs.

*2. About 65 mill. yrs. ago, a comet or asteroid crashed into the earth.

*3. The result was a huge crater about 10 km. (6.2 mi.) deep in the Gulf of Mex.

*4. Sharpton's new measurements suggest that the crater is 50 pct. larger than scientists had previously believed.

*5. Indeed, 20-yr.-old drilling cores reveal that the crater is about 186 mi. wide, roughly the size of Conn.

6. The space object was traveling more than 100,000 miles per hour and hit earth with the impact of 100 to 300 megatons of TNT.

7. On impact, 200,000 cubic km. of rock and soil were vaporized or thrown into the air.

8. That's the equivalent of 2.34 bill. cubic ft. of matter.

9. The impact would have created 400-ft. tidal waves across the Atl. Ocean, temps. higher than 20,000 degs., and powerful earthquakes.

10. Sharpton theorizes that the dust, vapor, and smoke from this impact blocked the sun's rays for mos., cooled the earth, and thus resulted in the death of the dinosaurs.

num
50

50 Numbers

Is it *28* or *twenty-eight*?

Expressing numbers in numerals (*28*) or in words (*twenty-eight*) is often a matter of style in a discipline: the technical disciplines more often prefer numerals, and the nontechnical disciplines

http://www.ablongman.com/littlebrown ▶

Visit the companion Web site for more help
and an electronic exercise on numbers.

more often prefer words. All disciplines use many more numerals in source citations than in the document text.

Note Grammar and style checkers will flag numerals beginning sentences and can be customized to ignore or to look for numerals. But they can't tell you whether numerals or spelled-out numbers are appropriate for your writing situation.

50a   Use numerals according to standard practice in the field you are writing in.

Always use numerals for numbers that require more than two words to spell out:

> The leap year has <u>366</u> days.
> The population of Minot, North Dakota, is about <u>32,800</u>.

In nontechnical academic writing, spell out numbers of one or two words:

> <u>Twelve</u> nations signed the treaty.
> The ball game drew <u>forty-two thousand</u> people. [A hyphenated number may be considered one word.]

In much business writing, use numerals for all numbers over ten: *five reasons, 11 participants*. In technical academic and business writing, such as in science and engineering, use numerals for all numbers over ten, and use numerals for zero through nine when they refer to exact measurements: *2 liters, 1 hour*. (Consult one of the style guides listed on pp. 478–79 for more details.)

Note Use a combination of numerals and words for round numbers over a million: *26 million, 2.45 billion*. And use either all numerals or all words when several numbers appear together in a passage, even if convention would require a mixture.

CULTURE LANGUAGE In standard American English, a comma separates the numerals in long numbers (*26,000*), and a period functions as a decimal point (*2.06*).

50b   Use numerals according to convention for dates, addresses, and other information.

Days and years		The time of day	
June 18, 1985	AD 12	9:00 AM	3:45 PM
456 BC	2010		

num
50b

Addresses
355 Clinton Avenue
Washington, DC 20036

Exact amounts of money
$3.5 million $4.50

Scores and statistics
21 to 7   a ratio of 8 to 1
a mean of 26

Decimals, percentages, and
fractions

22.5   3½
48% (*or* 48 percent)

Pages, chapters, volumes, acts,
scenes, lines

Chapter 9, page 123
Hamlet, act 5, scene 3

Exceptions Round dollar or cent amounts of only a few words may be expressed in words: *seventeen dollars; sixty cents*. When the word *o'clock* is used for the time of day, also express the number in words: *two o'clock* (not *2 o'clock*).

50c   Spell out numbers that begin sentences.

For clarity, spell out any number that begins a sentence. If the number requires more than two words, reword the sentence so that the number falls later and can be expressed as a numeral.

Not   3.9 billion people live in Asia.
But   The population of Asia is 3.9 billion.

EXERCISE 50.1
Revising: Numbers

Revise the following sentences so that numbers are used appropriately for nontechnical writing. If a sentence is already correct as given, mark the number preceding it. Answers to starred items appear at the end of the book. (You can do this exercise online at *ablongman.com/littlebrown*.)

Example:

Addie paid two hundred and five dollars for used scuba gear.
Addie paid $205 for used scuba gear.

*1. The planet Saturn is nine hundred million miles, or nearly one billion five hundred million kilometers, from the sun.
*2. A year on Saturn equals almost thirty of our years.
*3. Thus, Saturn orbits the sun only two and four-tenths times during the average human life span.
*4. It travels in its orbit at about twenty-one thousand six hundred miles per hour.
*5. 15 to 20 times denser than Earth's core, Saturn's core measures 17,000 miles across.

num
50c

6. The temperature at Saturn's cloud tops is minus one hundred seventy degrees Fahrenheit.

7. In nineteen hundred thirty-three, astronomers found on Saturn's surface a huge white spot 2 times the size of Earth and 7 times the size of Mercury.

8. Saturn's famous rings reflect almost seventy percent of the sunlight that approaches the planet.

9. The ring system is almost forty thousand miles wide, beginning 8,800 miles from the planet's visible surface and ending forty-seven thousand miles from that surface.

10. The Cassini-Huygens spacecraft traveled more than eight hundred and twenty million miles to explore and photograph Saturn.

7

Research and Documentation

How should I approach and manage a research project?

Like many writers, you may find it helpful to approach research writing as a detective approaches a new case. The mystery is the answer to a question you care about. The search for an answer leads you to consider what others think about your subject, but you do more than simply report their views. You build on them to develop and support your own opinion.

Your investigation will be more productive and enjoyable if you take some steps described in this chapter: plan your work (below), keep a research journal (facing page), find an appropriate subject and research question (p. 418), set goals for your research (p. 420), and keep a working, annotated bibliography (p. 422).

51a Plan the research process.

Research writing is a *writing* process:

- **You work within a particular situation of subject, purpose, audience, and other factors** (see Chapter 1).
- **You gather ideas and information about your subject** (Chapter 2).
- **You focus and arrange your ideas** (Chapter 3).
- **You draft to explore your meaning** (Chapter 4).
- **You revise and edit to develop, shape, and polish** (Chapter 5).

Although the process seems neatly sequential in this list, you know from experience that the stages overlap—that, for instance, you may begin drafting before you've gathered all the information you expect to find, and then while drafting you may discover a source that causes you to rethink your approach. Anticipating the process of research writing can free you to be flexible in your search and open to discoveries.

A thoughtful plan and systematic procedures can help you follow through on the diverse activities of research writing. One step is to make a schedule like the one opposite that apportions the available time to the necessary work. You can estimate that each segment marked off by a horizontal line will occupy *roughly* one-

51a

http://www.ablongman.com/littlebrown ▶

Visit the companion Web site for more help and an electronic exercise on research strategy.

quarter of the total time—for example, a week in a four-week assignment. The most unpredictable segments are the first two, so it's wise to get started early enough to accommodate the unexpected.

Complete
by:

———   1. Setting a schedule and beginning a research journal (here and below)
———   2. Finding a researchable subject and question (next page)
———   3. Setting goals for sources (p. 420)
———   4. Finding print and electronic sources (p. 425), and making a working, annotated bibliography (p. 422)

———   5. Evaluating and synthesizing sources (pp. 446, 457)
———   6. Gathering information from sources (p. 459), often using summary, paraphrase, and direct quotation (p. 460)
———   7. Taking steps to avoid plagiarism (p. 470)

———   8. Developing a thesis statement and creating a structure (p. 480)
———   9. Drafting the paper (p. 481), integrating summaries, paraphrases, and direct quotations into your ideas (p. 465)

——— 10. Revising and editing the paper (p. 481)
——— 11. Citing sources in your text (p. 477)
——— 12. Preparing the list of works cited or references (p. 477)
——— 13. Preparing the final manuscript (p. 482)
——— Final paper due

You can download the schedule from *ablongman.com/littlebrown*. Use a duplicate to plan and time the specific steps of each research project you work on.

51b   Keep a research journal.

While working on a research project, carry index cards or a notebook with you at all times to use as a **research journal,** a place to record your activities and ideas. (See p. 10 on journal keeping.) In the journal's dated entries, you can write about the sources you consult, the leads you want to pursue, and any difficulties you encounter. Most important, you can record your thoughts about sources, leads, difficulties, new directions, relationships, and anything else that strikes you. The very act of writing in the journal can expand and clarify your thinking.

Note The research journal is the place to track and develop your own ideas. To avoid mixing up your thoughts and those of others, keep separate notes on what your sources actually say, using one of the methods discussed on pages 459–60.

51c   Find a researchable subject and question.

Before reading this section, you may want to review the suggestions given in Chapter 1 for finding and narrowing a writing subject (pp. 4–6). Generally, the same procedure applies to writing any kind of research paper. However, selecting and limiting a subject for a research paper can present special opportunities and problems. And before you proceed with your subject, you'll want to transform it into a question that can guide your search for sources.

1 • Appropriate subject

Seek a research subject that interests you and that you care about. (It may be a subject you've already written about without benefit of research.) Starting with your own views will motivate you, and you will be a participant in a dialog when you begin examining sources.

When you settle on a subject, ask the following questions about it. For each requirement, there are corresponding pitfalls.

- **Are ample sources of information available on the subject?**

  Avoid very recent subjects, such as a newly announced medical discovery or a breaking story in today's newspaper.

- **Does the subject encourage research in the kinds and number of sources required by the assignment?**

  Avoid (*a*) subjects that depend entirely on personal opinion and experience, such as the virtues of your hobby, and (*b*) subjects that require research in only one source, such as a straight factual biography.

- **Will the subject lead you to an objective assessment of sources and to defensible conclusions?**

  Avoid subjects that rest entirely on belief or prejudice, such as when human life begins or why women (or men) are superior. Your readers are unlikely to be swayed from their own beliefs.

- **Does the subject suit the length of paper assigned and the time given for research and writing?**

Avoid broad subjects that have too many sources to survey adequately, such as a major event in history.

2 • Research question

Asking a question about your subject can give direction to your research by focusing your thinking on a particular approach. To discover your question, consider what about your subject intrigues or perplexes you, what you'd like to know more about. (See the next page for suggestions on using your own knowledge.)

Try to narrow your research question so that you can answer it in the time and space you have available. The question *How is the Internet affecting business?* is very broad, encompassing issues as diverse as electronic commerce, information management, and employee training. In contrast, the question *How does Internet commerce benefit consumers?* or *How, if at all, should Internet commerce be taxed?* is much narrower. Each question also requires more than a simple yes-or-no answer, so that answering, even tentatively, demands thought about pros and cons, causes and effects.

As you read and write, your question will undoubtedly evolve to reflect your increasing knowledge of the subject, and eventually its answer will become your main idea, or thesis statement (see p. 480).

EXERCISE 51.1
Finding a subject and question

Choose three of the following broad subjects (or three subjects of your own), and narrow each of them to at least one subject and question suitable for beginning work on a research paper. For more sample subjects, see Chapter 1, page 6.

1. Business espionage
2. The effect of television on professional sports
3. Stem-cell research
4. Immigrants in the United States
5. Hazardous substances in the workplace
6. Science fiction
7. Alternative fuels
8. Successes in cancer research
9. Comic film actors
10. An unsolved crime
11. Immunization of children
12. Male and female heroes in modern fiction
13. Computers and the privacy of the individual
14. Gothic or romance novels in the nineteenth and twenty-first centuries
15. The social responsibility of business

51c

51d Set goals for your sources.

Before you start looking for sources, consider what you already know about your subject and where you are likely to find information on it.

1 • Your own knowledge

Discovering what you already know about your subject will guide you in discovering what you don't know and need to research. Take some time to spell out facts you have learned, opinions you have heard or read elsewhere, and of course your own opinions. Use one or more of the discovery techniques discussed in Chapter 2 to explore and develop your ideas: keeping a journal, observing your surroundings, freewriting, brainstorming, clustering, asking questions, and thinking critically.

When you've explored your thoughts, make a list of questions for which you don't have answers, whether factual (*What laws govern taxes in Internet commerce?*) or more open-ended (*Who benefits from a tax-free Internet? Who doesn't benefit?*). These questions will give you clues about the sources you need to look for first.

2 • Kinds of sources

For many research projects, you'll want to consult a mix of sources, as described below. You may start by seeking the outlines of your subject—the range and depth of opinions about it—in reference works and articles in popular periodicals or through a Web search. Then, as you refine your views and your research question, you'll move on to more specialized sources, such as scholarly books and periodicals and your own interviews or surveys. (See pp. 429–46 for more on each kind of source.)

Library and Internet sources

The print and electronic sources available through your library —mainly reference works, periodicals, and books—have two big advantages over most of what you'll find on the Internet: they are cataloged and indexed for easy retrieval; and they are generally reliable, having been screened first by their publishers and then by the library's staff. In contrast, the Internet's retrieval systems are more difficult to use effectively, and Internet sources tend to be less reliable because most do not pass through any screening before being posted. (There are many exceptions, such as online scholarly journals and reference works. But these sources may be available through your library's Web site as well.)

Most instructors expect research writers to consult library sources. But they'll accept Internet sources, too, if you have used them judiciously. Even with its disadvantages, the Internet can be a valuable resource for primary sources, current information, and a diversity of views. For guidelines on evaluating both library and Internet sources, see pages 447–56.

Primary and secondary sources

As much as possible, you should rely on **primary sources,** or firsthand accounts: historical documents (letters, speeches, and so on), eyewitness reports, works of literature, reports on experiments or surveys conducted by the writer, or your own interviews, experiments, observations, or correspondence.

In contrast, **secondary sources** report and analyze information drawn from other sources, often primary ones: a reporter's summary of a controversial issue, a historian's account of a battle, a critic's reading of a poem, a physicist's evaluation of several studies. Secondary sources may contain helpful summaries and interpretations that direct, support, and extend your own thinking. However, most research-writing assignments expect your ideas to go beyond those in such sources.

Scholarly and popular sources

The scholarship of acknowledged experts is essential for depth, authority, and specificity. Most instructors expect students to emphasize scholarly sources in research. But the general-interest views and information of popular sources can help you apply more scholarly approaches to daily life.

- **Check the title.** Is it technical, or does it use a general vocabulary?
- **Check the publisher.** Is it a scholarly journal (such as *Education Forum*) or a publisher of scholarly books (such as Harvard University Press), or is it a popular magazine (such as *Time* or *Newsweek*) or a publisher of popular books (such as Little, Brown)?
- **Check the length of periodical articles.** Scholarly articles are generally much longer than magazine and newspaper articles.
- **Check the author.** Have you seen the name elsewhere, which might suggest that the author is an expert?
- **Check the electronic address.** Addresses, or URLs, for Internet sources often include an abbreviation that tells you something about the origin of the source: *edu* means the source comes from an educational institution, *gov* from a government body,

51d

org from a nonprofit organization, *com* from a commercial organization such as a corporation. The abbreviation is not a firm guide to the kind of source—*edu* sites, for instance, may include student papers and Web logs as well as works by scholars—but it can indicate the context. (See pp. 449–50 for more on types of online sources.)

Older and newer sources

Check the publication date. For most subjects a combination of older, established sources (such as books) and current sources (such as newspaper articles, interviews, or Web sites) will provide both background and up-to-date information. Only historical subjects or very current subjects require an emphasis on one extreme or another.

Impartial and biased sources

Seek a range of viewpoints. Sources that attempt to be impartial can offer an overview of your subject and trustworthy facts. Sources with clear biases can offer a diversity of opinion. Of course, to discover bias, you may have to read the source carefully (see pp. 448–56); but even a bibliographical listing can be informative.

- **Check the author.** You may have heard of the author as a respected researcher (thus more likely to be objective) or as a leading proponent of a certain view (less likely to be objective).
- **Check the title.** It may reveal something about point of view. (Consider these contrasting titles: "Keep the Internet Tax-Free" and "Taxation of Internet Commerce: Issues and Questions.")

Note Sources you find on the Internet must be approached with particular care. See pages 448–56.

Sources with helpful features

Depending on your topic and how far along your research is, you may want to look for sources with features such as illustrations (which can clarify important concepts), bibliographies (which can direct you to other sources), and indexes (which can help you develop keywords for electronic searches; see p. 427).

51e

51e   Keep a working, annotated bibliography.

To track where sources are and what they are, make a **working bibliography,** a file of books, articles, Web sites, and other possibilities. When you have a substantial file—say, ten to thirty sources—you can decide which ones seem most promising and look them up first.

1 • Source information

When you turn in your paper, you will be expected to attach a list of the sources you have used. So that readers can check or follow up on your sources, your list must include all the information needed to find the sources, in a format readers can understand. (See pp. 477–78.) The box below shows the information to record for each type of source so that you will not have to retrace your steps later.

Information for a working bibliography

For books

Library call number
Name(s) of author(s), editor(s), translator(s), or others listed
Title and subtitle
Publication data:
  Place of publication
  Publisher's name
  Date of publication
Other important data, such as edition or volume number

For periodical articles

Name(s) of author(s)
Title and subtitle of article
Title of periodical
Publication data:
  Volume number and issue number (if any) in which article appears
  Date of issue
  Page numbers on which article appears

For electronic sources

Name(s) of author(s)
Title and subtitle
Publication data for books and articles (see above)
Date of release, online posting, or latest revision

Medium (online, CD-ROM, etc.)
Format of online source (Web site, Web page, e-mail, etc.)
Date you consulted the source
Complete URL (unless source was obtained through a subscription service and has no permanent address)
For sources obtained through a subscription service:
  Name of database
  Name of service
  URL of the service's home page or search terms used to reach the source

For other sources

Name(s) of author(s), government department, recording artist, photographer, or others listed
Title of the work
Format, such as unpublished letter, live performance, or photograph
Publication or production data:
  Publisher's or producer's name
  Date of publication, release, or production
  Identifying numbers (if any)

You can download these lists from *ablongman.com/littlebrown*. Copy the appropriate list for each source you're using, and fill in the required information.

51e

Note Whenever possible, record source information in the correct format for the documentation style you will be using. Then you will be less likely to omit needed information or to confuse numbers, dates, and other data when it's time to write your citations. This book describes two styles: MLA (p. 483) and APA (p. 531). For others, consult one of the guides listed on pages 478–79.

2 • Annotations

Creating annotations for a working bibliography converts it from a simple list into a tool for assessing sources. When you discover a possible source, record not only its publication information but also the following:

- **What you know about the content of the source.** Periodical databases and book catalogs generally include abstracts, or summaries, of sources that can help with this part of the annotation.
- **How you think the source may be helpful in your research.** Does it offer expert opinion, statistics, an important example, or a range of views? Does it place your subject in a historical, social, or economic context?

Taking the time with your annotations can help you discover gaps that may remain in your sources and will later help you decide which sources to pursue in depth. One student annotated a bibliography entry on his computer with a summary and a note on the source features he thought would be most helpful to him:

Entry for an annotated working bibliography

Publication and access information for source	United States. Dept. of Education. National Center for Education Statistics. <u>Internet Access in US Public Schools and Classrooms</u>. 24 Feb. 2006. 12 Mar. 2006 <http://nces.ed.gov/ pubsearch/pubsinfo.asp?pubid=2005015>.
Summary of source Ideas on use of source	Report on the annual NCES survey of the quantity and quality of technology used in K-12 classrooms. Includes important statistics on trends—student-to-computer ratios, teacher training, computer availability to students in different socio-economic brackets.

As you become more familiar with your sources, you can use your initial annotated bibliography to record your evaluations of them and more detailed thoughts on how they fit into your research.

52 Finding Sources

How can I locate ideas and information about my research subject?

Your library and a computer connected to the Internet give you access to an almost infinite range of sources. The challenge, of course, is to find the most worthy and appropriate sources for your needs and then to use them effectively. This chapter shows you how to conduct electronic searches (below) and take advantage of the print and electronic sources available to you: reference works (p. 429), books (p. 432), periodicals (p. 432), the Web (p. 437), other on-line sources (p. 441), government publications (p. 443), and your own interviews, surveys, and other primary sources (p. 445). Judging the appropriateness of sources and using them effectively are covered in Chapters 53–54.

52a Plan electronic searches.

1 • Your library's Web site

As you conduct research, the World Wide Web will be your gateway to ideas and information. Always start with your library's Web site, not with a public search engine such as *Google*. (*Google Scholar*, a new tool that searches for scholarly articles, is discussed on p. 434.) The library site will lead you to vast resources, including books, periodical articles, and reference works. More important, every source you find on the library site will have passed through filters to ensure its value. A scholarly journal article, for instance, undergoes at least three successive reviews: subject-matter experts first deem it worth publishing in the journal; then a database vendor deems the journal worth including in the database; and finally your school's librarians deem the database worth subscribing to.

Google and other search engines may seem more user-friendly than the library's Web site and may seem to return plenty of sources for you to work with. Many of the sources may indeed be reliable and relevant to your research, but many more will not be. In the end, a library Web search will be more efficient and more effective than a direct Web search. (For help with evaluating sources from any resource, see pp. 447–56.)

52a

http://www.ablongman.com/littlebrown ▶

Visit the companion Web site for more help and an electronic exercise on finding sources.

A tip for researchers

Take advantage of two valuable resources offered by your library:

- **An orientation,** which introduces the library's resources and explains how to reach and use the Web site and the print holdings.
- **Reference librarians,** whose job it is to help you and others navigate the library's resources. Even very experienced researchers often consult reference librarians.

Note Start with the library's Web site, but don't stop there. Many books, periodicals, and other excellent sources are available only on library shelves, not online, and most instructors expect research papers to be built to some extent on these resources. When you spot promising print sources while browsing the library's online databases, make records of them and then look them up at the library.

2 • Kinds of electronic sources

Your school's library and the Web offer several kinds of electronic resources that are suitable for academic research:

- **The library's catalog of holdings** is a database that lists all the resources that the library owns or subscribes to: books, journals, magazines, newspapers, reference works, and more. The catalog may also include the holdings of other school libraries nearby or in your state.
- **Online databases** include indexes, bibliographies, and other reference works. They are your main route to articles in periodicals, providing publication information, summaries, and often full text. Your library subscribes to the databases and makes them available through its Web site. (You may also discover databases directly on the Web, but, again, the library is a more productive starting place.)
- **Databases on CD-ROM** include the same information as online databases, but they must be read at a library computer terminal. Increasingly, libraries are providing CD-ROM databases through their Web sites or are moving away from CD-ROMs in favor of online databases.
- **Full-text resources** contain the entire contents of articles, book chapters, even whole books. The library's databases provide access to the full text of many listed sources. In addition, the Web

52a

sites of many periodicals and organizations, such as government agencies, offer the full text of articles, reports, and other publications.

3 • Keyword searches

Probably the most important element in an electronic search is appropriate **keywords,** or **descriptors,** that name your subject for databases and Web search engines.

Databases vs. the Web

To develop keywords it helps to understand an important difference in how library databases and the open Web work:

- **A database indexes sources by authors, titles, publication years, and its own subject headings.** The subject headings reflect the database's directory of terms and are assigned by people who have read the sources. You can find these subject headings by using your own keywords until you locate a promising source. The information for the source will list the headings under which the database indexes it and other sources like it. (See p. 436 for an illustration.) You can then use those headings for further searches.

- **A Web search engine seeks your keywords in the titles and texts of sites.** The process is entirely electronic, so the performance of a search engine depends on how well your keywords describe your subject and anticipate the words used in sources. If you describe your subject too broadly or describe it specifically but don't match the vocabulary in relevant sources, your search will turn up few relevant sources and probably many that aren't relevant.

Keyword refinement

Every database and search engine provides a system that you can use to refine your keywords for a productive search. The basic operations appear in the box on the next page, but resources do differ. For instance, some assume that *AND* should link two or more keywords, while others provide options specifying "Must contain all the words," "May contain any of the words," and other equivalents for the operations described in the box. You can learn a search engine's system by consulting the Advanced Search page.

52a

Trial and error

You will probably have to use trial and error in developing your keywords, sometimes turning up few or no sources and sometimes

Ways to refine keywords

Most databases and search engines work with **Boolean operators,** terms or symbols that allow you to expand or limit your keywords and thus your search.

- Use *AND* or + **to narrow the search** by including only sources that use all the given words. The keywords *Internet AND tax* request only the sources in the shaded area:

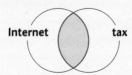

- Use *NOT* or – **("minus") to narrow the search** by excluding irrelevant words. *Internet AND tax NOT access* excludes sources that use the word *access.*

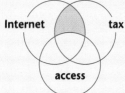

- Use *OR* **to broaden the search** by giving alternative keywords. *Internet OR (electronic commerce) AND tax* allows for sources that use *Internet* or *electronic commerce* (or both) along with *tax.*

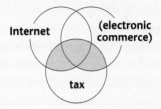

52a

- Use parentheses or quotation marks to form search phrases. For instance, *(electronic commerce)* requests the exact phrase, not the separate words.
- Use *NEAR* **to narrow the search** by requiring the keywords to be close to each other—for instance, *Internet NEAR tax.* Depending on the resource you're using, the words could be directly next to each other or many words apart. Some resources use *WITHIN ___* so that you can specify the exact number of words apart—for instance, *Internet WITHIN 10 tax.*

- **Use wild cards to permit different versions of the same word.** In *child**, for instance, the wild card * indicates that sources may include *child, children, childcare, childhood, childish, childlike,* and *childproof.* If a wild card opens up your search too much (as with the example *child**), you may be better off using *OR* to limit the options: *child OR children.* (Note that some systems use ?, :, or + for a wild card instead of *.)
- **Be sure to spell your keywords correctly.** Some search tools will look for close matches or approximations, but correct spelling gives you the best chance of finding relevant sources.

turning up thousands of mostly irrelevant sources. But the process is not busywork—far from it. It can teach you a great deal about your subject: how you can or should narrow it, how it is and is not described by others, what others consider interesting or debatable about it, and what the major arguments are.

See pages 440–41 for a sample keyword search of the Web.

52b Consult reference works.

Reference works, often available online or on CD-ROM, include encyclopedias, dictionaries, bibliographies, indexes, and handbooks. Your research *must* go beyond these sources, but they can help you decide whether your topic really interests you and whether it meets the requirements for a research paper (p. 418). Reference works can also help you develop keywords for electronic searches and can direct you to more detailed sources on your topic.

You'll find many reference works through your library and directly on the Web. The following lists give general and specific Web references for a range of disciplines. For updates of these sources and URLs, visit *ablongman.com/littlebrown.*

All disciplines

Internet Public Library (ipl.org)
Library of Congress (lcweb.loc.gov)
LSU Libraries Webliography (lib.lsu.edu/weblio.html)
World Wide Web Virtual Library (vlib.org)

Humanities

General

BUBL Information Service (bubl.ac.uk)
EDSITEment (edsitement.neh.gov)
Voice of the Shuttle (vos.ucsb.edu)

52b

Art

Artnet (*artnet.com*)
World Wide Arts Resources (*wwar.com/browse.html*)

Dance

BUBL Link: Dance (*bubl.ac.uk/link/d/dance.htm*)
Google Directory: Dance Links (*directory.google.com*)

Film

Internet Resources for Film Studies (*www2.lib.udel.edu/subj/film/
internet.htm*)
Internet Movie Database (*imdb.com*)

History

Best of History Web Sites (*besthistorysites.net*)
Librarians' Index to the Internet: History (*lii.org/search/file/history*)

Literature

American and English Literature Internet Resources (*library.scsu.ctstateu.edu/
litbib.html*)
EServer (*eserver.org*)
Internet Public Library: Online Literary Criticism (*ipl.org/div/litcrit*)
Key Sites on American Literature (*usinfo.state.gov/products/pubs/oal/
amlitweb.htm*)
Voice of the Shuttle: Drama, Theater, and Performance Art Studies
(*vos.ucsb.edu/browse.asp?id=782*)
Voice of the Shuttle: Literature (in English) (*vos.ucsb.edu/
browse.asp?id=3*)
Voice of the Shuttle: Literatures (Other than English) (*vos.ucsb.edu/
browse.asp?id=2719*)
Yahoo Directory: Literature (*dir.yahoo.com/Arts/humanities/literature*)

Music

American Music Resource (*amrhome.net*)
Web Resources Research in Music (*www.music.ucc.ie/wrrm*)

Philosophy

Guide to Philosophy on the Internet (*www.earlham.edu/~peters/gpi*)
Intute: Philosophy (*www.intute.ac.uk/artsandhumanities/philosophy*)

52b

Religion

Academic Info: Religion Gateway (*academicinfo.net/religindex.html*)
Virtual Religion Index (*religion.rutgers.edu/vri*)

Theater

*McCoy's Brief Guide to Internet Resources in Theatre and Performance
Studies* (*stetson.edu/departments/csata/thr_guid.html*)
Theater Connections (*uncc.edu/jvanoate/theater*)

Social Sciences

General

Data on the Net (*3stages.org/idata*)
Intute: Social Sciences (*www.intute.ac.uk/social sciences/*
   lost.html)
WWW Virtual Library: Social and Behavorial Sciences (*vlib.org*)

Anthropology

Anthro.Net (*anthro.net*)
Anthropology Resources on the Internet (*anthropologie.net*)

Business and economics

Resources for Economics on the Internet (*rfe.org*)
Virtual International Business and Economic Sources (*library.uncc.edu/*
   display/?dept=reference&format=open&page=68)

Education

Educator's Reference Desk (*eduref.org*)
US Department of Education (*ed.gov*)

Ethnic and gender studies

Diversity and Ethnic Studies (*www.public.iastate.edu/~savega/*
   divweb2.htm)
Voice of the Shuttle: Gender Studies (*vos.ucsb.edu/browse.asp?id=2711*)

Political science and law

Librarians' Index to the Internet: Law (*lii.org*)
Political Science Resources (*www.psr.keele.ac.uk*)

Psychology

Psychology Online Resource Central (*psych-central.com*)
PsychWeb (*psywww.com*)

Sociology

SocioWeb (*socioweb.com*)
WWW Virtual Library: Sociology (*socserv2.mcmaster.ca/w3virtsoclib*)

Natural and applied sciences

General

Google Directory: Science Links (*directory.google.com*)
Librarians' Index to the Internet: Science (*lii.org*)
WWW Virtual Library: Natural Sciences and Mathematics (*vlib.org*)

Biology

Biology Online (*biology-online.org*)
National Biological Information Infrastructure (*nbii.gov*)

52b

Chemistry
Chemistry.org (*chemistry.org/portal/a/c/s/1/home.html*)
WWW Virtual Library: Links for Chemists (*liv.ac.uk/Chemistry/Links/
links.html*)

Computer science
IEEE Computer Society (*computer.org*)
University of Texas Virtual Computer Library (*utexas.edu/computer/vcl*)

Engineering
BUBL: Technology (*bubl.ac.uk*)
Internet Guide to Engineering, Mathematics, and Computing (*eevl.ac.uk*)

Environmental science
EE-link: Environmental Education on the Internet (*eelink.net*)
EnviroLink (*envirolink.org*)

Geology
American Geological Institute (*www.agiweb.org*)
US Geological Survey Library (*usgs.gov*)

Health sciences
Hardin MD (*www.lib.uiowa.edu/hardin/md*)
World Health Organization (*who.int*)

Mathematics
Math on the Web (*www.ams.org*)
BUBL: Natural Sciences and Mathematics (*bubl.ac.uk*)

Physics and astronomy
American Institute of Physics (*aip.org*)
PhysicsWeb (*physicsweb.org*)

52c Consult books.

Your library's book catalog is searchable at a terminal in the library and via the library's Web site. You can search the catalog by author, by title, by your own keywords, or by the headings found in *Library of Congress Subject Headings* (*LCSH*). The screen shot on the facing page shows the complete record for a book, including the *LCSH* headings that can be used to find similar sources.

52d Consult periodicals.

Periodicals include newspapers, journals, and magazines. Newspapers, the easiest to recognize, are useful for detailed accounts of

Book catalog full record

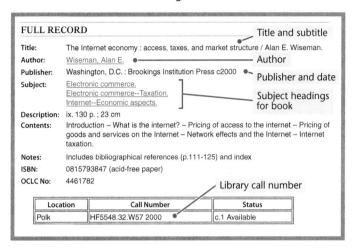

FULL RECORD ······································ Title and subtitle

Title:	The Internet economy : access, taxes, and market structure / Alan E. Wiseman.
Author:	Wiseman, Alan E. ● ──────── Author
Publisher:	Washington, D.C. : Brookings Institution Press c2000 ●~ Publisher and date
Subject:	Electronic commerce.
	Electronic commerce--Taxation. ─── Subject headings
	Internet--Economic aspects. ─ for book
Description:	ix. 130 p. ; 23 cm
Contents:	Introduction – What is the internet? – Pricing of access to the internet – Pricing of goods and services on the Internet – Network effects and the Internet – Internet taxation.
Notes:	Includes bibliographical references (p.111-125) and index
ISBN:	0815793847 (acid-free paper)
OCLC No:	4461782 ──── Library call number

Location	Call Number	Status
Polk	HF5548.32.W57 2000 ●	c.1 Available

past and current events. Journals and magazines can be harder to distinguish, but their differences are important. Most college instructors expect students' research to rely more on journals than on magazines.

Journals	Magazines
Examples: *American Anthropologist, Journal of Black Studies, Journal of Chemical Education, American Journal of Psychology*	Examples: *The New Yorker, Time, Rolling Stone, People, National Review*
Available mainly through college and university libraries.	Available in public libraries, on newsstands, and in bookstores.
Articles are intended to advance knowledge in a particular field.	Articles are intended to express opinion, inform, or entertain.
Writers and readers are specialists in the field.	Writers may or may not be specialists in their subjects. Readers are members of the general public or a subgroup with a particular interest.
Articles always include source citations.	Articles rarely include source citations.
Articles are usually long, ten pages or more.	Articles are usually short, fewer than ten pages.

52d

Journals	Magazines
Appearance is bland, with black-only type, little or no decoration, and only illustrations that directly amplify the text, such as graphs.	Appearance varies but is generally lively, with color, decoration (headings, sidebars, and other elements), and illustrations (drawings, photographs).
Issues may appear quarterly or less often.	Issues may appear weekly, biweekly, or monthly.
Issues may be paged separately (like a magazine) or may be paged sequentially throughout an annual volume, so that issue 3 (the third issue of the year) could open on page 327. (The method of pagination affects source citations. See p. 502.)	Issues are paged separately, each beginning on page 1.

1 • Indexes to periodicals

How indexes work

Periodical databases index the articles in journals, magazines, and newspapers. Often these databases include abstracts, or summaries, of the articles, and they may offer the full text of the articles as well. Your library subscribes to many periodical databases and to services that offer multiple databases. (See p. 437 for a list.) Most databases and services will be searchable through the library's Web site.

Note The search engine *Google* is developing *Google Scholar*, an engine at *scholar.google.com* that seeks out scholarly articles. Although it could eventually prove a valuable research tool, at this point *Google Scholar* produces results that are far from complete and include more from science and engineering than from the humanities and social sciences. If you find an article through *Google Scholar*, search for it specifically on your library's site.

Selection of databases

To decide which databases to consult, you'll need to consider what you're looking for:

- **How broadly and deeply should you search?** Periodical databases vary widely in what they index. Some, such as *ProQuest Research Library*, cover many subjects but don't index the full range of periodicals in each subject. Others, such as *Business Periodicals Index*, cover a single subject but then include most of the available periodicals. If your subject ranges across disciplines, then start with a broad database. If your subject fo-

52d

cuses on a particular discipline, then start with a narrower database.

- **Which databases most likely include the kinds of resources you need?** The Web sites of most libraries allow you to narrow a database search to a particular kind of periodical (such as newspapers or journals) or to a particular discipline. You can then discover each database's focus by checking the description of the database (sometimes labeled "Help" or "Guide") or the list of indexed resources (sometimes labeled "Publications" or "Index"). The description will also tell you the time period the database covers, so you'll know whether you also need to consult older print indexes at the library.

Database searches

When you first search a database, use your own keywords to locate sources. The procedure is illustrated in the three screen shots below and on the next page. Your goal is to find at least one source that seems just right for your subject, so that you can then see what subject headings the database itself uses for such sources. Using one or more of those headings will focus and speed your search.

Note Many databases allow you to limit your search to so-called peer-reviewed or refereed journals—that is, scholarly journals whose articles have been reviewed before publication by experts in the field and then revised by the author. Limiting your search to peer-reviewed journals can help you navigate huge databases that might otherwise return scores of unusable articles.

1. Initial keyword search of periodical database

52d

2. Partial keyword search results

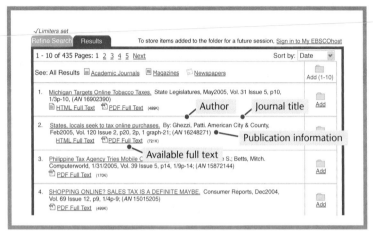

3. Full article record with abstract

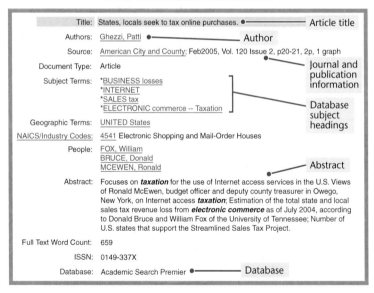

52d

The use of abstracts

In screen 3 above, the full article record shows a key feature of many databases' periodical listings: an **abstract** that summarizes the article. By describing research methods, conclusions, and other information, an abstract can tell you whether you want to pursue an article and thus save you time. However, the abstract cannot replace the actual article. If you want to use the work as a source, you must consult the full text.

Helpful databases

The list below includes databases to which academic libraries commonly subscribe. Some of these databases cover much the same material, so your library may subscribe to several of them but not all.

EBSCOhost Academic Search. A periodical index covering magazines and journals in the social sciences, sciences, arts, and humanities. Many articles are available full-text.

InfoTrac Expanded Academic. The Gale Group's general periodical index covering the social sciences, sciences, arts, and humanities as well as national news periodicals. It includes full-text articles.

LexisNexis Academic. An index of news and business, legal, and reference information, with full-text articles. *LexisNexis* includes international, national, and regional newspapers, news magazines, legal and business publications, and court cases.

Nineteenth-Century Masterfile. Perhaps the only electronic database for periodicals from the nineteenth century.

ProQuest Research Library. A periodical index covering the sciences, social sciences, arts, and humanities, including many full-text articles.

Wilson Databases. A collection of indexes, often provided in a package, including *Business Periodicals Index, Education Index, General Science Index, Humanities Index, Readers' Guide to Periodical Literature,* and *Social Sciences Index.*

2 • Locations of periodicals

If an index listing does not include or link directly to the full text of an article, you'll need to consult the periodical itself. Recent issues of periodicals are probably held in the library's periodical room. Back issues are usually stored elsewhere, either in bound volumes or on film that requires a special machine to read. A librarian will show you how to operate the machine.

52e   Search the Web.

52e

As an academic researcher, you enter the World Wide Web in two ways: through your library's Web site, and through public search engines such as *Yahoo!* and *Google.* The library entrance, covered in the preceding sections, is your main path to the books and periodicals that, for most subjects, should make up most of your sources. The public entrance, discussed here, can lead to a wealth of information, but it also has a number of disadvantages:

- **The Web is a wide-open network.** Anyone with the right hardware and software can place information on the Internet, and even a carefully conceived search can turn up sources with widely varying reliability: journal articles, government documents, scholarly data, term papers written by high school students, sales pitches masked as objective reports, wild theories. You must be especially diligent about evaluating Internet sources (see p. 449).

- **The Web changes constantly.** No search engine can keep up with the Web's daily additions and deletions, and a source you find today may be different or gone tomorrow. Generally, you should not put off consulting an online source that you think you may want to use.

- **The Web provides limited information on the past.** Sources dating from before the 1980s or even more recently probably will not appear on the Web.

- **The Web is not all-inclusive.** Most books and many periodicals are available only via the library, not directly via the Web.

Clearly, the Web warrants cautious use. It should not be the only resource you work with.

1 • Search engines

To find sources on the Web, you use a **search engine** that catalogs Web sites in a series of directories and conducts keyword searches (see p. 427). Generally, use a directory when you haven't yet refined your topic or you want a general overview. Use keywords when you have refined your topic and you seek specific information.

Current search engines

The box on the next page lists the currently most popular search engines. To reach any one of them, enter its address in the Address or Location field of your Web browser.

Note For a good range of reliable sources, try out more than a single search engine, perhaps as many as four or five. No search engine can catalog the entire Web—indeed, even the most powerful engine may not include half the sites available at any given time, and most engines include only a fifth or less. In addition, most search engines accept paid placements, giving higher billing to sites that pay a fee. These so-called sponsored links are usually marked as such, but they can compromise a search engine's method for arranging sites in response to your keywords.

52e

Web search engines

The features of search engines change often, and new ones appear constantly. For the latest on search engines, see the links collected by Search Engine Watch at *searchenginewatch.com/links*.

Directories that review sites
BUBL Link (*bubl.ac.uk*)
Internet Public Library (*ipl.org/div/subject*)
Internet Scout Project (*scout.wisc.edu/archives*)
Librarians' Index to the Internet (*lii.org*)

Most advanced and efficient engines
AlltheWeb (*alltheweb.com*)

One of the fastest and most comprehensive engines, *AlltheWeb* updates its database frequently so that it returns more of the Web's most recent sites. It allows searches for news, pictures, and audio and video files.

Google (*google.com*)

Also fast and comprehensive, *Google* ranks a site based not only on its content but also on the other sites that are linked to it, thus providing a measure of a site's usefulness. *Google* also allows searches for news, discussion groups, and images.

Other engines
AltaVista (*altavista.com*)
Ask.com (*ask.com*)
Dogpile (*dogpile.com*)
Excite (*excite.com*)
Lycos (*lycos.com*)
MetaCrawler (*metacrawler.com*)
Yahoo! (*yahoo.com*)

A sample search engine

On the next page, a screen shot from *Google* shows the features common to most search engines. Note especially the Advanced Search option, which allows you to customize your search (for instance, by selecting a date range, a language, or a number of results to see) and to limit or expand your keywords (for instance, by using *AND, NOT*, and other operators). The Advanced Search page may also tell you how the search engine determines the order in which it presents results. (Criteria include the number of times your

52e

Google home page

keywords appear on a site, whether the terms appear in the site's title or address, and, in *Google*'s case, which other sites link to the site.)

Search records

Your Web browser includes functions that allow you to keep track of Web sources and your search:

- *Favorites* or *Bookmarks* **save site addresses as links.** Click one of these terms near the top of the browser screen to add a site you want to return to. A favorite or bookmark remains on file until you delete it.

- *History* **records the sites you visited over a certain period,** such as a single online session or a week's sessions. (After that period, the history is deleted.) If you forgot to bookmark a site, you can click History or Go to locate your search history and recover the site.

2 • A sample search

The following sample Web search illustrates how the refinement of keywords can narrow a search to maximize the relevant hits and minimize the irrelevant ones. Kisha Alder, a student researching the taxes on Internet commerce, first used the keywords *Internet taxes* on *Google*. But, as shown in the first screen shot on the next page, the search produced more than *13 million* hits, an unusably large number and a sure sign that Alder's keywords needed revision.

After several tries, Alder arrived at *"sales tax" Internet states reform* to describe her subject more precisely. These keywords still

52e

produced 5,000 hits (second illustration below), but many potential sources appeared on the first few screens.

1. First *Google* search results

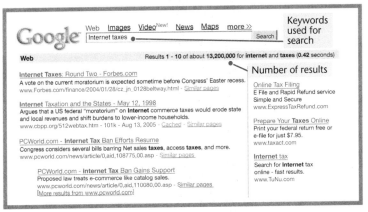

2. *Google* results with refined keywords

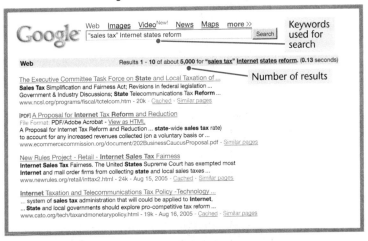

52f

52f   Explore other online sources.

Several online sources can put you directly in touch with experts and others whose ideas and information may inform your research. Because these sources, like Web sites, are unfiltered, you must always evaluate them carefully. (See pp. 454–56.)

1 • Using Web logs

Web logs, or **blogs,** are personal sites on which an author posts time-stamped comments, generally centering on a common theme, in a format that allows readers to respond to the author and to each other. You can find a directory of blogs at *bloglines.com* or *blogwise.com.*

Web logs consulted as potential sources must be evaluated carefully. Some are reliable sources of opinion, news, or evolving scholarship, and many refer to worthy books, articles, Web sites, and other resources. But lots of blogs are little more than outlets for their authors' gripes and prejudices. See pages 454–56 for tips on telling the good from the bad.

2 • Using electronic mail

As a research tool, e-mail allows you to communicate with others who are interested in your topic. You might, for instance, carry on an e-mail conversation with a teacher at your school or with other students. Or you might interview an expert in another state to follow up on a scholarly article he or she published. (See pp. 158–61 for more on using e-mail.)

3 • Using discussion lists

A **discussion list** (sometimes called a **listserv** or just a **list**) uses e-mail to connect individuals who are interested in a common subject, often with a scholarly or technical focus. By sending a question to an appropriate list, you may be able to reach scores of people who know something about your topic. For an index of discussion lists, see *tile.net/lists.*

When conducting research on a discussion list, follow the guidelines for e-mail etiquette on pages 158–61 as well as these:

- *Lurk for a while*—read without posting messages. Make sure the discussion is relevant to your topic, and get a sense of how the group interacts.
- **Don't ask for information you can find elsewhere.** Most list members are glad to help with legitimate questions but resent messages that rehash familiar debates or that ask them to do someone else's work.
- **Evaluate messages carefully.** Many list subscribers are passionate experts with fair-minded approaches to their topics, but almost anyone with an Internet connection can post a message to a list. See pages 454–56 on evaluating online sources.

52f

4 • Using Web forums and newsgroups

Web forums and newsgroups are more open and less scholarly than discussion lists, so their messages require even more diligent evaluation. **Web forums** allow participants to join a conversation simply by selecting a link on a Web page. For a directory of forums, see *delphiforums.com*. **Newsgroups** are organized under subject headings such as *soc* for social issues and *biz* for business. For a directory of newsgroups, see *groups.google.com*.

5 • Using synchronous communication

Synchronous (or simultaneous) **communication** allows conversation in real time, the way you talk on the phone. Synchronous programs include instant-messaging applications, Web courseware, Internet relay chat (IRC), and virtual environments called MOOs.

Synchronous communication can be used to conduct interviews or hold debates. Your instructor may ask you to use it for your coursework or research and will provide the software and instructions to get you started. You can also find out more about synchronous communication at *du.org/cybercomp.html* or *Internet101 .org/chat.html*.

52g   Consult government publications.

Government publications provide a vast array of data, compilations, reports, policy statements, public records, and other historical and contemporary information. For US government publications, consult the Government Printing Office's *GPO Access* at *gpoaccess .gov/index.html*. Many federal, state, and local government agencies post important publications—legislation, reports, press releases—on their own Web sites. You can find lists of sites for various federal agencies by using the keywords *United States federal government* with a search engine. In addition, two Web sites are useful resources: *fedstats.gov* (government statistics) and *infoplease.com/us.html* (links to information on federal, state, and local governments).

52h   Locate images.

52h

To find images that can support your ideas, you have a number of options. (The Web links in the following lists are available online at *ablongman.com/littlebrown*.)

- **Scout for images while reading sources.** Your sources may include charts, graphs, photographs, and other images that can support your ideas. When you find an image you may want to use, photocopy or download it so you'll have it available later.

- **Create your own images,** such as photographs or charts. See pages 78–82 for examples.
- **Use an image search engine.** *Google, Yahoo!, AlltheWeb,* and some other search engines conduct specialized image searches. They can find scores of images, but the results may be inaccurate or incomplete because the sources surveyed often do not include descriptions of the images. (The engines will search file names and any text accompanying the images.)
- **Use a public image database.** The following sites generally conduct accurate searches because their images are filed with information such as a description of the image, the artist's name, and the image's date:

  Adflip (adflip.com): Historical and contemporary print advertisements
  Duke University, *Ad*Access (scriptorium.lib.duke.edu/adaccess)*: Print advertisements spanning 1911–55
  Library of Congress, *American Memory (memory.loc.gov/ammem)*: Maps, photographs, and prints documenting the American experience
  Library of Congress, *Prints and Photographs Online Catalog (loc.gov/rr/print/catalog.html)*: Images from the library's collection, including those available through *American Memory*
  New York Public Library Digital Gallery (digitalgallery.nypl.org/nypldigital): Maps, drawings, photographs, and paintings from the library's collection
  Political Cartoons (politicalcartoons.com): Cartoons on contemporary issues and events

- **Use a public image directory.** The following sites collect links to image sources:

  Art Source (ilpi.com/artsource/general.html): Sources on art and architecture
  ARTstor (artstor.org): Museum collections and a database of images typically used in art history courses
  Museum Computer Network (mcn.edu/resources/sitesonline.htm): Museum collections
  Washington State University, *Popular Culture: Resources for Critical Analysis (wsu.edu/%7Eamerstu/pop/tvrguide.html)*: Sources on advertising, fashion, magazines, toys, and other artifacts of popular culture
  Yale University Arts Library, *Image Resources (library.yale.edu/art/imageresources.html)*: Sources on the visual and performing arts

- **Use a subscription database.** Your library may subscribe to the following resources:

  Associated Press, *AccuNet/AP Multimedia Archives:* Historical and contemporary news images

Grove Art Online: Art images and links to museum sites

Many images you find will be available for free, but some sources do charge a fee for use. Before paying for an image, check with a librarian to see if it is available elsewhere for free.

Note You must cite every image source fully in your paper, just as you cite text sources, with author, title, and publication information. In addition, some sources will require that you seek permission from the copyright holder, either the source itself or a third party such as a photographer. Permission is especially likely to be required if you are submitting your paper on the public Web. See pages 476–77 for more about online publication.

52i Generate your own sources.

Academic writing will often require you to conduct primary research for information of your own. For instance, you may need to analyze a poem, conduct an experiment, survey a group of people, or interview an expert.

An interview can be especially helpful for a research project because it allows you to ask questions precisely geared to your topic. You can conduct an interview in person, over the telephone, or online using electronic mail (see p. 442) or a form of synchronous communication (see p. 443). A personal interview is preferable if you can arrange it, because you can see the person's expressions and gestures as well as hear his or her tone and words.

Here are a few guidelines for interviews:

- **Call or write for an appointment.** Tell the person exactly why you are calling, what you want to discuss, and how long you expect the interview to take. Be true to your word on all points.
- **Prepare a list of open-ended questions to ask**—perhaps ten or twelve for a one-hour interview. Plan on doing some research for these questions to discover background on the issues and your subject's published views on the issues.
- **Give your subject time to consider your questions.** Don't rush into silences with more questions.
- **Pay attention to your subject's answers** so that you can ask appropriate follow-up questions and pick up on unexpected but worthwhile points.
- **Take care in interpreting answers,** especially if you are online and thus can't depend on facial expressions, gestures, and tone of voice to convey the subject's attitudes.
- **Keep thorough notes.** Take notes during an in-person or telephone interview, or tape-record the interview if you have the

52i

equipment and your subject agrees. For online interviews, save the discussion in a file of its own. (A synchronous discussion may require that you activate a Log or Archive function before you begin your interview in order to save it afterward.)

- **Verify quotations.** Before you quote your subject in your paper, check with him or her to ensure that the quotations are accurate.

- **Send a thank-you note immediately after the interview.** Promise your subject a copy of your finished paper, and send the paper promptly.

EXERCISE 52.1
Finding sources

Using your library and three Web search engines, locate at least ten promising sources for one of the topics you selected in the previous chapter (Exercise 51.1, p. 419). Begin by developing a list of keywords, revising it as needed to focus your research. Consider the sources "promising" if they seem directly to address your central research question. Following the guidelines on pages 422–24, make a working, annotated bibliography of the sources. Be sure to include all the information you would need to acknowledge the sources in a final paper.

---

53 Working with Sources

How can I use sources critically and effectively?

Research writing is much more than finding sources and reporting their contents. The challenge and interest come from *interacting* with sources, reading them critically to discover their meanings, judge their relevance and reliability, and create relationships among them.

This chapter offers help with this crucial phase of research writing. It discusses evaluating and synthesizing sources (opposite and p. 457); gathering information from sources (p. 459); using summary, paraphrase, and direct quotation when borrowing from sources

---

http://www.ablongman.com/littlebrown ▶

Visit the companion Web site for more help and electronic exercises on working with sources.

(p. 460); and integrating source material into your text (p. 465). The next chapter (p. 470) discusses avoiding plagiarism and documenting sources.

⟨ **CULTURE** ⟩ Interacting with sources requires thinking critically about them and developing independent ideas. These goals may at first be uncomfortable for you if your native culture emphasizes understanding and respecting established authority over questioning and enlarging it. The information here will help you work with sources so that you can become an expert in your own right and convincingly convey your expertise to others.

53a   Evaluate sources.

Before you gather ideas and information from your sources, scan them to evaluate what they offer and how you might use them.

Note In evaluating sources, you need to consider how they come to you. The sources you find through the library, both print and online, have been previewed for you by their publishers and by the library's staff. They still require your critical reading, but you can have some confidence in the information they contain. With online sources you reach directly, however, you can't assume similar previewing, so your critical reading must be especially rigorous. Special tips for evaluating Web sites and other online sources appear on pages 448–56.

1 • Relevance and reliability

Not all the sources you find will prove worthwhile: some may be irrelevant to your topic, and others may be unreliable. Gauging the relevance and reliability of sources is the essential task of evaluating them. If you haven't already done so, read this book's Chapter 10 on critical reading and writing. It provides a foundation for answering the questions in the following box.

Questions for evaluating sources

For online sources, supplement these guidelines with those on pages 449 and 454.

Relevance

- **Does the source devote some attention to your subject?** Check whether the source focuses on your subject or covers it marginally, and compare the source's coverage to that in other sources.

(continued)

Questions for evaluating sources

(continued)

- **Is the source appropriately specialized for your needs?** Check the source's treatment of a topic you know something about, to ensure that it is neither too superficial nor too technical.
- **Is the source up to date enough for your subject?** Check the publication date. If your subject is current, your sources should be, too.

Reliability

- **Where does the source come from?** It matters whether you found the source through your library or directly on the Internet. (If the latter, see below and p. 454.) Check whether a library source is popular or scholarly. Scholarly sources, such as refereed journals and university press books, are generally deeper and more reliable.
- **Is the author an expert in the field?** The authors of scholarly publications tend to be experts. To verify expertise, check an author's credentials in a biography (if the source includes one), in a biographical reference, or by a keyword search of the Web.
- **What is the author's bias?** Every author has a point of view that influences the selection and interpretation of evidence. How do the author's ideas relate to those in other sources? What areas does the author emphasize, ignore, or dismiss? When you're aware of sources' biases, you can attempt to balance them.
- **Is the source fair and reasonable?** Even a strongly biased work should present sound reasoning, adequate evidence, and a fair picture of opposing views—all in an objective, calm tone. The absence of any of these qualities should raise a warning flag.
- **Is the source well written?** A logical organization and clear, error-free sentences indicate a careful author.

You can download these questions from *ablongman.com/littlebrown* and use a copy of the file for each source you are evaluating, providing written answers between the questions.

53a

2 • Web sites

To a great extent, the same critical reading that helps you evaluate library sources will help you evaluate Web sites. But most Web sites have not undergone prior screening by editors and librarians. On your own, you must distinguish scholarship from corporate promotion, valid data from invented statistics, well-founded opinion from clever propaganda.

The strategy summarized in the following box can help you make such distinctions. We'll apply the strategy to the Web site shown on page 451, *Global Warming Information Center,* which turned up in a search for views and data on global warming.

Questions for evaluating Web sites

Supplement these questions with those in the box opposite.

- **What type of site are you viewing?** What does the type lead you to expect about the site's purpose and content?
- **Who is the author or sponsor?** How credible is the person or group responsible for the site?
- **What is the purpose of the site?** What does the site's author or sponsor intend to achieve?
- **What does context tell you?** What do you already know about the site's subject that can inform your evaluation? What kinds of support or other information do the site's links provide?
- **What does presentation tell you?** Is the site's design well thought out and effective? Is the writing clear and error-free?
- **How worthwhile is the content?** Are the site's claims well supported by evidence? Is the evidence from reliable sources?

You can download these questions from *ablongman.com/littlebrown.* Use a copy of the file for each source you are evaluating, providing written answers between the questions.

Note To evaluate a Web document, you'll often need to travel to the site's home page to discover the author or sponsoring organization, date of publication, and other relevant information. The page you're reading may include a link to the home page. If it doesn't, you can find it by editing the URL in the Address or Location field of your browser. Working backward, delete the end of the URL up to the last slash and hit Enter. Repeat this step until you reach the home page. There you may also find a menu option, often labeled "About," that will lead you to a description of the site's author or sponsor.

Determine the type of site.

When you search the Web, you're likely to encounter various types of sites. Although they overlap—a primarily informational site may include scholarship as well—the types can usually be identified by their content and purposes. Here are the main types:

53a

- Sites focusing on scholarship: These sites have a knowledge-building interest and include research reports with supporting data and extensive documentation of scholarly sources. The

URLs of the sites generally end in *edu* (originating from an educational institution), *org* (a nonprofit organization), or *gov* (a government department or agency). Such sites are more likely to be reliable than the others described below.

- **Sites with an informational purpose:** Individuals, nonprofit organizations, schools, corporations, and government bodies all produce sites intended to centralize information on subjects as diverse as astronomy, hip-hop music, and zoo design. The sites' URLs may end in *edu, org, gov,* or *com* (originating from a commercial organization). Such sites generally do not have the knowledge-building focus of scholarly sites and may omit supporting data and documentation, but they can provide useful information and often include links to scholarly sources.

- **Sites focusing on advocacy:** Many sites present the views of individuals or organizations that advocate certain policies or actions. Their URLs usually end in *org,* but they may end in *edu* or *com.* Some advocacy sites include serious, well-documented research to support their positions, but others select or distort evidence.

- **Sites with a commercial purpose:** Corporations and other businesses maintain Web sites to explain or promote themselves or to sell goods and services. The URLs of commercial sites end in *com.* The information on such a site furthers the sponsor's profit-making purpose, but it can include reliable data.

- **Personal sites:** The sites maintained by individuals range from diaries of a family's travels to opinions on political issues to reports on evolving scholarship. The sites' URLs usually end in *com* or *edu.* Personal sites are only as reliable as their authors, but some do provide valuable eyewitness accounts, links to worthy sources, and other usable information. A particular kind of personal site, the Web log, is discussed on pages 454–56.

On the home page of the *Global Warming Information Center* (facing page), the URL and the site's title give some information that can be used to tell the site's type.

53a

Identify the author or sponsor.

A reputable site will list the author or group responsible for the site and will provide information or a link for contacting the author or group. If none of this information is provided, you should not use the source. If you have only the author or group name, you may be able to discover more in a biographical dictionary or through a keyword search. You should also look for mentions of the author or group in your other sources.

1. Home page of the *Global Warming Information Center*

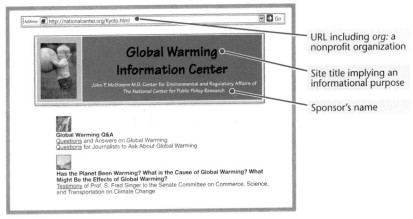

As the above screen shot shows, the site *Global Warming Information Center* names its sponsor right up front: the John P. McGovern M.D. Center for Environmental and Regulatory Affairs. The bottom of this home page gives links to information about the McGovern Center and its parent organization, the National Center for Public Policy Research. Their names imply that both groups are involved in research, so the site does indeed seem to be informational or possibly even scholarly.

Gauge purpose.

A Web site's purpose determines what ideas and information it offers. Inferring that purpose tells you how to interpret what you see on the site. If a site is intended to sell a product or an opinion, it will likely emphasize favorable ideas and information while ignoring or even distorting what is unfavorable. In contrast, if a site is intended to build knowledge—for instance, a scholarly project or journal—it will likely acknowledge diverse views and evidence.

Determining the purpose of a site often requires looking beneath the surface of words and images and beyond the first page. On the *Global Warming* page, the title and the photo of a child carrying a globe through a field of grass—suggest an environmentalist purpose of informing readers about the theory and consequences of rising earth temperatures caused by pollution. The site's purpose is actually different, though. The home-page links lead to statements about the aims of the McGovern Center and its parent, the National Center. The McGovern Center states that it was launched in the

53a

1900s "to counter misinformation being spread to the public and policymakers by the environmental left." The National Center states its purpose more broadly:

> The National Center for Public Policy Research is a communications and research foundation supportive of a strong national defense and dedicated to providing free market solutions to today's public policy problems. We believe that the principles of a free market, individual liberty, and personal responsibility provide the greatest hope for meeting the challenges facing America in the 21st century.

These two statements imply that the purpose of the McGovern Center's *Global Warming* site is to inform readers about the evidence against global warming in the interest of reducing or overturning environmental regulations.

Consider context.

Your evaluation of a Web site should be informed by considerations outside the site itself. Chief among these is your own knowledge: What do you already know about the site's subject and the prevailing views of it? In addition, you can follow some of the site's links to see how they support, or don't support, the site's credibility. For instance, links to scholarly sources lend authority to a site—but *only if* the scholarly sources actually relate to and back up the site's claims.

The *Global Warming* site has a clear anti-regulatory bias, but this view is a significant one in the debates over global warming. That is, the bias does not necessarily disqualify the site as a source on global warming. The question is how reliable its information is: does it come from trustworthy, less-biased sources? All the site's links lead to publications of the McGovern Center or the National Center, so the question can be answered only by looking more deeply at these publications.

Look at presentation.

Considering both the look of a site and the way it's written can illuminate its intentions and reliability. Are the site's elements all functional and well integrated, or is the site cluttered with irrelevant material and graphics? Does the site seem carefully constructed and well maintained, or is it sloppy and outdated? Does the design reflect the apparent purpose of the site, or does it undercut or conceal that purpose in some way? Is the text clearly written, or is it difficult to understand? Is it error-free, or does it contain typos and grammatical errors?

At first glance, as noted earlier, the *Global Warming* site casts a pro-environmentalist image that turns out not to coincide with its

53a

purpose. Otherwise, the site is cleanly designed, with minimal elements laid out clearly. The text on other pages is straightforward and readable. Apparently, the sponsor takes its purpose seriously and has thought out its presentation.

Analyze content.

With information about a site's author, purpose, and context, you're in a position to evaluate its content. Are the ideas and information slanted and, if so, in what direction? Are the views and data authoritative, or do you need to balance them—or even reject them? These questions require close reading of the text and its sources.

The *Global Warming* site links to a wealth of reports and prominently features "Questions and Answers on Global Warming." The following screen shots show two of the items from this page and the footnotes citing sources for the answers.

---

2. Content and documentation from the site

Questions and Answers on Global Warming

1. Is global warming occurring? Have the forecasts of global warming been confirmed by actual measurements?

There is no serious evidence that man-made global warming is taking place. The computer models used in U.N. studies say the first area to heat under the "greenhouse gas effect" should be the lower atmosphere - known as the troposphere.1 Highly accurate, carefully checked satellite data have shown absolutely no such tropospheric warming. There has been surface warming of about half a degree Celsius, but this is far below the customary natural swings in surface temperatures.2

2. Are carbon dioxide emissions from burning fossil fuels the primary cause of climate change? Can the Earth's temperature be expected to rise between 2.5 and 10.4 degrees Fahrenheit in this century as has been reported?

There are many indications that carbon dioxide does not play a significant role in global warming. Richard Lindzen, Ph.D., professor at the Massachusetts Institute of Technology and one of the 11 scientists who prepared a 2001 National Academy of Sciences (NAS) report on climate change, estimates that a doubling of carbon dioxide in the atmosphere would produce a temperature increase of only one degree Celsius.3 In fact, clouds and water vapor appear to be far more important factors related to global temperature. According to Dr. Lindzen and NASA scientists, clouds and water vapor may play a significant role in regulating the Earth's temperature to keep it more constant.4

> Assertions about the validity and causes of global warming, citing data and expert opinion as evidence

Footnotes

1 James K. Glassman and Sallie Baliunas, *The Weekly Standard*, June 25, 2001.
2 *Ibid.*
3 Richard Lindzen, professor of meteorology, Massachusetts Institute of Technology and member of the National Academy of Sciences, "Scientists' Report Doesn't Support The Kyoto Treaty," *The Wall Street Journal*, June 11, 2001.
4 Glassman and Baliunas.

> Footnotes citing an article in the conservative magazine *The Weekly Standard* and a newspaper report, not scholarly publications that explain methods of gathering and interpreting the data used as evidence

The source mix shown in the preceding screen shot is similar in the other publications found through the *Global Warming* site. Scholars do disagree over many aspects of global warming, such as how fast temperatures are rising, whether human-made pollution is an important cause, how serious the consequences may be, and how to solve the problem. Because the *Global Warming* site does not offer or refer to the scholarly research, its claims and evidence must be viewed suspiciously and probably rejected for use in a research paper. A usable source need not be less biased, but it must be more substantial.

3 • Evaluating other online sources

Web logs and the postings to online discussions require the same critical scrutiny as Web sites do. Web logs can be sources of in-depth information and informed opinion, but they can also be virtually useless. Web forums and newsgroups are similarly suspect. Even if a reliable blog or discussion-group message provides very current information or eyewitness testimony, it will not have the authority of a scholarly publication. An e-mail discussion list may be more trustworthy if its subscribers are professionals in the field, but you will still find wrong or misleading data and skewed opinions.

Use the following strategy for evaluating blogs and messages in online discussions.

Questions for evaluating Web logs and online discussions

Supplement these questions with those on pages 447–48.

- **Who is the author?** How credible is the person writing?
- **What is the author's purpose?** What can you tell about why the author is writing?
- **What does the context reveal?** What do others' responses on a blog or the other messages in a discussion thread indicate about the source's balance and reliability?
- **How worthwhile is the content?** Are the author's claims supported by evidence? Is the evidence from reliable sources?
- **How does the blog or message compare with other sources?** Do the author's claims seem accurate and fair given what you've seen in sources you know to be reliable?

You can download these questions from *ablongman.com/littlebrown*. Use a copy of the file for each source you are evaluating, providing written answers between the questions.

53a

Identify the author.

Checking out the author of a blog or online message can help you judge the reliability of the posting. If the author uses a screen name, write directly to him or her requesting full name and credentials. Do not use the message as a source if the author fails to respond. Once you know an author's name, you may be able to obtain background information from a keyword search of the Web or a biographical dictionary.

Analyze the author's purpose.

As with Web sites, you can use cues in the author's writing to figure out *why* he or she is writing and thus how to position the blog or message among your other sources. The claims, use (or not) of evidence, and treatment of opposing views all convey the author's stand on the subject and general fairness.

Consider the context.

Web logs and discussion-group postings are often difficult to evaluate in isolation. Looking outside a particular contribution to the responses of others will give you a sense of how the author's view is regarded. On a blog, look at the comments others have posted. Do the same with discussion-group messages, going back to the initial posting in the discussion thread and reading forward.

Analyze content.

A reliable source will offer evidence for claims and sources for evidence. If you don't see such supporting information, ask the author for it. (If he or she fails to respond, don't use the source.) Then verify the sources with your own research: are they reputable?

The tone of the writing can also be a clue to its purpose and reliability. Blogs and online discussions tend to be more informal and often more heated than other kinds of dialog, but look askance at writing that's contemptuous, dismissive, or shrill.

Compare with other sources.

Always consider blogs and discussion-group messages in comparison to other sources so that you can distinguish singular, untested views from more mainstream views that have been subject to verification. Don't assume that a blog author's information and opinions are mainstream just because you see them on other blogs. The technology allows content to be picked up instantly by other blogs, so widespread distribution indicates only popularity, not reliability.

53a

Be wary of blogs or messages that reproduce periodical articles, reports, or other publications. Try to locate the original version of the publication to be sure it has been reproduced fully and accurately, not quoted selectively or distorted. If you can't locate the original version, then don't use the publication as a source.

EXERCISE 53.1
Evaluating a source

Imagine that you are researching a paper on the advertising techniques that are designed to persuade consumers to buy products. You have listed the following book in your working bibliography:

Vance Packard, *The Hidden Persuaders,* revised edition, 1981.

On your own or with your classmates (as your instructor wishes), obtain this book from a library and evaluate it as a source for your paper. Use the guidelines in the box on pages 447–48. (You can do this exercise online at *ablongman.com/littlebrown.*)

EXERCISE 53.2
Evaluating Web sites

Find and evaluate three Web sites: a commercial site, such as Microsoft's or Apple's; a site for a nonprofit organization, such as the American Medical Association or Greenpeace; and the personal site of an individual. What do you know or can you infer about each site's author or sponsor? What seems to be the site's purpose or purposes? What do the site's links contribute? How effective is the site's design? How reliable do you judge the site's information to be? How do the three types of sites differ in these respects?

EXERCISE 53.3
Evaluating a Web log

Visit *bloglines.com* or *blogwise.com* to find a Web log on a controversial subject such as stem-cell research or online sharing of music files. Who is responsible for the blog? What can you tell about its purpose? How reliable do you judge its ideas and information to be?

EXERCISE 53.4
Evaluating an online discussion

Using *groups.google.com,* locate a newsgroup on a subject that interests you. (If you already participate in an online discussion group, you can use it instead.) Pick one series of at least ten related messages on a single topic. Write a brief summary of each message (see pp. 96–97 on summarizing). Then analyze and synthesize the messages to develop a one- or two-paragraph evaluation of the discussion. Which messages seem reliable? Which don't? Why?

53a

53b Synthesize sources.

When you begin to locate the differences and similarities among sources, you move into the most significant part of research writing: forging relationships for your own purpose. This **synthesis** is an essential step in reading sources critically, and it continues through the drafting and revision of a research paper. As you infer connections—say, between one writer's opinions and another's or between two works by the same author—you create new knowledge.

Your synthesis of sources will grow more detailed and sophisticated as you proceed through the research-writing process. Unless you are analyzing primary sources such as the works of a poet, at first read your sources quickly and selectively to obtain an overview of your topic and a sense of how the sources approach it. Don't get bogged down in taking detailed notes, but *do* record your ideas about sources in your research journal (p. 417) or your annotated bibliography (p. 424).

Respond to sources.

Write down what your sources make you think. Do you agree or disagree with the author? Do you find his or her views narrow, or do they open up new approaches for you? Is there anything in the source that you need to research further before you can understand it? Does the source prompt questions that you should keep in mind while reading other sources?

Connect sources.

When you notice a link between sources, jot it down. Do two sources differ in their theories or their interpretations of facts? Does one source illuminate another—perhaps commenting or clarifying or supplying additional data? Do two or more sources report studies that support a theory you've read about or an idea of your own?

Heed your own insights.

Apart from ideas prompted by your sources, you are sure to come up with independent thoughts: a conviction, a point of confusion that suddenly becomes clear, a question you haven't seen anyone else ask. These insights may occur at unexpected times, so it's good practice to keep a notebook handy to record them.

Use sources to support your own ideas.

As your research proceeds, the responses, connections, and insights you form through synthesis will lead you to answer your

53b

starting research question with a statement of your thesis (see p. 480). They will also lead you to the main ideas supporting your thesis—conclusions you have drawn from your synthesis of sources, forming the main divisions of your paper. When drafting the paper, make sure each paragraph focuses on an idea of your own, with the support for the idea coming from your sources. In this way, your paper will synthesize the others' work into something wholly your own.

EXERCISE 53.5
Synthesizing sources

The following three passages address the same issue, the legalization of drugs. What similarities do you see in the authors' ideas? What differences? Write a paragraph of your own in which you use these authors' views as a point of departure for your own view about drug legalization. (You can do this exercise online at *ablongman.com/littlebrown*.)

Perhaps the most unfortunate victims of drug prohibition laws have been the residents of America's ghettos. These laws have proved largely futile in deterring ghetto-dwellers from becoming drug abusers, but they do account for much of what ghetto residents identify as the drug problem. Aggressive, gun-toting drug dealers often upset law-abiding residents far more than do addicts nodding out in doorways. Meanwhile other residents perceive the drug dealers as heroes and successful role models. They're symbols of success to children who see no other options. At the same time the increasingly harsh criminal penalties imposed on adult drug dealers have led drug traffickers to recruit juveniles. Where once children started dealing drugs only after they had been using them for a few years, today the sequence is often reversed. Many children start using drugs only after working for older drug dealers for a while. Legalization of drugs, like legalization of alcohol in the 1930s, would drive the drug-dealing business off the streets and out of apartment buildings and into government-regulated, tax-paying stores. It also would force many of the gun-toting dealers out of the business and convert others into legitimate businessmen.

—Ethan A. Nadelmann, "Shooting Up"

Statistics argue against legalization. The University of Michigan conducts an annual survey of twelfth graders, asking the students about their drug consumption. In 1980, 56.4 percent of those polled said they had used marijuana in the past twelve months, whereas in 2005 only 45.7 percent had done so. Cocaine use was also reduced in the same period (22.6 percent to 15.4 percent). At the same time, twelve-month use of legally available drugs—alcohol and nicotine-containing cigarettes—remained constant at about 75 percent and 55 percent, respectively. The numbers of illegal drug users haven't declined nearly enough: those teenaged marijuana and cocaine users are still vulnerable to addiction and even death, and they threaten to infect their impressionable peers.

But clearly the prohibition of illegal drugs has helped, while the legal status of alcohol and cigarettes has not made them less popular.
—Sylvia Runkle, "The Case Against Legalization"

I have to laugh at the debate over what to do about the drug problem. Everyone is running around offering solutions—from making drug use a more serious criminal offense to legalizing it. But there isn't a real solution. I know that. I used and abused drugs, and people, and society, for two decades. Nothing worked to get me to stop all that behavior except just plain being sick and tired. Nothing. Not threats, not ten-plus years in prison, not anything that was said to me. I used until I got through. Period. And that's when you'll win the war. When all the dope fiends are done. Not a minute before.
—Michael W. Posey, "I Did Drugs Until They Wore Me Out. Then I Stopped."

53c Gather information from sources.

You can accomplish a great deal of synthesis while gathering information from your sources. This information gathering is not a mechanical process. Rather, as you read you assess and organize the information in your sources.

Researchers vary in their methods for working with sources, but all methods share the same goals:

- **Keep accurate records of what sources say.** Accuracy helps prevent misrepresentation and plagiarism.
- **Keep accurate records of how to find sources.** These records are essential for retracing steps and for citing sources in the final paper. (See pp. 422–24 on keeping a working bibliography.)
- **Interact with sources.** Reading sources critically leads to an understanding of them, the relationships among them, and their support for one's own ideas.

To achieve these goals, you can take handwritten notes, type notes into your computer, annotate photocopies or printouts of sources, or annotate downloaded documents. On any given project, you may use all the methods. Each has advantages and disadvantages.

- **Handwritten notes:** Taking notes by hand is especially useful if you come across a source with no computer or photocopier handy. But handwritten notes can be risky. It's easy to introduce errors as you work from source to note card. And it's possible to copy source language and then later mistake and use it as your own, thus plagiarizing the source. Always take care to make accurate notes and to place big quotation marks around any passage you quote.

53c

- **Notes on computer:** Taking notes on your computer can streamline the path of source to note to paper because you can import the notes into your draft as you write. However, computer notes have the same disadvantages as handwritten notes: the risk of introducing errors and the risk of plagiarizing. As with handwritten notes, strive for accuracy, and use quotation marks for quotations.

- **Photocopies and printouts:** Photocopying from print sources or printing out online sources each has the distinct advantages of convenience and reduction in the risks of error and plagiarism during information gathering. But each method has disadvantages, too. The busywork of copying or printing can distract you from the crucial work of interacting with sources. And you have to make a special effort to annotate copies and printouts with the publication information for sources. If you don't have this information for your final paper, you can't use the source.

- **Downloads:** Researching online, you can usually download full-text articles, Web pages, discussion-group messages, and other materials into your word processor. While drafting, you can import source information from one file into another. Like photocopies and printouts, though, downloads can distract you from interacting with sources and can easily become separated from the publication information you must have in order to use the sources. Even more important, directly importing source material creates a high risk of plagiarism. You must keep clear boundaries between your own ideas and words and those of others.

53d   Use summary, paraphrase, and quotation.

As you take notes from sources or work source material into your draft, you can summarize, paraphrase, quote, or combine methods. The choice should depend on why you are using a source.

Note Summaries, paraphrases, and quotations all require source citations in your paper. A summary or paraphrase without a source citation or a quotation without quotation marks is plagiarism. (See pp. 470–77 for more on plagiarism.)

53d

1 • Summary

When you **summarize,** you condense an extended idea or argument into a sentence or more in your own words. (See pp. 96–97 for tips.) Summary is most useful when you want to record the gist of an author's idea without the background or supporting evidence. Following is a passage from a government report on the so-called digital divide between US residents with and without access to the Internet. Then a sample computer note shows a summary of the passage.

Original quotation
        The following examples highlight the breadth of the digital divide today:

- Those with a college degree are more than *eight times* as likely to have a computer at home, and nearly *sixteen times* as likely to have home Internet access, as those with an elementary school education.

- A high-income household in an urban area is more than *twenty times* as likely as a rural, low-income household to have Internet access.

- A child in a low-income white family is *three times* as likely to have Internet access as a child in a comparable black family, and *four times* as likely to have access as children in a comparable Hispanic household.

                                        —US Department of Commerce,
                                        Falling Through the Net:
                                        Toward Digital Inclusion, p. 7

Summary of source

Digital divide

Dept. of Commerce 7

US residents who are urban, white, college educated, and affluent are much more likely to be connected to the Internet than those who are rural, black or Hispanic, not educated past elementary school, and poor.

2 • Paraphrase

When you **paraphrase**, you follow much more closely the author's original presentation, but you still restate it in your own words and sentence structures. Paraphrase is most useful when you want to present or examine an author's line of reasoning but don't feel the original words merit direct quotation. Here is a paraphrase of the quotation from the Department of Commerce report given above:

53d°

Paraphrase of source

Digital divide

Dept. of Commerce 7

Likelihood of being connected to the Internet among US groups:

Home connection, elementary education vs. college education: 1/16 as likely.

Any access, rural setting and low-income household vs. urban setting and afflu-ent household: 1/20 as likely.

Any access, low-income black child vs. low-income white child: 1/3 as likely.

Any access, low-income Hispanic child vs. low-income white child: 1/4 as likely.

Notice that the paraphrase follows the original but uses differ-ent words and different sentence structures. The paraphrase needs a source citation because it borrows ideas from the source, but it does not need quotation marks. In contrast, an unsuccessful paraphrase—one that plagiarizes—copies the author's words or sen-tence structures or both *without quotation marks*. (See p. 475 for ex-amples.)

Paraphrasing a source

- **Read the relevant material several times to be sure you under-stand it.**
- **Restate the source's ideas in your own words and sentence struc-tures.** You need not put down in new words the whole passage or all the details. Select what is relevant to your topic, and restate only that. If complete sentences seem too detailed or cumbersome, use phrases, as in the example above.
- **Be careful not to distort meaning.** Don't change the source's empha-sis or omit connecting words, qualifiers, and other material whose ab-sence will confuse you later or cause you to misrepresent the source.

53d

CULTURE LANGUAGE If English is your second language and you have difficulty paraphrasing the ideas in sources, try this. Before at-tempting a paraphrase, read the original passage several times. Then, instead of "translating" line by line, try to state the gist of the passage without looking at it. Check your effort against the original to be sure you have captured the source author's meaning and em-phasis without using his or her words and sentence structures. If you need a synonym for a word, look it up in a dictionary.

3 • Direct quotation

Your notes from sources may include many quotations, especially if you rely on photocopies, printouts, or downloads. Whether to use a quotation in your draft, instead of a summary or paraphrase, depends on whether the source is primary or secondary and on how important the exact words are:

- **Quote extensively when you are analyzing primary sources**—firsthand accounts such as literary works, eyewitness reports, and historical documents. The quotations will often be both the target of your analysis and the chief support for your ideas.
- **Quote selectively when you are drawing on secondary sources**—reports or analyses of other sources, such as a critic's view of a poem or a historian's synthesis of several eyewitness reports. Favor summaries and paraphrases over quotations, and put every quotation to each test in the box below. Most papers of ten or so pages should not need more than two or three quotations that are longer than a few lines each.

Tests for direct quotations from secondary sources

The author's original satisfies one of these requirements:

- The language is unusually vivid, bold, or inventive.
- The quotation cannot be paraphrased without distortion or loss of meaning.
- The words themselves are at issue in your interpretation.
- The quotation represents and emphasizes a body of opinion or the view of an important expert.
- The quotation emphatically reinforces your own idea.
- The quotation is an illustration such as a graph, diagram, or table.

The quotation is as short as possible:

- It includes only material relevant to your point.
- It is edited to eliminate examples and other unneeded material, using brackets and ellipsis marks (pp. 385–88.)

53d

When you quote a source, either in your notes or in your draft, take precautions to avoid plagiarism or misrepresentation of the source:

- **Copy the material carefully.** Take down the author's exact wording, spelling, capitalization, and punctuation.
- **Proofread every direct quotation at least twice.**

- **Use quotation marks around the quotation** so that later you won't confuse it with a paraphrase or summary. Be sure to transfer the quotation marks into your draft as well, unless the quotation is long and is set off from your text. For advice on handling long quotations, see pages 523–24 (MLA style) and 550 (APA style).

- **Use brackets** to add words for clarity or to change the capitalization of letters (see pp. 388, 400–01).

- **Use ellipsis marks** to omit irrelevant material (see pp. 385–87).

- **Cite the source of the quotation in your draft.** See pages 477–79 on documentation.

EXERCISE 53.6
Summarizing and paraphrasing

Prepare two source notes, one summarizing the entire paragraph below and the other paraphrasing the first four sentences (ending with the word *autonomy*). Use the format for a note illustrated on pages 461 and 462, omitting only the subject heading. (You can do this exercise online at *ablongman.com/littlebrown.*)

Federal organization [of the United States] has made it possible for the different states to deal with the same problems in many different ways. One consequence of federalism, then, has been that people are treated differently, by law, from state to state. The great strength of this system is that differences from state to state in cultural preferences, moral standards, and levels of wealth can be accommodated. In contrast to a unitary system in which the central government makes all important decisions (as in France), federalism is a powerful arrangement for maximizing regional freedom and autonomy. The great weakness of our federal system, however, is that people in some states receive less than the best or the most advanced or the least expensive services and policies that government can offer. The federal dilemma does not invite easy solution, for the costs and benefits of the arrangement have tended to balance out.

—Peter K. Eisinger et al., *American Politics,* p. 44

EXERCISE 53.7
Combining summary, paraphrase, and direct quotation

Prepare a source note containing a combination of paraphrase or summary and direct quotation that states the main idea of the passage below. Use the format for a note illustrated on pages 461 and 462, omitting only the subject heading. (You can do this exercise online at *ablongman.com/littlebrown.*)

Most speakers unconsciously duel even during seemingly casual conversations, as can often be observed at social gatherings where they show less concern for exchanging information with other guests than for asserting their own dominance. Their verbal dueling often employs very subtle weapons like mumbling, a hostile act which defeats the listener's desire to understand what the speaker claims he is trying to say (but is really not saying because he is mumbling!). Or the verbal dueler may keep talking after someone has passed out of hearing range—which is often an aggressive challenge to the listener to return and acknowledge the dominance of the speaker.

—Peter K. Farb, *Word Play*, p. 107

53e   Integrate sources into your text.

The evidence of others' information and opinions should back up, not dominate, your own ideas. To synthesize evidence, you need to smooth the transitions between your ideas and words and those of your sources, and you need to give the reader a context for interpreting the borrowed material.

Note The examples in this section use the MLA syle of source documentation and also present-tense verbs (such as *disagrees* and *claims*). See pages 468–69 for specific variations in documentation style and verb tense within the academic disciplines. Several other conventions governing quotations are discussed elsewhere in this book:

- Using commas to punctuate signal phrases (pp. 361–62).
- Placing other punctuation marks with quotation marks (pp. 381–82).
- Using brackets and the ellipsis mark to indicate changes in quotations (pp. 385–88).
- Punctuating and placing parenthetical citations (pp. 489–91).
- Formatting long prose quotations and poetry quotations (MLA style, pp. 523–24; APA style, p. 550).

1 • Introduction of borrowed material

Readers will be distracted from your point if borrowed material does not fit into your sentence. In the passage below, the writer has not meshed the structures of her own and her source's sentences:

Awkward   One editor disagrees with this view and "a good reporter does not fail to separate opinions from facts" (Lyman 52).

In the following revision the writer adds words to integrate the quotation into her sentence:

Revised   One editor disagrees with this view, <u>maintaining that</u> "a good reporter does not fail to separate opinions from facts" (Lyman 52).

53e

To mesh your own and your source's words, you may sometimes need to make a substitution or addition to the quotation, signaling your change with brackets:

Words added	"The tabloids [of England] are a journalistic case study in bad reporting," claims Lyman (52).
Verb form changed	A bad reporter, Lyman implies, is one who "[fails] to separate opinions from facts" (52). [The bracketed verb replaces *fail* in the original.]
Capitalization changed	"[T]o separate opinions from facts" is the work of a good reporter (Lyman 52). [In the original, *to* is not capitalized.]
Noun supplied for pronoun	The reliability of a news organization "depends on [reporters'] trustworthiness," says Lyman (52). [The bracketed noun replaces *their* in the original.]

2 • Interpretation of borrowed material

Even when it does not conflict with your own sentence structure, borrowed material will be ineffective if you merely dump it in readers' laps without explaining how you intend it to be understood. Reading the following passage, we must figure out for ourselves that the writer's sentence and the quotation state opposite points of view:

Dumped	Many news editors and reporters maintain that it is impossible to keep personal opinions from influencing the selection and presentation of facts. "True, news reporters, like everyone else, form impressions of what they see and hear. However, a good reporter does not fail to separate opinions from facts" (Lyman 52).

In the following revision, the underlined additions tell us how to interpret the quotation:

Revised	Many news editors and reporters maintain that it is impossible to keep personal opinions from influencing the selection and presentation of facts. Yet not all authorities agree with this view. One editor grants that "news reporters, like everyone else, form impressions of what they see and hear." But, he insists, "a good reporter does not fail to separate opinions from facts" (Lyman 52).

53e

Signal phrases

The words *One editor grants* and *he insists* in the preceding revised passage are **signal phrases:** they tell readers who the source is and what to expect in the quotations that follow. Signal phrases usually contain (1) the source author's name (or a substitute for it, such as *One editor* and *he*) and (2) a verb that indicates the source author's attitude or approach to what he or she says.

Some verbs for signal phrases appear below. These verbs are in the present tense, typical of writing in the humanities. In the social and natural sciences, the past tense (*asked*) or present perfect tense (*has asked*) is more common. See pages 468–69.

Author is neutral	Author infers or suggests	Author argues	Author is uneasy or disparaging
comments	analyzes	claims	belittles
describes	asks	contends	bemoans
explains	assesses	defends	complains
illustrates	concludes	holds	condemns
notes	considers	insists	deplores
observes	finds	maintains	deprecates
points out	predicts		derides
records	proposes	Author	disagrees
relates	reveals	agrees	laments
reports	shows	admits	warns
says	speculates	agrees	
sees	suggests	concedes	
thinks	supposes	grants	
writes			

Vary your signal phrases to suit your interpretation of borrowed material and also to keep readers' interest. A signal phrase may precede, interrupt, or follow the borrowed material:

Precedes   Lyman insists that "a good reporter does not fail to separate opinions from facts" (52).

Interrupts "However," Lyman insists, "a good reporter does not fail to separate opinions from facts" (52).

Follows   "[A] good reporter does not fail to separate opinions from facts," Lyman insists (52).

Background information

You can add information to a signal phrase to inform readers why you are using a source. In most cases, provide the author's name in the text, especially if the author is an expert or readers will recognize the name:

Author   Harold Lyman grants that "news reporters, like everyone
named   else, form impressions of what they see and hear." But, Lyman insists, "a good reporter does not fail to separate opinions from facts" (52).

53e

If the source title contributes information about the author or the context of the quotation, you can provide it in the text:

Title
given

Harold Lyman, in his book *The Conscience of the Journalist,* grants that "news reporters, like everyone else, form impressions of what they see and hear." But, Lyman insists, "a good reporter does not fail to separate opinions from facts" (52).

If the quoted author's background and experience reinforce or clarify the quotation, you can provide these credentials in the text:

Credentials
given

Harold Lyman, a newspaper editor for more than forty years, grants that "news reporters, like everyone else, form impressions of what they see and hear." But, Lyman insists, "a good reporter does not fail to separate opinions from facts" (52).

You need not name the author, source, or credentials in your text when you are simply establishing facts or weaving together facts and opinions from varied sources. In the following passage, the information is more important than the source, so the name of the source is confined to a parenthetical acknowledgment:

To end the abuses of the British, many colonists were urging three actions: forming a united front, seceding from Britain, and taking control of their own international relations (Wills 325–36).

3 • Discipline styles for integrating sources

The preceding guidelines for introducing and interpreting borrowed material apply generally across academic disciplines, but the disciplines do differ in verb tenses and documentation style.

English and some other humanities

Writers in English, foreign languages, and related disciplines use MLA style for documenting sources (see Chapter 56) and generally use the present tense of verbs in signal phrases. In discussing sources other than works of literature, the present perfect tense is also sometimes appropriate:

Lyman insists . . . [present].
Lyman has insisted . . . [present perfect].

In discussing works of literature, use only the present tense to describe both the work of the author and the action in the work:

Kate Chopin builds irony into every turn of "The Story of an Hour." For example, Mrs. Mallard, the central character, finds joy in the death of

53e

her husband, whom she <u>loves</u>, because she <u>anticipates</u> "the long procession of years that would belong to her absolutely" (23).

Avoid shifting tenses in writing about literature. You can, for instance, shorten quotations to avoid their past-tense verbs.

Shift Her freedom <u>elevates</u> her, so that "she <u>carried</u> herself unwittingly like a goddess of victory" (24).

No shift Her freedom <u>elevates</u> her, so that she <u>walks</u> "unwittingly like a goddess of victory" (24).

History and other humanities

Writers in history, art history, philosophy, and related disciplines generally use the present tense or present perfect tense of verbs in signal phrases.

Lincoln persisted, as Haworth <u>has noted</u>, in "feeling that events controlled him."[3]

What Miller <u>calls</u> Lincoln's "severe self-doubt"[6] undermined his effectiveness on at least two occasions.

The raised numbers after the quotations are part of the Chicago documentation style, used in history and other disciplines. See this book's Web site (*ablongman.com/littlebrown*) for information on Chicago style.

Social and natural sciences

Writers in the sciences generally use a verb's present tense just for reporting the results of a study (*The data suggest* . . .). Otherwise, they use a verb's past or present perfect tense in a signal phrase, as when introducing an explanation, interpretation, or other commentary. (Thus when you are writing for the sciences generally convert the list of signal-phrase verbs on p. 467 from the present to the past or present perfect tense.)

Lin (2001) <u>has suggested</u> that preschooling may significantly affect children's academic performance not only in elementary school but through high school (pp. 22–23).

In an exhaustive survey of the literature published between 1990 and 2005, Walker (2006) <u>found</u> "no proof, merely a weak correlation, linking place of residence and rate of illness" (p. 121).

These passages conform to APA documentation style, discussed in Chapter 57. APA style, or one quite similar to it, is also used in sociology, education, nursing, biology, and many other social and natural sciences.

53e

EXERCISE 53.8
Introducing and interpreting borrowed material

Drawing on the ideas in the following paragraph and using examples from your own observations and experiences, write a paragraph about anxiety. Integrate at least one direct quotation and one paraphrase from the following paragraph into your own sentences. In your paragraph identify the author by name and give his credentials: he is a professor of psychiatry and a practicing psychoanalyst. (You can do this exercise on-line at *ablongman.com/littlebrown*.)

> There are so many ways in which human beings are different from all the lower forms of animals, and almost all of them make us uniquely susceptible to feelings of anxiousness. Our imagination and reasoning powers facilitate anxiety; the anxious feeling is precipitated not by an absolute impending threat—such as the worry about an examination, a speech, travel—but rather by the symbolic and often unconscious representations. We do not have to be experiencing a potential danger. We can experience something related to it. We can recall, through our incredible memories, the original symbolic sense of vulnerability in childhood and suffer the feeling attached to that. We can even forget the original memory and be stuck with the emotion—which is then compounded by its seemingly irrational quality at this time. It is not just the fear of death which pains us, but the anticipation of it; or the anniversary of a specific death; or a street, a hospital, a time of day, a color, a flower, a symbol associated with death.
>
> —Willard Gaylin, "Feeling Anxious," p. 23

54 Avoiding Plagiarism and Documenting Sources

How can I use sources honestly?

Honest use of sources underpins the knowledge building that is the focus of academic writing. The work of an author is his or her intellectual property: if you use that work, you must acknowledge the author's ownership. At the same time, source acknowledgments tell readers what your own writing is based on, creating the trust that knowledge building requires.

Plagiarism (from a Latin word for "kidnapper") is the presentation of someone else's ideas or words as your own. Whether deliberate or accidental, plagiarism is a serious offense.

plag
54

---

http://www.ablongman.com/littlebrown ▶

Visit the companion Web site for more help and an electronic exercise on avoiding plagiarism and documenting sources.

- *Deliberate* plagiarism:

  Copying or downloading a phrase, a sentence, or a longer passage from a source and passing it off as your own by omitting quotation marks and a source citation.

  Summarizing or paraphrasing someone else's ideas without acknowledging your debt in a source citation.

  Handing in as your own work a paper you have bought, copied off the Web, had a friend write, or accepted from another student.

- *Accidental* plagiarism:

  Forgetting to place quotation marks around another writer's words.

  Carelessly omitting a source citation for a paraphrase.

  Omitting a source citation for another's idea because you are unaware of the need to acknowledge the idea.

In most colleges a code of academic honesty calls for severe consequences for deliberate or accidental plagiarism: a failing grade, suspension from school, or even expulsion.

The way to avoid plagiarism is to acknowledge your sources by documenting them. This chapter discusses plagiarism and the Internet, shows how to distinguish what doesn't require acknowledgment from what does, and provides an overview of source documentation.

◖ CULTURE LANGUAGE ◗ The concept of intellectual property and thus the rules governing plagiarism are not universal. In some other cultures, for instance, students may be encouraged to copy the words of scholars without acknowledgment, in order to demonstrate their mastery of or respect for the scholars' work. In the United States, however, using an author's work without a source citation is considered theft. When in doubt about the guidelines in this chapter, ask your instructor for advice.

54a Beware of plagiarism from the Internet.

The Internet has made it easier to plagiarize than ever before, but it has also made plagiarism easier to catch.

Even honest students risk accidental plagiarism by downloading sources and importing portions into their drafts. Dishonest students may take advantage of downloading to steal others' work. They may also use the term-paper businesses on the Web, which offer both ready-made research and complete papers, usually for a fee. **Paying for research or a paper does not make it the buyer's work.** Anyone who submits someone else's work as his or her own is a plagiarist.

Checklist for avoiding plagiarism

Type of source

Are you using

- your own independent material,
- common knowledge, or
- someone else's independent material?

You must acknowledge someone else's material.

Quotations

- Do all quotations exactly match their sources? Check them.
- Have you inserted quotation marks around quotations that are run into your text?
- Have you shown omissions with ellipsis marks and additions with brackets?
- Does every quotation have a source citation?

Paraphrases and summaries

- Have you used your own words and sentence structures for every paraphrase and summary? If not, use quotation marks around the original author's words.
- Does every paraphrase and summary have a source citation?

The Web

- Have you obtained any necessary permission to use someone else's material on the Web?

Source citations

- Have you acknowledged every use of someone else's material in the place where you use it?
- Does your list of works cited include all the sources you have used?

You can download this checklist from *ablongman.com/littlebrown*. Working with a copy of the list, question every use you make of someone else's material.

Students who plagiarize from the Internet both deprive themselves of an education in honest research and expose themselves to detection. Teachers can use search engines to locate specific phrases or sentences anywhere on the Web, including among scholarly publications, all kinds of Web sites, and term-paper collections. They can search the term-paper sites as easily as students can, looking for similarities with papers they've received. Increasingly, teachers can use special detection programs that compare students' work with other work anywhere on the Internet, seeking matches as short as a few words.

Some instructors suggest that their students use plagiarism-detection programs to verify that their own work does not include accidental plagiarism, at least not from the Internet. Links to such programs appear on this book's Web site at *ablongman.com/littlebrown.*

54b   Know what you need not acknowledge.

1 • Your independent material

Your own observations, thoughts, compilations of facts, or experimental results—expressed in your words and format—do not require acknowledgment. You should describe the basis for your conclusions so that readers can evaluate your thinking, but you need not cite sources for them.

2 • Common knowledge

Common knowledge consists of the standard information on a subject as well as folk literature and commonsense observations.

- **Standard information** includes the major facts of history, such as the dates of Charlemagne's rule as emperor of Rome (800–14). It does not include interpretations of facts, such as a historian's opinion that Charlemagne was sometimes needlessly cruel in extending his power.
- **Folk literature,** such as the fairy tale "Snow White," is popularly known and cannot be traced to a particular writer. Literature traceable to a writer is not folk literature, even if it is very familiar.
- **Commonsense observations** are things most people know, such as that inflation is most troublesome for people with low and fixed incomes. However, an economist's argument about the effects of inflation on Chinese immigrants is *not* a commonsense observation.

If you do not know a subject well enough to determine whether a piece of information is common knowledge, make a record of the source as you would for any other quotation, paraphrase, or summary. As you read more about the subject, the information may come up in other people's work without any source citation, in which case it is probably common knowledge. But if you are still in doubt when you finish your research, always acknowledge the source.

plag
54b

54c Know what you *must* acknowledge.

You must always acknowledge other people's independent material—that is, any facts or ideas that are not common knowledge or your own. The source may be anything, including a book, an article, a movie, an interview, a microfilmed document, a Web page, a newsgroup posting, or an opinion expressed on the radio. You must acknowledge summaries or paraphrases of ideas or facts as well as quotations of the language and format in which ideas or facts appear: wording, sentence structures, arrangement, and special graphics (such as a diagram). You must acknowledge another's material no matter how you use it, how much of it you use, or how often you use it.

1 • Using copied language: Quotation marks and a source citation

The following example baldly plagiarizes the original quotation from Jessica Mitford's *Kind and Usual Punishment,* page 9. Without quotation marks or a source citation, the example matches Mitford's wording (underlined) and closely parallels her sentence structure:

Original quotation	"The character and mentality of the keepers may be of more importance in understanding prisons than the character and mentality of the kept."
Plagiarism	But the character of prison officials (the keepers) is more important in understanding prisons than the character of prisoners (the kept).

To avoid plagiarism, the writer has two options: (1) paraphrase and cite the source (see the revised examples opposite) or (2) use Mitford's actual words *in quotation marks* and *with a source citation* (here, in MLA style):

Revision (quotation)	According to one critic of the penal system, @The character and mentality of the keepers may be of more importance in understanding prisons than the character and mentality of the kept@ (Mitford 9).

Even with a source citation and with a different sentence structure, the next example is still plagiarism because it uses some of Mitford's words (underlined) without quotation marks:

Plagiarism	According to one critic of the penal system, the psychology of the kept may say less about prisons than the psychology of the keepers (Mitford 9).
Revision (quotation)	According to one critic of the penal system, the psychology of @the kept@ may say less about prisons than the psychology of @the keepers@ (Mitford 9).

2 • Using paraphrase or summary: Your own words and sentence structure and a source citation

The example below changes the sentence structure of the original Mitford quotation, but it still uses Mitford's words (underlined) without quotation marks and without a source citation:

Plagiarism   In understanding prisons, we should know more about the character and mentality of the keepers than of the kept.

To avoid plagiarism, the writer has two options: (1) use quotation marks and cite the source (opposite) or (2) *use his or her own words* and still *cite the source* (because the idea is Mitford's, not the writer's):

Revision   Mitford holds that we may be able to learn more about
(paraphrase)   prisons from the psychology of the prison officials than from that of the prisoners (9).

Revision   We may understand prisons better if we focus on the
(paraphrase)   personalities and attitudes of the prison workers rather than those of the inmates (Mitford 9).

In the next example, the writer cites Mitford and does not use her words but still plagiarizes her sentence structure:

Plagiarism   One critic of the penal system maintains that the psychology of prison officials may be more informative about prisons than the psychology of prisoners (Mitford 9).

Revision   One critic of the penal system maintains that we may be
(paraphrase)   able to learn less from the psychology of prisoners than from the psychology of prison officials (Mitford 9).

EXERCISE 54.1
Recognizing plagiarism

The numbered items below show various attempts to quote or paraphrase the following passage. Carefully compare each attempt with the original passage. Which attempts are plagiarized, inaccurate, or both, and which are acceptable? Why?

I would agree with the sociologists that psychiatric labeling is dangerous. Society can inflict terrible wounds by discrimination, and by confusing health with disease and disease with badness.
                    —George E. Vaillant, *Adaptation to Life,* p. 361

1. According to George Vaillant, society often inflicts wounds by using psychiatric labeling, confusing health, disease, and badness (361).
2. According to George Vaillant, "psychiatric labeling [such as 'homosexual' or 'schizophrenic'] is dangerous. Society can inflict terrible wounds by . . . confusing health with disease and disease with badness" (361).
3. According to George Vaillant, when psychiatric labeling discriminates between health and disease or between disease and badness, it can inflict wounds on those labeled (361).

4. Psychiatric labels can badly hurt those labeled, says George Vaillant, because they fail to distinguish among health, illness, and immorality (361).
5. Labels such as "homosexual" and "schizophrenic" can be hurtful when they fail to distinguish among health, illness, and immorality.
6. "I would agree with the sociologists that society can inflict terrible wounds by discrimination, and by confusing health with disease and disease with badness" (Vaillant 361).

54d Take care with online sources.

Online sources are so accessible and so easy to download into your own documents that it may seem they are freely available, exempting you from the obligation to acknowledge them. They are not. Acknowledging online sources is somewhat trickier than acknowledging print sources, but no less essential. Further, if you are publishing your work online, you need to take account of sources' copyright restrictions as well.

1 • Online sources in an unpublished project

When you use material from an online source in a print or online document to be distributed just to your class, your obligation to cite sources does not change: you must acknowledge someone else's independent material in whatever form you find it. With online sources, that obligation can present additional challenges:

- **Record complete publication information each time you consult an online source.** Online sources may change from one day to the next or even disappear entirely. See page 423 for the information to record, such as the electronic address and the publication date. Without the proper information, you *may not* use the source.
- **Acknowledge linked sites.** If you use not only a Web site but also one or more of its linked sites, you must acknowledge the linked sites as well. The fact that one person has used a second person's work does not release you from the responsibility to cite the second work.
- **Seek the author's permission before using an e-mail message, Web-log contribution, or discussion-group posting.** Obtaining permission advises the author that his or her ideas are about to be distributed more widely and lets the author verify that you have not misrepresented the ideas.

2 • Print and online sources in a Web composition

When you use material from print or online sources in a composition for the Web, you must not only acknowledge your sources but also take the additional precaution of observing copyright restrictions.

A Web site is a medium of publication just as a book or magazine is and so involves the same responsibility to obtain reprint permission from copyright holders. The exception is a password-protected site (such as a course site), which many copyright holders regard as private. You can find information about copyright holders and permissions on the copyright page of a print publication (following the title page) and on a page labeled something like "Terms of Use" on a Web site. If you don't see an explicit release for student use or publication on private Web sites, assume you must seek permission.

The legal convention of fair use allows an author to reprint a small portion of copyrighted material without obtaining the copyright holder's permission, as long as the author acknowledges the source. The online standards of fair use differ for print and online sources and are not fixed in either case. The guidelines below are conservative:

- **Print sources:** Quote without permission fewer than fifty words from an article or fewer than three hundred words from a book. You'll need the copyright holder's permission to use any longer quotation from an article or book; any quotation at all from a play, poem, or song; and any use of an entire work, such as a photograph, chart, or other illustration.

- **Online sources:** Quote without permission text that represents just a small portion of the whole—say, forty words out of three hundred. Follow the print guidelines above for plays, poems, songs, and illustrations, adding multimedia elements (audio or video clips) to the list of works that require reprint permission for any use.

- **Links:** You may need to seek permission to link your site to another one—for instance, if you rely on the linked site to substantiate your claims or to provide a multimedia element.

54e   Document sources carefully.

Every time you borrow the words, facts, or ideas of others, you must **document** the source—that is, supply a reference (or document) telling readers that you borrowed the material and where you borrowed it from.

Editors and teachers in most academic disciplines require special documentation formats (or styles) in their scholarly journals and in students' papers. All the styles share common features:

- **Citations in the text** signal that material is borrowed and refer readers to detailed information about the sources.

- **Detailed source information,** either in footnotes or at the end
  of the paper, tells how to locate the sources.

Together, the citations and detailed information allow readers to find
both the sources and the places in them where borrowed material
appears.

Aside from these essential similarities, the disciplines' documentation styles differ markedly in citation form, arrangement of
source information, and other particulars. Each discipline's style reflects the needs of its practitioners for certain kinds of information
presented in certain ways. For instance, the currency of a source is
important in the social sciences, where studies build on and correct
each other; thus in-text citations in the social sciences include a
source's date of publication. In the humanities, however, currency is
less important, so in-text citations do not include date of publication.

The disciplines' documentation formats are described in style
guides, including those in the following list. This book presents the
styles of the guides marked *: the *MLA Handbook* and the *APA Publication Manual*. In addition, the styles of two of the other guides
are detailed on this book's Web site at *ablongman.com/littlebrown*:
The Chicago Manual of Style (for the humanities) and *Scientific Style
and Format: The CSE Manual for Authors, Editors, and Publishers*
(for the natural sciences).

Humanities
The Chicago Manual of Style. 15th ed. 2003. (See this book's Web site.)
*Gibaldi, Joseph. *MLA Handbook for Writers of Research Papers.* 6th ed.
  2003. (See pp. 483–530.)
Turabian, Kate L. *A Manual for Writers of Term Papers, Theses, and Disser-
  tations.* 6th ed. Rev. John Grossman and Alice Bennett. 1996.

Social sciences
American Anthropological Association. "AAA Style Guide." 2002.
  http://www.aaanet.org/pubs/style_guide.htm.
American Management Association. *The AMA Style Guide for Business
  Writing.* 1996.
American Political Science Association. *Style Manual for Political Science.*
  2001.
*American Psychological Association. *Publication Manual of the American
  Psychological Association.* 5th ed. 2001. (See pp. 531–54.)
American Sociological Association. *ASA Style Guide.* 2nd ed. 1997.
Linguistic Society of America. "LSA Style Sheet." Published every Decem-
  ber in *LSA Bulletin.*
A Uniform System of Citation (law). 17th ed. 2001.

Sciences and mathematics
American Chemical Society. *ACS Style Guide: A Manual for Authors and
  Editors.* 2nd ed. 1997.

American Institute of Physics. *Style Manual for Guidance in the Preparation of Papers.* 4th ed. 1990.

American Mathematical Society. *The AMS Author Handbook: General Instructions for Preparing Manuscripts.* Rev. ed. 1996.

American Medical Association Manual of Style. 9th ed. 1998.

Bates, Robert L., Rex Buchanan, and Marla Adkins-Heljeson, eds. *Geowriting: A Guide to Writing, Editing, and Printing in Earth Science.* 5th ed. 1995.

Council of Science Editors. *Scientific Style and Format: The CSE Manual for Authors, Editors, and Publishers.* 7th ed. 2006. (See this book's Web site.)

Always ask your instructor which documentation style you should use. If your instructor does not require a particular style, use the one in this book that's appropriate for the discipline you're writing in. Do follow a single system for citing sources so that you provide all the necessary information in a consistent format.

Note Bibliography software—*Biblio, Refworks, Endnote, Procite,* and others—can help you format your source citations in the style of your choice. Always ask your instructors if you may use such software for your papers. The programs prompt you for needed information (author's name, book title, date of publication, and so on) and then arrange, capitalize, and punctuate the information as required by the style. But no program can anticipate all varieties of source information or substitute for your own care and attention in giving your sources accurate and complete acknowledgment in the required form.

55 Writing the Paper

What are the stages of writing research?

Like other kinds of writing, research writing involves focusing on a main idea, organizing ideas, expressing ideas in a draft, revising and editing drafts, and formatting the final paper. Because research writing draws on others' work, however, its stages also require attention to interpreting, integrating, and citing sources.

This chapter complements and extends the detailed discussion of the writing situation and the writing process in Chapters 1–5,

55

---

http://www.ablongman.com/littlebrown

Visit the companion Web site for more help on writing and revising a research paper.

which also include many tips for using a word processor. If you haven't already done so, you may want to read Chapters 1–5 before this one.

55a   Focus and organize the paper.

Before you begin using your source notes in a draft, give some thought to your main idea and your organization.

1 • Thesis statement

You began research with a question about your subject (see p. 419). Though that question may have evolved during research, you should be able to answer it once you've consulted most of your sources. Try to state that answer in a **thesis statement,** a claim that narrows your subject to a single idea. Here, for example, are the research question and thesis statement of Kisha Alder, whose final paper appears on pages 526–30:

Research question
How, if at all, should the Internet be taxed?

Thesis statement
To improve equity between online and traditional stores and between consumers with and without Internet access, tax laws should be revised to allow collection of sales taxes on Internet purchases.

A precise thesis statement will give you a focus as you organize and draft your paper. For more on thesis statements, see pages 18–20.

2 • Organization

To structure your paper, you'll need to synthesize, or forge relationships among ideas (see pp. 457–58). Here is one approach:

- **Arrange source information in categories.** Each group should correspond to a main section of your paper: a key idea of your own that supports the thesis.
- **Review your research journal** for connections between sources and other thoughts that can help you organize your paper.
- **Look objectively at your categories.** If some are skimpy, with little information, consider whether you should drop the categories or conduct more research to fill them out. If most of your information falls into one or two categories, consider whether they are too broad and should be divided. (If any of this rethinking affects your thesis statement, revise it accordingly.)

55a

- **Within each group, distinguish between the main idea and the supporting ideas and evidence.** Only the support should come from your sources. The main idea should be your own.

See pages 21–25 for more on organizing a paper, including samples of both informal and formal outlines.

55b Draft, revise, and format the paper.

1 • First draft

In drafting your paper, you do not have to proceed methodically from introduction to conclusion. Here are some tips for writing a draft:

- **Work section by section.** Draft your paper in sections, beginning with the one you feel most confident about. Each section should center on a principal idea contributing to your thesis, a conclusion you have drawn from reading and responding to sources. Start the section by stating the idea; then support it with information, summaries, paraphrases, and quotations from your notes. Remember to insert source information from your notes as well.
- **Weave the sections together with transitions and other signposts.** As the sections of your paper develop, you will see relationships emerging among them. Spell these relationships out, and highlight them with transitions (see pp. 56–57 and 69–70). Headings may be appropriate to highlight your organization and signal direction. These signposts will help create a coherent whole.
- **Track source citations.** As you draft your paper, insert the source of each summary, paraphrase, and quotation in parentheses in the text—for instance, "(Frankel 42)," referring to page 42 in a work by Frankel. If you are conscientious about inserting these notes and carrying them through successive drafts, you will be less likely to plagiarize accidentally and you will have little difficulty documenting your sources in the final paper.

2 • Revision and editing

For a complex project like a research paper, you'll certainly want to revise in at least two stages—first for thesis, structure, and other whole-paper issues, and then for clarity, grammar, and similar sentence-level issues. Chapter 5 supports this two-stage approach

55b

with checklists for revision (p. 32) and editing (p. 37). The box below provides additional steps to take when revising a research paper.

Checklist for revising a research paper

Assignment
How does the draft satisfy all of the criteria stated in your instructor's assignment?

Thesis statement
How well does your thesis statement describe your subject and your perspective as they emerged during drafting?

Structure
(Outlining your draft can help you see structure at a glance. See p. 24.)
How consistently does borrowed material illuminate and support—not lead and dominate—your own ideas? How well is the importance of ideas reflected in the emphasis they receive? Will the arrangement of ideas be clear to readers?

Evidence
Where might supporting evidence seem weak or irrelevant to readers?

Reasonableness and clarity
How reasonable will readers find your argument? (See pp. 127–37.) Where do you need to define terms or concepts that readers may not know or may dispute?

You can download this checklist from *ablongman.com/littlebrown*. Copy the checklist for each research paper, answering the questions in writing.

---

3 • Format

The final draft of your paper should conform to the document format recommended by your instructor or by the style guide of the discipline in which you are writing (see pp. 478–79). This book details two common formats: Modern Language Association (opposite) and American Psychological Association (p. 531).

In any discipline you can use a word processor to present your ideas effectively and attractively with readable type fonts, headings, illustrations, and other elements. See pages 74–84 for ideas.

55b

56 MLA Documentation and Format

How do I cite sources and format papers in English and other humanities?

The style guide for English, foreign languages, and some other humanities is the *MLA Handbook for Writers of Research Papers* (6th ed., 2003), published by the Modern Language Association. In the documentation system of the *MLA Handbook*, you twice acknowledge the sources of borrowed material:

- In your text, a brief parenthetical citation adjacent to the borrowed material directs readers to a complete list of all the works you cite.
- At the end of your paper, the list of works cited includes complete bibliographical information for every source.

Every entry in the list of works cited has at least one corresponding citation in the text, and every in-text citation has a corresponding entry in the list of works cited.

This chapter describes MLA documentation: writing text citations (below), placing citations (p. 489), using supplementary notes (p. 491), and preparing the list of works cited (p. 491). A detailed discussion of MLA document format (p. 521) and a sample MLA paper (p. 524) conclude the chapter.

56a Use MLA parenthetical citations in your text.

1 • Citation formats

In-text citations of sources must include just enough information for the reader to locate the following:

- The *source* in your list of works cited.
- The *place in the source* where the borrowed material appears.

For any kind of source, you can usually meet both these requirements by providing the author's last name and (if the source uses them) the page numbers where the borrowed material appears. The reader can find the source in your list of works cited and find the borrowed material in the source itself.

The following models illustrate the basic text-citation forms and also forms for more unusual sources, such as those with no named

MLA parenthetical text citations

1. Author not named in your text *484*
2. Author named in your text *484*
3. A work with two or three authors *485*
4. A work with more than three authors *485*
5. A work with numbered paragraphs or screens instead of pages *485*
6. An entire work or a work with no page or other reference numbers *485*
7. A multivolume work *486*
8. A work by an author of two or more cited works *486*
9. An anonymous work *486*
10. A government publication or a work with a corporate author *487*
11. An indirect source *487*
12. A literary work *487*
13. The Bible *488*
14. An electronic source *488*
15. Two or more works in the same citation *488*

author or no page numbers. See the box above for an index to all the models.

Note Models 1 and 2 below show the direct relationship between what you include in your text and what you include in a parenthetical citation. If you do *not* name the author in your text, you include the name in parentheses before the page reference (model 1). If you *do* name the author in your text, you do not include the name in parentheses (model 2).

1. Author not named in your text

When you have not already named the author in your sentence, provide the author's last name and the page number(s), with no punctuation between them, in parentheses:

> One researcher concludes that "women impose a distinctive construction on moral problems, seeing moral dilemmas in terms of conflicting responsibilities" (Gilligan 105-06).

2. Author named in your text

If the author's name is already given in your text, you need not repeat it in the parenthetical citation. The citation gives just the page number(s):

> Carol Gilligan concludes that "women impose a distinctive construction on moral problems, seeing moral dilemmas in terms of conflicting responsibilities" (105-06).

3. A work with two or three authors

If the source has two or three authors, give all their last names in the text or in the citation. Separate two authors' names with and:

As Frieden and Sagalyn observe, "The poor and the minorities were the leading victims of highway and renewal programs" (29).

According to one study, "The poor and the minorities were the leading victims of highway and renewal programs" (Frieden and Sagalyn 29).

With three authors, add commas and also and before the final name:

The textbook by Wilcox, Ault, and Agee discusses the "ethical dilemmas in public relations practice" (125).

One textbook discusses the "ethical dilemmas in public relations practice" (Wilcox, Ault, and Agee 125).

4. A work with more than three authors

If the source has more than three authors, you may list all their last names or use only the first author's name followed by et al. (the abbreviation for the Latin "and others"). The choice depends on what you do in your list of works cited (see p. 495).

It took the combined forces of the Americans, Europeans, and Japanese to break the rebel siege of Beijing in 1900 (Lopez et al. 362).

It took the combined forces of the Americans, Europeans, and Japanese to break the rebel siege of Beijing in 1900 (Lopez, Blum, Cameron, and Barnes 362).

5. A work with numbered paragraphs or screens instead of pages

Some electronic sources number each paragraph or screen instead of each page. In citing passages in these sources, give the paragraph or screen number(s) and distinguish them from page numbers: after the author's name, put a comma, a space, and the abbreviation par. (one paragraph), pars. (more than one paragraph), screen, or screens.

Twins reared apart report similar feelings (Palfrey, pars. 6-7).

6. An entire work or a work with no page or other reference numbers

When you cite an entire work rather than a part of it, the citation will not include any page or paragraph number. Try to work the author's name into your text, in which case you will not need a parenthetical citation. But remember that the source must appear in the list of works cited.

MLA
56a

> Boyd deals with the need to acknowledge and come to terms with our fear of nuclear technology.

Use the same format when you cite a specific passage from a work that has no page, paragraph, or other reference numbers, such as an online source.

If the author's name does not appear in your text, put it in a parenthetical citation:

> Almost 20 percent of commercial banks have been audited for the practice (Friis).

7. A multivolume work

If you consulted only one volume of a multivolume work, your list of works cited will say so (see p. 498), and you can treat the volume as any book.

If you consulted two or more volumes of a multivolume work, your citation must indicate which one you are referring to. In the example the number 5 indicates the volume from which the quotation was taken; the number 438 indicates the page number in that volume.

> After issuing the Emancipation Proclamation, Lincoln said, "What I did, I did after very full deliberations, and under a very heavy and solemn sense of responsibility" (5: 438).

8. A work by an author of two or more cited works

If your list of works cited includes two or more works by the same author, then your citation must tell the reader which of the author's works you are referring to. Give the title either in the text or in a parenthetical citation. In a parenthetical citation, give the full title only if it is brief; otherwise, shorten the title to the first one, two, or three main words (excluding *A, An,* or *The*). For the following source, the full book title is *The Arts and Human Development:*

> At about age seven, most children begin to use appropriate gestures to reinforce their stories (Gardner, <u>Arts</u> 144-45).

9. An anonymous work

Anonymous works are alphabetized by title in the list of works cited. In the text they are referred to by full or shortened title. The next citation refers to an unsigned article titled "The Right to Die." (A page number is omitted because the article is only one page.)

> One article notes that a death-row inmate may demand his own execution to achieve a fleeting notoriety ("Right").

If two or more anonymous works have the same title, distinguish them with additional information in the text citation, such as the publication date.

10. A government publication or a work with a corporate author

Some works list as author a government body, association, committee, company, or other group. Cite such a work by that organization's name. If the name is long, work it into the text to avoid an intrusive citation.

A 2005 report by the Hawaii Department of Education predicts an increase in enrollments (6).

11. An indirect source

When you want to use a quotation that is already in quotation marks—indicating that the author you are reading is quoting someone else—try to find the original source and quote directly from it. If you can't find the original source, then your citation must indicate that your quotation of it is indirect. In the following citation, qtd. in ("quoted in") says that Davino was quoted by Boyd:

George Davino maintains that "even small children have vivid ideas about nuclear energy" (qtd. in Boyd 22).

The list of works cited then includes only Boyd (the work consulted), not Davino.

12. A literary work

Novels, plays, and poems are often available in many editions, so your instructor may ask you to provide information that will help readers find the passage you cite no matter what edition they consult.

- **Novels:** the page number comes first, followed by a semicolon and then information on the appropriate part or chapter of the work.

  Toward the end of James's novel, Maggie suddenly feels "the thick breath of the definite—which was the intimate, the immediate, the familiar, as she hadn't had them for so long" (535; pt. 6, ch. 41).

- **Poems that are not divided into parts:** You may omit the page number and supply the line number(s) for the quotation. To prevent confusion with page numbers, precede the number(s) with line or lines in the first citation; then use just the number(s).

In Shakespeare's Sonnet 73 the speaker identifies with the trees of late autumn, "Bare ruined choirs, where late the sweet birds sang" (line 4). "In me," Shakespeare writes, "thou seest the glowing of such fire / That on the ashes of his youth doth lie . . ." (9-10).

- **Verse plays and poems that are divided into parts:** Omit a page number and cite the appropriate part—act (and scene, if any), canto, book, and so on—plus the line number(s). Use Arabic numerals for parts, including acts and scenes (3.4 in the example).

  Later in King Lear the disguised Edgar says, "The prince of darkness is a gentleman" (3.4.147).

- **Prose plays:** Provide the page number followed by the act and scene, if any (see the citation of *Death of a Salesman* on pp. 490–91).

13. The Bible

When you cite passages of the Bible in parentheses, abbreviate the title of any book longer than four letters—for instance, Gen. (Genesis), 1 Sam. (1 Samuel), Ps. (Psalms), Matt. (Matthew). Then give the chapter and verse(s) in Arabic numerals.

  According to the Bible, at Babel God "did . . . confound the language of all the earth" (Gen. 11.9).

14. An electronic source

Cite an electronic source as you would any other source: usually by author's name or, if there is no author, by title.

  Business forecasts for the fourth quarter tended to be optimistic (White 4).

This example cites a source with page numbers. For a source with other numbering or no numbering, see models 5 and 6 (pp. 485–86).

15. Two or more works in the same citation

If you use a single parenthetical citation to refer to more than one work, separate the references with a semicolon.

  Two recent articles point out that a computer badly used can be less efficient than no computer at all (Gough and Hall 201; Richards 162).

Since long citations in the text can distract the reader, you may choose to cite several or more works in an endnote or footnote rather than in the text. See page 491.

2 • Placement and punctuation of parenthetical citations

The following guidelines will help you place and punctuate text citations to distinguish between your and your sources' ideas and to make your own text readable. See also pages 465–68 on editing quotations and using signal phrases to integrate source material into your sentences.

Where to place citations

Position text citations to accomplish two goals: (1) make it clear exactly where your borrowing begins and ends; (2) keep the citation as unobtrusive as possible. You can accomplish both goals by placing the parenthetical citation at the end of the sentence element containing the borrowed material. This sentence element may be a phrase or a clause, and it may begin, interrupt, or conclude the sentence. Usually, as in the examples below, the element ends with a punctuation mark.

> The inflation rate might climb as high as 30 percent (Kim 164), an increase that could threaten the small nation's stability.

> The inflation rate, which might climb as high as 30 percent (Kim 164), could threaten the small nation's stability.

> The small nation's stability could be threatened by its inflation rate, which, one source predicts, might climb as high as 30 percent (Kim 164).

In the last example the addition of *one source predicts* clarifies that Kim is responsible only for the inflation-rate prediction, not for the statement about stability.

When your paraphrase or summary of a source runs longer than a sentence, clarify the boundaries by using the author's name in the first sentence and placing the parenthetical citation at the end of the last sentence.

> Juliette Kim studied the effects of acutely high inflation in several South American and African countries since World War II. She discovered that a major change in government accompanied or followed the inflationary period in 56 percent of cases (22-23).

MLA
56a

When you cite two or more sources in the same paragraph, position authors' names and parenthetical citations so that readers can see who said what. In the following example, the beginnings and ends of sentences clearly mark the different sources with authors' names, transitional expressions, and parenthetical citations:

For some time, schools have been using computers extensively for drill-and-practice exercises, in which students repeat specific skills such as spelling words or using the multiplication facts. But many education experts criticize such exercises for boring students and failing to engage their critical thinking and creativity. Jane M. Healy, a noted educational psychologist and teacher, takes issue with "interactive" software for children as well as drill-and-practice software, arguing that "some of the most popular 'educational' software . . . may be damaging to independent thinking, attention, and motivation" (20). Another education expert, Harold Wenglinsky of the Educational Testing Service, found in a well-regarded 1998 study that fourth and eighth graders who used computers frequently, including for drill and practice, actually did worse on tests than their peers who used computers less often (Does It Compute? 21). In a later article, Wenglinsky concludes that "the quantity of use matters far less than the quality of use." In schools, he says, high-quality computer work, involving critical thinking, is still rare ("In Search" 17).

How to punctuate citations

Generally place a parenthetical citation *before* any punctuation required by your sentence, as in the preceding examples. If the borrowed material is a quotation, place the citation *between* the closing quotation mark and the punctuation.

Spelling argues that during the 1970s American automobile manufacturers met consumer needs "as well as could be expected" (26)⊙

The exception is a quotation ending in a question mark or exclamation point. Then use the appropriate punctuation inside the closing quotation mark, and follow the text citation with a period.

"Of what use is genius," Emerson asks, "if the organ . . . cannot find a focal distance within the actual horizon of human life⑦" ("Experience" 60)⊙ Mad genius is no genius.

When a citation appears at the end of a quotation set off from the text, place it one space *after* the punctuation ending the quotation. Do not use additional punctuation with the citation or quotation marks around the quotation.

In Arthur Miller's Death of a Salesman, the most poignant defense of Willie Loman comes from his wife, Linda:

⊙He's not the finest character that ever lived. But he's a human being, and a terrible thing is happening to him. So attention must be paid. He's not to be allowed to fall into his grave like an old dog. Attention, attention must finally be paid to such a person.(56; act 1)

(This citation of a play includes the act number as well as the page number. See p. 488.)

3 • Footnotes or endnotes in special circumstances

Footnotes or endnotes may replace parenthetical citations when you cite several sources at once, when you comment on a source, or when you provide information that does not fit easily in the text. Signal a footnote or endnote in your text with a numeral raised above the appropriate line. Then write a note with the same numeral.

Text   At least five studies have confirmed these results.[1]

Note   [1] Abbott and Winger 266-68; Casner 27; Hoyenga 78-79; Marino 36; Tripp, Tripp, and Walk 179-83.

In a note, the raised numeral is indented one-half inch or five spaces and is followed by a space. If the note appears as a footnote, place it at the bottom of the page on which the citation appears, set it off from the text with quadruple spacing, and single-space the note itself. If the note appears as an endnote, place it in numerical order with the other endnotes on a page between the text and the list of works cited. Double-space all the endnotes.

56b   Prepare the MLA list of works cited.

At the end of your paper, a list titled Works Cited includes all the sources you quoted, paraphrased, or summarized in your paper. (If your instructor asks you to include sources you examined but did not cite, title the list Works Consulted.)

The list of works cited always begins a new page, numbered in sequence with the preceding pages. Format the list as in the sample on the next page. Arrange all your sources in alphabetical order by the last name of the author—or by the last name of the first author if there is more than one. If a source has no named author, alphabetize it by the first main word of the title (excluding *A*, *An*, or *The*). Use *only* alphabetical order to arrange sources, not another principle such as type of source or date of publication.

An index to all the following models appears on the next two pages. Use your best judgment in adapting the models to your particular sources. If you can't find a model that exactly matches a source you used, locate and follow the closest possible match. You

MLA works-cited page

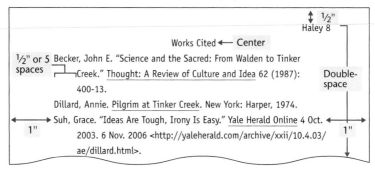

Haley 8

½"

Works Cited ← Center

½" or 5 spaces Becker, John E. "Science and the Sacred: From Walden to Tinker Creek." Thought: A Review of Culture and Idea 62 (1987): 400-13.

Double-space

Dillard, Annie. Pilgrim at Tinker Creek. New York: Harper, 1974.

Suh, Grace. "Ideas Are Tough, Irony Is Easy." Yale Herald Online 4 Oct. 2003. 6 Nov. 2006 <http://yaleherald.com/archive/xxii/10.4.03/ae/dillard.html>.

1"

1"

will certainly need to combine formats—for instance, drawing on model 2 ("A book with two or three authors") and model 26 ("An article in a daily newspaper") for a newspaper article with two authors.

MLA works-cited models

Books

1. A book with one author *494, 495*
2. A book with two or three authors *494*
3. A book with more than three authors *494*
4. Two or more works by the same author(s) *494*
5. A book with an editor *496*
6. A book with an author and an editor *496*
7. A translation *496*
8. A book with a corporate author *496*
9. An anonymous book *496*
10. The Bible *497*
11. A later edition *497*
12. A republished book *497*
13. A book with a title in its title *497*
14. A work in more than one volume *498*
15. A work in a series *498*

16. Published proceedings of a conference *498*
17. An anthology *498*
18. A selection from an anthology *499*
19. Two or more selections from the same anthology *499*
20. An introduction, preface, foreword, or afterword *500*
21. An article in a reference work *500*

Periodicals

22. An article in a journal with continuous pagination throughout the annual volume *501, 502*
23. An article in a journal that pages issues separately or that numbers only issues, not volumes *502*
24. An article in a monthly or bimonthly magazine *502*
25. An article in a weekly or biweekly magazine *502*

MLA

56b

MLA

56b

1 • Books

The next page shows the basic format for a book and the location of the required information in a book. When other information is required for a reference, it generally falls either between the author's name and the title or between the title and the publication information, as in the following models.

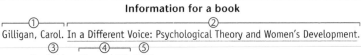

Information for a book

Gilligan, Carol. In a Different Voice: Psychological Theory and Women's Development.

Cambridge: Harvard UP, 1982.

Title page

② **Title,** underlined. Give the full title and any subtitle, separating them with a colon. End the title with a period.

In a Different Voice

Psychological Theory and Women's Development

① **Author.** Give the full name—last name first, a comma, first name, and any middle name or initial. Omit *Dr., PhD,* or any other title. End the name with a period.

Carol Gilligan

④ **Publisher's name.** Shorten most publishers' names ("UP" for University Press, "Little" for Little, Brown). Give both imprint and publisher's names when they appear on the title page: e.g., "Vintage-Random" for Vintage Books and Random House.

③ **City of publication.** Precede the publisher's name with its city, followed by a colon. Use only the first city if the title page lists more than one.

Harvard University Press
Cambridge, Massachusetts, and London, England

Copyright page

⑤ **Date of publication.** If the date doesn't appear on the title page, look for it on the next page. End the date with a period.

Copyright © 1982 by Carol Gilligan
All rights reserved
Printed in the United States of America

1. A book with one author

Gilligan, Carol. <u>In a Different Voice: Psychological Theory and Women's Devel-</u>
<u>opment</u>. Cambridge: Harvard UP, 1982.

2. A book with two or three authors

Lifton, Robert Jay, and Greg Mitchell. <u>Who Owns Death: Capital Punishment, the</u>
<u>American Conscience, and the End of Executions</u>. New York: Morrow, 2000.

Wilcox, Dennis L., Phillip H. Ault, and Warren K. Agee. <u>Public Relations:</u>
<u>Strategies and Tactics</u>. 6th ed. New York: Irwin, 2006.

Give the authors' names in the order provided on the title page. Reverse the first and last names of the first author *only,* not of any other authors. Separate two authors' names with a comma and and; separate three authors' names with commas and with and before the third name.

3. A book with more than three authors

Lopez, Geraldo, Judith P. Salt, Anne Ming, and Henry Reisen. <u>China and the</u>
<u>West</u>. Boston: Little, 2005.

Lopez, Geraldo, et al. <u>China and the West</u>. Boston: Little, 2005.

You may, but need not, give all the authors' names if the work has more than three authors. If you choose not to give all the names, provide the name of the first author only, and follow the name with a comma and the abbreviation et al. (for the Latin *et alii,* meaning "and others").

4. Two or more works by the same author(s)

Gardner, Howard. <u>The Arts and Human Development</u>. New York: Wiley, 1973.

---. <u>The Quest for Mind: Piaget, Lévi-Strauss, and the Structuralist Movement</u>.
New York: Knopf, 1973.

If you cite two or more works by the same author, give the author's name only in the first entry. For the second and any subsequent works by the same author, substitute three hyphens for the author's name, followed by a period. (If you are citing two or more works by the same editor, editors, or translator, follow the hyphens with a comma and ed., eds., or trans. as appropriate. See models 5, 6, and 7.) Note that the three hyphens stand for *exactly* the same name or names. If the second source above were by Gardner and somebody else, both names would have to be given in full.

Place an entry or entries using three hyphens immediately after the entry that names the author. Within the set of entries by the same author, arrange the sources alphabetically by the first main

MLA
56b

word of the title (excluding *A, An,* or *The*), as in the preceding examples (Arts, then Quest).

5. A book with an editor

Holland, Merlin, and Rupert Hart-Davis, eds. The Complete Letters of Oscar
Wilde. New York: Holt, 2000.

Handle editors' names like authors' names (models 1–3), but add a
comma and the abbreviation ed. (one editor) or eds. (two or more
editors) after the last editor's name.

6. A book with an author and an editor

Mumford, Lewis. The City in History. Ed. Donald L. Miller. New York: Pantheon,
1986.

When citing the work of the author, give his or her name first,
and give the editor's name after the title, preceded by Ed. (singular only, meaning "Edited by"). When citing the work of the editor,
use model 5 for a book with an editor, adding By and the author's
name after the title: Miller, Donald L., ed. The City in History. By Lewis Mumford.

7. A translation

Alighieri, Dante. The Inferno. Trans. John Ciardi. New York: NAL, 1971.

When citing the work of the author, give his or her name first, and
give the translator's name after the title, preceded by Trans. ("Translated by"). When citing the work of the translator, give his or her
name first, followed by a comma and trans.; then follow the title
with By and the author's name: Ciardi, John, trans. The Inferno. By Dante
Alighieri.

When a book you cite by author has a translator and an editor,
give the translator's *and* editor's names in the order used on the
book's title page.

8. A book with a corporate author

Lorenz Research, Inc. Research in Social Studies Teaching. Baltimore: Arrow,
2005.

Corporate authors include associations, institutions, government
bodies, companies, and other groups. List the name of the group as
author when a source gives only that name and not an individual's.

9. An anonymous book

The Dorling Kindersley World Reference Atlas. London: Dorling, 2005.

List a book that names no author—neither an individual nor a group—by its full title. Alphabetize the book by the title's first main word (here Dorling), excluding *A, An,* or *The.*

10. The Bible

The Bible. King James Version.

The New English Bible. London: Oxford UP and Cambridge UP, 1970.

When citing a standard version of the Bible (as in the first example), do not underline the title or the name of the version, and you need not provide publication information. For an edition of the Bible (as in the second example), underline the title and give full publication information.

11. A later edition

Bolinger, Dwight L. Aspects of Language. 3rd ed. New York: Harcourt, 1981.

For any edition after the first, place the edition number after the title. (If an editor's name follows the title, place the edition number after the name. See model 18.) Use the appropriate designation for editions that are named or dated rather than numbered—for instance, Rev. ed. for "Revised edition."

12. A republished book

James, Henry. The Golden Bowl. 1904. London: Penguin, 1966.

Republished books include paperbound editions of books originally released in hard bindings and books reissued under new titles. Place the original date of publication (but not the place of publication or the publisher's name) after the title, and then provide the full publication information for the source you are using. If the book was originally published under a different title, add this title at the end of the entry and move the original publication date to follow the title—for example, Rpt. of Thomas Hardy: A Life. 1941.

13. A book with a title in its title

Eco, Umberto. Postscript to The Name of the Rose. Trans. William Weaver. New York: Harcourt, 1983.

When a book's title contains another book title (as here: *The Name of the Rose*), do not underline the second title. When a book's title contains a quotation or the title of a work normally placed in quotation marks, keep the quotation marks and underline both titles: Critical Response to Henry James's "The Beast in the Jungle." (Note that the underlining extends under the closing quotation mark.)

14. A work in more than one volume

Lincoln, Abraham. The Collected Works of Abraham Lincoln. Ed. Roy P. Basler.
    8 vols. New Brunswick: Rutgers UP, 1953.

Lincoln, Abraham. The Collected Works of Abraham Lincoln. Ed. Roy P. Basler.
    Vol. 5. New Brunswick: Rutgers UP, 1953. 8 vols.

If you use two or more volumes of a multivolume work, give the work's total number of volumes before the publication information (8 vols. in the first example). Your text citation will indicate which volume you are citing (see p. 486). If you use only one volume, give that volume number before the publication information (Vol. 5 in the second example). You may add the total number of volumes to the end of the entry (8 vols. in the second example).

If you cite a multivolume work published over a period of years, give the inclusive years as the publication date: for instance, Cambridge: Harvard UP, 1978-90.

15. A work in a series

Bergman, Ingmar. The Seventh Seal. Mod. Film Scripts Ser. 12. New York:
    Simon, 1995.

Place the name of the series (not quoted or underlined) just before the publication information. Abbreviate common words such as *modern* and *series*. Add any series number after the series title.

16. Published proceedings of a conference

Watching Our Language: A Conference Sponsored by the Program in Architec-
    ture and Design Criticism. 6-8 May 2006. New York: Parsons School of
    Design, 2006.

Whether in or after the title of the conference, supply information about who sponsored the conference, when it was held, and who published the proceedings. Treat a particular presentation at the conference like a selection from an anthology (model 18).

17. An anthology

Kennedy, X. J., and Dana Gioia, eds. Literature: An Introduction to Fiction,
    Poetry, and Drama. 9th ed. New York: Longman, 2005.

Cite an entire anthology only when citing the work of the editor or editors or when your instructor permits cross-referencing like that shown in model 19. Give the name of the editor or editors (followed by ed. or eds.) and then the title of the anthology.

18. A selection from an anthology

Mason, Bobbie Ann. "Shiloh." <u>Literature: An Introduction to Fiction, Poetry, and</u>
<u>Drama</u>. Ed. X. J. Kennedy and Dana Gioia. 9th ed. New York: Longman,
2005. 643-54.

The essentials of this listing are these: author of selection; title of selection (in quotation marks); title of anthology (underlined); editors' names preceded by Ed. (meaning "Edited by"); publication information for the anthology; and inclusive page numbers for the selection (without the abbreviation "pp."). In addition, this source requires an edition number for the anthology. If you wish, you may also supply the original date of publication for the work you are citing, after its title. See model 12 on page 497.

If the work you cite comes from a collection of works by one author and with no editor, use the following form:

Auden, W. H. "Family Ghosts." <u>The Collected Poetry of W. H. Auden</u>. New York:
Random, 1945. 132-33.

If the work you cite is a scholarly article that was previously printed elsewhere, provide the complete information for the earlier publication of the piece, followed by Rpt. in ("Reprinted in") and the information for the source in which you found the piece:

Molloy, Francis C. "The Suburban Vision in John O'Hara's Short Stories."
<u>Critique: Studies in Modern Fiction</u> 25.2 (1984): 101-13. Rpt. in <u>Short</u>
<u>Story Criticism: Excerpts from Criticism of the Works of Short Fiction</u>
<u>Writers</u>. Ed. David Segal. Vol. 15. Detroit: Gale, 1989. 287-92.

San Juan, E. "Theme Versus Imitation: D. H. Lawrence's 'The Rocking-Horse
Winner.'" <u>D. H. Lawrence Review</u> 3 (1970): 136-40. Rpt. in <u>From Fiction</u>
<u>to Film: D. H. Lawrence's "The Rocking-Horse Winner."</u> Ed. Gerald R.
Barrett and Thomas L. Erskine. Dickenson Literature and Film Ser.
Encino: Dickenson, 1974. 70-74.

19. Two or more selections from the same anthology

Chopin, Kate. "The Storm." Kennedy and Gioia 127-31.

Kennedy, X. J., and Dana Gioia, eds. <u>Literature: An Introduction to Fiction,</u>
<u>Poetry, and Drama</u>. 9th ed. New York: Longman, 2005.

O'Connor, Flannery. "Revelation." Kennedy and Gioia 443-58.

When you are citing more than one selection from the same source, your instructor may allow you to avoid repetition by giving the source in full (as in the Kennedy and Gioia entry) and then simply cross-referencing it in entries for the works you used. Thus, instead of full information for the Chopin and O'Connor works, give Kennedy and Gioia and the appropriate pages in that book. Each entry appears in its proper alphabetical place among other works cited.

20. An introduction, preface, foreword, or afterword

Donaldson, Norman. Introduction. The Claverings. By Anthony Trollope. New

York: Dover, 1977. vii-xv.

An introduction, foreword, or afterword is often written by someone other than the book's author. When citing such a piece, give its name without quotation marks or underlining. (If the piece has a title of its own, provide it, in quotation marks, between the name of the author and the name of the piece.) Follow the title of the book with By and its author's name. Give the inclusive page numbers of the part you cite. (In the preceding example, the small Roman numerals refer to the front matter of the book, before page 1.)

When the author of a preface or introduction is the same as the author of the book, give only the last name after the title:

Gould, Stephen Jay. Prologue. The Flamingo's Smile: Reflections in Natural History. By Gould. New York: Norton, 1985. 13-20.

21. An article in a reference work

Mark, Herman F. "Polymers." The New Encyclopaedia Britannica: Macropaedia.

15th ed. 1991.

"Reckon." Merriam-Webster's Collegiate Dictionary. 11th ed. 2003.

List an article in a reference work by its title (second example) unless the article is signed (first example). For works with entries arranged alphabetically, you need not include volume or page numbers. For well-known works like those listed above, you may also omit the editors' names and all publication information except any edition number and the year of publication. For works that are not well known, give full publication information:

"Hungarians in America." The Ethnic Almanac. Ed. Stephanie Bernardo. New

York: Doubleday, 2001. 109-11.

2 • Periodicals: Journals, magazines, and newspapers

The facing page shows the basic format for an article in a periodical (a journal) and the location of the required information.

Note The treatment of volume and issue numbers and publication dates varies depending on the kind of periodical being cited, as

Information for a journal article

①
Selwyn, Neil. "The Social Processes of Learning to Use Computers." Social Science
②   ③

④   ⑤   ⑥
Computer Review 23.1 (2005): 122-35.

Journal cover

④ **Volume and/or issue number**, in Arabic numerals.

SPRING 2005   VOLUME 23   NUMBER 1

⑤ **Year of publication**, in parentheses and followed by a colon.

SOCIAL SCIENCE COMPUTER REVIEW

③ **Title of periodical**, underlined. Omit any *A*, *An*, or *The* from the beginning of the title. Do not end with a period.

② **Title of article**, in quotation marks. Give the full title and any subtitle, separating them with a colon. End the title with a period inside the final quotation mark.

First page of article

The Social Processes of Learning to Use Computers

NEIL SELWYN
Cardiff School of Social Sciences

① **Author.** Give the full name—last name first, a comma, first name, and any middle name or initial. Omit *Dr.*, *PhD*, or any other title. End the name with a period.

Specia
New C

The ability to use a computer is assumed to be a cornerstone of effective citi Age, with a range of initiatives and educational provisions being introduc become competent with information technology (IT). Despite such provision, levels of computer use and competence have been found to vary widely throughout the general population, and we know little of how different ways of learning to use computers contribute to people's eventual use of IT. Based on data from in-depth interviews with 100 adults in the United Kingdom, this article examines the range and social stratification of formal and informal learning about computers that is taking place, suggesting that formal computer instruction orientated toward the general public may inadvertently widen the digital knowledge gap. In particular, the data highlight the importance of informal learning about IT and of encouraging such learning, especially in the home.

AUTHOR'S NOTE: This article is based on a project funded by the Economic and Social Research Council (R000239518). I would like to thank the other members of the Adults Learning@ Home project (Stephen Gorard and John Furlong) as well as the individuals who took part in the in-depth interviews. Correspondence concerning this article may be addressed to Neil Selwyn, School of Social Sciences, Cardiff University, Glamorgan Building, King Edward VII Avenue, Cardiff CF10 3WT, UK; e-mail: selwynnc@cardiff.ac.uk.

122

MLA
56b

⑥ **Inclusive page numbers of article**, without "pp." Go to the end of the article for the last page number. Provide only as many digits in the last number as needed for clarity, usually two.

the following models indicate. For the distinction between journals and magazines, see pages 433–34.

22. An article in a journal with continuous pagination throughout the annual volume

Lever, Janet. "Sex Differences in the Games Children Play." Social Problems 23 (1996): 478-87.

Some journals number the pages of issues consecutively throughout a year, so that each issue after the first in a year begins numbering where the previous issue left off—say, at page 132 or 416. For this kind of journal, give the volume number after the title (23 in the preceding example) and place the year of publication in parentheses. The page numbers will be enough to guide readers to the issue you used.

23. An article in a journal that pages issues separately or that numbers only issues, not volumes

Selwyn, Neil. "The Social Processes of Learning to Use Computers." Social Science Computer Review 23.1 (2005): 122-35.

Some journals page each issue separately (starting each issue at page 1). For these journals, give the volume number, a period, and the issue number (as in 23.1 in the Selwyn entry above and on the previous page). When citing an article in a journal that numbers only issues, not annual volumes, treat the issue number as if it were a volume number, as in model 22.

24. An article in a monthly or bimonthly magazine

Garber, Marjorie. "Our Genius Problem." Atlantic Monthly Dec. 2002: 46-53.

Follow the magazine title with the month and the year of publication. (Abbreviate all months except May, June, and July.) Don't place the date in parentheses, and don't provide a volume or issue number.

25. An article in a weekly or biweekly magazine

Talbot, Margaret. "The Bad Mother." New Yorker 5 Aug. 2005: 40-46.

MLA
56b

Follow the magazine title with the day, the month, and the year of publication. (Abbreviate all months except May, June, and July.) Don't place the date in parentheses, and don't provide a volume or issue number.

26. An article in a daily newspaper

Zeller, Tom, Jr. "To Go Global, Do You Ignore Censorship?" New York Times 24 Oct. 2006, natl. ed.: C3+.

Give the name of the newspaper as it appears on the first page (but without *A, An,* or *The*). If the name of the city is not in the title of a local newspaper, add the city name in brackets after the title, without underlining: Gazette [Chicago]. Then follow model 25, with two differences: (1) If the newspaper lists an edition at the top of the first page, include that information after the date and a comma. (See natl. ed. in the example.) (2) If the newspaper is divided into lettered or numbered sections, provide the section designation before the page number when the newspaper does the same (C3+ in the example); otherwise, provide the section designation before the colon— for instance, sec. 1: 1+. The plus sign here and with C3+ indicates that the articles do not run on consecutive pages but start on page 1 or C3 and continue later.

27. An anonymous article

"The Right to Die." Time 11 Oct. 1996: 101.

For an article with no named author, begin the entry with the title of the article. In the list of works cited, alphabetize an anonymous source by the first main word of the title ("Right" in this model).

28. An editorial or letter to the editor

"Dualing Power Centers." Editorial. New York Times 14 Jan. 2006, natl. ed.:
    A16.

Add the word Editorial or Letter after the title if there is one or after the author's name, as follows:

Dowding, Michael. Letter. Economist 5-11 Jan. 2005: 4.

(The numbers 5-11 in this entry are the publication days of the periodical: the issue spans January 5 through 11.)

29. A review

Nelson, Cary. "Between Anonymity and Celebrity." Rev. of Anxious Intellects:
    Academic Professionals, Public Intellectuals, and Enlightenment Values,
    by John Michael. College English 64 (2002): 710-19.

Rev. is an abbreviation for "Review." The name of the author of the work being reviewed follows the title of the work, a comma, and by. If the review has no title of its own, then Rev. of and the title of the reviewed work immediately follow the name of the reviewer.

30. An abstract of a dissertation or article

Steciw, Steven K. "Alterations to the Pessac Project of Le Corbusier." Diss. U of
    Cambridge, England, 1986. DAI 46 (1986): 565C.

MLA

56b

For an abstract appearing in *Dissertation Abstracts* (*DA*) or *Dissertation Abstracts International* (*DAI*), give the author's name and the title, Diss. (for "Dissertation"), the institution granting the author's degree, the date of the dissertation, and the publication information. See model 58, page 517, for listing an entire dissertation rather than an abstract.

For an abstract of an article, first provide the publication information for the article itself, followed by the information for the abstract. If the abstract publisher lists abstracts by item rather than page number, add item before the number.

> Lever, Janet. "Sex Differences in the Games Children Play." Social Problems 23
>
> (1996): 478-87. Psychological Abstracts 63 (1996): item 1431.

3 • Electronic sources

Electronic sources include those you find online (either through the library Web site or directly over the Internet) and those you find on CD-ROM (see pp. 515–16). The following list, adapted from the *MLA Handbook*, itemizes the possible elements of an online source, in order of their appearance in a works-cited entry. *No source will include all the elements.*

1. **Name of author, editor, compiler, or translator,** arranged and punctuated as in models 1–3, page 495. Use ed., comp., or trans. after the name as appropriate, as shown in models 5 and 7, page 496.

2. **Title of a short work,** in quotation marks. Short works include poems, articles, documents or pages on a Web site, Web log entries, and postings to discussion groups. (Follow the last with Online posting.)

3. **Title of a book,** underlined.

4. **Name of editor, compiler, or translator of the source,** if not cited before, preceded by Ed., Comp., or Trans. as appropriate. See models 6 and 7, page 496.

5. **Publication information for any print version of the source,** following earlier models for books and periodical articles. For a periodical article, the publication information includes the periodical title.

6. **Title of the online site,** underlined. The title might be that of a periodical (if not already given), a scholarly project, a database, a Web log, and so on. For a site with no title, add Home page, Course home page, or another description.

7. **Name of site editor,** if any, preceded by Ed.

8. **Version number, if any, or volume/issue numbers for an online journal.** See models 22–23, pages 501–02, for journals.
9. **Date of electronic publication, latest revision, or posting.**
10. **Title of a subscription database, name of the subscription service, and name and location of the subscriber.**
11. **Title of a discussion group.**
12. **Inclusive page numbers, number of paragraphs, or other identifying numbers,** if any.
13. **Name of site sponsor,** such as an institution or organization, if not cited before.
14. **Date you consulted the source.**
15. **URL of the source.** To ensure the accuracy of URLs, use Copy and Paste to duplicate them in a file or an e-mail to yourself. In the list of works cited, break URLs *only* after slashes—do not hyphenate. Unless you are submitting your paper online, use the Tools menu of your word processor to eliminate hyperlinks in works-cited entries (click on AutoCorrect in *Microsoft Word,* Settings in *WordPerfect*).

Note A URL does not always provide a usable route to a source, especially with subscription services. See the explanations of models 31 (below) and 32 (next page).

31. A work from an online service to which your library subscribes

Gorski, Paul C. "Privilege and Repression in the Digital Era: Rethinking the Sociopolitics of the Digital Divide." Race, Gender and Class 10.4 (2003): 145-76. Ethnic NewsWatch. ProQuest. U of Minnesota, Twin Cities, Wilson Lib. 24 July 2006 <http://proquest.umi.com>.

See the following page for an analysis of the preceding model and the location of the required information on the subscription service.

Note Many subscription services provide source URLs that are temporary, specific to the library, or too long to copy with certain accuracy. If any of these applies to the URL of the source you're consulting, you can use the service's home page URL instead or omit a URL. Some services provide a "Permanent link" or "Document URL" on each source record: a URL for finding the source from within the library's system (not from the open Web). You can see such a link on the database source shown on the next page. Like the one in the example, permanent links are often unmanageably long and complex. In that case, use the service's home-page URL, which runs through *com* in the permanent link.

MLA
56b

Information for an article from a subscription service

Gorski, Paul C. "Privilege and Repression in the Digital Era: Rethinking the Sociopolitics of the Digital Divide." Race, Gender and Class 10.4 (2003): 145-76. Ethnic
NewsWatch. ProQuest. U of Minnesota, Twin Cities, Wilson Lib. 24 July 2006
<http://proquest.umi.com>.

⑤ **Name of the service**, not underlined, ending with a period.

④ **Name of the database**, underlined, ending with a period.

⑥ **Names of the subscribing institution and library**, separated by a comma and ending with a period.

② **Title of the article**, in quotation marks. End the title with a period inside the final quotation mark.

③ **Publication information for any print version.** If the site gives information for a print version of the source, give it after the source title, following an appropriate model on pp. 500–04.

① **Author.** Give the full name—last name first, a comma, first name, and any middle name or initial. Omit *Dr., PhD,* or any other title. End with a period.

⑧ **URL**, enclosed in angle brackets. But if the source URL is temporary, unique to your search, or too long (as in the example), use the URL of the site's home page. See the note on the previous page.

⑦ **Date of your access.** Give the day first, then month, then year. Abbreviate all months except May, June, and July. Do not end the date with a period. (Since this date does not appear on the site, record it separately.)

MLA
56b

Image published with permission of ProQuest Information and Learning Company. Further reproduction is prohibited without permission.

32. A work from an online service to which you subscribe

"China—Dragon Kings." The Encyclopedia Mythica. America Online. 6 Jan.

2006. Path: Research and Learn; Encyclopedia; More Encyclopedias; (4)
Encyclopedia Mythica.

If you find a source through America Online, MSN, or another personal online service and you do not see a usable URL or any URL, provide the path you used to get to the source, as in the example above: ① Title of source, in quotation marks, and title of larger work, underlined. ② Name of the service, neither underlined nor quoted. ③ Date of your access, followed by a period. ④ Path: and the sequence of topics required to reach the source, with the topics separated by semicolons.

If you used a keyword instead of a path to reach the source, give that information instead: Keyword: Chinese dragon kings.

33. An entire online site (scholarly project, professional site, personal site, etc.)

A scholarly project or professional site:

American Verse Project. 16 May 2001. U of Michigan Humanities Text Initiative. 21 July 2006 <http://www.hti.umich.edu/a/amverse>.

When citing a scholarly project or professional site, include the following: ① Title of the site, underlined. ② Date of publication or most recent update. ③ Name of any organization or institution that sponsors the site. ④ Date of your access. ⑤ URL. If the project or site has an editor or compiler, add the name, preceded by Ed. or Comp., after the site title. See the Conrad entry on page 508.

A personal site:

Lederman, Leon. Topics in Modern Physics—Lederman. 28 Aug. 2005. 12 Dec. 2006 <http://www-ed.fnal.gov/samplers/hsphys/people/lederman.html>.

Cite a personal site with this information: ① Author's name, if any. ② Title, if any, underlined. If the site has no title, describe it with a label such as Home page, without quotation marks or underlining. ③ Date of last revision. ④ Date of your access. ⑤ URL.

A business site:

Prius. 2007. Toyota Motor Corp. 2 Feb. 2007 <http://www.toyota.com/prius>.

For the site of a corporation or other business, give the following: ① Site title, underlined. ② Date of site. ③ Name of sponsoring business. ④ Date of your access. ⑤ URL.

34. A poem, essay, or other short work from an online site

Wheatley, Phillis. "On Virtue." <u>Poems on Various Subjects, Religious and Moral</u>.
London: A. Bell, 1773. <u>American Verse Project</u>. 16 May 2001. U of Michigan Humanities Text Initiative. 21 July 2006 <http://
name.umdl.umich.edu/BAP5379>.

See the model and screen shots on the facing page for an analysis of
this entry and the location of the required information on the Web
site.

35. An online book

An entire book:

Austen, Jane. Emma. 1816. Ed. R. W. Chapman. Oxford: Clarendon, 1926. Oxford
Text Archive. 2004. Oxford U. 15 Dec. 2006 <http://ota.ahds.ac.uk/
Austen/Emma.1519>.

For a book published online, give the following information: ① Author and title. ② Date of original publication of the book if not given
in item 4. ③ Name of any editor or translator. ④ Any publication information for the original print version of the book, following one
of models 1–17 (pp. 495–98). ⑤ Title of the site, underlined. ⑥ Date
of electronic publication. ⑦ Name of any sponsoring organization
or institution. ⑧ Date of your access. ⑨ URL for the book. If the site
has an editor, add the name after the site's title (see the following
model).

A part of a book:

Conrad, Joseph. "A Familiar Preface." Modern Essays. Ed. Christopher Morley.
New York: Harcourt, 1921. Bartleby.com: Great Books Online. Ed. Steven
van Leeuwan. Nov. 2000. 21 Jan. 2007 <http://www.bartleby.com/237/
8.html>.

For a part of a book published online, provide this information:
① Author of the part. ② Title of the part, in quotation marks. (Do not
use quotation marks for Introduction, Foreword, or another standard
part.) ③ Title of the book (underlined), editor of the book (if any),
and publication information for the print version of the book. ④
Title of the site (underlined) and editor of the site (if any). ⑤ Date of
electronic publication. ⑥ Date of your access. ⑦ URL for the part of
the book. If the site as a whole has a sponsoring organization, give
the name between the date of electronic publication and the date of
your access (see the Austen model above).

Information for a short work from an online site

① ② ③
Wheatley, Phillis. "On Virtue." Poems on Various Subjects, Religious and Moral. Lon-
④ ⑤ ⑥
don: A. Bell, 1773. American Verse Project. 16 May 2001. U of Michigan Human-
⑦ ⑧
ities Text Initiative. 21 July 2006 <http://name.umdl.umich.edu/BAP5379>.

Home page of site

University of Michigan Humanities Text Initiative
**American
Verse
Project**

The American Verse Project is a collaborative project between the University of Michigan Humanities Text Initiative (HTI) and the University of Michigan Press. The project is assembling an electronic archive of volumes of American poetry prior to 1920. The full text of each volume of poetry is being converted into digital form and coded in Standard Generalized Mark-up Language (SGML) using the TEI Guidelines, with various forms of access provided through the WWW. In recognition of the effort involved in selecting, editing, encoding, and maintaining online texts in this archive, we expect all users to abide by the conditions of use.

- Basic Searches: Single word and phrase searches throughout the entire corpus.
- Proximity Searches: Find the co-occurrence of two or three words or phrases.
- Boolean Searches: Find combinations of two or three words in a given paragraph or verse.
- Word Index: Browse through lists of all unique words in the texts.
- Bibliographic Searches: Identify works by author and title.
- Browse the American Verse Project Texts
- About the American Verse Project

Go to UMDL Texts to search multiple collections.

Powered by DLXS
To comment or inquire about content, contact HTI Info

Last content update May 16, 2001.

⑥ **Name of the sponsor,** ending with a period.

④ **Site title,** underlined and ending with a period.

⑤ **Date of electronic publication or last update.** Give the day first, then month, then year. Abbreviate all months except May, June, and July. End the date with a period.

Source record for poem

**Print
Source:** Poems on various subjects, religious and moral
Phillis Wheatley
A. Bell
London
1773
URL: http://name.umdl.umich.edu/BAP5379

③ **Publication information for any print version.** If the site gives information for a print version of the source, as here, provide it after the source title, following an appropriate model on pp. 495–504.

Poem

File Edit View Go Bookmarks Tools Help
http://name.umdl.umich.edu/BAP5379

American Verse Project   UMDL Texts home
Home
Wheatley, Phillis, 1753-1784: Poems on various subjects, religious and moral [electronic text]
table of contents | view text | add to bookbag
ON VIRTUE
previous section | next section

O Thou bright jewel in my aim i strive
To comprehend thee. Thine own words declare
Wisdom is higher than a fool can reach.
I cease to wonder, and no more attempt
Thine height t' explore, or fathom thy profound.
But, O my soul, sink not into despair,
Virtue is near thee, and with gentle hand
Would now embrace thee, hovers o'er thine head.
Fain would the heav'n-born soul with her converse,
Then seek, then court her for her promis'd bliss.

Auspicious queen, thine heav'nly pinions spread,
And lead celestial Chastity along;
Lo! now her sacred retinue descends,
Array'd in glory from the orbs above.
Attend me, Virtue, thro' my youthful years!
O leave me not to the false joys of time!
But guide my steps to endless life and bliss.

⑦ **Date of your access.** Give the day first, then month, then year. Abbreviate all months except May, June, and July. Do not end the date with a period. (Since this date does not appear on the site, record it separately.)

⑧ **URL of the short work,** enclosed in angle brackets. If the URL is long, temporary, or unique to your search, use the URL of the site's home page.

① **Author.** Give the full name—last name first, a comma, first name, and any middle name or initial. Omit Dr., PhD, or any other title. End the name with a period. If you don't see the author's name at the top of the page, look at the bottom. If no author is listed, begin with the title.

② **Title of the short work,** in quotation marks. End the title with a period inside the final quotation mark.

36. An article in an online journal

Palfrey, Andrew. "Choice of Mates in Identical Twins." <u>Modern Psychology</u> 4.1
(2003): 26-40. 25 Feb. 2006 <http://www.liasu.edu/modpsy/
palfrey4(1).htm>.

Give the following information for an online scholarly article that you reach directly: ① Author, article title, journal title, volume and any issue numbers, and publication date, as in model 22 or 23 (pp. 501–02). ② Page numbers in the journal or total number of pages, paragraphs, or sections, if any of these are given. Omit reference numbers if the source does not use them. ③ Date of your access. ④ URL for the article.

For a journal article reached through a subscription service, see model 31 (pp. 505 and 506).

37. An online abstract

Palfrey, Andrew. "Choice of Mates in Identical Twins." <u>Modern Psychology</u> 4.1
(2003): 26-40. Abstract. 25 Feb. 2006 <http://www.liasu.edu/modpsy/
abstractpalfrey4(1).htm>.

Treat an online abstract like an online journal article (model 36), but add Abstract (without quotation marks or underlining) between the publication information and the date of your access.

38. An article in an online newspaper or on a newswire

Still, Lucia. "On the Battlefields of Business, Millions of Casualties." <u>New York
Times on the Web</u> 3 Mar. 2006. 27 Jan. 2007 <http://www.nytimes.com/
specials/downsize/06down1.html>.

Provide the following information for an online newspaper article that you reach directly: ① Author, article title, newspaper title, and publication date as in model 26 (p. 502). Give section, page, or paragraph numbers if the newspaper does. ② Date of your access. ③ URL for the article.

Treat a newswire article similarly, substituting the title of the wire service for the newspaper title (this article is anonymous):

"Film, Fashion Asked to Stop Glamorizing Smoking." <u>Reuters</u> 2 Feb.
2007. 10 Feb. 2007 <http://www.reuters.com/
newsArticle.jhtml?type=industryNewsID2246811>.

See model 31 (pp. 505 amd 506) when citing a newspaper or newswire article that you reached through a subscription service.

39. An article in an online magazine

Lewis, Ricki. "The Return of Thalidomide." Scientist 22 Jan. 2001: 5. 24 Jan.

2007 <http://www.the-scientist.com/yr2001/jan/lewis_pl_010122. html>.

Provide the following information for an online magazine article that you reach directly: ① Author's name, article title, magazine title, and publication date, as in model 24 or 25 (p. 502). ② Any page, paragraph, or other reference numbers. ③ Date of your access. ④ URL for the article.

See model 31 (pp. 505 and 506) when citing a magazine article that you reached through a subscription service.

40. An online review

Detwiler, Donald S., and Chu Shao-Kang. Rev. of Important Documents of the

Republic of China, ed. Tan Quon Chin. Journal of Military History 56.4

(1992): 669-84. 16 Sept. 2006 <http://www.jstor.org/fcgi-bin/jstor/

viewitem.fcg/08993718/96p0008x>.

Cite an online review as follows: ① Author, any review title, Rev. of and the title of the reviewed book, author or editor of the reviewed book, and publication information—all as in model 29 (p. 503). ② Date of your access. ③ URL for the review.

See model 31 (pp. 505 and 506) when citing a review that you reached through a subscription service.

41. An online government publication

United States. Dept. of Commerce. National Telecommunications and Informa-

tion Admin. A Nation Online: Entering the Broadband Age. Feb. 2005.

1 Feb. 2007 <http://www.ntia.doc.gov/reports/anol/index.html>.

Follow the models of printed government publications on page 516, adding the facts of electronic publication. The model above includes the following: ① Names of government, department, and agency. ② Title of publication, underlined. ③ Date of publication. ④ Date of your access. ⑤ URL for the publication.

42. An article in an online encyclopedia or other information database

Dull, Jack L. "Wu-ti." Encyclopaedia Britannica Online. 2004 Encyclopaedia

Britannica. 23 Dec. 2006 <http://www.britannica.com/eb/

article?tocid:9077599>.

For an article in an encyclopedia or other information database, provide the following: ① Author's name, if any is given. ② Title of the article, in quotation marks. ③ Title of the database, underlined. ④ Date of electronic publication. ⑤ Name of sponsoring organization or publisher. ⑥ Date of your access. ⑦ URL for the article.

See models 31 and 32 (pp. 506–07) when citing an information database that you reached through a library or personal subscription service. For encyclopedias and other reference works that you find in print or on CD-ROM, see pages 500 and 515, respectively.

43. An online image (artwork, advertisement, graph, etc.)

In general, you can base citations of online images on the examples in model 59 (pp. 517–18), adding information for the online source, particularly site title, date of your access, and URL. The following examples show a range of possibilities:

A work of art:

> Pollock, Jackson. Shimmering Substance. 1946. Museum of Modern Art, New York. WebMuseum. 12 Mar. 2006 <http://www.ibiblio.org/wm/paint/auth/Pollock/pollock.shimmering.jpg>.

A photograph:

> Curtis, Edward S. Canyon de Chelly—Navaho. 1904. Lib. of Congress. American Memory. 21 July 2005 <http://hdl.loc.gov/loc.award/iencurt.cp01028>.

An advertisement:

> Absolut Vodka. Advertisement. Vanity Fair Jan. 2003. Adflip. 18 Nov. 2006 <http://adflip.com/php?adID=14714>.

A cartoon or comic strip:

> Keefe, Mike. "Suspicious Package." Cartoon. Denver Post 21 July 2005. PoliticalCartoons.com. 6 Jan. 2007 <http://www.politicalcartoons.com>.

A map, chart, graph, or diagram:

> Hamilton, Calvin J. "Components of Comets." Diagram. Space Art. 2003. 20 Dec. 2006 <http://solarviews.com/eng/comet.htm>.

44. An online television or radio program

Base citations of online television and radio programs on model 60, page 518, adding your access date and the URL.

> Gross, Terry, host. Fresh Air. National Public Radio. 11 Jan. 2007. 12 Jan. 2007 <http://discover.npr.org/freshair/day_fa.html?display=January/11/2007>.

45. An online sound recording or clip

Base citations of online sound recordings or clips on model 61, page 518, adding your access date and the URL.

> Reagan, Ronald W. State of the Union Address. 26 Jan. 1982. Vincent Voice
> Library. Digital and Multimedia Center, U of Michigan. 6 May 2006
> <http://www.lib.msu.edu/vincent/presidents/reagan.htm>.

46. An online film or film clip

Base citations of online films or film clips on model 62, page 519, adding your access date and the URL.

> Stewart, Leslie J. 96 Ranch Rodeo and Barbecue. 1951. Lib. of Congress.
> American Memory. 7 Jan. 2007 <http://lcweb2.loc.gov/ammem/
> afc96ran_v034>.

47. The home page for a course or department

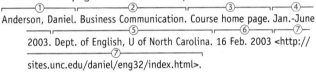

> Anderson, Daniel. Business Communication. Course home page. Jan.-June
> 2003. Dept. of English, U of North Carolina. 16 Feb. 2003 <http://
> sites.unc.edu/daniel/eng32/index.html>.

For the home page of a course, provide this information: ① Instructor's name. ② Course title, without quotation marks or underlining. ③ The description Course home page. ④ Inclusive dates of the course. ⑤ Names of the department and the school, separated by a comma. ⑥ Date of your access. ⑦ URL for the home page.

For a department home page, give the department name first, followed by Dept. home page, the name of the school, your access date, and the URL:

> Computer Engineering. Dept. home page. Santa Clara U School of Engineering.
> 12 Oct. 2006 <http://www.cse.scu.edu>.

48. An entry on a Web log

> Daswani, Susheel. "Hollywood vs. Silicon Valley." Berkeley Intellectual Prop-
> erty Weblog. 16 Mar. 2006. 22 Aug. 2006 <http://www.biplog.com/
> archive/cat_hollywood.html>.

To cite an entry on a Web log, give the following: ① Author's name. ② Title of the entry, in quotation marks. ③ Title of the Web log, underlined. ④ Date of the entry. ⑤ Date of your access. ⑥ URL for the entry.

49. Electronic mail

Millon, Michele. "Re: Grief Therapy." E-mail to the author. 4 Jan. 2007.

For e-mail, give the following: ① Writer's name. ② Title, if any, from the e-mail's subject heading, in quotation marks. ③ Description of the transmission, including to whom it was sent. ④ Date of posting.

50. A posting to an e-mail discussion list

Tourville, Michael. "European Currency Reform." Online posting. 6 Jan. 2007. International Finance Discussion List. 12 Jan. 2007 <http:// www.weg.isu.edu/finance-dl/archive/46732>.

Whenever possible, cite an archived version of a posting to an e-mail discussion list so that readers can find it without difficulty. Give this information for the posting: ① Author's name. ② Title, if any, from the e-mail's subject heading, in quotation marks. ③ Online posting. ④ Date of posting. ⑤ Name of the discussion list, without quotation marks or underlining. ⑥ Date of your access. ⑦ URL, if known, or e-mail address for the list's moderator or supervisor.

51. A posting to a newsgroup or Web forum

A newsgroup:

Cramer, Sherry. "Recent Investment Practices in US Business." Online posting. 26 Mar. 2006. Young Entrepreneurs. 3 Apr. 2006 <http:// finance.groups.yahoo.com/group/youngentrepreneurs3>.

For a posting to a newsgroup that you read on the Web, give the following: ① Author's name. ② Title from the subject heading, in quotation marks. ③ Online posting. ④ Date of posting. ⑤ Name of the newsgroup, without quotation marks or underlining. ⑥ Date of your access. ⑦ URL for the group. If you read the posting on a news server instead of on the Web, omit the group name before your access date and give the group name in the URL, preceded by news: <news:biz.startups.youngentrepreneurs.2700>.

MLA

56b

A Web forum:

Razi, N. M. "Hypothyroidism." Online posting. 6 July 2006. Homeopathy Forum. 28 Jan. 2007 <http://www.hpathy.com/homeopathy/forums/ forum_topics.asp?FID=328>.

For a posting to a Web forum, provide this information: ① Author's name. ② Title, if any, in quotation marks. ③ Online posting. ④ Date of posting. ⑤ Name of the forum, without quotation marks or underlining. ⑥ Date of your access. ⑦ URL for the forum.

52. A synchronous communication

Bruckman, Amy. MediaMOO Symposium: Virtual Worlds for Business? 20 Jan. 2006. MediaMOO. 26 Feb. 2006 <http://www.co.gatech.edu/fac/ Amy.Bruckman/MediaMOO/cscw-symposium-06.html>.

Whenever possible, cite an archived version of a synchronous communication so that readers can find it without difficulty. Provide this information: ① Speaker's name. ② Description of the event, without quotation marks or underlining. ③ Date of the event. ④ Forum, without quotation marks or underlining. ⑤ Date of your access. ⑥ URL for the archive.

53. A source on a periodical CD-ROM database

Hakim, Danny. "Iacocca, Away from the Grind, Still Has a Lot to Say." New York Times 19 July 2006, natl. ed.: C1+. New York Times Ondisc. CD-ROM. UMI-ProQuest. Sept. 2006.

Databases on CD-ROM are issued periodically—for instance, every six months or every year. The journals, newspapers, and other publications included in such a database are generally available in print as well, so your works-cited entry should give the information for both formats: ① Information for the print version, following models on pages 500–04. ② Title of the CD-ROM, underlined. ③ Medium, CD-ROM. ④ Name of the vendor (or distributor) of the CD-ROM. ⑤ Date of electronic publication.

54. A source on a nonperiodical CD-ROM

Nunberg, Geoffrey. "Usage in the Dictionary." The American Heritage Dictionary of the English Language. 4th ed. CD-ROM. Boston: Houghton, 2005.

Single-issue CD-ROMs may be encyclopedias, dictionaries, books, and other resources that are published just once, like printed books. Use this format: ① Author's name, if any. ② Title of the source. Use quotation marks for short works, such as an article. Underline the title if it is a book. ③ Title of the entire CD-ROM, underlined. Note that this CD-ROM also includes an edition number. ④ Medium, CD-ROM. ⑤ CD-ROM's place of publication, publisher, and date of publication.

See also pages 500 and 511, respectively, for models of print and online reference works.

55. Computer software

Project Scheduler 9000. Vers. 5.1. Orlando: Scitor, 2007.

For software, provide the following: ① Title, underlined. ② Version number. ③ Publication information, including place of publication, publisher, and date. If the software has a listed author, give his or her name first in the entry. If you consulted or obtained the software online, replace the publication information with the date of your access and the URL, as in earlier examples.

4 • Other print and nonprint sources

56. A government publication

Board of Governors. US Federal Reserve System. Federal Reserve Bulletin Aug. 2006: 20-21.

Hawaii. Dept. of Education. Kauai District Schools, Profile 2005-06. Honolulu: Hawaii Dept. of Education, 2006.

Stiller, Ann. Historic Preservation and Tax Incentives. US Dept. of Interior. Washington: GPO, 2003.

United States. Cong. House. Committee on Ways and Means. Medicare Payment for Outpatient Occupational Therapy Services. 109th Cong., 1st sess. Washington: GPO, 2005.

If an author is not listed for a government publication, give the appropriate agency as author, as in the first, second, and last examples. Provide information in the order illustrated, separating elements with a period: the name of the government, the name of the agency (which may be abbreviated), and the title and publication information. For a congressional publication (last example), give the house and committee involved before the title, and give the number and session of Congress after the title. In the last two examples, GPO stands for the US Government Printing Office.

57. A pamphlet

Medical Answers About AIDS. New York: Gay Men's Health Crisis, 2006.

Most pamphlets can be treated as books. In the preceding example, the pamphlet has no listed author, so the title comes first. If the pamphlet has an author, list his or her name first, followed by the title and publication information as given in the example.

58. An unpublished dissertation or thesis

Wilson, Stuart M. "John Stuart Mill as a Literary Critic." Diss. U of Michigan,
1990.

The title is quoted rather than underlined. Diss. stands for "Dissertation." U of Michigan is the institution that granted the author's degree.

59. An image (artwork, advertisement, graph, etc.)

A work of art:

Hockney, David. Place Furstenberg, Paris. 1985. College Art Gallery, New Paltz,
New York. David Hockney: A Retrospective. Ed. Maurice Tuchman and
Stephanie Barron. Los Angeles: Los Angeles County Museum of Art,
1988. 247.

For a work of art, name the artist and give the title (underlined), the date of creation, and the name and location of the owner. For a work you see only in a reproduction, provide the complete publication information, too, as in the Hockney model. Omit such information only if you examined the actual work.

A photograph:

Heinz, Thomas A. Fallingwater: Exterior Detail. Frank Lloyd Wright: Architect.
Ed. Terence Riley. New York: Museum of Modern Art, 2000. 236.

Treat a photograph you find in a collection or book like a work of art, with photographer's name (if known), photograph title (underlined), and date. Add the owner's name (as in the Hockney entry above) if the photograph is an artwork and not an illustration. Give the publication information unless you examined an actual print of the photograph.

For a personal photograph by you or someone else, describe the subject (without quotation marks or underlining), say who took the photograph, and add the date:

Children in Central Park. Personal photograph by the author. 16 Mar. 2006.

An advertisement:

Jetta by Volkswagen. Advertisement. New Yorker 24 July 2006: 31.

MLA
56b

Cite an advertisement with the name of the product or company advertised, the description Advertisement, and the publication information.

A cartoon or comic strip:

> Trudeau, Garry. "Doonesbury." Comic strip. San Francisco Chronicle 28 Aug.
>
> 2006: E6.

Cite a cartoon or comic strip with the artist's name, the title (in quotation marks), the description Cartoon or Comic strip, and the publication information.

A map, chart, graph, or diagram:

> Women in the Armed Forces. Map. Women in the World: An International Atlas.
>
> By Joni Seager and Ann Olson. New York: Touchstone, 2007. 44-45.

List the image by its title (underlined) unless its creator is credited on the source. Provide a description (Map, Chart, and so on) and then the publication information.

60. A television or radio program

> "I'm Sorry, I'm Lost." By Alan Ball. Dir. Jill Soloway. Six Feet Under. HBO.
>
> 2 July 2005.

Start with the title unless you are citing the work of a person or persons. The example here includes an episode title (in quotation marks), the writer's and director's names, the program title (underlined), the name of the network, and the date. If the program aired on a local TV station, identify the station between the network and the date—for example, WGBH, Boston.

61. A sound recording

> Brahms, Johannes. Piano Concerto no. 2 in B-flat, op. 83. Perf. Artur Rubin-
>
> stein. Cond. Eugene Ormandy. Philadelphia Orch. LP. RCA, 1972.
>
> Springsteen, Bruce. "Empty Sky." The Rising. Columbia, 2002.

Begin with the name of the individual whose work you are citing. If you're citing a song or song lyrics, give the title in quotation marks. Then provide the title of the recording, not underlined if it identifies a composition by form, number, and key (first example). After the title, provide the names of any other artists it seems appropriate to mention, the manufacturer of the recording, and the date of release. If the medium is other than compact disk, provide it immediately before the manufacturer's name—for instance, LP (as in the first example) or Audiocassette.

62. A film, DVD, or video recording

The Lord of the Rings: The Return of the King. Dir. Peter Jackson. New Line,

2003.

Start with the title of the work you are citing, unless you are citing the contribution of a particular individual (as in the next model). Give additional information (director, writer, lead performers, and so on) as you judge appropriate. For a film, end with the distributor and date.

For a DVD or videocassette, include the original release date (if any) and the medium (DVD, videocassette) before the distributor's name:

George Balanchine, chor. Serenade. Perf. San Francisco Ballet. Dir. Hilary Bean.

1991. Videocassette. PBS Video, 1997.

63. A musical composition

Fauré, Gabriel. Sonata for Violin and Piano no. 1 in A Major, op. 15.

Don't underline musical compositions, such as the one above, that are identified only by form, number, and key. Do underline titled operas, ballets, and compositions (Carmen, Sleeping Beauty).

64. A performance

Barenboim, Daniel, cond. Chicago Symphony Orch. Symphony Center, Chicago.

22 Jan. 2005.

The English Only Restaurant. By Silvio Martinez Palau. Dir. Susana Tubert.

Puerto Rican Traveling Theater, New York. 27 July 2005.

As with films and television programs, place the title first unless you are citing the work of an individual (first example). Provide additional information about participants after the title, as well as the theater, city, and date. Note that the orchestra name in the first example is neither quoted nor underlined.

65. A letter

Buttolph, Mrs. Laura E. Letter to Rev. and Mrs. C. C. Jones. 20 June 1857. In

The Children of Pride: A True Story of Georgia and the Civil War. Ed.

Robert Manson Myers. New Haven: Yale UP, 1972. 334-35.

List a published letter under the writer's name. Specify that the source is a letter and to whom it was addressed, and give the date on which it was written. Treat the remaining information like that for a selection from an anthology (model 18, p. 499). (See also p. 503 for the format of a letter to the editor of a periodical.)

For a letter in the collection of a library or archive, specify the writer, recipient, and date, as in the previous example, and give the name and location of the archive as well:

> James, Jonathan E. Letter to his sister. 16 Apr. 1970. Jonathan E. James
> Papers. South Dakota State Archive, Pierre.

For a letter you receive, give the name of the writer, note the fact that the letter was sent to you, and provide the date of the letter:

> Packer, Ann E. Letter to the author. 15 June 2006.

Use the form above for personal e-mail as well, substituting E-mail for Letter: E-mail to the author (see model 49, p. 514).

66. A lecture or address

> Carlone, Dennis. "Architecture for the City of the Twenty-First Century." Symposium on the City. Urban Issues Group. Cambridge City Hall, Cambridge.
> 22 May 2006.

Give the speaker's name, the title (in quotation marks), the title of the meeting, the name of the sponsoring organization, the location of the lecture, and the date. If the lecture has no title, use Lecture, Address, or another description instead.

Although the *MLA Handbook* does not provide a specific style for classroom lectures in your courses, you can adapt the preceding format for this purpose:

> Chang, Julia. Class lecture on the realist novel. Homans College. 20 Jan. 2006.

67. An interview

> Graaf, Vera. Personal interview. 5 Feb. 2007.
> Rumsfeld, Donald. Interview. Frontline. PBS. WGBH, Boston. 10 Oct. 2005.

Begin with the name of the person interviewed. For an interview you conducted, specify Personal interview or the medium (such as Telephone interview or E-mail interview), and then give the date. For an interview you read, heard, or saw, provide the title if any or Interview if there is no title, along with other bibliographic information and the date.

EXERCISE 56.1
Writing works-cited entries

Prepare works-cited entries from the following information. Follow the models of the *MLA Handbook* given in this chapter unless your instructor specifies a different style. For titles, use underlining (as here) unless your instructor requests italics. Arrange the finished entries in alphabetical order, not numbered. Answers to the starred items appear at the end of the book. (You can do this exercise online at *ablongman.com/littlebrown*.)

*1. A journal article titled "Networking the Classroom" by Christopher Conte. The article appears in volume 5 of CQ Researcher, a journal that pages issues continuously throughout each annual volume. Volume 5 is dated 2005. The article runs from page 923 to page 943.

*2. A magazine article on a database that is also available in print. The author is Larry Irving. The title is "The Still Yawning Divide." The article appears in the March 12, 2006, issue of Newsweek, a weekly magazine, and starts on page 64. You consulted the article on November 14, 2006, through the database Expanded Academic ASAP from the service InfoTrac (http://www.galegroup.com). You reached the database through Southeast State University's Polk Library.

*3. A government document you consulted on November 12, 2006, over the Internet. The author is the National Center for Education Statistics, an agency within the United States Department of Education. The title of the document is Internet Access in Public Schools. It was published February 24, 2005, and can be accessed at http://www.ed.gov/nces/edstats.

*4. A book called Failure to Connect: How Computers Affect Our Children's Minds—For Better and Worse, written by Jane M. Healy and published in 2000 by Simon & Schuster in New York.

5. An article in the October 9, 2005, issue of the magazine The Nation titled "The Threat to the Net." The article is by Jeff Chester and appears on pages 6 to 7 of the magazine. You found it through Polk Library at Southeast State University on November 14, 2006, using the database Expanded Academic ASAP from the service InfoTrac. The home page URL for the database is http://www.galegroup.com.

6. A pamphlet titled Bridging the Digital Divide, with no named author. It was published in 2006 by the ALA in Chicago.

7. An article titled "MyPyramid.gov: Achieving E-Health for All?" on the Web site Digital Divide Network at http://www.digitaldivide.net/articles. The Web site is sponsored by the Benton Foundation. The article is by Andy Carvin and is dated February 22, 2005. You found it on November 10, 2006.

8. An e-mail interview you conducted with Mary McArthur on October 31, 2006.

MLA
56c

56c Format the paper in MLA style.

The document format recommended by the *MLA Handbook* is fairly simple, with just a few elements. See also pages 74–84 for guidelines on type fonts, headings, lists, and other features that are not specified in MLA style.

The following illustrations show the formats for the first page and a later page of a paper. For the format of the list of works cited, see pages 491–92.

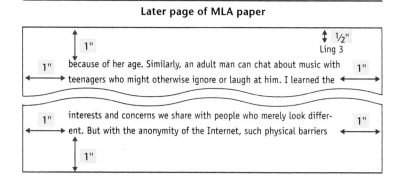

Margins Use minimum one-inch margins on all sides of every page.

Spacing and indentions Double-space throughout. Indent paragraphs one-half inch or five spaces. (See the facing page for indention of set-off quotations.)

Paging Begin numbering on the first page, and number consecutively through the end (including the list of works cited). Type Arabic numerals (1, 2, 3) in the upper right about one-half inch from the top. Place your last name before the page number in case the pages later become separated.

Identification and title MLA style does not require a title page for a paper. Instead, give your name, your instructor's name, the course title, and the date on separate lines in the upper left of the first page—one inch from the top and the left of the paper. (See the sample on the facing page.) Double-space between all lines of this identification.

Double-space also around the title, and center it. If the title runs two lines, center both lines and double-space between them. Use capital and small letters for the title, capitalizing according to the guidelines on page 403. Don't type the title in all-capital letters, underline it, or enclose it in quotation marks. (See the sample on the facing page.)

Poetry and long prose quotations Treat a single line of poetry like any other quotation, running it into your text and enclosing it in quotation marks. You may run in two or three lines of poetry as well, separating the lines with a slash surrounded by space.

> An example of Robert Frost's incisiveness is in two lines from "Death of the Hired Man": @"Home is the place where, when you have to go there (/) They have to take you in" (119-20).

Always set off quotations of more than three lines of poetry and more than four typed lines of prose. (See pp. 463–64 for guidelines on when to use such long quotations.) Use double spacing above and below the quotation and for the quotation itself. Indent the quotation one inch or ten spaces from the left margin. *Do not add quotation marks to set-off quotations.*

> Emily Dickinson stripped ideas to their essence, as in this description of "A narrow Fellow in the Grass," a snake:
>
>> I more than once at Noon
>> Have passed, I thought, a Whip lash
>> Unbraiding in the Sun
>> When stopping to secure it
>> It wrinkled, and was gone (12-16)

> In Talley's Corner, his influential 1967 study of the urban poor, Elliot Liebow observes that "unskilled" construction work requires more experience and skill than is generally assumed:
>
>> A healthy, sturdy, active man of good intelligence requires from two to four weeks to break in on a construction job. . . . It frequently happens that his foreman or the craftsman he services is not willing to wait that long for him to get into condition or to

learn at a glance the difference in size between a rough 2 x 8 and
a finished 2 x 10.(62)

Do not use a paragraph indention for a quotation of a single
complete paragraph or a part of a paragraph. Use paragraph indentions of one-quarter inch or three spaces only for a quotation of two
or more paragraphs.

56d   A sample paper in MLA style

The sample paper beginning on page 526 follows the guidelines
of the *MLA Handbook* for overall format, parenthetical citations,
and the list of works cited. Marginal annotations highlight features
of the paper.

Note Because the sample paper addresses a current Internet
controversy, many of its sources come from the Internet and do not
use page or other reference numbers. Thus the in-text citations of
these sources do not give reference numbers. In a paper relying
solely on printed journals, books, and other traditional sources,
most if not all in-text citations would include page numbers.

A note on outlines

Some instructors ask students to submit an outline of the final
paper. For advice on constructing a formal or topic outline, see
pages 24–25. Below is an outline of the sample paper following,
written in complete sentences. Note that the thesis statement precedes either a topic or a sentence outline.

Thesis statement

To improve equity between online and traditional stores and between consumers with and without Internet access, tax laws should be revised to allow
collection of sales taxes on Internet purchases.

I. A Supreme Court ruling and congressional legislation presently govern
Internet taxation.

   A. A 1992 Supreme Court decision frees vendors from collecting sales
   taxes from customers in states where the vendors have no physical
   presence.

   B. A 1998 law, extended in 2004, placed a moratorium on Internet
   taxes.

II. A tax-free Internet is unfair to traditional brick-and-mortar stores.

   A. Sales taxes can make brick-and-mortar purchases significantly more
   expensive than online purchases.

   B. Sales taxes exceed online merchants' shipping charges.

III. A tax-free Internet is unfair to consumers who lack Internet access.

   A. A government report shows a huge "digital divide" among US residents.

      1. The affluent are much more likely to have Internet access than the poor.

      2. Whites who are college educated are much more likely to have Internet access than nonwhites with elementary educations.

   B. The digital divide means the poor must pay sales taxes while the affluent can avoid the taxes by shopping online.

IV. The three main arguments against Internet taxation do not rebut the issue of fairness.

   A. Taxes on Internet commerce would not, as claimed, undermine the freedom of the Internet.

   B. Internet commerce does not, as claimed, deserve special protection and encouragement that is not given to traditional commerce.

   C. The very real complexities of Internet taxation do not, as claimed, justify a permanent ban on taxation.

Identification: writer's name, instructor's name, course title, date.	Kisha Alder Ms. Savarro English 101 15 December 2006
Title centered.	Who Pays the Bill for Internet Shopping?

Going to the mall may soon go out of style. These days more and more people are shopping from home over the Internet. In 2002 electronic commerce (e-commerce) took in approximately $40 billion from shoppers; by 2007 that amount is expected to be $105 billion or more ("Sales Tax"). These numbers are good news for the online stores and for online shoppers, who can anticipate increasing variety in e-commerce offerings. But because taxes are not collected on Internet sales as they are on purchases in almost all states, online stores compete unfairly with traditional "brick-and-mortar" stores, and shoppers with Internet access have an unfair advantage over shoppers with no such access. To improve equity between online and traditional stores and between consumers with and without Internet access, tax laws should be revised to allow collection of sales taxes on Internet purchases.

Internet commerce is regulated by the same tax laws that govern other commerce. However, in 1992 the Supreme Court ruled that vendors do not have to collect taxes on behalf of states where they do not have a physical presence, because such collection would place an unconstitutional burden on interstate commerce (Quill Corp. v. North Dakota 5-8). Buyers are supposed to send the correct taxes to their state governments voluntarily, but they rarely do and states currently have no way to collect (Zimmerman and Hoover 45). In a decision addressing mail-order sales but considered applicable to Internet sales, the Court's majority urged Congress to reexamine the tax laws governing interstate commerce:

> The underlying issue is not only one that Congress may be better qualified to resolve, but also one that Congress has the ultimate power to resolve. . . . Accordingly, Congress is now free to decide whether, when, and to what extent the States may burden interstate mail-order concerns with a duty to collect use taxes. (Quill Corp. v. North Dakota 18-19)

Margin annotations:

- Double-space throughout.
- Introduction: gives background to establish the issue.
- Citation form: shortened title for anonymous source; online source has no page number.
- Thesis statement.
- Background on Internet taxation (next two paragraphs).
- Citation form: law case; case name underlined in the text citation.
- Citation form: source with two authors.
- Quotation over four lines set off without quotation marks. See p. 523.
- Ellipsis mark signals omission from quotation.
- Citation form: after displayed quotation, citation follows sentence period and one space.

Alder 2

Because of this decision, Congress has been wrestling with whether and how to tax Internet commerce.

Congress did take some action in 1998, when e-commerce was blossoming, by placing a temporary moratorium on new Internet taxes and by creating the Advisory Commission on Electronic Commerce to study the taxation issue and recommend solutions. A majority of the commission recommended extending the moratorium for another five years, through 2006, so that the taxation issue could be studied further and the state and local taxing authorities could simplify their complex and overlapping tax systems (US Advisory Commission). Congress agreed and voted in 2002 and again in 2004 to extend the moratorium, which now runs through 2007. Meanwhile, the debate over taxing e-commerce continues to heat up. On one side are state and local governments that are attempting to regain lost revenue with a uniform tax rate that would apply to Internet purchases. On the other side are those who would transform the moratorium on Internet sales taxes into a permanent ban ("Congress").

As long as the moratorium is in effect, Internet shopping is essentially tax-free. Yet in almost all states, traditional shopping is subject to sales tax. Brick-and-mortar stores that are required by law to charge and collect sales taxes are at a distinct disadvantage compared to the online stores with no such burden. The local bookstore, music store, and drugstore must charge sales tax; their competitors Barnes&Noble.com, CDNOW.com, and PlanetRx.com do not, though some, like Amazon.com, have begun voluntarily collecting sales tax under pressure from the states. The tax burden can be significant: for instance, California and New York State charge residents at least 7 percent to shop in their own neighborhoods (Wiseman 60).

Some online merchants claim that the shipping costs they charge offset the sales taxes they don't charge (Granfield 57). However, many online companies offer free shipping and handling as an incentive to online shoppers. And even without such promotions, state and local sales taxes far exceed most shipping costs. As one frequent online consumer said, "If I buy more than three CDs . . . , the shipping cost is less than the sales tax would have been" (James). On balance, the traditional purchase just costs more.

Common knowledge of congressional votes does not require source citations.

Source: corporate author. Citation form: corporate author only, because online source has no page or other reference numbers.

Citation form: shortened title for anonymous source; no page number for one-page source.

Contrast between online and traditional commerce (next two paragraphs).

Selective use of data, with summary of source acknowledged.

Paragraph integrates evidence from two sources.

Primary source: e-mail interview. Citation form: source name only, because interview has no page or other reference numbers.

Contrast between shoppers with and without Internet access (next two paragraphs).	The Internet's tax-free shopping is also damaging to equality among groups of people. Governments, scholars, and businesspeople express concern about the "digital divide" between the affluent who have Internet access and the poor who do not. According to <u>A Nation Online</u>, the most recent US Department of Commerce study of Internet access, "Households with incomes of $75,000 and higher are more than <u>twice</u> as likely to have access to the Internet as those at the lowest income levels [below $15,000]" (24; emphasis added).
Source named in the text, so not named in parenthetical citations that follow.	
Brackets signal words added to clarify the quotation. Citation form: "emphasis added" indicates underlining was not in original quotation.	The same study shows that Internet access is two times more common among whites than among African Americans or Latinos (72) and twelve times more common among those with college educations than among those with elementary school educations (71).
Writer's own conclusions from preceding data.	The digital divide has implications for the relative abilities of people in different groups to function effectively in an increasingly electronic world. But where sales taxes are concerned, it does further harm to the disadvantaged. For the most part, white, educated, and affluent consumers can shop tax-free because they can shop on the Internet, whereas nonwhite, uneducated, and poor consumers have no choice but to shop locally and pay the required taxes.
Statement and rebuttal of three opposing views (next five paragraphs).	Equity thus requires sales taxes on e-commerce, but there are many who argue strongly against such taxes. The writing about Internet taxation (in articles and discussion groups and on Web sites) reveals three major arguments against it. (A fourth, against any new taxes of any kind, is not specifically relevant to Internet commerce.)
Signal phrase interrupts quotation and is set off by commas.	The first argument holds that Internet freedom is sacred and should be protected. "To me," writes one discussion participant, "the Internet is . . . freedom of thought. We can't have the government meddling in the ability of its citizens to read, speak, and, yes, conduct free enterprise online" (Angeles). But Internet commerce is commerce, after all. Even if the network often serves as a site for free thought and communication, when it serves as a place of business it should be subject to the same rules as other businesses.
Citation form: author's name only, because online source has no page or other reference numbers.	
Rebuttals are writer's own ideas and do not require source citations.	
Citation form: no parenthetical citation because author is named in the text and online source has no page or other reference numbers.	The second major argument against Internet taxes, related to the first, is expressed in this statement by a major opponent of the taxes, US Senator Ron Wyden: "State and local taxes could do irreparable harm to the Internet, killing the goose that could lay billions of dollars in golden eggs." But this argument, like the first one, assumes that Internet commerce deserves special protection and

Alder 4

encouragement—even at the expense of brick-and-mortar commerce. In fact, both kinds of commerce contribute to the health of the economy, and they should be protected, or taxed, equally.

Finally, the third major argument against Internet taxes holds that the issue is too complex to be resolved, a "logistical nightmare," in the words of a taxation opponent (Granfield 57). As outlined by more neutral observers—members of the respected accounting firm of Deloitte Touche Tohmatsu—the main complexities are very real: the existence of more than 3000 state and local taxing authorities in the United States, each with its own regulations and rates; the need to bring these jurisdictions into agreement on how to rationalize and simplify their systems; the concern that any federally imposed solution might violate states' rights; and finally the uncertainty about whether an online vendor conducts taxable business where its office, its server, its customer, or all three are located (67-72).

The complexities do seem nightmarish, as tax opponents claim, but change is underway. In October 2005 nineteen states launched a voluntary program, the Streamlined Sales Tax Project, to tax Internet transactions using a uniform tax system. Online merchants who participate receive free collection and remittance software and services (Krebs). Stephen Kranz of the Council on State Taxation says that "states, local governments, and businesses interested in reducing the complexity of sales taxes have created a plan that might work nationwide" (qtd. in Krebs). The states hope that the success of the pilot will lead Congress to pass into law a mandatory national sales tax program.

The Internet has introduced many improvements in our lives, including the ability to make purchases with the click of a mouse. But at the same time the tax-free status of Internet commerce has allowed it to compete unfairly with traditional businesses and given an unfair financial advantage to those who most likely already have plenty of advantages. Congress and Internet businesses must recognize these inequities and must work with state and local taxing authorities to remedy them.

Annotations (right margin):

Citation form: author not named in the text.

Citation form (here and end of paragraph): corporate author named in the text.

Summary reduces six pages in the source to a list of four points.

Position of citation indicates that all preceding information comes from the Deloitte source.

Citation form: author's name only, because online source has no page or other reference numbers.

Citation form: indirect source (Kranz quoted by Krebs).

Conclusion: summary and a call for action.

New page.	
Heading centered.	Works Cited
Sources are alphabetized by authors' last names.	Angeles, Lemuel. "Internet Freedom." Online posting. 8 Oct. 2006. ZDNet Talkback. 18 Nov. 2006 <http://www.zdnet.com/ tklbck/comment/22/0,7056.html>.
Second and subsequent lines of each source are indented one-half inch.	"Congress Votes to Ban States from Taxing Internet." New York Times 20 Nov. 2004, late ed.: C4. LexisNexis Academic. LexisNexis. Southeast State U, Polk Lib. 14 Nov. 2006 <http:// www.lexisnexis.com>.
	Deloitte Touche Tohmatsu. Establishing a Framework to Evaluate E-Commerce Tax Options. Berkeley: U of California P, 2004.
A magazine article.	Granfield, Anne. "Taxing the Internet." Forbes 17 Dec. 2004: 56-58.
An e-mail interview.	James, Nora. E-mail interview. 26 Nov. 2006.
An online newspaper article.	Krebs, Brian. "States Move Forward on Internet Sales Tax." washingtonpost.com 1 July 2005. 18 Nov. 2006 <http:// www.washingtonpost.com/wp-dyn/content/article/2005/07/01>.
A law case: name not underlined in list of works cited.	Quill Corp. v. North Dakota. 504 US 298. 1992.
An anonymous article listed and alphabetized by title. Source obtained through a library subscription service.	"Sales Tax on Internet Buys Could Help Fill Budget Gaps." Associated Press State and Local Wire. 26 Aug. 2006. LexisNexis Academic. LexisNexis. Southeast State U, Polk Lib. 18 Nov. 2006 <http://www. lexisnexis.com>.
A government publication with no named author, so government body given as author.	United States. Advisory Commission on Electronic Commerce. Report to Congress. Apr. 2000. 25 Nov. 2006 <http:// www.ecommercecommission.org/report.htm>.
Second source by author of two or more cited works: three hyphens replace author's name (United States).	---. Dept. of Commerce. National Telecommunications and Information Admin. A Nation Online: Entering the Broadband Age. Sept. 2004. 22 Nov. 2006 <http://www.ntia.doc.gov/reports/ anol/index/html>.
A book.	Wiseman, Alan E. The Internet Economy: Access, Taxes, and Market Structure. Washington: Brookings, 2006.
A page on a Web site.	Wyden, Ron. "Statement on the Internet Tax Non-Discrimination Act." Ron Wyden Online. 7 Jan. 2003. 16 Nov. 2006 <http:// wyden.senate.gov/media/speeches/2003/ 01072003_internettax_statement.html>.
An article from a journal that pages each issue separately. A source with two authors.	Zimmerman, Malai, and Kent Hoover. "Use of Third Parties to Collect State and Local Taxes on Internet Sales." Pacific Business Journal 26.2 (2005): 45-48.

57 APA Documentation and Format

How do I cite sources and format papers in the social sciences?

The most widely used style guide in the social sciences is the *Publication Manual of the American Psychological Association* (5th ed., 2001). In the APA documentation style, you acknowledge each of your sources twice:

- In your text, a brief parenthetical citation adjacent to the borrowed material directs readers to a complete list of all the works you refer to.
- At the end of your paper, the list of references includes complete bibliographical information for every source.

Every entry in the list of references has at least one corresponding citation in the text, and every in-text citation has a corresponding entry in the list of references.

This chapter describes APA text citations (below) and references (p. 535), details APA document format (p. 547), and concludes with a sample APA paper (p. 550).

57a Use APA parenthetical citations in your text.

In the APA documentation style, parenthetical citations within the text refer the reader to a list of sources at the end of the text. See the next page for an index to the models of parenthetical citations.

Note Models 1 and 2 show the direct relationship between what you include in your text and what you include in a parenthetical citation. The citation always includes a publication date and may include a page number. It also includes the author's name if you do *not* name the author in your text (model 1). It does not include the author's name if you *do* name the author in your text (model 2).

1. Author not named in your text

One critic of Milgram's experiments said that the subjects "should have been fully informed of the possible effects on them" (Baumrind, 1998, p. 34).

APA
57a

When you do not name the author in your text, place in parentheses the author's last name and the date of the source. Separate the

http://www.ablongman.com/littlebrown ▶

Visit the companion Web site for more help and an electronic exercise on APA documentation and format.

APA parenthetical text citations

elements with commas. Position the reference so that it is clear what material is being documented *and* so that the reference fits as smoothly as possible into your sentence structure. (See pp. 489–90 for guidelines.) The following would also be correct:

> In the view of one critic of Milgram's experiments (Baumrind, 1998), the subjects "should have been fully informed of the possible effects on them" (p. 34).

Unless none is available, the APA requires a page or other identifying number for a direct quotation (as in the preceding examples) and recommends an identifying number for a paraphrase. Use an appropriate abbreviation or symbol before the number—for instance, p. for *page* and ¶ for *paragraph* (or para. if you do not have the symbol). The identifying number may fall with the author and date (example on the previous page) or by itself in a separate pair of parentheses (example above). See also model 11 (p. 534).

2. Author named in your text

> Baumrind (1998) said that the subjects in Milgram's study "should have been fully informed of the possible effects on them" (p. 34).

When you use the author's name in the text, do not repeat it in the reference. Place the source date in parentheses after the author's name. Place any page or paragraph reference either after the borrowed material (as in the example) or with the date: (1998, p. 34). If you cite the same source again in the paragraph, you need not repeat the reference as long as it is clear that you are using the same source.

3. A work with two authors

> Pepinsky and DeStefano (2000) demonstrated that a teacher's language often reveals hidden biases.

One study (Pepinsky & DeStefano, 2000) demonstrated hidden biases in teachers' language.

When given in the text, two authors' names are connected by and. In a parenthetical citation, they are connected by an ampersand, &.

4. A work with three to five authors

Pepinsky, Dunn, Rentl, and Corson (2001) further demonstrated the biases evident in gestures.

In the first citation of a work with three to five authors, name all the authors, as in the example above. In the second and subsequent references to the work, generally give only the first author's name, followed by et al. (Latin abbreviation for "and others"):

In the work of Pepinsky et al. (2001), the loaded gestures included head shakes and eye contact.

However, two or more sources published in the same year could shorten to the same form—for instance, two references shortening to Pepinsky et al., 2001. In that case, cite the last names of as many authors as you need to distinguish the sources, and then give et al.: for instance, Pepinsky, Dunn, et al., 2001 and Pepinsky, Bradley, et al., 2001.

5. A work with six or more authors

One study (Rutter et al., 2004) attempted to explain these geographical differences in adolescent experience.

For six or more authors, even in the first citation of the work, give only the first author's name, followed by et al. If two or more sources published in the same year shorten to the same form, follow the instructions with model 4.

6. A work with a group author

An earlier prediction was even more somber (Lorenz Research, 2003).

For a work that lists an institution, agency, corporation, or other group as author, treat the name of the group as if it were an individual's name. If the name is long and has a familiar abbreviation, you may use the abbreviation in the second and subsequent citations. For example, you might abbreviate American Psychological Association as APA.

7. A work with no author or an anonymous work

One article ("Right to Die," 2001) noted that a death-row inmate may crave notoriety.

APA

57a

For a work with no named author, use the first two or three words of the title in place of an author's name, excluding an initial *The*, *A*, or *An*. Italicize book and journal titles, place quotation marks around article titles, and capitalize the significant words in all titles cited in the text. (In the reference list, however, do not use quotation marks for article titles, and capitalize only the first word in all but periodical titles. See p. 536.)

For a work that lists "Anonymous" as the author, use this word in the citation: (Anonymous, 1999).

8. One of two or more works by the same author(s)

At about age seven, most children begin to use appropriate gestures to reinforce their stories (Gardner, 1973a).

If your reference list includes two or more works published by the same author(s) *in the same year*, the works should be lettered in the reference list (see p. 539). Then your parenthetical citation should include the appropriate letter, as in 1973a in the example.

9. Two or more works by different authors

Two studies (Herskowitz, 1999; Marconi & Hamblen, 2006) found that periodic safety instruction can dramatically reduce employees' accidents.

List the sources in alphabetical order by their first authors' names. Insert a semicolon between sources.

10. An indirect source

Supporting data appeared in a study by Wong (cited in Marconi & Hamblen, 2006).

The phrase cited in indicates that the reference to Wong's study was found in Marconi and Hamblen. Only Marconi and Hamblen then appears in the list of references.

11. An electronic source

Ferguson and Hawkins (2000) did not anticipate the "evident hostility" of participants (¶ 6).

Electronic sources can be cited like printed sources, usually with the author's last name and the publication date. When quoting or paraphrasing electronic sources that number paragraphs instead of pages, provide the paragraph number preceded by the symbol ¶ if you have it, or by para. Even if the source does not number its paragraphs, you can still direct readers to a specific location by listing the heading under which the quotation appears and then (counting paragraphs yourself) the number of the paragraph in which the quotation appears—for example, (Morrison & Lee, 2004, Method section, ¶ 4). When the source does not number pages or paragraphs or provide frequent headings, omit any reference number.

57b   Prepare an APA reference list.

In APA style, the in-text parenthetical citations refer to the list of sources at the end of the text. This list, titled References, includes full publication information on every source cited in the paper. The list falls at the end of the paper, numbered in sequence with the preceding pages. The sample below shows the elements and their spacing.

APA reference list

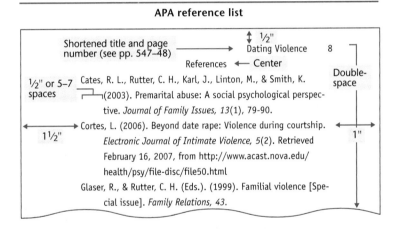

Arrangement Arrange sources alphabetically by the author's last name. If there is no author, alphabetize by the first main word of the title. Do *not* group sources by type (books, journals, and so on).

Spacing Double-space everything in the references, as shown in the sample, unless your instructor requests single spacing. (If you do single-space the entries themselves, always double-space *between* them.)

Indention As illustrated in the sample above, begin each entry at the left margin, and indent the second and subsequent lines five to seven spaces or one-half inch.

Punctuation Separate the parts of the reference (author, date, title, and publication information) with a period and one space. Do not use a final period in references to electronic sources, which conclude with an electronic address (see pp. 541–45).

Authors For works with up to six authors, list all authors with last name first, separating names and parts of names with commas. Use initials for first and middle names. Use an ampersand (&) before the last author's name. See model 3 (p. 538) for the treatment of seven or more authors.

Publication date Place the publication date in parentheses after the author's or authors' names, followed by a period. Generally this date is the year only, though for some sources (such as magazine and newspaper articles) it includes month and sometimes day as well.

Titles In titles of books and articles, capitalize only the first word of the title, the first word of the subtitle, and proper nouns; all other words begin with small letters. In titles of journals, capitalize all significant words. Italicize the titles of books and journals. Do not italicize or use quotation marks around the titles of articles.

City of publication For print sources that are not periodicals (such as books or government publications), give the city of publication. The following US cities do not require state names as well: Baltimore, Boston, Chicago, Los Angeles, New York, Philadelphia, and San Francisco. Follow their names with a colon. For most other cities, add a comma after the city name, give the two-letter postal abbreviation of the state, and then add a colon. (You may omit the state if the publisher is a university whose name includes the state name, such as University of Arizona.)

Publisher's name For nonperiodical print sources, give the publisher's name after the place of publication and a colon. Use shortened names for many publishers (such as Morrow for William Morrow), and omit "Co.," "Inc.," and "Publishers." However, give full names for associations, corporations, and university presses (such as Harvard University Press), and do not omit "Books" or "Press" from a publisher's name.

Page numbers Use the abbreviation p. or pp. before page numbers in books and in newspapers. Do *not* use the abbreviation for journals and magazines. For inclusive page numbers, include all figures: 667-668.

An index to the following models appears opposite. If you don't see a model listed for the kind of source you used, try to find one that comes close, and provide ample information so that readers can trace the source. Often you will have to combine models to provide the necessary information on a source—for instance, combining "A book with two to six authors" (model 2) and "An article in a journal" (model 12) for a journal article with two or more authors.

APA references

Books

1. A book with one author *538*
2. A book with two to six authors *538*
3. A book with seven or more authors *538*
4. A book with an editor *538*
5. A book with a translator *538*
6. A book with a group author *538*
7. A book with no author or an anonymous book *539*
8. Two or more works by the same author(s) published in the same year *539*
9. A later edition *539*
10. A work in more than one volume *539*
11. An article or chapter in an edited book *540*

Periodicals

12. An article in a journal with continuous pagination throughout the annual volume *540*
13. An article in a journal that pages issues separately *540*
14. An abstract of a journal article *540*
15. An article in a magazine *541*
16. An article in a newspaper *541*
17. An unsigned article *541*
18. A review *541*

Electronic sources

19. A journal article that is published online and in print *542*

20. An article in an online journal *542*
21. A journal article retrieved from an electronic database *542*
22. An abstract retrieved from an electronic database *543*
23. An article in an online newspaper *543*
24. An entire Web site *543*
25. An independent document on the Web *543*
26. A document from the Web site of a university or government agency *543*
27. An online government report *543*
28. A multipage online document *544*
29. A part of an online document *544*
30. An entry on a Web log *544*
31. A retrievable online posting *544*
32. Electronic mail or a non-retrievable online posting *544*
33. Software *544*

Other sources

34. A report *545*
35. A government publication *545*
36. A doctoral dissertation *545*
37. An interview *546*
38. A motion picture *546*
39. A musical recording *546*
40. A television series or episode *547*

APA
57b

1 • Books

1. A book with one author

Rodriguez, R. (1982). *A hunger of memory: The education of Richard Rodriguez.*
    Boston: Godine.

The initial R appears instead of the author's first name, even though the author's full first name appears on the source. In the title, only the first words of title and subtitle and the proper name are capitalized.

2. A book with two to six authors

Nesselroade, J. R., & Baltes, P. B. (1999). *Longitudinal research in the study of behavioral development.* New York: Academic Press.

An ampersand (&) precedes the last author's name.

3. A book with seven or more authors

Wimple, P. B., Van Eijk, M., Potts, C. A., Hayes, J., Obergau, W. R., Zimmer, S.,
    et al. (2001). *Case studies in moral decision making among adolescents.*
    San Francisco: Jossey-Bass.

Substitute et al. (Latin abbreviation for "and others") for all authors' names after the first six.

4. A book with an editor

Dohrenwend, B. S., & Dohrenwend, B. P. (Eds.). (1999). *Stressful life events: Their nature and effects.* New York: Wiley.

List the editors' names as if they were authors, but follow the last name with (Eds.)—or (Ed.) with only one editor. Note the periods inside and outside the final parenthesis.

5. A book with a translator

Trajan, P. D. (1927). *Psychology of animals* (H. Simone, Trans.). Washington,
    DC: Halperin.

The name of the translator appears in parentheses after the title, followed by a comma, Trans. and a closing parenthesis, and a final period. Note also the absence of periods in DC.

6. A book with a group author

Lorenz Research (2005). *Research in social studies teaching.* Baltimore: Arrow
    Books.

For a work with a group author—such as a research group, government agency, institution, or corporation—begin the entry with the group name. In the reference list, alphabetize the work as if the first main word (excluding *The, A,* and *An*) were an author's last name.

7. A book with no author or an anonymous book

Merriam-Webster's collegiate dictionary (11th ed.). (2003). Springfield, MA: Merriam-Webster.

When no author is named, list the work under its title, and alphabetize it by the first main word (excluding *The, A, An*).

For a work whose author is actually given as "Anonymous," use this word in place of the author's name and alphabetize it as if it were a name:

Anonymous. (2007). *Teaching research, researching teaching.* New York: Alpine Press.

8. Two or more works by the same author(s) published in the same year

Gardner, H. (1973a). *The arts and human development.* New York: Wiley.

Gardner, H. (1973b). *The quest for mind: Piaget, Lévi-Strauss, and the structuralist movement.* New York: Knopf.

When citing two or more works by exactly the same author(s), published in the same year—as in the preceding examples—arrange them alphabetically by the first main word of the title (here *arts,* then *quest*) and distinguish the sources by adding a letter to the date. Both the date *and* the letter are used in citing the source in the text (see p. 534).

When citing two or more works by exactly the same author(s) but *not* published in the same year, arrange the sources in order of their publication dates, earliest first.

9. A later edition

Bolinger, D. L. (1981). *Aspects of language* (3rd ed.). New York: Harcourt Brace Jovanovich.

The edition number in parentheses follows the title and is followed by a period.

10. A work in more than one volume

Lincoln, A. (1953). *The collected works of Abraham Lincoln* (R. P. Basler, Ed.). (Vol. 5). New Brunswick, NJ: Rutgers University Press.

Lincoln, A. (1953). *The collected works of Abraham Lincoln* (R. P. Basler, Ed.). (Vols. 1-8). New Brunswick, NJ: Rutgers University Press.

APA
57b

The first entry cites a single volume (5) in the eight-volume set. The second cites all eight volumes. Use the abbreviation Vol. or Vols. in parentheses, and follow the closing parenthesis with a period. In the absence of an editor's name, the description of volumes would follow the title directly: *The collected works of Abraham Lincoln* (Vol. 5).

11. An article or chapter in an edited book

Paykel, E. S. (1999). Life stress and psychiatric disorder: Applications of the clinical approach. In B. S. Dohrenwend & B. P. Dohrenwend (Eds.), *Stressful life events: Their nature and effects* (pp. 239-264). New York: Wiley.

Give the publication date of the collection (1999 above) as the publication date of the article or chapter. After the article or chapter title and a period, write In and then provide the editors' names (in normal order), (Eds.) and a comma, the title of the collection, and the page numbers of the article in parentheses.

2 • Periodicals: Journals, magazines, newspapers

12. An article in a journal with continuous pagination throughout the annual volume

Emery, R. E. (2006). Marital turmoil: Interpersonal conflict and the children of discord and divorce. *Psychological Bulletin, 92,* 310-330.

See page 502 for an explanation of journal pagination. Note that you do not place the article title in quotation marks and that you capitalize only the first words of the title and subtitle. In contrast, you italicize the journal title and capitalize all significant words. Separate the volume number from the title with a comma, and italicize the number. Do not add "pp." before the page numbers.

13. An article in a journal that pages issues separately

Dacey, J. (2005). Management participation in corporate buy-outs. *Management Perspectives, 7*(4), 20-31.

Consult page 502 for an explanation of journal pagination. In this case, place the issue number in parentheses after the volume number without intervening space. Do *not* italicize the issue number.

14. An abstract of a journal article

Emery, R. E. (2006). Marital turmoil: Interpersonal conflict and the children of discord and divorce. *Psychological Bulletin, 92,* 310-330. Abstract obtained from *Psychological Abstracts,* 2005, *69,* Item 1320.

When you cite the abstract of an article, rather than the article it-self, give full publication information for the article, followed by Abstract obtained from and the information for the collection of abstracts, including title, date, volume number, and either page number or other reference number (Item 1320 above).

15. An article in a magazine

William, N. (2005, October 24). Beethoven's late quartets. *The New York Review of Books*, 16-19.

If a magazine has volume and issue numbers, give them as in models 12 and 13. Also give the full date of the issue: year, followed by a comma, month, and day (if any). Give all page numbers even when the article appears on discontinuous pages, without "pp."

16. An article in a newspaper

Kolata, G. (2007, January 7). Kill all the bacteria! *The New York Times*, pp. B1, B6.

Give month *and* date along with year of publication. Use *The* in the newspaper name if the paper itself does. Precede the page number(s) with p. or pp.

17. An unsigned article

The right to die. (2001, October 11). *Time, 126,* 101.

List and alphabetize the article under its title, as you would a book with no author (model 7, p. 539).

18. A review

Dinnage, R. (1987, November 29). Against the master and his men [Review of the book *A mind of her own: The life of Karen Horney*]. *The New York Times Book Review,* 10-11.

If the review is not titled, use the bracketed information as the title, keeping the brackets.

3 • Electronic sources

In general, the APA's electronic-source references begin as those for print references do: author(s), date, title. Then you add information on when and how you retrieved the source. For example, an online source might end Retrieved January 8, 2006, from http://www.isu.edu/finance-dl/46732 (in APA style, no period follows a URL at the end of the reference).

Using the following models for electronic sources, you may have to improvise to match your source to a model. Try to locate all the information required by a model, referring to pages 506 and 509 for help. However, if you search for and still cannot find some information, then give what you can find. If a source has no publication date, use n.d. (for *no date*) in place of a publication date (see model 28, p. 544).

Note When you need to divide a URL from one line to the next, APA style calls for breaking *only* after a slash or before a period. Do not hyphenate a URL.

19. A journal article that is published online and in print

Palfrey, A. (2005). Choice of mates in identical twins [Electronic version].
   Modern Psychology, 4(1), 26-40.

If you consulted the online version of a journal article that appears the same way both online and in print, follow model 12 or 13 (p. 540) for a print journal article, and insert [Electronic version] between the article title and the following period.

If you believe that the online version you consulted differs in some way from the print version, omit the bracketed insert and provide a retrieval statement with the date of your access and the complete URL for the article:

Grady, G. F. (2005). The here and now of hepatitis B immunization. *Today's
   Medicine, 13*, 145-151. Retrieved December 27, 2006, from http://
   www.fmrt.org/todaysmedicine/Grady050203.html

20. An article in an online journal

Wissink, J. A. (2007). Techniques of smoking cessation among teens and
   adults. *Adolescent Medicine, 2.* Retrieved January 16, 2007, from
   http://www.easu.edu/AdolescentMedicine/2-Wissink.html

If the article has an identifying number, give it after the volume number and a comma.

21. A journal article retrieved from an electronic database

Wilkins, J. M. (1999). The myths of the only child. *Psychology Update, 11*(1),
   16-23. Retrieved December 20, 2006, from ProQuest Direct database.

Many reference works and periodicals are available full-text from electronic databases to which your library subscribes, such as ProQuest Direct or LexisNexis Academic. Your reference need not specify how you reached the database—for instance, through a Web site or on a CD-ROM. However, it should provide the appropriate information for the source itself—in the preceding example, for a journal article—and it should conclude with a retrieval statement giving the date of your access and the name of the database.

22. An abstract retrieved from an electronic database

Wilkins, J. M. (1999). The myths of the only child. *Psychology Update, 11*(1), 16-23. Abstract retrieved December 20, 2006, from ProQuest Direct database.

23. An article in an online newspaper

Pear, R. (2007, January 23). Gains reported for children of welfare to work families. *The New York Times on the Web.* Retrieved January 23, 2007, from http://www.nytimes.com/2006/01/23/national/23/WELF.html

24. An entire Web site (text citation)

The APA's Web site provides answers to frequently asked questions about style (http://www.apa.org).

Cite an entire Web site (rather than a specific page or document) by giving the URL in your text, not in your list of references.

25. An independent document on the Web

Anderson, D. (2005, May 1). *Social constructionism and MOOs.* Retrieved August 6, 2006, from http://sites.unc.edu/~daniel/social_constructionism

Treat the title of an independent Web document like the title of a book. If the document has no named author, begin with the title and place the publication date after the title.

26. A document from the Web site of a university or government agency

McConnell, L. M., Koenig, B. A., Greeley, H. T., & Raffin, T. A. (2004, August 17). *Genetic testing and Alzheimer's disease: Has the time come?* Retrieved September 1, 2006, from Stanford University, Project in Genomics, Ethics, and Society Web site: http://sebe.stanford.edu/pges

Provide the name of the host organization and any sponsoring program as part of the retrieval statement.

27. An online government report

U.S. Department of Commerce. National Telecommunications and Information Administration. (2005, February). *A nation online: Entering the broadband age.* Retrieved January 22, 2007, from http://www.ntia.doc.gov/reports/anol/index.html

APA
57b

28. A multipage online document

Elston, C. (n.d.). *Multiple intelligences.* Retrieved June 6, 2006, from
http://education.com/teachspace/intelligences

For an Internet document with multiple pages, each with its own URL, give the URL of the document's home page. Note the use of n.d. after the author's name to indicate that the document provides no publication date.

29. A part of an online document

Elston, C. (n.d.). Logical/math intelligence. In *Multiple intelligences.* Retrieved
June 6, 2006, from http://education.com/teachspace/intelligences/
logical.jsp

If the part of a document you cite has a label (such as "chapter 6" or "section 4"), provide that in parentheses after the document title: *Multiple intelligences* (chap. 6).

30. An entry on a Web log

Daswani, S. (2006, March 16). Hollywood vs. Silicon Valley. *Berkeley intellectual property Weblog.* Retrieved October 22, 2006, from http://www
.biplog.com/archive/cat_hollywood.html

31. A retrievable online posting

Tourville, M. (2007, January 6). European currency reform. Message posted to
International Finance electronic mailing list, archived at http://www
.isu.edu/finance-dl/46732

Include postings to discussion lists and newsgroups in your list of references *only* if they are retrievable by others. The source above is archived (as the reference makes plain) and is thus retrievable at the address given.

32. Electronic mail or a nonretrievable online posting (text citation)

At least one member of the research team has expressed reservations about
the design of the study (L. Kogod, personal communication, February 6,
2007).

Personal electronic mail and other online postings that are not retrievable by others should be cited only in your text, as in the preceding example, not in your list of references.

33. Software

Project scheduler 9000 [Computer software]. (2007). Orlando, FL: Scitor.

Provide an author's name for the software if an individual has the rights to the program. If you obtain the software online, you can generally replace the producer's city and name with a retrieval statement that includes the URL.

4 • Other sources

34. A report

Gerald, K. (2004). *Medico-moral problems in obstetric care* (Report No. NP-71). St. Louis, MO: Catholic Hospital Association.

Treat a report like a book, but provide any report number in parentheses immediately after the title, with no punctuation between them.

For a report from the Educational Resources Information Center (ERIC), provide the ERIC document number in parentheses at the end of the entry:

Jolson, M. K. (2002). *Music education for preschoolers* (Report No. TC-622). New York: Teachers College, Columbia University. (ERIC Document Reproduction Service No. ED 264488)

35. A government publication

Hawaii. Department of Education. (2006). *Kauai district schools, profile 2005-06.* Honolulu, HI: Author.

Stiller, A. (2002). *Historic preservation and tax incentives.* Washington, DC: U.S. Department of the Interior.

U.S. House. Committee on Ways and Means. (2005). *Medicare payment for outpatient physical and occupational therapy services.* 109th Cong., 1st Sess. Washington, DC: U.S. Government Printing Office.

If no individual is given as the author, list the publication under the name of the sponsoring agency. When the agency is both the author and the publisher, use Author in place of the publisher's name.

36. A doctoral dissertation

A dissertation abstracted in DAI *and obtained from UMI:*

Steciw, S. K. (1986). Alterations to the Pessac project of Le Corbusier. *Dissertation Abstracts International, 46,* 565C. (UMI No. 6216202)

A dissertation abstracted in DAI *and obtained from the university:*

Chang, J. K. (2003). Therapeutic intervention in treatment of injuries to the hand and wrist (Doctoral dissertation, University of Michigan, 2003). *Dissertation Abstracts International, 50,* 162.

APA

57b

An unpublished dissertation:

Delaune, M. L. (2005). *Child care in single-mother and single-father families: Differences in time, activity, and stress.* Unpublished doctoral dissertation, University of California, Davis.

37. An interview

Brisick, W. C. (2006, July 1). [Interview with Ishmael Reed]. *Publishers Weekly,* 41-42.

List a published interview under the interviewer's name. Provide the publication information for the kind of source the interview appears in (here, a magazine). Immediately after the date, in brackets, specify that the piece is an interview and give the subject's name if necessary. For an interview with a title, add the title (with an initial capital letter, no quotation marks, and no closing period) before the bracketed information.

An interview you conduct yourself should not be included in the list of references. Instead, use an in-text parenthetical citation, as shown in model 32 (p. 544.)

38. A motion picture

American Psychological Association (Producer). (2001). *Ethnocultural psychotherapy* [Motion picture]. (Available from the American Psychological Association, 750 First Street, NE, Washington, DC 20002-4242, or online from http://www.apa.org/videos/4310240.html)

Spielberg, S. (Director). (1993). *Schindler's list* [Motion picture]. United States: Viacom.

A motion picture may be a film, DVD, or video. Depending on whose work you are citing, begin with the name or names of the creator, director, producer, or primary contributor, followed by the function in parentheses. (The second model above would begin with the producer's name if you were citing the motion picture as a whole, not specifically the work of the director.) Add [Motion picture] after the title. For a motion picture in wide circulation (second example), give the country of origin and the name of the organization that released the picture. For a motion picture that is not widely circulated (first example), give the distributor's name and address in parentheses.

39. A musical recording

Springsteen, B. (2002). My city of ruins. *The rising* [CD]. New York: Columbia.

Begin with the name of the writer or composer. (If you cite another artist's recording of the work, provide this information after the title of the work—for example, [Recorded by E. Davila].) Give the medium in brackets ([CD], [Cassette recording], and so on). Finish with the city and name of the recording label.

40. A television series or episode

Cleveland, R., Andries, L., & Taylor, C. (Producers). (2005). *Six feet under* [Television series]. New York: HBO.

Cleveland, R. (Writer), & Engler, M. (Director). (2005). Dillon Michael Cooper [Television series episode]. In R. Cleveland, L. Andries, & C. Taylor (Producers), *Six feet under*. New York: HBO.

For a television series, begin with the producers' names and identify their function in parentheses. Add [Television series] after the series title, and give the city and name of the network. For an episode, begin with the writer and then the director, identifying the function of each in parentheses, and add [Television series episode] after the episode title. Then provide the series information, beginning with In and the producers' names and function, giving the series title, and ending with the city and name of the network.

57c Format the paper in APA style.

The APA *Publication Manual* distinguishes between documents intended for publication (which will be set in type) and those submitted by students (which are the final copy). The following guidelines apply to most undergraduate papers. Check with your instructor for any modifications to this format.

Note See pages 535–36 for the APA format of a reference list. And see pages 74–84 for guidelines on type fonts, lists, tables and figures, and other elements of document design.

Margins Use one-inch margins on the top, bottom, and right side. Add another half-inch on the left to accommodate a binder.

Spacing and indentions Double-space your text and references. (See p. 550 for spacing of displayed quotations.) Indent paragraphs and displayed quotations one-half inch or five to seven spaces.

Paging Begin numbering on the title page, and number consecutively through the end (including the reference list). Type Arabic numerals (1, 2, 3) in the upper right, about one-half inch from the top.

Place a shortened version of your title five spaces to the left of the page number.

Title page Include the full title, your name, the course title, the instructor's name, and the date. Type the title on the top half of the page, followed by the identifying information, all centered horizontally and double-spaced. Include a shortened form of the title along with the page number at the top of this and all other pages.

APA title page

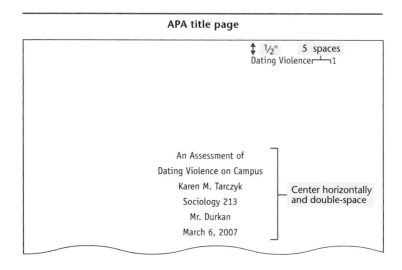

Abstract Summarize (in a maximum of 120 words) your subject, research method, findings, and conclusions. Put the abstract on a page by itself. (See the sample below.)

APA abstract

½"   5 spaces
Dating Violence   2

No indention   Abstract   Double-
space
Little research has examined the patterns of abuse and violence
occurring within couples during courtship. With a questionnaire
administered to a sample of college students, the extent and na-
1½"   1"

Body Begin with a restatement of the paper's title and then an introduction (not labeled). The introduction concisely presents the problem you researched, your research method, the relevant background (such as related studies), and the purpose of your research.

First page of APA body

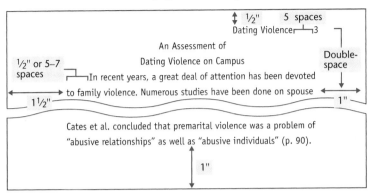

The next section, labeled Method, provides a detailed discussion of how you conducted your research, including a description of the research subjects, any materials or tools you used (such as questionnaires or surveys), and the procedure you followed. In the illustration below, the labels Method and *Sample* are first-level and second-level headings, respectively. When you need one, two, or three levels of headings, use the following formats, always double-spacing above and below:

First-Level Heading

Second-Level Heading

Third-level heading. Run this heading into the text paragraph.

Later page of APA body

Dating Violence   4
All the studies indicate a problem that is being neglected.
My objective was to gather data on the extent and nature of premarital violence and to discuss possible interpretations.

Method ← Double-space
Sample ←
I conducted a survey of 200 students (134 females, 66 males) at a large state university in the northeastern United States. The sample consisted of students enrolled in an introductory sociology

The Results section (labeled with a first-level heading) summarizes the data you collected, explains how you analyzed them, and
presents them in detail, often in tables, graphs, or charts.

The Discussion section (labeled with a first-level heading) inter-
prets the data and presents your conclusions. (When the discussion
is brief, you may combine it with the previous section under the
heading Results and Discussion.)

The References section, beginning a new page, includes all your
sources. See pages 535–36 for an explanation and sample.

Long quotations Run into your text all quotations of forty
words or less, and enclose them in quotation marks. For quotations
of more than forty words, set them off from your text by indenting
all lines one-half inch or five to seven spaces, double-spacing above
and below. For student papers, the APA allows single-spacing of displayed quotations:

> Echoing the opinions of other Europeans at the time, Freud (1961) had a poor
> view of Americans:
>
> ○The Americans are really too bad. . . . Competition is much more pun-
> gent with them, not succeeding means civil death to every one, and
> they have no private resources apart from their profession, no hobby,
> games, love or other interests of a cultured person. And success means
> money.○(p. 86)

Do not use quotation marks around a quotation displayed in this
way.

Illustrations Present data in tables and figures (graphs or
charts), as appropriate. (See pp. 533 and 79–82 for examples.) Begin each illustration on a separate page. Number each kind of illustration consecutively and separately from the other (Table 1, Table 2,
etc., and Figure 1, Figure 2, etc.). Refer to all illustrations in your text—
for instance, (see Figure 3). Generally, place illustrations immediately
after the text references to them.

57d   A sample paper in APA style

The following excerpts from a sociology paper illustrate elements of a research paper using the APA style of documentation
and format.

[Title page.]

An Assessment of

Dating Violence on Campus

Karen M. Tarczyk

Sociology 213

Mr. Durkan

March 6, 2007

[New page.]

Abstract

Little research has examined the patterns of abuse and violence occurring within couples during courtship. With a questionnaire administered to a sample of college students, the extent and nature of such abuse and violence were investigated. The results, interpretations, and implications for further research are discussed.

[New page.]

An Assessment of

Dating Violence on Campus

In recent years, a great deal of attention has been devoted to family violence. Numerous studies have been done on spouse and child abuse. However, violent behavior occurs in dating relationships as well, yet the problem of dating violence has been relatively ignored by sociological research. It should be examined further since the premarital relationship is one context in which individuals learn and adopt behaviors that surface in marriage.

The sociologist James Makepeace (1989) contended that courtship violence is a "potential mediating link" between violence in one's family of orientation and violence in one's later family of procreation (p. 103). Studying dating behaviors at Bemidji State University in Minnesota, Makepeace reported that one-fifth of the respondents had had at least one encounter with dating violence. He then extended these percentages to students nationwide, suggesting the existence of a major hidden social problem.

Dating Violence   4

Citation form:
source with
three to five au-
thors, named in
the text.

Citation form:
author not
named in the
text.

More recent research supports Makepeace's. Cates, Rutter, Karl, Linton, and Smith (2003) found that 22.3% of respondents at Oregon State University had been either the victim or the perpetrator of premarital violence. Another study (Cortes, 2006) found that so-called date rape, while much more publicized and discussed, was reported by many fewer woman respondents (2%) than was other violence during courtship (21%).

[The introduction continues.]

All these studies indicate a problem that is being neglected. My objective was to gather data on the extent and nature of premarital violence and to discuss possible interpretations.

First- and
second-level
headings.

"Method" sec-
tion: discussion
of how research
was conducted.

Method

Sample

I conducted a survey of 200 students (134 females, 66 males) at a large state university in the northeastern United States. The sample consisted of students enrolled in an introductory sociology course.

[The explanation of method continues.]

The Questionnaire

A questionnaire exploring the personal dynamics of relationships was distributed during regularly scheduled class. Questions were answered anonymously in a 30-minute period. The survey consisted of three sections.

[The explanation of method continues.]

Section 3 required participants to provide information about their current dating relationships. Levels of stress and frustration, communication between partners, and patterns of decision making were examined. These variables were expected to influence the amount of violence in a relationship. The next part of the survey was adopted from Murray Strauss's Conflict Tactics Scales (1992). These scales contain 19 items designed to measure conflict and the means of conflict resolution, including reasoning, verbal aggression, and actual violence. The final page of the questionnaire contained general questions on the couple's use of alcohol, sexual activity, and overall satisfaction with the relationship.

"Results" sec-
tion: summary
and presenta-
tion of data.

Results

The questionnaire revealed significant levels of verbal aggression and threatened and actual violence among dating couples. A high num-

ber of students, 50% (62 of 123 subjects), reported that they had been
the victim of verbal abuse, either being insulted or sworn at. In addition, almost 14% (17 of 123) of respondents admitted being threatened
with some type of violence, and more than 14% (18 of 123) reported
being pushed, grabbed, or shoved. (See Table 1.)

Reference to table.

[The explanation of results continues.]

[Table on a page by itself.]

Table 1

Incidence of Courtship Violence

Table presents data in clear format.

Type of violence	Number of students reporting	Percentage of sample
Insulted or swore	62	50.4
Threatened to hit or throw something	17	13.8
Threw something	8	6.5
Pushed, grabbed, or shoved	18	14.6
Slapped	8	6.5
Kicked, bit, or hit with fist	7	5.7
Hit or tried to hit with something	2	1.6
Threatened with a knife or gun	1	0.8
Used a knife or gun	1	0.8

Discussion

"Discussion" section: interpretation of data and presentation of conclusions.

Violence within premarital relationships has been relatively ignored. The results of the present study indicate that abuse and force do
occur in dating relationships. Although the percentages are small, so
was the sample. Extending them to the entire campus population of
5,000 would mean significant numbers. For example, if the nearly 6%
incidence of being kicked, bitten, or hit with a fist is typical, then 300
students might have experienced this type of violence.

[The discussion continues.]

If the courtship period is characterized by abuse and violence,
what accounts for it? The other sections of the survey examined some
variables that appear to influence the relationship. Level of stress and

frustration, both within the relationship and in the respondent's life, was one such variable. The communication level between partners, both the frequency of discussion and the frequency of agreement, was another.

[The discussion continues.]

The method of analyzing the data in this study, utilizing frequency distributions, provided a clear overview. However, more tests of significance and correlation and a closer look at the social and individual variables affecting the relationship are warranted. The courtship period may set the stage for patterns of married life. It merits more attention.

[New page.]

New page for reference list.

References

An article in a print journal.

Cates, R. L., Rutter, C. H., Karl, J., Linton, M., & Smith, K. (2003). Premarital abuse: A social psychological perspective. *Journal of Family Issues, 13*(1), 79-90.

An article in an online journal.

Cortes, L. (2006). Beyond date rape: Violence during courtship. *Electronic Journal of Intimate Violence, 5*(2). Retrieved February 16, 2007, from http://www.acast.nova.edu/health/psy/file-disc/file50.html

Glaser, R., & Rutter, C. H. (Eds.). (1999). Familial violence [Special issue]. *Family Relations, 43.*

Makepeace, J. M. (1989). Courtship violence among college students. *Family Relations, 28*, 97-103.

A book. ("Tactics Scales" is part of a proper name and so is capitalized.)

Strauss, M. L. (1992). *Conflict Tactics Scales.* New York: Sociological Tests.

Glossary of Usage

This glossary provides notes on words or phrases that often cause problems for writers. The recommendations for standard American English are based on current dictionaries and usage guides. Items labeled **nonstandard** should be avoided in speech and especially in writing. Those labeled **colloquial** and **slang** occur in speech and in some informal writing but are best avoided in the more formal writing usually expected in college and business. (Words and phrases labeled *colloquial* include those labeled by many dictionaries with the equivalent term *informal.*)

Note Two lists in the text supplement this glossary: idioms with prepositions, such as *part from* and *part with* (p. 209); and words that are pronounced the same or similarly but spelled differently, such as *heard* and *herd* (pp. 392–93).

a, an   Use *a* before words beginning with consonant sounds, including those spelled with an initial pronounced *h* and those spelled with vowels that are sounded as consonants: *a historian, a one-o'clock class, a university.* Use *an* before words that begin with vowel sounds, including those spelled with an initial silent *h: an organism, an L, an honor.*

The article before an abbreviation depends on how the abbreviation is to be read: *She was once an AEC undersecretary* (*AEC* is to be read as three separate letters). *Many Americans opposed a SALT treaty* (*SALT* is to be read as one word, *salt*).

See also pp. 313–15 on the uses of *a/an* versus *the.*

accept, except   *Accept* is a verb meaning "receive." *Except* is usually a preposition or conjunction meaning "but for" or "other than"; when it is used as a verb, it means "leave out." *I can accept all your suggestions except the last one. I'm sorry you excepted my last suggestion from your list.*

advice, advise   *Advice* is a noun, and *advise* is a verb: *Take my advice; do as I advise you.*

affect, effect   Usually *affect* is a verb, meaning "to influence," and *effect* is a noun, meaning "result": *The drug did not affect his driving; in fact, it seemed to have no effect at all.* But *effect* occasionally is used as a verb meaning "to bring about": *Her efforts effected a change.* And *affect* is used in psychology as a noun meaning "feeling or emotion": *One can infer much about affect from behavior.*

agree to, agree with   *Agree to* means "consent to," and *agree with* means "be in accord with": *How can they agree to a treaty when they don't agree with each other about the terms?*

all ready, already   *All ready* means "completely prepared," and *already* means "by now" or "before now": *We were all ready to go to the movie, but it had already started.*

all right *All right* is always two words. *Alright* is a common misspelling.

all together, altogether *All together* means "in unison" or "gathered in one place." *Altogether* means "entirely." *It's not altogether true that our family never spends vacations all together.*

allusion, illusion An *allusion* is an indirect reference, and an *illusion* is a deceptive appearance: *Paul's constant allusions to Shakespeare created the illusion that he was an intellectual.*

almost, most *Almost* means "nearly"; *most* means "the greater number (or part) of." In formal writing, *most* should not be used as a substitute for *almost: We see each other almost [not most] every day.*

a lot *A lot* is always two words, used informally to mean "many." *Alot* is a common misspelling.

among, between In general, use *among* for relationships involving more than two people or for comparing one thing to a group to which it belongs. *The four of them agreed among themselves that the choice was between New York and Los Angeles.*

amount, number Use *amount* with a singular noun that names something not countable (a noncount noun): *The amount of food varies.* Use *number* with a plural noun that names more than one of something countable (a plural count noun): *The number of calories must stay the same.*

and/or *And/or* indicates three options: one or the other or both (*The decision is made by the mayor and/or the council*). If you mean all three options, *and/or* is appropriate. Otherwise, use *and* if you mean both, *or* if you mean either.

ante-, anti- The prefix *ante-* means "before" (*antedate, antebellum*); *anti-* means "against" (*antiwar, antinuclear*). Before a capital letter or *i*, *anti-* takes a hyphen: *anti-Freudian, anti-isolationist.*

anxious, eager *Anxious* means "nervous" or "worried" and is usually followed by *about. Eager* means "looking forward" and is usually followed by *to. I've been anxious about getting blisters. I'm eager [not anxious] to get new running shoes.*

anybody, any body; anyone, any one *Anybody* and *anyone* are indefinite pronouns; *any body* is a noun modified by *any; any one* is a pronoun or adjective modified by *any. How can anybody communicate with any body of government? Can anyone help Amy? She has more work than any one person can handle.*

any more, anymore *Any more* means "no more"; *anymore* means "now." Both are used in negative constructions. *He doesn't want any more. She doesn't live here anymore.*

are, is Use *are* with a plural subject (*books are*), *is* with a singular subject (*book is*).

as   Substituting for *because, since,* or *while, as* may be vague or ambiguous: *As the researchers asked more questions, their money ran out.* (Does *as* mean "while" or "because"?) *As* should never be used as a substitute for *whether* or *who. I'm not sure whether* [not *as*] *we can make it. That's the man who* [not *as*] *gave me directions.*

as, like   In formal speech and writing, *like* should not introduce a full clause (with a subject and a verb) because it is a preposition. The preferred choice is *as* or *as if: The plan succeeded as* [not *like*] *we hoped. It seemed as if* [not *like*] *it might fail. Other plans like it have failed.*

assure, ensure, insure   *Assure* means "to promise": *He assured us that we would miss the traffic. Ensure* and *insure* often are used interchangeably to mean "make certain," but some reserve *insure* for matters of legal and financial protection and use *ensure* for more general meanings: *We left early to ensure that we would miss the traffic. It's expensive to insure yourself against floods.*

awful, awfully   Strictly speaking, *awful* means "awe-inspiring." As intensifiers meaning "very" or "extremely" (*He tried awfully hard*), *awful* and *awfully* should be avoided in formal speech or writing.

a while, awhile   *Awhile* is an adverb; *a while* is an article and a noun. *I will be gone awhile* [not *a while*]. *I will be gone for a while* [not *awhile*].

bad, badly   In formal speech and writing, *bad* should be used only as an adjective; the adverb is *badly. He felt bad because his tooth ached badly.* In *He felt bad,* the verb *felt* is a linking verb and the adjective *bad* describes the subject. See also p. 306.

being as, being that   Colloquial for *because,* the preferable word in formal speech or writing: *Because* [not *Being as*] *the world is round, Columbus never did fall off the edge.*

beside, besides   *Beside* is a preposition meaning "next to." *Besides* is a preposition meaning "except" or "in addition to" as well as an adverb meaning "in addition." *Besides, several other people besides you want to sit beside Dr. Christensen.*

better, had better   *Had better* (meaning "ought to") is a verb modified by an adverb. The verb is necessary and should not be omitted: *You had better* [not just *better*] *go.*

between, among   See *among, between.*

bring, take   Use *bring* only for movement from a farther place to a nearer one and *take* for any other movement. *First take these books to the library for renewal; then take them to Mr. Daniels. Bring them back to me when he's finished.*

but, hardly, scarcely   These words are negative in their own right; using *not* with any of them produces a double negative (see p. 310). *We have but* [not *haven't got but*] *an hour before our plane leaves. I could hardly* [not *couldn't hardly*] *make out her face.*

Usage

but, however, yet Each of these words is adequate to express contrast. Don't combine them. *He said he had finished, yet [not but yet] he continued.*

can, may Strictly, *can* indicates capacity or ability, and *may* indicates permission or possibility: *If I may talk with you a moment, I believe I can solve your problem.*

censor, censure To *censor* is to edit or remove from public view on moral or other grounds; to *censure* is to give a formal scolding. *The lieutenant was censured by Major Taylor for censoring the letters her soldiers wrote home from boot camp.*

cite, sight, site *Cite* is a verb usually meaning "quote," "commend," or "acknowledge": *You must cite your sources. Sight* is both a noun meaning "the ability to see" or "a view" and a verb meaning "perceive" or "observe": *What a sight you see when you sight Venus through a strong telescope. Site* is a noun meaning "place" or "location" or a verb meaning "situate": *The builder sited the house on an unlikely site.*

climatic, climactic *Climatic* comes from *climate* and refers to the weather: *Last winter's temperatures may indicate a climatic change. Climactic* comes from *climax* and refers to a dramatic high point: *During the climactic duel between Hamlet and Laertes, Gertrude drinks poisoned wine.*

complement, compliment To *complement* something is to add to, complete, or reinforce it: *Her yellow blouse complemented her black hair.* To *compliment* something is to make a flattering remark about it: *He complimented her on her hair. Complimentary* can also mean "free": *complimentary tickets.*

conscience, conscious *Conscience* is a noun meaning "a sense of right and wrong"; *conscious* is an adjective meaning "aware" or "awake." *Though I was barely conscious, my conscience nagged me.*

continual, continuous *Continual* means "constantly recurring": *Most movies on television are continually interrupted by commercials. Continuous* means "unceasing": *Some cable channels present movies continuously without commercials.*

could of See *have, of.*

credible, creditable, credulous *Credible* means "believable": *It's a strange story, but it seems credible to me. Creditable* means "deserving of credit" or "worthy": *Steve gave a creditable performance. Credulous* means "gullible": *The credulous Claire believed Tim's lies.* See also *incredible, incredulous.*

criteria The plural of *criterion* (meaning "standard for judgment"): *Our criteria are strict. The most important criterion is a sense of humor.*

data The plural of *datum* (meaning "fact"). Though *data* is often used as a singular noun, many readers prefer the plural verb, and it is always correct: *The data fail [not fails] to support the hypothesis.*

device, devise   *Device* is the noun, and *devise* is the verb: *Can you devise some device for getting his attention?*

different from, different than   *Different from* is preferred: *His purpose is different from mine.* But *different than* is widely accepted when a construction using *from* would be wordy: *I'm a different person now than I used to be* is preferable to *I'm a different person now from the person I used to be.*

differ from, differ with   To *differ from* is to be unlike: *The twins differ from each other only in their hairstyles.* To *differ with* is to disagree with: *I have to differ with you on that point.*

discreet, discrete   *Discreet* (noun form *discretion*) means "tactful": *What's a discreet way of telling Maud to be quiet?* *Discrete* (noun form *discreteness*) means "separate and distinct": *Within a computer's memory are millions of discrete bits of information.*

disinterested, uninterested   *Disinterested* means "impartial": *We chose Pete, as a disinterested third party, to decide who was right.* *Uninterested* means "bored" or "lacking interest": *Unfortunately, Pete was completely uninterested in the question.*

don't   *Don't* is the contraction for *do not*, not for *does not: I don't care, you don't care,* and *he doesn't* [not *don't*] *care.*

due to the fact that   Wordy for *because.*

eager, anxious   See *anxious, eager.*

effect   See *affect, effect.*

elicit, illicit   *Elicit* is a verb meaning "bring out" or "call forth." *Illicit* is an adjective meaning "unlawful." *The crime elicited an outcry against illicit drugs.*

emigrate, immigrate   *Emigrate* means "to leave one place and move to another": *The Chus emigrated from Korea. Immigrate* means "to move into a place where one was not born": *They immigrated to the United States.*

ensure   See *assure, ensure, insure.*

enthused   Used colloquially as an adjective meaning "showing enthusiasm." The preferred adjective is *enthusiastic: The coach was enthusiastic* [not *enthused*] *about the team's victory.*

et al., etc.   Use *et al.*, the Latin abbreviation for "and other people," only in source citations: *Jones et al.* Avoid *etc.*, the Latin abbreviation for "and other things," in formal writing, and do not use it to refer to people or to substitute for precision, as in *The government provides health care, etc.*

everybody, every body; everyone, every one   *Everybody* and *everyone* are indefinite pronouns: *Everybody* [*Everyone*] *knows Tom steals. Every one* is a pronoun modified by *every*, and *every body* a noun modified by *every*. Both refer to each thing or person of a specific group and are typically followed by *of: The game commissioner has stocked every body of fresh water in the state with fish, and now every one of our rivers is a potential trout stream.*

everyday, every day   *Everyday* is an adjective meaning "used daily" or "common"; *every day* is a noun modified by *every: Everyday problems tend to arise every day.*

everywheres   Nonstandard for *everywhere.*

except   See *accept, except.*

except for the fact that   Wordy for *except that.*

explicit, implicit   *Explicit* means "stated outright": *I left explicit instructions. Implicit* means "implied, unstated": *We had an implicit understanding.*

farther, further   *Farther* refers to additional distance (*How much farther is it to the beach?*), and *further* refers to additional time, amount, or other abstract matters (*I don't want to discuss this any further*).

fewer, less   *Fewer* refers to individual countable items (a plural count noun), *less* to general amounts (a noncount noun, always singular). *Skim milk has fewer calories than whole milk. We have less milk left than I thought.*

flaunt, flout   *Flaunt* means "show off": *If you have style, flaunt it. Flout* means "scorn" or "defy": *Hester Prynne flouted convention and paid the price.*

flunk   A colloquial substitute for *fail.*

fun   As an adjective, *fun* is colloquial and should be avoided in most writing: *It was a pleasurable* [not *fun*] *evening.*

further   See *farther, further.*

get   This common verb is used in many slang and colloquial expressions: *get lost, that really gets me, getting on. Get* is easy to overuse: watch out for it in expressions such as *it's getting better* (substitute *improving*) and *we got done* (substitute *finished*).

good, well   *Good* is an adjective, and *well* is nearly always an adverb: *Larry's a good dancer. He and Linda dance well together. Well* is properly used as an adjective only to refer to health: *You look well.* (*You look good,* in contrast, means "Your appearance is pleasing.")

good and   Colloquial for "very": *I was very* [not *good and*] *tired.*

had better   See *better, had better.*

had ought   The *had* is unnecessary and should be omitted: *He ought* [not *had ought*] *to listen to his mother.*

hanged, hung   Though both are past-tense forms of *hang, hanged* is used to refer to executions and *hung* is used for all other meanings: *Tom Dooley was hanged* [not *hung*] *from a white oak tree. I hung* [not *hanged*] *the picture you gave me.*

hardly   See *but, hardly, scarcely.*

have, of   Use *have*, not *of*, after helping verbs such as *could, should, would, may,* and *might: You should have* [not *should of*] *told me.*

he, she; he/she   Convention has allowed the use of *he* to mean "he or she": *After the infant learns to creep, he progresses to crawling.* However, many writers today consider this usage inaccurate and unfair because it seems to exclude females. The construction *he/she,* one substitute for *he,* is awkward and objectionable to most readers. The better choice is to make the pronoun plural, to rephrase, or, sparingly, to use *he or she.* For instance: *After infants learn to creep, they progress to crawling. After learning to creep, the infant progresses to crawling. After the infant learns to creep, he or she progresses to crawling.* See also pp. 210 and 298–99.

herself, himself   See *myself, herself, himself, yourself.*

hisself   Nonstandard for *himself.*

hopefully   *Hopefully* means "with hope": *Freddy waited hopefully for a glimpse of Eliza.* The use of *hopefully* to mean "it is to be hoped," "I hope," or "let's hope" is now very common; but since many readers continue to object strongly to the usage, try to avoid it. *I hope* [not *Hopefully*] *the law will pass.*

idea, ideal   An *idea* is a thought or conception. An *ideal* (noun) is a model of perfection or a goal. *Ideal* should not be used in place of *idea: The idea* [not *ideal*] *of the play is that our ideals often sustain us.*

if, whether   For clarity, use *whether* rather than *if* when you are expressing an alternative: *If I laugh hard, people can't tell whether I'm crying.*

illicit   See *elicit, illicit.*

illusion   See *allusion, illusion.*

immigrate, emigrate   See *emigrate, immigrate.*

implicit   See *explicit, implicit.*

imply, infer   Writers or speakers *imply,* meaning "suggest": *Jim's letter implies he's having a good time.* Readers or listeners *infer,* meaning "conclude": *From Jim's letter I infer he's having a good time.*

incredible, incredulous   *Incredible* means "unbelievable"; *incredulous* means "unbelieving": *When Nancy heard Dennis's incredible story, she was frankly incredulous.* See also *credible, creditable, credulous.*

individual, person, party   *Individual* should refer to a single human being in contrast to a group or should stress uniqueness: *The US Constitution places strong emphasis on the rights of the individual.* For other meanings *person* is preferable: *What person* [not *individual*] *wouldn't want the security promised in that advertisement? Party* means "group" (*Can you seat a party of four for dinner?*) and should not be used to refer to an individual except in legal documents. See also *people, persons.*

infer   See *imply, infer.*

in regards to   Nonstandard for *in regard to, as regards,* or *regarding.*

insure   See *assure, ensure, insure.*

irregardless   Nonstandard for *regardless.*

is, are   See *are, is.*

is because   See *reason is because.*

is when, is where   These are faulty constructions in sentences that define: *Adolescence is a stage* [not *is when a person is*] *between childhood and adulthood. Socialism is a system in which* [not *is where*] *government owns the means of production.* See also p. 340.

its, it's   *Its* is the pronoun *it* in the possessive case: *That plant is losing its leaves. It's* is a contraction for *it is* or *it has: It's* [*It is*] *likely to die. It's* [*It has*] *got a fungus.* Many people confuse *it's* and *its* because possessives are most often formed with *-'s;* but the possessive *its,* like *his* and *hers,* never takes an apostrophe.

kind of, sort of, type of   In formal speech and writing, avoid using *kind of* or *sort of* to mean "somewhat": *He was rather* [not *kind of*] *tall.*
    Kind, sort, and *type* are singular and take singular modifiers and verbs: *This kind of dog is easily trained.* Agreement errors often occur when these singular nouns are combined with the plural adjectives *these* and *those: These kinds* [not *kind*] *of dogs are easily trained. Kind, sort,* and *type* should be followed by *of* but not by *a: I don't know what type of* [not *type* or *type of a*] *dog that is.*
    Use *kind of, sort of,* or *type of* only when the word *kind, sort,* or *type* is important: *That was a strange* [not *strange sort of*] *statement.*

lay, lie   *Lay* means "put" or "place" and takes a direct object: *We could lay the tablecloth in the sun.* Its main forms are *lay, laid, laid. Lie* means "recline" or "be situated" and does not take an object: *I lie awake at night. The town lies east of the river.* Its main forms are *lie, lay, lain.* (See also p. 254.)

leave, let   *Leave* and *let* are interchangeable only when followed by *alone; leave me alone* is the same as *let me alone.* Otherwise, *leave* means "depart" and *let* means "allow": *Jill would not let Sue leave.*

less   See *fewer, less.*

lie, lay   See *lay, lie.*

like, as   See *as, like.*

like, such as   Strictly, *such as* precedes an example that represents a larger subject, whereas *like* indicates that two subjects are comparable. *Steve has recordings of many great saxophonists such as Ben Webster and Lee Konitz. Steve wants to be a great jazz saxophonist like Ben Webster and Lee Konitz.*

literally   This word means "actually" or "just as the words say," and it should not be used to qualify or intensify expressions whose words are not to be taken at face value. The sentence *He was literally climbing the walls* describes a person behaving like an insect, not a person who is restless or anxious. For the latter meaning, *literally* should be omitted.

lose, loose   *Lose* means "mislay": *Did you lose a brown glove?* *Loose* means "unrestrained" or "not tight": *Ann's canary got loose.* *Loose* also can function as a verb meaning "let loose": *They loose the dogs as soon as they spot the bear.*

lots, lots of   Colloquial substitutes for *very many, a great many,* or *much.* Avoid *lots* and *lots of* in college or business writing.

may, can   See *can, may.*

may be, maybe   *May be* is a verb, and *maybe* is an adverb meaning "perhaps": *Tuesday may be a legal holiday. Maybe we won't have classes.*

may of   See *have, of.*

media   *Media* is the plural of *medium* and takes a plural verb: *All the news media are increasingly visual.* The singular verb is common, even in the media, but many readers prefer the plural verb, and it is always correct.

might of   See *have, of.*

moral, morale   As a noun, *moral* means "ethical conclusion" or "lesson": *The moral of the story escapes me. Morale* means "spirit" or "state of mind": *Victory improved the team's morale.*

most, almost   See *almost, most.*

must of   See *have, of.*

myself, herself, himself, yourself   The *-self* pronouns refer to or intensify another word or words: *Paul helped himself; Jill herself said so.* The *-self* pronouns are often used colloquially in place of personal pronouns, but that use should be avoided in formal speech and writing: *No one except me* [not *myself*] *saw the accident. Our delegates will be Susan and you* [not *yourself*]. See also p. 290 on the unchanging forms of the *-self* pronouns in standard American English.

nowheres   Nonstandard for *nowhere.*

number   See *amount, number.*

of, have   See *have, of.*

off of   *Of* is unnecessary. Use *off* or *from* rather than *off of: He jumped off* [or *from,* not *off of*] *the roof.*

OK, O.K., okay   All three spellings are acceptable, but avoid this colloquial term in formal speech and writing.

on the other hand   This transitional expression of contrast should be preceded by its mate, *on the one hand: On the one hand, we hoped for snow. On the other hand, we feared that it would harm the animals.* However, the two combined can be unwieldy, and a simple *but, however,* *yet,* or *in contrast* often suffices: *We hoped for snow. Yet we feared that it would harm the animals.*

owing to the fact that   Wordy for *because.*

party   See *individual, person, party.*

people, persons   In formal usage, *people* refers to a general group: *We the people of the United States.* . . . *Persons* refers to a collection of individuals: *Will the person or persons who saw the accident please notify.* . . . Except when emphasizing individuals, prefer *people* to *persons.* See also *individual, person, party.*

per   Except in technical writing, an English equivalent is usually preferable to the Latin *per: $10 an* [not *per*] *hour; sent by* [not *per*] *parcel post; requested in* [not *per* or *as per*] *your letter.*

percent (per cent), percentage   Both these terms refer to fractions of one hundred. *Percent* always follows a number (*40 percent of the voters*), and the word should be used instead of the symbol (%) in general writing. *Percentage* stands alone (*the percentage of voters*) or follows an adjective (*a high percentage*).

person   See *individual, person, party.*

persons   See *people, persons.*

phenomena   The plural of *phenomenon* (meaning "perceivable fact" or "unusual occurrence"): *Many phenomena are not recorded. One phenomenon is attracting attention.*

plenty   A colloquial substitute for *very: The reaction occurred very* [not *plenty*] *fast.*

plus   *Plus* is standard as a preposition meaning "in addition to": *His income plus mine is sufficient.* But *plus* is colloquial as a conjunctive adverb: *Our organization is larger than theirs; moreover* [not *plus*], *we have more money.*

precede, proceed   The verb *precede* means "come before": *My name precedes yours in the alphabet.* The verb *proceed* means "move on": *We were told to proceed to the waiting room.*

prejudice, prejudiced   *Prejudice* is a noun; *prejudiced* is an adjective. Do not drop the *-d* from *prejudiced: I knew that my parents were prejudiced* [not *prejudice*].

pretty   Overworked as an adverb meaning "rather" or "somewhat": *He was somewhat* [not *pretty*] *irked at the suggestion.*

principal, principle   *Principal* is an adjective meaning "foremost" or "major," a noun meaning "chief official," or, in finance, a noun meaning "capital sum." *Principle* is a noun only, meaning "rule" or "axiom." *Her principal reasons for confessing were her principles of right and wrong.*

proceed, precede   See *precede, proceed.*

question of whether, question as to whether Wordy substitutes for *whether.*

raise, rise *Raise* means "lift" or "bring up" and takes a direct object: *The Kirks raise cattle.* Its main forms are *raise, raised, raised. Rise* means "get up" and does not take an object: *They must rise at dawn.* Its main forms are *rise, rose, risen.* (See also p. 254.)

real, really In formal speech and writing, *real* should not be used as an adverb; *really* is the adverb and *real* an adjective. *Popular reaction to the announcement was really* [not *real*] *enthusiastic.*

reason is because Although colloquially common, this expression should be avoided in formal speech and writing. Use a *that* clause after *reason is: The reason he is absent is that* [not *is because*] *he is sick.* Or: *He is absent because he is sick.* (See also p. 340.)

respectful, respective *Respectful* means "full of (or showing) respect": *Be respectful of other people. Respective* means "separate": *The French and the Germans occupied their respective trenches.*

rise, raise See *raise, rise.*

scarcely See *but, hardly, scarcely.*

sensual, sensuous *Sensual* suggests sexuality; *sensuous* means "pleasing to the senses." *Stirred by the sensuous scent of meadow grass and flowers, Cheryl and Paul found their thoughts growing increasingly sensual.*

set, sit *Set* means "put" or "place" and takes a direct object: *He sets the pitcher down.* Its main forms are *set, set, set. Sit* means "be seated" and does not take an object: *She sits on the sofa.* Its main forms are *sit, sat, sat.* (See also p. 254.)

shall, will *Will* is the future-tense helping verb for all persons: *I will go, you will go, they will go.* The main use of *shall* is for first-person questions requesting an opinion or consent: *Shall I order a pizza? Shall we dance? Shall* can also be used for the first person when a formal effect is desired (*I shall expect you around three*), and it is occasionally used with the second or third person to express the speaker's determination (*You shall do as I say*).

should of See *have, of.*

sight, site, cite See *cite, sight, site.*

since *Since* mainly relates to time: *I've been waiting since noon.* But *since* is also often used to mean "because": *Since you ask, I'll tell you.* Revise sentences in which the word could have either meaning, such as *Since you asked, I've researched the question.*

sit, set See *set, sit.*

site, cite, sight See *cite, sight, site.*

so Avoid using *so* alone or as a vague intensifier: *He was so late. So* needs to be followed by *that* and a clause that states a result: *He was so late that I left without him.*

somebody, some body; someone, some one *Somebody* and *someone* are indefinite pronouns; *some body* is a noun modified by *some;* and *some one* is a pronoun or an adjective modified by *some. Somebody ought to invent a shampoo that will give hair some body. Someone told Janine she should choose some one plan and stick with it.*

sometime, sometimes, some time *Sometime* means "at an indefinite time in the future": *Why don't you come up and see me sometime? Sometimes* means "now and then": *I still see my old friend Joe sometimes. Some time* means "a span of time": *I need some time to make the payments.*

somewheres Nonstandard for *somewhere.*

sort of, sort of a See *kind of, sort of, type of.*

such Avoid using *such* as a vague intensifier: *It was such a cold winter. Such* should be followed by *that* and a clause that states a result: *It was such a cold winter that Napoleon's troops had to turn back.*

such as See *like, such as.*

supposed to, used to In both these expressions, the *-d* is essential: *I used to* [not *use to*] *think so. He's supposed to* [not *suppose to*] *meet us.*

sure Colloquial when used as an adverb meaning *surely: James Madison sure was right about the need for the Bill of Rights.* If you merely want to be emphatic, use *certainly: Madison certainly was right.* If your goal is to convince a possibly reluctant reader, use *surely: Madison surely was right.*

sure and, sure to; try and, try to *Sure to* and *try to* are the correct forms: *Be sure to* [not *sure and*] *buy milk. Try to* [not *Try and*] *find some decent tomatoes.*

take, bring See *bring, take.*

than, then *Than* is a conjunction used in comparisons, *then* an adverb indicating time: *Holmes knew then that Moriarty was wilier than he had thought.*

that, which *That* introduces an essential clause: *We should use the lettuce that Susan bought* (*that Susan bought* limits the lettuce to a particular lettuce). *Which* can introduce both essential and nonessential clauses, but many writers reserve *which* only for nonessential clauses: *The leftover lettuce, which is in the refrigerator, would make a good salad* (*which is in the refrigerator* simply provides more information about the lettuce we already know of). Essential clauses (with *that* or *which*) are not set off by commas; nonessential clauses (with *which*) are. See also pp. 353–55.

that, which, who Use *that* for animals, things, and sometimes collective or anonymous people: *The rocket that failed cost millions. Infants that walk need constant tending.* Use *which* only for animals and things:

The river, which flows south, divides two countries. Use *who* only for people and for animals with names: *Dorothy is the girl who visits Oz. Her dog, Toto, who accompanies her, gives her courage.*

their, there, they're   *Their* is the possessive form of *they: Give them their money. There* indicates place (*I saw her standing there*) or functions as an expletive (*There is a hole behind you*). *They're* is a contraction for *they are: They're going fast.*

theirselves   Nonstandard for *themselves.*

them   In standard American English, *them* does not serve as an adjective: *Those* [not *Them*] *people want to know.*

then, than   See *than, then.*

these kind, these sort, these type, those kind   See *kind of, sort of, type of.*

this, these   *This* is singular: *this car* or *This is the reason I left. These* is plural: *these cars* or *These are not valid reasons.*

thru   A colloquial spelling of *through* that should be avoided in all academic and business writing.

to, too, two   *To* is a preposition; *too* is an adverb meaning "also" or "excessively"; and *two* is a number. *I too have been to Europe two times.*

too   Avoid using *too* as a vague intensifier: *Monkeys are too mean.* When you do use *too,* explain the consequences of the excessive quality: *Monkeys are too mean to make good pets.*

toward, towards   Both are acceptable, though *toward* is preferred. Use one or the other consistently.

try and, try to   See *sure and, sure to; try and, try to.*

type of   See *kind of, sort of, type of.* Don't use *type* without *of: It was a family type of* [not *type*] *restaurant.* Or better: *It was a family restaurant.*

uninterested   See *disinterested, uninterested.*

unique   *Unique* means "the only one of its kind" and so cannot sensibly be modified with words such as *very* or *most: That was a unique* [not *a very unique* or *the most unique*] *movie.*

usage, use   *Usage* refers to conventions, most often those of a language: *Is "hadn't ought" proper usage? Usage* is often misused in place of the noun *use: Wise use* [not *usage*] *of insulation can save fuel.*

use, utilize   *Utilize* can be used to mean "make good use of": *Many teachers utilize computers for instruction.* But for all other senses of "place in service" or "employ," prefer *use.*

used to   See *supposed to, used to.*

wait for, wait on   In formal speech and writing, *wait for* means "await" (*I'm waiting for Paul*) and *wait on* means "serve" (*The owner of the store herself waited on us*).

ways   Colloquial as a substitute for *way: We have only a little way* [not *ways*] *to go.*

well   See *good, well.*

whether, if   See *if, whether.*

which, that   See *that, which.*

which, who, that   See *that, which, who.*

who, whom   *Who* is the subject of a sentence or clause (*We don't know who will come*). *Whom* is the object of a verb or preposition (*We do not know whom we invited*). (See also pp. 292–93.)

who's, whose   *Who's* is the contraction of *who is* or *who has: Who's* [*Who is*] *at the door? Jim is the only one who's* [*who has*] *passed. Whose* is the possessive form of *who: Whose book is that?*

will, shall   See *shall, will.*

would have   Avoid this construction in place of *had* in clauses that begin *if* and state a condition contrary to fact: *If the tree had* [not *would have*] *withstood the fire, it would have been the oldest in town.* See also p. 276.

would of   See *have, of.*

you   In all but very formal writing, *you* is generally appropriate as long as it means "you, the reader." In all writing, avoid indefinite uses of *you,* such as *In one ancient tribe your first loyalty was to your parents.* See also p. 304.

your, you're   *Your* is the possessive form of *you: Your dinner is ready. You're* is the contraction of *you are: You're bound to be late.*

yourself   See *myself, herself, himself, yourself.*

Credits

Text and Illustrations

American Verse Project: From HTI American Verse Project. Copyright © 2005 by the University of Michigan Press. Reprinted by permission.

"At what point do national security and common sense collide? Join the conversation." Ad in *Time*, October 7, 2002. Reprinted by permission of *Time*.

Brooks: "The Bean Eaters" from *Blacks* by Gwendolyn Brooks. Copyright © 1991 by Gwendolyn Brooks. Reprinted by consent of Brooks Permissions.

Campbell and Reece: Excerpt from *Biology*, 7th Edition, by Neil A. Campbell and Jane B. Reece. Copyright © 2005 by Pearson/Benjamin Cummings. Reprinted with permission.

CNN: "War Against Terror, Flight Risk, Airport Wage." Copyright © 2001 Cable News Network, LP, LLLP. Reprinted courtesy of CNN.

Davies: "Unemployment Rates of High School Graduates and College Graduates, 1984–2004," from "The Economics of College Tuition" by Antony Davies. Copyright © 2005. Reprinted by permission.

Dickinson: Lines from "A narrow fellow in the Grass" by Emily Dickinson. From *The Poems of Emily Dickinson*, edited by Thomas H. Johnson. Cambridge, MA: The Belknap Press of Harvard University Press. Copyright © 1951, 1955, 1979 by the President and Fellows of Harvard College. Reprinted by permission of the publishers and the Trustees of Amherst College.

Dyson: Excerpt from *Disturbing the Universe* by Freeman J. Dyson. Copyright © 1979 by Freeman J. Dyson. Reprinted by permission of Basic Books, a member of Perseus Books, LLC.

EBSCOhost: Screen images of EBSCOhost database used with permission from EBSCOhost Publishing.

Eisinger et al.: Excerpt from *American Politics: The People and the Polity* by Peter Eisinger et al. Copyright © 1978 by Little, Brown and Company. Reprinted by permission of the author.

Gaylin: Excerpt from "Feeling Anxious" in *Feelings: Our Vital Signs* by Willard Gaylin. Copyright © 1979 by Willard Gaylin. Reprinted by permission of William Morris Agency, LLC, on behalf of the Author.

Google: Screen images used by permission from *Google*.

Goreau: Excerpt from "Worthy Women Revisited" by Angeline Goreau. *The New York Times*, December 11, 1986. Copyright © 1986 by *The New York Times*. Reprinted by permission.

Hartmann: "How Dangerous Is Your Computer?" by Thomas Hartmann, available at http://www.atariarchives.org/deli/how_dangerous.php.

King: Excerpt from "I Have a Dream" by Martin Luther King, Jr. Reprinted by arrangement with the Estate of Martin Luther King, Jr., c/o Writer's House as agent for the proprietor, New York, NY. Copyright 1963 Martin Luther King, Jr., copyright renewed 1991 by Coretta Scott King.

Photos

Answers to Selected Exercises

These pages provide answers to all exercise items and sentences that are labeled with a star ($*$) in the book.

Exercise 8.1, p. 91

Possible revision

The stereotype that women talk more on cell phones than men do turns out to be false. In a five-year survey of 1021 cell phone owners, a major wireless company found that men spend 35 percent more time on their phones.

Exercise 11.4, p. 132

1. A reasonable generalization.
2. An unreasonable generalization that cannot be inferred from the evidence.

Exercise 11.5, p. 132

Possible answers

1. **Premise:** Anyone who has opposed pollution controls may continue to do so.
   Premise: The mayor has opposed pollution controls.
   Conclusion: The mayor may continue to do so.
   The statement is valid and true.
2. **Premise:** Corporate Web sites are sponsored by for-profit entities.
   Premise: Information from for-profit entities is unreliable.
   Conclusion: Information on corporate Web sites is unreliable.
   The statement is untrue because the second premise is untrue.

Exercise 11.6, p. 133

Possible answers

1. Primarily emotional appeal. Ethical appeal: knowledgeable, concerned, reasonable (at least in the two uses of *may*), slightly sarcastic (*most essential of skills*).
2. Primarily rational appeal. Ethical appeal: knowledgeable, reasonable.

Exercise 11.8, p. 137

Possible answers

1. Sweeping generalization and begged question.
   A revision: A successful marriage demands a degree of maturity.

2. Hasty generalization and non sequitur.
   A revision: Students' persistent complaints about the unfairness of the grading system should be investigated.

3. Reductive fallacy.
   A revision: The United States got involved in World War II for many complex reasons. The bombing of Pearl Harbor was a triggering incident.

4. Either/or fallacy and hasty generalization.
   A revision: People watch television for many reasons, but some watch because they are too lazy to talk or read or because they want mindless escape from their lives.

5. Reductive fallacy and begged question.
   A revision: Racial tension may occur when people with different backgrounds live side by side.

Exercise 15.1, p. 178

Possible answers

1. Many heroes helped to emancipate the slaves.
2. Harriet Tubman, an escaped slave herself, guided hundreds of other slaves to freedom on the Underground Railroad.

571

Exercise 15.2, p. 180

Possible answers

1. Pat Taylor strode into the packed room, greeting students called "Taylor's Kids" and nodding to their parents and teachers.
2. This wealthy Louisiana oilman had promised his "Kids" free college educations because he was determined to make higher education available to all qualified but disadvantaged students.

Exercise 15.3, p. 183

Possible answers

1. Because soldiers admired their commanding officers, they often gave them nicknames containing the word *old*, even though not all of the commanders were old.
2. General Thomas "Stonewall" Jackson was also called "Old Jack," although he was not yet forty years old.

Exercise 15.4, p. 186

Possible answers

1. Genaro González is a successful writer whose stories and novels have been published to critical acclaim.
2. Although he loves to write, he has also earned a doctorate in psychology.

Exercise 15.5, p. 186

Possible revision

Sir Walter Raleigh personified the Elizabethan Age, the period of Elizabeth I's rule of England, in the last half of the sixteenth century. Raleigh was a courtier, a poet, an explorer, and an entrepreneur. Supposedly, he gained Queen Elizabeth's favor by throwing his cloak beneath her feet at the right moment, just as she was about to step over a puddle.

Exercise 16.1, p. 190

Possible answers

1. The ancient Greeks celebrated four athletic contests: the Olympic Games at Olympia, the Isthmian Games near Corinth, the Pythian Games at Delphi, and the Nemean Games at Cleonae.
2. Each day of the games consisted of either athletic events or ceremonies and sacrifices to the gods.
3. In the years between the games, competitors were taught wrestling, javelin throwing, and boxing.
4. Competitors ran sprints, participated in spectacular chariot and horse races, and ran long distances while wearing full armor.
5. The purpose of such events was developing physical strength, demonstrating skill and endurance, and sharpening the skills needed for war.

Exercise 16.2, p. 190

Possible answers

1. People can develop post-traumatic stress disorder (PTSD) after experiencing a dangerous situation and fearing for their survival.
2. The disorder can be triggered by a wide variety of events, such as combat, a natural disaster, or a hostage situation.

Exercise 17.1, p. 195

Possible revision

After being dormant for many years, the Italian volcano Vesuvius exploded on August 24 in the year AD 79. The ash, pumice, and mud from the volcano buried two towns—Herculaneum and the more famous Pompeii—which lay undiscovered until 1709 and 1748, respectively.

Exercise 18.1, p. 202

Possible answers

1. Acquired immune deficiency syndrome (AIDS) is a <u>serious threat</u> all over the world.
2. The disease <u>is transmitted</u> primarily by sexual intercourse, exchange of bodily fluids, shared needles, and blood transfusions.
3. Those who think the disease is limited to <u>homosexuals</u>, <u>drug users</u>, and foreigners are quite mistaken.
4. <u>Statistics</u> suggest that in the United States one in every five hundred college <u>students</u> carries the HIV virus that causes AIDS.
5. <u>People</u> with HIV or full-blown AIDS <u>do</u> not deserve <u>others' exclusion</u> or callousness. Instead, <u>they need</u> all the compassion, medical care, and financial assistance due <u>the seriously ill</u>.

Exercise 18.2, p. 202

Possible answers

1. When <u>people apply</u> for a job, <u>they</u> should represent <u>themselves</u> with the best possible résumé.
2. A person applying for a job as a <u>mail carrier</u> should appear to be honest and responsible.
3. <u>Applicants</u> for a position as an in-home nurse should also represent <u>themselves</u> as honest and responsible.
4. Of course, <u>the applicant</u> should also have a background of capable nursing.
5. The business <u>executive</u> who is scanning a stack of résumés will, of necessity, read them all quickly.

Exercise 18.4, p. 206

1. Maxine Hong Kingston was <u>awarded</u> many prizes for her first two books, *The Woman Warrior* and *China Men*.
2. Kingston <u>cites</u> her mother's tales about ancestors and ancient Chinese customs as the sources of these memoirs.
3. Two of King's <u>progenitors</u>, her great-grandfathers, are focal points of *China Men*.
4. Both men led rebellions against <u>oppressive</u> employers: a sugar-cane farmer and a railroad-construction engineer.
5. In her childhood Kingston was greatly <u>affected</u> by her mother's tale about a pregnant aunt who was ostracized by villagers. [*Ostracized* is correct.]

Exercise 18.5, p. 207

1. AIDS is a serious health <u>problem</u>.
2. Once the virus has entered the blood system, it <u>destroys</u> T-cells.

Exercise 18.7, p. 210

1. As Mark and Lana waited <u>for</u> the justice of the peace, they seemed oblivious <u>to</u> [*or* of] the other people in the lobby.
2. But Mark inferred <u>from</u> Lana's glance at a handsome man that she was no longer occupied <u>by</u> him alone.

Exercise 18.8, p. 211

1. The Eighteenth Amendment <u>to</u> the Constitution <u>of</u> the United States was ratified <u>in</u> 1919.
2. It prohibited the "manufacture, sale, or transportation <u>of</u> intoxicating liquors."

Exercise 18.10, p. 213

Possible answers

1. The <u>disasters</u> of the war have shaken the small nation <u>severely</u>.
2. Prices for food have <u>risen markedly</u>, and citizens <u>suspect</u> that others are <u>profiting</u> on the black market.

3. Medical supplies are so <u>scarce</u> that even <u>very sick</u> civilians cannot get treatment.
4. With most men fighting or injured or killed, women have had to <u>take men's places</u> in farming and manufacturing.
5. <u>Finally</u>, the war's <u>high cost</u> has <u>destroyed the nation's economy.</u>

Exercise 19.1, p. 215

1. The first ice cream, eaten <u>in</u> China in about 2000 BC, was lumpier than modern ice cream.
2. The Chinese made their ice cream of milk, spices, and overcooked rice and packed <u>it</u> in snow to solidify.

Exercise 20.1, p. 221

Possible answers

1. If sore muscles after exercising are a problem for you, there are some <u>things you can do</u> to ease the discomfort.
2. First, <u>apply cold immediately</u> to reduce inflammation.
3. <u>Cold constricts</u> blood vessels <u>and keeps</u> blood away from the injured muscles.
4. <u>Avoid</u> heat for the first day.
5. <u>Applying</u> heat within the first twenty-four hours <u>can increase</u> muscle soreness and stiffness.

Exercise 20.2, p. 221

Possible answers

<u>After much thought</u>, he <u>concluded</u> that carcinogens <u>could be treated like automobiles</u>. Instead of giving in to <u>a fear</u> of cancer, we should <u>balance</u> the benefits <u>we receive</u> from potential carcinogens (<u>such as</u> plastic <u>and pesticides</u>) against the damage <u>they do.</u>

Exercise 21.1, p. 228

1. Ancestors of the ginkgo tree, a relic from the age of the dinosaurs, lived 175 to 200 million years ago.
2. The tree sometimes grows to over a hundred feet in height.
3. It has fan-shaped leaves about three inches wide.
4. A deciduous tree, the ginkgo loses its leaves in the fall after they turn bright yellow.
5. The ginkgo tree is esteemed in the United States and Europe as an ornamental tree.

Exercise 21.2, p. 229

1. You can reduce stress by making a few simple changes.
2. Get up fifteen minutes earlier than you ordinarily do.
3. Eat a healthy breakfast, and eat it slowly so that you enjoy it.
4. Do your unpleasant tasks early in the day.
5. Every day, do at least one thing you really enjoy.

Exercise 21.3, p. 231

1. Just about everyone has heard the story <u>of</u> the Trojan Horse.
2. This incident happened at the city of Troy <u>and</u> was planned by the Greeks.
3. The Greeks built a huge wooden horse; <u>inside</u> it was a hollow space big enough to hold many men.
4. At night, they rolled the horse to the gate of Troy <u>and</u> left it there before sailing their ships out to sea.
5. <u>In</u> the morning, the Trojans were surprised to see the enormous horse.

Exercise 22.1, p. 234

1. The <u>horse</u> / <u>has</u> a long history of serving humanity but today <u>is</u> mainly a show and sport animal.

2. A member of the genus *Equus*, the domestic <u>horse</u> / <u>is</u> related to the wild Przewalski's horse, the ass, and the zebra.
3. The domestic <u>horse</u> and its <u>relatives</u> / <u>are</u> all plains-dwelling herd animals.
4. An average-sized adult <u>horse</u> / <u>may require</u> twenty-six pounds or more of pasture feed or hay per day.
5. <u>Racehorses</u> / <u>require</u> grain for part of their forage.

Exercise 22.2, p. 237

1. The number of serious crimes in the United States decreased.
2. A decline in serious crimes occurred each year.
3. The Crime Index measures serious crime.
4. The FBI invented the index.
5. The four serious violent crimes are murder, robbery, forcible rape, and aggravated assault.

Exercise 22.3, p. 240

1. <u>Milo Addica and Will Rokos cowrote</u> the screenplay for *Monster's Ball*.
2. <u>Marc Foster directed</u> the film.

Exercise 23.1, p. 244

1. Because of its many synonyms, or words with similar meanings, English can make it difficult to choose the exact word.
2. Borrowing words from other languages such as French and Latin, English acquired an unusual number of synonyms.
3. Having so many choices, how does a writer decide between *motherly* and *maternal* or among *womanly, feminine,* and *female?*
4. Some people prefer longer and more ornate words to avoid the flatness of short words.
5. During the Renaissance a heated debate occurred between the Latinists, favoring Latin words, and the Saxonists, preferring native Anglo-Saxon words.

Exercise 23.2, p. 246

1. The Prophet Muhammad, <u>who was the founder of Islam</u>, was born about 570 CE in the city of Mecca.
2. He grew up in the care of his grandfather and an uncle <u>because both of his parents had died</u>.
3. His family was part of a powerful Arab tribe <u>that lived in western Arabia</u>.
4. <u>When he was about forty years old</u>, he had a vision in a cave outside Mecca.

5. He believed <u>that God had selected him to be the</u> ^N <u>prophet of a true religion for the Arab people.</u>

Exercise 24.1, p. 248

1. ┌──main clause──┐ ┌──main clause──┐
   Our world has many sounds, but they all have one thing in common. [Compound.]

2. ┌────main clause────┐
   The one thing that all sounds share is that they are produced by vibrations.
   [Complex.]   └─subordinate clause─┘   └────subordinate clause────┘

3. ┌────main clause────┐ ┌────main clause────┐
   The vibrations make the air move in waves, and these sound waves travel to the ear.
   [Compound.]

4. ┌────subordinate clause────┐ ┌────main clause────┐
   When sound waves enter the ear, the brain has to interpret them. [Complex.]

5. ┌────main clause────┐
   Sound waves can also travel through other material, such as water and even the solid earth. [Simple.]

Exercise 25.1, p. 253

1. The world population has <u>grown</u> by two-thirds of a billion people in less than a decade. [Past participle.]
2. Recently it <u>broke</u> the 6 billion mark. [Past tense.]
3. Experts have <u>drawn</u> pictures of a crowded future. [Past participle.]
4. They predict that the world population may have <u>slid</u> up to as much as 10 billion by the year 2050. [Past participle.]
5. Though the food supply <u>rose</u> in the last decade, the share to each person <u>fell</u>. [Both past tense.]

Exercise 25.2, p. 254

1. Yesterday afternoon the child <u>lay</u> down for a nap.
2. The child has been <u>raised</u> by her grandparents.

Exercise 25.3, p. 256

1. A teacher sometimes <u>asks</u> too much of a student.
2. In high school I was once <u>punished</u> for being sick.
3. I had <u>missed</u> a week of school because of a serious case of the flu.
4. I <u>realized</u> that I would fail a test unless I had a chance to make up the class work.
5. I <u>discussed</u> the problem with the teacher.

Exercise 25.4, p. 261

1. Each year thousands of new readers <u>have</u> been discovering Agatha Christie's mysteries.
2. The books <u>were</u> written by a prim woman who had worked as a nurse during World War I.

Exercise 25.5, p. 261

1. A report from the Bureau of the Census has <u>confirmed</u> a widening gap between rich and poor.
2. As suspected, the percentage of people below the poverty level did <u>increase</u> over the last decade.

Exercise 25.6, p. 264

1. A program called HELP Wanted tries to encourage citizens <u>to</u> take action on behalf of American competitiveness.
2. Officials working on this program hope <u>to improve</u> education for work.

Exercise 25.7, p. 266

1. American movies treat everything from going out with [correct] someone to making up [correct] an ethnic identity, but few people <u>look into their significance</u>.
2. While some viewers stay away from [correct] topical films, others <u>turn up at the theater</u> simply because a movie has sparked debate.

Exercise 26.1, p. 271

The 1960 presidential race between Richard Nixon and John F. Kennedy was the first to feature a televised debate. [Sentence correct.] Despite his extensive political experience, Nixon <u>perspired</u> heavily and <u>looked</u> haggard and uneasy in front of the camera. By contrast, Kennedy <u>projected</u> cool poise and <u>provided</u> crisp answers that made him seem fit for the office of President.

Exercise 26.2, p. 271

E. B. White's famous children's novel *Charlotte's Web* is a wonderful story of friendship and loyalty. [Sentence correct.] Charlotte, the wise and motherly spider, <u>decides</u> to save her friend Wilbur, the young and childlike pig, from being butchered by <u>his</u> owner. She <u>makes</u> a plan to weave words into her web that <u>describe</u> Wilbur.

Exercise 26.3, p. 274

1. Diaries that Adolf Hitler <u>was supposed</u> to have written <u>had surfaced</u> in Germany.
2. Many people <u>believed</u> that the diaries <u>were</u> authentic because a well-known historian <u>had declared</u> them so.

Exercise 26.4, p. 274

1. When an athlete <u>turns</u> professional, he or she commits to a grueling regimen of mental and physical training.
2. If athletes <u>were</u> less committed, they <u>would disappoint</u> teammates, fans, and themselves.
3. If professional athletes <u>are</u> very lucky, they may play until age forty.
4. Unless an athlete achieves celebrity status, he or she <u>will have</u> few employment choices after retirement.
5. If professional sports <u>were</u> less risky, athletes <u>would have</u> longer careers and more choices after retirement.

Exercise 27.1, p. 276

1. If John Hawkins <u>had known</u> of all the dangerous side effects of smoking tobacco, would he have introduced the dried plant to England in 1565?
2. Hawkins noted that if a Florida Indian man <u>were</u> to travel for several days, he <u>would smoke</u> tobacco to satisfy his hunger and thirst.

Exercise 28.1, p. 279

Possible answers

1. Many <u>factors</u> <u>determine</u> water quality.
2. All natural <u>waters</u> <u>contain</u> suspended and dissolved substances.
3. The <u>environment</u> <u>controls</u> the amounts of the substances.
4. <u>Pesticides</u> <u>produce</u> some dissolved substances.
5. <u>Fields, livestock feedlots, and other sources</u> <u>deposit</u> sediment in water.

Exercise 28.2, p. 279

Possible answers

1. When <u>engineers</u> <u>built</u> the Eiffel Tower in 1889, the <u>French</u> <u>thought</u> it to be ugly.
2. At that time, industrial <u>technology</u> <u>was</u> still <u>resisted</u> <u>by</u> many people.

Exercise 29.1, p. 287

1. Weinstein & Associates <u>is</u> a consulting firm that <u>tries</u> to make businesspeople laugh.
2. Statistics from recent research <u>suggest</u> that humor relieves stress.

3. Reduced stress in businesses in turn reduces illness and absenteeism.
4. Reduced stress can also reduce friction within an employee group, which then works together more productively.
5. In special conferences held by one consultant, each of the participants practices making others laugh.

Exercise 29.2, p. 287

The Siberian tiger is the largest living cat in the world, much bigger than its relative the Bengal tiger. It grows to a length of nine to twelve feet, including its tail, and to a height of about three and a half feet. It can weigh over six hundred pounds. This carnivorous hunter lives in northern China and Korea as well as in Siberia. During the long winter of this Arctic climate, the yellowish striped coat gets a little lighter in order to blend with the snow-covered landscape. The coat also grows quite thick, since the tiger has to withstand temperatures as low as −50°F.

Exercise 30.1, p. 292

1. Jody and I had been hunting for jobs.
2. The best employees at our old company were she and I, so we expected to find jobs quickly.

Exercise 30.2, p. 293

1. The school administrators suspended Jurgen, whom they suspected of setting the fire.
2. Jurgen had been complaining to other custodians, who reported him.
3. He constantly complained of unfair treatment from whoever happened to be passing in the halls, including pupils.
4. "Who here has heard Mr. Jurgen's complaints?" the police asked.
5. "Whom did he complain most about?"

Exercise 30.3, p. 295

1. Sentence correct.
2. Sentence correct.
3. Immediately, he and Gilgamesh wrestled to see who was more powerful.
4. Sentence correct.
5. The friendship of the two strong men was sealed by their fighting.

Exercise 31.1, p. 300

Possible answers

1. Each girl raised in a Mexican American family in the Rio Grande valley of Texas hopes that one day she will be given a *quinceañera* party for her fifteenth birthday.
2. Such a celebration is very expensive because it entails a religious service followed by a huge party. [*Or:* Such celebrations are very expensive because they entail a religious service followed by a huge party.]
3. A girl's immediate family, unless it is wealthy, cannot afford the party by itself.
4. The parents will ask each close friend or relative if he or she can help with the preparations. [*Or:* The parents will ask close friends or relatives if they can help with the preparations.]
5. Sentence correct.

Exercise 32.1, p. 304

Possible answers

1. "Life begins at forty" is a cliché many people live by, and this saying may or may not be true.
2. Living successfully or not depends on one's definition of success.
3. When Pearl Buck was forty, her novel *The Good Earth* won the Pulitzer Prize.
4. Buck was raised in a missionary family in China, which [*or* whom] she wrote about in her novels.

5. In *The Good Earth* the characters have to struggle, but fortitude is rewarded.

Exercise 32.2, p. 305

Possible revision

In Charlotte Brontë's *Jane Eyre*, Jane is a shy young woman who takes a job as governess. Her employer is a rude, brooding man named Rochester. [Sentence correct.] He lives in a mysterious mansion on the English moors, and both the mansion and the moors contribute an eerie quality to Jane's experience. Eerier still are the fires, strange noises, and other unexplained happenings in the house; but Rochester refuses to discuss them.

Exercise 33.1, p. 307

1. The eighteenth-century essayist Samuel Johnson fared badly in his early life.
2. Sentence correct.
3. After failing as a schoolmaster, Johnson moved to London, where he did well.
4. Johnson was taken seriously as a critic and dictionary maker.
5. Johnson was really surprised when he received a pension from King George III.

Exercise 33.2, p. 310

1. Interest in books about the founding of the United States is not [*or* is hardly] consistent among Americans: it seems to vary with the national mood.
2. Sentence correct.

Exercise 33.3, p. 312

1. Several critics found Alice Walker's *The Color Purple* to be a fascinating book.
2. Sentence correct.

Exercise 33.4, p. 316

From the native American Indians who migrated from Asia 20,000 years ago to the new arrivals who now come by planes, the United States is a nation of foreigners. It is a country of immigrants who are all living under a single flag.

Back in the seventeenth and eighteenth centuries, at least 75 percent of the population came from England. However, between 1820 and 1975 more than 38 million immigrants came to this country from elsewhere in Europe.

Exercise 33.5, p. 317

1. Americans often argue about which professional sport is best: basketball, football, or baseball.
2. Basketball fans contend that their sport offers more action because the players are constantly running and shooting.
3. Because it is played indoors in relatively small arenas, basketball allows fans to be closer to the action than the other sports do.
4. Football fanatics say they hardly stop yelling once the game begins.
5. They cheer when their team executes a really complicated play well.

Exercise 34.1, p. 322

1. People who are right-handed dominate in our society.
2. Hand tools, machines, and even doors are designed for right-handed people.
3. However, nearly 15 percent of the population may be left-handed.
4. When they begin school, children often prefer one hand or the other.
5. Parents and teachers should not try deliberately to change a child's preference for the left hand.

Exercise 34.2, p. 322

1. A young Chinese computer specialist developed image controls.
2. A skeptical American engineer assisted the specialist.
3. Several university researchers are carrying out further study.

4. The controls depend on a hand-sized, T-shaped object connected by wires to the computer.
5. The image allows a biochemist to walk into a gigantic holographic display of a molecule.

Exercise 34.3, p. 324

Possible answers

1. After Andrew Jackson had accomplished many deeds of valor, his fame led to his election to the presidency in 1828 and 1832.
2. When Jackson was fourteen, both of his parents died.
3. To aid the American Revolution, Jackson chose service as a mounted courier.
4. Sentence correct.
5. Though not well educated, Jackson proved his ability in a successful career as a lawyer and judge.

Exercise 35.1, p. 330

Possible answers

1. Human beings who perfume themselves are not much different from other animals.
2. Animals as varied as insects and dogs release pheromones chemicals that signal other animals.
3. Human beings have a diminished sense of smell and do not consciously detect most of their own species' pheromones.
4. No sentence fragment.
5. Some sources say that people began using perfume to cover up the smell of burning flesh during sacrifices to the gods.

Exercise 35.2, p. 331

Possible answers

People generally avoid eating mushrooms except those they buy in stores. But in fact many varieties of mushrooms are edible. Mushrooms are members of a large group of vegetation called nonflowering plants including algae, mosses, ferns, and coniferous trees even the giant redwoods of California. Most of the nonflowering plants prefer moist environments such as forest floors, fallen timber, and still water. Mushrooms, for example prefer moist, shady soil. Algae grow in water.

Exercise 36.1, p. 336

Possible answers

1. Some people think that dinosaurs were the first living vertebrates but fossils of turtles go back 40 million years or further.
2. Although most other reptiles exist mainly in tropical regions turtles inhabit a variety of environments worldwide.
3. Turtles do not have teeth; their jaws are covered with a sharp, horny sheath.
4. Turtles cannot expand their lungs to breathe air; as a result they make adjustments in how space is used within the shell.
5. Some turtles can get oxygen from water; therefore they don't need to breathe air.

Exercise 36.2, p. 337

Possible answers

1. Money has a long history. It goes back at least as far as the earliest records.
   Money has a long history; it goes back at least as far as the earliest records.
2. Many of the earliest records concern financial transactions. Indeed, early history must often be inferred from commercial activity.
   Many of the earliest records concern financial transactions; indeed, early history must often be inferred from commercial activity.

3. Sentence correct.
4. Sometimes the objects have had real value⨀ however⨀ in modern times their value has been more abstract.

  Although sometimes the objects have had real value, in modern times their value has been more abstract.
5. Cattle, fermented beverages, and rare shells have served as money⨀ and each one had actual value for the society.

  Cattle, fermented beverages, and rare shells have served as money⨀ Each one had actual value for the society.

Exercise 36.3, p. 338

Possible answers

  What many call the first genocide of modern times occurred during World War I, when the Armenians were deported from their homes in Anatolia, Turkey. The Turkish government assumed that the Armenians were sympathetic to Russia, with whom the Turks were at war. Many Armenians died because of the hardships of the journey, and many were massacred. The death toll was estimated at between 600,000 and 1 million.

Exercise 37.1, p. 341

Possible answers

1. A hurricane occurs when the winds in a tropical depression rotate counterclockwise at more than seventy-four miles per hour.
2. Because hurricanes can destroy so many lives and so much property, people fear them.
3. Through high winds, storm surge, floods, and tornadoes, hurricanes have killed thousands of people.
4. Storm surge occurs when the hurricane's winds whip up a tide that spills over seawalls and deluges coastal islands.
5. Sentence correct.

Exercise 37.2, p. 343

1. Archaeologists and other scientists can often determine the age of their discoveries by means of radiocarbon dating.
2. This technique can be used on any material that once was living.
3. This technique is based on the fact that all living organisms contain carbon.
4. The most common isotope is carbon 12, which contains six protons and six neutrons.
5. A few carbon atoms are classified as the isotope carbon 14, where the nucleus consists of six protons and eight neutrons.

Exercise 38.1, p. 348

  When visitors first arrive in Hawaii, they often encounter an unexpected language barrier. Standard English is the language of business and government, but many of the people speak Pidgin English⨀ Instead of an excited "Aloha⦿" the visitors may be greeted with an excited Pidgin "Howzit⦿" or asked if they know "how fo' find one good hotel⨀"

Exercise 39.1, p. 351

1. Parents once automatically gave their children the father's last name⨀ but some no longer do.
2. Parents were once legally required to give their children the father's last name⨀ but these laws have been contested in court.
3. Parents may now give their children any last name they choose⨀ and the arguments for choosing the mother's last name are often strong and convincing.
4. Sentence correct.
5. The child's last name may be just the mother's⨀ or it may link the mother's and the father's with a hyphen.

Exercise 39.2, p. 353

1. Veering sharply to the right⊙ a large flock of birds neatly avoids a high wall.
2. Sentence correct.
3. With the help of complex computer simulations⊙ zoologists are learning more about this movement.
4. Because it is sudden and apparently well coordinated⊙ the movement of flocks and schools has seemed to be directed by a leader.
5. Almost incredibly⊙ the group could behave with more intelligence than any individual seemed to possess.

Exercise 39.3, p. 357

1. Italians insist that Marco Polo⊙ the thirteenth-century explorer⊙ did not import pasta from China.
2. Pasta⊙ which consists of flour and water and often egg⊙ existed in Italy long before Marco Polo left for his travels.
3. Sentence correct.
4. Most Italians dispute this account⊙ although their evidence is shaky.
5. Wherever it originated, the Italians are now the undisputed masters◯in making and cooking pasta.

Exercise 39.4, p. 359

1. Shoes with high heels were originally designed to protect feet from mud⊙ garbage⊙ and animal waste in the streets.
2. Sentence correct.
3. The heels were worn by men and made of colorful silk fabrics⊙ soft suedes⊙ or smooth leathers.
4. High-heeled shoes became popular when the short⊙ powerful King Louis XIV of France began wearing them.
5. Louis's influence was so strong that men and women of the court⊙ priests and cardinals⊙ and even household servants wore high heels.

Exercise 39.5, p. 364

1. An important source of water◯is underground aquifers.
2. Underground aquifers are deep◯and sometimes broad layers of water◯that are trapped between layers of rock.
3. Porous rock◯or sediment holds the water.
4. Deep wells drilled through the top layers of solid rock◯produce a flow of water.
5. Such wells are sometimes called◯artesian wells.

Exercise 39.6, p. 364

Ellis Island⊙ New York⊙ reopened for business in 1990⊙ but now the customers are tourists⊙ not immigrants. This spot⊙ which lies in New York Harbor⊙ was the first American soil seen◯or touched by many of the nation's immigrants. Though other places also served as ports of entry for foreigners⊙none has the symbolic power of◯ Ellis Island. Between its opening in 1892 and its closing in 1954, over 20 million people⊙ about two-thirds of all immigrants⊙ were detained there before taking up their new lives in the United States. Ellis Island processed over 2000 [or 2⊙000] newcomers a day when immigration was at its peak between 1900 and 1920.

Exercise 40.1, p. 367

Possible answers

1. Electronic instruments are prevalent in jazz and rock music⊙ <u>however</u>⊙ they are less common in classical music.
2. Jazz and rock change rapidly⊙ they nourish experimentation and improvisation.
3. The notes and instrumentation of traditional classical music were established by a composer writing decades or centuries ago⊙ <u>therefore</u>⊙ such music does not change.

4. Contemporary classical music not only can draw on tradition⊙ it can also respond to innovations such as jazz rhythms and electronic sounds.

5. Much contemporary electronic music is more than just jazz, rock, or classical⊙ it is a fusion of all three.

Exercise 40.2, p. 369

The set, sounds, and actors in the movie captured the essence of horror films. The set was ideal⊙ dark, deserted streets⊙ trees dipping their branches over the sidewalks⊙ mist hugging the ground and creeping up to meet the trees⊙ looming shadows of unlighted, turreted houses. The sounds, too, were appropriate⊙ especially terrifying was the hard, hollow sound of footsteps echoing throughout the film.

Exercise 41.1, p. 372

1. Sunlight is made up of three kinds of radiation⊙ visible rays; infrared rays, which we cannot see; and ultraviolet rays, which are also invisible.

2. Especially in the ultraviolet range⌒ sunlight is harmful to the eyes.

3. Ultraviolet rays can damage the retina⊙ furthermore, they can cause cataracts on the lens.

4. Infrared rays are the longest⌒ measuring 700 nanometers and longer, while ultraviolet rays are the shortest⌒ measuring 400 nanometers and shorter.

5. The lens protects the eye by⌒absorbing much of the ultraviolet radiation and thus protecting the retina.

Exercise 42.1, p. 375

1. In the myths of the ancient Greeks, the goddesses' roles vary widely.

2. Demeter's responsibility is the fruitfulness of the earth.

3. Athena's role is to guard the city of Athens.

4. Artemis's function is to care for wild animals and small children.

5. Athena and Artemis's father, Zeus, is the king of the gods

Exercise 42.2, p. 377

Landlocked Chad is among the world's most troubled countries. The people's of Chad are poor: their average per capita income equals $1000 per year. Just over 30 percent of Chad's population is literate, and every five hundred people must share only two teachers.

Exercise 43.1, p. 382

In one class we talked about a passage from "I Have a Dream," the speech delivered by Martin Luther King, Jr., on the steps of the Lincoln Memorial on August 28, 1963:

When the architects of our republic wrote the magnificent words of the Constitution and the Declaration of Independence, they were signing a promissory note to which every American was to fall heir. This note was a promise that all men would be guaranteed the unalienable rights of life, liberty, and the pursuit of happiness.

"What did Dr. King mean by this statement?" the teacher asked. "Perhaps we should define 'promissory note' first."

Exercise 44.1, p. 387

1. "To be able to read the Bible in the vernacular was a liberating experience . . . ."

Exercise 44.2, p. 389

"Let all the learned say what they can, / 'Tis ready money makes the man." These two lines of poetry by the Englishman William Somerville (1645–1742) may apply to a current American economic problem. Non-American investors with "ready money" pour some of it—as much as $1.3 trillion in recent years—into the United States. Stocks and bonds, savings deposits, service companies, factories, artworks, political campaigns⊟the investments of foreigners are varied and grow more numerous every day.

Exercise 45.1, p. 396

1. Science <u>affects</u> many <u>important</u> aspects of our lives.
2. Many people have a <u>poor</u> understanding of the <u>role</u> of scientific breakthroughs in <u>their</u> health.
3. Many people <u>believe</u> that <u>doctors</u> are more <u>responsible</u> for <u>improvements</u> in health care than scientists are.
4. But scientists in the <u>laboratory</u> have made crucial steps in the search for <u>knowledge</u> about human health and <u>medicine</u>.
5. For example, one scientist <u>whose</u> discoveries have <u>affected</u> many people is Ulf Von Euler.

Exercise 45.2, p. 397

The <u>weather</u> <u>affects</u> all of us, though <u>its</u> <u>effects</u> are different for different people. Some people love a <u>fair</u> day with warm temperatures and sunshine. They revel in spending a <u>whole</u> day outside without the threat of <u>rain</u>.

Exercise 46.1, p. 399

1. Sentence correct.
2. Sentence correct.
3. The non⊖African elephants of south⊖central Asia are somewhat smaller.
4. A fourteen⊖ or fifteen⊖year-old elephant has reached sexual maturity.
5. The elephant life span is about sixty⊖five or seventy years.

Exercise 47.1, p. 403

1. San Antonio, <u>T</u>exas, is a thriving city in the <u>S</u>outhwest.
2. The city has always offered much to tourists interested in the roots of <u>S</u>panish settlement of the <u>N</u>ew <u>W</u>orld.
3. The <u>A</u>lamo is one of five Catholic <u>m</u>issions built by <u>p</u>riests to convert <u>N</u>ative <u>A</u>mericans and to maintain <u>S</u>pain's claims in the area.
4. But the <u>A</u>lamo is more famous for being the site of an 1836 battle that helped to create the <u>R</u>epublic of Texas.
5. Many of the nearby <u>s</u>treets, such as Crockett <u>S</u>treet, are named for men who died in that <u>b</u>attle.

Exercise 48.1, p. 407

1. Of the many Vietnam veterans who are writers, Oliver Stone is perhaps the most famous for writing and directing the films <u>Platoon</u> and <u>Born on the Fourth of July</u>.
2. Tim O'Brien has written short stories for <u>Esquire</u>, <u>GQ</u>, and <u>Massachusetts Review</u>.
3. <u>Going After Cacciato</u> is O'Brien's dreamlike novel about the horrors of combat.
4. The word <u>Vietnam</u> is technically two words (<u>Viet</u> and <u>Nam</u>), but most American writers spell it as one word. [*Viet* and *Nam* were correctly highlighted. Highlighting removed from *one*.]
5. American writers use words or phrases borrowed from Vietnamese, such as <u>di di mau</u> ("go quickly") or <u>dinky dau</u> ("crazy").

Exercise 49.1, p. 411

1. Sentence correct.
2. About 65 <u>million years</u> ago, a comet or asteroid crashed into the earth.
3. The result was a huge crater about 10 <u>kilometers</u> (6.2 <u>miles</u>) deep in the Gulf of <u>Mexico</u>.
4. Sharpton's new measurements suggest that the crater is 50 <u>percent</u> larger than scientists had previously believed.
5. Indeed, 20-<u>year</u>-old drilling cores reveal that the crater is about 186 <u>miles</u> wide, roughly the size of <u>Connecticut</u>.

Exercise 50.1, p. 413

1. The planet Saturn is <u>900</u> million miles, or nearly <u>1.5 billion</u> kilometers, from the sun.
2. Sentence correct.
3. Thus, Saturn orbits the sun only <u>2.4</u> times during the average human life span.
4. It travels in its orbit at about <u>21,600</u> miles per hour.
5. <u>Fifteen</u> to <u>twenty</u> times denser than Earth's core, Saturn's core measures <u>seventeen thousand</u> miles across.

Exercise 56.1, p. 520

The entries below follow the order of the exercise and so are not alphabetized.

Conte, Christopher. "Networking the Classroom." <u>CQ Researcher</u> 5 (2005): 923-43.

Irving, Larry. "The Still Yawning Divide." <u>Newsweek</u> 12 Mar. 2006: 64. <u>Expanded Academic ASAP</u>. InfoTrac. Southeast State U, Polk Lib. 14 Nov. 2006 <http://www.galegroup.com>.

United States. Dept. of Education. National Center for Education Statistics. <u>Internet Access in Public Schools</u>. 24 Feb. 2005. 12 Nov. 2006 <http://www.ed.gov/nces/edstats>.

Healy, Jane M. <u>Failure to Connect: How Computers Affect Our Children's Minds—For Better and Worse</u>. New York: Simon, 2000.

Index

evidence in, 125–26
fallacies in, 133–37
inductive reasoning in, 127–28
organization of, 138
oversimplifications in, 135–37
reasonable, 127–37
sample of, 139–42
as writing assignment, 9
Art, Web sources on, 430. *See also*
  Illustrations and artworks
Articles (*a, an, the*)
  a vs. *an,* 555
  capitalization in titles, 403
  careless omission of, 215
  defined, 312
  grammar/style checkers for, 313
  rules for use of, 313–15
Articles in periodicals
  on computerized databases, 437
  documenting: APA style, 540–41;
    MLA style, 500–04, 510, 515
  finding bibliographic information
    for, 501, 505–06
  indexes to, 434–37
  peer-reviewed or refereed, 425, 435
  as research sources, 432–37
  titles, quotation marks for, 380
  in working bibliographies, 422–24
Art Source directory, 444
ARTstor directory, 444
Art works. *See* Illustrations and artworks
as
  vs. *like,* 557
  misuse for *because, since, while,*
    whether, who, 557
  parallelism with, 189
  pronoun after, 295
as . . . as, 231
as a result, punctuation with, 335–36
ascent, assent, 392
Ask.com, 439
Assignment, writing, 9
Associations, capitalization of names
  of, 401
Assumptions
  interpreting, in critical reading,
    110–11, 117–18
  used in argument, 126–27
assure, ensure, insure, 557
Astronomy, Web sources on, 432
at, in, on, 209–10
at last, punctuation with, 335–36
at length, punctuation with, 335–36
Audience
  for academic writing, 87
  consideration of, 3, 6–8
  disabilities, designing for, 83–84,
    164, 168

for illustrations, 113–14
for oral presentations, 169
for public writing, 162, 164
purpose and, 9
questions about, 3, 8
subject and, 5
Audio sources. *See* Sound recordings
Authors
  APA style: parenthetical citations,
    531–35; reference list, 535–47
  determining in online sources,
    450–51, 455
  information about, in critical read-
    ing, 106
  MLA style: list of works cited,
    493–520; parenthetical citations,
    483–91
  providing names of, in signal
    phrases, 467–68
Auxiliary verbs. *See* Helping verbs
  (auxiliary verbs)
aware of, 209
awful, awfully, 557
a while, awhile, 557

B
Background information, in signal
  phrases, 467–68
bad, badly, 306, 557
Bandwagon fallacy, 135
bare, bear, 392
based on, 209
BC, AD, 409
BCE, CE, 409
be
  forms of, 177–78, 227, 269–70
  as helping verb, 227, 258–59
  illogical equation with, 340
  as linking verb, 307–08
  omission of, 328
  past participle and forms of,
    258–59, 277
  present participle and forms of,
    258
  -s forms of, 255
  in subjunctive mood, 275–76
  as weak verb, 177–78
bear, bare, 392
Begging the question, 134
Beginnings of sentences
  for emphasis, 179–80
  variety and, 193–94
being as, being that, 557
Beliefs
  as claim in argument, 125
  critical thinking and, 110–11
beside, besides, 557
besides, 56, 335–36
better, had better, 557

Index

Index

Editing Symbols

Boldface numbers and letters refer to chapters and sections of the handbook.

ab	Faulty abbreviation, **49**		$\overset{\wedge}{,}$	Comma, **39**
ad	Misused adjective or adverb, **33**		;	Semicolon, **40**
agr	Error in agreement, **29**, **31**		:	Colon, **41**
ap	Apostrophe needed or misused, **42**		$\overset{,}{\vee}$	Apostrophe, **39**
appr	Inappropriate word, **18a**		`` "	Quotation marks, **40**
arg	Faulty argument, **11b–d**		— () … [] /	Dash, parentheses, ellipsis mark, brackets, slash, **44**
awk	Awkward construction		par, ¶	Start new paragraph, **6**
cap	Use capital letter, **47**		¶ coh	Paragraph not coherent, **6b**
case	Error in case form, **30**		¶ dev	Paragraph not developed, **6c**
cit	Missing source citation or error in form of citation, **54e**		¶ un	Paragraph not unified, **6a**
coh	Coherence lacking, **3b-3**, **6b**		pass	Ineffective passive voice, **28a**
con	Be more concise, **20**		pn agr	Error in pronoun-antecedent agreement, **31**
coord	Coordination needed, **15c**		ref	Error in pronoun reference, **32**
crit	Think or read more critically, **10a–b**		rep	Unnecessary repetition, **20c**
cs	Comma splice, **36**		rev	Revise or proofread, **5**
d	Ineffective diction (word choice), **18**		run-on	Run-on (fused) sentence, **36**
			shift	Inconsistency, **26d**, **27b**, **28b**, **32f**
des	Ineffective or incorrect document design, **7**		sp	Misspelled word, **45**
			spec	Be more specific, **6c**, **18b-2**
det	Error in use of determiner, **33f**		sub	Subordination needed or faulty, **15d**
dm	Dangling modifier, **34b**		t	Error in verb tense, **26**
emph	Emphasis lacking or faulty, **15**		t seq	Error in tense sequence, **26e**
exact	Inexact word, **18b**		trans	Transition needed, **6b-6**
frag	Sentence fragment, **35**		und	Underline or italicize, **48**
fs	Fused sentence, **36**		usage	See Glossary of Usage, p. 555
gram	Error in grammar, **21–24**		var	Vary sentence structure, **17b**
hyph	Error in use of hyphen, **46**		vb	Error in verb form, **25**
inc	Incomplete construction, **19**		vb agr	Error in subject-verb agreement, **29**
ital	Italicize or underline, **48**		w	Wordy, **20**
k	Awkward construction		ww	Wrong word, **18b-1**
lc	Use lowercase (small) letter, **47**		//	Faulty parallelism, **16**
mixed	Mixed construction, **37**		#	Separate with a space
mm	Misplaced modifier, **34a**		⌒	Close up the space
mng	Meaning unclear		℘	Delete
no cap	Unnecessary capital letter, **47**		t͟h͟e	Capitalize, **47**
no $\overset{\wedge}{,}$	Comma not needed, **39h**		T̷he	Use a small letter, **47**
no ¶	No new paragraph needed, **6**		t⊖b	Transpose letters or words
num	Error in use of numbers, **50**		x	Obvious error
p	Error in punctuation, **38–44**		∧	Something missing, **19**
. ? !	Period, question mark, exclamation point, **38**		??	Document illegible or meaning unclear

Throughout this handbook, the symbol 〖CULTURE LANGUAGE〗 signals topics for students whose first language or dialect is not standard American English. These topics can be tricky because they arise from rules in standard English that are quite different in other languages and dialects. Many of the topics involve significant cultural assumptions as well.

No matter what your language background, as a college student you are learning the culture of US higher education and the language that is used and shaped by that culture. The process is challenging, even for native speakers of standard American English. It requires not just writing clearly and correctly but also mastering conventions of developing, presenting, and supporting ideas. The challenge is greater if, in addition, you are trying to learn standard American English and are accustomed to other conventions. Several habits can help you succeed:

- **Read.** Besides course assignments, read newspapers, magazines, and books in English. The more you read, the more fluently and accurately you'll write.
- **Write.** Keep a journal in which you practice writing in English every day.
- **Talk and listen.** Take advantage of opportunities to hear and use English.
- **Ask questions.** Your instructors, tutors in the writing lab, and fellow students can clarify assignments and help you identify and solve writing problems.
- **Don't try for perfection.** No one writes perfectly, and the effort to do so can prevent you from expressing yourself fluently. View mistakes not as failures but as opportunities to learn.
- **Revise first; then edit.** Focus on each essay's ideas, support, and organization before attending to grammar and vocabulary. See the revision and editing checklists on pages 32 and 37.
- **Set editing priorities.** Concentrate first on any errors that interfere with clarity, such as problems with word order or subject-verb agreement. The following index can help you identify the topics you need to work on and can lead you to appropriate text discussions. The pages marked * include exercises for self-testing.

Contents

◄───   "Editing Symbols" and " CULTURE LANGUAGE Guide"